Lecture Notes in Computer Science 8520

Commenced Publication in 1973
Founding and Former Series Editors:
Gerhard Goos, Juris Hartmanis, and Jan van Leeuwen

Aaron Marcus (Ed.)

Design, User Experience, and Usability

User Experience Design Practice

Third International Conference, DUXU 2014
Held as Part of HCI International 2014
Heraklion, Crete, Greece, June 22-27, 2014
Proceedings, Part IV

 Springer

Volume Editor

Aaron Marcus
Aaron Marcus and Associates, Inc.
1196 Euclid Avenue, Suite 1F, Berkeley, CA 94708-1640, USA
E-mail: aaron.marcus@AMandA.com

ISSN 0302-9743   e-ISSN 1611-3349
ISBN 978-3-319-07637-9   e-ISBN 978-3-319-07638-6
DOI 10.1007/978-3-319-07638-6
Springer Cham Heidelberg New York Dordrecht London

Library of Congress Control Number: 2014939619

LNCS Sublibrary: SL 3 – Information Systems and Application, incl. Internet/Web and HCI

Typesetting: Camera-ready by author, data conversion by Scientific Publishing Services, Chennai, India

Printed on acid-free paper

Springer is part of Springer Science+Business Media (www.springer.com)

Foreword

The 16th International Conference on Human–Computer Interaction, HCI International 2014, was held in Heraklion, Crete, Greece, during June 22–27, 2014, incorporating 14 conferences/thematic areas:

Thematic areas:

- Human–Computer Interaction
- Human Interface and the Management of Information

Affiliated conferences:

- 11th International Conference on Engineering Psychology and Cognitive Ergonomics
- 8th International Conference on Universal Access in Human–Computer Interaction
- 6th International Conference on Virtual, Augmented and Mixed Reality
- 6th International Conference on Cross-Cultural Design
- 6th International Conference on Social Computing and Social Media
- 8th International Conference on Augmented Cognition
- 5th International Conference on Digital Human Modeling and Applications in Health, Safety, Ergonomics and Risk Management
- Third International Conference on Design, User Experience and Usability
- Second International Conference on Distributed, Ambient and Pervasive Interactions
- Second International Conference on Human Aspects of Information Security, Privacy and Trust
- First International Conference on HCI in Business
- First International Conference on Learning and Collaboration Technologies

A total of 4,766 individuals from academia, research institutes, industry, and governmental agencies from 78 countries submitted contributions, and 1,476 papers and 225 posters were included in the proceedings. These papers address the latest research and development efforts and highlight the human aspects of design and use of computing systems. The papers thoroughly cover the entire field of human–computer interaction, addressing major advances in knowledge and effective use of computers in a variety of application areas.

This volume, edited by Aaron Marcus, contains papers focusing on the thematic area of Design, User Experience and Usability, addressing the following major topics:

- DUXU in the enterprise
- Design for diverse target users

- Emotional and persuasion design
- User experience case studies

The remaining volumes of the HCI International 2014 proceedings are:

- Volume 1, LNCS 8510, Human–Computer Interaction: HCI Theories, Methods and Tools (Part I), edited by Masaaki Kurosu
- Volume 2, LNCS 8511, Human–Computer Interaction: Advanced Interaction Modalities and Techniques (Part II), edited by Masaaki Kurosu
- Volume 3, LNCS 8512, Human–Computer Interaction: Applications and Services (Part III), edited by Masaaki Kurosu
- Volume 4, LNCS 8513, Universal Access in Human–Computer Interaction: Design and Development Methods for Universal Access (Part I), edited by Constantine Stephanidis and Margherita Antona
- Volume 5, LNCS 8514, Universal Access in Human–Computer Interaction: Universal Access to Information and Knowledge (Part II), edited by Constantine Stephanidis and Margherita Antona
- Volume 6, LNCS 8515, Universal Access in Human–Computer Interaction: Aging and Assistive Environments (Part III), edited by Constantine Stephanidis and Margherita Antona
- Volume 7, LNCS 8516, Universal Access in Human–Computer Interaction: Design for All and Accessibility Practice (Part IV), edited by Constantine Stephanidis and Margherita Antona
- Volume 8, LNCS 8517, Design, User Experience, and Usability: Theories, Methods and Tools for Designing the User Experience (Part I), edited by Aaron Marcus
- Volume 9, LNCS 8518, Design, User Experience, and Usability: User Experience Design for Diverse Interaction Platforms and Environments (Part II), edited by Aaron Marcus
- Volume 10, LNCS 8519, Design, User Experience, and Usability: User Experience Design for Everyday Life Applications and Services (Part III), edited by Aaron Marcus
- Volume 12, LNCS 8521, Human Interface and the Management of Information: Information and Knowledge Design and Evaluation (Part I), edited by Sakae Yamamoto
- Volume 13, LNCS 8522, Human Interface and the Management of Information: Information and Knowledge in Applications and Services (Part II), edited by Sakae Yamamoto
- Volume 14, LNCS 8523, Learning and Collaboration Technologies: Designing and Developing Novel Learning Experiences (Part I), edited by Panayiotis Zaphiris and Andri Ioannou
- Volume 15, LNCS 8524, Learning and Collaboration Technologies: Technology-rich Environments for Learning and Collaboration (Part II), edited by Panayiotis Zaphiris and Andri Ioannou
- Volume 16, LNCS 8525, Virtual, Augmented and Mixed Reality: Designing and Developing Virtual and Augmented Environments (Part I), edited by Randall Shumaker and Stephanie Lackey

- Volume 17, LNCS 8526, Virtual, Augmented and Mixed Reality: Applications of Virtual and Augmented Reality (Part II), edited by Randall Shumaker and Stephanie Lackey
- Volume 18, LNCS 8527, HCI in Business, edited by Fiona Fui-Hoon Nah
- Volume 19, LNCS 8528, Cross-Cultural Design, edited by P.L. Patrick Rau
- Volume 20, LNCS 8529, Digital Human Modeling and Applications in Health, Safety, Ergonomics and Risk Management, edited by Vincent G. Duffy
- Volume 21, LNCS 8530, Distributed, Ambient, and Pervasive Interactions, edited by Norbert Streitz and Panos Markopoulos
- Volume 22, LNCS 8531, Social Computing and Social Media, edited by Gabriele Meiselwitz
- Volume 23, LNAI 8532, Engineering Psychology and Cognitive Ergonomics, edited by Don Harris
- Volume 24, LNCS 8533, Human Aspects of Information Security, Privacy and Trust, edited by Theo Tryfonas and Ioannis Askoxylakis
- Volume 25, LNAI 8534, Foundations of Augmented Cognition, edited by Dylan D. Schmorrow and Cali M. Fidopiastis
- Volume 26, CCIS 434, HCI International 2014 Posters Proceedings (Part I), edited by Constantine Stephanidis
- Volume 27, CCIS 435, HCI International 2014 Posters Proceedings (Part II), edited by Constantine Stephanidis

I would like to thank the Program Chairs and the members of the Program Boards of all affiliated conferences and thematic areas, listed below, for their contribution to the highest scientific quality and the overall success of the HCI International 2014 Conference.

This conference could not have been possible without the continuous support and advice of the founding chair and conference scientific advisor, Prof. Gavriel Salvendy, as well as the dedicated work and outstanding efforts of the communications chair and editor of *HCI International News*, Dr. Abbas Moallem.

I would also like to thank for their contribution towards the smooth organization of the HCI International 2014 Conference the members of the Human–Computer Interaction Laboratory of ICS-FORTH, and in particular George Paparoulis, Maria Pitsoulaki, Maria Bouhli, and George Kapnas.

April 2014   Constantine Stephanidis
                                        General Chair, HCI International 2014

Organization

Human–Computer Interaction

Program Chair: Masaaki Kurosu, Japan

Jose Abdelnour-Nocera, UK
Sebastiano Bagnara, Italy
Simone Barbosa, Brazil
Adriana Betiol, Brazil
Simone Borsci, UK
Henry Duh, Australia
Xiaowen Fang, USA
Vicki Hanson, UK
Wonil Hwang, Korea
Minna Isomursu, Finland
Yong Gu Ji, Korea
Anirudha Joshi, India
Esther Jun, USA
Kyungdoh Kim, Korea

Heidi Krömker, Germany
Chen Ling, USA
Chang S. Nam, USA
Naoko Okuizumi, Japan
Philippe Palanque, France
Ling Rothrock, USA
Naoki Sakakibara, Japan
Dominique Scapin, France
Guangfeng Song, USA
Sanjay Tripathi, India
Chui Yin Wong, Malaysia
Toshiki Yamaoka, Japan
Kazuhiko Yamazaki, Japan
Ryoji Yoshitake, Japan

Human Interface and the Management of Information

Program Chair: Sakae Yamamoto, Japan

Alan Chan, Hong Kong
Denis A. Coelho, Portugal
Linda Elliott, USA
Shin'ichi Fukuzumi, Japan
Michitaka Hirose, Japan
Makoto Itoh, Japan
Yen-Yu Kang, Taiwan
Koji Kimita, Japan
Daiji Kobayashi, Japan

Hiroyuki Miki, Japan
Shogo Nishida, Japan
Robert Proctor, USA
Youngho Rhee, Korea
Ryosuke Saga, Japan
Katsunori Shimohara, Japan
Kim-Phuong Vu, USA
Tomio Watanabe, Japan

Engineering Psychology and Cognitive Ergonomics

Program Chair: Don Harris, UK

Guy Andre Boy, USA
Shan Fu, P.R. China
Hung-Sying Jing, Taiwan
Wen-Chin Li, Taiwan
Mark Neerincx, The Netherlands
Jan Noyes, UK
Paul Salmon, Australia

Axel Schulte, Germany
Siraj Shaikh, UK
Sarah Sharples, UK
Anthony Smoker, UK
Neville Stanton, UK
Alex Stedmon, UK
Andrew Thatcher, South Africa

Universal Access in Human–Computer Interaction

Program Chairs: Constantine Stephanidis, Greece, and Margherita Antona, Greece

Julio Abascal, Spain
Gisela Susanne Bahr, USA
João Barroso, Portugal
Margrit Betke, USA
Anthony Brooks, Denmark
Christian Bühler, Germany
Stefan Carmien, Spain
Hua Dong, P.R. China
Carlos Duarte, Portugal
Pier Luigi Emiliani, Italy
Qin Gao, P.R. China
Andrina Granić, Croatia
Andreas Holzinger, Austria
Josette Jones, USA
Simeon Keates, UK

Georgios Kouroupetroglou, Greece
Patrick Langdon, UK
Barbara Leporini, Italy
Eugene Loos, The Netherlands
Ana Isabel Paraguay, Brazil
Helen Petrie, UK
Michael Pieper, Germany
Enrico Pontelli, USA
Jaime Sanchez, Chile
Alberto Sanna, Italy
Anthony Savidis, Greece
Christian Stary, Austria
Hirotada Ueda, Japan
Gerhard Weber, Germany
Harald Weber, Germany

Virtual, Augmented and Mixed Reality

Program Chairs: Randall Shumaker, USA, and Stephanie Lackey, USA

Roland Blach, Germany
Sheryl Brahnam, USA
Juan Cendan, USA
Jessie Chen, USA
Panagiotis D. Kaklis, UK

Hirokazu Kato, Japan
Denis Laurendeau, Canada
Fotis Liarokapis, UK
Michael Macedonia, USA
Gordon Mair, UK

Jooc San Martin, Spain   Christopher Stapleton, USA
Tabitha Peck, USA   Gregory Welch, USA
Christian Sandor, Australia

Cross-Cultural Design

Program Chair: P.L. Patrick Rau, P.R. China

Yee-Yin Choong, USA   Sheau-Farn Max Liang, Taiwan
Paul Fu, USA   Katsuhiko Ogawa, Japan
Zhiyong Fu, P.R. China   Tom Plocher, USA
Pin-Chao Liao, P.R. China   Huatong Sun, USA
Dyi-Yih Michael Lin, Taiwan   Emil Tso, P.R. China
Rungtai Lin, Taiwan   Hsiu-Ping Yueh, Taiwan
Ta-Ping (Robert) Lu, Taiwan   Liang (Leon) Zeng, USA
Liang Ma, P.R. China   Jia Zhou, P.R. China
Alexander Mädche, Germany

Online Communities and Social Media

Program Chair: Gabriele Meiselwitz, USA

Leonelo Almeida, Brazil   Anthony Norcio, USA
Chee Siang Ang, UK   Portia Pusey, USA
Aneesha Bakharia, Australia   Panote Siriaraya, UK
Ania Bobrowicz, UK   Stefan Stieglitz, Germany
James Braman, USA   Giovanni Vincenti, USA
Farzin Deravi, UK   Yuanqiong (Kathy) Wang, USA
Carsten Kleiner, Germany   June Wei, USA
Niki Lambropoulos, Greece   Brian Wentz, USA
Soo Ling Lim, UK

Augmented Cognition

**Program Chairs: Dylan D. Schmorrow, USA,
and Cali M. Fidopiastis, USA**

Ahmed Abdelkhalek, USA   Rosario Cannavò, Italy
Robert Atkinson, USA   Joseph Cohn, USA
Monique Beaudoin, USA   Andrew J. Cowell, USA
John Blitch, USA   Martha Crosby, USA
Alenka Brown, USA   Wai-Tat Fu, USA

Rodolphe Gentili, USA
Frederick Gregory, USA
Michael W. Hail, USA
Monte Hancock, USA
Fei Hu, USA
Ion Juvina, USA
Joe Keebler, USA
Philip Mangos, USA
Rao Mannepalli, USA
David Martinez, USA
Yvonne R. Masakowski, USA
Santosh Mathan, USA
Ranjeev Mittu, USA

Keith Niall, USA
Tatana Olson, USA
Debra Patton, USA
June Pilcher, USA
Robinson Pino, USA
Tiffany Poeppelman, USA
Victoria Romero, USA
Amela Sadagic, USA
Anna Skinner, USA
Ann Speed, USA
Robert Sottilare, USA
Peter Walker, USA

Digital Human Modeling and Applications in Health, Safety, Ergonomics and Risk Management

Program Chair: Vincent G. Duffy, USA

Giuseppe Andreoni, Italy
Daniel Carruth, USA
Elsbeth De Korte, The Netherlands
Afzal A. Godil, USA
Ravindra Goonetilleke, Hong Kong
Noriaki Kuwahara, Japan
Kang Li, USA
Zhizhong Li, P.R. China

Tim Marler, USA
Jianwei Niu, P.R. China
Michelle Robertson, USA
Matthias Rötting, Germany
Mao-Jiun Wang, Taiwan
Xuguang Wang, France
James Yang, USA

Design, User Experience, and Usability

Program Chair: Aaron Marcus, USA

Sisira Adikari, Australia
Claire Ancient, USA
Arne Berger, Germany
Jamie Blustein, Canada
Ana Boa-Ventura, USA
Jan Brejcha, Czech Republic
Lorenzo Cantoni, Switzerland
Marc Fabri, UK
Luciane Maria Fadel, Brazil
Tricia Flanagan, Hong Kong
Jorge Frascara, Mexico

Federico Gobbo, Italy
Emilie Gould, USA
Rüdiger Heimgärtner, Germany
Brigitte Herrmann, Germany
Steffen Hess, Germany
Nouf Khashman, Canada
Fabiola Guillermina Noël, Mexico
Francisco Rebelo, Portugal
Kerem Rızvanoğlu, Turkey
Marcelo Soares, Brazil
Carla Spinillo, Brazil

Distributed, Ambient and Pervasive Interactions

**Program Chairs: Norbert Streitz, Germany,
and Panos Markopoulos, The Netherlands**

Juan Carlos Augusto, UK
Jose Bravo, Spain
Adrian Cheok, UK
Boris de Ruyter, The Netherlands
Anind Dey, USA
Dimitris Grammenos, Greece
Nuno Guimaraes, Portugal
Achilles Kameas, Greece
Javed Vassilis Khan, The Netherlands
Shin'ichi Konomi, Japan
Carsten Magerkurth, Switzerland

Ingrid Mulder, The Netherlands
Anton Nijholt, The Netherlands
Fabio Paternó, Italy
Carsten Röcker, Germany
Teresa Romao, Portugal
Albert Ali Salah, Turkey
Manfred Tscheligi, Austria
Reiner Wichert, Germany
Woontack Woo, Korea
Xenophon Zabulis, Greece

Human Aspects of Information Security, Privacy and Trust

**Program Chairs: Theo Tryfonas, UK,
and Ioannis Askoxylakis, Greece**

Claudio Agostino Ardagna, Italy
Zinaida Benenson, Germany
Daniele Catteddu, Italy
Raoul Chiesa, Italy
Bryan Cline, USA
Sadie Creese, UK
Jorge Cuellar, Germany
Marc Dacier, USA
Dieter Gollmann, Germany
Kirstie Hawkey, Canada
Jaap-Henk Hoepman, The Netherlands
Cagatay Karabat, Turkey
Angelos Keromytis, USA
Ayako Komatsu, Japan
Ronald Leenes, The Netherlands
Javier Lopez, Spain
Steve Marsh, Canada

Gregorio Martinez, Spain
Emilio Mordini, Italy
Yuko Murayama, Japan
Masakatsu Nishigaki, Japan
Aljosa Pasic, Spain
Milan Petković, The Netherlands
Joachim Posegga, Germany
Jean-Jacques Quisquater, Belgium
Damien Sauveron, France
George Spanoudakis, UK
Kerry-Lynn Thomson, South Africa
Julien Touzeau, France
Theo Tryfonas, UK
João Vilela, Portugal
Claire Vishik, UK
Melanie Volkamer, Germany

HCI in Business

Program Chair: Fiona Fui-Hoon Nah, USA

Andreas Auinger, Austria
Michel Avital, Denmark
Traci Carte, USA
Hock Chuan Chan, Singapore
Constantinos Coursaris, USA
Soussan Djamasbi, USA
Brenda Eschenbrenner, USA
Nobuyuki Fukawa, USA
Khaled Hassanein, Canada
Milena Head, Canada
Susanna (Shuk Ying) Ho, Australia
Jack Zhenhui Jiang, Singapore
Jinwoo Kim, Korea
Zoonky Lee, Korea
Honglei Li, UK
Nicholas Lockwood, USA
Eleanor T. Loiacono, USA
Mei Lu, USA

Scott McCoy, USA
Brian Mennecke, USA
Robin Poston, USA
Lingyun Qiu, P.R. China
Rene Riedl, Austria
Matti Rossi, Finland
April Savoy, USA
Shu Schiller, USA
Hong Sheng, USA
Choon Ling Sia, Hong Kong
Chee-Wee Tan, Denmark
Chuan Hoo Tan, Hong Kong
Noam Tractinsky, Israel
Horst Treiblmaier, Austria
Virpi Tuunainen, Finland
Dezhi Wu, USA
I-Chin Wu, Taiwan

Learning and Collaboration Technologies

Program Chairs: Panayiotis Zaphiris, Cyprus, and Andri Ioannou, Cyprus

Ruthi Aladjem, Israel
Abdulaziz Aldaej, UK
John M. Carroll, USA
Maka Eradze, Estonia
Mikhail Fominykh, Norway
Denis Gillet, Switzerland
Mustafa Murat Inceoglu, Turkey
Pernilla Josefsson, Sweden
Marie Joubert, UK
Sauli Kiviranta, Finland
Tomaž Klobučar, Slovenia
Elena Kyza, Cyprus
Maarten de Laat, The Netherlands
David Lamas, Estonia

Edmund Laugasson, Estonia
Ana Loureiro, Portugal
Katherine Maillet, France
Nadia Pantidi, UK
Antigoni Parmaxi, Cyprus
Borzoo Pourabdollahian, Italy
Janet C. Read, UK
Christophe Reffay, France
Nicos Souleles, Cyprus
Ana Luísa Torres, Portugal
Stefan Trausan-Matu, Romania
Aimilia Tzanavari, Cyprus
Johnny Yuen, Hong Kong
Carmen Zahn, Switzerland

External Reviewers

Ilia Adami, Greece
Iosif Klironomos, Greece
Maria Korozi, Greece
Vassilis Kouroumalis, Greece

Asterios Leonidis, Greece
George Margetis, Greece
Stavroula Ntoa, Greece
Nikolaos Partarakis, Greece

HCI International 2015

The 15th International Conference on Human–Computer Interaction, HCI International 2015, will be held jointly with the affiliated conferences in Los Angeles, CA, USA, in the Westin Bonaventure Hotel, August 2–7, 2015. It will cover a broad spectrum of themes related to HCI, including theoretical issues, methods, tools, processes, and case studies in HCI design, as well as novel interaction techniques, interfaces, and applications. The proceedings will be published by Springer. More information will be available on the conference website: http://www.hcii2015.org/

General Chair
Professor Constantine Stephanidis
University of Crete and ICS-FORTH
Heraklion, Crete, Greece
E-mail: cs@ics.forth.gr

Table of Contents – Part IV

DUXU in the Enterprise

Design for Diverse Target Users

Emotional and Persuasion Design

User Experience Case Studies

DUXU in the Enterprise

Methodological Framework for Control Centres Evaluation and Optimization

Ana Almeida[1,2,3], Francisco Rebelo[1,2], and Paulo Noriega[1,2]

[1] Centre for Architecture, Urban Planning and Design (CIAUD)
Rua Sá Nogueira, Pólo Universitário, Alto da Ajuda, 1349-055 Lisboa, Portugal
[2] Ergonomics Laboratory, FMH-Universidade de Lisboa
Estrada da Costa 1499-002, Cruz Quebrada – Dafundo, Portugal
[3] CAPES Foundation, Ministry of Education of Brazil, Brasília - DF 70040-020, Brazil
analuciaalmeida1@yahoo.com.br, Frebelo@fmh.ulisboa.pt,
paulonoriega@gmail.com

Abstract. Workers in control centers often pay attention to a large amount of information from several sources and must be able to identify, at all times, the system state to, in an emergency, take correct decisions. In this context, this article aims to present a preliminary framework for the development of a virtual reality simulator for the study of control centres in order to prevent Human errors occurrence. It will also be presented an example of the framework use to study the excessive number of alarms in a railway control centres. The paper discuss the next steps of this work, the evaluation of it sensitivity and the usability characteristics of the VR simulator inside to our framework.

Keywords: framework, virtual reality, control centre, simulator.

1 Introduction

Control centres are complex structures where the operator performs to maintain the routine of the process, being extremely important identify factors that may lead to errors that affect the process and define actions to reduce its occurrence. People in control must often pay attention to a large amount of information from a variety of sources and must be able to identify, at all times, the system state to, in a contingency, take correct decisions. While technologies for control and supervision make operator's work more efficient and proactive, the requirement for a rapid response to the high volume of information available in modern control centres may impose heavy demands on the operator's, influencing its performance. The amount of physical and mental resources that the operator applies when performing a specific refers to that task workload [1]. The workload resources that are available are fundamental concept when considering individual performance within complex systems [2].

Some factors have particular relevance in control centers as an intervening condition to failure. Aspects related to the physical, organizational and personal environment may interfere with the operator performance. Literature highlights problems,

A. Marcus (Ed.): DUXU 2014, Part IV, LNCS 8520, pp. 3–11, 2014.

such as: high workload [2],[3],[4],[5],[6],[7] and temporal pressure [8]; fatigue and stress, regarding personal aspects; poor design equipment, temperature [9],[10]; lighting [11]; noises [10],[11], among other aspects. In this context, the motivation for the development of this paper comes from the occurrence of those problems in control centres that can lead to errors that result in accidents and incidents [9]. This article aims to present a preliminary framework for the development of a simulator for the study of control centres in order to prevent errors occurrence. It will also be presented an example of the framework use to study the excessive number of alarms in a railway control centres.

2   Framework

The preliminary framework (figure 1) of a Virtual Reality (VR) based simulator development for evaluation and control centers optimization can be summarized in four steps:

2.1   Data Gathering

This phase aims to characterize the control centers, in order to know the operation modes of devices, the working conditions and the major issues that may be responsible for accidents.

This phase is dependent on the nature of the study being undertaken. In experimental studies, data may be used from literature that report problems and conditions related to accidents occurrence. In field studies within organizations, data refer to real condition from the work tasks and activities analysis. It should, however, be, whenever possible, a balance between the data obtained from the literature and those obtained in a real work situation.

Diverse methods may be used to assess the control center work conditions. In particular, the following techniques can be applied: physiological measurements - to provide information about physiological states of the controllers; subjective rating scales - to provide information on how employees subjectively assess different aspects of work conditions and mental workload; performance assessment - to evaluate human mental and psychomotor performance under given work conditions, e.g. in order to assess decrements or variations in performance due to the effects of increasing mental workload; task analysis - to assess task elements, physical and psychosocial work conditions.

2.2   Problem Occurrence

This phase aims at defining the problem under study. Based on the analysis of data collected in the previous phase, the issues that might endanger persons, workers and control center safety are ranked. Relationship chains are also established among identified problems by defining a set of problems. At the end, relations are established among the problems and the characteristics of the control center.

This phase culminates in the identification of a problem or a set of interrelated problems and their association with the following aspects:

- Objects and equipment's size – (e.g. geometrical characteristics of objects and control center equipment);
- Environmental aspects – (e.g. lighting, noise, temperature, color);
- Personal aspects – (e.g. operational modes and level of stress, fatigue, motivation, operators experience);
- Organizational aspects – (e.g. workload, company polices, time pressure).

It is important to state which are only considered those aspects that have a significant impact on the consequences of the problems identified.

2.3 Simulator

This phase aims at developing a simulator to study the problems identified in the previous phase. Elements and variables number, to consider in modeling, are dependent on the type of problem to be studied and optimization sought. In this context, the simulator does not have the entire control centre and operations elements and functionality; it is only an adequate representation of the problem to be studied.

A simulator is composed of two components, the virtual environment and scenery. The virtual environment corresponds to the characteristics of the simulator that can be experienced by the participants, by sight, hearing or tactile, for example: furniture, machinery, types of control devices; displays with information; sound and lighting. It is very important that the virtual environment has consistent reactions to participant actions, allowing high levels of interaction.

The scenario corresponds to the narrative that will be presented to the participant and should be associated with the type of problem to be studied. Is usually associated with a framework in the form of a narrative, which includes the context of the problem occurring and tasks that must be performed by the participants. The scenario creates a quasi real environment of interaction and must allow the participant feel in the situation, so as to have a similar behavior to real situation. For this goal to be achieved, it is necessary that:

- The scenario has levels of detail consistent with the real situation;
- Be created a stream of increasing interaction, that in the beginning, the participant becomes involved with everyday tasks and at the end, is faced with the problem.

The simulations should include abnormal events, such as a fire, which cannot be reproduced in reality. Controlling the amount of time and intensity of the simulated events is a vital necessity for research [12].

Simulators have been used in recent and countless experiments in the railway sector, mostly in studies focused on train drivers. It is an important tool for evaluation, measure of performance or training, under normal conditions or at risk situations [12],[13],[14],[15],[16],[17],[18],[19], being relevant to answer issues about attention, situation awareness, workload, vigilance and fatigue [12].

There are different kinds of simulators, the most advanced represents the whole system and allow interactions very close to the one experienced in real systems, such as aircraft simulators. These models allow the training of pilots and the study of complex situations; however, its financial cost does not justify the development of such simulators for all situations, in particular, as regards control centers. An economic and effective solution is the use of Virtual Reality (VR), because allows the development of effective solutions and cost more bearable by organizations.

VR is an advanced computer interface that involves real-time simulation and interactions through multisensory channels [20]. It allows user to examine from different angles, three-dimensional spaces using three unique features of the RV, the so-called three "Is": Imagination, Interaction and Immersion.

- Imagination – is related to involvement meaning the degree of motivation for the engagement of a person with a certain activity. This involvement can be passive, where there is only the exploitation of the environment; or active, where there is environment interaction.
- Interaction – or manipulation, which is the system's ability to detect user input and respond to its real time commands.
- Immersion – is the feeling of being inside the virtual environment and not just feels watching from outside environment.

According to the official encyclopedic definition, VR is

"the use of computer modeling and simulation that enables a person to interact with an artificial three-dimensional (3D) visual or other sensory environment. VR applications immerse the user in a computer-generated environment that simulates reality through the use of interactive devices, which send and receive information and are worn as goggles, headsets, gloves, or body suits. In a typical VR format, a user wearing a helmet with a stereoscopic screen views animated images of a simulated environment." [21]

VR presents features such:

- Works with multisensory information (dynamic images, spatial sound, touch and force reaction, etc.) produced and manipulated in real-time;
- Prioritizes real time interaction;
- Requires high graphics, sound and haptics processing capability;
- Uses techniques and resources for graphic, sound and haptic rendering in real time;
- Promotes user actions in 3D environment;
- Uses special devices to multisensory interaction;
- Requires adaptation.

It is in this context that the framework presented in this paper is developed.

2.4   Solution

This phase aims to optimize the control centre characteristics that allow the improvement of the situation responsible for the problem. Thus, changes are implemented in the virtual environment characteristics (e.g.: type or number of commands, number and amount of information on the displays, sound information). Behavioral responses of the participants to these situations, allow checking whether, or not, there are improvements in modeled system performance. This information will be used to propose new changes in the simulator characteristics, until a satisfactory level of performance is achieved.

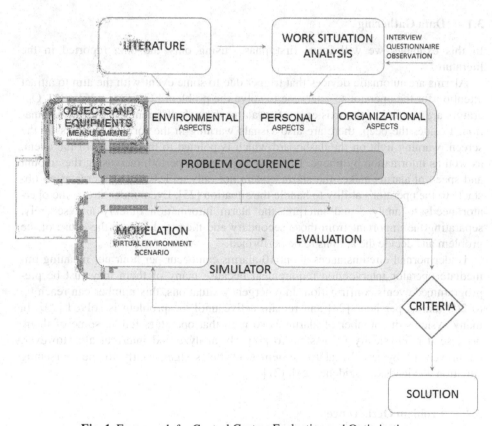

Fig. 1. Framework for Control Centres Evaluation and Optimization

3   One Framework Application: Alarms in a Railway Control Centre

Railway control centre operators actions is to maintain separation between trains on the network [22], then, his/her basic task is monitoring and supervising trains movement, in normal condition, and, intervention when problems occur. In these moments, it is necessary that the operator make the process back to normal using manual skills, mobilizing knowledge to develop strategies to act on diagnosis, fault detection, alarm management and problem resolution.

The context to be addressed refers to the physical environment, including noise and in particular alarms. Noise can arise from several devices installed in control centers, which, although not high, may cause disturbances [10], [11]; however alarms are the most common form of discomfort reported by operators [23].

In this item we will contextualize the use of framework with an example related to a problem that is reported in the literature in railway traffic control centres, the excessive number of alarms at certain times.

3.1   Data Gathering

In this example, we will focus first phase, using only the data reported in the literature.

Alarms are automatic devices that trigger due to some event with the aim to attract attention for the operator to intervene to solve the problem [23], [24], [25], [26]. Operators are notified of the existence of an alarm through different sources of information. Besides the beep, there are also visuals warning in the form of banners on the screen, warning light on the dashboard which is pointed to the location of the event, as well as information by phone. During a contingency period, increasing the amount and speed of alarms makes the alarm system not only useless but also creates an obstacle to the operator's ability to handle the situation [25]. Even under stress, the operator needs to analyze and interpret the alarm information quickly and securely, separating the important from those secondary and then to diagnose the cause of the problem and decide the actions to be performed.

Under normal circumstances about 10 alarms can occur per hour not meaning immediate operator intervention requirement because many of them may just be pre-programmed events confirmation. In emergency situations, this number can reach up to 200 alarms per hour [24] and remain active until the problem is solved [23]. In many systems the number of alarms is so high that operators ignore some of them, because it is physically impossible to properly analyze and interpret all. However, circumvent or bypass the alarm system contributes significantly to the worsening situation and leads to accidents [25], [27].

3.2   Problem Occurrence

"The alarm system must be reserved for events that require operator action" [28]. According to Hollifield and Habibi, one of the main reasons of alarm problems results from systems where alarms are configured without taking into account its main purpose which is to inform the operator that some action is necessary to prevent or mitigate a process disturbance. Problems arise during critical periods, where alarms are denser, where several alarms occur at the same time and among them occur alarms that do not give useful information about the detected anomaly or only indicate system status. In those moments false alarms will distract the operator and stop other tasks where the search for diagnosis is more difficult and requires the prioritization of information processing [29].

3.3   Simulator

What kind of alarm is best suited for the operator to make a decision in a critical situation?

Based on the following assumption will be made modeling scenarios and virtual environment will be taken.

Critical Situation Scenario. After a normal situation, a running over occurred on a line and consequent stoppage of the rail vehicle. Two more vehicles traveling in the same line and approach the vehicle is stopped. Two vehicles are urging to get in line, on grounds of delay. This triggers multiple alarms simultaneously.

The Elements Modeling in Virtual Environment. Considering the previous scenario is modeled a traditional control centre workstation, with table and with information line displays, control commands and audible alarms.

The behaviors to be observed correspond to the actions carried out to solve the problem.

Situation to Optimize. In the first phase is modeled the alarms typically used in control centres to evaluate the possible controllers performance degradation. After evaluating these results, strategies are developed for the modification of the alarms and evaluated the possible increases in operators' performance.

4   Conclusion

This paper described a preliminary framework for the development of a simulator for the study of control centers in order to prevent errors occurrence. An example was presented of the framework using a problem study in the railway control centers, particularly the alarm problem.

The next steps of this work will be the evaluation of it sensitivity and the usability characteristics of the VR simulator. The sensitivity of VR simulator shall be demonstrated by reproducing experimentally controlled variations of a problem. For example, a human error related with a high mental workload, associated with a particular work condition (i.e. number of actions to be performed, or the time constraints, under which the task has to be performed). In the VR simulator, this variation can be developed; creating conditions that can produce different degrees of mental work stress. The efficiency and user satisfaction is an important usability issue of the RV simulator. The efficiency is related with the effort required to create a VR simulator. In practice, we don't need to create a VR simulator with all characteristics of a control center situation, which involve huge resources that could disrupt the study. In addition, the

VR simulator should satisfy the requirements of the users. In this context is important to evaluate in an iterative way the performance of the simulator, against the user requirements.

Acknowledgements. This work was supported by grants BEX 0660-13/2 to Ana Almeida from CAPES Foundation Ministry of Education of Brazil.

References

1. Cañas, J.: Ergonomía en los sistemas de trabajo. UGT-CEC. Granada (2011)
2. Wilms, M.S., Zeilstra, M.P.: Subjective mental workload of Dutch train dispatchers: Validation of IWS in a practical setting. In: Dadashi, N., Scott, A., Wilson, J.R., Mills, A. (eds.), pp. 641–650. Taylor & Francis, London (2013)
3. Balfe, N., Wilson, J.R., Sharples, S., Clarke, T.: Effects of Level of Signalling Automation on Workload and Performance. In: Wilson, J.R., Mills, A., Clarke, T., Rajan, J., Dadashi, N. (eds.), pp. 404–411. Taylor & Francis (2012)
4. Hayden-Smith, N.: The Future of Signaller Workload Assessments in Automated World. In: Dadashi, N., Scott, A., Wilson, J.R., Mills, A. (eds.), pp. 419–426. Taylor & Francis, London (2013)
5. Shanahan, P., Gregory, D., Lowe, E.: Signaller Workload Exploration and Assessment Tool (SWEAT). In: Wilson, J.R., Mills, A., Clarke, T., Rajan, J., Dadashi, N. (eds.), pp. 434–443. Taylor & Francis (2012)
6. Weeda, C., Zeilstra, M.: Prediction of Mental Workload of Monitoring Task. In: Dadashi, N., Scott, A., Wilson, J.R., Mills, A. (eds.), pp. 633–640. Taylor & Francis, London (2013)
7. Zeilstra, M., Bruijn, D.W., Van Der Weide, R.: Development and Implementation of a Predictive Tool for Optimizing Workload of Train Dispatcher. In: Wilson, J.R., Mills, A., Clarke, T., Rajan, J., Dadashi, N. (eds.), pp. 444–453. Taylor & Francis (2012)
8. Read, G.J.M., Lenné, M.G., Moss, S.A.: Association Between Task, Training and Social Environmental Factors and Error Types Involved in Rail Incidents and Accidents. Accident Analysis and Prevention 48, 416–422 (2012)
9. Baysari, M.T., Mcintoch, A.S., Wilson, J.R.: Understanding the Human Factors Contribution to Railway Accidents and Incidents in Australia. Accident Analysis and Prevention 40, 1750–1757 (2008)
10. Nicholl, A.: Environmental Factors in the Control Room. In: Ivergard, T., Hunt, B. (eds.), 2nd edn., pp. 177–199 (2009)
11. Hénique, E., Lindegaard, S., Hunt, B.: Design of Large and Complex Display Systems. In: Ivergard, T., Hunt, B. (eds.), 2nd edn., pp. 83–130 (2009)
12. Maag, C., Schmitz, M.: Assessment of Train Drivers' Performance in a Driving Simulator. In: Wilson, J.R., Mills, A., Clarke, T., Rajan, J., Dadashi, N. (eds.), pp. 136–145. Taylor & Francis (2012)
13. Albrecht, T., Gassel, C.: Efficient Control of Passenger Railways: Testing Advice and Information System in a Driving Simulator. In: Wilson, J.R., Mills, A., Clarke, T., Rajan, J., Dadashi, N. (eds.), pp. 117–125. Taylor & Francis (2012)
14. Egea, B.G., Holgado, P.C., Suárez, C.G.: Human Factors Integration in Rail Simulators. In: Wilson, J.R., Mills, A., Clarke, T., Rajan, J., Dadashi, N. (eds.), pp. 188–193. Taylor & Francis (2012)

15. Hammerl, M., et al.: From a Testing Laboratory for Railway Technical Components to a Human Factors Simulation Environment. In: Wilson, J.R., Mills, A., Clarke, T., Rajan, J., Dadashi, N. (eds.), pp. 154–164. Taylor & Francis (2012)
16. Naweed, A., Hockey, G.R.J., Clarke, S.D.: Designing Simulator Tools for Rail Research: The Case Study of a Train Driving Microworld. Applied Ergonomics 44, 445–454 (2013)
17. Rentzch, M., et al.: Simulator Tests of a Harmonised European Driver's Desk. In: Wilson, J.R., Mills, A., Clarke, T., Rajan, J., Dadashi, N. (eds.), pp. 146–153. Taylor & Francis (2012)
18. Wada, K., Ueda, M.: Emotional Responses to Trouble Events on a Train-Driving Simulator. In: Human Factors and Ergonomics Society 56th Annual Meeting, pp. 1997–2001 (2012)
19. Yates, T.K., Sharples, S.: Determining the Effect of Simulator Configuration in a VR Train Driver System. In: Wilson, J.R., Mills, A., Clarke, T., Rajan, J., Dadashi, N. (eds.), pp. 107–116. Taylor & Francis (2012)
20. Burdea, G., Coiffet, P.: Virtual Reality Technology, 2nd edn. John Wiley & Sons (2003)
21. Encyclopædia Britannica,
    http://www.britannica.com/EBchecked/topic/630181/
    virtual-reality-VR
22. Patrick, C., Balfe, N., Wilson, J.R., Houghton, R.: Signaller information use in traffic regulation decisions. In: Dadashi, N., Scott, A., Wilson, J.R., Mills, A. (eds.), pp. 409–418. Taylor & Francis, London (2013)
23. Bransby, M.L., Jenkinson, J.: The Management of Alarm System: A Review of Current Practice in the Procurement, Design and Management of Alarm System in the Chemical and Power Industries. Health and Safety Executive (1998)
24. Dadashi, N., Wilson, J.R., Golightly, D., Sharples, S., Clarke, T.: Practical use of Work Analysis to Support Rail Electrical Control Rooms: A Case of Alarm Handling. J. Rail and Rapid Transit. 227, 148–160 (2012)
25. Hollifield, B.R., Habibi, E.: The History and Nature of the Alarm Problem. In: Hollifield, B.R., Habibi, E. (eds.), pp. 7–12 (2007)
26. Huang, F.-H., et al.: Evaluation and comparison of alarm reset modes in advanced control room of nuclear power plants. Safety Science 44, 935–946 (2006)
27. Hollifield, B.R., Habibi, E.: How do you Justify Alarm Management? In: Hollifield, B.R., Habibi, E. (eds.), pp. 13–18 (2007)
28. Hollifield, B.R., Habibi, E.: What Should be an Alarm? In: Hollifield, B.R., Habibi, E. (eds.), pp. 19–26 (2007)
29. Woods, D.D.: The Alarm Problem and Directed Attention in Dynamic Fault Management. Ergonomics 38, 2371–2393 (1995)

A UX Maturity Model: Effective Introduction of UX into Organizations

Lorraine Chapman and Scott Plewes

Macadamian Technologies
Gatineau, Quebec. Canada
{lorraine,scott}@macadamian.com

Abstract. Getting products out the door with a fantastic user experience (UX) is becoming increasingly more important in all aspects of the business world. Large companies have raised the bar in consumer products in terms of UX design, which has leaked into non-consumer organizations and contexts. The same people, who are also consumers, are now going to work with equally high expectations in their enterprise applications or even using their "consumer" product at work. Naturally, organizations that create products have responded by hiring consultants or professional UX designers. Yet, despite having the right skills, organizations are not necessarily getting the results they want. Achieving great UX design is not just a function or talent of *individuals*, it is an organizational characteristic. Understanding the organization's "maturity" level is a necessary first step for improving the effective delivery of UX design and for enabling the organization to advance to the proverbial "next level."

Keywords: UX maturity, maturity models usability, user-centered design, user satisfaction.

1 Introduction

"I think in order to design great products, you need to have the culture in place."

Cordell-Ratzlaff, 2010

Organizations are more and more seeing the value of hiring user experience (UX) professionals and incorporating user-centered design. More and more programs at universities are cropping up than ever before, to meet the demands in industry. Large name companies such as Google and Apple have incorporated UX design as a centerpiece of their successes. There have been a number of well-known treatises on the introduction of usability into an organization. For example Shaffer's work [1] documents some of the key components organizations must have in place to institutionalize usability. While not in conflict with Shaffer's ideas, here we focus more on how to effectively recognize what stage and organization is in with regards to usability and the key areas of focus for transitioning to the next stage.

A. Marcus (Ed.): DUXU 2014, Part IV, LNCS 8520, pp. 12–22, 2014.
© Springer International Publishing Switzerland 2014

There is a belief in the business value of UX design that simply did not exist 15 – 20 years ago [2]. There are more individuals trained and capable of excellence in UX design. However, beliefs and skilled UX resources are not enough to ensure that the UX design aspirations and goals for an organization are met. The user experience of a product is not the result of a UX designer alone – it is a result of how the organization as a whole executes on the product creation. There are a number of ways of decomposing the elements of user experience design and success. For the purposes of this paper, we will consider the following construct: Product value and user experience largely comes from two essential values.

1. An *emotional* value ("I love my new smartphone.")
2. A *utilitarian* value ("I can call and text my friends from anywhere.")

These two values are linked for most products in the sense that attaining a positive emotional response – over the long term – is difficult without at least some utilitarian value. We see emotional and utilitarian values delivered by three aspects of design:

1. Aesthetics
The product literally "looks good." People will often describe the aesthetics in non-scientific terms such as "slick," "clean," and "cool." When explored more deeply, these characteristics indicate at least some elements of aesthetics influencing their responses [3].

2. Functionality
The product allows the user to accomplish a goal that they value. For example, a user can scan their computer for a virus, make a phone call, or print a document. However, having functionality that is of value by no means ensures that it is easy to accomplish, easy to discover, more efficient or satisfying to use.

3. Usability
Usability is the manner in which functionality is delivered and experienced by the user. Is it effective, efficient, satisfying, and simple? [4]

It is not uncommon for some companies to focus primarily on the utilitarian value of the product and, in particular, on the functional aspect of the product design. For many product development program, success is defined by the number features that can be fit into each release cycle. Yet a great product delivers a user experience that combines aesthetics, functionality and usability to meet both the user's emotional and utilitarian needs. In discussing UX maturity, we are really postulating the following two key points:

- Organizations higher up on the UX maturity scale are more able to deliver effectively to the combination of functionality, aesthetics, and usability that is appropriate for their business goals.
- Organizations at certain levels of maturity implement processes, capabilities directed towards improved success in UX design that is appropriate for their level of maturity. That is a "stage 2" company, cannot jump to a "stage 5" design process.

There is an evolutionary process associated to moving through the different stages of UX maturity.

Knowing and understanding an organization's true UX goals and its level of maturity can guide decisions ranging from where an organization seeks help (by hiring internally or using consultants), to what processes they use and implement, and how decisions are made.

In our experience, there are six key indicators of UX maturity.

1. The *timing of UX* involvement in the design and development process. The earlier UX is involved, the more mature the company.
2. The *UX expertise and resources* in house and/or ability to bring in UX expertise quickly as needed.
3. The use of appropriate *techniques and deliverables* to obtain and understand user input and capture UX design.
4. The *leadership and culture* in the company. How well the leaders and company as a whole appreciate the value and necessity of UX design from a business perspective.
5. The degree to which UX processes are *connected and integrated with other* corporate processes that enable individuals to work together to create the user experience of the product(s).
6. *Design thinking is applied in the broadest perspective* possible to drive consistent customer experience.

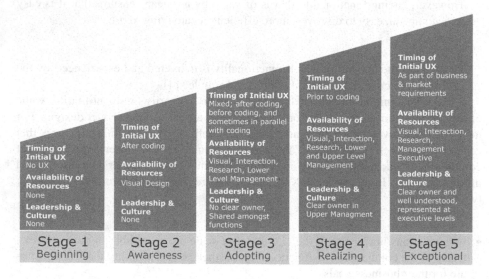

Fig. 1. The Stages of UX Maturity Model

Considering these criteria, we have created a model for assessing an organizations level of UX maturity (see Fig. 1). This is one model by which organizations can assess their level of UX maturity; however, there are other ways of looking at the UX maturity of a company, other factors or weighting of factors that could be considered [5]. The key factor is using models that can help with understanding a complex situation, making decisions and gaining insights [6]. The relevance in this model is less about exactly what stage an organization is in, and more about the insights and ideas decision-makers and influencers can utilize by applying this model to their own organization. For this reason, rather than focusing on absolutely measuring maturity, the model focuses on indicators of maturity and relating these indicators to stages of UX maturity. The intention is that the indicators will spur decision makers into action. If an organization aspires to "stage 5" UX goals, but there are several indicators that suggest the organization is at "stage 2," decision-makers can use the indicators to assess how they may progress to the next level.

2   Stage 1: Beginning

To the extent an organization thinks about UX design at all, at this stage an organization will typically see it simply as visual design. Design is perceived as something to be applied on top of the product's functionality. For software, it is generally addressed at or near the end of coding. There are no professional UX designers in house; often developers are responsible for the UX design. There may not even be product management, or product management is relegated to making suggestions about the design or functionality to developers. Essentially this means all the key indicators are "dark"; there is no expertise, techniques, or design-thinking culture that would suggest UX design is even being attempted in a meaningful way.

2.1   Implications

Products must differentiate themselves primarily on functionality or other factors outside of the direct user experience. This includes customer support, salesmanship, or the ability to technically integrate with other products or systems. Products created in this way are at high risk of displacement if competitors are able to match their primary value propositions while differentiating through a superior user experience. For example, an information management system at a hospital may be valued and purchased because it can "hook into" other hospital management systems. However, if it is cumbersome to use and causes significant overhead to the personnel who are interacting with it, another compatible product offering a better experience of information management could eventually displace it.

2.2   Key Signs of an Organization at This Stage

- UX design is almost never talked about or it is discussed only in terms of graphical design.
- Users are not consulted in the product design and development process.
- If any user suggestions or complaints are gathered, they are not critically evaluated. They are either dismissed or implemented verbatim.
- Any UX design activities have very little formal structure (developers do the necessary elements of screen layout) and are probably not considered part of a UX design activity.
- There are no UX design goals tied to business objectives.
- Product management may be non-existent or minimal.

2.3   Critical Success Factor to Achieve the Next Stage

Taking the first step towards UX design involves ensuring that the relevant business issues are correctly identified as being UX design-related. This awareness is often created through a combination of a significant "shock" event (for example a competitor wins a major sale because of their UX design) along with some degree of education and awareness occurring within the organization.

3   Stage 2: Awareness

At this stage, the organization may be considering UX design, but applying very little structure around UX activities. Often there is a significant amount of misunderstanding surrounding the real nature of UX design. Therefore, usually there are no UX professionals employed in the organization, though an outside "guru" may be brought in or consulted. UX design improvements or insights gained during the product design phase are often implemented in bits and pieces in the final product.

3.1   Implications

Out in the marketplace, the products must still differentiate themselves primarily on functionality or other aspects of the business beyond the direct product experience. The risk of competitive displacement remains high if competitors can match the key value propositions while differentiating themselves on user experience. Organizations at this stage must decide to what extent they wish to invest in introducing formal UX processes and practices in order to forestall the competition.

3.2   Key Signs of an Organization at This Stage

- UX design is a "hot" topic of debate for at least some projects.
- People are starting to make design decisions or suggestions based on articles, a conference or seminar attended or a personal interpretation of UX.

- Employees conduct design reviews with considerable discussion, yet become frustrated with the limited progress being made and disagreement on how to actually resolve UX design issues.
- Most user requirements are confined to marketing input or functional improvements.
- There is little user feedback or it is limited to asking users their opinions on design or functionality.
- UX design goals are general or hard to measure (for example, "the interface should be intuitive and straightforward").
- A UX professional is consulted during a projects too late in the process.
- There is inconsistent awareness and buy-in to making UX design investments, such as training, beyond a few people.

3.3 Critical Success Factor to Achieve the Next Stage

In this stage, organizations have an awareness of UX design having potential business value, but minimal to little understanding of what that means. Education is required to pivot the organization to higher maturity. While training is useful, it typically does not include decision makers and, therefore, an organizational understanding of UX design is not achieved. At this stage, organizations should seek to launch a pilot project, overseen by experts, with a clear connection between UX design goals and a business objective. It is this connection that pulls in the key decision makers and allows them to see the value of UX design; otherwise, organizational maturity may stagnate.

In our experience the transition from this stage to the next is the most difficult and most crucial, largely because it requires the most significant change in company. As the Director of Product for a company in the aircraft industry put it, "this is simply not in our DNA". Not only was it necessary to determine the right activities and projects to focus on, but also at least as much time has been (and is being) spent understanding individual challenges, agendas, concerns and perspectives of key decision makers and stakeholders. The effort is less on understanding what the right logistics are, and more about incorporating and dealing with change in roles and perspectives.

4   Stage 3: Adopting

An organization at this stage is experiencing the growing pains of adopting more sophisticated UX practices; some projects run smoothly and experience successful outcomes, while others fail miserably. Typically, there is growing belief among the leadership team of the value of design (although the leaders themselves may have little knowledge of UX or mixed knowledge of UX) and investments are being made in professional hires or contractors/firms. The prospects for using UX design as a competitive differentiator are positive; however, there is a high risk of getting stuck at this stage, or worse, "regressing" to old product design habits. This happens if the occasional project does not go well or new leadership comes in and acts to revert progress in maturity. This stage definitely has expertise in house or consultants involved, although it may not always be making the best use of the resources or UX resources are significantly overloaded in terms of deliverables and responsibilities.

4.1   Implications

Some products are now distinguishing themselves based on UX design, or at least they are not losing to competitive alternatives because of UX shortcomings. Success is still inconsistent across the brand (as is the design), and customers may not associate the company itself with excellence in UX design. However, the organization is starting to realize tangible difference to the business because of the benefits of an improved UX to their products.

4.2   Key Signs of an Organization at This Stage

- There have been some successful products recently where the UX design has clearly had positive business impacts.
- UX goals are measurable and clear on some projects. For example, the organization may be establishing user error rate targets, efficiency measurements, and user satisfaction goals.
- Users are regularly consulted on many projects; although perhaps not always in the right ways or in time to inform design decisions.
- The organization still experiences some issues with UX projects. It may be that good UX design is created on paper, but not fully realized in the product.
- There is no senior leadership or management in UX. The UX function may report into Marketing, Product Management or Engineering or is distributed between individuals across projects.
- There is no standard design and development process being practiced across the organization. For example, some projects or parts of the organization may insist on usability testing of products, while others do not.
- Similarly, roles are not standardized throughout the organization. On one project a business analyst may be responsible for understanding user context and motivations; on another project it is a UX researcher.
- There is a lot of discussion about UX design within the organization. Successful products/projects that involved UX design, and competitors who have used UX design as a differentiator, have made executive decision makers take notice. These executives and influence leaders now have strong and differing opinions on product design.
- A common perspective on UX design does not exist throughout the organization. The expertise exists within the company at the project delivery level, not at the executive level.

4.3   Critical Success Factor to Achieve the Next Stage

When it comes to organizations at this stage, moving to the next level means setting clear UX goals for teams on products/projects and requiring accountability from UX experts, as well as assigning empowerment to UX experts. However, the UX experts only are one key component. Related roles need to be defined so that everyone on a project/product feels they can contribute to UX outcomes on a project. Obviously senior leadership and experience is required to help align and co-ordinate UX resources and other functions. Among the best next steps is to augment the management and executive team with senior UX leadership and understanding. If this is not done, then while a desire for quality UX results may be in place, the lack of understanding at the decision-making level can undermine the experts at the less senior levels.

Moving through this stage through to stage 4 and even beyond is less of a challenge of people and change management and more about refining and adding nuances. As a medical company we worked with – who already had a well defined UX process – pointed out, our real value came in enhancing aspects of requirements gathering, subtleties in research methodologies and interpretation of data. This is significantly less challenging than a fundamental change to process and roles. It was more about additional skill sets and methodologies. They then could then incorporate and further on their own for future work.

5   Stage 4: Realizing

Stage 4 organizations, those displaying excellence in their UX design maturity, have moved far beyond discussing and arguing about whether or not it should be part of design and development. They are now more concerned with the nuances or particulars of improvement in UX. UX goals are clearly embedded with the organization's mindset and people understand their roles in the process.

5.1   Implications

The company has a reputation for UX excellence in their products and often wins on this point. It is used as a selling proposition and a differentiator. The company brand is clearly linked to great UX design.

5.2   Key Signs of an Organization at This Stage

- Many examples of successful products where the UX design has clearly had positive business impacts.
- UX goals are measurable and clear on almost all projects.
- UX is no longer viewed as hot topic, rather it has become table stakes. Discussion around UX is more likely to be about the latest techniques, process improvement and how to better incorporate it at all levels of the organization. Discussions amongst key stakeholders are no longer about where UX fits in a process or who is responsible for making design decisions.

- There is senior management leadership and accountability for UX at the same level as product management, development, marketing, sales, and other functions.
- A strong set of practices, processes and guidelines exist that are consistently utilized by project teams.
- If excellence in UX design is sacrificed, it is an intentional trade-off driven by business goals with well-understood consequences.
- Users are regularly consulted for product/projects. Design research with target end users is done consistently with correct techniques.
- UX design is considered at a "product family" or portfolio level and the decision-making processes and development are organized in recognition of this need. Each product is designed with other products that the customer might also use in mind so that the transition is seamless because consistent UX designs are used.
- All functional areas (such as Product Management, UX, Marketing, Engineering) are certain about their roles in the UX design process and understand each other's roles. While UX design experts make UX design decisions, ideas and innovation come from the entire team involved in product design and development.

5.3   Critical Success Factor to Achieve the Next Stage

Organizations at this level have a highly effective level of UX design and it is difficult to move beyond this level of maturity. We do believe, however, there is a natural evolution a company can make. Whether or not it is strictly an evolution of UX design is debatable, but we include it here for completeness. The next step beyond excellence is when the organization realizes that the product experience is just one part of a larger experience delivered to customers. Organizations must start planning complete customer experiences that include, but go beyond, the UX of the product alone. However, to move beyond stage four means understanding from a customer point of view what the experience is with the company as a whole and how the product fits in with that experience. This includes all of the touch points and processes that happen around the product such as, discovering it, buying it, installing it, using it, upgrading it and "sun setting" it.

6   Stage 5: Exceptional

When an organization is exceptional in its strategic implementation of UX design principles, UX design is firmly integrated into all aspects of customer experience – these organizations have fully realized their UX maturity goals and design thinking truly permeates all aspects of the organization. The same type of thinking that went into designing the product experience is present across the board in all customer touch points, although different experts and roles, not just UX designers, will implement it.

6.1   Implications

The company has a "gold standard" reputation for excellence in all aspects of customer experience (for example, marketing, sales, support, product design). This reputation is significant in achieving business goals and maintaining a competitive advantage.

6.2   Key Signs of an Organization at This Stage

- All aspects of Stage 4 product-orient UX excellence are strongly entrenched.
- When designing a product, the whole "ecosystem" of a user's experience with the company/brand is considered.
- UX goals are linked to business objectives with the total customer experience in mind.
- The first thought on UX design in a project is probably more about the overall customer experience rather then the intended user experience for just the product. This manifests itself in up front UX and customer experience research and the creation of artifacts such as customer experience maps.
- There are senior leaders accountable for customer experience and this part of the organization works with all functional groups that create/deliver customer touch points such as, UX designers, marketing, sales, and support.
- Research in UX is strongly coordinated with other customer experience feedback processes.

7   Conclusion

As discussed in the introduction, this 5-stage framework may not exactly match the specifics of a particular organization. In the real world, organizations may display a mix of characteristics from different stages across their organization. Nevertheless, we believe assessing a company against some of these key indicators can provide insights into opportunities and issues that will allow a company to adjust its trajectory and attain its business aspirations that are dependent or related to successful user experiences practices and their execution. Organizations, like people, learn by doing. And to do properly experts need to be hired or consulted. Identifying projects, deliverables, activities are key to progressing. Training, attending talks, reading books, is certainly helpful, but not enough. UX design is no different than any other function in this regard.

References

1. Shaffer, E.: The Institutionalization of Usability: A Step-By-Step Guide. Addison Wesley, New York (2004)
2. Trenner, L., Bawa, J. (eds.): The Politics of Usability: A Practical Guide to Designing Usable Systems in Industry. Springer, Berlin (1998)

3. Lavie, T., Tractinsky, N.: Assessing Dimensions of Perceived Visual Aesthetics of Web Sites. International Journal Human-Computer Studies 60, 269–298 (2004)
4. International Organization for Standardization: Ergonomic requirements for office work with visual display terminals (VDTs) – Part 11: Guidance on usability (ISO Reference No. 9241-11:1998(E)) (1998)
5. Vetrov, Y.: Applied UX Strategy, Part 1: Maturity Models. UX Matters (2013), http://www.uxmatters.com/mt/archives/2013/12/applied-ux-strategy-part-1-maturity-models.php
6. HIMSS Usability TaskForce.: Promoting Usability in Health Organizations: Initial Steps and Progress Toward a Healthcare Usability Maturity Model. Health Information and Management Systems Society (2011)

A Perception Oriented Approach for Usable and Secure Interface Development

Mehmet Göktürk and İbrahim Şişaneci

Gebze Institute of Technology, Gebze, Kocaeli, Turkey
{Gokturk,sisaneci}@gyte.edu.tr

Abstract. Developers generally try to make their systems secure by adding Information Security measures and components to User Interfaces. While applying these measures, usability of interfaces may decrease seriously. Developing secure and usable user interfaces became a necessity due to the fact that security and usability are both indispensable for users. To develop secure and usable interfaces, first, users' perception of information security is analyzed. In this study, An Enhanced Users' Perception of Information Security Model (EUPoIM) and Perception Oriented Usable & Secure Interface Development Model (POSUIDM) are proposed to empower developers in developing both secure and usable user interfaces.

Keywords: Enterprise UX structure and process, security perception, usable security, perception oriented approach.

1 Introduction

With the rapid developments in Information Technology, more complicated information security threats occur in every part of digital life. Many computers and digital devices are exposed to these threats via their interfaces. In order to cope with these, developers generally try to make their systems secure by adding Information Security (InfoSec) measures and components to User Interfaces (UI). As these measures are applied, usability of interfaces may decrease seriously. Developing secure and usable user interfaces became a necessity due to the fact that security and usability are both indispensable requirements for users. To develop secure and usable interfaces, first, users' perception of InfoSec (PoI) must be analyzed. Then, constructing a users' perception model according to the analysis is necessary.

The organization of this paper is as follows. In Section 2, usability and security related work is reviewed briefly. Next, methodology is presented in Section 3. In Section 4, Perception Oriented Approach and motivation of the approach are explained. Moreover, an Enhanced Users' Perception of Information Security Model (EUPoIM) is described with relation among features of user interface design, usability principles and EUPoIM. Next, in Section 5, Perception Oriented Usable & Secure Interface Development Model (POSUIDM) is proposed to empower developers in developing both secure and usable user interfaces. Finally, the conclusions and future work are presented in Section 6.

A. Marcus (Ed.): DUXU 2014, Part IV, LNCS 8520, pp. 23–31, 2014.
© Springer International Publishing Switzerland 2014

2   Literature Review

Usable and Secure Interface Development is an interdisciplinary issue that is closely related with human computer interaction (HCI), information security (InfoSec) and psychology disciplines. Research related this topic can be grouped into three categories such as Usability & Security, Privacy & Security and Perception of information security.

Computers are essential for people, yet most users have a tendency to use easy one regardless of its security. Unfortunately, unsecured systems aren't usable for long due to possible security compromises. Most studies agree that it's necessary to design both secure and usable systems, but there is less agreement about how to reach this goal [1-4].

A balance must be established between these two needs. To provide a balance, a systematic usability analysis and taxonomy are revealed under the main titles of "human factors in information security" and "user resistance against the information security measures" by Schultz in 2001[5].

Two methods have been developed; applying usability to secure systems and applying security to usable systems. However, since both methods do not reach the goal, user-centric security and usability approach has been used by Zurko's rule based user-centric authentication engine, by Fidas's password management and "human in the loop" framework [6-9].

From the perspective of privacy & security studies, an excessive amount of anonymity on the web and in particular the increase in the information sharing issue comes many privacy problems together. Many studies are emphasized why studies on privacy and security is critical today [10, 11].

From the perspective of perception of information security, Huang's study in 2010, one of the important studies on perception of information security, stated that understanding of the people's perception of information security may be possible with revealing how individuals perceive different threats and which factors affect them. In Huang's study, threat based perception of information security can be expressed under the main factors such as knowledge, impact, severity, controllability, possibility and awareness. Computer experience of users also affects their perception significantly where users with more experience concern less security issues. Another output of their work is that users' understandings of type of loss are very different [12].

In addition to above, an interesting e-commerce study proposed design elements that might positively affect user' perception of information security and tested on e-commerce web application [13, 14].

3   Methodology

Usability and Security, both of which are not functional requirements for many applications, cannot be measured directly. As information security can be measured by risk assessment, Usability can be evaluated by usability testing, cognitive walkthrough, heuristic evaluation, paper prototyping and empirical methods such as surveys.

The validity of proposed models, derived from literature research, is tested with usability tests/experiments and surveys in a case study through preparing sample user interfaces as future work.

4   Perception Oriented Approach

Perception is defined as "a major part of human intelligence and a key component in understanding human behavior"[15]. In other words, it is the mechanism with which a person evaluates external inputs, which, in turn, determines the behavioral response. As many human oriented efforts, perception, a key component of human behavior, should be effectively directed [16]. Perception of information security must be taken into account by developers in order to be successful when security & usability components to user interface are applied. Otherwise, these efforts could be ignored by user. Users can be the weakest link in information security chain or a victim of cyber threats. Moreover, they also give up using the system easily. The relationship among users, user interfaces and information security is depicted in the Figure 1. Users' perception varies according to threats and countermeasures on user interfaces. Accordingly, a user interface is evaluated as "secure perceived interface" or "insecure perceived interface" by users usually [17].

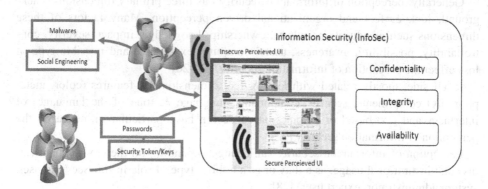

Fig. 1. Users, Threats, Countermeasures, User Interfaces and Information Security Relationship Diagram

4.1   Motivation and Axioms

With guidance of research questions listed below, sample axioms in Table 1 were derived and put forward to evaluate the relationship between user interfaces and perception of information security [18-23].

- How computer users' perception of InfoSec is formed? Which factors affect this perception?
- How will users react as a result of this perception?
- Which design elements/components are related to this perception model and what extent?
- Which factors are supported and what features are included by interfaces?

Table 1. Sample Axioms

Axioms
Education, culture and ownership factors affect the perception of information security.
Interfaces with full of security components or security elements come to the fore has low usability.
I/O components used in the UI and the status of them whether are usable by mouse/keyboard influences the perception of information security.
Color usage in interfaces affects the perception of information security
Metaphor usage in interfaces affects the perception of information security
Whether user interface components are text-based or graphics-based, affects the perception of InfoSec
Perception of information security can be expressed under the main factors such as knowledge, impact, severity, controllability, possibility and awareness.
Factors of users' computer experience and possible type of loss affects the perception of InfoSec
The language and tone of the language used in user interfaces influences the perception of InfoSec
Whether there is a privacy notification in the interface, perception of information security.

Generally, perception of information security has three primary dimensions: background, look & feel and organizational driven perception. Many factors of these dimensions such as education, culture, ownership, knowledge, impact, severity, controllability, possibility, awareness, users' computer experience and possible type of loss affect the perception of information security. [24-26]

In UI side, mostly related with look & feel dimension, UI features (color, metaphor, I/O components, security components, language & tone of the language) of interfaces and text-based or graphics-based design have particular influence on the perception of information security [27].

Perception of information security can change depending on the environment (individual/institutional usage, as a duty or as a hobby) type of role in InfoSec (end user, system administrator, expert user) [28].

4.2   Enhanced Users' Perception of InfoSec Model (EUPoIM)

Enhanced Users' Perception of InfoSec Model (EUPoIM) has been constructed by integrating threat based perception of information security factors with the additional factors expressing the case of "human as an actor in the information security".

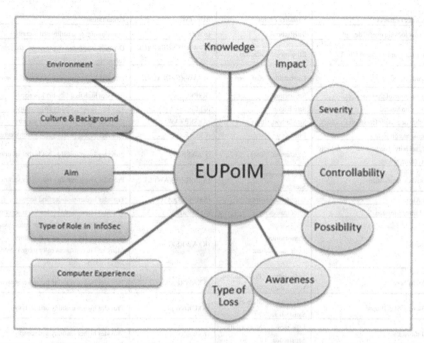

Fig. 2. Enhanced Users' Perception of Information Security Model

These additional factors derived from environment of usage, the role in information security and sample user behaviors such as violating InfoSec rules and operating incorrect actions. For example, many people can respond very diversely to InfoSec notification in the private usage and business environments. In other words, the EU-PoIM deals with both the threat based perception of information security and counter measure based perception of information security.

Relationship among features of user interface design, usability principles and EU-PoIM is shown in Table 2 in short [29-31].

The main factors of usability are learnability[1], utility[2], efficiency[3], memorability[4], error management[5] and satisfaction[6].

---

[1] The ability of the user to discover and understand product capabilities and how to use them.
[2] The completeness and appropriateness of the product in achieving end-user goals.
[3] The ease of use of the product in helping end-users to accomplish their critical tasks.
[4] The extent to which a casual user can remember how a product works and retain proficiency with it.
[5] The degree to which users enjoy using and interacting with the product.
[6] How errors are prevented, recovered from, and managed to minimize loss and user frustration.

Table 2. Relation among features of UI design, usability principles and EUPoIM

Components/Features	Usability Factor	EUPoIM[7]	Explanation
Professional looking overall design	Satisfaction	(AW)(E)(A)	Provides higher usability and security
Text-based or graphics-based UI	Efficiency, Satisfaction	(K)(AW)(E)(CE)(R)(C)(P)(A)	Depends computer experiences and environments.
Self learning features	Learnability, Satisfaction	(K)(AW)(E)(CE)(C)(R)	Provides higher usability but lower security
Language & tone of the language	Satisfaction	(K)(P)(C)(AW)	Provides high usability but low security
Sense of being limited	Satisfaction	(C)(E)	Provides lower usability and security
Availability or State Information Feedback	Satisfaction, Utility	(K)(S)(P)(AW)	Provides higher usability and security
Fast operation completion	Efficiency	(C)(L)(E)(R)	Provides higher usability and lower security
Full of security components or security elements come to fore	Satisfaction, Utility	(K)(I)(S)(C)	Provides lower usability but higher security
Using privacy notification	Error management, Satisfaction	(K)(S)(C)(P)(AW)(L)	Provides lower usability but higher security
Correct Alert	Error management,	(S)(I)(L)(P)(AW)	Provides higher usability and security
Detailed Error Message	Error management	(S)(I)(P)(AW)	Provides higher usability but lower security
Color usage	Memorability, Error management	(K)(AW)(S)(P)(A)	Several different and proper color usage provides higher usability and security. Many and in consistent color usage provides lower usability and security.
Using Metaphors	Learnability, Predictability, Memorability, Satisfaction	(K)(AW)(P)(A)	Provides higher usability but lower security
Using Step by Step Wizard	Efficiency, Memorability, Satisfaction	(K)(C)(AW)	Provides higher usability and security
Using Tabbed Panels	Efficiency, Memorability, Satisfaction	(K)(C)(AW)(A)	Provides higher usability and security
Using Confirmation Dialog	Satisfaction, Error management	(I)(S)(C)(P)(AW)	Provides lower usability but higher security
Using Graphical Password	Memorability, Satisfaction	(C)(AW)(A)	Provides lower usability but higher security
Using virtual keyboard	Memorability, Utility	(C)(AW)(E)	Provides lower usability but higher security
Using components which are able to hide input value	Satisfaction	(S)(C)(AW)(L)(E)	Provides lower usability but higher security
Using components which deactivates keyboard shortcuts or can be controllable by keyboard/mouse	Efficiency, Utility, Memorability	(C)(E)(R)	Provides lower usability but higher security
Using components which are able auto complete/recommend possible values	Learnability, Efficiency	(K)(P)(AW)(E)	Provides higher usability and security

5   Perception Oriented Usable and Secure Interface Development Model (POSUIDM)

Perception Oriented Usable & Secure Interface Development Model (POSUIDM) is based on user-centric security and usability approach (in Figure 3). It starts with identification the need and requirements. First, the aim of UI should be specified and the idea of the product and design requirements should be studied. Then, following stages are listing possible end users and finding a group of sample end users. Then, analyzing the

---

[7] (C) Controllability, (K) Knowledge, (S) Severity, (I) Impact, (P) Possibility, (A) Aim, (AW) Awareness, (E) Environment, (L) Type of Loss, (R) Type of Role, (CE) Computer Experiences.

perception of information security of possible end users is the most important stage in POUIDM. In this stage, background driven, look & feel driven and organizational perceptions of possible end users must be extracted with the help of EUPoIM.

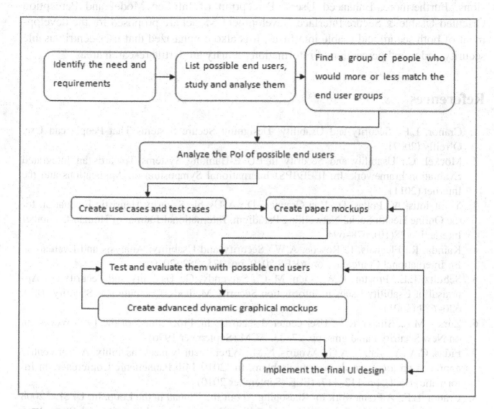

Fig. 3. Perception Oriented Usable & Secure Interface Development Model (POSUIDM)

POUIDM flow continues with creating use cases and test cases including usability test and perception of information security analysis and paper mockups dealing with the result of the perception of information security analysis. Next, testing and evaluation which includes the usability test and perception of information security analysis reviews besides functionality tests and creating advanced dynamic graphical mockups are iterative stages which provide good feedbacks to previous stages. Finally, implementation is performed based on the Usable & Secure perceived UI design.

6   Discussion/Conclusion

It is apparent that perception in look & feel dimension can only be manipulated by UI developers. To vary other dimensions, additional efforts (awareness, education etc.) must be spent by different actors other than UI developers such as back end developers. In general, UI side mainly deals with look & feel driven perception of perception of information security. In this study, relationship among features of UI design, usability principles and EUPoIM are demonstrated concisely. It is evident that perception oriented security is an interesting parameter to focus and consists of multiple dimensions. Furthermore, Enhanced Users' Perception of InfoSec Model and Perception Oriented Usable & Secure Interface Development Model are proposed for the development of both secure and usable interfaces. It is also emphasized that user-centric usable security and users' perception of information security are fertile research areas.

References

1. Cranor, L.F.: Security and Usability: Designing Secure Systems That People can Use. O'reilly (2007)
2. Möckel, C.: Usability and Security in EU E-Banking Systems Towards an Integrated Evaluation Framework. In: IEEE/IPSJ International Symposium on Applications and the Internet (2011)
3. Yeratziotis, A., Pottas, D., Van Greunen, D.: A Usable Security Heuristic Evaluation for the Online Health Social Networking Paradigm. International Journal of Human-Computer Interaction 28(10), 678–694
4. Kainda, R., Flechais, I., Roscoe, A.W.: Security and Usability: Analysis and Evaluation. In: International Conference on ARES 2010, pp. 275–282 (2010)
5. Schultz, E.E., Proctor, R.W., Lien, M.-C., Salvendy, G.: Usability and Security An Appraisal of Usability Issues in Information Security Methods. Computers & Security 20(7), 620–634 (2001)
6. Zurko, M.E., Simon, R.T.: User-centered security. In: Proceedings of the 1996 Workshop on New Security Paradigms, pp. 27–33. ACM (September 1996)
7. Fidas, C.A., Voyiatzis, A.G., Avouris, N.M.: When security meets usability: A user-centric approach on a crossroads priority problem. In: 2010 14th Panhellenic Conference on Informatics (PCI), pp. 112–117. IEEE (September 2010)
8. Cranor, L.F.: A Framework for Reasoning About the Human in the Loop. In: UPSEC 2008 Proceedings of the 1st Conference on Usability, Psychology, and Security, vol. 8, pp. 1–15 (2008)
9. Stanton, J.M., Stam, K.R., Mastrangelo, P., Jolton, J.: Analysis of end user security behaviors. Computers & Security 24(2), 124–133 (2005)
10. Flinn, S., Lumsden, J.: User perceptions of privacy and security on the web. In: Privacy Security and Trust (2005)
11. Chin, E., Felt, A.P., Sekar, V., Wagner, D.: Measuring User Confidence in Smartphone Security and Privacy. In: Symposium on Usable Privacy and Security (SOUPS), Washington, DC, USA, July 11-13 (2012)
12. Huang, D.L., Rau, P.L.P., Salvendy, G.: Perception of Information Security. Behaviour & Information Technology 29(3), 221–232 (2010)
13. Kamoun, F., Halaweh, M.: User Interface Design and E-Commerce Security Perception: An Empirical Study. International Journal of E-Business Research 8(2), 15 (2012)
14. Chanko, E.: Factors that influence users' perceptions of trust in e-commerce. School of Humanities and Informatics, University of Skövde, SWEDEN, M.Sc. dissertation in Computer Science (2004)
15. Salvendy, G.: Handbook of Human Factors and Ergonomics. Wiley-Interscience, New York (1997)

16. Cooper, D.: Psychology, Risk & Safety: Understanding How Personality & Perception can Influence Risk Taking. Professional Safety 48, 39–46 (2003)
17. Parsons, K., McCormac, A., Butavicius, M., Ferguson, L.: Human Factors and Information Security: Individual, Culture and Security Environment. Australian Goverment, Department of Defence, Defence Science and Technology Organization, Command, Control, Communications and Intelligence Division (2010)
18. Arteaga, J.M., Gonzáleza, R.M., Martinb, M.V., Vanderoncktc, J., Álvarez-Rodrígueza, F.: A Methodology For Designing Information Security Feedback Based On User Interface Patterns. Advances in Engineering Software 40, 1231–1241 (2009)
19. Fléchais, I.: Designing Secure and Usable Systems. PhD Thesis, University College London Department of Computer Science (February 2005)
20. Kuo, H.M., Chen, C.W.: Study Of Merchandise Information And Interface Design On B2C Websites. Journal of Marine Science and Technology 19(1), 15–25 (2011)
21. Liu, Y., Huang, D., Zhu, H., Rau, P.L.P.: Users' Perception of Mobile Information Security. In: 2011 International Conference for Internet Technology and Secured Transactions (ICITST), December 11-14, pp. 428–435 (2011)
22. Kim, C., Tao, W., Shin, N., Kim, K.: An Empirical Study of Customers' Perceptions of Security and Trust in E-Payment Systems. Electronic Commerce Research and Applications 9(1), 84–95 (2010); Special Issue: Social Networks and Web 2.0
23. Morris, M.G., Dillon, A.: How User Perceptions Influence Software Use. IEEE Software 14(4), 58–65 (1997)
24. Faily, S.: A Framework for Usable and Secure System Design. In: PhD Thesis, University of Oxford Wolfson College (2011)
25. González, R.M., Muñoz-Arteaga, J., Martin, M.V., Álvarez-Rodriguez, F., Calleros, J.G.: A Pattern Methodology to Specify Usable Security in Websites. In: IEEE 20th International Workshop on Database and Expert Systems Application (2009)
26. Cyr, D., Bonanni, C., Bowes, J., Ilsever, J.: Beyond Trust: Website Design Preferences Across Cultures. Journal of Global Information Management (January 2005)
27. Chiasson, S., Forget, A., Biddle, R., van Oorschot, P.C.: User Interface Design Affects Security: Patterns in Click-Based Graphical Passwords. Int. J. Inf. Secur. 8, 387–398 (2009)
28. Egger, F.N.: Affective Design of E-Commerce User Interfaces: How to Maximize Perceived Trustworthiness. In: Proceedings of the International Conference on Affective Human Factors Design, London (2001)
29. Chang, H.H., Chen, S.W.: Consumer perception of interface quality, security, and loyalty in electronic commerce. Information & Management 46, 411–417 (2009)
30. Radke, K., Boyd, C., Brereton, M., Nieto, J.G.: How HCI Design Influences Web Security Decisions. In: OZCHI 2010, Brisbane, Australia, November 22-26 (2010)
31. Fogg, B.J., Soohoo, C., Danielson, D.: How Do People Evaluate a Web Sites Credibility? Report. Persuasive Technology Lab Stanford University (2002)

Activities to Improve System Integration and Service Quality and Add Additional Values - Reducing the Cost in Applying Human-Centered-Design Process -

Rieko Hamachi, Ichiro Tsukida, and Hisashi Noda

NEC Soft, Ltd.
{hamachi@mxh,tsukida@mxf,noda-hisashi@mxd}nes.nec.co.jp

Abstract. NEC Soft has organized a team of Human-Centered-Design (HCD) specialists who have been engaging in activities to apply the HCD process to system integration (SI) and service projects for improving usability since 2007. HCD is an effective method for improving usability in SI and services. However, many engineers do not focus on improve usability because of the difficulty measuring the effectiveness of its benefits, unlike quality control actions such as eliminating bugs. In this paper, we will propose a method for applying the HCD process for minimal cost to convince engineers of the quantitative effects of using the HCD process for improving usability.

Keywords: HCD, cost benefit, system integration, small start, reducing HCD cost.

1   Introduction

Definitions of Terms

- Human-Centered-Design (HCD) specialist: knows about HCD and usability for designing system UI
- Designer: knows about artistic coloring and designing
- Engineer: receives customer requirements and does programing

NEC Soft has organized a team of Human-Centered-Design (HCD) specialists who have been engaging in activities to apply the HCD process to system integration (SI) and service projects for improving usability since 2007.

HCD is an effective method for improving usability in SI and services. However, many engineers do not focus on improving usability because of difficulty measuring the effectiveness of its benefits, unlike quality control actions such as eliminating bugs.

A. Marcus (Ed.): DUXU 2014, Part IV, LNCS 8520, pp. 32–38, 2014.

As costs are reduced and delivery deadlines are shortened for SI and service projects, further cost reduction efforts are needed to improve usability. Thus, the HCD process is applied.

Since NEC Soft started applying the HCD process to SI and service projects in 2007, the application rate has remained steady at approximately 10% or less of the total number of projects within NEC Soft.

We have hypothesized that the reason for this low take-up rate is the engineers' reluctance to apply the HCD process to their projects. They have not been convinced to apply the process due to uncertainty about the cost effectiveness and the cost benefits of HCD.

In this paper, we will propose a method for using the HCD process for minimal cost to convince the engineers of the quantitative effects of using the HCD process for improving usability.

2   Engineers' Opinions towards Improving Usability

HCD effectively improves usability at SI and service projects and customer satisfaction. However, its effectiveness is difficult to explain quantitatively to engineers and stakeholders, so we started to let the engineers experience improved usability.

2.1   Understanding Engineers' Attitudes

We wanted to know what the engineers' thoughts and objectives are, who the other stakeholders are, and what their projects involve. To find these out, we held a seminar for and meet with engineers.

Seminar for Engineers

In the seminar, we gave the engineers a questionnaire.

<Example questions >

- What do you know about HCD?
- How necessary do you think usability is and why?
- What, if any, are the problems with your project?
- In what ways, if any, does your product/service need its usability improved?
- How much you would pay to improve usability?

Meeting Engineers to Introduce Our HCD Activities

After explaining our organization's HCD activities for 15 to 30 minutes, we discussed with the engineers about their projects.

<Example questions >

- What kind of customers do you have (e.g. manufacturing, retail, etc.)?
- What is your current project?
- What was your previous project?
- How necessary do you think it is to improve your product/service usability?

We interviewed more than 100 engineers in the seminar and the meeting. We noticed that most engineers rejected focusing on improving usability and applying HCD for various reasons.

2.2   Results of Interviews with the Engineers

The results of the questionnaires and interviews revealed the following reasons the engineers did not want to improve usability or apply HCD.

- The engineers did not have any ideas for improving usability.
- Quality, cost, and delivery times (QCD) are the top priorities, so the engineers did not want to do more than necessary for meeting QCD requirements.
- We made a usability checklist that is available commonly, but it has too many items for the engineers to check.
- The engineers cannot clearly imagine how to improve usability and apply HCD because they have no experience of doing so. They also have no idea how much they would pay to do so.

We finally hypothesized that to promote improving usability, it is important to let the engineers experience applying HCD and realizing its effectiveness. To do so, we proposed a "small start" for applying HCD while aiming to minimize the necessary HCD cost. In this paper, we explain our method and describe two case studies.

3   Case Studies

We applied HCD for improving usability for more than 100 projects over seven years. Two such cases are described below.

3.1   Case 1: Improving Usability of Service (SAAS) for Telephone Shopping Call Center

1.   Stakeholders: sales division, the engineers, designers, and HCD specialists.
2.   The engineers' motivation for improving usability: medium. They want to differentiate themselves by improving usability. However, differentiation by adding functions is the top priority.
3.   Users: temporary employees at call centers, mostly female.

4. Frequency of use: one to five times a week. One user handles several dozen calls.
5. Recognized aim: minimizing operation time.
6. Experience of applying HCD: none.
7. Ingenuity point: finish system operation without speaking, only using a keyboard. Less UI interaction is needed, and all functions are incorporated onto one screen.
8. Cost for HCD: 3% of project budget.

3.2   Case 2: Improving Usability of Automatic Ticket Machines in Cinema Complex

1. Stakeholders: sales division, engineers, designers, and HCD specialists.
2. The engineers' motivation for improving usability: high. Because of customer requirements, they have to improve usability and consider UX.
3. Users: movie goers from 10 to 80 years old.
4. Frequency of use: inconsistent. From once a year to several times a week.
5. Recognized aim: buying movie tickets using automatic ticket machine without employees' help.
6. Experience of applying HCD: none
7. Ingenuity point: operable for first-time user. Attractive design matching cinema atmosphere.
8. Cost for HCD: 5% of project budget
1.
2. The contents of both cases are shown in Table 1.
3.
4.

Table 1.

5.	6. Case 1	7. Case 2
8. Project outline	9. Service (SAAS) for telephone shopping call center	10. Automatic ticket machine in cinema complex
11. Hardware	12. Personal computer	13. Automatic ticket machine
14. Stakeholders	15. Sales division, engineers, designers, and HCD specialist	16. Sales division, engineers, designers, and HCD specialist

Table 1. (*Continued*)

17. Engineers' motivation for improving usability	18. Medium. They want to differentiate themselves by improving usability. However, differentiation by adding function is top priority.	19. High. Because of customer requirements, they have to improve usability and consider UX.
20. User Location	21. Call center for telephone shopping	22. Cinema complex
23. Users	24. Temporary employees, mostly female.	25. Movie goers.
26. User age	27. From 18 to 40	28. From 10 to 80.
29. Frequency of use	30. One to 5 times a week. One user handles several dozen calls.	31. Inconsistent. From once a year to several times a week.
32. Recognized aim	33. Minimizing operation time.	34. Buying movie tickets using automatic ticket machine without employees' help.
35. Experience of applying HCD	36. None	37. None
38. Ingenuity point	39. Finish system operation without speaking, only using a keyboard.	40. Operable for first–time users. Attractive design matching cinema atmosphere.
41. Cost for HCD	42. 3% of project6 budget	43. 5% of project budget

4   Application of HDC

4.1   Engineer's Understanding in Both Cases

The commonality of both cases is that there was no experience of applying HCD. Thus, the engineers' understanding was as follows.

A)   They had no idea what to do.
B)   They had no image of what improved usability would be like.
C)   They did not know how much to spend to improve usability.
D)   They wanted to reduce the risk of applying HCD.

4.2   "Small Start" for Applying HCD

We proposed that the engineers do a "small start" for applying HCD.

ISO09241-210 Process of Design Solutions Production Activities

To improve operability for minimal cost and also improve the attractiveness of design, we had to make the engineers realize the effectiveness of HCD. Therefore, we concentrated resources on Design Solutions Production Activities. However, other processes also needed to be applied effectively, so we applied processes using different methods.

— Understand and specify the context of use
— Specify user and organizational requirements
— Evaluate designs on the basis of requirements [1]

<Example methods >.

— User interviews

After we collected information that engineers had received from customers, we concentrated on filling in gaps in information by interviewing users.

— Heuristic evaluation method

The heuristic evaluation method checklist has too many items. To evaluate usability better, we devised a shorter checklist for each project.

— Select standard screens as formats

We selected standard screens for formats, such as a selection menus and input screens.

Project Management Techniques for Maximizing Cost-Effectiveness of HCD

To maximize cost benefits of applying all HCD processes, especially Design Solutions Production Activities, engineers, designers, and HCD specialists need to collaborate. Below is what HCD specialists should do to manage projects effectively.

What HCD specialist should do.

1. Watch over the progress of the project.
2. Clarify the agreed on responsibilities of the engineers, designers, and HCD specialists.
3. Understand programming restrictions.
4. Reduce the budget for designing screens by using standard formats.
5. Understand the details of the each task, production costs, output, and technical terms and act as an intermediary between the engineers and designers.

6. Work with offshore designers by illustrating ideas with pictures, not only words.

5   Results and Discussion

5.1   Quantitative Effectiveness

• Costs were reduced after inclusion of HCD specialists and the subsequent application of the method. The costs were reduced by 10% to 40% in cases where a domestic designer participated in the project and 30% to 60% in cases where a domestic designer was replaced by an offshore designer.
• In both projects, the cost for applying the HCD process fell by one to two million yen regardless of the size of the project.

5.2   Qualitative Effectiveness

After the HCD process had been applied:

•   End user's satisfaction level improved.
•   The results of heuristic evaluation improved.

The initial target was demonstrating qualitative effectiveness for improving usability by applying HCD, but we also demonstrated quantitative effectiveness.

6   Conclusion

We applied Human-Centered-Design (HCD) for minimal cost to projects at the outline design phase (or later). We found that the cost for applying the HCD process can be reduced by the HCD specialists playing an effective role. By applying only relevant activities of the HCD process, it was proven that usability improvements, as assessed through heuristic evaluation, can be ensured.

In this study, we concentrated on letting engineers experience improving usability through HCD. We proposed a "small start" for applying HCD, especially Design Solutions Production Activities.

We will study more effective ways for improving usability.

Reference

1. ISO standards. Usability Partners,
   http://www.usabilitypartners.se/about-usability/iso-standards
   (retrieved)

ISO 9241-210 and Culture? – The Impact of Culture on the Standard Usability Engineering Process

Rüdiger Heimgärtner

Intercultural User Interface Consulting (IUIC), Germany
ruediger.heimgaertner@iuic.de

Abstract. In this paper, some ideas are presented regarding the question of whether standards can be valid internationally, i.e. worldwide and independent of the different cultures in the world, and how this question can be tackled. Exemplified by the standard usability engineering process in ISO 9241-210, the impact of culture on the main steps in the usability engineering process is analyzed. The output of the process is influenced by the process. If the process of usability engineering is culturally influenced and different for different cultures, the output of the usability engineering process, i.e. the user interface of the product, is also culturally influenced and different. Furthermore, the results are possibly not those as expected by the desired target culture. The presented ideas represent a first step towards deeper research in this area.

Keywords: User-Centered Design, ISO 9241-210, Culture, HCI, Approach, Process, Structure, Intercultural, Intercultural User Interface Design, Standard, Usability Engineering, Intercultural Usability Engineering.

1 Introduction

Globalization led to the development of products for other cultures. Therefore, intercultural product development and intercultural usability engineering is needed ([1]). The usability of user interfaces (UI) depends on the cultural context of use as well as on the cultural imprint of the users (age, sex, language, education, knowledge, experience, religion, self-conception, dealing with power, politics, wealth, income, infrastructure) (cf. [1], [2], [3]). To reach intercultural usability for a product, detailed cultural knowledge of the specific user habits is necessary for a designer in order to develop products that fit all customer needs in cultural contexts. Even if it is impossible that one UI designer has all this specific information from all relevant user groups worldwide, he must have a profound knowledge of the circumstances in his own cultural environment in order to be sensitive to the relevant aspects in other cultures (cf. [4]). In addition, the people involved in intercultural UI design should at least know the basic structures and principles from cultural studies in order to consider other cultures in their work (cf. [4]) such as quantitative cultural models (cf. [5]). This is augmented by working within an intercultural HCI designer team (cf. [6], [7]) using the usability engineering process for interactive systems which is defined in the

A. Marcus (Ed.): DUXU 2014, Part IV, LNCS 8520, pp. 39–48, 2014.

European Standard EN ISO 9241-210:2010 (cf. [8]). In this paper, I raise the question of how standards acknowledged by CEN and ISO can be internationally valid, i.e. if they apply independently of (national) cultures. An analysis of this process is done in order to identify aspects that are influenced by culture and to decide if it is necessary to change or adapt this ISO standard in order to work in different cultural contexts. First, cultural influences that affect interactive systems and their usage are presented followed by the description of the resulting discipline called "intercultural usability engineering". Then the process for designing utilizable interactive systems is shown and the influence of culture on the main aspects of the process in ISO 9241-210 are identified using the cultural models introduced before. Finally, the implications of these relationships are listed for further research.

2   Influence of Culture on User's Interaction with the UI

Culture as a set of facts, rules, values and norms (structural conditions) representing an orientation system (cf. [4]) established by collective programming of the mind (cf. [5]) within a group of individuals can influence Human-Machine Interaction (HMI) in different ways. Masao Ito and Kumiyo Nakakoji already demonstrated in 1996 the influence of culture on UI design for the modes „hear" and „speak" between user and system (cf. [9]). In the „hear mode", the presentation of information from the system to the user takes place within the phases perception, association and inference. From the first to the last phase, cultural dependency increases: colors and forms in the perception phase depend less strongly on culture than standards in language and metaphors within the phase of associating meaning. Finally, the inference mechanisms in the last phase that are based on logic and social norms depend strongly on culture. In the „speak mode", instructing the system by the user happens in four phases. First, the user recognizes the possibilities of system usage. For example, he grasps the meaning of the layout, selects alternatives, or initiates functions. Then he tests their applicability by checking semantic consistency using trial and error. In the third phase, he determines the expectations of the system regarding his actions and acknowledges the system instructions in the final phase. These process phases involve the perception of time, which is strongly dependent on culture (cf. [10]). In addition, cultural dependence increases from phase to phase. For example, in Japan, on the one hand, short system response time is very important. On the other hand, Japanese users are obviously more patient doing long-winded tasks than users from European countries (cf. [11]). Moreover, culture influences HMI on all levels of the interaction model (cf. acting level model according to [12]). Following [5], during the intensive learning phase in childhood, primary culture imprints the human being with certain rules, norms and desired ways of behavior to which the members of the group adhere. Figure 1 shows cultural models based on the compilation from literature by [13] that can be used to analyze the influence of culture on the behavior of users with interactive systems.

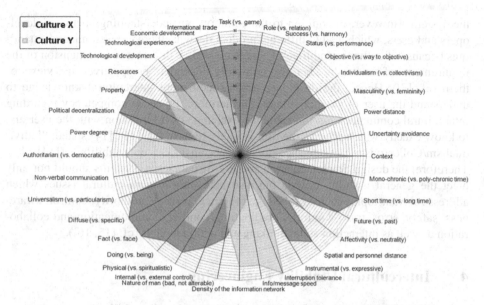

Fig. 1. Many cultural models can be used to analyze the influence of culture on the behavior of users with interactive systems (indexes are only valid for the cultural models of [5])

One type of cultural model are cultural dimensions, which serve to describe the behavior and values of members of certain cultures like uncertainty avoidance, individualism or collectivism or even power distance ([5]). For HCI, those cultural dimensions are most interesting that are directly connected to communication, information, interaction and dialogue design, i.e. the cultural dimensions concerning the culturally different concepts of space, time and communication (cf. chapters 1, 5 and 10 in [10]). Space and time are physical variables influencing the communicative behavior of human beings, which form the social processes of a group of humans and their culture: by learning certain kinds of behavior, the human being matures according to his cultural environment. The influence of cultural imprinting of the user on his behavior in interactions with other communication partners is immense. This is also valid for HMI because communication in HMI is determined by the interaction between the user and the system (cf. [3]). Hence, cultural differences in interpersonal communication can and must be transferred to the interaction with technical devices ([2]). Cultural dependencies in user system interactions (HMI) particularly concern interaction and dialog design (cf. [2]). Culture influences the interaction of the user with a computer system or a machine because of the movement of the user in cultural surroundings (cf. [2]). Therefore, culture has a direct influence on the interaction of the user with the system.

3   Influence of Culture on Usability and Usability Engineering

The usability of a system strongly depends on how the user can cope with the system (cf. [8]). The user articulates his desires and hence his needs regarding the usability of the system. However, in addition to the common misunderstandings between developers and users, which lead to different product designs, there are also misunderstandings because of cultural conditions. There is not only a different comprehension of the requirements of the product but also culturally dependent perspectives and views of them (cf. [7]). Hence, the developer needs much more intercultural knowledge to understand the user of another culture. Furthermore, he needs competency regarding intercultural communication to enable the exchange of information with the user and to know exactly which product the user is likely to have (cf. [1]). [14] stated, "Individualism/Collectivism is connected to and has an effect on usability." ([14]: 17). Therefore, the design, implementation and use of interactive systems should not only meet the general usability criteria but also take into account cultural issues which address relevant topics such as schedule, presence, privacy, authority, control, awareness, safety, error, trust, comfort, coordination, conflict, communication and collaboration as well as interaction style, thinking and action models (cf. [15, 16]).

4   Intercultural Usability Engineering

As explained above, the preconditions for intercultural usability engineering are knowledge about the cultural differences in HMI and its considerations in product design and product realization ([1]; [2]; [3]). "Intercultural" usability engineering is a method for designing products of good usability for users from different cultures. "Intercultural" in this context refers to the special methods that are necessary to do usability engineering for different cultures (cf. [1]). The "interculturally overlapping situation" arranged by a technical system is the most interesting (cf. [1]). [1] made the approach of [4] using "overlapping interaction situations" available for HMI design. These situations arise if a product is defined and formed within one culture and this product is then transferred and used in another culture. A change of cultural environment takes place at the transfer of a technology or a product from the developer's country to another country (cf. e.g., [1], [2], [17], [18]). Therefore, the work of [1] deals with the question of whether there is a reduction of the fit between user and product if products of one culture are used in another. Furthermore, the same data can have different meanings in different cultures due to the experiences within one's own, since every culture has its own values, symbols and behavior patterns with meanings and interpretations connected to them. These aspects have an effect on the coding or decoding of news during communication (cf. [2]). Miscommunication has negative effects on the usability of the product. Therefore, at the collection of culture specific user requirements and culture specific assessment of the concepts used, it has to be examined how far approved methods of usability engineering are suitable. The existing cultural models should be taken into account in the process of product design in the context of intercultural usability engineering. First, the product developers must be sensitized to the difficulties of cultural influences on product development and product use. Then cultural factors influencing HMI must be provided to the developers and considered in the product. This requires knowledge in software ergonomics and intercultural UI design as well as the application of usability engineering methods in the intercultural context. In contrast, if the currently implemented functionality of a system of a certain culture is used as a basis for the analysis of UI characteristics, it may lead to erroneous or simply wrong design guidelines because those requirements need not necessarily match the real needs of the user. Therefore, the user's needs must be collected for every user or at least for the desired user groups (e.g., Chinese and German users).

5   Cultural Influences on the Standard Process for Designing Utilizable Interactive Systems

Questions concerning the interaction level, the mind and the cognition as well as behavior in using usability engineering methods and applying the usability engineering process itself within cultural contexts are either not answered or only partly answered until now. How do different cultures interfere and affect the navigation within applications? Are there significant improvements when comparing an application without taking into account intercultural differences with the adapted version of the application? Can users from different cultures have different experiences when interacting with applications from their own or other cultures? Such questions must be answered by research to acquire useful hints for designers and developers of user interfaces for the cultural context. Some of the questions are already answered (cf. e.g., [14]), but many of them are still open especially regarding the compatibility of processes in different cultural contexts. In the following, some ideas will be presented concerning the question where cultural influences affect the usability engineering process.

5.1   Process for Designing Utilizable Interactive Systems

Figure 2 shows an overview of the process for designing utilizable interactive systems according to the European Standard EN ISO 9241-210:2010. This process contains

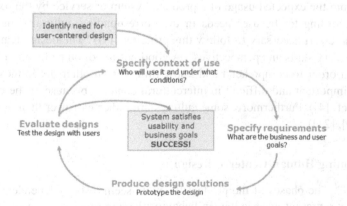

Fig. 2. Usability Engineering Process according to ISO 9241-210

several main steps, which will be analyzed in the following concerning their applicability in intercultural contexts. The weaknesses in every process step if used in intercultural contexts are identified in order to define and determine recommendations for improvement. Every process step is briefly described, followed by an idea of the possible cultural impact on the step and sometimes by implications from it on the process, the factual products and the total product where appropriate or presently achieved respectively.

5.2   Principles of Human-Centered Design

(i) "The design is based upon an explicit understanding of users, tasks and environments". Explicit understanding of users, tasks and environments is one of the most difficult tasks especially in intercultural contexts because of different explicit and implicit or tacit factual and procedural knowledge resulting from different world views, assumptions, methods and processes (cf. [7]). (ii) "The users are involved throughout design and development". However, there is cultural behavior in opposition to the expected and required user behavior throughout design and development (cf. [5]). Users from different cultures grasp things differently and behave accordingly in certain design and development situations (cf. [1]), which also impairs the next principle of human-centered design: (iii) "The design is driven and refined by user-centered evaluation". Here, there are cultural differences in reacting to questions and being observed (cf. [18], cf. also face saving aspect, [19]), which must be considered in order to adapt or change evaluation methods accordingly. (iv) "The process is iterative" seems not to be a problem on first sight for different cultures because iterative learning is necessary for all users all over the world. However, it has to be checked if there are hurdles when diving into details. For instance, there may be different styles of learning also concerning the iteration cycles such as iteration time and iteration frequency. (v) "The design addresses the whole user experience". This principle seems to be generally valid for all users of any culture. However, the perceptions and reactions from the expected usage of a product, system or service by the users can be different according to the user needs in the corresponding cultural context, which increases the effort necessary to follow this principle. (vi) "The design team includes multidisciplinary skills and perspectives". A good portion of empathy and frankness is necessary in order to comprehend and know things from other disciplines, which is even more important and difficult in intercultural contexts because of the complexity of culture (cf. [4]). Furthermore, some cultures are rather narrower than open minded (cf. [5], [20], [21]).

5.3   Planning Human-Centered Design

(i) "General". The phases of the product lifecycle seem to be independent of culture because they represent generic human behavior: having an idea (conception), gathering the necessary things to realize the idea (analysis), thinking about the physical realization of idea (design), physically realizing the idea (implementation), checking if the realization of the idea represents the idea (test), supporting your realized idea until you do not like it anymore (maintenance). Every human being has to do these steps independent of their culture. Nevertheless, also here are cultural differences. For example, Japanese plan very long before the realize things in contrast to Germans (cf. [22]). (ii) "Responsibility". In contrast, responsibility is strongly culturally influenced. Cultures with high power distance and high uncertainty avoidance do have a different attitude about accepting responsibility than cultures with low power distance and low uncertainty avoidance (cf. [5]). (iii) "Content of plan" and (iv) "Integration with project plan". According to the Weltanschauung, different methods have to be used in order to obtain reasonable results (cf. [7]). For instance, the plan can be very detailed or very loose and agile. Their acceptance depends on culture. Negotiation and contracting is another issue along with agreement about time prescriptions for the iterative process cycles that can be problematic in different cultures according to mono-causal or multi-causal thinking (cf. [2]). (v) "Timing and resources". Here there are cultural influences described by the cultural models of time behavior (cf. [21], mono-chronic vs. poly-chronic) and usage of resources (cf. [13]).

5.4   Human-Centered Design Activities

(i) "Understanding the context of use". The objective of this process step is to collect all needs, interests, expectations and behavior patterns of the different user groups. In an international context, it is important to determine that there is not one homogeneous user group but that there are thousands or even millions of individual users worldwide. To specify the individual cultural context of use in the relevant usage situations it is important to develop a profound understanding of the individual culture specific needs of the users. The current process does not cover this aspect fully for the intercultural context because there is not sufficient focus on the profound analysis of the cultural aspects and their influences represented by HCI dimensions, UI characteristics, intercultural variables and cultural dimensions. HCI dimensions describe the style of human machine interaction expressed by information frequency and density and order as well as interaction frequency and speed. User interface characteristics capture the most relevant attributes of user interfaces containing metaphors, presentation, navigation, interaction and mental models ([13]). Intercultural variables cover the localization levels function, interaction and presentation ([23]). Direct intercultural variables concern HCI directly such as color, icons, language and layout as well as interaction speed and frequency. Indirect intercultural variables embrace HCI related topics such as service manual or packaging. [20] defined cultural dimensions that are related to human interaction such as universalism, neutrality, specification, continuity and control. They can be related to HCI dimensions to establish a link between the cultural imprint of users to their HCI style ([15]) in order to describe the analytical basis to specify the context of use in the intercultural context as well as to support the next activity: (ii) "Specifying the user requirements". The task is to acquire a deep understanding of the complexity of the task and its requirements (cf. [6]) by analyzing the current market situation concerning existing products, main competitors, environmental factors like politics, new legislation, economic trends, sociologic and technological developments of the target markets. The implications for optimization of ISO 9241-210 can be extended to the tasks and the roles in this standard for its application in intercultural contexts. Here also elements from usage-centered design process such as cultural specific user tasks and roles as well as an additional cultural model can be applied in order to systemize the intercultural usability engineering process (cf. [24]). (iii) "Producing design solutions". In this process step a culturally diverse UI design team has the task to generate new innovative design solutions. The better and more precise the product targets are defined at the beginning of the development project, the easier it is to compare them with the current state of design. Thereby, communication is a challenge in diverse teams as mentioned before: misunderstandings caused by talking the same language which is, however, not the mother tongue for most of the team members will happen frequently and can lead to anger and frustration. Thereby, also task distribution and feedback loops are strongly affected negatively, which possibly drives the final activity ad absurdum because of wrong or lacking (interpretation of) feedback: (iv) "Evaluating the design". In addition, in intercultural context, it is important to evaluate the design status from the perspectives of the different cultural user groups defined to ensure that the design fits the different and sometimes even contradictory requirements of all stakeholders.

6   Discussion and Conclusion

Even if these initial ideas provide a basis for further research, they are just preliminary and must be detailed and investigated in depth in order to become general statements. Hence, an even more profound discussion is outstanding. Nevertheless, some ideas indicate that the existing HMI development process defined in ISO 9241-210 could be extended by roles and tasks in order to be successful in all cultural contexts worldwide and to fulfill the expected validity at least internationally (cf. also [6]). Furthermore, the user interface design methods should be systematically complemented with cultural aspects to ensure that new systems can be designed right from the beginning for one or more cultures while designers better accommodate the diverse global user requirements and respond faster to change using agile methods and modules from usage-centered design (cf. also [24]). In any case, it is reasonable that experts in international standardization committees related to HMI have intercultural experience and knowledge in intercultural user interface design as well as intercultural usability engineering.

References

1. Honold, P.: Cross-cultural Usability Engineering: Development and State of the art. In: Proceedings of HCI International (The 8th International Conference on Human-Computer Interaction) on Human-Computer Interaction: Ergonomics and User Interfaces-Volume I, pp. 1232–1236. L. Erlbaum Associates Inc. (1999)
2. Röse, K.: The Development of Culture-Oriented Human Machine Systems: Specification, Analysis and Integration of Relevant Intercultural Variables. In: Kaplan, M. (ed.) Cultural

Ergonomics, Advances in Human Performance and Cognitive Engineering Research. Elsevier, Netherlands (2005)

3. Heimgärtner, R.: Cultural Differences in Human-Computer Interaction. Paperback B: Einband - flex(Paperback) ed. vol. 1. 2012: Oldenbourg Verlag. XVIII, 325 S. - 24,0 x 17,0 cm

4. Thomas, A., Kinast, E.-U., Schroll-Machl, S.: Handbook of intercultural communication and cooperation. Basics and Areas of Application. Vandenhoeck & Ruprecht, Göttingen (2010)

5. Hofstede, G.H., Hofstede, G.J., Minkov, M.: Cultures and organizations: Software of the mind, 3rd edn. McGraw-Hill, Maidenhead (2010)

6. Schoper, Y., Heimgärtner, R.: Lessons from Intercultural Project Management for the Intercultural HCI Design Process. In: Marcus, A. (ed.) DUXU/HCII 2013, Part II. LNCS, vol. 8013, pp. 95–104. Springer, Heidelberg (2013)

7. Heimgärtner, R., Tiede, L.-W., Windl, H.: Empathy as Key Factor for Successful Intercultural HCI Design. In: Marcus, A. (ed.) Design, User Experience, and Usability, Pt II, HCII 2011. LNCS, vol. 6770, pp. 557–566. Springer, Heidelberg (2011)

8. DIN, DIN EN ISO 9241-210 Ergonomische Anforderungen der Mensch-System-Interaktion Teil 210: Prozess zur Gestaltung gebrauchstauglicher Systeme. BeuthVerlag, Berlin (2010)

9. Masao, I., Kumiyo, N.: Impact of culture on user interface design. In: International Users Interface, pp. 105–126. John Wiley & Sons, Inc., New York (1996)

10. Hall, E.T.: The silent language (2006)

11. Lee, Y.: Introduction (2012) (November 19, 2002), http://www.csulb.edu/web/journals/jecr/issues/20024/paper3.pdf

12. Heinecke, A.M.: Mensch-Computer-Interaktion. 2. überarb. u. erw. Aufl, ed. 2011: Springer Verlag. 386 (2012)

13. Marcus, A., Baumgartner, V.-J.: Mapping User-Interface Design Components vs. Culture Dimensions in Corporate Websites. Visible Language Journal MIT Press 38(1), 1–65 (2004)

14. Vöhringer-Kuhnt, T.: The Influence of Culture on Usability. Freie Universität Berlin (2002)

15. Heimgärtner, R.: Reflections on a Model of Culturally Influenced Human Computer Interaction to Cover Cultural Contexts in HCI Design. International Journal of Human-Computer Interaction (2013)

16. Liang, S.F.M.: Cross-Cultural Issues in Interactive systems. In: Proceedings of the International Ergonomics, Ergonomics in the Digital. Age (2003)

17. Hermeking, M.: Kulturen und Technik. Waxmann, München (2001)

18. Clemmensen, T., Goyal, S.: Cross cultural usability testing: The relationship between evaluator and test user. Copenhagen Business School, C. B. S. Institut for Informatik I. N. F. Department of Informatics I. N. F (2005)

19. Victor, D.A.: International business communication, 7th edn., p. 280. Harper Collins, New York (1998)

20. Trompenaars, F., Hampden-Turner, C.: Riding the waves of culture: Understanding diversity in business. rev. and updated, 3rd edn. Nicholas Brealey Publ., London (2012)

21. Hall, E.T., Hall, M.R.: Understanding cultural differences: Germans, French and Americans. Intercultural Press, Boston (2009)

22. Kuhnert, I.: Business with the Japanese, p. 125. GABAL, Offenbach (2004)

23. Röse, K., Zühlke, D.: Culture-Oriented Design: Developers' Knowledge Gaps in this Area. In: 8th IFAC/IFIPS/IFORS/IEA Symposium on Analysis, Design, and Evaluation of Human-Machine Systems, September 18-20, Pergamon, Kassel (2001)
24. Windl, H., Heimgärtner, R.: Intercultural Design for Use - Extending Usage-Centered Design by Cultural Aspects. In: Marcus, A. (ed.) DUXU 2013, Part II. LNCS, vol. 8013, pp. 139–148. Springer, Heidelberg (2013)

Design, Deployment and Evaluation of a Social Tool for Developing Effective Working Relationships in Large Organizations

Athanasios Karapantelakis[1] and Yonghui Guo[2]

[1] Ericsson Research, Färögatan 6, 164 40, Stockholm, Sweden
[2] Ericsson Competence Readiness, Torshamnsgatan 23, 164 83, Stockholm, Sweden

Abstract. In an attempt to raise public awareness and promote their objectives, organizations increasingly strive for social media presence. Similarly to using social media tools to communicate externally, organizations are starting to adopt such tools internally to promote information exchange. This is especially the case for large technology companies with a skilled workforce, where exchange of knowledge and ideas can help establish working relationships and eventually improve organizational performance. Past experience shows that successful adoption of social media tools differs between cases, and is closely related to organizational culture. In this paper, we present an application designed to arrange custom lunches between randomly-selected employees and argue that a study of the organizational culture and subsequent application of the findings of this study to the design of the application has contributed to it's success. We determine success by exposing the application to trial use and evaluating feedback from real users.

Keywords: social media, enterprise, organizational culture.

1 Introduction

Driven by rapid growth, social media today are widely used and represent a significant share of the Internet's user base; an eMarketer report titled "Worldwide Social Network Users: 2013 Forecast and Comparative Estimates" and published in June 2013 indicates that one in four internet users worldwide connects to some kind of social media platform at least once per month, while the number of users is projected to reach 2.55 billion by 2017.

Originally, social media were targeted at private individuals, and were perceived as tools for communicating their personal interests; with organizations frowning upon or even banning their use (well known examples for prohibitive social media policies were the sports network ESPN and US Marine Corps). However, as their popularity rose, the perception of their usefulness in the enterprise changed.

Ployhart observes that as organizations are becoming increasingly aware of the value of social media in the enterprise, they are starting to include them as part

A. Marcus (Ed.): DUXU 2014, Part IV, LNCS 8520, pp. 49–60, 2014.

of their corporate strategy. At the same time, he proposes different approaches for external social presence expansion and internal adoption [1].

Many organizations have already created and are executing strategies for managing their social media presence. In a recent survey, approximately 75% of the 110 respondents indicated that their organization has already deployed and is improving it's external social media presence [2]. However, in the same survey only 32% of the respondents indicated that their organization has deployed social media for internal use.

The results of this survey are not incidental, and are based on the fact that the success factors for internal social media introduction are more complex than the ones for establishing external social media presence (thus requiring additional effort to understand all parameters). The latter case typically involves an external relations group publishing content in a controlled manner. Successful execution in this case depends on how well the goals outlined in the organization's social media strategy are communicated and how the organization diffuses feedback from social media users. The former requires a careful examination of the observable patterns of behaviour of the employees in the organization - also known as organizational culture - prior to any attempt of deployment. Empirical findings from previous deployments support this claim. NASA's social network for example failed to gain traction because employees had very specific job roles with repetitive tasks and thus not having the need to update their online profiles [3]. Findings from the evaluation of an instant messaging system in an organization also indicated that employees were reluctant to use it for communicating with their superiors because they were concerned about conveying inappropriate impressions [4].

In this paper, we present ConnectedLunch, an application designed to arrange lunches between employees of an organization. This application introduces employees previously unknown to each other and allows them to discuss at a mutually convenient time. In the long term, some of this discussions may lead to establishment of working relationships. After a review of previous research on the importance of working relationships in organizations and comparison of similar applications to ConnectedLunch (section 2), we show how the application was designed to be compatible with the culture of the organization it was deployed in (see section 3), describe it's architecture (section 4) and determine its successful deployment (see section 5). We conclude by discussing the benefits of ConnetedLunch in greater detail as well as reviewing organizational learnings.

2   Background Work

The goal of ConnectedLunch is to introduce employees to one another over lunch. This is seen as a first step in establishing working relationships, which are proven to produce short and/or long-term benefits for the organization (for further analysis on the benefits there relations produce see section 5) [5]. Working relationships in the context of this study, are professional relationships employees have with each other, irrespective of their position in the organizational structure. In contradiction to formal interactions such as scheduled meetings, ConnectedLunch arranges for people to meet in informal environments such as restaurants or cafés. Such informal meetings are important for building working relationships: previous research shows that informal communication strengthens working relationships by building trust [6] and aligning perspectives [7] of the people involved.

Table 1. Comparison of ConnectedLunch with other Lunch-pairing applications

	Lunch Pairing	Pair Lunch	Lunch Roulette	ZinkUz	ConnectedLunch
Pairing rules	no	no	simple	complex	complex
Scale	small	small	large	unknown	large
IT Integration	potentially	potentially	potentially	potentially	yes
Charges	no	no	no	yes	no

The idea of pairing people for lunch is not new. There exist a number of approaches, such as "Lunch Pairing" [8], "Pair Lunch" [9], "Lunch Roulette" [11] and "ZinkUz" [10]. Table 1 compares these solutions with ConnectedLunch, against four basic criteria.

The first criterion is the complexity of the pairing rules. Applications use these rules to decide if any constraints will be applied when matching employees for lunch. Small-scale solutions such as "Lunch Pairing" and "Pair Lunch", which target companies of 30-40 employees have no pairing rules, meaning that the matching process is completely random. The absence of rules in this case is not a technical limitation of the applications, but it is a conscious design choice taken in order to maximise lunch arrangements, given the small user base. "Lunch Roulette" provides simple choices such as time of lunch and restaurant of choice. Finally, "ZinkUz" provides a customisable ruleset, according to the company's webpage [10]. In the case of ConnectedLunch, we also offer users sone control over the choice of lunch partner by optionally allowing choice of a partner's work area and work experience. Given the large user base of the application (see section 3), offering these choices was not only reasonable in terms of matching lunch partner availability, but it also increased application desirability (as validated by our measurements in section 5).

We also compare the applications by their capability to scale in order to serve organizations of thousands of employees. For cost reasons, it is important that the application is designed in such a way that it is easily accessible and does not require excessive maintenance, other than provisioning for the required IT resources. As per previous, "Lunch Pairing" and "Pair Lunch" were designed for small companies, and require manual maintenance by an administrator rendering them cost-ineffective for large-scale deployments. "Lunch Roulette" has a proven record of successful, large-scale deployments as mentioned in the application's website [11], while we could not find any account of deployments of ZinkUz in the company's website[10]. ConnectedLunch was designed from the beginning to scale to serve a large user base, requiring limited maintenance. The scalability capabilities of the application were evaluated during the trial launch period (see section 5).

Scalability also relates to the degree the applications can interface with existing enterprise software systems deployed in the organization. By interfacing with these systems, scalability risks can be mitigated as functionality can be delegated to already-deployed enterprise applications. In ConnectedLunch, we minimised the application's maintenance costs by delegating user and lunch calendar management to existing enterprise software. In addition to cost-cutting, we reduced the learning curve of the application for new users (see section 4). Although they offer no direct support for interfacing with existing enterprise software, all other applications could be extended to provide such functionality. In this case, the additional cost of implementing these interfaces has to be factored in to the deployment costs.

Finally, all applications except "ZinkUz" are free of charge and their authors provide access to the source code. However, when all four of the aforementioned criteria are considered, we find that ConnectedLunch offers a unique combination of low-cost, high-scalability, rule customisation and integration with existing enterprise software, which cannot be provided from another tool.

The next section describes the thought process we followed on identifying the factors contributing to a successful lunch experience, and subsequently how these factors were interpreted as requirements in the application design.

3 From Analysis of Customer Experience to Creating Application Design Constraints

Prior to implementing ConnectedLunch, we investigated the work environment and culture of the organization in which the application was to be deployed. We started by considering the contributing factors for a successful lunch experience (i.e. one where all lunch partners satisfy their personal expectations). We have managed to reduce the number of factors contributing to this success to three:

- Spatial Proximity: Since business lunches take place during working time, all lunch partners must be close to a lunch venue to reduce time spent in reaching the venue.
- Temporal Alignment: All lunch partners must meet for lunch at a mutually convenient time. Given that lunches take place during work-time lunch reservations are more prone to being cancelled bilaterally, or unilaterally due to overlaps (e.g. more important meetings, deadlines, etc.).
- Personal Preference: Employees participating in a business lunch may have a personal preference on the type of person they would like to have as a lunch partner. Based on their preferences, they might be looking to establish a working relationship for expanding their professional network, exchanging knowledge, seeking to receive or provide mentorship, engaging in synergies and professional collaborations or a combination of the above. Furthermore, employees may also have a personal preference on the lunch venue.

We subsequently filtered the success factors through an organizational culture lens, which allowed us to deduct a number of constraints our application should operate in, when matching employees for lunch (see table 2).

Table 2. This table shows the factors for a successful lunch experience and how they relate to the organization's culture. The application design constraints are requirements on the application design and are derived from the aforementioned relationship.

Success Factor	Organizational Context and Culture	Application Design Constraint
Spatial Proximity	ConnectedLunch was designed to serve employees of a large telecommunications organization located in Kista, a suburb of the city of Stockholm in Sweden, where approximately 11.000 employees are occupying workplaces inside an approximately squared area of 0.87 by 0.9 km (or roughly 0.78 km^2).	The spatial proximity of the potential users means that all restaurants in the area were accessible by everyone; therefore, we made all the restaurants in the area available to all users to choose from. It is worth noting that due to the same spatial proximity reasons we did not consider user location as a determining factor when pairing users.
Lunch Time	Lunchtime for the majority of employees is between 11:30 - 12:00 every day	Two fixed timeslots for booking lunch each day, 11:30 to 12:30 and 12:00 to 13:00.
Lunch Reservation Routine	Users usually make lunch arrangements between a few days and a few hours before lunchtime.	Lunch reservations possible for any date within the current work week but not for subsequent week(s), as users could schedule more important meetings over the lunch meetings in the interim, which could lead to cancellations.
Personal Preference	User base from all parts of the organization, experience ranging from newly hired employees to experienced people. Large selection of lunch venues to suit personal taste (in terms of cuisine, environment and lunch cost).	Desired work area (e.g. finance, marketing, supply, research and development, human relations) and level of experience of lunch partner as well as preferred lunch venue can be optionally set (see section 4).

The next section describes the architecture of ConnectedLunch and a typical lunch booking use-case from a hypothetical user.

4   Application Implementation

4.1   Development Lifecycle

The idea for creating ConnectedLunch was a result of a round-table discussion between employees of a large telecommunications organization located in Kista, Stockholm, Sweden, in mid-October 2012. The application was developed part-time by one employee, tested by a team of 6 people and was ready for use 3.5 months after the original discussion, in the beginning of February 2013. The total development time was 83 man hours, 40 of which were spent in programming the application, 35 on testing it, and the remaining 8 on deploying and configuring the application in the corporate cloud environment.

4.2   Architecture

The design of the application is based on a standard client-server model (see figure 1). Users are able to book lunches using their preferred web browser, while server side software modules manage user authentication, match users for lunch and notify them on a successful match via e-mail. The rest of this subsection describes the software modules and their interactions in greater detail.

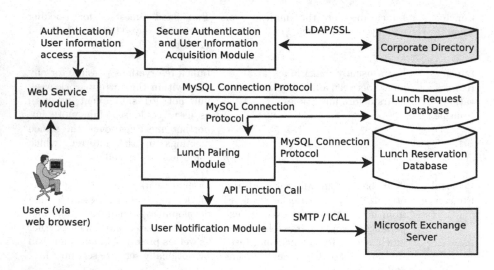

Fig. 1. This figure illustrating the block components of the application and their interactions. The components filled with grey colour are already existing enterprise assets (databases, servers, etc.) interfacing with ConnectedLunch.

The "Web Service" module contains a web server running a user interface (presented in section 4.3) which is accessed by users (i.e. employees). Using this interface, employees can create new lunch requests, view their lunch reservations for the current week, or cancel pending lunch requests that have not yet been matched to a colleague. Internally, the "Web Service" module interfaces with the "Secure Authentication and User Information Acquisition" module, which in turn interfaces with the "Corporate Directory" module.

The "Corporate Directory" is a database which contains information about the employees of the organization, such as their real names, email addresses, work phone numbers, job roles and exact office addresses. This information is used when employees submit new lunch requests, so that when they eventually get a lunch reservation confirmation they also receive a few useful information about their lunch partner (e.g. a phone number in case they want to call each other before lunch). Additionally, this directory contains the corporate credentials of employees, which are used by the "Web Service" module to authenticate them before using ConnectedLunch. The "Corporate Directory" predates Connected-Lunch and is managed by the Human Resources (HR) group of the organization, thus it did not add any additional costs to the development and maintenance of the application.

Triggered by an employee lunch reservation request, the "Web Service" module stores the request to a "Lunch Request Database". The request stores information about the employees preferences such as desired time to have lunch and optionally lunch venue and preferences about the potential lunch partner. As mentioned previously in this subsection, it is possible to cancel a lunch request, in which case the reservation request entry is removed from the "Lunch Request Database".

The "Lunch Pairing" module is software running independently in the background. It executes a pairing algorithm which periodically polls the "Lunch Request Database" incoming lunch reservation requests (a detailed description of the algorithm is provided at [12]). In case of a match of two requests, the "Lunch Pairing" module removes those requests from the "Lunch Request Database" and creates a reservation entry in the "Lunch Reservation Database". It also calls the "User Notification Module" to send a meeting invitation in ICAL format to the two lunch partners.

4.3   Lunch Reservation Use-Case

This section describes a typical ConnectedLunch usage scenario, according to which a hypothetical user logs in to the application, creates a new lunch reservation request and receives an email from the system when he/she was successfully matched against a lunch partner and a reservation has been made. Figure 2 illustrates the process.

Notice how the requirement for fixed timeslots, as shown in table 2, has been implemented in figure 2b. The fixed timeslots significantly increase the number of paired lunches, compared to allowing users to specify arbitrary times explicitly, while at the same time they serve the majority of the employees in the organization who traditionally go for lunch between 11:00 and 12:30.

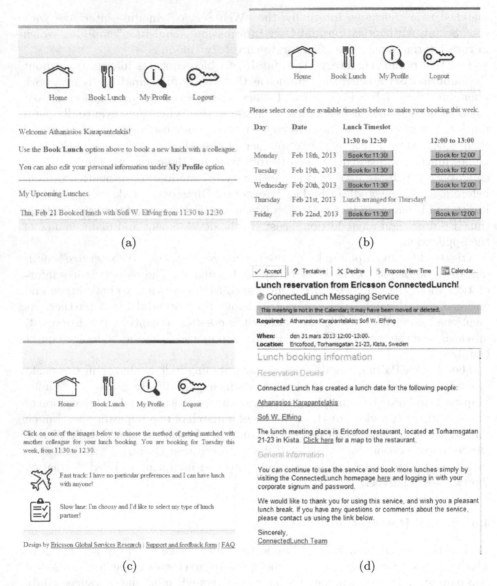

(a)   (b)

(c)   (d)

Fig. 2. This figure illustrates the lunch reservation process in ConectedLunch. Upon successful authentication, users are greeted by the "home screen" of the application which shows their arranged lunches for the week, if any. Bookings are done from the "book lunch" option. In the first step of the booking process, users select an available timeslot for a day of the week (b). Subsequently, they are presented with the choice of entering their preferences about their lunch partner (work area and years of experience) and/or lunch venue, or choosing a completely random match (c). Finally, (d) shows a calendar invitation sent via email to lunch partners upon successful match.

Also note the wording "fast track" and "slow lane", for matching with a random lunch partner, or a preferred one respectively (figure 2c). These words were chosen intentionally, as we wanted employees to choose to be randomly matched as we believed that this approach would increase the appeal of the application, as it stired the curiosity of the employees to try it out.

5   Application Deployment and Evaluation

ConnectedLunch was deployed for trial use in a large telecommunications organization located in Kista, a suburb of Stockholm, Sweden from end of February 2013 until middle of September 2013. The application was initially announced to a small number of employees via email using a distribution list for event communication and its use was expanded through word of mouth. The user group was heterogeneous, as employees who joined had different work backgrounds and years of experience (see tables 3 and 4).

Table 3. Number of ConnectedLunch users categorised by work area

Work Area	Number of Users
Research and Development (R&D), Product Management	113 (55%)
Service Delivery, Other Services	16 (8%)
Supply and Sourcing	17 (9%)
Business Development, Sales, Marketing, Commercial Management	16 (8%)
General Management, Operational Development, Competence Development, Human Resources (HR)	14 (7%)
Finance, IT, Communications, Other Jobs	29 (13%)

Table 4. Number of ConnectedLunch users categorised by work experience

Years of Experience	Number of Users
Up to one five of experience	68 (33.2%)
Between five and ten years of experience	85 (41.4%)
More than ten years of experience	52 (25.4%)

Although the overwhelming majority of users of ConnectedLunch had R&D and product management roles, other functions of the organization had a fair amount of representation in the user base. This is something we expected, given the fact that the number of employees from R&D represent the majority of total employee number, in the area were ConnectedLunch was deployed. Interestingly enough, all levels of years of experience in the organization, from newly hired to long-time employees had substantial representation. We therefore consider that ConnectedLunch had universal appeal to the organization's employees.

In total, during the trial period, 205 users booked 384 lunches. From these users, approximately 64% used the service more than once. From the lunch reservations, 186 were between managers and employees with a non-management role (roughly 48%). This is a positive result showing that ConnectedLunch facilitates communication between employees of different levels in the organizational structure. Although communication was happening before ConnectedLunch horizontally (i.e. on the same level - for example, between engineers from different groups), vertical communication between leaders and managed employees was limited to formal interactions.

Another one of our observations was that the majority of lunch reservations (334 lunches or 87% of total) was done using the "slow lane" approach, where users preferred specifying the profile of person they wanted to have lunch with (work area and years of experience) and/or the lunch venue over a random match (see figure 2c). This came as a surprise result to us, especially since we chose the wording "slow lane" intentionally to encourage users to use the random matching option "fast track" to promote random matching of employees. These results show that users had specific intentions when booking lunches, as they provided specific requirements on the profile of the desired lunch partner.

In order to gain more insight into these intentions as well as the whether the application fulfilled it's original goal of bringing people together to establish working relationships, we carried out a qualitative study after the trial phase concluded. An electronic questionnaire was made available to ConnectedLunch users on the application webpage. The questions focused on the perceived value of ConnectedLunch. 168 users (or 60% of the user-base) participated in the survey. 143 users (or 85% of those that participated) reported that the application was easy to use, while 147 (or 87.5%) reported that their lunch experience was overall positive.

Some users also reflected on how it helped them create and grow working relationships, in particular:

- 44 users stated that they rescheduled a lunch with the same lunch partner after the first meeting.
- 68 users stated that they maintained contact with their lunch partner over email, instant messaging, or using the company's internal social network.
- 32 newly-hired employees stated that ConnectedLunch helped them to expand their network and facilitate their introduction within the company.
- 18 users stated that they scheduled a professional meeting with their lunch partner (e.g. for knowledge exchange and/or potential collaboration).

In addition to the above, 50 users recommended ConnectedLunch to their colleagues. Users also suggested ways for improving the application. For instance, some mentioned that it would be beneficial if we provided a reward system for application use - which could help spread the application even further (some suggested examples were arranging random lunches with the company CEO, providing a "high score" page, where users with the most lunches would be clearly visible, etc.).

6   Contribution and Learnings

ConnectedLunch was a simple idea for enhancing dialogue in large organizations. It was rapidly prototyped and tested from employees of such an organization. The next paragraph summarises the benefits of ConnectedLunch, as observed from a 6-month period of trial use.

- Enhancing organizational cohesion by breaking traditional communication barriers between senior leadership and managed employees.
- Facilitating introduction of new employees to the organization by expanding their network of contacts.
- Benefitting seasoned professionals in the organization who can use ConnectedLunch as a means to expand their knowledge and engage in potential collaborations with other senior colleagues.
- ConnectedLunch does not affect the daily performance of employees, as lunchtime is typically a planned activity during a working day.
- Easy to learn and use, ConnectedLunch follows the organization's UI design guidelines (see figure 2) and reuses already existing, managed IT infrastructure and enterprise software to minimize maintenance costs.
- ConnectedLunch is a good return-on-investment, given the relatively small cost of implementation (see section 4.1) and maintenance (see section 4.2) and the promising results of the evaluation of the trial phase (see section 5).

Our experience with the application has also resulted in a number lessons learned. These could be considered by any organization planning to design similar tools.

- Organizational Flexiblity for Innovation: The organization must be flexible enough to support materialization of promising ideas, no matter from which part they originate. There are two dimensions for such flexibility, which, in our experience, the organizations need to have in place; namely, leadership commitment and resource procurement.
  Albeit small, ConnectedLunch required an up-front investment from the organization in order for the idea to materialize. Given that the application was outside of the designated work tasks of both authors, commitment was required both from the leadership team, who had to make a decision whether or not to proceed and the authors, who had to carry out their designated work tasks in tandem with implementing the application. Mutual understanding of the value of the application, which implies communication of justification of how the application would benefit the organization in clear terms to the leadership team, was the success factor in our case.
  Additionally, the organization must provide for the resources required for the idea to materialize, without stalling provisioning of such resources through

tedious, bureaucratical processes. A virtual environment in the corporate cloud platform, which automatically handled authorisation for accessing other enterprise software and specifically designed for prototyping new small-scale applications was in our case the catalyst for accelerating development.

– Users Desire Tailored Experiences: Another lesson learned for us was that the users actually preferred spending more time in the application to profile their lunch partner when reserving lunches, ignoring the option of random matching, which we believed would be the most popular one.

References

1. Ployhart, R.E.: Social Media in The Workplace: Issues and Strategic Questions. SHRM Foundation Executive Briefing
2. Kolsky, E., Pombriant, D.: Social Media 2012: State of Adoption. Beagle Research Group LLC and thinkJar LLC (August 10, 2012)
3. Faas, R.: NASA's internal social network was a flop, Here's how to make sure yours isn't
   http://www.citeworld.com/social/20611/successful-enterprise-social-network-needs-be-steeped-corporate-culture
4. Cho, H.-K., Trier, M., Kim, E.: The Use of Instant Messaging in Working Relationship Development: A Case Study. Journal of Computer-Mediated Communication 10(4) (July 2005)
5. Lowe, G.S., Schellenberg, G.: What's a Good Job? The Importance of Employment Relationships CPRN study no. W/05, Canadian Policy Research Networks, Ottawa
6. Gabarro, J.J., John, P.: Managing Your Boss. Harvard Business Review 83(1) (January 2005)
7. Kraut, R.E., Fish, R.S., Root, R.W., Chalfonte, B.L., Oskamp, I.S.: Informal communication in organizations: Form, function, and technology. In: Human Reactions to Technology: Claremont Symposium on Applied Social Psychology (1990)
8. Kusleika, D.: (2012) Lunch Pairings:
   http://dailydoseofexcel.com/archives/2012/04/03/lunch-pairings/
9. Erickson, C.: Pair Lunch: An Inexpensive, Effective Benefit to Strengthen Company Bonds,
   http://greatnotbig.com/2013/04/pair-lunch-an-inexpensive-effective-benefit-to-strengthen-company-bonds/ (visited on February 7, 2014)
10. ZinkUz, http://zinkuz.com/ (visited on February 7, 2014)
11. Roulette, L.: http://lunchroulette.us/index.htm (visited on February 7, 2014)
12. Lunch Pairing Algorithm Description, http://thanosk.info/papers/lpgalg.html (visited on February 7, 2014)

Humanizing the Enterprise

Delivering Best in Class User Experience to Business Software Users

Janaki Kumar

3410 Hillview Ave., Palo Alto, CA, 94304, USA
janaki.kumar@sap.com

Abstract. To deliver best in class user experiences to business users, design practitioners need to consider not just the user interface of applications, but the end-to-end customer experience. The enterprise software industry is undergoing a transformation as users ex-pect simple, easy-to-use experiences from their business software. However, to deliver on this expectation, enterprise software vendors face three primary hur-dles: The complexity of their customer's information technology land-scapes, Complexity of business processes in their customer's organizations, and Lack of design skills in customer's IT organizations. This paper describes these changing expectations and unique challenges in enterprise software user experience design. It outlines the user experience strategy that SAP, a leading enterprise software company, SAP, has developed to overcome these challenges, and deliver best in class user experiences to business users.

Keywords: User Experience, UX, Strategy, UX Management, UX Leadership, Customer Experience, Human Centered Design, Information Technology,

1   Introduction

User Centered design practitioners are trained to study user needs and deliver well designed, efficient, effective and satisfactory user interfaces to address these needs. When designing enterprise software, however, such practitioners need to go beyond the user interface, and consider the end-to-end experience of both customers and business user.

Enterprise software refers to a software suite comprised of common business applications such as Human Resources, Financials, Supply Chain Management, Customer Relationship Management etc., along with tools for modeling how the entire organization works (e.g. task flows and business process flows). Enterprise software is typically purchased by companies and made available to its employees. Consumer software is typically acquired by an individual for his or her personal use, such as social networking apps, email, word processing, instant messenger, web browsing.

A. Marcus (Ed.): DUXU 2014, Part IV, LNCS 8520, pp. 61–70, 2014.

Business users have an increasing expectation for simple, easy-to-use, consumer grade experiences from their information technology landscapes. While this is the goal of enterprise software vendors as well, there are some unique challenges in delivering such designs into the hands of the end users.

This paper describes these changing expectations and unique challenges in enterprise software design. It also outlines the User Experience strategy of an enterprise software company SAP, to overcome these challenges, and deliver best in class user experiences to business users.

2   Changing Expectations

Consumerization is rapidly transforming businesses and business users expect simple, easy-to-use experiences from their business software. There are three main drivers for this trend:

2.1   Changing Technology

Not long ago, office workers experienced the latest technology at work, and older technologies at home. Today with the advances in mobile technology and the prevalence of social media and consumer websites, the situation is reversed. People use the latest technology in their consumer grade apps via mobile devices, consumer websites, social media and game consoles. Whereas, the business software that they use at work lags behind.

2.2   Changing Work Practices

The line between work and personal life is blurring. People work at home and shop at work. For example, it is possible that a person will make a personal purchase, and a business related purchase, on the same day, and perhaps on the same device. They cannot help but compare the two experiences. They click on "buy" on their consumer website, and the product arrives at their doorstep the next day. For their business purchases, the catalog is limited to only the company approved vendors, searching is not as convenient, they have to go through a multi-step approval process, and the item may take weeks to arrive. Furthermore, they may pay more for their business purchases. Why is the shopping experience on consumer websites so much better than their company's procurement website?

2.3   Changing User Base

Another important factor is that the demographics of the enterprise worker are changing. The so-called digital natives[1] have entered the workplace. According to

---

[1] http://en.wikipedia.org/wiki/Digital_native

Wikipedia, a digital native is a person who was born after 1960, during or after the general introduction of digital technologies and who, through interacting with digital technology from an early age, has a greater understanding of its concepts. They have grown up with access to highly engaging video games and consumer software, and have similar expectations of enterprise software.

3   Unique Challenges to Enterprise Users

Enterprise software vendors, such as SAP are committed to meeting and exceeding these expectations. However, they need to overcome certain challenges that are unique to enterprise software industry.

3.1   Complexity of Technology Landscapes

According to CIO Magazine[2] organization's technology landscapes are increasing in complexity. This is primarily due to the heterogeneous and distributed nature of IT systems, which are facing increased pressure to adopt consumer technologies, support a mobile workforce, manage technical architectures, govern this workforce and ensure security in a distributed environment.

Accordingly to Mark McDonald, Garner's vice president of executive programs[3], "the challenge of (IT) complexity is exacerbated by the fact that many organizations have technology systems built over time, or acquired through acquisitions or complicated by many waves of vendor consolidations. For these companies, moving forward requires an almost archaeological effort to unearth, understand and work with all these layers of sedimentary technology."

Therefore, even a simple upgrade to business software has a ripple effect on the already complex landscape. They need to go through a rigorous process of planning, implementation and testing such software upgrades, to ensure that the integration between systems is intact, and business reporting is still accurate.

From a user experience perspective, business software designers face the challenge of considering not only the efficacy of the user interface, but also the cost of adoption, and the additional technical complexity it introduces into the landscape.

3.2   Business Complexity

Businesses are becoming more complex, and the rate of change is faster than ever. Due to increasing globalization, a company's customers, suppliers, manufacturers, distributors may span the world. With globalization comes increased regulatory pressure and penalties of non-compliance.

---

[2] http://www.cio.com/article/158250/
Consumer_Tech_The_New_Complexity_Add
[3] http://cxo-talk.com/mark-p-mcdonald-group-vp-gartner/

While enterprise software is delivered to fit standard business processes, each company may have unique workflows. Business software designers are faced with the task of recognizing these unique needs of the customer, while enabling a simple, easy-to use experience for end users.

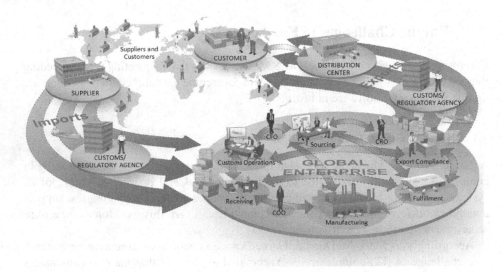

Fig. 1. Business is complex

3.3   Lack of Design Skills in IT Organizations

To address the technical and business complexity, enterprise software is customized and configured, by teams of consultants and IT staff. While these teams are typically comprised of people with technical skills who might also have knowledge of the business domain, they usually lack design skills. Therefore, they consider the technical and business requirements of the organization, but ignore the overall user experience. This leads to software that may be functionally complete, but does not take into consideration a human being who needs to use it to get their job done.

4   SAP's User Experience Strategy

Headquartered in Walldorf, Germany, with locations in more than 130 countries, SAP, is a world leader in enterprise software and software-related services. Founded in June 1972, its flagship product is SAP R/3, an Enterprise Resource Planning (ERP) application that manages business operations.

Based on the client-server model, SAP R/3 was introduced over 20 years ago. While SAP introduced many new products with modern user interface technologies, these products have not reached the adoption level of R/3, primarily due to the challenges described above. From a user experience perspective, many end-users of SAP, experience SAP's user interface through technology that was a couple of decades old.

Many SAP users still use **SAP GUI**

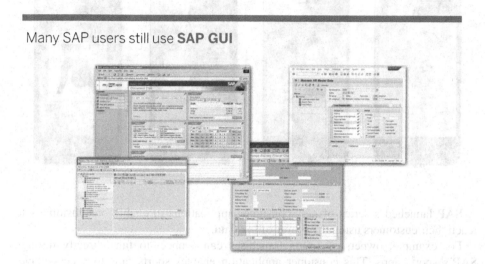

Fig. 2. SAP R/3 user interface

In 2013, to address these adoption issues and deliver best in class user experiences to their end users, the SAP decided to focus on three areas:

- Provide consumer-grade user experience for **new** applications for new business scenarios
- **Renew** existing applications by improving the user experience of the most broadly and frequently used business scenarios
- **Enable** customers to configure and customize the user experience to meet their own unique business processes

This product experience strategy is complemented by a cohesive services strategy. SAP offers Design Services to translate their UX strategy to the needs of the customers, and transform the experience for their business users.

5   New

Have you seen these **consumer apps** from SAP?

| Recalls Plus | PhotoTribe | Fan Experience | MyRunway |

SAP launched a series of new consumer applications to enable our customers to reach their customers using the power of big data.

For example, owners of sports franchises can connect to fans directly through SAP's sports apps. This consumer application enables sports fans to access player statistics and buy fan merchandise through their smart phone. For the first time, this application enables sport arenas to know exactly who attended their sporting events. Ticket sales are an unreliable indicator, since tickets can be purchased on behalf of others. Additionally, a typical fan who is engrossed in the game is less likely to leave their seat and buy sports merchandise even if they may want to. This app provides options for fans to make purchases without leaving their seat.

5.1   Renew

The strategy is also driving the renewal of the experience for the most broadly used SAP functions. SAP introduced Fiori in 2013—a collection of apps with a simple and easy to use experience for broadly and frequently used SAP software functions that work seamlessly across devices desktop, tablet, or smartphone.

Fiori allows enterprises to leverage their existing investment in SAP and deliver easy to use, responsive applications to the end-users of these applications.

These applications are architected to be introduced into the customer's landscape with minimal disruption. The user interface design is based on the following principles:

Role Based. While traditional business software attempts to maximize features and do all things for all people, Fiori starts with a clear definition of the user and their role in the organization.

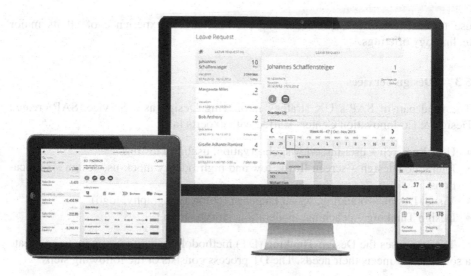

Fig. 3. Fiori

Responsive. Using HTML5 technology for the front-end, Fiori code is written once, and can be accessed via a desktop, tablet and mobile device. It is vendor agnostic and works with Apple, Microsoft and Google devices. This reduces complexity for SAP and the customer. The level of user experience degradation in using HTML5 verses a native technology is minimal.

Simple. Fiori applications strive for simplicity. The designer's rule of thumb is 1:1:3 – one user, one use case and three screens. While this is not absolute, it gives designers a framework to analyze business requirements. If the business team wants to cram multiple use cases onto the UI and the application is expanding to many screens, it may be time to pause and break up the app into its simpler parts. The team is encouraged to design multiple applications instead of combining all functionality into one.

Coherent. All Fiori apps have a single navigational paradigm and layout. This has obvious benefits to end users who can leverage this across multiple apps. While the navigation and layout remain consistent, designers are free to design the application content in the best way to fit the use case

Instant Value. Fiori apps must provide immediate value to customers without a lengthy implementation process. By leveraging the existing investment as much as possible, Fiori rapidly delivers value into the hands of end-users in days instead of the typical months.

5.2   Enable

SAP UX strategy recognizes that no matter how good the standard design, each customer has unique business needs. SAP delivers a set of robust and a set of easy to use tools to customize, configure and personalize the experience of all its major technology offerings.

5.3   Design Services

The final part of SAP's UX strategy is offering Design as a Service. SAP created Design & Co-Innovation Centers staffed with experts in:

- User Research – user interviews, observation, usability testing
- Interaction design – screen flows, low and high fidelity mock-us, design specifications
- Visual Design – branding, visual language (color, typography, logo)
- Design Thinking – coaching, moderation, storyboarding

The team uses the Design Thinking (DT) methodology with customers to co-create a solution that meets their needs. The DT process consists of the following steps:

- Understand the business objective
- Observe the end users
- Define a point-of-view
- Ideate on design solutions to the problems identified
- Prototype a design solution
- Test the prototype with customers and iterate based on feedback

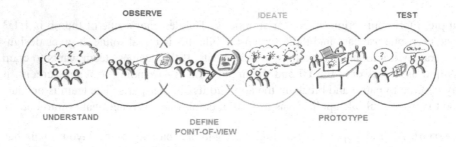

Fig. 4. Design Thinking process

The Design Thinking method is iterative and allows the customers and end-users to play an active role in shaping the design outcome. This increases the ultimate adoption of the new implementation since the business users are more invested in the results.

Here are a couple of examples that illustrate this aspect.

An Example – Redesigning a Financial Dashboard. In this project, the customer's IT Department received requirements for a financial dashboard from their stakeholders. As is typical for IT departments, they did not have any user experience designers on staff. The IT staff implemented the dashboards based on the technical specification with minimal interaction with the end users. Upon launch, end-users did not adopt these dashboards readily. They complained about usability and look-and feel.

The customer engaged the SAP Design Services team to remedy the situation. Since there was minimal user involvement in the earlier attempt, the designers from SAP leveraged the design thinking methodology and engaged the end user community. They interviewed them to understand their information needs. They observed how these users analyzed the information and how end users resolved issues that they identified. Based on insights, from these observations, the SAP design services team redesigned the dashboards. They gave visual prominence to the most important information; they organized the information to make it easy for analysis, and changed the visual look and feel to match the customer's brand.

The Line of Business (LOB) welcomed these changes and the introduction of design thinking and human centered design practices, helped remedy the relationship between the LOB and IT Department.

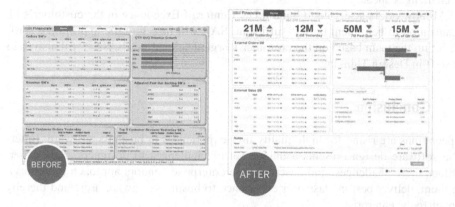

Fig. 5. Redesigning a Financial Dashboard

Reduced number of clicks by 43% from 45 to 26 clicks

Fig. 6. Increasing user productivity through simplification

Increased User Productivity through Simplification. In this example, the end users needed a system for a specific set of use cases. The standard implementation that IT had created exposed significantly more functionality than required by the end-user. The large number of errors and the resulting loss in productivity frustrated users.

The SAP Design Services team analyzed the usage patterns of the customers. This lead them to simplify the experience by removing unnecessary information. These changes reduced the number of clicks by 43% thereby reducing the error rate and significantly increased productivity.

6   Next Steps and Challenges Ahead

The initial reaction has been positive, and there are significant opportunities to expand the scope of design services for SAP. However, scaling these offerings to meet the increased demand from customers, while ensuring uncompromised quality is one of the challenges ahead.

SAP now offers a service to build a UX Center of Excellence in the customer's IT organization to help them be self-sufficient. SAP will help hire the appropriate staff, and set up the team based on the customer's organizational needs. SAP will also train the staff in Design Thinking.

7   Conclusion

Expectations are rising for high quality user experiences in business software. Enterprise software design presents a unique set of challenges to designers. This paper, outlines these challenges, and describes one enterprise vendors approach to addressing them, deliver best in class user experience to business software users and thereby humanize the enterprise.

Designing Financial Literacy and Saving Tools
for the Unbanked and under-banked in Brazil

Ananya Mukherjee[1], Catherine Winfield[1], Shan He[1],
Federico Casalegno[1], and Wilson Ruggiero[2]

[1] Mobile Experience Laboratory, Massachusetts Institute of Technology,
E15-320, 20 Ames Street, Cambridge, MA- 02139, United States of America
{ananya_m,winfield,shanhe,casalegno}@mit.edu
[2] Computer Engineering Department, Escola Politecnica, University of Sao Paolo,
Rua Prof. Luciano Gualberto, Travessa 3, no. 158, 05508-010, Sao Paolo, Brasil
wilson@larc.usp.br

Abstract. In this paper, we are interested in designing a novel approach to financial learning and saving for the unbanked and under-banked populations in emerging economies, more specifically in Brazil. Despite efforts by governments, non-profits and privately held banks, unbanked and under-banked populations remain prone to unfavorable financial habits and are ill equipped to utilize financial services. In proposing new modes of engagement with the topic of financial literacy and saving, we evaluate 1) social and behavioral aspects of financial lives of said populations 2) productive learning models 3) results from an ethnographic study, to finally demonstrate potential applications.

Keywords: Design for behavioral change, financial literacy, user experience design for financial products.

1 Introduction

In this paper, we are interested in designing a novel approach to financial learning and saving for the unbanked and under-banked populations in emerging economies, more specifically in Brazil.

By definition, unbanked customers have no checking, savings, credit, or insurance account with a traditional, regulated depository institution. Under-banked customers on the other hand, have one or more of these accounts, but conduct most of their financial transactions with alternative service providers, such as check-cashing services, salary accounts, payday lenders, and pawnshops - and still primarily use cash for most transactions. Estimates suggest that close to 2.5 billion people the world over remain un-served or underserved by formal or informal financial services [1]. While issues like accessibility, literacy and motivation are frequently recognized as the chief obstacles to mainstream banking for the rural poor, urban low-income groups grapple with deeper social and economic problems, especially in the context of Brazil.

Brazil has a unique position in this– the Brazilian Government has actively worked on bringing financial services to people's homes through an ambitious network of

A. Marcus (Ed.): DUXU 2014, Part IV, LNCS 8520, pp. 71–80, 2014.

banking correspondents. Approximately 2,200 of Brazil's 5,500 municipalities, representing 20 million people (more than 10% of the total population), had no bank branches and therefore no access to financial services in the year 2000. Within a span of ten years, an ambitious network of banking correspondents was able to reach all but 30 municipalities in Brazil [2]. Additionally, programs like the Bolsa Familia have played a monumental role in increasing the cash flow of families in need through Conditional Case Transfer Programs [3]. Despite the scale of effort in bringing said populations within mainstream banking, and this is of specific interest to the problem we pose, because of a culture of historically normalized credit and the valuation of goods over money due to inflation, the efforts of the government and the central bank have yielded limited results. Personal financial attitudes are not encouraging -in 2010, 53% of Brazilian households were spending more than they were earning. In 2012, the default rate on credit cards was 16% of the GDP, up from 6% in just a decade [4]. Some estimates suggest that the number of economically active unbanked and under-banked comprise 36% of the population [5].

In this paper, we present the process and results of a design research project aimed at producing new modes of financial literacy and developing applications and tools to assist the under-banked and the unbanked.

2   Methodology

The exploration of this topic was conducted in three distinct phases as presented in the following sections. A study of related works in the area of financial education, especially among under-banked and unbanked populations laid the groundwork for further engagement. Upon identifying and understanding key issues surrounding this topic, we led an ethnographic study in the city of Rio de Janeiro in Brazil. Finally, the insights gathered from these phases were used to inform design decisions and led to the creation of three functional prototypes demonstrating the conceptual and operational scope.

3   Related Works

3.1   Financial Behaviors among the Unbanked and under-banked

In their influential study, Dupas and Robinson [6] conducted field experiments among unbanked populations in Kenya to understand operational and behavioral barriers towards saving more. Using data from field experiments, Dupas and Robinson show that providing informal and simple saving technologies can substantially increase savings. For instance, simply offering a place to put away cash away from sight helped in inculcating a persistent saving habit. The act of putting an amount of cash away each month forced the user to keep a monthly mental account of their money, thereby influencing positive financial behavior and awareness. Additionally, earmarking savings had a tremendous impact on positive saving behavior. Users were able to anticipate their monetary needs for the future and save towards them rather than saving for the sake of saving. In the long run, savings that were associated with a specific financial goal were much more likely to succeed than those without. The only drawback observed here was the loss of liquidity. Users wanted to be able to save towards specific financial goals without losing out on the liquidity of un-allotted cash.

Social saving mechanisms were especially popular and successful in maintaining long term saving habits. ROSCA or rotating savings and credit associations are widely found as a way of saving in under-banked and unbanked populations across the world. Typically, a ROSCA is run by trusted members of the community and relies on social pressure and commitment to make sure that every member saves in accordance to the scheme they are a part of.

Studies published by the Innovations for Poverty Action (IPA) [7] have shown that the desire to save more is as common for the unbanked or under-banked poor as it is for the banked individual. One of the reasons, and one that is especially important for the scope of this paper, is the fact that services for the unbanked or under-banked poor are most often not designed to align with their financial behaviors. For instance, maintaining liquidity while saving towards specific goals is a priority among said populations. In a simple experiment, members of the IPA created jigsaw puzzles with pictures of clients' savings goals, such as a student in school, a picture of a home, or a vehicle. Every time clients made a deposit, they received a piece of the jigsaw puzzle. The 1,200 people randomly assigned to receive the jigsaw puzzle pieces were 2.3 percentage points more likely to meet their commitment of making a deposit every month for one year than were the 879 participants who were randomly assigned to the control group. This two-percentage point difference may seem like a small number, but it shows that a strikingly cheap and easy intervention can have a significant effect on savings.

Similar experiments like sending reminders, emphasizing losses over gain, binding accounts where customers are unable to withdraw money until they reach their financial goal and compartmentalizing savings have gone a long way in influencing positive saving behaviors.

3.2   Financial Literacy Programs

Although financial behavior seems to be positively affected by financial literacy, the long-term effects of financial education on financial behavior are less certain. Lusardi and Mitchell [8] show that households with low levels of financial literacy tend not to plan for retirement. They also tend to borrow at higher interest rates [9], acquire fewer assets [10], and participate less in the formal financial system relative to their more financially literate counterparts [11]. In response to this evidence, financial literacy programs have been advanced as a low-cost intervention with the potential to improve household financial decision-making and ultimately increase savings and welfare on a large scale. Cole, Sampson and Zia [12], show however, via a survey and study in India and Indonesia that traditional financial literacy programs produce modest effects, increasing demand for mainstream banking only for those with existing albeit low levels of education or financial literacy.

3.3   Theoretical Framework

A key aspect of Papert's constructionist learning theory [13] is that of "learning by doing." Much like traditional educational models, financial literacy programs depend on instruction-based learning. The current approach towards financial literacy programs struggles with the same problem as traditional education models – knowledge is unidirectional and there is a spatio-temporal lag between the reception of knowledge and action. Papert challenged this model by proposing models where knowledge structures are produced as a result of active engagement. Borrowing from Papert, we are able to propose ways in which the user's engagement with financial literacy occurs in the plane of real financial action.

Considering that several problems in User Experience Design areas are likely to have little previous literature and existing theories to fall back upon, and context in which the experiences occur plays crucial role, Grounded Theory is a potent tool for generating new knowledge [14]. Grounded theory, though originally developed for application in social research, has gained wide acceptance in various other domains including consumer experience and information systems research [15]. This theory offers one the flexibility of relying on multiple, varied data points and extract theories that pertain to the phenomenon being observed. Since it is based on empirical data, theories and applications can always be traced back to the root of the hypothesis. In using this framework for designing a service for the unbanked and the under-banked, we have been able to draw from multiple sources of data to derive fundamental concepts. In this process, we have been able to use academic research, newspaper articles, interviews and ethnographic research. With each step of the process, new data is used to refine and inform the original theory until additional data do not impact fundamental theories. In this way, each concept is backed, or grounded in significant data.

4   Ethnographic Study

In an ethnographic study of Brazilian unbanked and under-banked populations, data were collected from ten unbanked and under-banked families in a favela in Rio de Janeiro, Brazil. Through audio interviews, we were able to gain insight into their financial lives, ambitions and pain points. The results showed that in addition to the culture of credit, a deep mistrust of banks and the banking system has led to negative associations with traditional financial instruments. Many families felt shunned by mainstream banks. Traditional bank offerings are not well suited to their needs and the priority for most was to be in complete control of their money. In this regard, Conta Salario or Salary Accounts have worked exceptionally well. A vast majority of the under-banked collects their monthly salaries through these accounts where they typically withdraw their entire salaries in cash. In this predominantly cash economy, people end up employing jars and 'under-the-mattress' saving solutions to be in better control of their money. Saving decisions and behaviors were focused on specific short-term financial goals.

Community plays a big role in the everyday lives of the unbanked and the under-banked. In this particular favela, ROSCA like informal saving institutions were common. People heavily relied on financial help from their peers in case of emergencies and social structures were built around a tacit agreement of stepping up to help one's neighbor in times of need. People are also known to trust their families and friends over more formal financial advice and strategies. None of the candidates in our study had ever considered approaching a bank to plan their financial life. Instead, they could relate easily to the experiences of those around them and preferred to follow their advice to a bank's.

To summarize, we learnt that the unbanked and the under-banked have a deep mistrust of banks. This is because said populations prefer to have complete control of their money; a behavior that can also be seen in their choice to operate only in cash. Saving decisions are motivated by short-term goals and the savings are typically kept under the mattress or in jars. Finally, financial decisions and exchange of knowledge is an activity that is highly centered within the community among one's peers. Not only is such financial knowledge valued over one offered by a bank or an institution, it is believed to be far more relevant and tailored to the seeker.

5   Results

The findings from our research and ethnographic study point to very specific problems in existing services for the unbanked and the under-banked. First and foremost, very few services are actually designed specifically for the unbanked and the under-banked. The barriers to mainstream banking for said populations range from simple things like a complicated account opening process, unclear information on banking practices and simply not having enough information. In the case of Brazil, these issues are compounded by a deep feeling of mistrust in banking institutions.

The design of the prototypes was informed primarily by the following findings:

1. Users need to be in control of their money- "Under-the-mattress" saving solutions are widespread among the unbanked and under-banked. Apart from more obvious benefits like maintaining liquidity of money and having access to cash at all times, there is a deeper behavioral aspect to this. These kinds of solutions make people feel like they are in control of their money. It is visible, accessible and there are no middlemen between them and their cash.
2. Recognize the power and influence of the community-When it comes to financial advice and planning, people from said populations are much more likely to follow their peers than seek information elsewhere.
3. Design productive learning environments - One of the directing principles, key to all three concepts, draws from the tenets of Papert's constructionism as a foundation for designing productive learning environments. The first "big idea" proposed by Papert is that of learning by doing as opposed to learning by being taught explicitly. He proposes that this way of learning is not only more engaging, but more productive and relevant to the individual's needs and goals. This is especially relevant to us since financial literacy is not productive when it is independent of finan-

cial action. Reducing or obliterating the distance between financial education and financial decision-making is one of the secondary goals of the project.

The complex arrangement of trust, motivation and cultural behaviors informed the design of the prototypes that place maximum trust and faith in the user, reinforcing ownership of money and financial futures, and thereby accountability.

6   Prototypes

Three high-fidelity prototypes were developed to showcase the conceptual and operational scope of the proposed solution.

1) *Luz* - *Luz* (Portuguese for "light") was developed as a response to the habit of appropriating household objects to store cash. *Luz,* in this case a lamp, is a utilitarian everyday object with the added functionality of a personalized, interactive safe that handholds the user through the process of saving. The user is able to define short-term financial goals and receives timely and relevant financial guidance in order to reach their goals. For instance, *Luz* reminds the user when it's time to make the next deposit on a financial goal. The user experience ensures maximum control over cash by keeping it in the house but is carefully designed to encourage reaching the saving goal, thus encouraging saving up for purchases rather than saving down or buying on credit. Using Dupas and Robinsons formulation, *Luz* both "hides" the cash while assuring the user of liquid cash if need be.

   Luz was built as an exploration into intelligent everyday objects. By adding a layer of intelligence over traditional saving devices like a box, the experience is markedly different. The device is now able to guide the user through the process of saving without alienating the original experience completely. Currently the prototype does not address security concerns.

2) *Smart Saving Envelopes*- A significant number of the under-banked in Brazil are owners of *Conta Salario* or Salary Accounts. Every payday, owners of such accounts are known to withdraw their entire salary in cash. *Smart Saving Envelopes* were designed to reach users at this touch point by offering simple, color coded saving envelopes with achievable saving goals (in denominations of R$100, 200 & 500). By using simple peel-off envelopes, the user is motivated to reach their saving goal by being reminded of the worth of their savings with each increment. The experience is supplemented with actionable saving tips sent via SMS on reaching notable milestones. The experience of saving with *Smart Saving Envelopes* is familiar in its use of the ubiquitous paper envelope as a saving device. By adding gamification to the process of saving and simple interactivity via SMS, *Smart Saving Envelopes* offer a clear vision and the steps in the process of reaching one's saving goal.

   This offers a low-cost, low-infrastructure solution that can be developed and applied easily by small-scale banks and financial institutions.

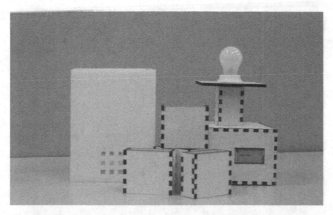

Fig. 1. Luz, front view. The modular structure of the device is designed to offer compartments for earmarked savings. The main parts of the device are 1) Saving compartments 2) E-ink display 3) Lamp bulb and facade.

Fig. 2. Luz, scanning envelope. Users scan goal specific envelopes with a set amount each month. The display is updated to show progress on a saving goal. The display also shows reminders and information relevant to the user and their saving goals transmitted over wi-fi.

Fig. 3. Luz, Goal specific saving compartment. Luz offers four goal specific saving compartments.

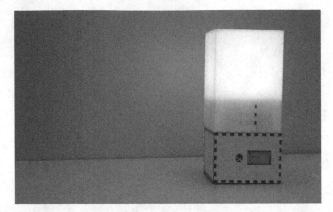

Fig. 4. Luz, as a lamp. When not in use, Luz is used as a lamp.

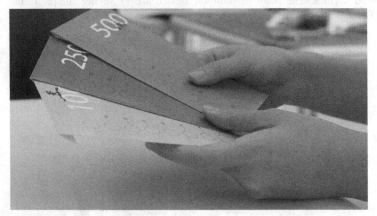

Fig. 5. Smart saving envelopes come in denominations of R$ 100, 250 and 500. With each saving increment, the user is shown the worth of their savings thereby encouraging them to save more.

3) *Realize- Realize* was conceived as an online space where users could learn about everyday finance from lived experiences of their peers and those around them. Supplemented with expert advice, *Realize* becomes a repository of crowd-sourced knowledge about everyday financial tips and advice. As a financial social network, *Realize* reverses the expert-novice relationship typical of financial literacy programs and relies on collective action to democratize financial knowledge. Additionally, it takes into account the need for a friendly space that offers relevant and credible financial advice. Users become part of communities that are like them and learn, and gain support from their peers.

Brazil is one of the fastest growing countries when it comes to social media. Our ethnographic study shows that most people in the favelas have an Internet connection and are active on social media. This is slated to grow in the future with social media companies investing heavily in Brazil. [15]

Fig. 6. Realize offers a safe and trustworthy place to ask financial questions most relevant to the user. Users can get advice from their peers as well as an experienced professional on the same platform.

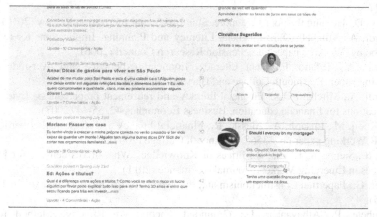

Fig. 7. Users can be part of topic specific groups like "First time home-buyers" or "Saving for college"

7   Conclusion

This study has aimed to produce an understanding of the behavioral and social under-pinnings of the financial lives of the unbanked and the under-banked. We have proposed novel and unprecedented solutions that aid said populations to acquire financial knowledge and directly act on that knowledge. All the proposed solutions have been driven by the single focus of making financial knowledge actionable. By embracing the principle of "learning by doing", we hope to reduce the gap between financial knowledge and financial decision-making. In our future work, we aim to conduct a user test among the unbanked and under-banked populations of Brazil.

Delivering financial services to the unbanked and under-banked remains a globally relevant problem, affecting 2.5 billion people worldwide by some estimates. This study can be applied to other emerging economies and adapted to specific contexts.

Acknowledgements. The authors would like to thank Karina Silvester, Andrew Johnson and Amar Boghani for their contributions to the project. We are thankful to our collaborators at Banco Bradesco, Rony Rogerio Martins Sakuragui and Fabio Muneratti Ortega of Scopus Tecnologia, Brazil.

References

1. Chaia, A., Goland, T.: Counting the world's unbanked. McKinsey Study (2010)
2. Consortium on Financial Systems and Poverty: Brazil's innovative banking correspondents' expand financial services to underserved areas (2012)
3. Soares, F.V., Ribas, R.P., Osorio, R.G.: Evaluating the Impact of Brazil's Bolsa Familia: Cash Transfer Programs in Comparative Perspective (2007)
4. Tekur, S., Eisenbeis, H.: BRIC Saving and Spending by the Letters. Iconoculture (2012)
5. Febraban: 36% of the population is unbanked (2012)
6. Dupas, P., Robinson, J.: Why don't the poor save more? Evidence from Health Savings (2011)
7. Karlan, D.: Helping the poor save more. Stanford Social Innovation Review (2010)
8. Lusardi, A., Mitchell, O.S.: Financial Literacy and Planning- Implications for retirement well-being. Working paper no.1. Pension Research Council (2006)
9. Lusardi, A., Tufano, P.: Debt Literacy, financial experience and over-indebtedness. Working paper. Dartmouth College and Harvard Business School (2008)
10. Lusardi, A., Mitchell, O.S.: Financial literacy and retirement preparedness- Evidence and implications for financial education. Business Economics 42, 35-44 (2007)
11. Van Rooij, M., Lusardi, A., Alessie, R.: Financial literacy and stock market participation. NBER Working paper no. 13565. Dartmouth College (2007)
12. Cole, S., Sampson, T., Zia, B.: Prices or Knowledge? What drives demand for Financial Services in Emerging Markets? Journal of Finance (2011)
13. Stager, G.: Papertian Constructionism and the Design of Productive Contexts for Learning (2005)
14. Khambete, P., Athavankar, U.: Grounded Theory: An Effective Method for User Experience Design Research. Design Thoughts (2010)
15. Eriksson, P., Kovalainen, A.: Qualitative Methods in Business Research, 1st edn. SAGE (2008)
16. Chao, L.: Brazil: The Social Media Capital of the World. Wall Street Journal (2013)

Enabling Better User Experiences across Domains: Challenges and Opportunities Facing a Human Factors Professional

Emrah Onal[1], Susan McDonald[1], Corey Morgan[1], and Olga Onal[2]

[1] SA Technologies, Inc. Marietta, GA, USA
{emrah,susan.mcdonald,corey.morgan}@satechnologies.com
[2] Marietta, GA, USA
olga@designers-int.com

Abstract. *Human Factors* is a multidisciplinary field studying the design of systems and equipment that fit the human physical and cognitive abilities. *Human factors* professionals are in a unique position to practice their trade within a variety of domains including government, industry, and military. Regardless of the domain, good *user experience*, as provided by a human factors practitioner, affords more effective human systems interaction. In this paper, we offer insights into the value of a good user experience and the consequences of not providing it; we discuss organizational and practical challenges that may lead to neglecting user experience; and finally, we offer ideas on how to bring human factors into projects and provide better user experience.

Keywords: user experience, human factors, domains, challenges, opportunities.

1 Introduction

ISO 9241-210 defines *user experience* as "a person's perceptions and responses that result from the use or anticipated use of a product, system or service" [1]. Good user experience, as provided by human factors practitioner, affords more effective human systems interaction where the user is an important part of the system (Fig. 1). Regardless of the domain, when humans are required to use technology to perform their daily tasks, their interaction and experience with the system or product will be the determining factor for overall efficiency, safety, and acceptance.

A host of people – e.g., cellphone users, on-line shoppers [2], drivers, healthcare professionals, gas & electric operators, oilfield engineers, mining operators [3], satellite operators, flight controllers [4], pilots [5], and soldiers – all interact with products and systems, and they all suffer if their experience is not pleasant, simple, efficient, or safe. As *human factors* practitioners, we are uniquely positioned to apply scientific principles to bring the best possible user experience to our users.

In this paper, our objective is to inform the reader on potential challenges and opportunities when designing a better user experience across a variety of domains. First, we explain the importance of providing a good user experience and how different

A. Marcus (Ed.): DUXU 2014, Part IV, LNCS 8520, pp. 81–89, 2014.

domains emphasize different aspects of a user's experience. Next, we discuss the reasons why user experience may be neglected and the consequences of not providing a good user experience. Finally, we offer ideas on how to bring human factors into projects and provide better user experience.

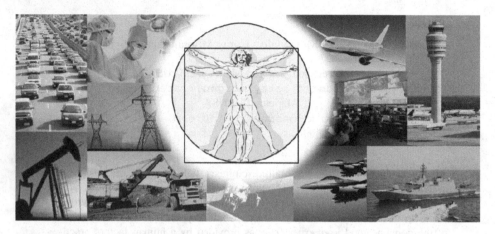

Fig. 1. In a variety of domains the human operator is the key element for success. A good user experience is essential to a successful product or system.

2   Background

2.1   The Importance of User Experience

The value of user experience is that it emphasizes all aspects of a user's interaction with the product, from beginning to end. This may include shopping, purchasing, unboxing, setup, learning, technical support, and usage of a particular product. A major goal of the *human factors* practitioner is to design and enable the best experience in all stages of product acquisition and use.

Fig. 2 shows the famous tree swing cartoon depicting a tire and rope swing in various states of dysfunction [6]. This cartoon, which has existed in many variations since the late 1960s [7], illustrates some of the pitfalls faced when working on a project. The cartoon has a simple premise: a customer needs a way to swing from a tree. There are many ways to design a tree swing, but a customer's explanation of their needs may not always be interpreted correctly. In his excitement, the customer may fail to provide key details or over-specify, leading the project leader to develop their own interpretation of the customer's needs. The project leader provides a simplified version of the design – a single bench connected to the tree. However, he misses the most important fact about the swing, which is that it should not swing across the tree trunk. The analyst, perceptively, fixes that problem by cutting the tree trunk and adding support so that the tree doesn't fall down. The programmer ignores both trunk cutting and supports, focusing instead on implementing his understanding of project requirements (a bench, some rope, and some relationship between rope and tree). From there things go spectacularly downhill. The business consultant promises a comfy padded armchair, yet the product that is installed lacks any resemblance to the customer's initial explanation. The customer is billed for a whole amusement park and is left with little to no documentation or support for how the product is to be used. In the end we see that all along what the customer really needed was the simplest solution of all: a tire swing. We laugh because, as users, we have seen products that function that way, and as product creators, we have experienced any or all of the misunderstandings implied.

A project may fail because of poor product design, poor customer service, or because of a failure to understand the user's needs. A failure in one step can ruin the whole experience. User experience emphasizes all aspects of user involvement and input. A well-designed user experience should help avoid many of the problems highlighted in this cartoon.

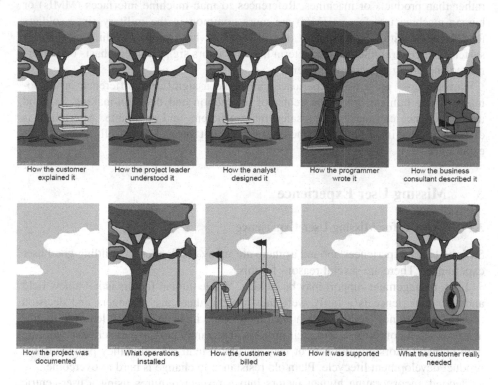

Fig. 2. The famous "tree swing cartoon". A well-designed user experience should help avoid many of the problems highlighted in this cartoon. *Creative Commons Attribution 3.0 Unported License,* http://www.projectcartoon.com/about [6].

2.2　Use and Emphasis across Domains

User experience can be seen as a component of the human factors (or *ergonomics*) discipline. The International Ergonomics Association defines human factors as "...the scientific discipline concerned with the understanding of interactions among humans and other elements of a system, and the profession that applies theory, principles, data and methods to design in order to optimize human well-being and overall system performance." [8] The term *user experience* was introduced by Donald Norman in the mid-1990s with the intention to emphasize all aspects of the person's experience with a system, including design, graphics, the interface, the physical interaction, and the manual. [9]

Different domains often emphasize different aspects of a user's experience. For example, the term user experience is more often used in consumer-oriented industries because of its strong emphasis on the user (who is making the purchase decision). Industries with an emphasis on computer systems, especially complex ones, tend to refer to human-computer interaction (HCI) or computer-human interaction (CHI) as an alternative term. HCI focuses more on users working specifically with computers, rather than products or machines. References to man-machine interfaces (MMIs) or human-machine interfaces (HMIs) are more common in the military since soldiers tend to work with a combination of software and hardware, including mechanical systems. In general, the use of the term human factors signals an emphasis on performance and safety aspects of a system.

Nevertheless, good user experience can make a significant difference in all domains where humans are at the center of interaction and decision-making, as good user experience can make things safer, more efficient, and enjoyable. After all, it is difficult to imagine a situation where users will not appreciate a well-designed user experience.

3   Missing User Experience

3.1   Reasons for Missing User Experience

Still, bad user experiences abound as there are many challenges to building good user experiences. There are several reasons for this.

First, management support may be lacking. While human factors is not a new field and user experience is a fairly well-known term, there are managers and decision makers who are not familiar with human factors and its benefits, or at least not familiar enough to incorporate it into their projects. They may not have experience working with human factors practitioners or may not understand the value they provide to the product development lifecycle. Plain old resistance to change is hard to overcome.

Second, incorporating human factors into a project requires using a user-centric design and development process, which includes human factors practitioners in all stages of design and development, from requirements gathering to validation and deployment. This in turn requires rethinking existing design and development processes. Project planning has to be done with upfront human factors focus, and the project timeline has to incorporate regular evaluations and usability testing. When budget and time are limited, the additional focus on human factors might be seen as merely an unnecessary increase to project duration and cost.

Third, human factors may be seen as an optional component, while software and hardware development are essential to shipping a product.

Fourth, some systems may be too complex to be redesigned from scratch. For example, improving the user experience in mining operations may require fundamental changes to a variety of hardware and software that were designed perhaps independently by different contractors or vendors [3].

Finally, management may not understand that creating a product without human factors is akin to building a house with only a hammer and saw. The final product may look fine, but on closer inspection is barely useful or completely unusable.

These issues are less common in consumer-facing industries where a lack of usability or good experience directly translates into lost revenue. For example, one cannot imagine a successful website without good design and usability. In other industries, however, it is harder to persuade managers or decision makers of the value in providing a good user experience unless it clearly translates into fewer accidents, increased productivity, or some other clearly quantifiable factor. It took airplane crashes to bring the usability of flight systems to public attention [10].

3.2   Consequences of Missing User Experience

While there are many aspects of user experience that can be neglected, this paper will address one specific, common failure – that of technology-centic design, where pieces of technology are cobbled together to perform a variety of functions, resulting in disarray from the user's perspective. This technology-driven approach can result in a collection of systems that gather and present their own data sources, with each new system being added alongside existing ones. The data are not integrated or transformed to take into account the user's needs. This causes significant challenges for the user experience, as they must gather disparate pieces of information from multiple systems or displays, then integrate these bits together mentally to develop an understanding of system functioning [11].

For example, Fig. 3 is a picture of the inside of an electric shovel cab used in mining operations. In addition to communication controls, mechanical controls, and a control panel, there are six computer monitors interfacing a variety of systems. This example is by no means atypical, especially in domains with complex systems (such as the military). Such systems may be built by multiple contractors or provided by multiple vendors, where each one delivers an isolated function that, at best, integrates loosely with the rest of the system. Each vendor usually understands a small part of the puzzle and may not be aware of the big picture.

Another example is in oil well drilling, where multiple systems are employed and each system has its own alarms. Since the multiple systems don't communicate with each other, alarms can go off during steps in the drilling process where they are not relevant (e.g., a "low flow" alarm goes off during breakout because the system that monitors flow doesn't know they have turned off the pumps to add new pipe).

Fig. 3. Example of a technology-centric design in an electric shovel cab. Six computer monitors, communication systems, mechanical shovel controls, and a control panel clutter the cab. Clearly, this is not a user-centric design.

Users are flexible, but they can adapt only so much. Information overload and increased workload brought by each additional system can quickly overwhelm and surpass human cognitive capabilities. This may result in more accidents, reduced safety, reduced customer acceptance, reduced productivity, and decreased performance. The science of human factors, particularly situation awareness and decision making research, is ideal for improving the user experience in this area.

4   Bringing Better User Experience

So, what can we do to bring good user experience to projects? Measuring and quantifying benefits of good user experience are good starting points for convincing decision-makers.

4.1   Measure Benefits

First, we need to demonstrate value – how user experience and human factors benefit the projects. We need to measure benefits such as increased system performance and usability, user acceptance and performance, and decreased workload and error rates. These are all parameters that will help management make informed decisions. If a product or system is not properly tested for usability pitfalls there will be significant uncertainty about the success of that product.

4.2   Quantify Benefits

It is even better to quantify those benefits in terms that directly affect decision-makers – potential profits or, equivalently, losses the project can suffer due to user experience issues. Translating what usability really means for a project's bottom line can help decision-makers understand the necessity of creating good user experiences. Clearly, poor safety and poor performance, driven by bad system design or integration, can cost money and lives. Below are some examples from the mining domain.

1. A large haul truck fully loaded with high-grade gold ore can be worth hundreds of thousands of dollars. Poor system integration (between shovels, dump trucks, and dispatch), poor visibility into system behavior, and poor UI feedback can (and does) result in haul trucks accidentally dumping valuable ore into waste areas.
2. At peak capacity, a crusher can grind thousands of metric tons of copper ore per hour, potentially worth hundreds of thousands of dollars. A lost bucket tooth, if undetected (either due to lack of alerts or to too many alerts that are ignored), can jam crushers and require dangerous repairs along with hours of downtime.
3. Mines operate on large scales: large volumes of material, mega-shovels, mega-trucks. Small incremental improvements can result in large profits. According to a study [12] a small increase in haul truck efficiency can translate into millions of dollars in yearly increased revenue.

4.3   Convince Decision-Makers

It is critical to be aware of what is important to decision-makers. In some situations, there is a special group of end users whose need for user-friendliness is paramount because their time is especially valuable. An example of this is the highly competitive field of e-commerce, where user experience can directly affect a user's decision or ability to purchase a product. Another example of this is manufacturing, where small improvements in usability for highly repetitive actions can translate to large increases in productivity. In other situations, the software must be completely error-proof because the cost of human error is very high; an example is cockpit software for airline pilots. Demonstrating added value in high visibility circumstances can inform and often influence decision-makers.

4.4   Improve Communication between Human Factors and Development

Another key to successfully completing a project that provides good user experience is effective communication and collaboration between human factors and development teams. While the human factors team focuses on the user, the development team focuses on the technical aspects of the project. These are clearly complementary functions with strong interdependencies. Both teams have the same goal: delivering a successful product. At the same time, there is an inherent conflict of interest because of the different focus areas of these teams. There is a clear tradeoff between the value certain features provide to the user versus the time and effort required to develop them, and effective communication makes yes / no decisions (whether to develop a feature) easier. Table 1 shows a simplified decision matrix for feature implementation.

Table 1. A simplified decision matrix showing the value of a feature to the user versus its development cost. 'Yes' indicates that it is probably worthwhile implementing the feature; 'No' indicates features with a high cost/benefit ratio; and 'Depends' is for those in-between cases.

		Development Cost		
		High	Medium	Low
Value to User	High	Yes	Yes	Yes
	Medium	Depends	Yes	Yes
	Low	No	Depends	Yes
	None	No	No	No

Good management facilitates communication between different areas of expertise and finds the right balance for the success of the project, especially when facing tight deadlines and limited budgets that inevitably impact most projects. Also, both teams need to understand how the other team operates rather than working independently. Human factors teams may not fully understand the intricacies of development, and development teams may not fully understand how incorporating the user's perspective leads to a better product. Good user experience is not easy to provide, and good development takes time and effort. If the teams are aware of each other's challenges, they will be more amenable to their differences. Obviously, there are many other teams involved in a project (business analysis, software testing, documentation, etc.), and good communication between all teams is important.

5   Conclusion and Future Work

To summarize, there are many reasons why user experience may be neglected; however, we propose a number of approaches to counteract this neglect.

- Clearly explain and quantify the benefits of human factors, preferably translating them to the bottom line (e.g., more satisfied users, more revenue, better sales, percent increase in performance or efficiency, reduced number of errors, etc.)
- Facilitate communication between teams to understand how each team works and understand the rationale behind their responses.
- Good management who appreciates all teams and their value, and who understands that good user experience is essential.

References

1. International Organization for Standardization: Ergonomics of human system interaction - Part 210: Human-centered design for interactive systems. ISO/FDIS 9241-210:2009. Geneva, Switzerland (2009)
2. McCarthy, J., Wright, P.: Technology as experience. Interactions 11(5), 42–43 (2004)
3. Onal, E., Craddock, C., Endsley, M.R., Chapman, A.: From theory to practice: Designing for situation awareness to transform shovel operator interfaces, reduce costs, and increase safety. Canadian Institute of Mining, Metallurgy and Petroleum (CIM) Journal 4(4) (2013)
4. Wickens, C.D., Mavor, A.S., McGee, J.P. (eds.): Flight to the future: Human factors in air traffic control. National Academies Press (1997)
5. Endsley, M.R., Garland, D.J., Shook, R.W., Coello, J., Bandiero, M.: Situation Awareness in General Aviation Pilots. In: Annual Report Prepared for NASA-Ames Research Center Under Contract #NAS2-99073 (2000)
6. The Project Cartoon, http://www.projectcartoon.com
7. Businessballs, http://www.businessballs.com/treeswing.htm
8. International Ergonomics Association, http://www.iea.cc/whats/index.html
9. Norman, D., Miller, J., Henderson, A.: What you see, some of what's in the future, and how we go about doing it: HI at Apple Computer. In: Conference Companion on Human Factors in Computing Systems, p. 155. ACM (1995)
10. Wiegmann, D.A., Shappell, S.A.: A Human Error Analysis of Commercial Aviation Accidents Using the Human Factors Analysis and Classification System (HFACS). In: Federal Aviation Administration Oklahoma City OK Civil Aeromedical Inst. (2001)
11. Endsley, M.R., Jones, D.G.: Designing for situation awareness: An approach to human-centered design. Taylor & Francis, London (2012)
12. Chapman, A.: Field Study on Haul Time Variability in Open Pit Mines. Thesis submitted to the Department of Mining Engineering. Queen's University, Kingston, Ontario, Canada (2012)

Brands Analysis Using Informational Ergonomics Concepts: A Proposal

João Carlos Riccó Plácido da Silva, Luis Carlos Paschoarelli,
and José Carlos Plácido da Silva

UNESP, Bauru, Brazil
joaocarlos_placido@hotmail.com,
{paschoarelli,plácido}@faac.unesp.br

Abstract. Currently, a lot of visual information present in all media is form vehemently, for example, in print media and interfaces used for publicity in conjunction with informational design. This visual information has great influence in the life of human beings, since the vision of these individuals is the most used sense. Studies on visual identity have not explored this issue in a satisfactory manner, favoring thus the subject of this small development projects in the area. It is noted the need for analyzes to enable implementation principles of project, making them accessible to the comprehension of most individuals. This study aimed to propose an evaluation of visual identities, which were analyzed by means of visual concepts of usability, design methodologies and Gestalt. We contacted design firms specialized in visual identity projects, places where interviews were conducted to collect the brands allowed for analysis. The results point to a frequent demand for the employment of visual usability principles, design methodologies and Gestalt design in visual identities.

Keywords: Ergonomic, Graphic Design, Guidelines, Visual Identities.

1 Introduction

Mankind uses brands to communicate since the prehistoric time. Over the time those brands have been more complex and with denser messages. The apex of the contemporary time are the institutional brands that use symbols or graphic language and typography to transmit their message. The lack of concern how those graphic projects are being applied, has caused a visual discomfort, which is called visual noise and consists in the excess of pre-organized information. According to Raposo (14), if the brand is not used in a coherent and consistent manner, or if the other elements of identity are not a unit, you end up losing the logic of graphic discourse that allows its recognition.

The solution, at first, is responsibility of graphic designers, since they have the knowledge and the methodology to analyze and organize the information in a more appropriate manner, aiming to positively affect the daily life of users. It is noteworthy, in this case, the development, definition and implementation of visual identities.

A. Marcus (Ed.): DUXU 2014, Part IV, LNCS 8520, pp. 90–101, 2014.

The lack of patterns for the development of the visual identity results in incomprehensible projects, and realization of the growing number of institutions seeking a place in the market; misconceptions in the use of colors and shapes result in informational overload, among others. Moreover, when the development of the brand is not well done, the visual element can end up in not summarizing the product or service, confusing the perception and reception of the consumer.

This study is based on a directed literature review, addressing factors that are around the visual identity, such as the fundamentals of design, nonverbal language, color, ergonomics and gestalt. Posteriorly, it was developed an analysis sheet based on the review and guided by the informational ergonomics, so brands were pooled to be surveyed by the analysis form, enabling to present some important parameters for evaluating visual identities.

2 Theoretical Foundation

2.1 Design

The conception of objects and information systems in today's world depends on several technological areas, however, the indication of the term design to denote this practice seems to be inherent in a scientific discussion in this area. Currently, after nearly a century of the initiative of the German school, the Bauhaus, the design is still a controversial term. It is noted a trivialization of the term design, sometimes by lack of knowledge, sometimes because it does not imply a unique career, as law, medicine or architecture. These jobs require a license or qualification, with established standards and protected by self-regulatory institutions. The design, on the other hand, widens increasingly new skills, but without any institutionalized specification, without organization or regulatory concept, which makes it capable of indiscriminate use (6).

2.2 Visual Identity

The visual identity is the set of formal elements that visually represents, by a systematic way, a name, idea, ideology, product, company, institution or service (16). The visual identity or brand is an appeal to the senses, it is possible to see, touch, grab, listen, observe and move. It feeds the user recognition and widen the differentiation of its products and ideas, as well as bringing together disparate elements, unifying them into integrated systems (18).

Raposo (14), says that if the brand is not used in a consistent and consistently way, or if the other elements of identity does not form a unit, you end up losing the logic of graphic discourse that allows its recognition. The brand cannot be regarded as advertising or comics, so it does not purport to convey all the corporate values. To demonstrate the quality of the product or service that the institution provides is the role of the publicity. It must explain the positioning of the brand and show its meanings or values. In the development of a visual identity, four main graphic elements must be considered: logo, symbol, color and alphabet.

2.3   Informational Ergonomics

The contemporary ergonomics has focused on studying systems where there is a predominance of sensory aspects, in other words, visual perception and other sensations that work together with the body for decision making (7). According to Chapanis (2), Ergonomics is a body of knowledge and analysis of human abilities, limitations and other relevant features for design projects, which includes the informational aspects.

The informational ergonomics uses the principles of information theory, send the right information to the right person at the desired time, in a more effectively and efficiently way, thus bringing satisfaction to the users and always respecting their diversity. To accomplish that aim, it contemplates the cognition and perception, and covers the aspects of verbal and nonverbal language (8).

This area of ergonomics is related to human cognition process. According to Preece (13) cognition is the event of the mind in carrying out daily tasks and involves interaction of cognitive processes, such as thinking, speaking, among others. This concept can be divided into two types: experimental and reflective, the first involves the action and reaction of the humans involved in certain activities while the second involves the act of thinking, compare and make decisions, this is the type that develops the ideas and rises the creativity (12).

Those models of cognition use some paradigms for their functionality as attention, perception, comprehension and memorization. The attention is related to the level of alertness of the body. Perception is the relation to the cultural context of the individual. Comprehension relates to the correspondence of the senses of the message assigned by the font and the memorization by selective retention of the message (11).

Ergonomics and usability of information systems deal with human-task-machine communication in other supports beyond computers, including, warnings, cautions on packaging, information systems, static graphics, instruction manual, color. It is highlighted in that item the readability issues, decoding focused to the logic of use instead of its operation (10). There is a concern of design professionals in understanding how the user communicates with the products, developing models to facilitate the connection of these with the system in which they are working. It also seeks to facilitate the rapprochement of the two parts, so that it is possible to be more intuitive and/or effective interactions from two situations: an ideal and other problematic.

The analysis of graphic design aims to determine whether the product instructs users efficiently, respecting each process and means of work, seeking as a result the user satisfaction, while respecting the limitations of each individual (9).

The informational ergonomics involves a number of aspects and principles, which deal especially with the whole relation in the human-technology interface, where visual and auditory means, in the information processing, are crucial to an action or activity. The informational ergonomics shall be responsible for visibility, readability, comprehension and quantification, prioritization and coordination, standardization, compatibility and consistency of symbolic components, such as alphanumeric characters and iconographic symbols, which are widely used in signaling, safety and guidance system (16). It is responsibility of the informational ergonomics the application of specific techniques that provide men the tight balance between themselves, their work and the environment around them. When applied and managed correctly in institutions, it enables the worker (or user), higher levels of perceived health, comfort and safety (18).

Usability as a concept deals with the suitability of the product to the task, where performance is destined to the suitability of the product with the user and the context in which it will be used. Concern with usability has usually occurred in the end of the design cycle, during the evaluation of the product already finished, which results in few changes due to the high cost. Therefore, since the beginning of the design activity, usability must be present in its development (10).

Usability tests are techniques that involve representative users in a certain population for a specific system. Users are assigned to perform typical and critical tasks, where the collection of data occurs for future analysis. Those tests are characterized by different techniques, intended for ergonomic evaluation of interactive systems, such as heuristic evaluation, ergonomic criteria, standards-based inspection, style guides or recommendations guides, checklist inspection, cognitive walkthrough (or inspection), empirical user test, interviews and questionnaires (3).

2.4   Informational Ergonomics and the Visual Identity

The human cognitive system is characterized by processing of symbolic information, in other words, humans create and develop images through mental models or representations of reality, which can be models or aspects of reality (3). In this sense, the cognitive system is the term used to refer to structured and formal representations grounded in theories of psychology.

There are several models of communication that can help understand how scholars have seen this problem, given the difficulty of understanding how individuals see and understand the information presented. The informational ergonomics is widely used in research that relates signaling sites and the recognition and comprehension of signs and information boards. The human structure and information processing are the main methods used to understand and organize studies of functionality and comprehension of the signs of warnings (20). One of the models of information processing is the one proposed by Alves, in 1985, which derived from the model of Welford in 1968, and which was later adapted by Whiting in 1979, comprised of five phases, since the appearance of the information to the motor response (Figure 01).

The models determine the individuals behavior and constitute their vision of reality, that can be modified or simplified by what is functionally significant for them. This process helps the individual to extend the relevant elements and eliminate the secondary ones, and they are usually connected to the knowledge already acquired (3).

This same model can be used in the comprehension of visual identities, which normally have information relating to the institution that is wanted to identify, so that the users can understand and associate with something already seen and processed by their cognitive system. The use of pictograms and icons in the visual identities can facilitate that comprehension.

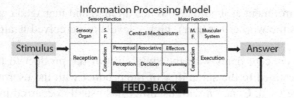

Fig. 1. Model of information processing (Source: Alves, 1985, adapted by the authors)

The visual identities seek to inform and identify in a simple way, just like sign-posts. Pictorial images are used in their symbols and logos to facilitate the approach of the user with the image being displayed.

A brand does not necessarily need a symbol. Another factor widely used in the development of visual identity is the typography, which is considered a technological element. The possibility of usability applied to the typography responds to the basic interface conditions between the elements and the readers, usually receivers of signs.

2.5   Gestalt

The studies related to Gestalt began in the late nineteenth century in Austria and Germany, and resulted in studies of perception, also known as Form Psychology, Gestalt Psychology and Gestalt. The first published work in the area, which dealt with the visual perception, was that of Max Wertheimer in 1912, in which Wolfgang Kohler and Kurf Koffka were his partners. These three researchers are considered the initiators of the Gestalt movement. They considered the psychological phenomena as a standalone set, indivisible and articulated in its configuration, organization and internal law, independent of individuals perception that formulate their own laws of human perception.

William James, American philosopher, greatly influenced the fundamentals of that school, considering that people do not observe the objects as packages made up of sensations, but as a unit, concluding that the perception of the whole is greater than the sum of its parts. The phenomenology of Emund Husser also influenced the Gestalt formation. It is based on the principle that all consciousness relates to something and, accordingly, it is not a substance, but rather an activity consisting of acts, perception, imagination, speculation, volition, passion, among others, with which it is possible to aim for something (4).

For Arnheim (1) the visual perception is organized through the establishment of total and central patterns in the comprehension of some laws. This pattern can be structured in the internal sense that is part of that image so that the appearance of any part depends on its greater or lesser extent inside the structure which is influenced by the nature of its parts. The act of note those relations is a more effective way to establish those differences and establish a set of perceptual tensions that highlights the contrasting elements in the image. From this premise, the comparisons among contrast, similarity, proximity and others share the study of mental comparisons and the relation with the existing one.

Those studies arose as a reaction to the established contemporary theories and were based only on the individual and sensory experience. They assume that the sensible object is not just a bundle of sensations for humans, because the perception is beyond the elements provided by the sensory organs. They were based on the statements of Kant, that the elements perceived by us are organized to make sense and not only by associations with what is known previously (5).

According to Gestalt principles, there are eight main aspects in the perception of objects and shapes: Unity, Segregation, Unification, Closure, Continuity, Proximity, Similarity and Pregnancy of Form (5).

3   Materials and Methods

Studies conducted through bibliographical references were applied directly to the analyzed objects in order to propose possible parameters for analysis and development of visual identities. Accordingly, we sought to demonstrate the range of related issues enabling a technical analysis of these projects. Thus, we tried to gather all the factors in a spreadsheet that enables the study of brands, seeking an equality among them on issues established by the review.

The next step was to select the brands that would be analyzed and compared to each other, not in order to show which one is superior or better, but rather seek and display the same factors that highlight the brands in the projects of the graphic area.

For this, it became necessary direct contact with companies and professionals, through personal contact, clarifying our intention, so that companies and professionals did not feel intimidated by the approach.

3.1   Proceedings

Analysis Sheet. In order to enable an effective analysis of the brands obtained, we opted for the development of an analysis sheet that seeks to address all or most of the important factors in the development of a brand. It was not found any line of analysis related to visual identities in national bibliographies. There are specific analyzes, such as those made by visual ergonomics or the gestalt. Based on literature review, we realized the existence of factors that could later allow the proposal of some parameters for the development and analysis of visual identities, among them it was seen the aspects related to visual ergonomics, the gestalt and colors, using techniques such as the verification of the golden ratio, number of colors, color psychology, and others. Analysis sheet, at first, was defined with the following items: company name, rank, range, brand, size, typography, symbol and composition. All those factors made it feasible the search for equality among the brands used, thus it was possible to propose parameters for analysis and development of the analysis sheet (Figure 02).

Company Name. The company name describes its fancy name, so that it becomes easier to identify to which company the brand belongs.

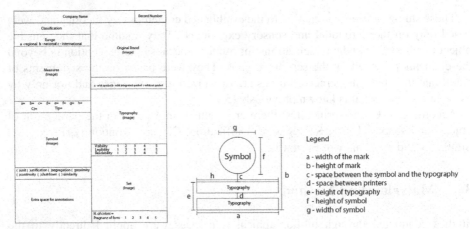

Fig. 2. Structure of the analysis sheet of brands (Source: authors)

Fig. 3. Template of measurements of the dimensions of the brands (Source: authors)

Sheet Number. The number of the analysis sheet enables data collection and analysis of results without the need to memorize the names of companies and the organization in each classification.

Classification. The classification refers to which market sector the brand is inserted. This item allows a division that allows a comparison of the same markets, and then among all the brands that will be analyzed. The brands were divided by the market to which they are intended: Industry, Commerce, Health, Education, Food, Transportation, Event; Offices; Product.

Range. As far as the brand reaches geographically. Brand is the original image or the desired object, divided in regional, national and international. To determine which definition the brand is inserted if researched on the internet the market it covers or if there is any relation outside the state or outside the country for each company.

Dimensions. In this section is where the search for some relations among proportion is inserted. In order to perform this analysis, the sheets were printed and measured. The established measures were always noted in one dimension, considering the largest brand length by setting a size of 63 mm, in its longest line, for example, if it is wider or higher, thus maintaining equality in measurements and subsequent existing comparisons. I was created a template for performing the measurement (Figure 03).

Typography. In typography we analyzed how the fonts and shapes were used to achieve their goal, highlighting aspects of visual ergonomics, such as visibility, legibility and readability. There are six aspects that can vary an alphabet: the case, weight, width, inclination, contrast and style. In those variables there is an unlimited number of spatial possibilities of expression and texture (15). Those aspects make the brand more visible or legible and these types of items will be considered in the analysis of the brands. The classification of each item of analysis occurs in a range of 1 to 5, considering an increasing scale, where 1 is terrible, 2 is bad, 3 is regular 4 is good and 5 is great.

Symbol. To analyze the symbol, the typography was excluded, isolating it from the symbol, and determining a degree of connection with its reference object. In the symbol we just consider the gestalt, using six laws, which are: Unity, Unification; Segregation; Closure; Proximity, Similarity. Performing a visual reading of the shape, as shown by Gomes Filho (5), we selected three items present in that shape.

Composition. Analyzing the composition, it is possible to see how is the brand set. First, the amount of existing colors, and then assess the level of pregnancy of the shape, which is another of the Gestalt laws. Thus the brand set was analyzed, in other words, symbol and logo which binds to visual ergonomics items discussed in typography. Regarding the pregnancy of the shape, we opted for a bar analysis, such as the one made in the typography, where an increasing scale was used, in which part 1 was terrible and 5 was great.

Space for Extra Notes. This space has been reserved in order to write down some existing problem in the sheet or any item that could not be analyzed by the established means in the literature review.

Brands. The interviews proved to be effective, because they enabled the comprehension of companies to the importance of the research and use of their projects in it, which means that they allowed the analysis of their graphic designs in this study. Five projects of 10 companies were sent, as defined previously, thus obtaining a total of 50 brands. Companies were numbered (concealing their names) and their respective brands.

4   Results

4.1   Results of the Analysis

After the analysis of the brands, it was possible to tabulate all the data to obtain the results in each item defined in the analysis. First it was necessary to divide them into categories, allowing a deeper and more complete data study comparing just the related brands to the same sector, in order to compare all the results of analyzes. Below, there is an example of sheet filled in (Figure 04).

The result was expressed in a table in which some items were placed in percentage and the others in numerical values, since it dealt with the selection of dimensions and quantities (see Table 01). The numerical values were used only on the dimensions in relation to the interval and the higher incidence (mode) and also in the total mean. It was also used in the gestalt section, since it reflects to the three ones that most often appear in symbols, and thus it is easier to analyze them by numbers.

The range of brands is present in the results, expressed in percentage. Regarding the dimensions, which are eight in total, measured from the brand, and two more that are the mean of the set and typography, it was analyzed the percentage that appears, the range of measures, the higher incidence and the full analysis of the mean. In typography it was analyzed the visibility, legibility and readability, expressed in percentage. In gestalt, it was listed the first three laws that appear in the brand symbol, whether integrated or only typography. In colors, it was quantified the different colors that appear, also expressed in percentage. In the symbol, we observed if it existed or not, and if it was integrated into the set, also expressed as a percentage. And lastly, the pregnancy of the shape, expressed in percentage.

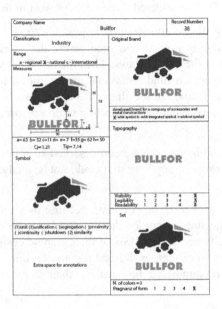

Fig. 4. Example of filling the analysis sheet (Source: authors)

Tables containing the results were also divided by color, to facilitate their identification and visualization. Each selected color refers to the category to which it was adopted, thus facilitating subsequent comparisons among categories.

In Gestalt is possible to verify a number below the statement, since this number corresponds to the number of brands multiplied by three, resulting in the amount of gestalt laws that would be present, and thus an easy access and comprehension of the resulting numbers.

General Analysis. The capture of the brands with the interviewed companies resulted in a total of 50 brands. In this table it is possible to see the comparative results of all brands obtained and analyzed, also joining the two brands which do not belong to either category, in other words, transport and product categories. The overall results presented here are very important to understand how the relevance of each item of the brand is treated for its development.

In range, there is a large percentage of 50% for national brands. Regarding typography is observed a great commitment in brand visibility, and 92% achieved the top score, and in relation to the legibility and readability, respectively, 70% and 66%. In Gestalt, the laws that prevail in relation to the symbols of the brands are in decreasing order: closure, similarity, unification, unity and continuity, segregation and proximity. In the colors, the use of only two is extensive, 76%. Regarding the symbol, it is confirmed the high percentage of 64% in the presence of the symbol. In the pregnancy of shape, it was proven that 74% were considered of great comprehension and fixation of the brand.

Table 1. Results of the analyzes of brands - Total

Results of the analysis of brands					Total						N of Brand
Range (%)	regional	national	international		Typography (%)	Filter	bad	regular	good	optimum	
	30	50	20		visibility	0	0	0	8	92	**50**
Dimensions					legibility	0	0	6	24	70	
	Incidence (%)	interval (mm)	mode (mm)	Mean (mm)	readability	0	0	4	30	66	
b	100	10-62	20	34,7	Gestalt	unification	unit	similarity		shutdown	
c	74	2-10	2	4		25	19	27		37	
d	56	1-5	2	2,8	**150**	continuity		proximity		segregation	
e	90	06-34	10	15,9		19		10		13	
f	84	10-47	20	24,5	Colors (%)	1	2	3			
g	84	10-63	20	30,7		16	76	6	Symbol (%)	w/ symbol: 64 / integrated: 30 / without symbol: 6	
h	100	33-63	63	56,4	Pz. of Form (%)	Filter	bad	regular	good	optimum	
CJ.	100	10,1-38,7	31,5	21,7		0	0	2	24	74	
Tip	100	14-63	63	41,1							

Regarding the dimensions, there is a high incidence of all of them, and the dimension "d" remains less incident, with 56%. In some items, extended intervals are observed, which have made mode very similar to the mean of those intervals. We chose not to use the symbol approximately in this mode, since it was exactly correct, without many variations. In the study of total brands, the mean was included as a complement to the mode, demonstrating that even with an extensive range, it remains in an approximate measure of the mean.

5   Discussion

The evolution of the methodology enabled several ways to develop a good design project for any type of product, but may be perceived that in companies there is not a specific methodology for the development of graphic brands. They showed that for most developers of this kind of project, the methodology is used in order to adapt to every professional and every type of team that the company has.

The analysis sheet showed to be very effective in the division and study of graphic brands. The sheet was developed using criteria of visual ergonomics in its division in order to enable a more thorough observation of the brands, separating the analysis into specific points, such as the existence of the symbol, whether it is used or is included on the brand, or even if it absent. The study showed that 64% of the brands analyzed contained symbol and 30% had the symbol integrated to the typography.

The study demonstrated the range of the brand which resulted in 50% of them having a national range, while 30% are regional. This showed us that the companies analyzed in this study are small and medium-sized, and they are in the same bracket, allowing a closer and comparative study among them.

The separation of the symbol was of utmost importance to study the laws of gestalt, because it was possible to check which laws were used for development. Applying the three major laws, verified in one order, it proved to be a concern of its comprehension through simplicity. It was observed in the results that the most active law was the Closure, just because this law is able to link the elements of the symbol, which enables us to understand its real sense, in second place was the Similarity, which allows the use of equal elements in order to simplify the shapes, facilitating the visibility, in third place was the Unification, which is the junction of different shapes to create a whole.

The analysis of typography, through the laws of visual ergonomics, showed a concern with the visibility, which background was the legibility and readability, as reported in some of the interviews. The result always relevant of that item showed that all companies seek a way to promote the comprehension of the brand, demonstrating that they seek the same pattern, working largely with the medium and small companies. Because the brands were provided by medium-sized companies, there was no major problems regarding the brand reading, where it was possible see that in the item visibility, 92% achieved the highest score, followed by legibility with 70%, and readability with 66%.

The analysis of the color showed to be very effective with the use of few colors in the development and implementation of brands, which was expected by the reports in the interviews. The result showed that two colors are usually used, with few variations in gradient, among other graphic accessories, which may hinder the visibility of the brand. This factor is directly related to the pregnancy of the shape, which is characterized by ease of reading and understanding. In this question 74% of the brands obtained maximum score.

The sheet also included the dimensions of brands and their relations, there are a lot of similar or very close dimensions followed by the higher incidence of the same dimension. This demonstrates the existence of a pattern for certain brands, which may facilitate less experienced professionals in the development of their first projects. There was a need to develop a more effective methodology, despite complaints from some interviewees in relation to newly graduated students, who do not use any method in product development.

6   Concluding Notes

For the proposed parameters in this study, it was used as a reference all the available theoretical background in order to provide means of analysis of visual identities for companies and public or civil institutions. The use of those references allowed reaching all the goals defined and established throughout the literature review, which covered subjects related to the world of brands. It was described: items related to the design, the project methodology, the visual identity, ergonomics, non verbal language, color, and gestalt, which provided the construction and a proposed of an analysis sheet, which aimed to study the brands selected with the companies surveyed, according to pre-established criteria and maintenance of the necessary ethics during this type of approach. The sheet covered all the necessary aspects demonstrated in the theoretical apparatus defined for the study, thus enabling those projects to be discussed in a depth and objective way. That provides new studies possibilities of analysis that permeate the field of informational ergonomics, since this is a new area of research applied directly to graphic design which so far have been based on intuition and experience of its designers, causing the scientific research to stay in the background, since those projects have a large intuitive load, which is hard to evaluate. The research contributed significantly to the design area studies, allowing it to be expanded, whereas the approach allowed different views on the development of projects, thus providing the opening of new horizons and new possibilities for future research in the area of visual identity, but also in other fields of graphic design. The use of an analysis sheet may expand the parameters on several other products of graphic design, as well as for product design. The methodology of the research presented here, proved to be adequately effective, obtaining concrete results and that might be used in order to analyze and develop new visual identity projects.

References

1. Arnheim, R.: Arte & percepção visual: uma psicologia da visão criadora. Pioneira, 13th edn. São Paulo (2000)
2. Chapanis, A.: A some reflection on progress. In: Human Factors Society. Proccedings Santa Monica, Santa Monica (1985)
3. Cybis, W.A., Betiol, A.H., Faust, R.: Ergonomia e Usabilidade – Conhecimentos, Métodos e Aplicações. NovatecEditora, São Paulo (2007)
4. Dondis, D.A.: A sintaxe da imagem visual. Editora Gustavo Gili, Barcelona (1997)
5. Gomes Filho, J.: Gestalt do Objeto: Sistema de Leitura Visual da Forma. Escrituras Editora, São Paulo (2000)
6. Heskett, J.: Design, Ática, São Paulo (2008)
7. IIDA, I. Ergonomia Projeto e Produção. EditoraEdgard Blucher LTDA, São Paulo (2005)
8. Martins, L.B., Moraes, A.: Ergonomia Informacional: algumas considerações sobre o sistema humano-mensagem visual. In: Gestão da Informação na Competitividade das Organizações, vol. 1, pp. 165–181. Editora Universitaria da UFPE, Recife (2002)
9. Melo, C.V.A., Cursino, R.M., Santos, V.M.V.: Estudo da Ergonomia Informacional Sobre o Uso de Mapa de Riscos e Sinalizações Voltados as Rotas de Fuga Existentes Numa Planta de Processamento. XXVII ENEGEP, Foz do Iguaçu (2007)
10. de Moraes, A., Frisoni, B.C.: Ergodesign: Produtos e processos. 2AB, Rio de Janeiro (2001)
11. Moraes, A.: Design e Avaliação de Interface: ergodesign e interaçãohumanocomputador / Organizadora: Anamaria de Moraes. iUsEr, Rio de Janeiro (2002)
12. Norman, D.A.: La Psicologia de los ObjetosCotidianos. Editora Nerea, Madrid (1990)
13. Preece, J.: Design no Brasil: Origens e Instalação. Editora 2AB, Rio de Janeiro (2007)
14. Raposo, D.: Design de Identidade e Imagem Corporativa. IPC, Lisboa/Portugal (2009)
15. Samara, T.: Evolução do design: da teoria à prática. Editora Bookman, São Paulo (2010)
16. Santos, N., Fialho, F.: Manual de Análise Ergonômica no Trabalho, 2nd edn. Gênesis Editora, Curitiba (1997)
17. Strunk, G.: Identidade visual: A direção do olhar. Editora Europa, Rio de Janeiro (1989)
18. Takeda, F., Xavier, A.A.P.: Ergonomia informacional: sistemas de informação e comunicação na gestão de riscos de acidentes numa planta de abate de frango. XV Simpep, Simpósio de engenharia de produção (2008)
19. Wheller, A.: Design de Identidade da Marca. Editora Bookman, Porto Alegre (2009)
20. Wogalter, M.S., Dejoy, D.M., Laughery, K.R.: Organizing theoretical framework: A consolidated communication-human information processing (C-HIP) model in Wogalter. In: Dejoy, L. (ed.) Warning ans Risk Communication. Taylor & Francis, Abington (1999)

Design for Diverse Target Users

The Design and Development of Empathetic Serious Games for Dyslexia: BCI Arabic Phonological Processing Training Systems

Arwa Al-Rubaian[1], Lama Alssum[1], Rawan Alharbi[1], Wafa Alrajhi[1], Haifa Aldayel[1],
Nora Alangari[1], Hadeel Al-Negheimish[1], Aljohara Alfayez[1], Sara Alwaalan[1],
Rania Aljindan[1], Ashwag Alshathri[1], Dania Alomar[1],
Ghada Alhudhud[1], and Areej Al-Wabil[1,2]

[1] Software and Knowledge Engineering Research Group,
King Saud University, Riyadh, Saudi Arabia
skerg@ksu.edu.sa
[2] Software Engineering Department, College of Computer and Information Sciences,
King Saud University; Riyadh, Saudi Arabia
aalwabil@ksu.edu.sa

Abstract. In this paper, we describe the User Interface (UI) design issues for serious games aimed at developing phonological processing skills of people with specific learning difficulties such as dyslexia. These games are designed with Brain-Computer Interfaces (BCI) which take the compelling and creative aspects of traditional computer games designed for Arabic interfaces and apply them for cognitive skills' development purposes. Immersion and engagement in the games are sought with novel interaction methods; the interaction mode for these games involved mind-control coupled with cursor-based selection. We describe the conceptual design of these serious games and an overview of the BCI software development framework.

Keywords: Brain-Machine Interface, BMI, SpLD, Learning Difficulty, Dyslexia, Brain-Computer Interface, BCI, Usability.

1   Introduction

Serious games have received increasing interest in Human- Computer Interaction (HCI) research [1,2]. Correspondingly, many accessibility researchers have taken up the challenge of establishing how to best design rehabilitation software and remedial software training programs for developing skills of people with cognitive disabilities and learning difficulties [2]. The development of serious games aimed at language processing skills in particular could contribute to the proliferation of immersive and engaging learning experiences for people with learning difficulties such as dyslexia.

Recent studies have shown compelling evidence in how traditional computer games enhance the learning experience [2]. Gamification in rehabilitation software for auditory processing difficulties and specific learning difficulties has been shown to be

A. Marcus (Ed.): DUXU 2014, Part IV, LNCS 8520, pp. 105–112, 2014.

effective with users across of the spectrum of difficulty levels [12, 13]. Exploiting existing novel interaction methods, such as mind-control and adaptation via affective computing, can impact the user experience in serious games by increasing levels of immersion and engagement [3, 5]. These user experiences have the potential to enhance the motivation, maintain the momentum of learning, and assist educators and practitioners in objectively monitoring the progress of the individuals as well as assessing the effectiveness of configurable remedial programs in these serious games [5, 8]. The concept of such emerging technologies, such as Brain Computer Interfaces (BCI) is leveraging the engaging aspect of using brainwaves, to control elements in an immersive environment, to enhance the learning experience [4, 5].

2   Brain-Computer Interaction in Serious Gaming

BCI research is a growing domain of interest for the design and development of assistive technologies, gaming, and applied contexts of affective computing. Much of the prior research in BCI for assistive technologies is aimed at individuals who have physical disabilities that hinder their ability to manipulate tangible controls (e.g. paralysis), attention deficit disorders (e.g. ADD, APD, and ADHD), and developmental disorders. The gaming paradigm is an interesting platform to employ BCI to further assist the aforementioned target user populations through the translation of user's mental activity into game controls and increasing engagement with nocel interaction modalities for the purpose of immersion in learning activities and improved accessibility.

In recent years, games are increasingly being designed with novel multimodal interaction [8, 10]. BCI games in this domain have leveraged the capability of detecting attention to develop the cognitive skills of players such as sustaining attention [10-11]. Studies examining the usability and user experience (UX) of BCI games have suggested increased levels of engagement and immersion in BCI games [14, 15]. However, the inaccuracy and complexity in controlling objects within the games have been noted as challenges for gamers [16]; these difficulties often hinder their ability to progress within the games and demand higher learning curves when compared to traditional modes of interaction.

3   Mind-Controlled Dyslexia Training

An application for cognitive training of phonological processing skills for Arabic-speaking children with SpLDs was developed. The serious game was designed for the Emotiv EPOC headset to detect patterns of brainwaves for controlling the selection mode in the game and to detect levels of basic affective states (e.g. frustration, excitement, boredom), with frustration levels being linked to controls within the game. The two channels of interaction are depicted in the model illustrated in Figure 1.

Mind Control for Selection   Affective States
(Brain Waves)   (Frustration)

Fig. 1. BCI game based on brainwaves for selection and affective states for adaptation

The electrical activity in the brain can be monitored using different ways. One of these methods is non-invasive; it involves detecting the signals from the human scalp without any surgical intervention. Electroencephalography (EEG) technology is a well-known method used to record brain signals in a non-invasive way.

Several companies have released devices For EEG brain computer interface (BCI). One of these devices is EPOC, it is produced by Emotiv Systems. EPOC is a headset that contains 16 sensors distributed over different areas on the brain to detect EEG signals [6]. This headset not only provides the capability to measure cognitive and expressive emotions, but it also provides a mechanism of detecting facial expressions [7]. The interaction modalities made available with the EPOC headset as well as its unobtrusive properties as an input modality have made it an attractive tool to consider in this project. In the following sections, we describe the design framework that guided the development of the BCI serious games.

3.1 Developing the Interaction Modalities for the BCI Application

To work with EPOC headsets, a bespoke application was developed using the Educational Emotiv Software Development Kit (SDK) which is a "toolset that allows development of applications and games to interact with Emotiv EmoEngine and Emotiv neuroheadsets" [6]. There are several components in the SDK that are essential for the design and development of BCI applications. The Control Panel provides an interface to detect the locations of the headset sensors and to train the EPOC on each user [6]. The EmoComposer is an emulator of EmoEngine which can be used without the headset. The Emotiv EmoEngine refers to the logical abstraction of the functionality that Emotiv provides and it streamlines the flow of data to the Emotiv headset as it "receives preprocessed EEG and gyroscope data, manages user-specific or application-specific settings, performs post- processing, and translates the Emotiv detection results into an easy-to-use structure called an EmoState" [6].

3.2   Software Architecture and Design of the BCI Application

In the development phase of the application C# was selected for the programming language and the composer was used to emulate interaction in iterative design cycles to facilitate rapid development and testing in a context with limited access to headsets for each member on the development team. When a user starts the game, a direct connection to the EmoEngine is established using the calling function of engine.Connect(); after the user logs in and before the user starts playing, functions are called for the different processes:

1. User Profile: This function checks whether the user has a previously existing profile. If the user is not new to the system, or a profile is found, then the user's training data is retrieved.
2. User training data: If the user is new, then the EPOC headset must be trained to understand the cognitive data for that specific user before moving on to the game. The training data often involves the individual's pattern of imagining an action such as push, pull or navigation directions. In our case, we were interested in the push signal only, so training was designed to be conducted for that specific signal.
3. Measure the frustration, boredom, and excitement: The Epoch headset detects affective states of an individual such as levels of frustration, boredom, excitement and meditative states. After retrieving the training data, the user may start the game. In each stage of the game, the EPOC headset will detect the frustration level of the user. When the serious games detect high levels of frustration for the player, the system automatically adapts by reducing the complexity of the game, such as the scenario depicted in Figure 4.
4. Push: After proper training, the EPOC headset should be able to recognize the push signal immediately. So, when the user thinks of pushing a button in the game, the push signal will be detected and matched with the signal learned during training. Thus, the button in the game was designed to trigger the action being detected by the neuroheadset and reflect the system's response.

3.3   Flow of Cognitive Training in the BCI Game Scenarios

The serious games developed in this project aim to develop the key skill of auditory language comprehension in Arabic-speaking individuals with developmental dyslexia. Phonological processing impairments are often experienced in people with dyslexia and these can be addressed in drill based exercises that aim to develop the skill in auditory and visual stimuli [7]. The use of serious games in rehabilitation and cognitive training programs has been considered by researchers and practitioners to optimize the rehabilitation of learning disabilities [10-11]. In addition, the innovative approach of BCI interaction that is considered in these games has been shown to provide the user with an enhanced user experience (UX) of motivation and enjoyment and better engagement levels in the gaming experience [14-16].

The BCI game was designed as a self-training tool that aims to improve the phonological language skills of people with developmental phonological dyslexia; their inability to map printed words onto their corresponding sounds of spoken words reinforces the need for a proper treatment, given that this language difficulty affects their reading and spelling skills [9].

In this BCI gaming application, the user is required to wear the neuroheadset while playing the game to detect subconscious emotional states and user-trained mental commands for proper control of objects presented within the game. The two channels of interaction we have chosen to be detected for this game are the "push" action and frustration levels, these are depicted in the model illustrated in Figure 1. A sample of the game's interface is shown in Figure 2; in which users listen to a spoken Arabic word by the program. Following the auditory trigger, users are expected to navigate the cursor to the correct word and then concentrate to make their selection.

Fig. 2. Mind-Controlled Selection of Words

The game consists of three different levels each containing five stages. The complexity and challenge of the game relies on the number and the weights of the presented words; the similarity between the weights of different Arabic words makes it more difficult for the dyslexic player to distinguish between their pronunciations correspondences. The difficulty of the game increases as the player proceeds to the following levels.

Figure 3 shows a sample of the three different levels. Level one presents three words with different weights as depicted in Figure (3.1). Level two presents five words (three words with the same weight (3.2), and level three presents seven words (five words with the same weight) as depicted in Figure (3.3).

At the beginning of each stage, the player will listen to the pronunciation of a word generated by the program and try to match it with its corresponding text. To choose an answer, the user is expected to move the cursor to the correct word and concentrate on it to trigger the push action from the headset. The games' ability to recognize human emotional states with physiological signals facilitated the design of an empathetic system in this learning contexts and thus maintaining the engagement level throughout the interaction in the games. For example, selection of the word is made by focusing the user's cognitive attention on the item of interest for a duration that is above the threshold which is configurable by the system administrator.

Fig. 3. Varying levels of difficulty in the game

The headset also detects affective and meditational states. The affective state relevant to the design of this specific game was 'frustration'; frustration levels of the player while interacting with the game. The result of this detection could help in reducing the anxiety experienced by the user when facing difficulties in choosing the correct answer. As higher levels of frustration are detected, the program responds by reducing the answer choices and eliminating one of the incorrect answers to adapt the level of difficulty in the game. Levels of difficulty are configurable by the administrator of the system and can be designed to adapt to users with SpLDs who have varying levels of abilities. One scenario of adaptation in response to affective states of the gamers is depicted in Figure 4.

Fig. 4. Empathetic Design Responding to the Gamer's Frustration Level by Systematically Reducing Complexity

The game was designed so that gamers would be required to answer at least 80% of the questions correctly in order to proceed to the next level. The number of incorrect attempts for each stage will be recorded to decide on the result that will be displayed at the end of each level. Furthermore, the time taken for each player to choose the correct answer will be recorded to test the performance and speed of phonological processing. Both the level of disability (mild, moderate or severe) and age will be taken into consideration for each user to further classify our results from this study.

The chosen words for the game were collected from previous projects that are targeted for users' with learning disabilities and were carefully studied and revised by specialists [12,13].

4 Conclusion

In this paper we described the design and development of a mind-controlled serious game for dyslexia. Despite the emerging BCI gaming field, there are few design frameworks that facilitate integrating emotion recognition and mind-control effectively by developers of rehabilitation software. The work reported here offers a first step towards addressing the inadequate understanding of how BCI can be utilized in configurable applications for specific learning difficulties. Future work involves usability evaluations of the application with users of varying levels of difficulties.

Acknowledgement. The authors extend their appreciation to the Deanship of Scientific Research at King Saud University for funding the work through the research group project number RGP-VPP-157.

References

1. Crookall, D.: Serious Games, Debriefing, and Simulation/Gaming as a Discipline. Simul. Gaming 41(6), 898–920 (2010)
2. Bragge, J., Thavikulwat, P., Töyli, J.: Profiling 40 Years of Research in Simulation & Gaming. Simulation and Gaming 41(6), 869–897 (2010)
3. Gürkök, H., Nijholt, A., Poel, M.: Brain- Computer interface games: towards a framework. In: Herrlich, M., Malaka, R., Masuch, M. (eds.) ICEC 2012. LNCS, vol. 7522, pp. 373–380. Springer, Heidelberg (2012)
4. Graimann, B., Allison, B., Pfurtscheller, G.: Brain- Computer Interfaces: Revolutionizing Human-Computer Interaction. Springer, Berlin (2011)
5. Gürkök, H., Nijholt, A.: Brain-computer interfaces for multimodal interaction. International Journal of Human-Computer Interaction 28(5), 292–307 (2012)
6. User Manual: Epocsdk Electroencephalography (EEG) headset Brain-Computer Interfaces (BCI), http://Emotiv.com
7. Mateer, C.A., Sohlberg, M.M. (eds.): Cognitive Rehabilitation: An Integrative Neuropsychological Approach, 2nd edn. The Guilford Press (2001)
8. Plass-Oude Bos, D., Reuderink, B., van de Laar, B., Gürkök, H., Mühl, C., Poel, M., Nijholt, A., Heylen, D.: Brain-computer interfacing and games. In: Brain-Computer Interfaces, pp. 149–178. Springer (2010)
9. Snowling, M.J., Griffiths, Y.M.: Individual differences in dyslexia. In: Nune, T., Bryant, P.E. (eds.) Handbook of Literacy. Kluwer Press, Dordrecht (2005)

10. Jiang, L., Guan, C., Zhang, H.: Brain computer interface based 3D game for attention training and rehabilitation. In: Proceedings of the 6th IEEE Conference on Industrial Electronics and Applications, ICIEA (2011)
11. Lim, C.G., Lee, T.S., Guan, C., Fung, D.S.S., Zhao, Y., et al.: A Brain-Computer Interface Based Attention Training Program for Treating Attention Deficit Hyperactivity Disorder. PLoS ONE 7(10), e46692 (2012), doi:10.1371/journal.pone.0046692
12. AlGhamdi, N., AlOhali, Y.: The Design and Development of an Interactive Aural Rehabilitation Therapy Program. In: Proceedings of the 12th International ACM ASSETS 2010 Conference, October 25-27 (2010)
13. Al-Wabil, A., Drine, S., Alkoblan, S., Alamoudi, A., Al-abdulrahman, R., Almuzainy, M.: The Use of Personas in the Design of an Arabic Auditory Training System for Children. In: Proceedings of the 13th International Conference on Computers Helping People with Special Needs (ICCHP 2012), Linz, Austria (July 2012)
14. Bos, D.P.-O., Reuderink, B., van de Laar, B., Gürkök, H., Mühl, C., Poel, M., Heylen, D., Nijholt, A.: Human-Computer Interaction for BCI Games: Usability and User Experience. In: 2010 International Conference on Cyberworlds (CW), October 20-22, pp. 277–281 (October 2010), doi:10.1109/CW.2010.22
15. Plass-Oude Bos, D., Gürkök, H., Van de Laar, B., Nijboer, F., Nijholt, A.: User Experience Evaluation in BCI: Mind the Gap. International Journal of Bioelectromagnetism 13(1), 48–49 (2011)
16. Al-Ghamdi, N., Al-Hudhud, G., Alzamel, M., Al-Wabil, W.: Trials and tribulations of BCI control applications. In: Science and Information Conference (SAI), pp. 212–217 (2013)

Considering People Living with Dementia When Designing Interfaces

Claire Ancient and Alice Good

School of Computing, University of Portsmouth
Buckingham Building, Lion Terrace, Portsmouth, UK, PO1 3HE
{claire.ancient,alice.good}@port.ac.uk

Abstract. Dementia is an escalating problem which is estimated to affect 35.6 million people worldwide. In an environment which is becoming increasingly dependent on technology, the interaction needs of people living with dementia is being ignored by interface designers. This paper aims to highlight the factors which should be considered when designing interfaces to be "dementia-friendly". The article draws on the limited previous research to suggest that interfaces need to consider two main factors: personalisation (which includes both accessibility and usability) and user acceptance (including the experience produced by the interfaces and barriers to technology adoption).

Keywords: Dementia, Interface Design, Personalisation, User Acceptance.

1 Introduction

The worldwide prevalence of dementia is rapidly increasing. In 2012, the World Health Organisation estimated a figure of 35.6 million people worldwide living with the condition, a number which is expected to rise by 7.7 million each year [1]. In the UK, 1 in 3 people over the age of 65 will develop a form of dementia [2].

Dementia is the term used for a collection of conditions including Alzheimer's disease and Vascular dementia. It is caused by damage to the brain, either due to diseases or a series of strokes. Alzheimer's disease is the most common form of dementia, affecting between 60% and 70% of diagnosed cases [1]. However, there are many rarer causes of dementia. Whilst each dementia-causing condition will have its own set of specific symptoms, people living with dementia will often experience short-term memory loss, problems with communication and difficulties with concentration [3].

The condition is progressive; therefore, the symptoms of dementia will get worse over time. In addition, every person living with dementia will experience the condition in their own way. This is dependent on a number of factors including (but not limited to): the type of dementia diagnosed, their personality, the medication prescribed and the support network around them [4].

A. Marcus (Ed.): DUXU 2014, Part IV, LNCS 8520, pp. 113–123, 2014.
© Springer International Publishing Switzerland 2014

1.1   Importance of Technology

Despite a lack of understanding and experience, previous research suggests older people are willing to utilise recent advances in technology, particularly when the device is considered beneficial [5].   In addition, research by Rosenberg et al. [6] suggests that people with dementia are able to utilise well-known technologies at a competent level. However, combining this reduced knowledge with interfaces that have been poorly designed and implemented can hinder the interaction and amplify pre-existing feelings of technical isolation and inadequacy [7, 8].

Technology, with special emphasis on assistive technology, when applied in an effective manner has the potential to improve the quality of life for both the person living with dementia and their caregiver allowing users the possibility of remaining in their own home longer; thus reducing the cost of residential care [5, 9-12].   Furthermore providing the opportunity to access therapeutic interventions in the users own time would provide people living with dementia an increased feeling of independence and improved levels of satisfaction [13].   However, there is often a stigma attached to the use of assistive devices [14].   Therefore, care needs to be taken to ensure the assistive device is appropriate for the needs of the person with dementia and mitigates any feelings of inadequacy.   Examples of assistive technology include devices to promote safer walking, telecare to ensure safety within the home environment and memory aids to compensate for a declining cognitive ability [9].

It is important to note, that when assistive technology is introduced it should aim to augment the daily caring activities, rather than replace them totally.   Whilst it is vital to find alternative methods to improve day-to-day life for both the person living with dementia and their caregiver, technology should not replace the vital human contact aspect of caring for someone [15].

By not considering the interaction needs of people living with dementia, interface designers may be isolating their intended users and hence negating the potential effectiveness of the developed technology.   This could lead to prospective users disregarding a technology which could enhance their quality of life, enabling them to remain within the community and increase their safety.

1.2   Objective

Using secondary research in the form of a literature review, this paper aims to investigate the factors which need to be considered when designing interfaces for people living with dementia.   By considering the interaction difficulties encountered due to dementia-related cognitive decline, designers can ensure technology is easily utilised by people living with the condition.

2   Method

In order to achieve the objectives of this paper, a literature search using the Discovery Service tool provided by the University of Portsmouth was conducted.   This tool allowed the search of multiple library resources, including ScienceDirect, IEEE Xplore and the ACM Digital Library, to be explored simultaneously (for a full database listing visit: http://www.port.ac.uk/library/infores/discovery/).

Boolean logic was used to combine the keywords listed in table 1. This allowed the search results to be narrowed and ensured each of the title, abstract and subject terms were investigated for the inclusion of all keyword combinations. The Discovery search engine provides the functionality to search within the full text of a publication. However, in order to minimise the possible number of redundant results, it was decided not to utilise this functionality.

All the searches were limited to articles which have been published between January 2008 and December 2013. This ensured that only recent articles were obtained as part of the searching algorithm so as to only consider the most up-to-date knowledge and to obtain recommendations for the latest advances in technology, such as tablet computers.

Table 1. Search Keywords, chosen for their relevance to the topic reviewed

Dementia	Interact*
Comput*	Technolog*
"User experience"	Experience
Accessib*	Usab*
"Design considerations"	"Design implications"
Impair*	Mobile
"Human factor"	"Human factors"
HCI	"Interface design"
Tablet	iPad
Ubiquitous	Pervasive
Interface	Accept*
"User Acceptance"	Personal*
Ergonom*	Adopt*

After the initial searches had been completed, the inclusion criteria described in section 2.1 was applied based upon the publication abstract and the subsequent duplicate articles removed.

2.1   Inclusion Criteria

The following inclusion criteria were applied to the abstracts of the articles found as a result of the initial searches:

- Publications written in English
- Articles published in Academic Journals, Conference Proceedings and Books
- Publications where the focus is ensuring interfaces are suitable for people living with dementia (including accessibility, usability, user experience and user acceptance theory)
    - Articles focusing on the technology rather than the design have been excluded from this current study, but have been reserved for future research.

3   Results

The results of this study showed that in the last six years minimal research has been carried out into the interaction needs of people living with dementia.   The diagram in figure 1 shows the process carried out in order to reduce the number of possible articles from 1670 publications after the initial search to just 16 relevant studies.

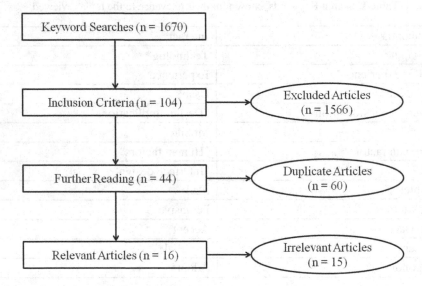

Fig. 1. Flowchart showing the process used to narrow the total number of articles

The initial searches yielded a total number of 1670 potential articles which could be relevant to the current study.   The application of the inclusion criteria (described in the previous section) to the article abstracts reduced the number of publications to 104. Table 2 shows the total number of results for each search term together with the number of potentially useful results.

Table 2. Search Results

Search Terms	Total Number of Results	Useful Results
dementia AND interact* AND technolog*	71	3
dementia AND interact* AND comput*	78	5
dementia AND "user experience"	0	0
dementia AND experience AND comput*	44	2
dementia AND experience AND technolog*	71	5
dementia AND accessib* AND comput*	21	3
dementia AND accessib* AND technolog*	24	2
dementia AND usab* AND comput*	17	6
dementia AND usab* AND technolog*	19	3
dementia AND "design considerations"	4	0
dementia AND "design implications"	0	0
dementia AND impair* AND technolog*	189	5
dementia AND impair* AND comput*	451	9
dementia AND mobile	96	4
dementia AND ("human factor" OR "human factors")	12	0
dementia AND hci	6	1
dementia AND "interface design"	1	1
dementia AND tablet AND comput*	4	1
dementia AND tablet AND technolo*	4	1
dementia AND iPad	6	0
dementia AND ubiquitous AND comput*	5	0
dementia AND ubiquitous AND technolog*	3	1
dementia AND pervasive AND comput*	9	3
dementia AND pervasive AND technolog*	5	3
dementia AND interface AND comput*	64	9
dementia AND interface AND technolog*	20	5
dementia AND accept* AND technol*	48	3
dementia AND accept* AND comput*	46	3
dementia AND "user acceptance"	3	1
dementia AND person* AND technolog*	55	4

Table 2. (*Continued*)

dementia AND person* AND comput*	64	6
dementia AND interact* AND person*	159	2
dementia AND interface AND person*	23	3
dementia AND ergonom* AND technolog*	2	1
dementia AND ergonom* AND comput*	6	3
dementia AND adopt* AND technolog*	31	5
dementia AND adopt* AND comput*	9	1

Once the inclusion criteria had been applied, the duplicate articles were removed to produce a final list of 44 articles to be further investigated. These articles were read to ensure they were applicable to the current study at which point 15 articles were excluded.

The final number of articles suitable for inclusion in this study was 16.

4   Discussion of Relevant Articles

In previous research, when designing interfaces three main factors were considered: accessibility, usability and user experience [16]. However, when designing for people living with dementia, two main ideas need to be considered holistically: personalisation and user acceptance, as shown by figure 2.

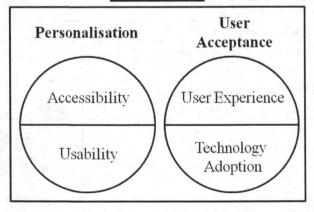

Fig. 2. Diagram to show the factors involved in interface design

4.1   Personalisation

The concept of personalisation involves the adaption of the user interface in order to specifically meet the needs of the user.   In this sense, personalisation would include features to ensure the interaction was both accessible and usable.   Personalisation would be an ideal solution to catering for a wide variety of needs within a single group of users, making the technique appropriate for use with people living with dementia at all stages of the condition's progression [13].

A diagnosis of dementia does not automatically imply the person is unable to utilise technology to its full potential.   Every person in different and should be treated as such.   Any perceived interaction difficulties should be assessed on a case by case basis rather than making generalised assumptions about the state of a person's cognitive ability [6, 17].

The amount of personalisation an interface requires is a delicate process.   Just like a human caregiver, it is important to ensure the right amount of support is provided in a timely manner.   Both the system and the caregiver must provide the appropriate amount of assistance to empower the person living with dementia to complete the task without deskilling taking place [18].   As the person living with dementia's cognitive ability declines, the amount of support which is required from the system will increase.   This leads to the requirement for the personalisation to be dynamic, and as such be able to adjust to the changing needs of the user over time [18].

In addition, the process of personalisation should tailor the interface to provide the necessary support to compensate for a person with dementia's declining abilities whilst maintaining the abilities which currently remain intact [5].   However, care needs to be taken that the interface is not simplified to a level which could patronise the person with dementia [10, 19].   Mihailidis et al. [13] argue that the interface should "start users with the most minimal possible starting point appropriate for their current level of abilities", reducing the likelihood of feeling overwhelmed. Rosenberg et al.'s study [5] showed that one concern of caregivers is that technology would be simplified to such an extent that it would "weaken a person's own abilities". By employing Mihailidis et al.'s approach to personalisation, the concerns of the caregivers would be allieviated.

The major downfall with the current user interface guidelines provided by the W3C WAI is the lack of flexibility and their apparent "one-size-fits-all" approach to design. The variability in the effects of dementia means that this approach to interface design will not work for this demographic.   Flexibility is perceived as a crucial design requirement [5, 15] to ensure the interface is appropriate for the user, but could in turn become a hindrance should the person living with dementia be able to manually change the settings [5].

4.2   User Acceptance

User acceptance can be considered a critical success factor for projects to implement assistive technologies [18].   This concept can be split into two sections: user experience and technology adoption.   These two aspects are inherently linked.   If the interface does not provide a pleasurable interaction experience, the user will be less inclined to maintain usage. An engaging interaction experience will encourage users to adopt novel technologies, which could lead to acceptance of the device into every-day usage.

People living with dementia and their caregivers are more likely to adopt a novel technology if they perceive a need requiring support [5, 17, 20]. This increased in-terest remains regardless of whether the users encountered difficulties which required further explanations from supervisors [20]. However, Rosenberg et al. [5] are keen to point out that the potential users still need to experience the current need for the technology. In addition, the technology would need to seamlessly integrate within the person with dementia and their caregiver's existing habits [5, 15].

Previous experience of computing is also an important consideration for user ac-ceptance. Research by deSant'Anna et al. [21] suggests that older users are reluctant to make use of IT through fear of causing irreparable damage to the system. This anxiety could jeopardise the effective use of the technology, negating its possible benefits [21]. In addition, the cognitive decline associated with dementia could di-minish the person's ability to learn and retain the information required to operate the technology. This effect is enhanced when follow-ups and supported practice sessions are not implemented, increasing the likelihood of the technology being abandoned, despite an on-going need for continued use [22].

Both Aloulou et al. [18] and Starkhammar & Nygard [22] argue that acceptance would be lower for people in the earlier stages of the dementia progression, when the perceived need is lower and higher in people whose abilities have significantly declined. Whilst people with a higher cognitive ability would find learning new interfaces easier, they may believe that they have no requirement for the system and therefore, may find the system (and the suggestion of implementation) both patronis-ing and stigmatizing [10].

Self image plays an important part in the adoption and acceptance of assistive technology [5, 17]. Karlsson et al. [17] found that people with dementia utilised the devices in a fashion which complemented their own self images. If the use of the device did not fit in with their preconceived image they lost interest in using the tech-nology.

Another important factor to consider when discussing technology adoption for people living with dementia is the influence of their caregivers. Research conducted by Karlsson et al. [17] suggests that spousal support for the integration of technology has an important influence over the person living with dementia's acceptance of novel devices. Whilst research carried out by both Hwang et al. [15] and McKenzie et al. [12] suggests that whilst caregivers are supportive of new technology aimed at reduc-ing the burden of caring, they are reluctant to adjust their responsibility to the mainte-nance of the new systems. In addition, caregivers are reluctant to provide support for new technologies which were either inconvenient or gave their home an "institu-tional" feel [12]. By avoiding assistive technologies which have an institutional look, the caregivers may be helping the person with dementia to maintain their own self-image and esteem.

5   Conclusion

In the last six years (January 2008 - December 2013) there has been minimal research focusing exclusively on ensuring interfaces are dementia-friendly. With the increasing number of people being diagnosed with the condition, this is a surprising conclusion. The increased prevalence of technology has the potential to provide multiple benefits, including enhanced independence and delaying the need for residential care. However, if the interfaces are not conducive to use by people living with dementia, the users may not be able to utilise assistive technologies to their full potential.

The research does, however, suggests that considering both personalisation and user acceptance is required to make an interface dementia-friendly. Due to the diverse nature of dementia, personalisation is particularly important for this demographic. By ensuring the interface adapts to the individual user's current circumstances, the interface would increase the accessibility and usability of the application. In addition, a dynamically adapting interface will allow the users to continue utilising the technology despite facing a progressive decline in their cognitive ability.

5.1   Limitations

This study has a number of limitations which will be addressed in future research.

Firstly, this study only includes papers which have been published in the last six years, between January 2008 and December 2013. As such, it will not include relevant papers which have been published in the preceding years. By including these articles increased awareness of the problems associated with utilising technology whilst living with the symptoms of dementia could be sought.

Secondly, people living with dementia also experience the natural effects of ageing [16]. Through the exclusion of articles which do not relate to dementia directly, this study has neglected to investigate important factors related to ageing which will also affect interaction with technology. The inclusion of research focused on the effects of ageing will serve to enhance the knowledge of impairments experienced by people living with a dementia diagnosis.

Finally, this study only included research where interaction with technology by people living with dementia is the main focus of the article. However, there are some studies where the main focus is on the use of technology and the design implications only briefly discussed. Through the inclusion of these studies, additional insights into interaction needs could be incorporated.

5.2   Future Research

The overall aim of the research, which includes this study, is to develop a set of guidelines with the goal of aiding interface designers to make interaction with technology dementia-friendly. This will allow the researchers to develop a smart application designed to be utilised by people living with dementia and their caregivers. The adherence to the developed set of guidelines will aim to ensure the application can be used to its full potential.

Further relevant articles, which are outside the January 2008 to December 2013 publication date range will be obtained through the reference harvesting (or snowballing) technique. This will ensure that earlier research will be included within the developed guidelines. As part of this process, additional relevant search terms will be added to the list of keywords.

Finally, additional searches of the literature will be conducted to include additional keywords such as: older, elderly ageing and aged. These searches will inform the guidelines and allow them to take into account the natural effects of ageing. In addition, considering the interface needs of older people will aid interaction with the developed smart application for the caregiver of the person living with dementia.

References

1. World Health Organisation, http://www.who.int/mediacentre/factsheets/fs362/en/
2. Alzheimer's Society, http://www.alzheimers.org.uk/infographic
3. Alzheimer's Society, http://www.alzheimers.org.uk/site/scripts/documents_info.php?documentID=106
4. Alzheimer's Society, http://www.alzheimers.org.uk/site/scripts/documents_info.php?documentID=133
5. Rosenberg, L., Kottorp, A., Nygard, L.: Readiness for Technology Use with People with Dementia: The Perspectives of Significant Others. Journal of Applied Gerontology 31, 510–530 (2012)
6. Rosenberg, L., Kottorp, A., Winblad, B., Nygard, L.: Perceived Difficulty in Everyday Technology Use Among Older Adults With or Without Cognitive Deficits. Scandinavian Journal of Occupational Therapy 16, 216–226 (2009)
7. Chou, J., Hsiao, S.: A Usability Study on Human-Computer Interface for Middle-aged Learners. Computers in Human Behavior 23, 2040–2063 (2007)
8. Ziefle, M.: Information Presentation in Small Screen Devices: The Trade Off between Visual Density and Menu Foresight. Applied Ergonomics 41, 719–730 (2010)
9. Alzheimer's Society, http://www.alzheimers.org.uk/site/scripts/documents_info.php?documentID=109
10. Nijhof, N., van Gemert-Pijnen, J., Burns, C., Seydel, E.: A Personal Assistant for Dementia to Stay at Home Safe at a Reduced Cost. Gerontechnology 11, 469–479 (2013)
11. Skillen, K., Chen, L., Nugent, C., Donnelly, M., Solheim, I.: A User Profile Ontology Based Approach for Assisting People with Dementia in Mobile Environments. In: 34th Annual International Conference of the IEEE EMBS, pp. 6390–6393 (2012)
12. McKenzie, B., Bowen, M., Keys, K., Bulat, T.: Safe Home Program: A Suite of Technologies to Support Extended Home Care of Persons with Dementia. American Journal of Alzheimer's Disease and Other Dementias 28, 348–354 (2013)
13. Mihailidis, A., Blunsden, S., Boger, J., Richards, B., Zutis, K., Young, L., Hoey, J.: Towards the Development of a Technology for Art Therapy and Dementia: Definition of Needs and Design Constraints. The Arts in Psychotherapy 37, 293–300 (2010)
14. Carrillo, M., Dishman, E., Plowman, T.: Everyday Technologies for Alzheimer's Disease Care: Research Findings, Directions and Challenges. Alzheimer's & Dementia 5, 479–488 (2009)

15. Hwang, A., Truong, K., Mihailidis, A.: Using Participatory Design to Determine the Needs of Informal Caregivers for Smart Home User Interfaces. In: 6th International Conference on Pervasive Computing Technologies for Healthcare (PervasiveHealth) and Workshops, pp. 41–48 (2012)
16. Ancient, C., Good, A.: Issues with Designing Dementia-Friendly Interfaces. In: Stephanidis, C. (ed.) HCII 2013, Part I. CCIS, vol. 373, pp. 192–196. Springer, Heidelberg (2013)
17. Karlsson, E., Axelsson, K., Zingmark, K., Savenstedt, S.: The Challenge of Coming to Terms with the Use of a New Digital Assistive Device: A Case Study of Two Persons with Mild Dementia. The Open Nursing Journal, 5, 102-110 (2011).
18. Aloulou, H., Mokhtari, M., Tiberghien, T., Biswas, J., Phua, C., Lin, J., Yap, P.: Deployment of Assistive Living Technology in a Nursing Home Environment: Methods and Lessons Learned. BMC Medical Informatics and Decision Making 13 (2013)
19. Mahmud, N., Vogt, J., Luyten, K., Slegers, K., Van den Bergh, J., Coninx, K.: Dazed and Confused Considered Normal: An Approach to Create Interactive Systems for People Living with Dementia. In: Bernhaupt, R., Forbrig, P., Gulliksen, J., Lárusdóttir, M. (eds.) HCSE 2010. LNCS, vol. 6409, pp. 119–134. Springer, Heidelberg (2010)
20. Gonzalez-Palau, F., Franco, M., Toribio, J., Losada, R., Parra, E., Bamidis, P.: Designing a Computer-based Rehabilitation Solution for Older Adults: The Importance of Testing Usability. PsychNology Journal 11, 119–136 (2013)
21. de Sant'Anna, M., Vallet, C., Kadouche, R., Stefanucci, D., Tomascakova, A., Morat, B., Rigaud, A.-S.: Computer Accessibility for Individuals Suffering from Mild to Moderate Alzheimer's Disease. European Geriatric Medicine 1, 186–192 (2010)
22. Starkhammar, S., Nygard, L.: Using a Timer Device for the Stove: Experiences of Older Adults with Memory Impairment or Dementia and their Families. Technology and Disability 20, 179–191 (2008)

Ergonomic Evaluation of Manual Force Levels of the Elderly in the Handling of Products: An Analysis Using Virtual Reality

Rafaela Q. Barros[1], Marcelo Márico Soares[1], and Maria Goretti Fernandes[2]

[1] Program of Post-graduation in Design, Federal University of Pernambuco, Recife, Brasil,
Av Academico Helio Ramos, S/No. Cidade Universitaria, 50.670-420, Recife, PE, Brazil
[2] Departament of Physiotherapy, Federal University of Sergipe, Aracaju, Brasil
{Rafaela Q.Barros,lotus100}@outlook.com

Abstract. Data from the World Health Organization - WHO [1] estimated that from 2000 to 2050, there will be a threefold increase in the population over 60-year-old population, which will rise to nearly 2 billion. It is important to designer understand the aging process and its peculiarities, such as those issues that affect cognitive issues and physical skills, thus enabling the understanding of products targeted on elderly people. The Virtual Reality via using haptic gloves to simulate everyday activities (EDAs) in a virtual environment. Thus, it is intended that this technology will enable the study of the measurement of forces applied in performing tasks. Data on measuring the levels of manual strength in the virtual environment were not found in the literature. Based on the data obtained in this review of the literature, the intention is to simulate elderly people´s manual activities with a view to quantifying levels of force.

Keywords: Virtual Reality, Manual strength and ergonomics.

1 Introduction

Data from the World Health Organization - WHO [1] estimated that from 2000 to 2050, there will be a threefold increase in the world population aged over 60, which will thus rise from 600 to nearly 2 billion people.

According to this source, the bulk of this growth is occurring in developing countries, like Brazil, where the number of elderly will grow from 400 million to 1.7 billion.

The World Health Organization (WHO) defines an elderly person being someone in the First World who is aged 65 and over, and 60 or over how old a limit of 65 or over the age of individuals in developed countries, and aged 60 or over for those from developing countries.

It is important to understand the aging process and its peculiarities, as those which affect cognitive and physical skills, thus enabling an understanding of products that will be targeted on the elderly.

A. Marcus (Ed.): DUXU 2014, Part IV, LNCS 8520, pp. 124–132, 2014.

Chaumon and Ciobanu [2] distinguish the aging process as being: normal (classic aging with degradation, certain human functions being maintained); pathological (various accidents or diseases increase or exacerbate the consequences of aging); optimal (identical or superior performance to that of younger people); and successful (when psychologically they adapt to change and/or accept their situation).

They report that the elderly may have different types of (permanent or temporary) deficiencies, namely those of: perception (hearing or vision); use (due to limitations in moving lower and/or upper limbs); psychological (greater psychological vulnerability), and so forth.

According to Paschoarelli et al. [3], the decline in levels of habitual physical activity for the elderly contributes to reducing functional fitness and to the manifestation of various diseases as a result of loss of functional capacity and decreasing motor performance in performing Every Day Activities (EDAs). Such problems may be related to inadequate demands on strength in packaging, particularly for vacuum-sealed products or which have child-proof safety seals.

Some tools, involving new technologies present themselves as suitable for handling everyday products. Among them Virtual Reality using haptic gloves stands out as this enables EDAs to be simulated in a virtual environment. Therefore, it is intended that this technology will enable the measurement of forces applied in performing tasks to be studied. Data on how to measure levels of manual strength in the virtual environment were not found in the literature.

2 Aging and Difficulties in Handling Products

The aging of the population is one of humanity's greatest triumphs and one of major challenges in terms of considering their abilities, needs and limitations when designing products and jobs.

As we enter the 21st century, global aging will cause an increase in social and economic demands worldwide. This demand is expressed on considering that this population will occupy jobs and use consumer products in their day-to-day lives. However, people of the Third Age are, in general, ignored with respect to their physical and cognitive demands being regarded as productive and active elements in our society.

It is important to understand the aging process and its peculiarities as those that affect cognitive issues and physical skills, thus enabling products targeted on the elderly to be understood.

According to Parente et al. [4], human aging, as well as other stages of life (development) is a transformation process of the organism that is reflected in its physical structures, in manifestations of cognition as well as in the subjective perception of these transformations.

Besides the problems of human beings' aging process, common complaints from the elderly are about the problems of inadequate demands when handling consumer products in relation to the sufficiency of the strength used when using for example, vacuum sealed packages. This type of situation is extremely important, taking into account the growth of the elderly population and increase in life expectancy [5].

Thus, according to Iida [6], the loss of the sense of touch is another important problem attributed to osteomuscular difficulties when handling objects. This is due to the difficulty in picking up or handling objects, while pointing out that the elderly´s notion of size or space stars to seem to be confused, thereby producing erroneous information about the strength and the environment to be used when performing tasks.

Both the strongest users, as well as the weakest ones, may perform actions that lead to accidents because they overload their ostemuscular systems when active, thus subjecting themselves to the risk of injury or simply of not managing to do the activity [7, 8].

Santos and Sala [9] point to the growth in the number of the elderly in relation to national population rates and medical advances, which prolong the current life expectancy of society. However, it would be useless to increase the satisfaction of these people if the limitations and progression of the quality of life were not taken into account.

The authors report that, over the years, the human body undergoes a natural aging process that induces functional and structural changes that impede the performance of daily activities independently. Although not fatal, these conditions generally tend to have a significant adverse effect on the quality of life of the elderly.

According to Smith [10], when a person gets older some changes may occur. Some characteristics and abilities of the elderly population differ considerably from those of younger people. It is extremely important that such changes are considered in the process of designing, planning and developing products that will be used by members of the elderly population.

Also according to Smith, the changes that occur with aging can be physical, such as changes in the size and shape of the body; or maximum strength decreasing; changes in the performance of the sensory functions such as vision and hearing; or they may be psychological, such as changes in cognitive or psychomotor functions.

Data from Brazil [11] and Duarte et al. [12] show that the life expectancy of the elderly population has been growing substantially due to improvements in their quality of life. Nevertheless, the aging process shows there is concern related to disabling events caused by problems about needing to maintain the functionalities of physical skills.

Duarte et al. [12], in their study, reveals that functionality can be interpreted as the individual's ability to perform activities or functions by making use of his/her abilities to engage on social interactions in leisure activities and in other conduct asked for in their everyday lives.

As a major part of the functionality considers the need to manipulate objects, the manipulation of objects is common in most ADLs, in which the hands, through the movement associated with the application of grip muscle strength action, perform the mechanical action. Incorrect sizing of the power demand of a product / activity can generate constraints on tasks.

The reduction in the strength to manipulate objects is one of the characteristics of aging. Thus, the purpose of this research study is to measure different levels of manual force of the physical demands on an elderly population manipulating everyday objects by means of Virtual Reality.

3   Ergonomics, Usability of Products

According to Campos et al [13], the intention of ergonomic design is to reduce the problems in the human-technology interface, and is based on the methods of usability analysis, which are applied in the production process of a product.

Falcao and Soares [14] consider usability as an important relationship for the individual that influences the choice of a particular product. Therefore, usability sets out to improve the user´s relationship with a product by making the interface clear, thereby making a good, effective and efficient interaction possible that might allow full control of the environment without problems appearing during the relationship.

In the studies of Voorbij and Steenbekkers [16], their analysis found that it is common for sizing strength in consumer products to be a problem especially in vacuum-sealed products or those that have child-proof safety seals. The reason for the difficulties was insufficient strength to use the packaging.

Exemplifying this context, Paschoarelli et al. [3] present studies reporting that in the UK in 1994, 550 accidents to the elderly occurred when glass bottles were opened and 610 accidents when the elderly opened plastic bottles. According to these authors, these episodes are related to the elderly using sharp instruments to assist in opening hard tops and complicated seals which are then manually removed.

According to Voorbij et al. [17], one study reports that nine packages available on the market were analyzed, six of which demanded strength higher than the capacity of the elderly and two made demands greater than the capacity of even young adults. Another study, presented by the same authors, found that 20% of subjects had difficulties in opening glass packaging.

Therefore, it is deemed necessary to understand the importance of the ability to use the hand as a clamp or claw, this position being called prehension or grip [18].

The study of the manipulative abilities of the hand began by analyzing holds and the forces involved. Hand grip positions are usually classified as prehensile or non-prehensile [19].

Most biomechanical research reports a range of manual force related to the age of the individual, there being increase in strength in young adulthood and a consecutive deficit until the onset of aging [15], [16].

Yoxall [20] says that certain types of packaging request the use of a certain force to open them and obtain access to the product, thereby determining that the consumer is able to exercise this strength, since packaging produced in the last 10 years has become more complex to open.

So it is important to stress the need for extreme efforts to open conserved food jars, since many users are unable to open them because they lack the appropriate strength. These packages were based on some studies covering an analysis of forces and torque related to gender and age. These are the key points for the proper use (or constraints) in opening a product [20].

Therefore, the biomechanical aspects of the human upper limbs are of utmost importance to the ergonomic design of hand tools so the following biomechanical and task factors must be taken into account: postures with flexions of the wrist; extreme postures and limitation the area which are disadvantageous to using strength. Regarding the design of grips and manipulations of objects that require greater effort, it is best to choose palm grips, flexion-extension movements to those of pronation-supination because they generate higher forces [21].

As to the object, according to Yoxall, account should be taken of size as this can significantly change the manual force needed. In product design and tasks, the grip position is favoured when done near shoulder height and force is applied in the horizontal direction.

Due to the reduction in manipulation strength, a characteristic of the elderly, performing tasks such as opening, closing, pulling and manipulating packaging becomes a challenge for these users. This research will identify limits of forces by simulating manual activities in virtual environments.

4   Virtual Reality and Simulation of Activities

In general terms, according to Rebelo et al. [22], virtual reality is a way to transport a person to a reality in which he/she is not physically present but it seems that he/she is there.

According to these authors, Virtual Reality (VR) is "the use of computer modeling and simulation that allows a person to interact with a three-dimensional (3-D) artificial environment that is visualized or in which there is other sensory involvement. In immersive VR situations, the user is located in an environment in which reality is simulated by using interactive devices. These send and receive information and can be used as goggles, headsets, gloves or body suits. In a typical VR environment, the user who wears a helmet with a stereoscopic screen sees animated images of a simulated environment".

Burdea and Coiffet (2003) divided VR technology into input devices (e.g., trackers, navigation and gesture interfaces) and output devices (e.g., graphics, sound and touch screens).

Rebelo et al. [22] present a description of VR applied to consumer products. The text below is mainly based on the analysis of these authors.

According to these authors, from the human point of view, input devices are activated by a user action (e.g., head movement, body movement and voice) and output devices activate the human senses (e.g., visual, auditory, tactile, proprioceptive). Therefore, an increase in inputs and outputs makes the system more immersive.

Immersion is also defined by its width (for example, several sensory modalities are stimulated) and depth (for example, with regard to the visual resolution). The greater the width and depth, the more immersive VR is.

Non- immersive VR, computers and an LCD monitor are often used. Sometimes, users can also wear 3-D glasses to enhance visual depth and create stereoscopic effects. Any input devices may be used, such as a joystick, a trackball, or a haptic glove.

Some tools that involve new technologies are suitable for identifying the strength limits when the elderly handle objects. Among these, Virtual Reality is suitable for simulating activities in digital and virtual environments. Most EDAs are performed by manual intervention and interaction with real world objects. Therefore, haptic gloves were designed to recognize the user's finger movements and transfer them to virtual environments. In general, a Haptics glove comprises an exoskeleton that enables information to be captured by flexing the fingers and the real location of the hand.

Force-feedback is implemented through a network of tendons that are directed towards the fingers. By using this equipment, what is offered is the sensation of the size and shape of an object that is being manipulated in a virtual reality environment. The processing system of the Instrumentation unit, a CyberGlove ®, communicates with the data of the CyberGrasp Force Control Unit (FCU). Figure 1 shows the haptic glove designed by the Immersion Corporation, and is called CyberGraspTM [24,25].

Fig. 1. CyberGrasp ™ haptic glove designed by Immersion Corporation

The CyberGrasp ™ may be used in conjunction with the CyberGlove ®, called CyberGrasp ™. The CyberGrasp ™ is a lightweight exoskeleton (16 oz) that fits under the CyberGlove ® device and can provide tactile feedback to the fingers. This is supplied to the fingers by means of a 24-"tendon" system or cables that run along the back of the hand and are attached to the tip of each finger. The CyberGrasp ™ can deliver a maximum of 12 newtons of force continuously to each finger [24].

In tactile feedback, tactile sensations such as the texture of a given surface are offered to the user. In feedback on strength, the device counterpoints itself to a given force applied by the user, thereby offering resistance and representing physical variables such as weight. Finally, thermal feedback seeks to represent the sensations of hot and cold [25].

According to Burdea and Coiffet [23] (2003), the user´s tactile perception is brought about by the concepts of touch and kinesthesia. Regarding touch, the user may feel different types of sensation such as temperature, pressure, vibration or pain and this will depend on the sensitivity of his/her kin. This sensitivity may vary according to the selected region where contact will be made. Kinesthesia, for its part, is related to the perception of the tensions exerted on muscles and joints. This perception is also called proprioception or force-feedback and is able to recognize the rigidity of objects.

While gloves are being used, the user may play, point to, manipulate and feel the object in the virtual environment. The gloves perform the behavior of a virtual hand within the environment, allowing the individual to undertake activities that the system will respond to [26].

The exoskeleton CyberGrasp ™, worn over a CyberGlove ® was originally created for the U.S. Navy for use in telerobotic applications. CyberGrasp ™ can be used apart from virtual reality simulation for handling hazardous materials and when using computer-aided design (CAD). In the experiment, the CyberGrasp ™ was used to aid the movement of the fingers of a 25-year-old person who suffered a stroke and whose ability to open a hand was diminished [24, 25].

In the study cited above, the individual studied had spasticity levels ranging from mild to moderate. However, on using the CyberGrasp ™, the flexion movement of the affected hand was improved and was worked in synchrony with the other hand during bilateral manual training. The results say that without this robotic assistance, hand tool has been improved and worked in sync with the other hand during bilateral training manual. The results describe that without robotic assistance, the subject would not have been able to develop simultaneous and bilateral movement adequately.

Thus, by using haptic systems it becomes possible to move or deform a virtual object - depending on the material that it is made of – by feeling its texture, weight, or the force resulting from this movement .To do so, the program must precisely calculate the force properties that the device should return to the user. If the force applied is excessive, the user will tire quickly and if it is very weak, the feelings will not seem true ones. The programmer must find a way to calibrate and balance these forces thus making the interface the most realistic one possible.

5   Conclusion

Based on this review of the literature, the intention is to formulate theoretical bases so as to apply Virtual Reality as an instrument for simulating manual activities of a population of elderly people that will enable the levels of forces used in manual activities to be quantified.

References

1. WHO – WORLD HEALTH ORGANIZATION. Questions and Answers. What are the public health implications of global ageing? (2011), http://www.nia.nih.gov/sites/default/files/nia-who_report_booklet_oct-2011_a4__112-12_5.pdf
2. Chaumon, M.E.B., Ciobanu, R.O.: Les Nouvelles Technologies au Service des PersonnesAgées: Entre Promesseset Interrogations – Une Revue de Questions. Psychologiefrançaise 54, 271–285 (2009)
3. Razza, B.M., Paschoarelli, M.C.: Avaliação de forças de preensão digital: parâmetrospara o design ergonômico de produtos. In: Pachoarelli, L.C., Menezes, M.S. (eds.) Design e Ergonomia: Aspectos Tecnológicos, p. 279. Editora UNESP. Cultura Acadêmica, São Paulo (2009) ISBN 978-85-7983-001-3
4. Parente, M.A.M.P.: Cognição e envelhecimento. Artmed, Porto Alegre (2006)
5. Voorbij, A.I.M., Steenbekkers, L.P.A.: The twisting force of aged consumers when opening a jar. Applied Ergonomics, 105–109 (2002)
6. Iida, I.: Ergonomia: Projeto e produção. E. Blucher, São Paulo (2005)
7. Pheasant, S.: Bodyspace: Anthropometry, ergonomics and the design of work, 3rd edn. Taylor & Francis, London (2005)
8. Mital, A., Kumar, S.: Human muscle strength definitions, measurement, and usage: Part I – Guidelines for the practitioner. International Journal of Industrial Ergonomics 22, 101–121 (1998); Human Muscle Strength Definitions, Measurement, and Usage: Part II – The Scientific Basis (Knowledge Base) for the Guide
9. Santos, F.A.N.V., Sala, S.F.: Ergonomia e terceira idade: aspectos relevantes para o projeto de produtos para pessoas idosas. In: Abergo 2010 –Ulaergo2010/ XVI Congresso Brasileiro de Ergonomia e III Congresso Latino de Ergonomia. Rio de Janeiro. Anais do Abergo 2010 –Ulaergo2010 / XVI Congresso Brasileiro de Ergonomia e III Congresso Latino de Ergonomia (2010)
10. Smith, S., Norris, B., Peebles, L.: OlderAdultdata: The Handbook of Measurements and Capabilities of the Older Adult. Nottingham. p. 4-9 (1998)
11. Brasil. Ministério da Saúde, Secretaria de Atenção à Saúde, Departamento de Atenção Básica. Envelhecimento e saúde da pessoa idosa. Brasília (2006)
12. Duarte, Y.A.O., Andrade, C.L., Lebrão, M.L.O.: Índex de Katz na avaliação da funcionalidade dos idosos. Revista Escola Enfermagem. 41(2), 317–325 (2007)
13. Campos, L.F.A., Paschoarelli, L.C., Silva, D.C., Muniz, F.J., Lanutti, J.N.L., Silva, J.C.P.: Análise física da força manual de torque: Contribuições para para o design de ferramentas manuais. In: XVI Congresso Brasileiro de Ergonomia, 2 a 6 de Agosto de 2010, ABERGO, Rio de Janeiro (2010)
14. Falcão, C.S., Soares, M.M.: Usability of Consumer Products: an analyses of concepts methods and applications. Estudos em Design (online). Rio de Janeiro 21(2), 1–26 (2013)
15. Mathiowetz, V., Rennells, C., Donahoc, L.: Effect of elbow position on grip and key pinch strength. The Journal of Hand Surgery, 694–697 (1985)
16. Voorbij, A.I.M., Steenbekkers, L.P.A.: The twisting force of aged consumers when opening a jar. Applied Ergonomics, 105–109 (2002)
17. Voorbij, A.I.M., Steenbekkers, L.P.A., Ramos, I.R., Toniolo, J., Cendoroglo, M., Garcia, J., Paola, C., Santos, F.: Two-year follow-up study of elderly residents in S. Methodology and preliminary. Revista de SaúdePública 32(63), 397–407 (1998)
18. Konin, J.: Cinesiologiaprática para fisioterapeutas, 1st edn. Guanabara Koogan, Rio de Janeiro (2006)

19. Cushman, W.H., Rosenberg, D.J.: Human factors in product design. Elsevier, New York (1991)
20. Yoxall, A.R., Janson, S.R., Bradubury, J., Langley, J., Wearn; Hayes, S.: Openability: Products design limits for consumer packaging Technology and Science. In: Khalid, H., Hedge, A., Tareq, Z. (eds.) Advances in Ergonomics Modeling and Usability Evaluation. Advances in Human Factors and Ergonomics Series, pp. 219–225. CRC Press, Boca Raton (2012)
21. Razza, B.M., Paschoarelli, L.C.: Hand strength and the product design: A review. Revista Tecnológica 18, 37–52 (2009)
22. Rebelo, F., Duarte, E., Noriega, P., Soares, M.: Virtual reality in consume products design: Methods and applications. In: Karwowski, W., Soares, M., Stanton, N. (eds.) Human Factors and Ergonomics in Consumer Product Design: Methods and Techniques, pp. 381–404. CRC Press, Boca Raton (2011)
23. Burdea, G., Coiffet, P.: Virtual Reality Technology, 2nd edn. Wiley-IEEE Press, New Brunswick (2003)
24. CyberGlove® Reference Manual v. 1, Virtual Technologies, Inc., Palo Alto (1991-1998)
25. CyberGrasp™ User's Guide v1.2, Immersion Corporation, San Jose C.A (2000-2003)
26. Rodello, I.A., Sanches, S.R.R., Sementille, A.C., Brega, J.R.F.: Realidade Misturada: Conceitos, Ferramentas e Aplicações. Revista Brasileira de Computação Aplicada 2(2), 2–16 (2010)

Accessibility of Mobile Platforms

Alireza Darvishy

ZHAW Zurich University of Applied Sciences, Zurich, Switzerland
dvya@zhaw.ch

Abstract. This paper compares accessibility features of two popular platforms from a user perspective. The comparison is based on accessibility features for different kinds of disabilities such as vision, hearing or physically challenged users. A section on accessibility in mobile applications follows. According to a survey [1], the use of mobile platforms by people with disabilities is dramatically increasing. New accessibility features are introduced for each release of these platforms which makes them an affordable assistive technology.

Keywords: Accessibility, mobile devices, screen-readers, people with disabilities, assistive technologies, accessible apps.

1   Introduction

The use of mobile devices is growing rapidly, and the way we use mobile devices continues to evolve. Use of mobile devices for shopping, banking and other apps is to increasing and opening more opportunities to how we use mobile devices in daily life.

The advantages to people with disabilities are potentially more effective than those for the general population. Accessible mobile devices increase the ability of people with disabilities to shop, communicate, study and do other activities. Commercially available mobile devices can replace specialized hardware that many people with disabilities rely on for applications such as way-finding, reading and others.

The use of accessible mobile devices has recently increased dramatically, according to the last survey carried out by WebAim Screen Reader Survey 4, which reported that 71.8 percent of respondents indicated they use a screen reader on a mobile device, a 600 percent increase in mobile screen reader usage since the first survey was conducted just over 1 year ago.

There are a number of mobile devices on the market which offer accessibility features, including as Apple iOS, Google Android and BlackBerry. This paper considers the most popular mobile platforms, namely Apple iOS 7 and Google Android 4.4 [2,3,4,5].

2   Comparing Accessibility Features of iPhone and Android

This section compares accessibility features of two popular mobile platforms: Apple iOS 7 and Google Android 4.4. The comparison is based on different senses such as

A. Marcus (Ed.): DUXU 2014, Part IV, LNCS 8520, pp. 133–140, 2014.

vision, hearing, and physical and motor. The comparison is probably not complete and might be extended to other features.

Apple provides a strong base of accessibility features just out of the box. With the release of the iPhone 3GS in 2009, Apple developed the first mobile screen reader for touch-based devices. The VoiceOver [6] screen reader which is built into the Mac desktop platform was introduced into the iPhone. Apple provided a unique set of gestures to allow a user to nonvisually control the iPhone using VoiceOver. As a user's finger moves over or taps an element, the name of the element is spoken. Double tapping on the screen then activates the element.

Google, on the other hand, has an open source philosophy and this had led to adoption of a more "wild west" model of accessibility where developers are expected to create accessibility solutions rather than having them provided centrally.

2.1 Vision

Feature(s)	iOS	Android
Screen Reader	VoiceOver	TalkBack
Zoom	Zoom	Magnification gestures
Text magnification	Large Text • 20pt • 24pt • 32pt • 40pt • 48pt • 56pt	Font Size • Tiny • Small • Normal • Large • Huge
Bold Text	Bold Text	
Colors	Invert Colors • White/Black • Black/White	
Contrast	Increase Contrast	
Speak Selected Text	Speak Selection	
Speech Rate	Speaking Rate	Speech Rate • Very slow • Normal • Fast • Faster • Very fast • Rapid • Very rapid • Fastest

Navigation	Rotor	
Handwriting	Handwriting • Writing • Navigation	
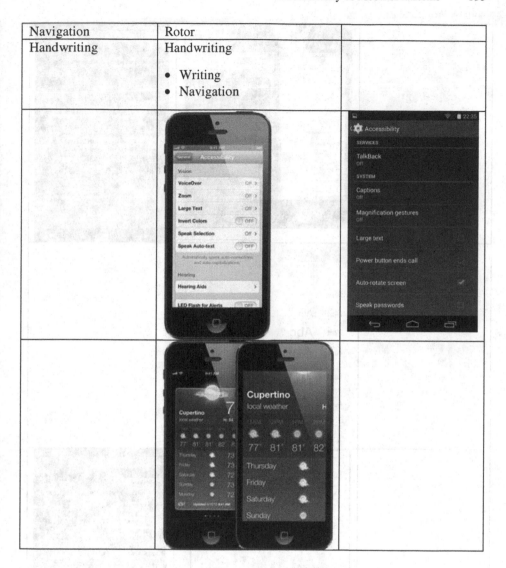		

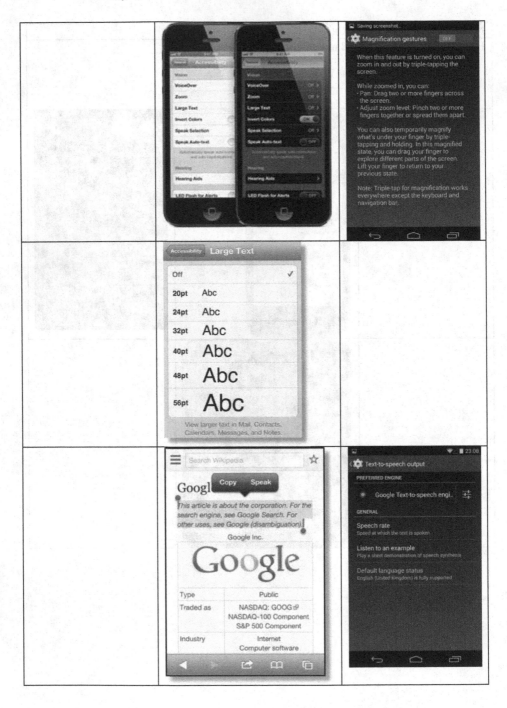

2.2   Hearing

Feature(s)	iOS	Android
Flash Alert	Led Flash Alert	Led Notification
Audio Balance	Mono Audio and Balance	Sound Balance • Adjusting sound Left/Right
Audio/Stereo	Mono Audio and Balance	Mono Audio • Mono/Stereo
Video Calls	FaceTime	Hangouts
Subtitles/Caption	Subtitles and caption option	Captions • Language • Text size • Caption style

2.3   Physical and Motor

Feature(s)	iOS	Android
Touch Assistant	Assistive Touch	
Incoming Calls	Incoming Calls • Default • Headset • Speaker	Answering/Ending Calls

Accessibility click speed	Home-click Speed • Default • Slow • Slowest	Touch and hold delay • Short • Medium • Long

2.4   Additional Features

Feature(s)	iOS	Android
Speech Input	SIRI • Send messages • Place phone calls • Schedule meetings • Set reminders • Look up movie times • Etc…	GoogleNow
Speak Password		Speak Password: When explored by touch is enabled, characters entered in password fields read out by the device
Answering/ending calls		Answering/ending calls: • The home key answers calls • Answer calls by tapping • Voice control • The power key ends calls
Enable/Disable Accessibility		Show shortcut: Press and hold the power key to use the shortcut of accessibility menu under phone options

Manage Accessibility Setting		• Export: Save the accessibility settings as a file • Update: Update your accessibility settings by importing the saved file • Share via: Share the accessibility settings • Android Beam: send the accessibility settings file via NFC
Accessibility Shortcut	Accessibility shortcut • VoiceOver • Invert Colors • Zoom • Switch Control • Assistive Touch	Accessibility shortcut • Press and hold the power key until you hear a sound or feel a vibration • Tap and hold with two fingers until you hear audio confirmation
Simultaneous use of Screen Reader and Zoom functionality	This feature is provided	
Support additional external devices	Bluetooth refreshable braille display	

2.5   Accessible Best Practices for Mobile Development

Many fundamental accessible best practices will apply to mobile applications. Here are some examples:

- Text and images must meet relevant requirements for sufficient color contrast
- Screens must be laid out in an order that permits intuitive sequential navigation
- User interface controls must respond to multiple modalities of input
- User interface components must communicate correct information about the name, state, role and value of each component.

For a comprehensive description of the best practices see [7] for iOS and Android.

3   Conclusion

This paper presented a comparison of accessibility features from two popular platforms. The presented features are not comprehensive, but it gives a good overview of currently available features. New trends and modalities such as force feedback [8] will provide good new accessibility features for users with disabilities in the future.

References

1. http://webaim.org/projects/screenreadersurvey/
2. http://support.apple.com/kb/HT5018?viewlocale=en_US
3. http://developer.android.com/design/patterns/accessibility.html
4. http://mobileapps.blackberry.com/devicesoftware/entry.do?code=bsr
5. http://docs.blackberry.com/en/smartphone_users/deliverables/21882/index.html?name=Hearing+Aid+Compatibility+with+BlackBerry+Smartphones+-+BlackBerry+Smartphones5.0&language=English&userType=1&category=BlackBerry+Smartphones&subCategory=Accessibility
6. https://www.webaccessibility.com/best_practices.php
7. http://eyes-free.googlecode.com/svn/trunk/documentation/android_access/services.html

TAC-ACCESS - Technologies to Support Communication from Interfaces Accessible and Multimodal for People with Disabilities and Diversity: Context-Centered Design of Usage

Cristiani de Oliveira Dias[1], Liliana Maria Passerino[1], Carlos de Castro Lozano[2], and Enrique García Salcines[2]

[1] Universidade Federal do Rio Grande do Sul, Brazil
{cristianideoliveiradias,lpasserino}@gmail.com
[2] Univerisidad de Córdoba, Spain
carlosdecastrolozano@gmail.com, egsalcines@uco.es

Abstract. The school and the family can use technological resources to provide the individual with disabilities the opportunity to obtain a good quality of life, autonomy and cognitive development. It is known that the process of inclusion of this subject in the school may not be enough to meet your needs. In both activities both in school and family, using digital services to more intensive monitoring may be a proposal to include homeschooling (Passerino, de Castro, 2013). It was thought therefore, a computing platform that assists subjetcts, family and school to participate in these scenarios, integrating them. A partnership between one University in Brazil and one University in Spain allow this integration. The research plans to join the Alternative Communication (AC) named SCALA and an operating system and platform in the cloud whose main goal is to give conditions for development to people who are dependent (elderly, disabled) Siesta Cloud software. This integration has aimed at creating opportunities for these people to obtain autonomy, communicative interaction and improvement in their quality of life. For this platform reach the largest number of people, it was necessary to choose the method of usability and we chose for Context-Centered Design of Usage and in this article the process that led to this choice are shown.

Keywords: Usablility, Alternative Comunication, Context-Centered Design of Usage.

1   Introduction

According to the United Nation Enable (2014) approximately 15% of the world population, 1 billion people, have some type of disability. Policies were necessary to get the equalization of rights and opportunities before and subtracted at the 1994 World Conference on Special Education with the presence of more than 80 governments signed the Declaration of Salamanca in Spain. Important for inclusion and access of

A. Marcus (Ed.): DUXU 2014, Part IV, LNCS 8520, pp. 141–151, 2014.

the society resources. The school such as the families can use technological resources that provide the individual with disabilities the opportunity to obtain a good quality of life, autonomy and cognitive development. It is known that the process of inclusion of this children in the school may not be enough to meet your needs. In both activities in school and family, using digital services to more intensive monitoring may be a proposal to include homeschooling (home and school) (Passerino, de Castro, 2013).

It was thought therefore, a computing platform that assists users, family and school to participate in these scenarios, integrating them. As a focus of research, we chose subjects with difficulties in social interaction as children with Autistic Spectrum Disorder more specific Syndrome of Autism, with motor and speech difficulties. Communication skills are fundamental in the development of social interaction, as they allow to establish reciprocity People who have deficits in communication often need to use additional supplementary means of communication or magnifiers, called Alternative Communication (AC) (Passerino, 2013 Bez and Passerino,2009).

2   SCALA and SiestaCloud

According to Von Tetzchner and Martinsen (2000) and Glennen (1997), alternative media is all communicative practice that differs from speech and that is used in contexts of communication face to face, replacing it. The concept of Alternative Communication aims to define the different forms of communication such as gestures, sign language, facial expressions, and even the use of software capable of supporting communication. The AC term is used in this study as all forms of communication to replace, supplement or extension of orality (Bez, 2012). A designed and developed to support the process of language development in individuals with autism, called SCALA (System of Literacy Alternative Communication for People with Autism) project is presented as an alternative in the care and support homeschooling this user with difficulty in communication and speech. The project SCALA began in 2009 and the main goal is to support the process of language development in children with autism and communication deficits, epistemologically grounded in theory. In 2011, SCALA becomes SCALA 2.01 being a multiplatform application (Passerino, de Castro, 2013). Initially tested with three autistic children and three different contexts: school, family and university research lab. The SCALA has two modules: board (Figure 1a) and stories (Figure 1b) and was developed under the GNU and Creative Commons licenses to ensure its open content. The pictograms used in the system were mostly developed by ARASAAC2 group. With the use of these images and the images themselves, the SCALA has over 4000 (four thousand) images, divided into the categories: People, Objects, Nature, Stock, Food, Feelings, Qualities and My Pictures, where the user has the option inserting own image on the system (Passerino, de Castro, 2013).

---

[1] http://scala.ufrgs.br
[2] The stock images used in SCALA were translated from pictographic symbols CATEDU (http://catedu.es/arasaac/) under the Creative Commons license.

(a) - Module Board Figure   1 (b) - History Module

Fig. 1. Interface Scale (Source: SBIE, 2013)

As result of over 25 years of research and development EATCO group at the University of Cordoba, Spain, the SiestaCloud is a cloud platform complemented with an operating system based on Siesta Local GNU / Linux installable on settop-box or computer (de Castro, 2011). For De Castro (2011) SiestaCloud is an ecosystem, because it is a set of applications, operating system and cloud platform whose main aim is to give conditions for development to people in situations of dependency as for example the elderly, people with disabilities, people hospitalized. For this reason, the SiestaCloud was developed following international standards for accessibility and usability (Bevan, 2012). The SiestaCloud, which can be seen in Figure 2, is part of an interface that aggregates multiple software, plus a user-friendly interface, with icons, taskbar, integration with other tools and software.

Fig. 2. Siesta Cloud Platform and the differents technological devices (Source: RED 32, p. 1-43)

The SiestaCloud has a model of homecare, using known feature of most people and internalized by them, like TV. The interaction is via a remote control with six colored keys and the interaction is reduced to six types of events that can be six movements, gestures and voices. Can be customized as for users(Castro,Burón,Sainz y García, 2011). This system was developed using criteria of usability, accessibility and is adaptive, so it is intended to cover the greatest number of people possible. Following the text this research presents usability and accessibility issues and the use of these criteria in the development of a software.

Supported by the Government of Brazil and Spain, both research groups and develop technologies for special education and teamed to integrate two of this mentioned platforms.

3   TAC-ACCESS - Assistive Technology for Communication to Accessible and Multimodal Interfaces for People with Disabilities and Diversity

The TAC-ACCESS-Assistive Technology for Communication Design from accessible and multimodal interfaces for people with disabilities and diversity, emerges as a research project and technology development of technology, information processing, multimodal applications and interfaces technologies applied to the field of inclusion (Passerino, Bez, de Castro, Salcines, 2013). It is also a cooperation research of the Brazilian Goverment and the Ministry of Education of Spain that aims to integrate this two software and share experiences and knowledgment.The methodology of this study consisted of a case study, supported by Yin (2005), unfolding in three stages, which will not occur in full sequence, because of the numerous resumptions of steps performed during the research (Passerino, 2011). The step of integration is still being modeled and designed. As both software already have the characteristic of being accessible and usable, it is thought to adding functionality. Add the public with communication difficulties served by SCALA and Siesta with its multi-platform tool. Following to the definition of a method for evaluating the usability and accessibility of integrated product (shown in this article), the next step is validation of the tool with the autistic children, with families and professionals/teachers and after applying questionnaires.The last step was a check on the system usability in inspections and usability tests. Some questions about integration are made and this articles elect one of the questions to be answered . What protocols usability analysis can be built to meet the diversity of Universal Design including usability and accessibility? To answer this question some research on which method to be applied in evaluating the usability of these two integrated software

> "A systematic review responds to a clearly formulated question using systematic and explicit methods to identify , select and critically Avalar relevant research and collect and analyze data from the studies included in the review (Clark , 2001)".

Was choosen three methods to avaluate usability. Based in methods already used in both of the projects, was studied what methods of evaluation that contemplates the process of development of software on which the comunity help in this process. The Methods of User Centered Design (UCD), the Think Aloud Protocol and Context-Centered Design of Usage (DCC) were investigated. With this, we intend to answer a corresponding question made by the project reported here and define the method that will be associated with the context of this research, the evaluation of the platform, the start of the integration to the application. Then we checked the table with the relationship of these methods (Table 1). To present the characteristics of each one of the methods was used the Human Computer Interaction concepts: requirement analysis, design, prototype and evaluation.

Table 1. Methods of evaluating usability analyzed

The User-Centered Design (UCD)	This system is design based on users necessities and uses his help in all the steps of development. *Requirements analysis*: Determine the target audience, platforms, targets the subject, technical requirements, the need of the subject and usability requirements. *Design:* Use cases, task analysis, navigation and search systems *Prototype:*Drawings,documents, storyboards, mock-ups, scenarios, videos. *Evaluation:* Inspection, testing and questionnaires, evaluating usability
Context-Centered Design of Usage (CCD)	It constitutes the basis of the subject in context, bringing a design that transcends the focus only on a profile of final user and shall also be concerned with the educational and family context that this subject is submerged (Passerino, 2011). *Requirements* analysis to define the profile of the user, profiling the living environment (family, school, community) which the skills of the user, how he interacts in the environment they live *Design:* observation, interviews, questionnaires (professional and family), analysis of documents, theoretical framework. *Prototype*: definition of the user's profile, communication strategies, building on the elements of the context, defining the steps to be gradually developed in the prototype interaction with the user *Avaliação:* interviews, step-by-step guide(containing a list of necessary equipment and aspects to be highlighted to previously user)
Think Aloud Protocol	This procedure is to encourage participants to verbalize during use of the product/system, all your thoughts. To make "visible" to the researcher, what is hidden within the mind of the participant. Thus, the researcher will have access in real-time, relevant information on the mental map of the users, their doubts, their difficulties, their reasoning, where they're looking at what they are feeling, etc. (Ericsson, Simon, 2010). *Requirements analysis:* Test program, mindmap *Design:* observation notes, video recording, audio recording, transcript *Prototype:* analysis by user software in a mental organization, pointing out every step and what their difficulties, doubts, improvements *Evaluation:* Reviewed from observations, notes, finally all of recorded documentation analyze what were the reviews.

3.1   Choosing the Method of Usability

The software of alternative communication SCALA such SiestaCloud which will be used by groups of people with disabilities. Scala does not need to be used only by autistic person but can be used by people who are illiterate, blind with motor disabilities. The Siesta covers a group of tools that can be used on any person in distress and with a friendly and comfortable interface being operable on multiple devices. With this, it is necessary joining methods and usability and accessibility protocols that will be important for the final product and mostly reach your goal. The studies related to the design of HCI (Human Computer Interaction) refer how to build interfaces with high quality. For this purpose, methods , models and guidelines are defined. The studies related to the assessment of HCI, in turn, seek to evaluate the quality of an interface design, both along the development process as when the software is ready (Barbosa and Prates, 2000). Within the project will be defined as the interactions between the user and the machine or as PREECE (et al . 1994) Interaction says is the process of communication between people and interactive systems. Have the interface is a part of the system in which the user will interact, use. Comprises both software and hardware.

The physical dimension includes the elements of the user interface can handle, while the perceptual dimension encompasses those that the user can understand. The conceptual dimension results from processes of interpretation and reasoning triggered by user interaction with the system, based on its physical and cognitive characteristics , their goals and their work environment (Barbosa and Prates,2000).

It is important to know the project is developing the software supports users in their tasks and work environment. As functionality tests are needed to verify the robustness of the implementation, evaluation of interface is needed to assess the quality of use of software. The earlier the problems are found interaction or interface, the lower the cost to repair them (Barbosa and Prates, 2000). After the project is ready, we need to attest to their quality.

Therefore, tests will be done, can be the designer or user defined and must be selected in the method of evaluation. This quality or quality of use is defined as "the ability and ease of users achieve their goals with efficiency and satisfaction (Barbosa and Prates, 2000)."

Within this general concept of quality of use, the most widely used is the usability. The definitions of the authors Pierce et al..

. **Ease of Learning:** Refers to the time and effort spent on each task . Should be taken into account the level of user knowledge as well as their level of training with the tool .

. **Ease of use:** It can be related to the cognitive effort to interact with the tool and with the mistakes made during the interaction .

. **Use efficiency and productivity:** is to analyze whether the system does well what it is intended . Have the productivity factor serves to evaluate whether the user can do what they need quickly and effectively (Barbosa and Prates, 2000) .

. **User satisfaction:** subjective user evaluation system utilization , emotions , pleasure , frustration , negative feelings or positive.

. **Flexibility:** how the system is able to adapt to the basic, intermediate and advanced user , but they reach the same goal .

. **Functionality:** set of features for user to perform a task .

. **Security Usage:** Be able to recover the information system in case of a problem.

For a typical system life cycle of software development steps: analysis-design-design-prototype-test-maintenance. These systems are not used the user opinion, and even was part of the development. New perspectives and paradigms in software development where the relationship to user interaction with the system, such as human-computer interaction. Within this methodology HCI appears the User Centered Design Method - DCU (Figure 3). This model does not replace a classic development methodology, but it is included in one of its phases. It is a cyclical process, focused on the user in each interaction produces a fully functional prototype design according to his analysis that undergo reviews by users. The results are taken to start the cycle again until the need to model and intended end-user.

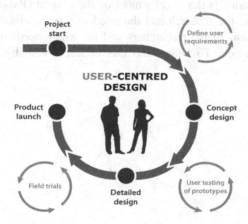

Fig. 3. Model of User-Centered Design. (Source : UCD process diagram (© Tom Wellings).

In this research study the epistemological basis of Scala and Siesta Cloud systems is socio-historical, both design development and implementation. This involves a conceptual reorganization of software development known as User Centered Design (UCD) for a Context-Centered Design of Usage (CCD) that exceeds the analysis only the user-object interaction and focuses on processes of user-object interaction process-user, wich the object is established as an instrument of mediation. (Passerino, Bez,2013; Avila, Passerino, 2011; Passerino, Bez and Avila, 2010; Bez, Passerino, 2009). The theoretical assumptions that guide the work the approach does not address only the user with disabilities, but this guy in interaction with others, which broadens the focus of research to:

(a) the social contexts in which

(b) cultural practices of communication and literacy are developed by

(c) other participants through

(d) mediating processes.

Thus, the general guidelines of CCD consider this macro context of human development in social interaction as the basis for the analysis of cases without isolating the characteristics and needs of individuals from their contexts. This difference is to avoid what usually happens in the development of Assistive Technology, which focuses on a functional view of human beings. The proposed system is not to ignore the functional aspects, but consider these within the cultural context in which an individual is inserted, preferably aiming its expansion (Passerino, Bez, Vicari, 2013). Thus, the focus is always the user in relation to their different contexts, in a mediation process that will learning to human development (Vygotsky, 1988). Each context sets our relations, so the possible mediations in a space-time dimension (Passerino, Bez, 2013). The configuration settings through the social-historic research, and is the macro research necessary for understanding the phenomenon of communication within the educational space level. On a micro level, the triads user-agent, non speaker-user and mediating processes are the starting point for understanding the processes of mediation technologies . Put another way, what people do in different contexts, with different goals and scenarios is the development of the system (Passerino, Bez, Vicari, 2013). Therefore, from the research and the need to use a method that is consistent with the theoretical basis of the researchers and the user's needs and its context, the CCD method was chosen. To understand this concepts visually, a figure is show (Figure 4).

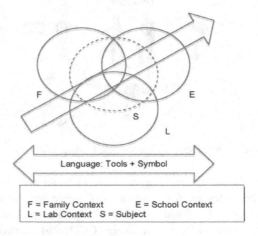

Fig. 4. Scheme of Context-Centered Design (CCD). (Passerino, Bez, 2014).

It is believed that learning and development of the user not only occurs for using one tool, but rather by the joint operating behind, supporting the person, like family, profiissionais, teachers. All of these contexts will be analyzed to form the design of the integration project. Throughout the construction process of integration between the SCALA plus SiestaCloud system occurs in parallel to a case study to develop strategies for communicating with a child with autism does not oral language. During this part of the research, collection instruments will be used as participant observation, interviews with people close to the child and document analysis which served to define not only communication strategies to be used, but as the Scala plus SiestaCloud should be built to contemplate the peculiarities of this user profile. Thus, in every interaction with the child, there will be new data that will be analyzed and put into discussion with the research group in charge of building the system. As well as strategies developed for communication with the child they help with the design and evaluation of SCALA plus Siesta, this served as a support for the inclusion in educational activities and homecare tool in a dialectical process where the interactions affecting the tool and this , in turn , directly affected the communication strategies (Avila, Passerino, 2011).

At the end of this part of the study, as seen in the closing of the research will be conducted the second part of the evaluation of Scala plus Siesta, which is geared specifically for educators who would work with the tool. During this stage, the usability evaluation of the prototype software will be made. The evaluation process will be divided into two parts: inspection and assessment tests. The inspection will be conducted usability, featuring a set of ten heuristics listed by Nielsen (1993) will be verified if the usability of the system is consistent with what would be expected by the research subjects. Already in the case of assessment tests, educators who work with children with deficits of communication who will be invited to review the system from the same set of heuristics are selected. Each participant will have an individual session inspection system, which mediates research, will lead participants along the proposed activities. The Think Aloud (Nielsen, 1993) method, which consists of the user speak aloud all the steps that runs in the system will also be used. Thus, the researcher has access not only to the results obtained by the user but also their cognitive structures established during the interaction with the tool.

A brief survey regarding the usability of sofware separated Siesta Scala and a start was made for analysis, shown in the description of each tool at the beginning of this article. The analysis in each software (Scala and Siesta), but at the time of integration believes that the concepts of usability and accessibility will be covered in full, using the principles of usability heuristics of Nielsen.

4   Results and Ongoing Research

Through this article showed the method and usability evaluation that will be used in the integration of two software programs that include diversity. Scala, a software alternative communication that purpores to be an aid in the process of developing language and communication in autistic children or person with communication defi-cit and SiestaCloud which is a set of applications, operating system and cloud plat-form whose main aim is to give conditions for development to people in situations of dependency as for example the elderly, disabled, hospitalized persons, among others. In this section we briefly describe our preliminary results and the progress that has been taking this survey.

At the moment, the SCALA is integrated to a TV Siesta beta, being used by both groups for validation of operational functionality. Adjustments are being made to ensure the integration of SiestaCloud interface model while retaining the essential settings. The colors of SCALA were also maintained to preserve the identity of the system and also because research has been done and the green color is the color that calms autistic users (information extract from graduate paper).With the requirements and modeling which are being developed, as a result we have also our first prototype to be evaluated in the field through the year 2014 (between February and March) .

The movements of this research provide a review of the software with children with autism who have not developed their orality and literacy in schools and in particular public service in the user's residence in the city of Córodoba in Spain, in a pilot project, after the analyzes and assessments apply in charter schools and in attendance at the residence of the user of Porto Alegre in Brazil. Making comparison between them. In parallel the same way, the application software will also be made with public school teachers and working with user. with autism, both of Spain, as in Brazil. In these interactions, strategies for the development of orality and literacy of the user, through the software should emerge as final results of this research.

References

1. Passerino, L.M.: Aprendizagem: estudo dos processos de Interação Social e Mediação. Tese (Doutorado em Informática na Educação) – UFRGS – Programa de Pós- Graduação em Informática na Educação. Porto Alegre (2005)
2. Avila, B.G., Passerino, L.M.: Comunicação Aumentativa e Alternativa para o Desenvolvimento da Oralidade de Pessoas com Autismo. Porto Alegre:PPGEDU da UFRGS, 2010. 103 p. Proposta de dissertação – Programa de Pós-graduação em Educação, Universidade Federal do Rio Grande do Sul (2010)
3. Bevan, N., Macleod, M.: Usability measurement in context. Behaviour and Information Technology 1&2(13)
4. Bez, M.R., Passerino, L.M.: Applying Alternative and Augmentative Communication to an inclusive group. In: WCCE 2009 - Education and Technology for a Better World Monday, Bento Gonçalves (2009)
5. Bez, M.R.: Sistema de Comunicação Alternativa Para Processos de Inclusão em Autismo: uma proposta integrada de desenvolvimento em contextos para aplicações móveis e web. 2012. 130 p. Proposta de Tese. Programa de Pós-Graduação em Informática na Educação, UFRGS, Porto Alegre (2012)
6. Clarke, K.R., Warwick, R.M.: Change in marine communities: An approach to statistical analysis and interpretation, 2nd edn. PRIMER-E, Plymouth (2001)
7. de Castro Lozano, C., Fernández, J.B., de Abajo, B.S., Salcines, E.G.: SIeSTA Project: Products and Results. In: Cipolla Ficarra, F.V., de Castro Lozano, C., Pérez Jiménez, M., Nicol, E., Kratky, A., Cipolla-Ficarra, M. (eds.) ADNTIIC 2010. LNCS, vol. 6616, pp. 171–181. Springer, Heidelberg (2011)
8. de Castro Lozano, C., Fernández, J.B., de Abajo, B.S., Salcines, E.G.: SIeSTA Project: Products and Results. In: Cipolla Ficarra, F.V., de Castro Lozano, C., Pérez Jiménez, M., Nicol, E., Kratky, A., Cipolla-Ficarra, M. (eds.) ADNTIIC 2010. LNCS, vol. 6616, pp. 171–181. Springer, Heidelberg (2011)
9. Glennen, S., Decoste, D.C.: The handbook of augmentative and alternative communication. Edition: illustrated. Publicado por Cengage Learning (1997)
10. Salviteri, G.I., Lores, T.: Engineering Process Model, Integration with Software Engineering. In: Proceedings of HCI Intl. 2003, Crete, Greece (2003)

11. Salviteri, G.I.: Toni. Mplu+a. Uma metodologia que integra la ingenieria del software, la interacción persona-ordenador y la accesibilidad en el contexto de equipos de desarrollo multidisciplinares. Tesis de doctorado, Universidad de Lleida, julio (2004)
12. Gregorc, A.F.: The mind styles model: Theory, principles and applications. Gregore associates, Columbia (1894)
13. Hassan Montero, Y.: Introducción a la Usabilidad. En: No Solo Usabilidad, vo.1 (2002) ISSN 1886-8592 - See more at:
    http://www.nosolousabilidad.com/articulos/introduccion_usabi lidad.htm#sthash.Dj1LzMpG.dpuf
14. IFIP WCCE Proceedings - Education and Technology for a Better World Monday, Germany, vol. 1, pp. 164–174 (2009)
15. de Castro Lozano, C.: El futuro de las tecnologías digitales aplicadas al aprendizaje de personas con necesidades educativas especiales - RED. Revista de Educación a Distancia (2012)
16. Mace, R., et al.: The Universal Design File: Designing for People of All Ages and Abilities (2002)
17. Miranda, T., Galvão Filho, T.: O professor e a educação inclusiva: Formação, práticas e lugares. Salvador/BA: Editora UFB 1, 217–240 (2012)
18. Montoya, S.R.: Capacidades visibles, tecnologías invisibles: Perspectivas y estudio de casos. nuevos escenarios, nuevas oportunidades. Murcia: Consejería de Educación y Cultura (2006)
19. Nielsen, J.: Usability Engineering. Morgan Kaufman, San Francisco (1993)
20. ONU – Organização das Nações Unidas, http://www.onu.org.br/ a-onu-em-acao/a-onu-e-as-pessoas-com-deficiencia/
21. Passerino, L.M.: Comunicacao alternativa, autismo e tecnologia: estudos.de caso a partir do Scala. SBIE (2013)
22. Avila, B.G., Passerino, L.M.: Comunicação Aumentativa e Alternativa e Autismo: desenvolvendo estratégias por meio do SCALA. In: Anais VI Seminário Nacional de Pesquisa em Educação especial: práticas pedagógicas na educação especial: multiplicidade do atendimento educacional especializado, vol. 1, pp. 1–10 (2011)
23. Passerino, L.M.: Anjos Tecnológicos na Torre de Babel: reflexões sobre o uso da Comunicação Alternativa em dispositivos móveis. In: Brito, M.C., Misquiatti, A (org.). Transtornos do Espectro do Autismo e Fonoaudiologia: atualização multiprofissional em saúde e educação
24. Prates, R.O., de Souza, C.S., Barbosa, S.D.J.: A Method for Evaluating the Communicability of User Interfaces. Interactions 7(1), 31–38 (2000)
25. Preece, J., Rogers, Y., Sharp, H.: Design de Interação: Além daInteração Homem-Computador. Bookman, Porto Alegre (2002)
26. Rodríguez, J., Montoya, R., Soto, F.J. (coords.): Las tecnologías en la escuela inclusiva:
27. Smith, T.F., Waterman, M.S.: Identification of Common Molecular Subsequences. J. Mol. Biol. 147, 195–197 (1981)
28. Tecnologia Assitiva, http://www.assistiva.com.br/tassistiva.html
29. UN – United Nation,
    http://www.un.org/disabilities/default.asp?id=18
30. Von Tetzchner, S., Martinsen, H.: Introdução à Comunicação Aumentativa e Alternativa. Porto, Portugal (2000)
31. Yin, R.K.: Estudo de Caso: Planejamento e Métodos, 3rd edn. Bookman, Porto Alegre (2005)
32. Vygotsky, L.S.: A Construção do Pensamento e da Linguagem (texto integral traduzido do russo). Martins Fontes, São Paulo (2001)
33. Passerino, L.M., Bez, M.R., Vicari, R.M.: Formação de professores em comunicação alternativa para crianças com TEA: Contextos em ação. Revista da Educação Especial 26(47), 619–638 (2013)

Designing with the User in Mind a Cognitive Category Based Design Methodology

Joseph Kramer[1] and Sunil Noronha[2]

[1] IBM Research, Hawthorne, NY, USA
kramerjo@us.ibm.com
[2] Yahoo Inc., Sunnyvale, CA, USA
noronha@yahoo-inc.com

Abstract. To design products and experiences that are highly intuitive and re-sonate with their target users the designer must have an accurate understanding of those users 'mental models'. New research in cognitive science, in particular in the area of cognitive category theory, provides clues how to better elicit and apply mental models in design. The resultant outcome is guaranteed to be more natural and understandable to its users. In this paper we will briefly review the cognitive science research and describe our resultant empirically grounded concept and definition of a `mental model'. We then explain how we use the mental model and related design principles to build intuitive designs.

Keywords: Mental model, psychology, cognitive category, design method.

1   Introduction

The design of an intuitive and familiar experience requires the mental model of the target audience to be embodied in the experience design. This is the reason why, for example, the folder icon is universally used as a metaphor in software interfaces as the container for electronic files. The folder mimics the user's real world mental model where paper documents are stored in files and folders. A user is then able to transfer their real world knowledge and experience to inform their expectations of the affordances provided in the virtual world.

Unfortunately we frequently encounter design errors that violate users' mental models. Figure 1. is an actual screenshot from a search engine serving millions of users, for the query "lady gaga". The module leads off with a big news article about the musician. We observed users skip past that article and then click on the second title under Related Stories: "Lady Gaga takes on John McCain...". And then the users were stumped— nothing seemed to happen when they clicked on the link!

Actually something did happen—the big title, "Lady Gaga releases video message" got replaced by "Lady Gaga takes on John McCain". I.e., the module was designed to replace the main article at the top by whichever Related Story was clicked by the user. However, the user didn't notice that. Their eyes had moved down, past the

A. Marcus (Ed.): DUXU 2014, Part IV, LNCS 8520, pp. 152–163, 2014.

Fig. 1. A design error

main title, which they weren't expecting would change. And they were expecting that a click on a blue-link article would open the article.

Unfortunately the designer had a different mental model. They viewed the module as highlighting a news story. When the user clicked on another title, the designer wanted to highlight that story, and therefore switched the two stories.

This module was an expensive failure—it was actually built and deployed into production—and was taken down a few months later. However the amazing part is that a very simple technique could have prevented the error; this module would not even have passed beyond a whiteboard sketch if the designer had employed the techniques we present in this paper. (See the View Design section.).

Capturing or eliciting an audience's mental model is thus instrumental in most of the design tasks performed by user experience professionals. Given that issues of item naming, classification, grouping, hierarchical structuring, navigation, understandability, `findability', brand promotion, etc., are all frequent concerns, in this paper we will focus on the elicitation, capture and application of mental models to support design. We will briefly review the latest research in cognitive science, in particular in the area of cognitive category theory and describe the empirically grounded concept of a mental model as developed in that field. We then explain how we use them and related design principles in all phases of design.

2   Background and Literature Review

2.1   Mental models in HCI and Traditional Psychology

In HCI the term 'mental model' is used rather loosely. For example mental models have been defined as a set of beliefs about how a system works and humans interact with systems based on these beliefs [1]; any type of mental representation that develops during the interaction with the system and enables and facilitates interaction with the system [2]; what the user believes about the system at hand [3]; an affinity diagram of user behaviors [4].

In psychology the term "mental model" was first mentioned by Craik as being "small-scale models of reality" that people carry in their minds to anticipate events, to reason, and to underlie explanation [5]. Subsequently Johnson-Laird [6] used the term to describe the process which humans go through to solve deductive reasoning problems and Gentner & Stevens [7] proposed that mental models provide humans with information on how physical systems work.

All those definitions of `mental model' are perfectly fine for their original purposes. However our objective is the following. We want to create designs that are extremely intuitive because the design `reflects the way the user thinks'. In other words, the design `speaks the user's language' or `mirrors what is in the user's mind'. This is the crucial design principle of mimicry: if the design only communicates in terms of "whatever is in the user's mind", the user will completely understand every part of the experience very easily.

This requires us to know "what's in the user's mind", whatever that means in a formal (psychological) and literal sense. We therefore define a "mental model" as simply a formal representation or documentation of the content in a user's head.

We are thus referring to a *literal dump* of everyday-knowledge that is inside the user's head, e.g., "my home is 5 miles from my office". We are *not* referring to the user's hypotheses about how some system work works, e.g., "what's your mental model of how a search engine works?" Nor are we referring to affinity based groupings of user activities.

In other words, for us the notion of a `mental model' is an empirical one: it's whatever biology tells us about the actual contents of the human brain. This introduces a rigor into the design process that is not present with the other definitions of `mental model'. Now the design task is to look inside the user's head, in a literal sense, and mimic the contents.

So what does empirical research tell us about the contents of human minds? What are the "units of content", and what is the "structure" that relates those units?

This has been the subject of much research in psychology, and the first generation of this work was based on weak experimental methods, yielding concepts such as "attitudes", "values", etc., which is of largely theoretical origin and has low validity.

However research in "second generation cognitive science" is grounded in biological experiments in neuroscience, and has produced major breakthroughs in our understanding of the "mind" and its contents, well summarized by Lakoff and Johnson [8].

2.2   New Research into Mental Models

This research recognizes the fundamental impact of the `mind' being physically situated in the body, i.e., recognizing that the "mind" is essentially a piece of fiction, just a way of describing the functioning of the brain, a physical entity that can be subjected to laboratory experiments in neuroscience. Those experiments yield insight into the fundamental `information' structures being processed by the brain.

The primary mental structures so identified include cognitive categories, emotions, images, scripts, and so on.   This area of study is very recent, and complete models of mental mechanisms are not yet available; however, the available components are already very useful for design.

In this paper we focus only on the mental structures known as cognitive categories. Cognitive categories roughly correspond to our everyday notion of "objects", e.g., "cars" and "cats" are cognitive categories, but "beautiful" is not.   Thus cognitive categories provide the basic foundation for how the brain 'sees' the world.

There are several types of cognitive categories . Most people have no problem distinguishing cats from elephants, but have difficulty distinguishing one species of elephant from another. In other words, some types of categories, called "basic-level" categories are fundamental to human perception and most human knowledge is organized in terms of these categories.   They are the most important ones for design.

The importance of the "basic-level" stems from the following properties [9];

1. It is the level at which most of our knowledge is organized
2. It is the level first named and understood by children
3. It is the level with the most commonly used labels for category members
4. It is the level at which category members have similarly perceived overall shapes
5. It is the level at which subjects are fastest at identifying category members
6. It is the highest level at which a single mental image can reflect the entire category. (We call this the "image marker rule")
7. It is the highest level at which a person uses similar motor programs for interacting with category members. (We call this the "action marker rule").

The first two points have a huge implication for design: they imply that the primary units of design for the general population should be basic-level cognitive categories. I.e., all objects that are surfaced in the design should correspond to this level if we wish to maximize intuitiveness and ease of use.

This point is reinforced by the other properties, each of which further increases the value of basic-level cognitive categories as the fundamental units of design.   E.g., point 4 implies that all objects that correspond to a given basic-level category can be illustrated by a single picture; this has huge benefits when illustrating a product catalog for example.   Point 5 implies that user effort is minimized at this level.   Points 6 and 7 give us a pair of powerful design tools that we discuss later in this paper.

Another valuable aspect of cognitive categories pertains to the relationship-structure between categories. For reasons of space, we refer the reader to [8] for the theory and touch upon the design implications briefly in the section on View Design

Returning to our goal in this section of formalizing the notion of a "mental model", we now define it as follows:

A 'mental model' is a representation of the cognitive categories in a user's head, along with relationships between those cognitive categories.   One way to represent a mental model on paper is to draw a graph comprising a node for each cognitive category, and an edge for each relationship linking cognitive categories.

Anyone familiar with software engineering will immediately think of the UML Class Diagram, which is indeed a perfectly suitable tool for capturing a mental model—as long as other baggage from object-oriented programming is left out.   It is important to recognize that this is meant to be a psychological diagram: it pictures the literal contents of the user's head, not a software system.   Therefore the only objects permissible in a mental model diagram are those elicited from the user.

3   A Cognitive Category Based Design Methodology

Over many projects we have honed a systematic approach to product design that not only reduces a complex challenge to relatively easier steps, but almost guarantees that the resulting product will be useful, highly intuitive, and easy to use. The methodology makes heavy use of scientific principles, especially cognitive category theory. Parts of this methodology have been documented elsewhere but we briefly recap it here, because a firm grasp of the big picture makes it easier to dive into the technical details of each step and relate the steps to each other.

From afar these steps may sound familiar — use cases, mental models, etc.— however there is an unusual engineering-like rigor and connectivity between the steps, arising out of the grounding in cognitive category theory, which seems to be new to most designers. We have rarely encountered anyone actually practicing the specifics described here unless they have been trained in this methodology.

Therein also lies the value of this methodology.   Over numerous projects at Yahoo, IBM and elsewhere, we've observed that the majority of design errors that we've encountered were due to the designer or product owner omitting one of these steps, or doing it partially.   When a designer has not trained themselves to instantly recognize the nature of an object, its relationships to other objects, and the corresponding design implications, they often miss errors that are instantly obvious to someone trained in these methods.   In fact when we explain how to observe this structure and to exploit it, the techniques seem so simple and the errors so obvious that it sometimes triggers a sheepish reaction.   We've observed that the learning curve for these techniques is very short, and most designers and product managers `get it' very quickly.   This is especially true of people who have had some engineering training, and they usually express a lot of delight in the power of the techniques.

The following section will provide an overview of the four major design phases, and the subsequent sections will do a deep dive into each phase.   Although this paper is meant to be primarily an aid to designers wanting to apply such techniques, we will also dive into the psychology underpinning these techniques for the benefit of researchers who want to understand why these techniques work as well as they do.

3.1   The Four Primary Phases of Design

Figure 2 is a birds-eye view of the four primary design steps. The primary function of these steps is to guarantee that a product will be `successful' in that sense that people will want to use it, it genuinely meets a need, and is highly intuitive and easy to use.

Those four steps are of course an over-simplification; there is a lot more to great product design than making a product useful, usable and intuitive. For example: how to build the product in a way that that people actually enjoy it and explicitly respond to it emotionally, and the product is perceived to be something truly different from its competitors.   However the four primary steps mentioned above here are the foundation of any design project and in our experience we've seen designers get a tremendous amount of value from focusing on these steps alone.

The first step is about unearthing user needs and documenting them.   It sounds straightforward, yet it's surprising how often product owners fail right at this step. When we have examined a product that failed and was shut down a few months after it launched, we have often found that the product had never documented a credible use case to begin with.

By "credible", we mean that the user needs must be (a) elicited from a typical user describing an actual situation or problem in their life and (b) documented entirely in the user's language.   We have often encountered product requirements documents violating those two rules, typically written by a product owner who felt that the `use cases' they wrote were perfectly plausible to themselves.   However we've learnt by watching failed and successful projects that the above criteria are hard rules. When they are violated there is a high risk of the product being designed for a `problem' that doesn't exist, leading to subsequent failure in the marketplace.

In theory one can argue that user language is not necessary for describing scenarios, since users may not be aware of their own need, or because a truly new product may create a need that previously didn't seem to exist.   However in practice we have observed that the absence of user language in use cases is a marker that no one has actually verified that the product addresses a real need, and predicts product failure. Therefore we have learnt to treat it as a red flag indicating high project risk.

In addition to ensuring that we are addressing genuine user needs, the principle of documenting literal user language has another benefit: it provides the primary data input for our second step, "mental models".

The second step is to document which objects `manifest themselves' in the user experience, and how these objects relate to each other. Again the crucial rule is that these objects must exist in the target users' heads—i.e., we cannot concoct new objects as an object-oriented computer programmer might do. For example, a "cluster of news articles" is not a valid object, even though they might be the typical output of clustering algorithms. The typical reader of news articles doesn't think in terms of "clusters", but thinks in terms of "topics". The latter might seem superficially like a `cluster', but is actually far more restricted—a user can readily select from list of common `topics' which ones interest them, but would struggle to deal with `clusters'

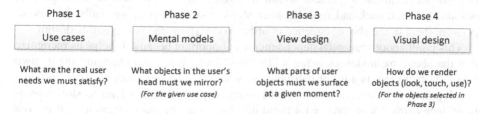

Fig. 2. The four phases of design

In order to determine which objects to surface within the user experience, we systematically walk through all the use cases from Step 1.   All the important nouns in the user-stories are extracted as `user objects'.   No other objects are introduced. That is why it was so important to elicit real use cases and document them in literal user language.   The literal-language rule protects us from injecting unintuitive content and structure into the design.

The third step, view design, corresponds to what is frequently called `wireframing' but again with a discipline that does not permit arbitrary wireframes.   In this step, each object from the user's head, which was elicited in Step 2, is now represented by a sketchy outline that specifies what attributes of the object are visible at a given point in the user experience.   This step is not about how the object looks; colors, sizes and other visual elements are not specified.   Only wireframe structure and visibility is decided.   The wireframe structure is set up to mimic that of the user object model. The choice of which attributes to show is determined by walking through the use cases to find out which details of each object must be present in order to successfully complete the use case.   This is done for all the use cases, and the attributes that are most frequently needed are selected for preferential treatment.

Clearly, this is in contrast to how typical wireframing is done.   Most designers jump straight from user stories to sketching out wireframes; this is often viewed as a free-form construction or *creative* process where anything be sketched out.   Instead in what we have described above is the wireframes are *derived* from the user-object model in a systematic way.   The user's mental model thus strongly constrains exploration of the design space to the `set of good designs', tacitly eliminating designs that would be unintuitive because they would not match the user's mental model.

The final step, visual design, determines exactly how each object looks, down to a pixel.   The primary function supported in this step is recognizability: with a quick glance a user must be able to recognize which object they're dealing with.   In other words, visuals that are more `typical' of the object are better than atypical renderings. This step also achieves several other secondary objectives, such as aesthetics, conformance to standards, brand recognition, etc.

Considering all four steps together, it should be obvious that there are sequential dependencies between the steps.   We cannot determine the right objects to surface unless we have first documented the use cases correctly.   We cannot determine the correct structure of the wireframes unless we have elicited the intrinsic properties of the objects they represent.   We cannot determine what kind of visuals to present unless we know what objects are represented by the visuals, and how much information we are required to present within a given space.   Therefore, although it is possible to jump back and forth between steps to some degree, we really do need to perform them in the above sequence in order to determine the best possible design.

This point about sequential dependencies is important because it helps us recognize that the above methodology is not a "Process" that we're recommending for its own sake.   In fact there is a lot of resistance to waterfall-like processes in `agile' product development paradigms, because unnecessary sequentiality can lead to slow execution; there is often a preference for rapid iteration as the primary means to figuring out the best design.   Rather, what we're pointing out is that there are intrinsic technical dependencies between the steps, much as one cannot install the roof before building the rest of the house. So the 4-step design methodology is not about executing a `process'; rather it is about respecting the intrinsic `logic of design'. The sooner we figure out that logic, the more time we spend exploring the best designs.

3.2   The Role of Cognitive Categories

The above outline briefly touched upon cognitive categories aka "user-objects" in each of the four steps. We now take a closer look at how this grounding in psychology increases the quality and robustness of designs.

Use Cases. Revisiting Step 1, eliciting user needs, it follows that use cases must be captured in their everyday language, else we risk departing from the basic-level to more abstract, unusable cognitive categories.   Sometimes however well intentioned designers introduce their own idealized or proposed means by which users could complete their tasks. The language introduced rapidly becomes part of the design team vernacular and ends up in the finished product, all whilst representing alien concepts that do not exist in the user's mental model.

User-objects, aka `Mental Models'. Step 2, documenting the user's mental model involves compiling a list of basic-level cognitive categories, when designing for the general population.   Other cognitive categories may be used when the product will only be used by a niche customer segment. E.g., collectors of antique furniture may have a knowledge of many different types of chairs at an almost `basic level', with a distinctive image springing to their mind when you say "Queen Anne chair".

In this step, the most common error we have seen is introducing objects into the design that do not correspond to a user's basic level. The usual cause is that the product manager, marketer and designer understand the product domain differently from the user, because the former are intimately familiar with the `sausage-making' involved in creating the product and have developed their own technical vocabulary.

When a designer then jumps straight from use cases to wireframing and skip formal documentation of the assumed mental model, they inject non-user objects that subsequently weaken the design.

In addition to documenting a list of the cognitive categories that manifest themselves in naturalistic conversations with target users, Step 2 is about documenting the attributes of these cognitive categories and the actions that users do with them.   It is common for an object to have numerous attributes, some concrete and some abstract, and not all attributes are equal from a user's perspective.   For example, a TV has a size and a black-screen level, and the size is critical since it affects not only how great the image feels but also whether the TV fits with rest of the user's furniture.

The most important attributes of a cognitive category are the ones that define it, because they give an object its identity and help users instantly recognize it when they encounter it.   Central to this are the image and action marker rules.

The Image Marker rule asks the question: When I say the word <chair>, does an image instantly spring to mind?   If the answer is yes, the object is probably a basic-level category, and the image is a definitional image which we should strive to use to represent the object.

The Action Marker rule asks the question: When I say the word <chair>, does an action instantly spring to mind? Do you instantly know what to do with the object? If so, the object is probably a basic-level category, and the actions define the object, helping give it its identity.

When both these rules produce a "Yes" answer, we know we have in our hands the right unit of design. We also have the right image to use in the design, and the minimal set of key actions that we need to support everywhere on the given object.

Sometimes only one of these rules turns out to have a "Yes" answer, in which case we are not quite at the basic-level, but might still have in our hands a usable object.

Because these two rules are so trivially easy to apply, they are among the most powerful everyday design tools we have encountered. More often than not, when designing for a general population we can apply these rules from our armchairs, and therefore within minutes cut through the clutter of confusing hypothetical objects and abstract concepts. The subsequent clarity of design is striking.

View Design. Since this step essentially derives wireframes from the previous step's documentation of the user's mental model, cognitive categories end up playing a key role in determining what content gets displayed during the user experience. No object, attribute, or action appears that has not been present previously in the mental model.

Furthermore, this step adds a focus on making sure that the right content is available at the right time during each moment of the user experience. Most cognitive categories have numerous attributes, and showing too many of them can overwhelm the user and needlessly clutter the experience. Too few and the user cannot actually complete the task they set out to do. The attributes and actions are prioritized based on their `definitional' nature (i.e., they are core to identifying the object) and their utility for the given use cases. The image and action marker rules mentioned above are useful guides. Frequency of use—what is the estimated probability that users will need the attribute?—is the other primary guide to optimizing this selection process.

Often different contexts (points in the user experience) will require the same object but with different attributes. E.g., when presenting the initial page of a product catalog, it may suffice to just mention the category name "TVs", i.e., a 'minimal view' with no further details. However deeper in the product catalog, many more details of the TVs will be needed. This implies developing multiple "views" of each cognitive category, selecting different sets of attributes and actions for each. This is an optimization problem using the same guidelines mentioned above: we strive to always present definitional attributes, and we rank other attributes by utility. Additionally, when there are multiple views we need to always provide an affordance for going from one view to another, e.g., to expand or collapse details. This preserves the "identity" of the cognitive category, and makes the user feel they are dealing with something they understand well.

As mentioned earlier, one important attribute of any cognitive category is its "Part-of" relationship to other cognitive categories. Recall the Lady Gaga example in the

Introduction, which baffled users with a strange mental model.   As we remarked there, a very simple test would have detected the errors and prevented them.   That example violates the structure connecting cognitive categories.

To see this, perform the following exercise: scrunch up your eyes until the picture looks like a bunch of blobs, and call out what objects you see. The first object that stands out is a Story, about Lady Gaga and the video message.   The next one is the 'List of   Stories', about Lady Gaga and John McCain, etc.

Then ask the question: what is the relationship between these two objects?   A Story is *Part-Of* a List of Stories.   Does the picture communicate that?   No, the List of Stories is inside the box depicting the main Story; the *Part-Of* relationship has been inverted. The list should have been outside, and the highlighted story inside the list.

As one structurally correct solution, the designer could have implemented these relationships by using an accordion widget for the list, showing one article expanded. Clicking on another article would expand it in-place, preserving the *Part-Of* relationships.

Clearly it is easy to detect these errors just by inspection once we develop sensitivity to the types of objects and their relationships to each other.   And it's almost as easy to come up with alternative correct designs by mimicking the correct structure.

This point about just following the underlying structure of the cognitive categories has huge implications.   E.g., it implies that efforts to "design the "navigation" of a site are misplaced.   Rather, navigation should be viewed a byproduct of cognitive category based design.   The actual design task is to ensure that all the attributes of an object can be accessed (at least indirectly) no matter where it appears.   The user will then automatically follow the relationships between objects (the links) and `good navigation' will be a side effect.

The Visual Design Phase. By the time we reach this step we have established the items that the user needs to interact with, and we have captured the particular meaning and actions that the users associate with those items. Now we need to visually render a design that reinforces that meaning and makes the content instantly recognizable.

A visual designer we worked with once described his job aptly that of a costume designer ensuring that an actor on stage is recognizable no matter which scene they are appearing in and no matter how significant a role they are playing.   The actor may change their garb and change their behavior in many ways; yet not so much that the audience struggles to recognize them in different scenes.   Likewise a designer needs to ensure that the design instantly brings out the identity of the objects present in the experience, whether they appear in a full or more compressed view.   While this advice seems intuitive and obvious, the numerous commonly found violations to this principle attest to the difficulty in adherence.

Consider for example the following illustration of three types of computers from a product catalog (Fig 3a).   Note that the visuals for desktops and workstations are rather similar; in fact in testing we observed that customers had difficulty determining which of the two they wanted. This is not an accident; the violation of the image marker rule predicts that users would have a hard time distinguishing the two products. In contrast, note that servers have a very different visual; the monitor is missing, and the image is cropped. The cropping neatly communicates scale; servers are apparently bigger than desktops and workstations. Users were much more easily able to tell whether they wanted a server or a desktop.

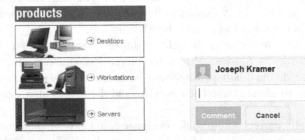

Fig. 3. A. Selecting a product category   B.   Adding a comment in Google Docs

An example from Google Docs (Fig 3b.) illustrates another point about deriving the visual design from the intrinsic nature of the object.   We have often heard users complaining that they entered comments into a Google Doc, but now can't find the comments.   Upon investigation it turns out that they never hit the "Comment" button on this widget after entering the text.   They assumed that since the yellow box was present on the page and didn't vanish when they clicked out of it, that it was saved. In truth the widget does not save comments unless the "Comment" button is clicked.

The root of the problem is that "comment" is both a noun and a verb.   The former is a cognitive category, and the widget correctly provides an object-like feel of a yellow sticky note on the page.   The verb "to comment" is an action.   It's an action performed by the user—it's not an action performed on the Comment object.   The actual action performed on the Comment object is "to save".   The button should therefore have been labeled "Save".   By labeling it "Comment", the design tacitly blinded the user to the fact that it was an action since the *object* comment was already in their head.   It didn't help that the button visuals were also changed; if both buttons were gray, there might have been a consistent cue that all actions are gray buttons, instead of one of them appearing to be a different type of entity. The inconsistent switching of visual cues about what constitutes an action versus what constitutes an object, compounded by the dual role of the word "comment" laid a trap for the unwary user.

This highlights the importance of understanding the nature of content in terms of the logic of cognitive categories, and systematizing visual design rules according to the nature of those objects and actions.

We discovered a powerful little trick to help us determine the best visual to use for any given object: just run an image search.   I.e., go to a major search engine such as Yahoo, enter the name of the object and click on the Images filter.   We are presented with numerous pictures matching the search query.   Frequently most the images are quite similar to each other, or fall into a few groups of similar images. Whatever is common about these images defines the object.

For example, a designer recently posed to us the challenge of how to visually represent a "favorite location". They were designing a map-based application and planned to use the standard upside-down teardrop as the symbol for a location. However they did not know how to mark some of those teardrops as 'favorites'.

We ran an image search for "favorite" and promptly discovered that two symbols are frequently used: the star and the red heart sign. That instantly gave us the clues we needed: one solution would be to insert a star inside the teardrop. The other solution would be to add a notch into the top the teardrop making it begin to resemble an elongated heart—and color it red.

Either way, we are exploiting the fact that cognitive categories have distinctive visuals in our brains, and search engines often pick up on those relationships by virtue of crunching tons of user-generated data from the real world.

4   Conclusions

Current research in neuroscience continues to yield fascinating insights into the nature of the human mind. In this paper we have illustrated how some of those insights, from cognitive category theory, can be transformed into powerful tools for designers.

When utilized within the framework of a systematic end-to-end design methodology as we described, it becomes very easy to build user experiences that are certain to be highly intuitive and useful. We now use these methods routinely in our design work and are frequently delighted by how much value we get in just minutes from comparing the structure of our design to the structure of the user's mental model.

References

1. Norman, D.A.: The design of everyday things, 1st Basic paperback. Basic Books, New York (2002)
2. van der Veer, G.C., del Carmen Puerta Melguizo, M.: The Human-computer Interaction Handbook. In: Jacko, J.A., Sears, A. (eds.), pp. 52–80. L. Erlbaum Associates Inc., Hillsdale (2003)
3. Mental Models and User Experience Design,
   http://www.nngroup.com/articles/mental-models/
   (accessed: February 20, 2014)
4. Young, I.: Mental models: Aligning design strategy with human behavior. Rosenfeld Media, Brooklyn (2008)
5. Craik, K.J.W.: The nature of explanation. Cambridge University Press, Cambridge (1967)
6. Johnson-Laird, P.N.: Mental Models. Harvard University Press (1983)
7. Gentner, D., Stevens, A.L.: Mental Models. Psychology Press (1983)
8. Lakoff, G., Johnson, M.: Philosophy in the flesh: The embodied mind and its challenge to Western thought. Basic Books, New York (1999)
9. Eco, U., Santambrogio, M., Violi, P.: Meaning and Mental Representations. Indiana University Press (1988)

The Impact of Human Likeness on the Older Adults' Perceptions and Preferences of Humanoid Robot Appearance[*]

Kerem Rızvanoğlu, Özgürol Öztürk, and Öner Adıyaman

Galatasaray University, Faculty of Communication,
Ciragan Cad. No: 36 Ortakoy 34357 Istanbul, Turkey
{ozozturk,krizvanoglu}@gsu.edu.tr, oner.adiyaman@gmail.com

Abstract. There's a growing interest towards human–robot interaction (HRI) as an area of research within human-computer interaction (HCI). Although nowadays robotics studies provide enough knowledge on social robots in major settings, there are still a limited number of studies that investigate expectations, attitudes and behaviors towards humanoid robots in the area of HRI. This study aims to investigate the older adults' perceptions and preferences of a humanoid robot appearance, which is planned to assist in healthcare activities. The preferences and the perceptions of a sample of 6 older adults are assessed through semi-structured in-depth interviews. By adopting a user-centered design process through the execution of techniques such as persona and user journeys, two different appearances are designed for the assessment: A cartoon-like, simplistic face with no specific gender and a more realistic feminine illustrative face. Findings support the notion that perceptions evoked in the users would depend on the human likeness of the robot's face. However, gender stereotypes also had impact on the perception and preference of the humanoid faces. A majority of older adults preferred a female human appearance for the robot by referring both to the human likeness and to the task of healthcare. The participants were able to understand the basic facial gestures in both appearances. However, they could not achieve to interpret the intensity of emotions in the expressions. In this context, when compared, simple cartoon-like faces seemed more affective to support detailed understanding of the expressions. Besides, the findings revealed that experience with technology and culture-specific aspects could also affect the perception of robot technology.

Keywords: Humanoid, Robot, Appearance, Perception, Older Adults.

1   Introduction

Nowadays the usage of robots widely spread from industry to domestic environments for end-users in their daily life. Autonomous robots may assist in a range of assistive

---

[*] This study was realized under the coordination of Assoc. Prof. Kerem Rızvanoğlu with the support of Galatasaray University Scientific Research Fund (Project ID: 12.300.001).

A. Marcus (Ed.): DUXU 2014, Part IV, LNCS 8520, pp. 164–172, 2014.

tasks for kids, elder and disabled users. In this context, it is obvious that in the coming future they will need to carry out social and intellectual tasks, as well as the physical ones. Humanoid robots, which adopt the strategy of anthropomorphism through the use of human faces, are the potential autonomous and domestic robots of the coming future. One of the recent search topics in relevant literature is whether perceptions evoked in different user groups would depend on the humanness of the robot's face [1].

The purpose of this study, which is part of a larger holistic study on social robot design, is to explore older adults' perceptions and preferences of robot faces that varied in terms of human likeness. In this context, by the adoption of a user-centered design process and relevant techniques such as persona and user journeys, two different appearances for a social humanoid robot, which is planned to assist in caregiving and nursing activities, are designed. The preferences and the perceptions of a sample of 6 older adults are investigated through semi-structured interviews. The remainder of this paper includes the theoretical background, methodology and results.

2   Theoretical Background

According to Goetz et al. appearance has a major influence on the assumptions people have about applications and functionalities of robots [2]. Relevant literature states that the appearance has to support the correct estimation of the robot's real competencies by the user [3].

Fong et al. (in [2]) proposed four types of social robots due to their appearance: Anthropomorphic, zoomorphic, caricatured, and functional robots. Studies emphasized that human-likeness has an impact on understanding nonverbal communication. Therefore an anthropomorphic appearance in robot design is highly valued since it may provide a better interaction with users [4]. Zoomorphic robots resemble animals to create the impression that a user may expect the robot to behave like an animal. Robots with a caricatured appearance are mainly based on specific facial features like mouth or eyes. The appearances in this category are used to prevent any expectations based on familiarity, which is caused by the realistic look. Functional robots focus on displaying the core functions of the robotic system [2].

In order to delve into anthropomorphism, it should be noted that anthropomorphism entails attributing human-like properties, characteristics, or mental states to real or imagined non-human agents and objects (Epley et al. in [2]). Blow et al. claimed that human form and functionality in robots would enhance and ease the quality of HRI [5]. Humanoid is an umbrella term for anthropomorphic robots whose structural compositions are based on the human form [1]. However, it will possess some human-like features, which are usually stylized, simplified or cartoon-like versions of the human equivalents, including some or all of the following: A head, facial features, eyes, ears, eyebrows, arms, hands, legs [6].

In this context, especially the human face plays an important role in social interactions by serving as a marker of identity and as a canvas for the display of non-verbal social cues [1]. Especially the design of a robot's face is an important issue within the field of HRI, because studies in recent literature prove the fact that most non-verbal cues were mediated through the face [5]. Lohse et al. stated that a robot is perceived as being anonymous without a face [24]. In this context the physiognomy of a robot changes the perception of its human-likeness, knowledge, and sociability. Therefore, people avoid robots behaving or looking negatively and prefer to interact with positive robots (Gockley et al. in [2]). In addition to that, Bruce et al. state that an expressive face indicating attention and imitating the face of a user makes a robot more compelling to interact with [2].

Briefly, the phenomenon of human-likeness is one of the most popular aspects concerning the theory of anthropomorphism in the field of robotics. This theory claims that the more a robot resembles a human being in appearance the more people expect it to have human-like qualities [2]. In this sense, the impact of human-likeness on robotic interface design is a challenging subject of research in the area of HRI [7].

Although there is ample literature on the design of robotic systems, investigation of the gender differences with respect to the visual aspects of the robotic interface design is limited. Even though gender stereotypes exists in society at large, current research has found few differences in how men and women perceive agents and how people perceive male and female agents [8]. For example, Koda and Maes [9] found no difference in perceptions of intelligence, likeability, and engagingness between visual forms of male and female agents.

Besides, the number of studies with older adults that focuses on the perception of robot appearance is also limited. Most research on robotic appearance has involved younger participants [6]. However, especially in the area of healthcare, this segment is the potential target group to benefit from the use of social humanoid robots.

3   Methodology

The purpose of this study, which is part of a larger holistic study on social robot design, is to investigate older adults' perceptions and preferences of robot faces that varied in terms of human likeness. Below is the research question of the study:

Due to which factors does human likeness affect the older adults' perception and preferences of humanoid robot appearance?

The study aimed to evaluate the human appearance of a humanoid robot, which will be designed to serve for the healthcare needs of older adults. Humanoid faces were designed to be presented on portable tablets, which would be located at the head of the domestic robot – namely *Medibot* - developed in *Galatasaray University*, as part of an ongoing research project (Fig. 1). In this context, two different humanoid faces were designed through a user centered design process. As part of the design process, two personas accompanied by user journeys referring to different healthcare scenarios were created. By referring to the categorization in the relevant literature it was aimed to design illustrative "anthropomorphic" and "caricature" faces, which provided different levels of human likeness [2]. The design process resulted in two different humanoid faces: A simplistic, cartoon-like renditions of human facial shape with no specific gender and a more realistic and sophisticated feminine appearance.

Fig. 1. Autonomous healthcare robot designed in Galatasaray University

Through diverse methodological approaches, researchers from different disciplines attempted to identify the so-called "basic emotions" and associate them with different physical forms of expression. By using psychological experiments, Scherer (in [10]) identified these so-called "basic emotions" and claimed that they could be observed on an intercultural level and supposedly have universal validity. These included: Angry, sad, happy, frightened, ashamed, proud, despairing. These feelings were related to a corresponding emotional state, which in turn had effects on interpersonal relations, attitudes and affective dispositions. There were also efforts to assign these emotions to particular postures and physical forms of expression. In another study, Becker focused on the emotions of astonishment, anger, sadness and happiness [10]. By referring to Becker, for this study three basic emotions, which presented a variation in terms of expression, were chosen for human appearances and the faces were visualized accordingly: Happiness, anger and astonishment.

This qualitative study was based on a semi-structured in-depth interview realized with 6 participants. The sample included 6 older adults with an age range of 40-70 (3 male, 3 female), which represented the target audience and the designed personas as well.

The study procedure was as follows: At the beginning of the study the participants were informed about the goal of the study by the presentation of a large set of face designs. The participants were told that they would be presented with different versions of two different face design models in three successive phases. Each phase included the comparative presentation of the expressions of a basic emotion for two models. Each presentation included both models expressing the same emotion in three different levels of intensity (Fig. 2, Fig. 3, Fig. 4). After each presentation, the participants were asked if they could understand the expressed emotion in the presented face models. In this context, the participants were also asked to define the level of intensity for each expression within a scale that ranges from 1 to 5. In the next stage of the interview, the participants were asked which face model was more appropriate in expressing the basic emotions. In order to investigate the relation between the human appearance and the task, participants were also asked to make an evaluation by referring to the intended task, namely healthcare. In this context, the participants were asked to choose the most appropriate face model due to the intended healthcare task. The interview was completed with the additional comments of each participant.

Fig. 2. Expressions for the "Happy Face" (The level of intensity increases from top to bottom)

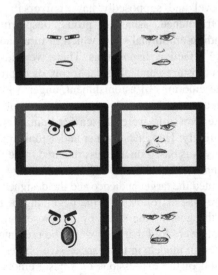

Fig. 3. Expressions for the "Angry Face" (The level of intensity increases from top to bottom)

Fig. 4. Expressions for the "Astonished Face" (The level of intensity increases from top to bottom)

4   Results and Discussion

The analysis framework of the study was derived from literature review presented above. It included three different axes: "Perception and Preference of Basic Emotions", "Experience with Technology" and "Trust issues as a Cultural Aspect".

4.1   Perception and Preference of Basic Emotions

The study provided findings on the perception and preference of basic emotions (happiness, anger, astonishment) derived from relevant literature presented above. It should be noted that the findings were analyzed qualitatively and rather than descriptive analysis, insights based on preliminary findings are presented to contribute to further research.

As it was mentioned in the methodology section above, before the interview, three different versions of two different face design models were presented to the participants in three successive phases.

Most of the participants (n=4) stated that the female model was more appropriate in expressing the basic emotions. Only two of the participants preferred cartoon-like models. This finding led us to believe the fact that the rendering of a robotic appearance might contribute to the acceptance of the robotic system by providing familiarity through human likeness.

The participants were able to understand the basic facial gestures, however, it was observed that they could not achieve to interpret the intensity of emotions in the expressions. When they were asked to define the level of intensity for each expression within a scale, surprisingly simplistic cartoon-like faces seemed more advantageous to support detailed understanding of the expressions. This issue might be related with the technical flaws in drawing some of the detailed expressions of the female model, which might cause confusion. On the other hand, this finding supported the notion that in order to enable the participants to understand diverse emotional expressions, the faces should be drawn in a simplistic style with optimal details that would not cause any confusion.

Finally when the participants were asked to make an evaluation by referring to the healthcare task, all the participants associated the female model with the relevant task. Gender stereotypes in Turkish society were affective in shaping people's expectation of the appearance of the robot. Participants clearly made a link between the nursing task and women, since supporting tasks like nursing are mostly professions associated with women in Turkey.

4.2   Experience with Technology

In the interviews, the participants' experience with computers and Internet were also investigated. The findings showed that 4 participants were regular users of computer technology and the Internet. However, 2 other participants had no prior experience with computer technology and the Internet. The answers revealed that the familiarity and experience with technology might positively influence the participants' approach towards robots. The more familiar and experienced they are with the computer technology, the faster they seem to adopt new innovative tech like social robots.

4.3   Trust Issues as a Cultural Aspect

Findings showed that certain cultural aspects could also have a role in the acceptance of social robotics.

Trust towards machines is one of the most important factors that affect the perception and acceptance of social robot and is frequently investigated in relevant literature. However, this study showed that besides trusting the robot itself, the trust issues about the offline medical community could also play an important role in the acceptance of robot technology in the hospital. This issue was considered as a cultural aspect specifically relating to the Turkish society.

Although patients are accustomed to the high technological environment in hospitals and may seem ready to accepting high-tech robots as well, it was observed that the problem mostly rooted in the prejudices towards the offline world. It was observed that negative trust issues addressing the offline medical community could be barriers in the adoption of the healthcare robots.

The findings revealed that there was a common dissatisfaction among the participants towards medical professionals in the offline world. The expressions of the participants confirmed this finding: *"The medical results should always be presented to a professor or another doctor for second opinion"*; *"You cannot trust the blood pressure results measured by a nurse"*, etc. This attitude became evident through the expressions of two participants who lived in Germany for long years. Having the chance to compare the Turkish and German medical ecosystem, they had difficulties in trusting to Turkish medical authorities. For example, one of those participants had a hearing problem. He clearly stated that he did not have any confidence in the hospital environment in Turkey and would rather prefer to be treated in Germany.

It is obvious that a healthcare robot will face these prejudices about trust towards medical professionals. It may be claimed that for users who have difficulties in trusting real doctors, it may also be difficult to trust a healthcare robot as well. It should be noted that this finding should be investigated in detail with further studies.

5   Conclusion

The purpose of this study, which was part of a larger holistic study on social robot design, was to investigate older adults' perceptions and preferences of robot faces that varied in terms of human likeness. Two different appearances for a healthcare robot were designed for the assessment through semi-structured in-depth interviews realized with 6 older adults. These appearances were as follows: A simplistic, cartoon-like renditions of human facial shape with no specific gender and a more realistic and sophisticated feminine appearance. Findings supported the notion that understanding user perceptions and preferences could enable the design of social robots suited for the extreme target user groups like older adults.

Findings showed that perceptions evoked in the users would depend on the human likeness of the robot's face. Making a robot look more like a real human, rather than a cartoon, was found to support understanding. Most of the participants stated that female appearance was more appropriate in expressing the basic emotions. This finding led us to believe the fact that the rendering of a robotic appearance might contribute to the acceptance of it by providing familiarity through human-likeness. This finding might also be associated with the age of the sample. Recent studies showed that [6] compared to younger adult sample, older adults had less familiarity and experience with robotic technologies. Our study also stated that the experience with technology affected the perception and thus acceptance of robot technology.

Besides, we believe that this finding might provide further information on how older adults perceive this technology. Recent studies showed that older adults' perceptions about a robot's appearance were more likely to be shaped by their expectations than by past experiences with such technology [6]. In this context, older adults' higher preference for a human appearance in our study could also be an outcome of such inexperience, as the most common reason given for the preference a human appearance was "familiarity" with such an appearance. Besides, by referring to the finding that simplistic cartoon-like faces seemed more affective to support detailed understanding of the expressions, it can be proposed that the human appearances should be drawn in a simplistic style with optimal details to enable the participants to understand diverse emotional expressions.

The gender stereotypes people have for individual tasks and social roles clearly influenced their preference for the robotic appearance. Given the fact that the robot would be used for healthcare, the participants linked this task to nursing and eventually to the feminine model. Participants clearly associated the supportive task the robot could perform with the gender stereotype of women playing more supporting roles.

Findings also showed that certain cultural aspects could also have a role in the acceptance of social robotics. It was found that the prejudices caused by the negative trust issues towards the offline Turkish medical community could be barriers in the adoption of the healthcare robots. In this sense, in order to design robotic interfaces, culture-specific aspects should be taken into account. This finding emphasized the importance of cross-cultural user studies in robotic interface design.

The study is only a first step of a larger study, which aims to explore the perception of humanoid robots' appearance. In the light of these preliminary findings, further research should include empirical studies with different robots appearances and larger / diverse user groups.

References

1. Prakash, A., Rogers, W.A.: Younger and Older Adults' Attitudes Toward Robot Faces: Effects of Task and Humanoid Appearance. Proceedings of the Human Factors and Ergonomics Society Annual Meeting 57(1), 114–118 (2013)
2. Lohse, M., Hegel, F., Wrede, B.: Domestic Applications for Social Robots - An Online Survey on the Influence of Appearance and Capabilities. Journal of Physical Agents 2, 21–32 (2008)
3. Kaplan, F.: Everyday Robotics: Robots as Everyday Objects. In: Proceedings of Soc-Eusai 2005, Grenoble, France, pp. 59–64 (2005)
4. Duffy, B.: Anthropomorphism and the Social Robot. Special Issue on Socially Interactive Robots, Robotics and Autonomous Systems 42, 3–4 (2003)
5. Blow, M., Dautenhahn, K., Appleby, A., Nehaniv, C.L., Lee, D.: The Art of Designing Robot Faces - Dimensions for Human-Robot Interaction. In: Proceedings of the 1st ACM SIGCHI/SIGART Conference on Human-Robot Interaction, Utah, USA, pp. 331–332 (2006)
6. Walters, M.L., Koay, K.L., Syrdal, D.S., Dautenhahn, K., Te Boekhorst, R.: Preferences and Perceptions of Robot Appearance and Embodiment in Human-Robot Interaction Trials. In: Proceedings of New Frontiers in Human-Robot Interaction: Symposium at AISB 2009 Convention, pp. 136–143 (2009)
7. Hackel, M., Schwope, M., Fritsch, J., Wrede, B., Sagerer, G.: Designing a Sociable Humanoid Robot for Interdisciplinary Research. Advanced Robotics 20(11), 1219–1235 (2006)
8. Zimmerman, J., Ayoob, E., Forlizzi, J., McQuaid, M.: Putting a Face on Embodied Interface Agents. Human- Computer Interaction Institute. Paper 229 (2005), http://repository.cmu.edu/hcii/229
9. Koda, T., Maes, P.: Agents with Faces: The Effect of Personification. In: Proceedings of IEEE Workshop on Robot and Human Communication, pp. 189–194 (1996)
10. Becker, B.: Social Robots – Emotional agents: Some Remarks on Naturalizing Man-Machine Interaction. International Review of Information Ethics 6(12), 37–45 (2006)

Aging and New Technologies: Challenges and Perspectives

Cláudia Stamato, Manuela Quaresma, and Cláudia Renata Mont'Alvão

PUC-Rio, Rua Marquês de São Vicente, 225, Gávea -
Rio de Janeiro, RJ - Brazil - 22451-900
stamatoclaudia@gmail.com,
{mquaresma,cmontalvao}@puc-rio.br

Abstract. This article discusses the results of an online questionnaire distributed to 393 participants residing in Brazil. The tool is an important part of the doctoral thesis of Design whose goal is to understand how older people socialize these days, when communication occurs much more virtually than in person. The world advocates that the elderly find it difficult to use technology and have little interest in using it. The relationship with technology can set about their inclusion or exclusion.

Keywords: Socialization, Elderly, Questionnaire, Active Aging, Social Relationship.

1 Introduction

This paper discusses the results from an online questionnaire distributed to 393 respondents living in Brazil. The tool is an important part of the doctoral thesis in progress at PUC-Rio on the relationship of the use of technological devices and socialization of seniors. A comparison between the responses given by seniors (60 or older) and by other age groups will be presented. With the results from this tool, the specific objectives of the thesis are intended to be reached. The objectives are the following:

— To clarify the concept of socialization of seniors;
— To list the technological communication devices that interfere with the human relationships of seniors;
— To understand the social behavior of seniors while using technological communication devices;

An online questionnaire was chosen, because in 2012, at the beginning of the research, it was found, through some theoretical references, and through 12 interviews among seniors, that this segment of the population has been using information and communication technologies. All respondents had a mobile phone or a smartphone and many of them wanted to buy more modern equipment. Among the three age groups (60 to 69, 70 to 79 and 80 to 89), all seniors from the first age group and half of the last age group had an email account [1]. Despite the interest in technology,

A. Marcus (Ed.): DUXU 2014, Part IV, LNCS 8520, pp. 173–184, 2014.

seniors have shown signs of difficulties with using such technology, either because of the fast technological developments or because of the natural aging losses or little experience with technological devices and built-in digital and virtual media. The interviews made clear that the older the user, the lower the number of features they know, recognize and use. [1]. [2] advocate that it takes longer for the seniors to execute a digital task than for other age groups. This study aims at learning how senior people use information and communication and how they socialize nowadays.

2   Theoretical References

2.1   Aging and Socializing

The world population is growing old! That is not new in Europe and in the USA, where it has been noticed a change in the population status in the last 150 years. In Brazil, that process occurred in 50 years only [3]. From 2000 to 2050, the 60-year old world population will grow from 605 million to 2 billion, and 80% of that will take place in developing countries. In 2025, Brazil will occupy fifth place with its 33.4 million senior citizens. [4]

The number of people who will not be able to take care of themselves will be four times higher by 2050 [5]. The incapacity to live in an independent and self-governing way brings with itself a drop in the self-esteem and an addition to social exclusion.

[6] saw that social isolation is associated with a higher rate of mortality in the senior population and that its reduction brings higher benefits against mortality than the reduction of loneliness, even though both are critical for a good life quality and well-being. The Active Aging is a project of the WHO – World Health Organization — and its purpose is to reach individuals and population groups through the dissemination of the idea of a good life quality throughout life by means of physical, social and mental well-being. The maintenance of self-governance and independence is related to the relationships inter-generations, and how the generations can and should cooperate with one another [5]. [7], [8], [9], and [10] state that a good quality aging depends on internal conditions such as environment and social relationships. [11] advocate that a key indicator to qualify the health condition of an old person is critical for a healthy and happy aging. "Social stimulation is based on: communication, affective exchange, coexistence, and the feeling of belonging to the groups they associate with" [9].

[12] in a research study about the aging process of 1,700 participants, tried to find out what people do to self-provide a "pleasant aging experience". As a general result, the study found out: "finding a life project, seeking the meaning of life, conquering freedom, craving happiness, cultivating friendship, living intensely the present, learning to say no, respecting their own will, allaying fears, accepting their age and giving lots of laughter." All these actions depend on an individual and internal process. However, most of these actions are only taken through social interactions.

"They (men and women) emphasize that, at a later age, they won the freedom to be "themselves." (...) By prioritizing the pursuit of meaning for their lives, they refused "symbolic death" or "social death," creating new positive representations of old age." [12]

2.2   Post-modern Socialization

The Post-Modernity of our world deeply modifies the social life: its dynamism, level of interference in the traditional habits and customs and the impact of the global reach [13]. [14] states that because the rhythm, extent and intensity in which the changes occur are so high, the end result is innovation prevailing over tradition. "The social process involves mutual and continuous interaction between an individual and the society", as in a two-way road [14]. A reflexivity ratio is established, building and modifying the individual and groups in a consecutive and simultaneous way. Technology is an important connection between the two ends, and its constant and rapid evolution directly contributes to the speed and depth of the modifications on the two sides [13]. Communication technology by means of digital tools, to control the functions and applications for the greatest variety of purposes, is constantly and uninterruptedly amplified in different devices such as smartphones, tablets, notebooks, netbooks, desktops, etc. Wireless connections, Bluetooth, Wi-Fi and Wi-Max networks interconnect everything in a friendly way offering both portability and mobility [15].Connectivity associated or not with portability has created a new way of interaction between people, that is, a new way to socialize.

[16] says that, despite the harms brought by the Internet such as "generating fragile and fleeting relationships, alienating the youth from family interactions and studies, generating separation of couples etc," considerable benefits are also enjoyed by the online population. Among the positive aspects, he mentions the variety of information sources, interaction with one or many users simultaneously from all parts of the world, fast retrieval of information, variety of media, etc. All this changed the way users think, act and interact. The world has become more agile, integrated, relativized, multitasking. This may easily explain the postmodern characteristic of immediacy [16]. There is an actual need to stay connected, especially for those in the labor market. Considering that the Internet was introduced in Brazil in the nineties, we can imagine that those about to retire at that time, are now older than 80 and have had little or no contact with the virtual world, except those who have worked in the IT business. In contrast, all other subsequent generations have been users of computers and the Internet.

3   The Problem

It is believed that the quality of aging is associated with the quality of individual socialization. If socializing ways have been changing according to the technological evolution of communication and information devices, what happens to that portion of seniors who theoretically find it harder to use this technology? Therefore, the subject matter of this doctoral thesis is the relationship between seniors and technological communication devices and the consequences on social relations. From the Problem, the following assumption was made: "The seniors' difficulty with interacting with technological devices of information and communication may interfere with the potential of their socialization process."

4   Questionnaire Results

The online questionnaire aims to start checking this assumption. In the future, the questionnaire will be answered by focal groups that include seniors, in order to prove this assumption. Before the questionnaire was sent out, ten tests were conducted with two users of each of the following age groups: 31 to 40, 41 to 50, 51 to 60, 61 to 70 and 71 to 80. Although the instrument accepted participants aged 18 and older, it was considered that testing the older ones was more important, based on the assumption that young people have an easier and more sophisticated interaction with the digital media than other age groups, except for IT experts.

Altogether, there were 393 respondents, but only 274 answered the questionnaire in full. Of these, 57 are distributed over the three groups of seniors aged 60 to 69, 70 to 79 and 80 and older. The overall analysis indicates a sample where 75.06% of respondents have enough experience using the Internet, i.e. at least eleven years to over fifteen years of experience, and a small portion of 5.34% have used the Internet for less than one year.

The seniors presented different sorts of experience. Yet, most of them have much experience. Among those aged 60 to 69 (n=42), 42.86% have used the Internet for more than fifteen years, 19.05% have use it for less than one year and 14.29% have used it for eleven to fourteen years. Among those aged 70 to 79 (n=11), 36.36% have used the Internet for over fifteen years, 27.27% have used the Internet for less than one year; 18.18% have used it for seven to ten years, and among those aged 80 and older (n=4), 50% have used it for less than one year, 25% have used for eleven to fourteen years and 25% have used it for more than fifteen years.

Preference for broadband connection was evident among the highest percentages, including private Wi-Fi, 3G and cable Internet, 76.08%, 57.25% and 53.69%, respectively. Almost 8% use the Edge mobile Internet, which consists in a basic mobile phone, i.e., one that offers a basic internet capability as its side function. It is believed that this audience seeks to keep up with technological developments as far as communication and information via the Internet is concerned. That is not different among the seniors. Among those aged 60 to 69 (n=42), 64.39% use private Wi-Fi broadband connection, 45.24% use 3G technology, 21.43% use public Wi-Fi and 11.9% already use the 4G technology, little widespread in Brazil. Among those aged 70 to 79 (n=11), 54.55% use private Wi-Fi, 45.45% use 3G technology, 36.36% use cable Internet and 18.8% use 4G technology. Among those aged 80 and older, there is a homogeneous distribution across dial-up Internet and private/public Wi-Fi and 3G technology. This is reaffirmed by the rates of daily use of mobile phones and smartphones, considering the whole sample: 35% against almost 69%, respectively. Nearly 55% of respondents do not use a mobile without internet, compared to only 24% who do not use smartphones. In this mobile context, a wide daily use of landline phones (wired or wireless) is perceived, reaching 58.52%. Among the seniors (n=57), 47.37% use mobile phones (without internet) and 43.86% use smartphones on a daily basis. But none of respondents aged 80 or older uses smartphones at any frequency. For the whole sample, digital TVs outnumber the daily use of conventional TVs by 54% against 38.6%. Almost 10% more of the respondents do not use conventional TV compared to those who do not use digital TV. Among the seniors (n=57), 63.16% use digital TV and 52.63% use conventional TV on a daily basis. A curious fact is that the seniors' rejection to the conventional TV is a bit higher than the digital TV. This means that even this group is open to a technological improvement. The only difference was the ever-beloved radio devices! One of the oldest information and communication technologies still resists in the conventional mode. The daily use of 32% is greater than two-fold compared to the digital version and non-use rates are higher compared to digital radio: 43.26% against 33%. Photo camera and recording features offered by mobile phones and smartphones are preferred to specific devices. The only variation that can be observed is the frequency of use, which is much lower in the older people. The figures show little difference in the daily use of desktop and notebook computers (64.63% and 60.05%, respectively). Among the seniors (n=57), 52.63% use desktop computers, and 49.12% use notebooks on a daily basis. Despite the percentage of acceptance of notebooks and desktops, the percentage of non-use of desktops is higher than that of notebooks (26.32% against 19.3%). This is a second sign of seniors' interest in technology. While only 29% of general respondents (n= 393) and 21.05% of senior respondents (n=57) use tablets, e-readers and the like on a daily basis, the general public, including the majority of senior respondents, gradually migrates to the most modern, lighter and, especially, mobile technologies. But the surprise is in 9.67% of all participants and 5.6% of older ones who reported not using landlines.

When asked about the preference for the means of communication, the respondents were clear in their preference for speed and record. Daily use of e-mails by 81.68% compared to almost 76% using voice calls via mobile phones, including smartphones, followed by the social media (62.85%) and instant messaging (60%). Text messaging is daily used by 45.55%. The result among the seniors (n=57) is similar: in first place, voice calls from landline phones and mobile ones on a daily basis by 73.68% and 70.18% respectively, followed by the use of e-mails by 64.91%, and 40.35% using the social media. 31.58% and 29.82% are the rates of instant messaging and text messaging, respectively. A little more than 50% of senior respondents do not use voice calls via the Internet, or and voice and video calls. Some seniors are starting to use these two latter means of communication at a rate of 5.26% and 7.02%, respectively. The figures, both considering the whole sample and the senior sample, are consistent with the ones shown in the preference of using broadband connection, Wi-Fi and 3G. Yet, voice calls are the most frequent communication means of all, over the entire sample. Over 20% of respondents do not use it yet, or have stopped using instant messaging. But the most valuable information comes from the absence of use of voice calls from landlines, which is almost 14%. This figure clearly demonstrates the migration of technologies.

When asked about the social groups in which they most communicate, the sample pointed out Love Partners, Family, Friends, Professional Groups and Acquaintances. Seniors answered in the following order: Family, Love Partners, Friends, Professional

Groups and Acquaintances. This small difference in the order of the first two groups may be explained by the interest in the grandchildren mentioned by some senior respondents. They help their kids raise their grandchildren, such as picking them up at school or looking after them when their parents are working. More than 50% has a love partner; the other half does not, and does not easily find a new love partner, especially senior women, which are the majority of seniors in Brazil. Men live four to seven years less than women do.

Among the activities carried out on a daily basis 80%, Work Activities are followed by Study Activities or Acquisition of New Pieces of Knowledge, with 57.39%. Taking Care of Family Members ranked third, whose daily rate reached 38.14%. Among the seniors (n=57), the order of daily activities mostly carried out is Work Activities (66.67%), Study Activities or Acquisition of New Pieces of Knowledge (49.12%), 45.61% for both Physical and Mental Healthcare Activities and Maintenance Activities (house and car) and 42.11% for Taking Care of Family Members. In the group of people aged 80 or older, the largest number of activities is done on a weekly basis. With the rate of 50% on a daily basis, this especial senior group elected Physical and Mental Healthcare Activities, Outside-Home Personal Care Activities, Maintenance Activities (house and car) and Leisure Activities.

Regarding the whole sample, Leisure Activities had their highest percentage on a weekly basis. This may be related to weekends. 36.43% reported performing Leisure Activities on a daily basis, thus ranking fourth. This came largely from the senior population in the sample (31.58%). The distribution of groups of social relations through activities with higher percentages of daily frequency is shown in the tables below. The first one shows the sample as a whole and the second one shows only the responses from the seniors. The first evidence is in the types of activities mostly performed by both samples. It suggests that the seniors, despite retirement, do not change completely their daily habits. The second evidence is the social groups with which the general respondents and senior participants performed the two first activities. They are exactly the same. It is at least interesting that such a sample of seniors, which includes 66.67% retirees, has Work Activities as the most frequent activity out of eleven different ones. It can be partly explained by 28.07% that are still working, despite retirement. 10.53% are self-employed and 3.51% are businesspersons.

These figures show that the population of seniors remains active in the market. It means they are still alive for finding meaning in life, which is important for them. For one to remain alive, one needs to have a social life. Being alive means being socially engaged in activities that benefit their emotional and physical well-being, establishing healthy relationships of exchange, to be always learning and teaching, feeling useful and being part of one or more groups of people. Being alive socially presupposes respecting and knowing oneself deeply in order to be able to interact with social groups with distinct characteristics without embarrassing oneself or the group. Having a work activity or any other kind of responsibility is key to emotional balance.

Table 1. Activity performed from higher to lower frequency (n= 393) X Social Groups with which he/she conducts activities

Activity performed from higher to lower frequency Sample of 393 respondents	Social Group 1	Social Group 2	Social Group 3
Work	42.71% Professional Group	23.61% Alone	14.37% Friends
Study or Acquisition of New Pieces of Knowledge	35.41% Alone	24.7% Professional Group	16.23% Friends
Taking Care of Family Members	50.12% Family	20.25% Alone	16.3% Love Partners
Leisure	27.91% Friends	25.75% Family	19.38% Love Partners

Table 2. Activity performed from higher to lower frequency (n= 57 Elderly) X Social Groups with which he/she conducts activities

Activity performed from higher to lower frequency Sample of 57 seniors	Social Group 1	Social Group 2	Social Group 3
Work	33.77% Professional Group	31.17% Alone	14.29% Friends
Study or Acquisition of New Pieces of Knowledge	35.79% Alone	27.37% Professional Group	14.74% Friends
Physical and Mental Healthcare Activities	44.16% Professional	36.36% Alone	9.09% Family
Maintenance Activities	47.76% Alone	20.09% Professional and Family	5.97% Lover Partner
Taking Care of Family Members	57.53% Family	15.07% Alone	13.7% Professional

The activities pointed out by the sample as those that most contribute to the acquisition of new social relations have much in common with the most frequent activities. There were no differences between the three activities that most contribute to the acquisition of new social relations and those that most contribute to the maintenance of existing social relations. These three activities are among the four activities mostly performed on a daily basis, as shown in the following table.

Table 3. Comparison between the activities most frequently carried out; those that most contribute to the acquisition of new social relations; and those that most contribute to the maintenance of existing social relations. (n=393)

Ranking in the Sample	Contribution to the acquisition of New Social Relations	Contribution to the Maintenance of Existing Social Relations	Activities most frequently performed
1st	Work Activities	Leisure Activities	Work Activities
2nd	Study Activities or Acquisition of New Pieces of Knowledge	Study Activities or Acquisition of New Pieces of Knowledge	Study Activities or Acquisition of New Pieces of Knowledge
3rd	Leisure Activities	Work Activities	Taking Care of Family Members
4th	Physical and Sports Activities	Taking Care of Family Members	Leisure Activities

Those activities are are critical for maintaining an active social life, whether to acquire new relationships or to maintain the existing ones.

Table 4. Comparison between the activities most frequently carried out; those that most contribute to the acquisition of new social relations; and those that most contribute to the maintenance of existing social relations. (n=57 Seniors)

Seniors' Ranking	Contribution to the acquisition of New Social Relations	Contribution to the Maintenance of Existing Social Relations	Activities most frequently performed
1st	Study Activities or Acquisition of New Pieces of Knowledge	Study Activities or Acquisition of New Pieces of Knowledge	Work Activities
2nd	Leisure Activities	Religious Activities	Study or Acquisition of New Pieces of Knowledge
3rd	Taking Care of Family Members	And Leisure Activities	Physical and Mental Healthcare Activities
4th	Physical and Sports Activities	Physical and Sports Activities and Physical and Mental Healthcare Activities	Maintenance Activities

Among the seniors, there were variations among their own preferences, as shown in the table above. The elderly sample points to two directions: Activities that promote socialization and those that are more frequent, regardless of social relations and interactions. They do not seem to think of socialization as any kind of interaction between at least two persons including work colleagues. The most frequent activities are working, but they are not listed among the most contributory for social relations.

It is a contradictory reasoning. Besides that, at least four out of five activities were mentioned as contributory for new social relations or for the maintenance the existing ones. Religious Activities were the difference; they were mentioned only for the maintenance of existing social relations. Religious Activities were most mentioned by the seniors aged 80 or older in both categories of contribution to socialization. The sample of this questionnaire presents the following variation of age:

Table 5. Table of sample's age distribution

	What is your gender?		
	Female	Male	All
Question	no.(%)	no.(%)	no.(%)
What is your age group?	100%	100%	100%
younger than 18	0%	0.88%	0.36%
18 to 29	20.5%	23.01%	21.53%
30 to 39	24.22%	17.7%	21.53%
40 to 49	14.91%	14.16%	14.6%
50 to 59	19.25%	23.89%	21.17%
60 to 69	16.77%	13.27%	15.33%
70 to 79	3.73%	4.42%	4.01%
older than 80	0.62%	2.65%	1.46%

The low number of senior respondents is in itself a result. Considering that e-mails are one of the most frequent forms of communication among the seniors, the low rate of replies may be due to some degree of distrust about sending out personal data over the Internet. During the tests, some participants were afraid of saying they lived alone, reporting their earnings and their daily activities. They even suggested that we invited their friends to participate in the survey, thus avoiding the embarrassment of informing their friends' e-mails without permission. In the overall sample (n=274), 46.72% are married and 20.07% are committed singles. Among the seniors (n=57) 54.39% are married and 12.28% are divorced with commitment. The sample as a whole presupposes high rates of cohabitation with love partners. 57.66% have at least one child and of these, 26.64% have two children against 42.34% with no children. Among the seniors, only 7.02% do not have children. According to the general sample, Taking Care of Family Members ranked sixth place out of eleven activities in the concept of contribution to the acquisition of new social relations and fourth place in the contribution to the maintenance of existing social relations. Surprisingly, though, among the seniors, this opinion is not supported. That is, to younger people, having children and taking care of them is conducive to their own socialization. The sample (n=274) presented a large majority with at least an undergraduate degree and only 12.06% with high school diplomas and 1.82% with elementary school diplomas. The rates of use of technological devices and the Internet in particular were high. One can consider the possibility of connecting education level to the use of the Internet and more advanced technological devices. Regarding the employment status of the sample, the vast majority still works and, among the seniors (n=57), although 66.67% of them are retired, 28.07% are still working. 54.39% is the percentage of all seniors of this sample who still work (retired or not). Among retirees, 63.16% had applied for retirement ten years before or more; 18.42% had applied three to six years before and 7.89% had retired less than one year before.

5   Conclusions

The sample of the online questionnaire exposed some lines of thought, sometimes in their own words, sometimes through open-ended questions. The great majority works. Working is critical for surviving and for social relations. The objective questions showed the Professional Group working only in their main occupation. However, the open-ended questions made this group emerge as a social relation that is also present for friendly interactions. Among the senior respondents, Professional groups were the most mentioned ones. This may be explained by the interaction through Physical and Sports Activities, Physical and Mental Healthcare Activities, Taking Care of Family Members and Work Activities. The older the user the bigger the need for special healthcare to perform daily activities. Back to the complete sample, when asked directly about how they socialize, "Friends" and "Family" were the two most mentioned words. Acquaintances, children and Love Partners also appeared after the Professional groups. Some interesting points are the statements about socialization with no comments on specific social interaction with parents, grandparents or uncles and aunts, and their detachment from the family group.

A recurrent data is socialization considered something strictly related to leisure. While "Friends" was the most mentioned word to explain how they socialize, the sample also brought back Work Activities with 13.86% followed by a full range of Leisure Activities, such as "Bars" (12.40%), "Parties" (11.67%), "Cinema" (9.12%) and "Traveling" (8.39%). Study Activities or Acquiring New Pieces of Knowledge through "Study/College/Courses/Classes" were in third place, with 10.21%. Physical Activities through "Sports/Hiking/Gym" ranked similar to "Traveling." All these activities require some level of planning, therefore, they should be performed with the social groups that most interest the participant. To perform all the aforementioned activities, the participants, regardless of their age, need to be informed and to communicate their own desire. That is where the technological devices and the means of communication (various media) come on the scene. The great majority of the sample wrote that they use the media to socialize virtually and to make arrangements to meet others in person. In the senior sample, it was noted that the older the participant, the lower the rate of complex technologies that they use. This difference is conspicuous in the group of seniors aged 80 or older. Besides that, most seniors try technological devices and some sorts of media communication, such as voice calls from landlines, mobiles or smartphones, e-mails from notebooks and desktops, social media such as Facebook, instant messaging from computers and text messaging from mobile phones. They even prefer digital TV instead of the conventional one and use more digital cameras from mobile phones than the camera equipment itself.

This sample noted that elderly people in Brazil are interested in using technology to be in touch with everybody, especially family members that live far and to receive information. Some of them wrote that, without an e-mail, nobody is able to reach you. They already prefer notebooks to desktops and there are more seniors who do not use desktops or landlines anymore than seniors that do not use notebooks or tablets yet. Very few use tablets, but the results pointed to a growing use of new technologies even by the elderly. They discovered and are invading Facebook, where they can make simple contacts and feel part of something bigger and up-to-date. It was observed that the older the participant the less complex the technology level he/she uses. The group aged 80 or older does not seem to use smartphones, notebooks or tablets. They still prefer desktops, mobiles and landlines. They complained about the extremely sensitive touch-screen technology. Religious activities are a very important way to socialize. This activity ranked at the highest contributory level, both to the acquisition of new social relations and to the maintenance of existing social relations.

Besides the interest in the Internet, Brazilian seniors are still afraid and not confident about using this media. This maybe because some of them do not consider virtual relationships as good, serious and reliable as the real ones. This opinion is shared by participants of other ages, but it is not the majority. This group (all ages) says the quality of the relationships is not the same; they are not deep enough. But this kind of social relations has its space in people's lives. Social Media are great for planning social events and quickly inviting everybody and to redeem lost friendships and maintain existing relationships, but not for making new friends. On the other hand, one group said they made good and new friends using the Internet and transformed virtual relationships into real ones. Across all ages, there are complaints about the exaggerations of some users of technological devices. They say that it is very important to make moderate use of any media or technological device, because virtual life or virtual relationships cannot replace the real ones. But if you do not have an e-mail, or at least a mobile phone, you are out, nobody will be able to find you when necessary. Post-modern life requires availability to be in touch.

Some senior respondents do not agree that there is a connection between socialization and technological devices. They defend that technology provides easy and speedy communication, but they do not provide socialization, which can only happen in person; not virtually or at a distance. Despite different opinions, most of them recognized the need for these technological devices and a range media options to be part of one or more groups and foster social relationships for a healthier personal life. It was evident that using a particular technology creates bonds or circles of relationships that can only be maintained if the users remain up to date, otherwise they may be left behind. The elderly, in particular, is discovering the immense social benefits brought by the use of these technological devices. The seniors' profile has changed considerably. Today, most of them are no longer in the residential "quarters." On the contrary, they are seeking new pieces of knowledge and social and romantic relationships through activities that they develop and technologies and media that they use. Along with the other age groups, they have been trying to keep up, to the extent possible, with the technological developments. Since the seniors are a population segment with rapid and irreversible growth, it is very important to look into their preferences of use in order to understand what encourages them to pursue better socialization options.

References

1. Stamato, Cláudia e Moraes, Anamaria de. Mobile Phone and elderly people: A noisy communication. IEA 2012 Congress/Recife. Work 41, 320–327 (2012), doi:10.3233/ WOR- 2012-1003-320
2. Pak, R., McLaughlin, A.: Designing Displays for Older Adults. Human Factors and Aging Series. CRC Press/ Taylor and Francis Group, New York (2011)
3. Pattison, M., Stemon, A.: Inclusive Design and Human Factors: Designing Mobile Phones for Older Users. SPECIAL ISSUE: Designing Technology to meet the needs of the Older User - Psychology Journal - The Other Side of Technology 4(3) (2002), http://www.psychnology.org (access on: March 23, 2011) ISSN 17207525
4. WHO. Care and independence in older age. Ageing and life course (May 30, 2013), http://www.who.int/ageing/en/ (access on June 23, 2013)
5. WHO – World Health Organization. Active ageing: a policy framework. Tradução Suzana Gontijo – Brasília: Organização Pan –Americana da saúde (2005)
6. Steptoe, A., Shankar, A., Demakakos, P., Wardle, J.: Social isolation, loneliness, and all-cause mortality in older men and women, vol. 110(15). University of California PNAS, Berkeley (2013)
7. Py, L., Pacheco, J.L., Sá, J.L.M., de e Goldman, S. N.: Tempo de Envelhecer: Percursos e dimensões psicossociais. Rio de Janeiro: NAU Editora (2004)
8. Rosenfeld, I.: Viva agora, envelheça depois. Maneiras comprovadas de desacelerar o tempo. Tradução Patrícia de Queiroz Carvalho Zimbres. São Paulo: Editora UNESP/ Editora SENAC (2002)
9. Zimerman, G.I.: Velhice: Aspectos biopsicossociais. Porto Alegre: Artmed (2000)
10. de Sant'anna, R.M., Camara, P., Braga, C.: Mobilidade na Terceira Idade: como planejar o futuro. Textos Envelhecimento, Rio de Janeiro 6(2) (2003), http://revista.unati.uerj.br/scielo.php?script=sci_arttext&p id=S151759282003000200002&lng=pt&nrm=iso (access on June 22, 2013)
11. Eliopoulos, C.: Enfermagem Gerontológica. 5ª edição. Artmed, Porto Alegre (2001)
12. Goldenber, M.: A Bela Velhice. Rio de Janeiro: Editora Record (2013)
13. Giddens, A.: Modernidade e Identidade. Rio de Janeiro, Jorge Zahar (2002)
14. Sell, C.E.: Sociologia Clássica. Itajaí: Editora UNIVALI (2002)
15. Siqueira, E.: Para compreender o mundo digital. Editora Globo: São Paulo (2008)
16. Nicolaci-Da-Costa, A.M. (org). Cabeças Digitais – O cotidiano na era da informação. Rio de Janeiro: Editora PUC-Rio (2006)

A Challenging Design Case Study for Interactive Media Design Education: Interactive Media for Individuals with Autism

Asım Evren Yantaç[1], Simge Esin Orhun[2], and Ayça Ünlüer Çimen[3]

[1] Koç University, Media and Visual Arts, Turkey
evren.yantac@gmail.com
[2] Özyeğin University, Dept. Of Communication Design, Turkey
esimge02@gmail.com
[3] Yıldız Technical University, Dept. Of Communication Design, Turkey
ayca.unluer@gmail.com

Abstract. Since 1999, research for creativity triggering education solutions for interactive media design (IMD) undergraduate level education in Yıldız Technical University leaded to a variety of rule breaking exercises. Among many approaches, the method of designing for disabling environment, in which the students design for the users with one or more of their senses disabled, brought the challenge of working on developing interactive solutions for the individuals with autism spectrum conditions (ASC). With the aim of making their life easier, the design students were urged to find innovative yet functional interaction solutions for this focused user group, whose communicational disability activate due to the deficiencies in their senses and/or cognition. Between 2011 and 2012, this project brief supported by participatory design method motivated 26 students highly to develop design works to reflect the perfect fit of interaction design to this challenging framework involving the defective social communication cases of autism.

Keywords: Autism, Interaction, Design Education, Innovation, Affordance.

1 Introduction

Research and design studies on assistive interaction design solutions for individuals with autism have been very popular for the last 20 years [1,2,3]. Autism is a disorder, which adversely affects individuals' cognitive abilities such as changing the perception mechanism, social communication abilities, recognizing and making facial expressions. Today's interactive technologies are on the verge of changing our lives by making the devices invisible so that we interact with them seamlessly and in a more natural manner. Many of these issues fall into the interests of interaction design field that works on the interaction between people-people or people-machines. Moreover, attentive user interface (AUI) studies [4] are looking for smart systems, which watch for people's needs and serves the information whenever needed. We believe that this

A. Marcus (Ed.): DUXU 2014, Part IV, LNCS 8520, pp. 185–196, 2014.

is potentially a sign of hope for individuals with autism. If we can design interactive experiences, which help IWA to be more naturally involved in everyday life in schools, offices, nomadic spaces, then we can all learn more from these experiences as well.

From another perspective, the facts mentioned above create very constructive design and design research challenges in relation to the creativity triggering exercises [5] Being related to lateral thinking ability of the designers and design researchers, making use of rule breaking methods by putting obstacles on the designer's way and presuming the users senses as disabled as a result of an environmental factor [6,7,8] has been used as one obstruction method. From this perspective, the features of autism may also be seen as challenging, and thus, valuable obstacles for design researchers and can be evolved as a particular case study along with interaction design students in studio classes where they can ideate, sketch and prototype interaction design solutions.

This paper shares our experiences from these studies we conducted with 26 students in 2011-13 concerning this case study of designing interactive solutions for individuals with autism in order to make their daily life easier. We used participatory design approach with the collaboration of professionals who are experienced in living with individuals with autism instead of working directly on autism. The studies were naturally directed into 3 different approaches: (a) wearable/tangible mobile; (b) spatially augmented; and (c) spatially organized interaction design solutions. The insights placed forward within this paper reflects how they are affected from these three different approaches and what kind of ideas came out of these exercises. Inline with our previous claim that disabling situations contribute to IMD education [5], we also believe that after this experience, autism and interaction design will work very well together in the near future.

2   Background

In this section, we will first discuss how the technology has been involved in autism related solutions in previous studies. Then we briefly discuss findings on affordance in relation with particular users with autism. Finally, we point out the similar approaches in design education in which autism is considered as a problem space.

2.1   Design Oriented Solutions for Autism

For the last 20 years in design practice, autism awareness has gradually been increasing within the design related fields such as architecture, visual communication, industrial product, and HCI. Architects explore guidelines for building autism-friendly living, working and education spaces. Psychologists and graphic design researchers focus on visual perception and representation methods. Industrial design domain discusses the tactile abilities of IWA and develops tangible solutions. As being one of the broadest inter-disciplinary domains of today, HCI researchers have also been leaning on this subject [9, 10]. IWA may lack abilities for planning actions [11], following social or one-to-one communications [12, 1], understanding facial expressions [13], cause-effect reasoning, and eye-contact [14]. In contradiction with above negativities, most IWA are good with structural information processing [15] and focusing on specific things such as mechanical systems. It is known that technology can help education, rehabilitation and daily life process of IWA [16] because the aforementioned features make them potentially good users of machines and technology [17]. But, when considering the fact that autism has a wide range of characteristics and effects regarding perception and representation abilities, smart and attentive interactive solutions aiming particular needs of different IWA cases should be developed [18].

Augmentative Alternative Communication (AAC) technology [19], is one leading method which uses visual or auditory messages to augment and regulate the intended communication. The emerging technologies in wearables, robotics and ubiquitous computing engage high potential for AAC studies. Furthermore, today we have the technological abilities to process the emotional states of people with motion and facial expression sensing technologies and help individuals understand emotions [3, 20] which can take the AAC subject to a next level. In one promising project, Kaliouby & Robinson [21] suggests a prosthetic solution; the "Emotional Hearing Aid", a system, which watches facial expressions of encountering persons and gives the information to the ASC individual providing feedback about facial expressions. However, it is also known that, ASC individuals don't like attachments in most cases. So we need further research on seamless technologies [22]. Another core focus for social involvement of IWA is about proximity information about socially challenged individuals. FeilSeifer & Mataric [9] used proximity information gathered through the observation of IWAs and robots to explore its effects on IWA. One of reasons why proximity is this important is that studies have shown that social involvement of IWA can be enhanced by the help of multi-user interfaces [14]. While some studied virtual reality (VR) solutions [23, 24, 2], some focused on and found positive effects of co-located collaboration using multi-user tangible tabletops [25]. Others also reached positive clues while exploring interaction with remote users through tangible interfaces [26]. Tangible interaction benefits affordance and hand-eye coordination abilities of IWA [22]. Moreover, most high functioning IWA can use tangible interfaces when written instructions, direct manipulation control devices, and keyboards are provided [27]. Based on the fact that Autism has an increasing worldwide prevalence [28], and HCI field is constantly developing more natural, intuitive, seamless and smart technologies every day, we believe that designing smart interactive user experience solutions for IWA is a promising topic within the area of IMD.

2.2   Affordance for Individuals with Autism

With above perspective, we've gone deeper into the subject of autism-specific affordance issues. One of the most important issues while designing a product that IWA are expected to use or interact in any way is the subject of affordance. In the physical world, objects communicate with the users. Healthy individuals, ones that are not suffering from ASD are supposed to predict how to use an object they encounter. Such clues that an object is giving out are called 'affordances'. Norman [29] implies that the idea of perceived affordances is that, when the designers expect the users to interact with an object -be it in real world or on a computer screen-, they have to make sure the users can easily comprehend, solve and understand what they can do with the object.

Yet, the designer has to be aware that the planned object and interaction scenarios might differ when a product is designed for IWA. Studies show that IWA may have a difficult time without the use of assistive equipment, when interacting with design objects and systems that are organized with metaphorical symbols, such as traffic systems, which healthy people may be familiar with [1]. This shows that metaphorical signs that are supposed to raise affordance may not work for IWA. On the other hand, many studies have shown that virtual environments that do not offer visual overload may be very well used by high-functioning IWA and may be used for reasons such as education or gaining various useful practices [23, 10]. Additionally, virtual reality is found to prove a safer environment for IWA, compared to physical educational spaces [1, 2]. As we mentioned above, IWA that experience communication difficulties with people because of their abnormalities in voice and face recognition [13], may easily embrace and adapt to control virtual avatars and puppet characters. They can get into interactions, which they may find difficult in real world, in virtual environments due to the high affordance that their visual resemblance to such avatars provides them.

IWA are known to have more success in using minimalistic interfaces that provide orderly and regular procedures, rather than multimodal interfaces that create cognitive overload [12]. IWA can also learn rules and restrictions of interfaces very well, as long as these are put clearly and not through metaphorical signs or speech [12, 1]. Also reward systems have proved to be useful in enhancing the educational level on IWA in such virtual systems [20]. Such reward systems also allow the IWA learn how to use more complicated interfaces. Another way to raise the affordance level for IWA is to design tangible interfaces and control devices that resemble real life objects [22]. While tangible interfaces are proven to be usable by IWA, the extents of what assistive designs can be made through such interfaces, is not researched adequately.

2.3   Autism as Problem Space for Design Education

Despite the presence of above summarized growing attention on autism among the whole design community and high relevance of autism's features for IMD education curriculum, we could not find any well-structured and rationalized attempt in the lite-rature. At first sight, it is not hard to encounter examples in the architectural design education. Heylighen et. al. [30] proposes design expertise on disability as comple-mental for architects' multi-sensory qualities in architectural design and claim that they are focusing on autism as a case study in this sense. Tang and Hsaio [26] ex-plains their experience about briefing interaction design graduate students on autism and collected insights from the students attended the studies, where they involved actual users for exploring user requirements. While they base their main objective on user involvement in a teamwork oriented studio, the influence on the autism case study is weakly considered in the paper. Island of ideas [24] is a collaborative virtual reality environment, which brings together students with autism; design students and researchers in order to develop user-centered design solutions with a participatory design approach. This ongoing study still questions if the creative and productive design research method called participatory design study, can also be used in studies with children with autism.

Autism research takes a very large share of worldwide research funding. Many universities all over the world have Autism related research groups and a significant amount of HCI research on Autism is being run. In 2011, Core77 and Autism Speaks Foundation have organized a worldwide design contest among undergraduate level design students. In contradiction with above facts, the results of focusing on autism as a case study in interaction design education had not been explored before.

3   Objectives

Our main objective in the study has been to draw upon the particular specifications of autism within the studio courses of IMD. Based on the previous findings in the literature, we believe that the specifications of autism listed above create very productive design challenges for interaction designers. We have been exploring "obstructive case studies" for triggering creativity in IMD education, and autism is promising to become the stage for yet another sophisticated case in the same manner.

With such goals in mind, we have been briefing IMD students with design challenges about autism. One of the priorities of our approach was to keep students from attempting to control or restrict the users' actions with their designs; but rather help others understand and interact with them, better. While we encourage the students to try to ease the life of individuals with autism, we also think this shouldn't be by trying to 'normalize' them from any point of view. This is not only because that the students don't study in a medical branch, but also we believe a designer should respect and try to enhance any individuals' features rather than limit them. Another criteria that we had advised the students to be sensible about was designing naturally usable interfaces (NUI), i.e. with high affordance, in order to stay away from trying to give detailed instructions to the users. This resulted in mobile, wearable, tangible or spatial solutions instead of graphical user interfaces (GUI) based applications.

As students began ideating on natural user interfaces (NUI), we wanted to take one step further to make them understand the variety of human interactions based on the performative skills of human body with respect to time and physical space. Originating from research, we have found out that visuospatial capabilities as well as spatial perception have not dramatically changed in IWA [1]. With reference to real objects and functions, the possibility to benefit from the use of solid and tangible user interfaces, was proved to be an effective way of helping with particular sensory features of IWA where the visual reference increases the affordance through the hand-eye coordination of IWA [22].

As the literature suggested, IWA may tend to suffer when they have to plan actions or make decisions and think for alternative solutions where these conditions trigger unexpected or inappropriate responses [11]. So we advised the students to base the spatial experience on a linear story with no alternative routes for navigation and no visual obstructions to provide informative and entertaining environments for IWA, especially for children, as the effects of this disorder begins in early childhood and persists throughout adulthood [14].

4   Method

The study mentioned above was conducted between 2010-2013 in the Department of Interactive Media Design of Yildiz Technical University with a total of 26 undergraduate students under design studio courses that focus on developing interaction design solutions for a variety of technological platforms, tools and user scenarios. Studio courses have been running with 4 hours studio sessions, 2 times a week, for a month. Although the outputs of each studio design course were different, general tendency to proceed could be defined from the steps given below:

Background Research: The students were advised to examine and investigate the information provided by movies, documentaries, interviews, the mission/vision and principles of associations concerned with IWA and autism disorder.

Disabling Environment Review: With the participation of experts on autism, the specific qualities and different behavioral aspects of IWA were discussed in order to understand the reactions they give to certain environmental factors, basic motor, emotional and cognitive tendencies and perceptual capabilities.

Assessing the Case Study Group: With reference to the investigation on different types of autism disorder, the students selected specific groups in terms of age and type, as their pilot group to work on.

Identifying the Problem: The problem was defined concerning the needs of IWA pilot group that does not refer to any prior psychiatric knowledge and existing tools, scenarios and technologies, which would not limit or prove disadvantageous for the individuals were discussed. Besides, the students were grouped to work on different technological platforms.

General Tendency for Design: The designed tool, service or application must be developed to ease the 2-way communication of the IWA with the outer world. While creating the automation in the design was favored, perceiving the designed tool as an exercise or a game is supposed to ease the use and increase the efficiency.

Preliminary Sketching: The students were guided to discover the different modes of interaction that would be beneficial for their projects. This process was important in order to discuss and dwell on the balance between the qualities of cognitive, emotive and motor skills that will be made use of. Meanwhile, they were also advised to take notice of the technological platforms. This process ends with developing alternative sketches for the combinations of the interface, interaction and technology.

Developing the Idea: Within this phase of the design studio, interaction scenarios were developed in parallel with the alternative forms in terms of activities, actions and operations [31]. This phase includes the detailed design and planning of interaction scenario together with maintaining the controls, movements and end results.

The interplay of action, interaction and controls were expected to be realized through the mapping correlations of the designs.

Evaluation: Experts from the area of autism studies and associations were invited for the assessment of the design works. In parallel with their experiences, the advantages and disadvantages of each design were discussed in parallel with the achievements of the design group.

5   Results

In parallel with the objectives and method proposed above, a variety of design problems were detected and design works with originality and versatility were obtained. It was interesting to see how each student perceived the disabling environment and disabling features of autism as an alien data set and reacted to find relevant solutions. As the students were used to solve interaction problems with complex information architecture, it was not easy for IMD students to understand how this user profile acts at the beginning of the design process. While some of the students focused on creating interactive solutions to transmit the physical conditions of the user profile, others tried to enhance the communicative skills of IWA using various tools and technologies. It became possible to separate them into 3 groups in terms of their physical specifications: (a) wearable and tangible mobile interactive (b) spatially augmented tangible interactive (c) spatially organized interaction solutions. Below we present some interesting student works based on this classification.

5.1   Wearable and Tangible Mobile Interactive Solutions

The project "Play Dough" by Yasemin Yıldırım (Fig. 1) addresses the mood changes of the children with ASC by a tactile sensor shaped as an ordinary looking play-dough. The dough senses changes in body temperature, sweat and hand vibration and reflects their mood by changing colors and shape, thus communicating with others. The dough also addresses tactile tendencies and changes in density according to the mood of the child to calm them when stressed or make them playful when happy.

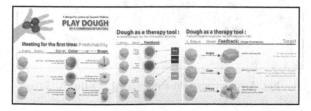

Fig. 1. Playdough (Yasemin Yıldırım, 2011)

The "Interactive Bracelet" project by Ozan Daniel Özışık (Fig. 2) consists of a wearable 2-way communication device for 3-6 year old children with autism. Firstly, the bracelet attracts the child by shining and vibrating whenever the child is called. Secondly it memorizes the child's specific movements before and during certain emergency conditions such as seizures, and contacts with the parents or nurse whenever these movements occur. In a third use, two children that are using the bracelet for a long time can communicate with each other by playing with their bracelets and changing colors of their companions.

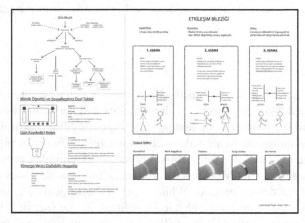

Fig. 2. Interactive Bracelet (Ozan Daniel Özışık, 2011)

5.2   Spatially Augmented Interactive Solutions

In her project (Fig. 3), Doğa Çorlu prefers to augment the proximity related information by mapping projected images on all surfaces. The objective here is to reflect the emotional states of each individual with and without autism within a room. Compared to previous suggestions, she explored different solutions where individuals might see or not see the projected visual messages with a different approach. For instance, when in a situation where the image should not distract IWA, image is projected at the back like a shadow or at the surfaces of the desk, which cannot be seen by the user, may be used to reflect emotional states.

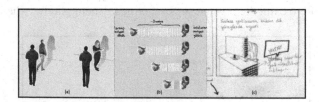

Fig. 3. Augmented Proximity (Doğa Çorlu, 2012)

In another spatially augmented interactive solution (Fig. 4), Gökalp Gönen projects abstract visual animation clues on surfaces or objects that visually inform the IWA about irregularities, warnings, and constructive clues. The main objective of the idea is to augment the environment according to the needs of the IWA in a natural way without putting physical obstructions in the space. This experimental idea explores if different visual representations can positively communicate with an IWA.

Fig. 4. Projected Assistance (Gökalp Gönen, 2012)

5.3   Spatially Organized Interaction Solutions

The design brief was based on the planning and design of a conceptual exhibition in a three-story building. This specific physical space was chosen as the working site so as to avoid linear configurations and storytelling and push the creative boundaries of students to find alternative combinations for the spatial configuration, interaction, navigational, storytelling and interface design solutions.

The interactive exhibition design project for children with autism (Fig. 5), by Mustafa Ahmet Kara named "Discrete Orchestra" focused on creating sounds by bodily interactions with tools and forming an overall orchestral music within the physical space. The tangible user interfaces of the tools were shaped with reference to the affordance design of original musical instruments. The information access tools on these tangible user interfaces were designed in an elaborated scale, so as to emphasize the affordance. Each instrument placed on different platforms connected by large stairs, the space was designed to be relaxing, distressful and transparent so as to prevent confusion, getting lost and becoming a challenge for IWA.

Fig. 5. An interactive exhibition for children with autism (Mustafa Ahmet Kara, 2011)

In his project named "Perceive" (Fig. 6), Berkin Nalbantli focused on the Gestalt principles of visual understanding and communication for the audience group of IWA with Asperger syndrome. Basic forms were used to explain how human buildings develop perception from childhood to adulthood, with matching interactions for IWA. One-way communication was favored with the touchscreens. In order to maintain the navigational and spatial unity, 3 floors were connected horizontally with ramps and vertically with a spiral that rotated in parallel with the action around it.

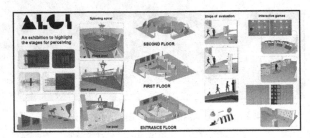

Fig. 6. An interactive exhibition for children with autism (Berkin Nalbantlı, 2011)

As a result, it is possible to say that, as the spatial connections and functional flowing of the interactions were supported by the storytelling, the navigational aspects of the designs were naturally solved within the physical space and was found to be successful in providing suitable physical conditions for IWA.

6   Discussions and Conclusion

In this paper, we share our insights from the experiences we had by briefing the IMD students with autism case study in their studio courses. This study has been a follow-up to our ongoing studies on teaching affordance so as to widen the students' creative limits while staying within the borders of accessibility. With this perspective, we wanted the students to explore the problem space relevant to interactive solutions for IWA where the features of the persona provides very valuable challenges and obstructions for the designer candidate in terms of the perceptual and mental models In order to adapt and understand the specific conditions of IWA, the students concentrated on specific problems for which they searched for attentive, smart, natural, and invisible real-life interventions using interactive media. The studies resulted in 3 different conceptual approaches in the end; (a) Mobile and wearable, (b) spatially augmented, (c) spatially organized solid solutions.

Solutions that can be categorized as "mobile and wearable" were less demanding, location-independent and partially seamless. Students tried to develop these devices as human-human communicators with the aim of avoiding the need for extra attention within the daily life of users, in addition to one other critical fact of bringing functionality to these devices to take-turn whenever needed, such as emergency situations. Consequently these designs didn't involve any form of screen. In a different approach, "spatially augmented" studies leaned on using the surfaces of the environment surrounding IWA and augmenting the environment by projecting interactive information on these surfaces. These smart systems watch for the needs and assist the communication between the co-located individuals. From the "spatially organized" interaction exercises, it was our experience to discover the potential of the solid user interface to give reference to predict the results of actions in terms of how things work. The students were able to create efficient conceptual models for the affordance design of information access elements with the appropriate use of form, sound and image. Moreover, based on the topological relationships structured in the 3rd dimension, students learned to consider the importance of the physical space to be an advantageous design element in order to shape the interactions naturally.

In summary, this has been a challenging and enlightening experience for both parties and the students with its rule-breaking results. We have seen that with the help of domain expert participation to the studios, students were very easily adapted to this challenging case study even though they were not familiar with autism beforehand. We also believe that they have learned a lot about affordance and accessibility due to many particular restrictions and special needs the autism case brings. However, it is too early to speak about the constructive results of our experiences for the student's education. We plan to run studies that question the effects for competence of students in design in order to further develop the structure of the case study.

References

1. Josman, N., Ben-Chaim, H.M., Friedrich, S., Weiss, P.L.: Effectiveness of virtual reality for teaching street-crossing skills to children and adolescents with autism. International Journal on Disability and Human Development 7(1), 49–56 (2008)
2. Parsons, S., Mitchell, P.: The potential of virtual reality in social skills training for people with autistic spectrum disorders. J. Intellect. Disabil. Res. 46, 430–443 (2002)
3. Sebrechts, M.M., Coleman, M., Finkelmeyer, A., Ramloll, R., Barker, L., Lathan, C., Vice, M., Pettersen, M.: Design trials of the Virtual Buddy: Progress report. Cyberpsychology & Behavior 7(3), 313–314 (2004)
4. Vertegaal, R., Shell, J.S., Chen, D., Mamuji, A.: Designing for augmented attention: Towards a framework for attentive user interfaces. Comp. in Human Behavior 22, 771–789 (2006)
5. Ozcan, O., Yantac, E.: Breaking the Rules in Interactive Media Design Education. Digital Creativity 17(2), 115–124 (2009)
6. Ünlüer, A., Özcan, O.: Learning Natural User Interface Design through Creative Drama Techniques: New Approaches to Design Education, School of Design, Northumbria University, Newcastle upon Tyne, UK (2012)
7. Yantaç, A.E.: A method for teaching affordance for user experience design in interactive media design education. In: Design, User Experience, and Usability. Design Philosophy, Methods, and Tools, pp. 630–638. Springer, Heidelberg (2013)
8. Yantac, A.E., Ozcan, O.: Participatory Study in Interactive Media Education: Disabling Environment and Augmented Reality Case. Digital Creativity 22(1), 40–48 (2011)
9. Feil-Seifer, D., Matarić, M.: Using proxemics to evaluate human-robot interaction. In: Proceedings of the 5th ACM/IEEE International Conference on Human-Robot Interaction, pp. 143–144. IEEE Press (March 2010)
10. Strickland, J.: Just the FAQs: An Alternative to Teaching the Research Paper. The English Journal 94(1), 23–28 (2004)
11. Russell, J.: Agency–itsroleinmentaldevelopment. Taylor & Francis, Erlbaum (1996)
12. Grynszpan, O., Martin, J.C., Nadel, J.: Multimedia interfaces for users with high functioning autism: An empirical investigation. International Journal of Human-Computer Studies 66(8), 628–639 (2008)
13. Adolphs, R., Sears, L., Piven, J.: Abnormal Processing of Social Information from Faces in Autism. J. of Cognitive Neuroscience. 13(2), 232–240 (2001)

14. Gal, E., Goren-Bar, D., Bauminger, N., Stock, O., Weiss, P.L.T.: Pilot study of enforced collaboration during computerized storytelling to enhance social communication of children with high-functioning autism. Cyberpsyc. & Beh. 9(6), 674–675 (2006)
15. Baron-Cohen, S., Wheelwright, S., Lawson, J., Griffin, R., Hill, J.: The exact mind: empathising and systemising in autism spectrum conditions. In: Handbook of Cognitive Development, pp. 491–508 (2002)
16. Moore, M., Calvert, S.: Brief report: Vocabulary acquisition for children with autism: Teacher or computer instruction. Jor. of Autism and Dev. Dis. 30(4), 359–362 (2000)
17. Baron-Cohen, S., Ring, H.A., Wheelwright, S., Bullmore, E.T., Brammer, M.J., Simmons, A., Williams, S.C.: Social intelligence in the normal and autistic brain: an fMRI study. European Journal of Neuroscience 11(6), 1891–1898 (1999)
18. Parés, N., Carreras, A., Durany, J., Ferrer, J., Freixa, P., Gómez, D., ... Sanjurjo, À.: Promotion of creative activity in children with severe autism through visuals in an interactive multisensory environment. In: Proceedings of the 2005 Conference on Interaction Design and Children, pp. 110–116. ACM (June 2005)
19. Bondy, A., Frost, L.: A Picture's Worth: PECS and Other Visual Communication Strategies in Autism. Topics in Autism (2002)
20. Trepagnier, C.Y., Sebrechts, M.M., Finkelmeyer, A., Stewart, W., Woodford, J.: Acceptance of a virtual social environment by pre-schoolers with autism spectrum disorder. Cyberpsychology & Behavior 9, 723 (2006)
21. El Kaliouby, R., Robinson, P.: Real-time inference of complex mental states from facial expressions and head gestures. In: Real-Time Vision for Human-Computer Interaction, pp. 181–200. Springer US (2005)
22. Jung, K.E., Lee, H.J., Lee, Y.S., Lee, J.H.: Efficacy of sensory integration treatment based on virtual reality-Tangible interaction for children with autism. Annual Review of Cyber Therapy and Telemedicine 4, 45–49 (2006)
23. Han, K., Ku, J., Kim, K., Park, J., Lee, H., Jang, H.J., ... Kim, S.I.: Analysis of VR-based head-motion to a virtual avatar: Characteristic of schizophrenia. Cyberpsychology& Behavior 9(6), 679–680 (2006)
24. Millen, L., Cobb, S.V.G., Patel, H., Glover, T.: Collaborative virtual environment for conducting design sessions with students with autism spectrum conditions. In: Proc. 9th Intl Conf. on Disability, Virtual Reality and Assoc. Technologies, pp. 269–278 (2012)
25. Piper, A.M., O'Brien, E., Morris, M.R., Winograd, T.: SIDES: a cooperative tabletop computer game for social skills development. In: Proceedings of the 2006 20th Anniversary Conference on Computer Supported Cooperative Work, pp. 1–10. ACM (2006)
26. Tang, H.H., Hsiao, E.: The advantages and disadvantages of multidisciplinary collaboration in design education. Paper presented at IASDR 2013, Tokyo (2013)
27. Jung, K.E., Lee, H.J., Lee, Y.S., Cheong, S.S., Choi, M.Y., Suh, D.S., Lee, J.H.: The Application of a Sensory Integration Treatment Based on Virtual Reality-Tangible Interaction for Children with Autistic Spectrum Disorder. Psyc. Journal 4(2), 145–159 (2006)
28. Rutter, M.: Incidence of autism spectrum disorders: Changes over time and their meaning. Acta Paediatrica 94(1), 2–15 (2005)
29. Norman, D.A.: The design of everyday things. Basic books (2002)
30. Heylighen, A., Devlieger, P., Strickfaden, M.: Design Expertise as Disability. Communicating (by) Design, 227–235 (2009)
31. Kaptelinin, V., Nardi, B.A.: Acting with technology. Mit Press (2006)

Emotional and Persuasion Design

Further Investigation of the Effects of Font Styles on Perceived Visual Aesthetics of Website Interface Design

Ahamed Altaboli

Industrial and Manufacturing Systems Engineering Department,
University of Benghazi, Benghazi, Libya
Altaboli.UOB@gmail.com

Abstract. Findings of an earlier study indicated that a webpage using the "Times New Roman" font type was perceived as having better visual aesthetics than a webpage using the "Calibri" font type. The current study is a continuation of this research, the purpose of the study is to investigate how using a mixture of the two font types in the same webpage would affect perception of visual aesthetics. Four webpage designs were compared in the current study; the two designs used in the earlier study and another two designs containing a mixture of both fonts. Results showed that mixing the two font types on the same page didn't improve perception of visual aesthetics. Still, the webpage design with only the Times New Roman font type perceived as having a better visual aesthetics than all the other three designs.

Keywords: font style, font type, perceived visual aesthetics, website interface design.

1   Introduction

Most of font types used in printing and on screen belong to two font styles: serif and sans-serif. A "serif" is a French term for a short decorative line (edge) at the start or finish of a stroke in a letter, and "sans-serif" is a French term meaning "without-serif". i.e. the serif style has edges that project from the main letter block, while the sans-serif style doesn't have these edges.

The effect of each style on readability and legibility is one concern of the field of document, screen and interface design, finding of related studies mostly agree that on printed papers the serif style gives better readability and legibility than the sans-serif style [2], while; on a computer screen this advantage of the serif types is reduced, and findings of several studies indicated that the sans-serif types have more readability and legibility [2, 4, 5 and 8]. This is due to the fact that on computer screens each character is displayed as dot-matrix (or pixels), which results on the character with the edges "serif" appears jagged. This effect increases with low resolution of the screen and should be reduced with higher screen resolutions. As screen resolution increases this jagged effect should be eventually eliminated [2].

A. Marcus (Ed.): DUXU 2014, Part IV, LNCS 8520, pp. 199–207, 2014.
© Springer International Publishing Switzerland 2014

Other than the issues of readability and legibility, there is the issue of which font style would be more aesthetically appealing for the users and how it would affect the overall visual appeal and aesthetics of the interface. An earlier study [1] compared the effects of the two font styles (serif and sans-serif) on the overall perception of visual aesthetics of website interface design. Two font types were tests in this study, namely: "Time News Roman" representing the "serif" style and "Calibri" representing the "sans-serif" style. Results indicated that the design with the Time New Roman font (the serif style) was perceived as having better visual aesthetics than the design with the Calibri font (sans-serif style).

The current study is a continuation of this research, the purpose of the current study is to investigate how using a mixture of the two font styles and font types in the same webpage (compared to the single styles and types used in the earlier study) would affect perception of visual aesthetics of the page design.

Four webpage designs were compared in the current study; the two designs used in the earlier study (one with the Time News Roman font and one with the Calibri font), and another two designs containing a mixture of both fonts.

2   Method

2.1   Design of the Experiment

An experiment was designed and conducted to test the effects of font type on participants' perceived visual aesthetics of website design.

A one- factor (font type) within participants design was utilized with four levels associated with the four conditions to be tested. Four designs of a webpage were prepared to represent the four levels. All designs have identical formats (colors, menus ...etc); the only difference is the font type(s) used in each design; in one design the Times New Roman font type was used in all text in the webpage, in the second design the Calibri font type was used. The third and fourth designs used a mixture of both types; in the third, the Times New Roman font type was used in the main title and in the navigation bar and menus, while the Calibri font type was used only for the main text on the page. With the fourth design the two font types were exchanged; Calibri was used in the main title, the navigation bar and menus, and the Times New Roman font was used for the main text.

Screen shots of the four designs of the webpage are presented in Fig1 to Fig 4. The webpage represents a homepage of a hypothetical website that talks about the ancient history of a certain region of North Africa.

User perception of visual aesthetics was measured using the VisAWI (Visual Aesthetics of Website Inventory) questionnaire [7]. The instrument is based on four interrelated facets of perceived visual aesthetics of websites: simplicity, diversity, colorfulness, and craftsmanship. Simplicity comprises visual aesthetics aspects such as balance, unity, and clarity. The Diversity facet comprises visual complexity, dynamics, novelty, and creativity. The colorfulness facet represents aesthetic impressions perceived from the selection, placement, and combination of colors. Craftsmanship comprises the skilful and coherent integration of all relevant design dimensions. Each of the first two facets is presented by five items in the questionnaire, while each of the last two facets has four items.

The font type(s) used in each design with its four conditions represents the independent variable. Questionnaire scores represent the dependent variable.

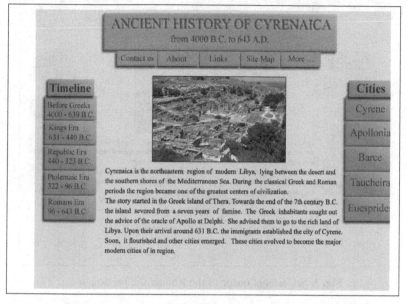

Fig. 1. Screen shot image The Times New Roman design

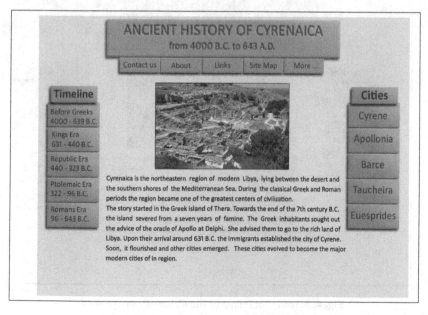

Fig. 2. Screen shot image the Calibri design

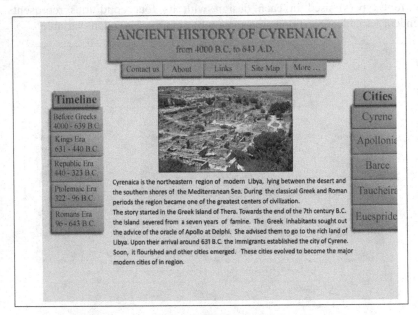

Fig. 3. Screen shot image of the Roman-Calibri design

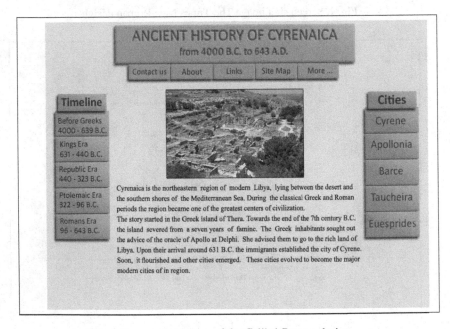

Fig. 4. Screen shot image of the Calibri-Roman design

2.2   Participants

Participants were recruited online. Email invitations were sent to audience within the United States with the choice of entering a lottery to win 100 US dollars. A total of 56 responses were received, from which 32 were valid responses. Average age of participants with valid responses is 47.9 years with a standard deviation of 7.4 years. 13 were males and 19 were females.

3   Results

Images of screen shots of the four designs were presented to each participant one at a time with an on screen size of 800X600 pixels. The questionnaire was placed under each image. Each participant had to answer the questionnaire for each design using a seven-point Likert scale. Both images and questionnaire items were presented in random orders for each participant.

Table 1 summarizes average scores per each scale (aesthetic facet) and for the total score. The averages were presented per each design (Roman, Calibri and the mixed Roman-Calibri and Calibri-Roman). Cronbach's α was used to measure reliability of the questionnaire. All calculated values were larger than 0.94 for the different scales of the questionnaire, indicating an acceptable level of reliability.

From the table it can be seen that with all scales and with the total, slightly higher average scores were recorded in the Roman design. However; the results of analysis of variance show that these differences are only significant with the craftsmanship scale and the total with p-values of 0.017 and 0.040 respectively. Pair-wise comparisons of average scores in both cases showed that the average score of the Roman design is significantly higher than the average scores of the other three designs. Participants perceived the Roman design as having better visual aesthetics than the Calibri design and the two mixed Roman/Calibri designs.

Statistically significant differences were found among the different scales with the total score (p-value = 0.02) and with both of the two mixed designs (Roman-Calibri and Calibri-Roman) with p-values of 0.012 and 0.018 respectively, as results of analysis of variance among the average scores of the scales for each design in Table 2 show. In all the significant cases, pair-wise comparisons were significant between the simplicity scale and all the other scales. The simplicity scale was given the highest average score in all the designs and the total. One can also note that with the craftsmanship scale, although not statistically significant, slightly higher average scores than the average scores of diversity and colorfulness scales were recorded in all cases.

Both of the simplicity scale and craftsmanship scale are related to the classical dimension of visual aesthetics, while the diversity and colorfulness are considered to be representatives of the expressive dimension of visual aesthetics [6]. The higher average scores given to the simplicity scale and the craftsmanship scale indicate that participants perceived the four deigns of the webpage as more classical than expressive.

Table 1. Average questionnaire scores and results of analysis of variance

Scale	Font Style	Average	Standard Deviation	F	P-value
Simplicity	Roman	4.94	1.63	1.19	0.316
	Calibri	4.76	1.53		
	Roman-Calibri	4.79	1.61		
	Calibri-Roman	4.82	1.57		
Diversity	Roman	4.45	1.57	0.39	0.754
	Calibri	4.39	1.62		
	Roman-Calibri	4.32	1.56		
	Calibri-Roman	4.42	1.61		
Colorfulness	Roman	4.72	1.85	2.53	0.062
	Calibri	4.41	1.81		
	Roman-Calibri	4.28	1.85		
	Calibri-Roman	4.33	1.84		
Craftsmanship	Roman	4.83	1.76	3.56	0.017
	Calibri	4.52	1.75		
	Roman-Calibri	4.47	1.68		
	Calibri-Roman	4.45	1.76		
Total	Roman	4.73	1.58	2.88	0.040
	Calibri	4.52	1.57		
	Roman-Calibri	4.47	1.58		
	Calibri-Roman	4.51	1.60		

Table 2. Results of analysis of variance for scales

Case	Scale	Average	Standard Deviation	F	P-value
Roman	Simplicity	4.94	1.63	2.47	0.067
	Diversity	4.45	1.57		
	Colorfulness	4.72	1.85		
	Craftsmanship	4.83	1.76		
Calibri	Simplicity	4.76	1.53	1.93	0.130
	Diversity	4.39	1.62		
	Colorfulness	4.41	1.81		
	Craftsmanship	4.52	1.75		
Roman-Calibri	Simplicity	4.79	1.61	3.84	0.012
	Diversity	4.32	1.56		
	Colorfulness	4.28	1.85		
	Craftsmanship	4.47	1.68		
Calibri-Roman	Simplicity	4.82	1.57	3.51	0.018
	Diversity	4.42	1.61		
	Colorfulness	4.33	1.84		
	Craftsmanship	4.45	1.76		
Total	Simplicity	4.83	1.55	3.46	0.020
	Diversity	4.39	1.53		
	Colorfulness	4.43	1.74		
	Craftsmanship	4.57	1.68		

4   Conclusions

This study was an extension of an earlier study [1], the purpose of the current study is to investigate how using a mixture of different font styles and font types in the same webpage (compared to the single styles and types used in the earlier study) would affect perception of visual aesthetics of the webpage design. Four webpage designs were compared; the two designs used in the earlier study (one with the Time News Roman font and one with the Calibri font), and another two designs containing a mixture of both fonts.

Analysis of results supports the findings of the earlier study; the "serif" style (represented by the Time New Roman design) was perceived as having better visual aesthetics than the "sans-serif" style (represented by the Calibri design). Furthermore analysis of results also showed that the Times New Roman was also perceived as having better visual aesthetics than both of the mixed designs; i. e. mixing both styles in the same page (serif and san-serif) didn't improve perception of visual aesthetics.

However, these results were only significant on the overall perception of visual aesthetics (the overall questionnaire score) and on the craftsmanship scale; it wasn't significant in each of the other three parts of the questionnaire (representing the facets of visual aesthetics).

As in the earlier study, results, here too, showed that participants perceived the design as more classical than expressive. It would be interesting to see if the above results (regarding font styles) would hold in cases of more aesthetically expressive designs.

Finally, the issue of a possible role of the context of use on perception of visual aesthetics of webpage design and how that might have affected the results of the current study need to be addressed in future research. Findings of several previous studies have indicated possible effects of context of use (serious context vs. funny and pleasurable context) on perception of visual aesthetics of webpage design [3 and 9]. The context of use in the current study can be considered as a more serious one. It would be interested to see if outcomes of the test would change in case of a more pleasurable context.

References

1. Altaboli, A.: Investigating the effects of font styles on perceived visual aesthetics of website interface design. In: Kurosu, M. (ed.) Human-Computer Interaction, Part I, HCII 2013. LNCS, vol. 8004, pp. 549–554. Springer, Heidelberg (2013)
2. Bernard, M., Chaparro, B., Mills, M., Halcomb, C.: Comparing the effects of text size and format on the readability of computer-displayed Times New Roman and Arial text. Int. J. Human-Computer Studies 59, 823–835 (2003)
3. De Angeli, A., Sutcliffe, A., Hartmann, J.: Interaction, usability and aesthetics: what influences users' preferences? In: Proceedings of the Sixth ACM Conference on Designing Interactive Systems, PA (June 2006)
4. Dix, A., Finlay, D., Abowd, G., Beale, R.: Human-Computer Interaction, 3rd edn. Pearson Education (2004)

5. Ling, J., Van Schaik, P.: The influence of font type and line length on visual search and information retrieval in web pages. Int. J. Human-Computer Studies 64, 395–404 (2006)
6. Laviea, T., Tractinsky, N.: Assessing dimensions of perceived visual aesthetics of web sites. Int. J. Human-Computer Studies 60, 269–298 (2004)
7. Moshagen, M., Thielsch, M.T.: Facets of visual aesthetics. Int. J. Hum.-Comput. Stud. 68(10), 689–709 (2010)
8. Sheedy, J., Subbaram, M., Zimmerman, A., Hayes, J.: Text Legibility and the Letter Superiority Effect. Human Factors 47(4), 797–815 (2005)
9. Van Schaik, P., Ling, J.: The role of context in perceptions of the aesthetics web pages over time. Int. J. Human-Computer Studies 67, 79–89 (2009)

You Can Interact with Your TV and You May Like It an Investigation on Persuasive Aspects for an iDTV Application

Samuel B. Buchdid, Roberto Pereira, and M. Cecília C. Baranauskas

Institute of Computing, University of Campinas,
Av. Albert Einstein N1251, Campinas-SP, Brazil
{buchdid,rpereira,cecilia}@.ic.unicamp.br

Abstract. Interactive Digital TV (iDTV) is a technology that has many challenges that surround it and that may discourage the passive viewers to interact with TV. To face the challenging scenario of designing for iDTV, we draw on the Social Aware Computing (SAC) approach to design, looking at the problem and proposing solutions on various abstraction levels (informal, formal and technical) according to the viewpoint of different stakeholders, including prospective end users. This paper presents a motivational analysis conducted through Analytical and Empirical evaluations and Questionnaires, to understand whether and how an iDTV application designed through the SAC motivates users to interact with it. As results, our analysis pointed out application features that are likely to motivate users to interact, and features that emerged during the design process and were reflected on the application prototype. Moreover, we discuss whether and how the SAC design process may support iDTV applications that make sense to users and motivate them to interact.

Keywords: Interactive Digital TV, Persuasive Design, HCI, Socially Aware Computing, Organizational Semiotics, Participatory Design, Design Patterns.

1 Introduction

The Interactive Digital TV (iDTV) is an emerging technology considered a promising medium for the dissemination of information, potentially contributing to social and digital inclusion by reducing barriers to knowledge. However, iDTV presents some problems that impact directly on iDTV usage and may discourage the viewer to change his/her passive posture in front of the TV. Examples of problems include: i) those inherent to iDTV technology (e.g., the interaction limited by the remote control, the limited processing resources and memory, the low transmission speed); ii) those inherited from the culture of using the analogical TV (e.g., the lack of habit to interact with television content, the usual presence of other viewers in the same physical space); and iii) those associated with technological convergence where the TV is inserted (e.g., devices can either support the television usage or compete with it) [5, 10]. Furthermore, every emergent technology suffers from a lack of references, processes and artifacts for supporting their application design [10].

A. Marcus (Ed.): DUXU 2014, Part IV, LNCS 8520, pp. 208–219, 2014.

To face these challenges, some authors point out the need for considering social, emotional and motivational issues in the design of iDTV applications, including the end user viewpoint and features of everyday life in order to promote the acceptance of this kind of application. Such elements include: i) design principles to support user interactivity during leisure pursuits in domestic settings [6]; ii) ethnographic studies in order to understand users' media behavior and expectations [2]; and iii) participatory design methodologies and interactive practices to propose design solutions [18]. We draw on Socially Aware Computing [1], grounded on Organizational Semiotics [11] and Participatory Design [14], to make a social responsible design of iDTV applications: a design that meets the needs of the different stakeholders involved and of the complex social context in which the application is/will be situated.

This paper presents and discusses results of an investigation on motivational aspects for promoting the use and adoption of iDTV applications. This investigation was grounded on the persuasive perspective proposed by Fogg [8], and considered three different kinds of evaluation: empirical evaluation, analytical evaluation, and questionnaires. As a result we have the intention to show motivational characteristics that emerged from iDTV application designed through the socially aware design.

The paper is organized as follows: Section 2 introduces the motivational theoretical and methodological background of our study; Section 3 shows the socially aware approach proposed to design an iDTV application in a TV Show's situated context; Section 4 describes the method for evaluating the prototype for an iDTV application; Section 5 presents and discusses the main findings from case study; and Section 6 presents our final considerations and directions for future research.

2   Theoretical and Methodological Foundation

By definition, motivation is "the act or process of giving someone a reason for doing something" [13]. Motivation emerges from internal needs (which are driven by an interest or enjoyment in the task) and external influences (which are influences of the environment to motivate the individual performing tasks to be rewarded or not to be punished) [17]. In this sense, there are several approaches investigating motivation from different theoretical viewpoints (e.g., biological, physiological, psychological, social) that complement or opposes each other. Some studies have proposed general theories to account for commonalities among all human motives, and others have studied specific motives such as hunger, sex, affiliation, and achievement [9].

According to Torning and Oinas-Kukkonen [21], there are at least four recognized key computer-based fields of research for persuasive systems and design: i) Human-computer interaction: investigates ways of designing computer systems that are usable and understandable, including how information can be gathered for such designs. ii) Computer-mediated communication: investigates how technology affects modes of communication (synchronous and asynchronous) and impacts on them. iii) Information systems: approaches the software, databases and the content provided for the user in a systemic way, looking for designing a system that will bring benefits to both the organization and the end user (often working in their habitat). iv) Affective computing: investigating the creation of systems in order to recognize, interpret, and process human emotions.

Literature also presents models for providing a systematic way to think about the factors underlying behavior change in the process of designing and evaluating persuasive systems, even for those who do not have an understanding on human psychology. For instance, Persuasive Systems Design (PSD) model [15] provides an extensive conceptualization of technology-mediated persuasion. It can be used to prescribe persuasive designs and software requirements; it also supports evaluations by categorizing and mapping persuasive elements. Reeve [17] proposes a framework to understand motivation and emotion which has been used, for example, in the HCI field for the design of Residential Energy Feedback Systems [16]. Other example is the work of Scialdone and Zhang [19] that present a theoretic-motivational model that helps to identify elements (from primitive human needs to formation and attainment of a specific behavior and goal) that can to inform design decisions of Information and Communication Technologies.

The Conceptual Persuasive Model used in this study is named "Fogg Behavior Model" (FMB) [8]. The FMB aggregates important aspects of behavior change (e.g., ability) that can be handled directly by HCI concepts (e.g., usability). It is also used to identify problems in systems that fail to achieve the intended outcomes (e.g., iDTV). Thus, it seems to be a theoretical framework suitable for our study.

2.1   Fogg Behavior Model

The FBM considers three main factors (motivation, ability and triggers) that influence people's behavior change. The *motivation* factor is related to elements such as pleasure, pain, hope, fear, and social acceptance to perform the target behavior. The *ability* factor is related to simplicity in design, which makes the system easy for the user to perform the target behavior. Finally, a *trigger* is something that tells/incites people to perform the behavior right now (e.g., prompts, cues, and calls to action). In summary, the model assumes that to perform a target behavior the person must have sufficient motivation and ability, and must be driven by an effective trigger. Moreover, all the three factors must be simultaneously present for the behavior to occur.

In this sense, in a design process of persuasive technology, the FBM may help the designer to direct his/her efforts more efficiently. For example, if the motivation factor is low, the designer can focus on this aspect during the design process. The same may happen to the ability and trigger factors. For clarifying the motivation, ability and trigger factors, Fogg [8] associated key elements to them – see Table 1.

People have different profiles: they can be more easily or hardly motivated, or have more or less abilities, or may be more or less stimulated by a same trigger. These factors vary according to the individual, but they also vary according to the context. Thus, designers should identify the audience and the context (e.g., media type, use time and location) because the more diverse they are, more complex is to design a motivational intervention [8].

Table 1. All three FMB's factors and their elements

Factors	Elements	Description
Motivation	Pleasure / Pain	They are (almost) an immediate motivator; It works as a primitive response and it is similar to activities related to self-preservation and propagation of our genes (e.g., hunger and sex).
Motivation	Hope / Fear	They are characterized by anticipation of an outcome (e.g., hope and fear are the expectation of something good or bad to happen, respectively).
Motivation	Social Acceptance / Rejection	They control our social behavior, from the clothes we wear to the language we use. In practice, people are motivated to maintain social accepted behaviors and avoid situations they are socially rejected.
Ability	Time	It refers to demand of time for a target behavior to occur; if we don't have available time, then, the behavior is not simple (e.g.; form that has 100 fields).
Ability	Money	It is associated with financial resources; if a target behavior costs money and we don't have money, then the behavior is not simple.
Ability	Physical Effort	It refers to physical effort to reach the target behavior, which may not be simple (e.g., travel long distances without transportation).
Ability	Brain Cycles	It refers to mental ability to reach the target behavior; If performing a target behavior causes us to think hard, that might not be simple (e.g., a hard math puzzle)
Ability	Social Deviance	It refers to the difficulty of getting a behavior that breaks society's rules (e.g., wearing pajamas to a city council meeting).
Ability	Non-Routine	Refers to the fact that a behavior becomes simpler if it is part of the people's daily routine (e.g., buying gas at the same station)
Trigger	Spark	It should be used when a person lacks motivation to perform a target behavior. It should be used in tandem with a motivational element (e.g., videos that inspire hope).
Trigger	Facilitator	It is proper for users that have high motivation but lack ability. The goal is to trigger the behavior while making the behavior easier to occur (e.g. one click can get the job done).
Trigger	Signal	It works best when people have both the ability and the motivation to perform the target behavior. The signal doesn't seek to motivate people or simplify the task, but to serve as a reminder (e.g., traffic light that turns red or green).

3   Situated Design

The Socially Aware Computing (SAC) [1] is an approach to make a socially responsible, participatory and universal design as a process and a product. The SAC draws on Organizational Semiotics (SO) [11] to understand the context in which the technical system is/will be inserted and the main forces that direct or indirectly act on it; and Participatory Design (PD) [14] to understand the situated context. Workshops involving heterogeneous groups of people who may influence and/or may be influenced by the problem being discussed and/or the solution to be designed are proposed within SAC.

SAC understands design as a wave that starts in the society and progresses through the informal and formal layers in order to build the technical system — see "SAC's instance" layers in Fig. 1. The informal level refers to social norms that regulate behavior, beliefs, values, habits, culture, etc., that drive people's behavior. The formal level involves rules and procedures created to explain mechanistic and repetitive tasks. The technical system is only part of the formal level of an organization, which can be automated. Once the technical system is projected, the wave returns impacting on the informal and formal layers, on society.

The study scenario was the "Terra da Gente" (TdG) program ("Our Land" in English), one of the several TV shows produced by EPTV: a Brazilian broadcasting company whose program reaches a region in Brazil that includes 300 cities and more than 10 million citizens [7]. The TdG program explores local fauna and flora, fishing and regional cuisine, and reaches people from all ages, mainly adults and elderly people [20]. The object of study is the design of an iDTV application for TdG, named iTG, which should reach the TV show's audience. For designing the iTG, we conducted different activities during four participatory workshops in the situated context of EPTV. Ten participants involved directly and indirectly in the problem domain, with different profiles (e.g., designer, engineers, researchers, TV program director and interns), participated in these workshops.

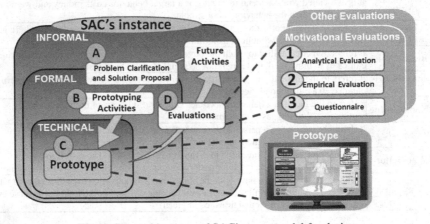

Fig. 1. Situated instance of SAC's meta-model for design

Fig. 1 presents Baranauskas' SAC approach to design [1] instantiated for the situated context of EPTV. In this context, we used artifacts from OS and created new practices for supporting participatory and situated design activities. For instance, activities encompassed the problem understanding and clarification, the analysis and organization of requirements for the application to be designed, and the generation of design ideas for the first prototype of the iTG (see "A" detail in Fig. 1). The produced ideas were materialized in prototyping activities through an adapted version of the Brain Draw participatory technique [3] ("B" detail) that made use of design patterns for iDTV [10]. Both *Balsamiq*® and *CogTool*® tools were used to create the interactive prototype ("C" detail). The final prototype (Fig. 2) was evaluated interactively by representatives from the target audience, by specialists in HCI, and also in a participatory practice with the workshops participants. These evaluation practices ("D" detail in Fig. 1) were important to identify problems and propose solutions before producing and broadcasting the first version of iTG application. The materials produced in these activities were reported in [3] and [4].

Fig. 2 highlights points that were reflected in the final prototype (from "A" to "F" details) and that emerged from different stages of the design process. For instance, "A" detail draws attention to a simple layout, which was suggested in problem clarification and solutions proposal stage, to prevent deviation of the television content and to complement it. The choice of remote control as the main interaction device, due to costs to viewers, also happened in the initial stage. The definitions of interface elements disposal and menu options emerged during the stage of drawing up ideas and prototyping ("B" detail). In this same stage, suggestions for the sub-page layouts ("D" and "E" details), and initial icon (see "F" detail) were made. The navigation project, which includes the remote control keys (see "C" detail), was defined in a design activity with Patterns and was refined during the construction of the final prototype.

Fig. 2. Application's screenshots

In addition to the situated and participatory activities, we applied questionnaires in each workshop. In the first we created a graph based on the FBM model, and asked the participants to represent the TdG viewer's behavior regarding the insertion/use of an iDTV application. Participants should mark an "X" to indicate where they think the behavior actually is, and a "Y" where they think the behavior should be (the desirable situation) (see Fig. 3).

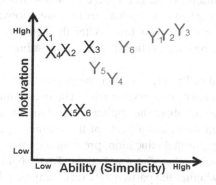

Fig. 3. Answers from the participants prospecting viewers behavior

Fig. 3 shows the answers of six participants: on the one hand, the "X" marks show that the participants believe the viewers to have high motivation to interact with an iDTV application because the audience's profile is exploratory and adventurous. However, the inexperience with iDTV applications indicates that viewers still have low skill. On the other hand, the "Y" marks indicate that participants believe the viewers will be motivated with the new technology and will acquire the necessary skill as soon as the application is available, achieving the activation line to promote the behavior change.

4   Motivational Evaluations

In this paper, we focus on the motivational evaluation of the interactive prototype from three different perspectives ("1", "2" and "3" details in Fig. 1) that were conducted to: *Goal 1*: indicate possible problems of interaction from motivational analysis. *Goal 2*: identify whether the prototyped application was able to motivate users to interact with it and watch the television program. *Goal 3*: prospect whether and how the socially aware design process is able to deal with persuasive issues that appeal the user. *Goal 4*: identify the motivational elements that appeared on the application, showing which of these elements appeared during the design process being reflected in the final prototype; and, *Goal 5*: raise useful ideas to promote the behavioral change on users of iDTV applications.

Analytical evaluation ("1" detail in Fig. 1): the prototype was analyzed according to 3 factors (motivation, ability and trigger) and theirs subfields (e.g., pleasure vs. pain, hope vs. fear, social acceptance vs. rejection) proposed in Fogg's model [8]. For this, HCI specialists explored all prototype screens and the possible interactions on them, mapping motivational features found in the prototype according to FBM.

Empirical evaluation ("2" detail in Fig. 1): an evaluation with prospective users interacting with the prototype was conducted for understanding the aspects that motivated, motivate, and supposedly will continue motivating them. The ease of use and triggers were also observed during the evaluation activity through the "Thinking Aloud" technique [12]. Participants' interaction and facial expressions were recorded under their informed consent. Here, users were invited to freely navigate through the prototype, and they were asked to say whatever they were looking at, thinking, doing, and feeling as they went about their task. After the activity, HCI experts analyzed the recordings and mapped motivational aspects according to FMB's factors and elements.

Questionnaires ("3" detail in Fig. 1): after the empirical evaluation, the prospective end users were asked to answer a questionnaire. The questionnaire aimed at identifying their general impressions about the application (subjective satisfaction), whether it discouraged or motivated them, and aspects of its usability. Questions were related to the user profile (e.g., age, formal education, previous experience using iDTV applications and mobiles, frequency that s/he watched the TdG program, etc.) and other general impressions (e.g.; whether the participants really enjoyed, liked moderately, were indifferent, didn't like so much or disliked the application; whether they had any suggestions for the application). The questionnaire also presented questions related to motivational issues, such as:

- **Motivational Axis:** What would be your main motivation to access the iTG application? And to continue accessing it? Do you consider that the iTG application will: i) motivate viewers to watch the TV Show, ii) indifferent (neither disturb nor motivate), or iii) disturb viewers when watching the TV Show. In what way?
- **Ability (simplicity) Axis:** Did you have any problem to interact with the iTG? Was (or was not) easy to interact with it? How? Why?

5   Results and Discussion

10 participants explored the prototype: 3 participants are 21-30 years old, 5 are 31-40 years old, 1 is 41-50 years old, and 1 participant is over 60 years old. Regarding their formal education: 1 has high school, 3 have bachelor's degree, 1 has specialization course, 3 have master's degree and 1 participant has a doctor's degree. None participant had previous experience using iDTV applications; 8 participants were aware of them, but had never seen any application; and 2 participants had seen them before. Furthermore, 6 have been watching the TdG program, although not often; 3 participants watch once a month; and 1 participant do not watch TdG.

The Analytical and Empirical Evaluations show that there are several pros and cons related to the motivational issues in the iTG context. Tables 2 and 3 present a summary of the results.

Table 2. Analytical and Empirical Evaluation – Motivational axis

Fac-tors	Ele-ments		Description	
			Analytical	*Empirical*
Motivation	Pleasure / Pain	pro	• Application content that complements the TV Shows • Entertainment features (e.g., Games and Pool) • iDTV application is an innovation	• Direct interaction with TV Show (e.g., Pools, Quiz, Fisherman Story) • Users feel motivated (happy) with formal (e.g., Localization/Mapp and Information/Curiosity) or informal (e.g., Fishing Game) content
		con		• When users want to use the application features, but they don't have the ability for it;
	Hope / Fear	pro	• "Help" and tips can minimize the fear of non-expert users to interact with a unknown technology	• Users hope that application content is related (or complement) the current TV Show. If necessary with next and previous TV Shows • The users feel motivated when they receive constant feedback from the application
		con	• Fear of iDTV application competes and distracts viewers from TV Show	• Non-technological users can be afraid to interact with new devices (cultural issues)
	Social Acceptance / Rejection	pro	• Simple application (allowing digital and social inclusion). • Content and language was designed to be familiar to TdG viewers	• Users are happy when they easily reach their goals (socially judged).
		con	• New technologies may be rejected by users	• Non-experts users are afraid of making mistakes (socially judged); they try to reach the goal by using trial and error approach. • Labels should be appropriate to target audience

In addition, the specialists understood that there are only 3 triggers in the application: i) initial icon: to call viewers to interact; ii) loading the application: to show that the application is starting; and iii) fishes appearing on the screen (in fishing game): to motivate viewers to continue watching the TV Show. All of them are trigger signals. The analysis of the prospective users interacting with the application indicated that the element designed to be the initial icon (see "F" detail in Fig. 1) would be sufficient for expert users, but not for the non-expert ones. Sparks and Facilitator triggers were not designed in the application because they are expected to come from the TdG magazine and the web portal.

Table 3. Analytical and Empirical Evaluation – Ability axis

Fac tors	Ele- ments		Description	
			Analytical	*Empirical*
Ability	Time	pro	• Simple application takes less time for interaction. • Structured and synthetic informations dispend less time from users.	• Having few information and requiring few interaction steps make it simple the use • Application allows taking notes (e.g., Localization/Maps and Receipt) without access to the internet. • User can open the applications only when and if they want. • Immediacy on TV of some features are important to application (e.g., Pool, Quiz, Informations)
		con	• Application will run just when TV show is running.	• Application is available only when the TV show is running • Non-expert users dispend time trying randomly options.
	Money	pro	• No money is necessary to access the application • Gifts can stimulate the users to interact	• Some users like when they earn gifts or money (e.g., a gift in the fishing game designed for the application)
	Physical Effort	pro	• Application has low hierarchical levels • Layout chosen to not disturb the TV content	• The application has few interaction levels: several interaction steps can disturb users from TV Show content.
		con	• Blind and handicapped users will have difficulties to interact	• Non-expert users will have difficulties to find uncommon remote control keys (e.g., the color keys).
	Brain Cycles	pro	• The application was designed to be simple (e.g., use of Arrows and OK keys)	• Intuitive layout favours the interaction
		con	• Remote control requires high cognitive abilities	• In the beginning non-experts feel lost interacting with the new technology
	Social Deviance	pro	• Remote control is the device more closer to viewers	
		con	• Interacting with TV is not in the culture of classic viewers (analogical TV)	• Elderly users suffer more influences from analogical TV habits (e.g., passivity)
	Non-Routine	pro		• Interacting with iDTV from second time makes the activity easier
		con	• Interact with iDTV applications is not part of the people's routine yet.	• The use of uncommon remote control keys (e.g., colour keys) may confuse non-expert users

The Questionnaire answered by the representatives from the target audience reinforced a favorable opinion about the interactive prototype. The 10 prospective users were able to understand and explore the prototype, indicating points related to both motivation and simplicity. From their responses to the Motivational axis on the evaluation questionnaire, 7 (70%) answered they consider that the iTG application would motivate viewers to watch the TV Show, and 3 (30%) answered it would be indifferent (neither disturb nor motivate). Participants suggested that their main motivation to access the iTG application would be: i) to access relevant content (curiosities, recipes, game fishing and exclusive content); ii) to view part of the content they missed in the TV Show; iii) to take note of information that is difficult to annotate during the TV show (e.g., recipe and directions); iv) to learn more about a new subject; v) to view the information quickly without watching the entire TV program. The last one conflicts with the TV Show interests. To continue accessing the iTG, users answered that the application should be updated for each new program with extra curiosities, new information, new games, and different recipes. From their responses related to the Ability axis, 8 (80%) answered they consider the iTG easy to interact, and 2 (20%) answered they had a few problems to interact with it. Problems were usually related to starting the application and choosing options referred by uncommon remote control keys (e.g., color and special keys).

5.1   Discussion

The evaluations presented in this paper were an important stage in the design process because they supported the understanding of motivational issues that were present or missing in the designed prototype. The three evaluations complemented each other, addressing specific points, from different perspectives, indicating possible problems of interaction (achieving our "*Goal 1*") and contributing to improve both the final application and the design process. For example, the evaluation conducted by HCI experts indicated possible problems of interaction and attention for the users (e.g., "The remote control requires high cognitive abilities"). These problems were reinforced in the evaluation with the prospective end users (e.g., "Non-expert users will have difficulties to find uncommon remote control keys, e.g., the color keys"), and other new issues emerged, such as "Labels should be appropriated to target audience".

The evaluation with prospective end users provided us information for achieving the "*Goal 2*" and showed a correct expectation from the professionals before design process – high motivation and a low ability (see Fig. 3). Although users found the application intuitive and easy to use, they had initial difficulties to interact with the prototype, in parts because of their lack of experience with iDTV applications. On the one hand, after a few interactions, users got more comfortable with the application and started to explore it, visiting its different features; this was reinforced by their answers to the questionnaire that stated the application is easy to interact and would motivate viewers to watch the TV Show. On the other hand, when some users feel lost, they try change the channel, turn off the TV device, try many remote key options or visit parts of application randomly. In general terms, this evaluation indicated that the prototype was able to motivate novice users to interact with it and watch to the television program.

As the answer to out *"Goal 3"*, the practices conducted according to the SAC perspective, favored the design of a prototype that is aware of the several iDTV challenges, including the technological ones and the diversity of the audience. The SAC holistic view, from the problem clarification to the prototype evaluation, allowed to deal with television problems (from technical to formal) and to propose an application that complies with technical questions and takes into account its target audience. The participatory activities, considering different stakeholders (e.g., designer, engineers, researches, and other stakeholders) encouraged the interaction among the participants and favored the existence of different views for the problem, where new solutions and ideas were contrasted and negotiated throughout the design process. For instance, the Fishing Game and the Pool were features that emerged from the design process (*"Goal 4"*) and generated controversy among workshop participants; nevertheless, they attracted attention from the users and pleased them. Because of its participatory and situated nature, the instance of SAC favored the design of features suitable to the TV Show (e.g., content and layout), and that motivated users during tests (*"Goal 5"*). This result suggests that the situated context favors the understanding of important aspects related to the values, habits, culture, needs, expectations, etc., from different stakeholders in the organization. These aspects would hardly be identified in a conventional design process detached from the organizational context.

During the design workshops, a resistance from participants to add motivational issues in the iTG application was identified. There are high investments from the company for producing and engineering content in order to please the audience, but as the iDTV application is still an evolving technology, the company believes it requires caution when investing.

6   Conclusion

While the iDTV comes as a promise to face social barriers to access the participatory and universal access to knowledge, it also suffers from problems that are inherent and that discourages user to interact with television applications. In this scenario, applications that promote behavior change and motivate viewers to interact are welcome. Design initiatives that understand the context in which the problem is inserted, the interests of key stakeholders and diversified audiences can be a differential to motivate viewers to interact effectively with the TV. In this paper, we explored the Fogg's persuasive approach on an iDTV application designed from a SAC [1] perspective.

The SAC approach generated an application with features in all motivational axes (motivation, ability and triggers), even without explicitly using any motivational artifact during the design process. In fact, most users responded positively to the questionnaire regarding their experience with the prototype. User also pointed out benefits in having an application that complements the television content. The analysis according to the FBM met the expectations for mapping motivational issues raised by the different evaluations and produced useful information for further design cycles. In future studies we intend to identify and adapt other persuasive techniques that can contribute along the SAC design process.

Acknowledgment. This research is partially funded by CNPq (#165430/2013-3) and FAPESP (#2013/02821-1). The authors specially thank the EPTV team, and the all participants who collaborated and authorized the use of their data in this paper.

References

1. Baranauskas, M.C.C.: Socially Aware Computing. In: VI International Conference on Engineering and Computer Education (ICECE 2009), pp. 1–5 (2009)
2. Bernhaupt, R., Weiss, A., Pirker, M., Wilfinger, D., Tscheligi, T.: Ethnographic Insights on Security, Privacy, and Personalization Aspects of User Interaction in Interactive TV. In: 8th International Interactive Conference on Interactive TV and Vide0 (EuroiTV 2010), pp. 187–196. ACM Press, New York (2010)
3. Buchdid, S.B., Pereira, R., Baranauskas, M.C.C.: Playing Cards and Drawing with Patterns: Situated and Participatory Practices for Designing iDTV Applications. In: 16th International Conference on Enterprise Information Systems (ICEIS 2014) (in press, 2014)
4. Buchdid, S.B., Pereira, R., Baranauskas, M.C.C.: Creating an iDTV Application from Inside a TV Company: A Situated and Participatory Approach. In: 15th International Conference on Informatics and Semiotics in Organisations (ICISO 2014) (in press, 2014)
5. Cesar, P., Chorianopoulos, K., Jensen, J.F.: Social Television and User Interaction. Computers in Entertainment-Social Television and User Interaction 6(1), 1–10 (2008)
6. Chorianopoulos, K.: Interactive TV Design That Blends Seamlessly with Everyday Life. In: Stephanidis, C., Pieper, M. (eds.) ERCIM Ws UI4ALL 2006. LNCS, vol. 4397, pp. 43–57. Springer, Heidelberg (2007)
7. EPTV Portal, http://www.viaeptv.com
8. Fogg, B.J.: A behavior model for persuasive design. In: 4th International Conference on Persuasive Technology (Persuasive 2009), Article No. 40, pp. 1–7. ACM Press (2009)
9. Kassin, S.: Essentials of Psychology. Prentice Hall, Upper Saddle River (2004)
10. Kunert, T.: User-Centered Interaction Design Patterns for Interactive Digital Television Applications. Springer, Berlin (2009)
11. Liu, K.: Semiotics in Information Systems Engineering. Cambridge University Press, Cambridge (2000)
12. Lewis, C.H.: Using the "Thinking Aloud" Method in Cognitive Interface Design. IBM Research Report RC-9265, Yorktown Heights, NY (1982)
13. Merriam-WebsterDictionary, http://www.merriam-webster.com
14. Muller, M.J., Haslwanter, J.H., Dayton, T.: Participatory Practices in the Software Lifecycle. In: Helander, M.G., Landauer, T.K., Prabhu, P.V. (eds.) Handbook of Human-Computer Interaction, 2nd edn., pp. 255–297. Elsevier, Amsterdam (1997)
15. Oinas-kukkonen, H., Harjumaa, M.: Persuasive Systems Design: Key Issues, Process Model, and System Features. Communications of the Association for Information Systems 24, article 28 (2009)
16. Piccolo, L.S.G., Baranauskas, M.C.C.: Basis and Prospects of Motivation Informing Design: Requirements for Situated Eco-feedback Technology. In: 11th Brazilian Symposium on Human Factors in Computer Systems (IHC 2012), pp. 137–146. ACM Press, New York (2012)
17. Reeve, J.: Understanding Motivation and Emotion, 5th edn. Wiley, Hoboken (2009)
18. Rice, M., Alm, N.: Designing new interfaces for digital interactive television usable by older adults. Computers in Entertainment-Social Television and User Interaction 6(1), article 6, 1–20 (2008)
19. Scialdone, M., Zhang, P.: Deconstructing Motivations of ICT Adoption and Use: A Theoretical Model and its Applications to Social ICT. In: iConference, University of Illinois (2010)
20. Terra da Gente Portal, http://www.terradagente.com.br
21. Torning, K., Oinas-Kukkonen, H.: Persuasive system design: state of the art and future directions. In: 4th International Conference on Persuasive (Persuasive 2009), article 30. ACM Press, New York (2009)

Mood Boards as a Universal Tool for Investigating Emotional Experience

Huang-Ming Chang[1,2,*], Marta Díaz[2], Andreu Català[2],
Wei Chen[1], and Matthias Rauterberg[1]

[1] Designed Intelligence Group, Department of Industrial Design, Eindhoven University of
Technology, Eindhoven, The Netherlands
[2] CETpD Research Center, Technical University of Catalonia, Vilanova i la Geltrú, Spain
{h.m.chang,w.chen,g.w.m.rauterberg}@tue.nl,
{marta.diaz,andreu.catala}@upc.edu

Abstract. Emotion is an essential part of user experience. While researchers are striving for new research tools for evaluate emotional experiences in design, designers have been using experience-based tools for studying emotions in practice, such as mood boards. Mood boards were developed for communicating emotional qualities between designers and clients, but have not yet been considered as an evaluation tool for investigating emotional experience. In t his study we examined whether design students and non-design students have similar criteria in evaluating these mood boards. The results showed that the inter-rater reliability among all participants were considerably high, which suggested that mood boards are potential to be used as an evaluation tool for research on emotion.

Keywords: mood boards, emotion, evaluation tool, user experience.

1 Introduction

In recent years, the focus of human-computer interaction (HCI) has shifted from functionality and usability to 'humans' [1]. The concept of user experience (UX) is widely embraced by the HCI community and raises many new challenges to researchers and designers [2]. As emotion is an essential part of our mental lives, one of the main challenges is to investigate the emotional aspect of user experience [3], and deliver these observed emotional qualities back to designers for initiating design processes [4]. While many researchers are striving for new tools to investigate emotions in design, designers have been using several experience-based tools for their work and some of these tools may be useful for evaluating emotions.

The use of mood boards is versatile. It has long been used for communicating emotional qualities between designers and clients [5], and the process of mood board making also serves as a resource for creative thinking [6]. While making mood boards has become an essential skill for design practice, we have seen its potential to be a research tool specifically for measuring non-verbal emotional experience. In the present study, we first review the current development of emotion evaluation tools in

A. Marcus (Ed.): DUXU 2014, Part IV, LNCS 8520, pp. 220–231, 2014.

design research, and revisit the procedure of making mood boards from a psychological perspective. Based on this framework, we conducted an experiment to examine the effectiveness of mood boards in expressing emotional qualities across interpretations of people with design and non-design backgrounds, and discuss how this new finding may inform future research on emotions.

2   A Psychological Perspective on Mood Boards

Since emotion is a psychological phenomenon that cannot be directly captured, research on emotion usually relies on a stimulus-response paradigm, which encompasses emotion elicitation and emotion recognition [7]. Researchers are able to infer the emotional quality that is induced in the subject according to the content of the stimuli and the corresponding emotional responses. For example, a subject might have experienced happiness because (1) the stimuli were funny pictures and (2) the subject also reported happiness. This stimulus-response paradigm has directed most of the contemporary psychological research on emotion, and also influenced other related areas, such as design research on emotions.

2.1   Emotion Evaluation Tools in the Design Field

Kansei Engineering [8] was developed as a consumer-oriented approach for new product development. Researchers in Kansei Engineering intend to investigate the relationship between consumers' psychological feelings and product features, such form, shape, color, and any perceptual qualities. Designers can thus generate new product concepts by manipulating product features. This method can also be used to evaluate qualities of new concept at the early stage of design process [9]. The Japanese word 'Kansei' encompasses broad concepts, referring to all of which are conceived as mental responses to external stimuli, including emotion, senses, and aesthetics [8]. Research in Kansei Engineering often uses semantic scales with perceptual and emotional qualities, which may give rise to some concerns about cultural differences and product categories [10]. For example, the expression in Japanese and English on certain perceptual qualities may differ; kitchen appliances and automobiles should use different sets of semantic scales.

Jordan [11] developed a questionnaire specifically for evaluating *positive* emotional experience about products. This questionnaire encompasses 14 questions about specific emotions, such as entertained, excited, and satisfaction. Taking into account the feasibility across products and cultures, this questionnaire provided optional open-ended questions that allowed the experimenter and the subject to add new words. While Kansei Engineering and Jordan's questionnaire focused on physical products, several new evaluation tools for measuring user experience were proposed in recent years. User experience questionnaire (UEQ) [12] used a similar approach to Kansei Engineering but shifted the focus from products to users. Thus, UEQ removed adjectives describing physical appearance of physical products (e.g. shape and color) and included more words for describing cognitive load, emotional feelings and preferences.

While most evaluation tools are intended to derive immediate responses from subjects, a tool called iScale [13] was developed for observing long-term, continuous user experiences. This tool requires users to recall their long-term experiences periodically while using a new product in their daily lives. Unlike other tools using likert scales, iScale takes a novel approach, asking users to draw a curve to indicate the changes in their emotional experiences related to the product. However, this curve-drawing approach does not aim to acquire exact emotional qualities, but to serve as a reference for tracing pleasant or unpleasant events that occurred, which allows designers to 'reconstruct' the past and solve potential problems of the product accordingly.

However, the abovementioned evaluation tools are language dependent. Although the interpretations in affective meaning is universal at a certain degree [14], various modalities of emotional responses are universally valid and might benefit non-verbal emotion communications, such as facial expressions [15]. PrEmo [16] was developed based on this assumption, using facial expressions and body gestures with animated cartoon characters to illustrate different emotional qualities. Subjects could thus fill this questionnaire through self-reports as an instrument for measuring consumers' emotional responses specifically to product appearance.

In addition to the abovementioned tools, there are more new tools released in recent years, e.g. [17, 18]. Most design researchers apply research-based approach to investigate product emotions [4] and endeavor to develop systematic procedures for evaluating emotional experience. However, how to study emotion in design practice is rarely discussed. Over the past years, designers have been using experience-based tools, such as mood boards, to study emotions. Comparing to systematic tools, experience-based tools are usually quick-and-dirty solutions and do not have strict term of use. On the other hand, the validity of experience-based tools is difficult to measure so that this kind of tool is rarely discussed in empirical studies

2.2   Revisiting 'Mood Boards'

Mood boards are a collection of visual images gathered together to represent an emotional responses to a design brief [19]. It is a visual and sensory instrument for designers to communicate with each other and also with the clients [6]. This tool functions as a non-verbal medium communicating complex and delicate emotional qualities that are difficult to express through languages. The process of mood board making can stimulate insightful discussions [6, 19], providing inspirations at the early stage of concept development [9]. In order to support mood board making, various modalities of interactive technologies were applied to developing digital mood board [20], which enable designers and clients to co-create mood boards effectively.

Traditionally, mood board making were solely for designers. Since mood board making is technically easy and simple, some researchers have tried to use mood boards as a catalyst in focus groups [21]. Similar to the *contextmapping* approach [22], mood board making may trigger more inputs from target users and help designers discover deeper insights about user needs and aspiration towards products. This has shown the potential of mood boards to be used as a tool for capturing emotional experiences in different contexts. Today, mood board making has become an essential skill for designers. Several studies have discussed how to teach and apply this technique in design education [5, 19, 23]. It appears that most designers are trained to translate emotional qualities into mood boards – a visual manifestation that associates with the given content, e.g. products and brands. However, this technique did not gain adequate credits in terms of scientific evidence. It is necessary to assess the validity of mood boards to be an effective tool for studying emotions in design research.

2.3   Mood Boards as an Emotion Evaluation Tool for Designers

A general context of use of mood boards can be illustrated as follows (see Fig. 1). In the early stage of the design process, one of the primary tasks is to define emotional qualities of the new product. To initiate this undertaking, designers usually start with the 'design theme' of the given project, such as the brand image of the client and the marketing position of the new product. After a thorough understanding of the theme, designers can thus make mood boards to visualize predefined emotional qualities. These mood boards serve as part of the key references for later stages of product development. Designers have to discuss with their clients about the mood boards to identify the common goal of the project, and also talk with target users in order to obtain useful insights.

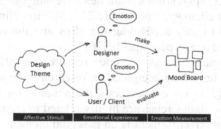

Fig. 1. A psychological perspective on mood board making in design practice

From a psychological perspective, the above process can be decomposed into two stimuli-response processes. The 'design theme' of the given project can be conceived as a mutual affective stimulus to bot designers and users/clients. After both of them have been primed with the emotional experience, designers make mood boards as a self-report outcome, and then users/clients provide their evaluation according to their subjective emotional experience. Designers need to modify their mood boards until a certain consensus has been built.

A preliminary studies have revealed that design students share a common perception of mood boards [23]. The author recruited a group of design students to create mood boards according to two general terms, 'masculine' and 'feminine', and asked them to give ratings to the mood boards created by other students depending on how well the mood boards represent the concept of masculine and feminine. The results suggested a consistency for both male and female students in terms of the concept of 'masculine' and 'feminine'. This finding is promising, but numbers of concerns need to be taken into account in order to prove the validity of mood boards as a useful tool in a more complex design task.

First of all, it is necessary to verify if mood boards are emotionally meaningful for both designers and users/clients (i.e. individuals who are not trained as a designer). While most designers are trained to make mood boards, they are also *experienced* in interpreting and justifying mood boards. Although mood boards are assumed to be a non-verbal emotional communication tool, it has not yet clarified if users share the same underlying criteria in justifying mood boards with designers. In order to apply mood boards as a universal tool for evaluating emotions for the general population, it is important to examine whether mood boards can be self-explained affective content to both designers and users.

Second, in the study of [23] the raters (i.e. the design students) also participated in the task of making mood boards. This would lead to a priming effect because the raters had thought attentively about the themes for creating mood boards, and would have anticipated what elements might be included in the final mood boards. We propose to include users as the role of rater in order to avoid priming effects, and this setting is also closer to how mood board making is applied in design practice.

Lastly, the stimuli for eliciting emotions in designers and users should be more immersive, emotionally rich, and generic. Most previous studies used static pictures to demonstrate the visual appearance of products, such as color, shape, and materials [8, 16]. However, this content is too feature specific, and is not suitable for the early stage of product development. Moreover, the selection of media type should also be taken into account. Several psychological studies have suggested that film clips are an effective media type for eliciting emotions [7, 24, 25]. Film clips are relatively short, intuitively powerful, and easily accessible; the clips and the procedure for viewing them can be standardized across participants [26].

We consider TV commercials as a proper resource for affective stimuli in our study. TV commercials have long been used in research on emotions specifically for consumer psychology [27]. TV commercials are suitable for our research because affective reactions to TV commercials are highly related to buying behaviors [28] and the symbolic meaning of advertisement is an essential element in visual communications between products and consumers [29]. Moreover, mood board making is closely related to the brand image of the product as it is often used in the early stage of product development [21].

The logic of our study is as follows. TV commercials of specific brands serve as affective stimuli. At the first stage, several professional designers would be recruited to create mood boards for each of the selected commercials. Mood board making in the present study should focus on the emotional qualities rather than design features. The mood boards are considered as representations of the emotional qualities delivered by the TV commercials. In the second stage – the experiment – participants are presented with the same TV commercials. After watching each commercial, participant need to compare their emotional feelings with the emotional qualities represented by the mood boards and gives rankings based on their subjective evaluation.

3   Making Mood Boards

The products of the TV commercials should belong to the same category in order that the results for the two commercials can be comparable. Two TV commercials of automobile brands, BMW [30] and Jeep [31], were selected as affective stimuli. Both of these two commercials were one minute long. The content of these two commercials represents feminine and masculine images based on the definition of Jungian theory of archetypes on Anima and Hero [32]. The selection process followed our previous work on analyzing symbolic meanings in modern movies [33].

Twelve Taiwanese professional designers were invited to participate in mood board making. They first watched one of the two commercials and created an image-only mood board, and repeated the same task for the other commercial. The display of the two commercials followed a random order. Designers were asked to make mood boards to describe their own emotional feelings about the content of the commercials and ignore their preoccupied impressions about the brand and its product features. In order to standardize the resources they used for creating mood boards, an online mood board making software called 'moodshare' [34] was used to perform the task. Therefore, 24 mood boards were created for the later experiment.

4   Experiment

While it has been revealed that mood boards are valid for designers, in this experiment we intended to verify whether non-design students and design students gave similar rankings over mood boards. If the answer was positive, mood boards could thus be useful for investigating emotional experience among individuals who were with or without a design background. A qualitative questionnaire was applied to collect more information about the criteria for justifying the quality of the mood boards.

Our experiment was conducted at the Usability Laboratory of CETpD research center at the Polytechnic University of Catalonia, and the design studio of the Department of Industrial Design at National Taiwan University of Technology. There were 36 design students and 16 non-design students, including 25 Females and 27 males, volunteered to participate in our experiment. The average age of the participants was 24.46 years old (SD = 4.96). The students were originally from 11 countries; 22 participants were from Asia; 26 were from Europe; 4 were from South America. The experiment followed a within-subject design. Each session accommodated one participant and thus every participant performed all the tasks respectively.

4.1   Procedure

The procedure of our experiment is as follows (see fig. 2). Firstly, an introduction was given to the participant and the participant needed to fill in an informed consent form for the experiment. After signing the agreement, the participant was seated in our laboratory, which was arranged as a usual living room to make the participant feel comfortable and relaxed. The visual part of the video was projected onto a white wall (display dimensions are 3m x 2m) while the audio part of the video was delivered via wireless headphones. When the above setting was ready, the light in the laboratory was dimmed in order to make the participant more immersed in the video presentations. The two TV commercials were play in random order. After finishing viewing one of the videos, the participant was then asked to fill the questionnaire. The questionnaire encompassed two parts; the first part was providing keywords to describe his or her emotional experience about the video; the second part was to rank mood boards according to the participant's own emotional experiences about the video.

Fig. 2. The procedure of the experiment. First, the participant watched one of the two commercials, wrote down keywords and then gave rankings for mood boards. The same order repeated for the other commercial.

The keywords served as qualitative data that represented the participant's perceived emotional qualities and denoted the prominent elements that attracted his or her attention. The participant was asked to focus on the content of the video rather than the brand of the commercial although the influence of the brand of the commercial might still affect the judgment of the participant. After this part of questionnaire was finished, the participant was led to the wall that presented mood boards corresponding to the given commercial. All the mood boards were presented at the same time in order to provide an overview, and the participant could look closer into each mood board to give rankings. The mood boards were created earlier by professional designers in the first stage, representing the emotional qualities that were perceived and expressed by them. The participant was asked to give rankings for the 12 mood boards for each commercial according to his or her overall viewing experience. The mood board that was most relevant should be ranked as number 1, and the second relevant as number 2, down to the least relevant which is number 12. The participant performed the same task for both the two commercials respectively.

4.2   Results

In most cases, a Pearson correlation is a valid estimator of inter-rater reliability, but only when meaningful pairings are available between two raters, but it is not suitable for more than two raters. An intra-class correlation (ICC) was developed for estimating inter-rater reliability on quantitative data [35]. We applied the analysis on intra-class correlation using a two-way-random, average-measure model. The results indicated that the inter-rater reliability among all rankings given by all participants is remarkably high (ICC(2, 52) = 0.939, F(23,1175) = 15.7 , p < 0.001, 95% confidence interval for ICC population values: 0.898 < ICC < 0.969), which indicates that design and non-design students showed similar opinions on how the mood boards matched their emotional experience. In order to examine if there are significant differences between the rankings of mood boards, we used a non-parametric repeated-measures analysis of variance, i.e. the Friedman Test. For the mood boards of BMW commercial, a Friedman test revealed a significant effect of Group on Value ($X^2(11) = 60.461$, $p < 0.001$). Similarly, the same test on the rankings for the mood boards of the Jeep commercial also revealed a significant effect ($X^2(11) = 198.855$, $p < 0.001$). The results suggested that there are significant main effects on the rankings of the mood boards for the two commercials respectively.

Table 1. The results of the descriptive analyses and the post-hoc test for pairwise comparison on the rankings for the mood boards. Twelve designers participated in this study (ID alphabetically ranging from A to L). Only the top 3 and the bottom 3 of the twelve mood boards are reported.

		BMW Commercial (Anima)			Jeep Commercial (Hero)	
	ID	Ranking	Post-hoc	ID	Ranking	Post-hoc
Top 3	K	4.80 (SD=3.23)	K-H: p = 0.003	G	3.65 (SD=2.79)	G-H: p < 0.001
	E	4.92 (SD=3.17)	K-B: p < 0.001	K	3.80 (SD=2.87)	G- I: p < 0.001
			K-C: p < 0.001			G-C: p < 0.001
	D	5.22 (SD=3.01)	E-H: p = 0.006	E	4.33 (SD=3.25)	K-H: p < 0.001
			E-B: p < 0.001			K- I: p < 0.001
Bottom 3	H	7.57 (SD=3.13)	E-C: p < 0.001	H	8.82 (SD=2.45)	K-C: p < 0.001
	B	8.02 (SD=3.25)	D-H: p = 0.028	I	9.55 (SD=2.60)	E-H: p < 0.001
			D-B: p = 0.002			E- I: p < 0.001
	C	8.43 (SD=2.68)	D-C: p < 0.001	C	9.88 (SD=2.44)	E-C: p < 0.001

Thus, we proceeded to post-hoc analyses. The Wilcoxon-Nemenyi-McDonald-Thompson test was developed specifically for a post-hoc test that enables pairwise comparisons for non-parametric repeated measures data [36]. In Table 1, we presented the results of descriptive analyses and the pairwise comparisons between the top three and bottom three mood boards for both two commercials. It needs to be noted that each of the top three mood boards is significantly better than any of the bottom three mood boards. It is noticeable that part of the top three and bottom three mood boards for BMW and Jeep commercials were made by the same designers (designer K and E in top 3; designer H and C in bottom 3). The top ranked mood boards for the two commercials are presented in Fig. 3 and 4. It can be seen that the numbers of the images included in each mood board are different. We performed Person's Chi-squared test to examine if there is a significant correlation between the number of the images in a mood board and its ranking. The results showed that there was a negative correlation between the numbers of images and rankings ($r = - 0.17$, $n = 1224$, $p < 0.001$). The results were reasonable because more images could accommodate richer information that communicates trivial emotional qualities.

Fig. 3. The top ranked mood board for the BMW commercial (by designer 'K' in Table 1.)

Fig. 4. The top ranked mood board for the Jeep commercial (by designer 'G' in Table 1.)

Table 2. The keywords provided by the participants for the two commercials, ordered by the average counts of the appearance of the words in the coding themes

BMW Commercial (Anima)		
Theme	Average Counts	Examples
Superior	1.31 (SD=1.39)	Modern, Admirable, Quality, Aesthetic, Stylish, Art
Home	1.25 (SD=1.19)	Relaxing, Happy, Comfort, Safe, Enjoy, Life, Warm
Sensual	1.19 (SD=1.34)	Breeze, Air, Floating, Soft, Vibration, Smooth, Gentle
Elegance	1.10 (SD=1.09)	Tranquil, Calm, Peace, Harmonious, Slow, Steady
Nature	1.08 (SD=1.45)	Freedom, Liberty, Adventure, Explore, Wild, Jump
Strength	1.00 (SD=1.07)	Velocity, Power, Momentum, Sprint, Streamline, Intense
Feminine	1.00 (SD=1.31)	Emotional, Attractive, Desire, Sexy, Dream, Reminiscing
Jeep Commercial (Hero)		
Craft	1.52 (SD=1.42)	Handmade, Perfection, Concentrate, Texture, Precision
Strength	1.25 (SD=1.52)	Fight, Strong, Rise, Tension, Heavy, Robust, Force
Trials	1.19 (SD=1.68)	Strive, Lonely, Challenge, Battle, Pain, Sweat, Frustrated
Hero	1.08 (SD=1.22)	Epic, Brave, Passion, Determination, Honest, Honor
Rebirth	0.79 (SD=1.04)	New life, Achievement, New horizon, Job well done
Mental	0.77 (SD=1.06)	Expectation, Projection, Motivation, Ambitious, Intention

The keywords given by the participants serve as references for inferring the underlying criteria that were used for ranking the mood boards. We applied the Ground theory to code the keywords in order to identify various themes [37]. After coding, we conducted a descriptive analysis on the numbers of appearance of words in each theme (see Table 2). It can be seen that the participants rarely refer to certain emotional qualities directly, but used a large amount of sensory words, analogies, and metaphors. Combining the keywords in the same theme allowed us to associate the emotional qualities perceived by the participants, e.g. the feeling of being home.

5   Discussion

These preliminary results have confirmed the reliability of using mood boards as a tool for investigating emotional experience among a general population. Furthermore, since the mood boards used in our study were made without adding any text, it has revealed the capability of mood boards to express non-verbal emotional qualities. Traditional research on emotion tends to use *direct* measurement, such as self-reports on specific emotional qualities, such as 'excited'. Although this approach is effective in most cases, it is prone to filter out trivial emotional qualities that are difficult to express through languages. It seems that mood boards are potential to be a useful alternative measure that applies an indirect approach, using visual images as cues for associating complex, trivial emotional qualities. Since mood boards are language independent, it may overcome the limitation of traditional approaches.

Designers are usually assumed to be more sensitive to affective content than users and clients because designers are more experienced in visualizing emotional qualities. However, it appears that users and clients also share similar criteria for judging visual affective content. This is probably because judging mood boards mainly relies on *association* and *intuition*. The nature of mood boards is sensorial, experiential and rich in content; interpreting the emotional qualities in mood boards cannot be logically reasoned. This also resonates with several psychological studies [38].

6   Conclusion

The present study has shown the potential of using mood boards as an evaluation tool for studying emotional experience. Mood boards are a generic tool that is applicable in various contexts of use and most designers are familiar with this tool. For future work, applying mood boards in research on user experience is a promising direction to proceed. Investigating the relationship between design content and corresponding emotional qualities is also another intriguing topic worth researching.

Acknowledgments. This work was supported in part by the Erasmus Mundus Joint Doctorate in Interactive and Cognitive Environments, which is funded by the EACEA Agency of the European Commission under EMJD ICE FPA n 2010-0012.

References

1. Redström, J.: Towards user design? On the shift from object to user as the subject of design. Des. Stud. 27, 123–139 (2006)
2. Law, E.L.-C., Roto, V., Hassenzahl, M., Vermeeren, A., Kort, J.: Understanding, scoping and defining user experience. In: Proceedings of the 27th International Conference on Human Factors in Computing Systems, CHI 2009, pp. 719–728. ACM Press, New York (2009)
3. Hassenzahl, M.: Emotions can be quite ephemeral; we cannot design them. Interactions 11, 46 (2004)

4. Desmet, P.M.A., Porcelijn, R., Dijk, M.B.: Emotional design; Application of a research-based design approach. Knowledge, Technol. Policy 20, 141–155 (2007)
5. Cassidy, T.D.: Mood boards: Current practice in learning and teaching strategies and students' understanding of the process. Int. J. Fash. Des. Technol. Educ. 1, 43–54 (2008)
6. McDonagh, D., Storer, I.: Mood boards as a design catalyst and resource: Researching an under-researched area. Des. J. 7, 16–31 (2004)
7. Rottenberg, J., Ray, R.D., Gross, J.J.: Emotion elicitation using films. In: Coan, J.A., Allen, J.J.B. (eds.) Handbook of Emotion Elicitation and Assessment, pp. 9–28. Oxford University Press, Oxford (2007)
8. Nagamachi, M.: Kansei Engineering: A new ergonomic consumer-oriented technology for product development. Int. J. Ind. Ergon. 15, 3–11 (1995)
9. Barnes, C., Lillford, S.P.: Decision support for the design of affective products. J. Eng. Des. 20, 477–492 (2009)
10. Khalid, H.M.: Customer emotional needs in product design. Concurr. Eng. 14, 197–206 (2006)
11. Jordan, P.W.: Designing Pleasurable Products. Taylor & Francis, London (2000)
12. Laugwitz, B., Held, T., Schrepp, M.: Construction and evaluation of a user experience questionnaire. In: Holzinger, A. (ed.) USAB 2008. LNCS, vol. 5298, pp. 63–76. Springer, Heidelberg (2008)
13. Karapanos, E., Martens, J.-B., Hassenzahl, M.: Reconstructing experiences with iScale. Int. J. Hum. Comput. Stud. 70, 849–865 (2012)
14. Osgood, C.E., May, W.H., Miron, M.S.: Cross-Cultural Universals of Affective Meaning. University of Illinois Press, Champaign (1975)
15. Ekman, P.: Strong evidence for universals in facial expressions: A reply to Russell's mistaken critique. Psychol. Bull. 115, 268–287 (1994)
16. Desmet, P.M.A., Monk, A.F., Overbeeke, K.: Measuring emotion: Development and application of an instrument to measure emotional responses to products. In: Blythe, M.A., Monk, A.F., Overbeeke, K., Wright, P.C. (eds.) Funology: From Usability to Enjoyment, pp. 111–123. Kluwer Academic Publishers, Dordrecht (2004)
17. Huisman, G., van Hout, M., van Dijk, B., van der Geest, T., Heylen, D.: LEMtool – Measuring emotions in visual interfaces. In: Proceedings of the SIGCHI Conference on Human Factors in Computing Systems, CHI 2013, pp. 351–360. ACM Press, New York (2013)
18. Hole, L., Williams, O.: The emotion sampling device (ESD). In: Proceedings of the 21st British HCI Group Annual Conference on People and Computers, pp. 177–178 (2007)
19. Garner, S., McDonagh-Philp, D.: Problem interpretation and resolution via visual stimuli: The use of "mood boards" in design education. Int. J. Art Des. Educ. 20, 57–64 (2001)
20. Lucero, A., Aliakseyeu, D., Martens, J.-B.: Funky wall: Presenting mood boards using gesture, speech and visuals. In: Proceedings of the Working Conference on Advanced Visual Interfaces, AVI 2008, pp. 425–428. ACM Press, New York (2008)
21. McDonagh, D., Bruseberg, A., Haslam, C.: Visual product evaluation: Exploring users' emotional relationships with products. Appl. Ergon. 33, 231–240 (2002)
22. Visser, F.S., Stappers, P.J., van der Lugt, R., Sanders, E.B.-N.: Contextmapping: experiences from practice. CoDesign 1, 119–149 (2005)
23. McDonagh, D., Denton, H.: Exploring the degree to which individual students share a common perception of specific mood boards: Observations relating to teaching, learning and team-based design. Des. Stud. 26, 35–53 (2005)
24. Philippot, P.: Inducing and assessing differentiated emotion-feeling states in the laboratory. Cogn. Emot. 7, 171–193 (1993)

25. Gross, J.J., Levenson, R.W.: Emotion elicitation using films. Cogn. Emot. 9, 87–108 (1995)
26. Lench, H.C., Flores, S.A., Bench, S.W.: Discrete emotions predict changes in cognition, judgment, experience, behavior, and physiology: A meta-analysis of experimental emotion elicitations. Psychol. Bull. 137, 834–855 (2011)
27. Edell, J.A., Burke, M.C.: The power of feelings in understanding advertising effects. J. Consum. Res. 14, 421–433 (1987)
28. Baumgartner, H., Sujan, M., Padgett, D.: Patterns of affective reactions to advertisements: The integration of moment-to-moment responses into overall judgments. J. Mark. Res. 34, 219–232 (1997)
29. Rompay, T., Pruyn, A., Tieke, P.: Symbolic meaning integration in design and its influence on product and brand evaluation. Int. J. Des. 3, 19–26 (2009)
30. Rathod, P.: BMW - Express your feeling, http://www.youtube.com/watch?v=OWDzRTMhSe0&hd=1
31. SistemasNormalesHD: Jeep Grand Cherokee - Official Commercial (2014), http://www.youtube.com/watch?v=UNaYZvJo4rQ&hd=1
32. Jung, C.G.: Man and His Symbols. Doubleday, Garden City (1964)
33. Chang, H.-M., Ivonin, L., Diaz, M., Catala, A., Chen, W., Rauterberg, M.: From mythology to psychology: Identifying archetypal symbols in movies. Technoetic Arts 11, 99–113 (2013)
34. Mooooodle Limited: MoodShare, http://www.moodshare.co/
35. Shrout, P.E., Fleiss, J.L.: Intraclass correlations: Uses in assessing rater reliability. Psychol. Bull. 86, 420–428 (1979)
36. Hollander, M., Wolfe, D.A.: Nonparametric Statistical Methods. Wiley-Interscience, Hoboken (1999)
37. Ryan, G.W., Bernard, H.R.: Techniques to identify themes. Field Methods 15, 85–109 (2003)
38. Kahneman, D.: Maps of Bounded Rationality: Psychology for Behavioral Economics. Am. Econ. Rev. 93, 1449–1475 (2003)

Cool in Business: Developing a Data-Based Instrument Measuring "Cool"

Carol Farnsworth[1], Karen Holtzblatt[2], Theo Held[3], and Shantanu Pai[1]

[1]SAP Labs, LLC, Palo Alto, CA, USA
carol.farnsworth@sap.com
[2]InContext Design, Concord, MA, USA
karen@incontextdesign.com
[3]SAP AG, Walldorf, Germany
theo.held@sap.com

Abstract. Cool products deliver a leap of value – so much so that people exclaim they are "cool". Cool products are transformative but cool can fade with time as people get used to them. Compared to other measures, the cool measures are assumed to be more subjective and qualitative in nature. Cool is being redefined all the time; what is cool today will probably not be cool in a few years. In extensive research activities, we identified "cool concepts" that are assumed to be quite independent from time and fashions. Impact on life is a strong element of coolness. For example, after many years the DVR continues to hold its position as a transformative, cool product that has had widespread positive impact and benefits on life. The seven constructs of cool, the Cool Concepts, and the 40 measures of coolness derived from them are grounded in data, with almost 900 consumers and over 2000 business professional participants in various research activities, conducted over 3 years.

Keywords: Cool, Field Research, Consumer Research, Measurement, Affinity Diagrams.

1 Introduction

After the release of the iPhone, something new seemed to be taking place that was different from other product releases. The iPhone release was all consuming, related to the overall user experience, social in nature, and something more than other innovative product releases over time. For designers it is crucial to understand what that "something" is and to understand what it means to design for a transformative experience. We want to identify principles that guide companies in designing "coolness" into their offerings.

Cool products provide a leap of value. They provide "I can't go back" and "I can't stop talking about it" experiences. Cool products can be transformative but can fade with time as expectations change over time—what is cool today will probably not be cool in a few years.

A. Marcus (Ed.): DUXU 2014, Part IV, LNCS 8520, pp. 232–243, 2014.

What is cool at any moment is not constant but we contend that the underlying cool factors define what contributes to the user's experience of coolness—independent of product, platform, and time. Whereas the initial experiences of cool may fade in excitement it points to the powerful impact and value products have on life. For example, after many years the digital video recorder (DVR) continues to hold its position as a transformative, cool product that has had widespread positive impact and benefits on life because it enables time-shifting of entertainment. The DVR has not been displaced because nothing better, easier, more impactful has been delivered over the last 12 years. But now with the rise of reliable streaming and off-the-TV entertainment services we are witnessing the upcoming challenger. The cool value delivered is the same, but reliable, easy to access streaming adds even more life flexibility: any time, any place, and any device entertainment. Life impact is central to the experience of coolness in technology products.

In the last two decades, much research has been conducted regarding various aspects of cool. Comprehensive overviews of this work are available in several publications. Interesting examples are the papers of Warren and Campbell [1], [2] as well as the recently published studies of Sundar, Tamul, and Wu [3].[1] In [1] and [2], the relationship between autonomy and social responsibility is considered a major factor influencing perceived coolness. "Bounded autonomy", meaning a grade of individual autonomy that avoids conformity but does not include aspects of antisocial behavior, is seen as the key for being perceived as cool. In [1] and [2] a couple of experimental studies are reported that investigate this assumption.

In contrast to that, in [3], an extensive literature review is presented where the authors try to extract the major characteristics and dimensions of cool. The identified dimensions are "uniqueness", "attractiveness", "subculture/counter-culture", and "genuineness". For each of those dimensions, a couple of potential measures (single adjectives or short statements) are identified. Participants of this study used those measures to rate a couple of mainstream digital devices. In an explorative factor analysis, the underlying factor structure is uncovered. It turned out that the concept of cool seems to be made up mainly by three factors called "appearance", "subculture", and "utility". The main factor appearance is constituted by attractiveness and uniqueness. It is also known from research in the area of user experience that perceived attractiveness of products seems to be a general factor that dominates most of the other identified dimensions in this area [5], [6]. The importance of appearance also points to the fact that perceived visual aesthetics has a big impact on rating products [7] (be it a rating as "cool", "attractive", or just as "good" or "bad"). Subculture as a factor goes into the direction of bounded autonomy as known from [1], [2]. The existence of utility as an extra factor fits quite well with results from user experience research, where a differentiation between pragmatic and hedonic factors is common [5], [6]. A second study with more participants unveiled an additional factor, "originality". Also this factor is closely related to known factor structures for user experience [6].

---

[1] We will not provide an exhaustive literature overview here. Instead we refer mainly to [3], [1], and also [4].

The discussion in the literature postulates that uniqueness, being different from the crowd, aesthetics, and usefulness are at the core of coolness. Whereas uniqueness and aesthetics may dominate art, clothing, even cars, do we have a deep enough understanding of what coolness means for technical consumer and business products? This project set about to determine the core factors that drive a cool user experience empirically and to develop a metric to measure it.

This paper presents a joint effort between SAP and InContext Design to answer this question: "What factors make devices and business software cool as perceived by business professionals?" The results of this project are seen as necessary prerequisites for designing cool business software and devices to be used in business. Apart from the known general concepts of cool, this special focus requires detailed and extensive research with business professionals to identify actionable attributes of products that can help design teams make transformative products. We assume that cool in business is not necessarily compliant with the known mainstream notion of cool described above. The fundamental ideas constituting the factors that influence coolness build upon the work of InContext Design and K. Holtzblatt identifying the Cool Concepts discussed here and described in previous work of K. Holtzblatt [8], [9].

The overall project consisted of several phases. In a first step, seven constructs as the core to the user experience of cool were uncovered by conducting extensive field research with consumers. Those constructs, termed the Cool Concepts, are represented as the "Wheel of Joy in life" and the "Triangle of Joy in use".

The Wheel includes

- Accomplishment of life,
- Connection to others that matter,
- Identity, celebrating what is core to self,
- Sensation, engaging in sensory delight and responding to design aesthetics.

The Triangle includes

- Direct into Action interfaces that achieve a focused intent like magic,
- The Hassle Factor, that removes technical and life hassle creating relief,
- The Learning Delta, that delivers value with little to no learning.[2]

In collaboration with InContext Design, SAP extended the consumer research conducted in 2010 into the world of business. The goal of this next step of the project was to understand how to apply the Cool Concepts developed by InContext Design for use in consumer settings to a business setting. In addition, SAP wanted to develop metrics for measuring the coolness of business products.

The seven constructs of Cool and the 40 measures of Coolness are grounded in data, with almost 900 consumers and over 2000 business professional participants in various research activities, conducted over 3 years. This paper focuses on the process

---

[2] Those constructs were developed by InContext Design before the cooperation with SAP was started.

followed and research conducted by SAP and InContext Design to develop the cool measures instrument. A condensed version of this report can be found in [10].

2   Capturing the Cool Concepts: Field Research Phase I and the First Set of Measures

In a first step, InContext Design wanted to understand what it means to design for a transformative experience. They wanted to identify principles to guide companies in designing cool into their offerings. Extensive field research with 65 consumers, as well as a survey with 800 consumers between the ages of 15 and 60 across multiple locations in the USA was run.

2.1   Consumer Field Research: Interviews

Invitations to take part in the consumer field research activity were sent to consumers throughout the USA. A total of 65 individuals took part in the interviews. The participants included 61% males and 39% females and ranged in age from 15-60 years. All interviews were face-to-face; all were conducted in the participants' home or place of residence.

During the two-hour session with the consumers, the consumer was asked to gather their most cool products that included technology. Then discussion was focused around the following topics for each cool product:

- What made it cool to them
- How it was used and experienced, unearthing impact on life and experience
- Observations of use and retrospective accounts of use and moments when the product delivered excitement

The data from the field interviews was organized into an affinity diagram (see [11] for methodic details) to raise themes and influences contributing to coolness. In this way the seven Cool Concepts were revealed. We also found that the most consistent products identified as cool across the population were smart phones including touch screens, MP3 players, DVR's, and a widely used social platform[3]. The Cool Concepts provide a conceptual framework for analyzing cool products.

2.2   Consumer Quantitative Research: Survey

To determine if the Cool Concepts were meaningful for differentiating products through a survey technique, invitations to take part in the consumer quantitative research activity were sent to consumers throughout the USA via craigslist. A total of 800 individuals took part in an online survey. The participants included 38% males

---

[3]   We will not refer to the names of products used in our investigations. Overall, it should be sufficient to name the type of product without disclosing the brand.

and 62% females and ranged in age from 15-60 years. All surveys were completed online.

People were asked to respond to statements representing the cool attributes that reflect the top five reasons why a product they own was cool. These statements mapped to the Cool Concepts. The online survey collected these findings, along with demographic data, from over 800 people in multiple cities across the US. These findings helped gauge product coolness and confirmed that the seven Cool Concepts could differentiate products.

2.3   Deriving the First Set of Measures

To create the original measures the cross-functional team consisting of representatives from SAP and InContext Design walked the affinity diagram using the data to stimulate the generation of key statements which could be measures for each of the Cool Concepts.

Examples of statements include:

- This product/service lets me do my work much faster as compared to life before I had this.
- This product/service makes me feel invisibly guided and confident when I try something new.
- Compared to what I had before, this is less complicated.

Similar statements were acceptable at this stage. We looked for phrases and statements that reflected the empirically collected consumer data in the affinity diagrams. Those phrases and statements served as a basis for the next step of the project where we investigated which statements and phrases work best for business professionals when they are asked to assess coolness of business software and electronic devices.

3   Refining the Cool Concepts: Field Research Phase II with Business Professionals

The business professional field research employed the same method as the initial consumer field research where InContext Design investigated the overall experience of cool for consumers. In addition, at the end of the interview interviewees were presented with the measures and asked to score 2 of the products discussed in the session.

3.1   Research Questions and Method

This phase of the project focused on the question, 'Do the cool principles derived from the consumer data also hold up in the business world?' As a prerequisite, we had to learn what the attributes and experience of a compelling business product are and how cool things fit into people's daily work lives, as well as how are they being used. This part of the field research was conducted as individual field interviews.

Another purpose of this phase was an initial validation of the Cool Concepts with business professionals in order to identify product attributes that excite people in their work. Based on the input given by the professionals, the phrasing of the measures was iterated. Through this process we also determined that longer phrases vs. shorter statements ensured that the meaning of the words was consistent with the Cool Concept it was referencing. Simple statements allowed the person to imagine what the words were referring to and so the resulting score had less meaning. The field interview was focused on the most memorable cool work products, the experience with their current work products, cool products from home and their personal life, and in general a typical day in their life and how they split up work and home activities over time and devices. This addition emerged from the overall findings of the consumer study suggesting a change in how activities were conducted. The day-in-life interview style allowed us to further validate the claim of how time was used.

To conclude the session, we asked the business professionals to complete the first version of the cool measures instrument and product/device comparison activities. In addition, we discussed how the measures reflect their actual experiences.

Invitations to take part in the field research activity were sent to business professionals (from the areas of Sales, Human Resources, Finance, and Procurement) in the Boston and San Francisco areas. A total of 28 individuals took part in the interviews and provided complete data sets. The participants included 65% males and 35% females and ranged in age from 30-55 years. All interviews were face-to-face; many were conducted in the participants' work office. The sessions lasted for two hours.

3.2 Interpretation of Results

The research team spent 2-3 hours after each interview documenting the details of each session in a Contextual Design interpretation session [11]. Data was captured on the following:

- Interpretation notes: Key issues and participant statements (30-75) from each interview session
- Detailed day-in-the-life description
- Results from the cool measures collection

In the subsequent analysis sessions, we looked at how work and consumer products support overall activities in and out of work in the context of our understanding of the structure of their day. We identified core intents and motivators and whether they were the same or different from our existing cool constructs. In addition, an affinity diagram was built from the field research data and the analysis of the cool measures data was completed.

The affinity diagram showed that the business data continued to map to the original Cool Concepts although the data also revealed that the construct could manifest somewhat differently from a business point of view. For example the cool of Accomplishment was also associated with anywhere anytime information and the Connection concept highlighted tools that enhanced team collaboration. But overall the qualitative data indicated that the framework held for business.

4   Construction of the Cool Measures

On the basis of the extensive field research described above, a set of 79 measures related to the seven dimensions of "cool" were assembled. For the establishment of an appropriate measurement tool, we have to investigate if (latent) factors or dimensions exist that correspond to the postulated dimensions or combinations of those components. In addition, we have to determine, which of the measures represent the respective dimensions most strongly. Consequently, the "strongest" measures for each dimension can be selected while such a selection can contribute to a significant reduction of the number of measures required for determining Coolness on all relevant dimensions. An appropriate methodic approach for those purposes is principal component analysis (PCA), a statistical technique for identifying structural properties of multidimensional data.

4.1   Studies

We conducted two extensive online studies for determining the underlying factorial structure and selecting the most suitable measures. In both studies, our set of 79 measures was presented in an online survey.

Procedure. In a first step, participants were asked to select their coolest devices from a given list. This list included the most important smartphones and tablet devices available at this point of time (Dec 2011-March 2012), e-readers, MP3 Players, a digital recording set-top device, and Flatscreen HDTV. Participants were asked to rank each of the selected devices with regards to its specific coolness. Then, the device ranked on top was used for conducting the rating on the 79 measures. Overall, two devices (one smartphone and one tablet) received the highest Coolness rankings and were therefore rated by the 79 measures most frequently.

Subsequently, the procedure was repeated with the same individuals with a set of given business applications including prominent cloud storage software, social platforms, and CRM systems. In case of business applications, participants could also select their own applications if none of the given apps was used by them or if they used applications that were more strongly associated with concept of "cool". For each participant, the measures were presented in randomized order.

Participants Study 1. Invitations to take part in the investigation were sent to business professionals in the USA (mainly from the areas of Sales, Human Resources, Procurement, and Finance). A total of 635 individuals, 25-65 years of age, took part in the online survey and provided complete data sets.

Participants Study 2. In contrast to study 1, we approached business professionals from outside the USA in order to identify and control effects that may be caused by drawing USA participants only. The 924 participants, 25-65 years of age, came from the United Kingdom, Germany, India, and Singapore. Again, participants are from the areas of Sales, Human Resources, Procurement, and Finance.

4.2   Results of Studies 1 and 2

Principal component analyses were conducted with the data-sets of both studies separately. Since we could not observe meaningful differences between the component structures of both samples and there were also no meaningful differences between the structures for devices and business applications, all subsequent analyses were conducted for the complete unified data set from 1559 global business professionals.

The analysis of the complete data set revealed a total of 7 factors. We found factors that are completely associated with measures belonging to one of the postulated Cool Concept dimensions. Those factors are "Accomplishment", "Identity", "Sensation", and "Learning Delta", while we found two separate factors associated with connection ("Connection-1", "Connection-2"). Factor Connection-1 includes measures that are targeting mainly on general aspects of connectedness, mainly in the private, personal, friends and family area, while Connection-2 is clearly focusing on aspects of work relationships and sharing work materials. This maps to the differences found in the qualitative data once we included a business tool focus. "Direct into Action" and "The Hassle Factor" are confounded within one common factor. This appears to be plausible if we consider those factors as the extremes of one common continuum. The above 7 factors explain 80% of variance, while the "strongest" factors are Direct into Action/Hassle (20%) and Accomplishment (14%).

Subsequently, the measures (i.e. the phrases) showing the highest correlations with the respective factor were selected for a final version of the Cool measures. In total, a set of 40 measures were selected. According to statistical properties of the measures we could even have reduced the measure set further, but decided to keep several measures because they were considered to be useful for deriving design implications. Whereas statistically we did not need all the measures for a reliable score we did need the measures to reflect the factor sufficiently to be meaningful to designers when they saw detailed results.

4.3   The Cool Measure Instrument

Based on the results of the studies reported above, a survey tool presenting the 40 measures has been constructed. The Cool Measures instrument is a 7-minute survey where users can compare their experience with a product at any stage of development (concept, prototype, product, etc.) with an individual benchmark (what they are using today or some specified product). Groups of measures are designated for each of the seven identified factors.

The cool score is derived by taking the average per cool measure across participants and multiplying it with the corresponding correlation coefficient. This score is then multiplied by the factor level weighting (i.e. weights for the cool constructs based on their contribution to variance explanation) and then rescaled on a 1-10 scale.

The Cool Measures instrument can be used during any user research activity where it makes sense and when we want to measure the coolness of a product. The Cool Measures instrument is presented to the test participant after they interact with a product. If the product is in the early stage of development, the test participant will need to imagine the finished product. In all cases, the test participant is asked to evaluate whether or not the product is/will be better than what they are using now.

The Cool Measures instrument helps us understand if this new product and/or product idea is better than what the test participant is using today. The slider scale allows the participant to state how much better than today. If there is 'No Change', then the participant does not move the slider bar and the measures result in a score of zero. The Cool Measures instrument also allows the test participant to say that the product they are evaluating is worse than what they are using today. Selecting 'Worse than today' results in negative scores for the measure (see Fig. 1).

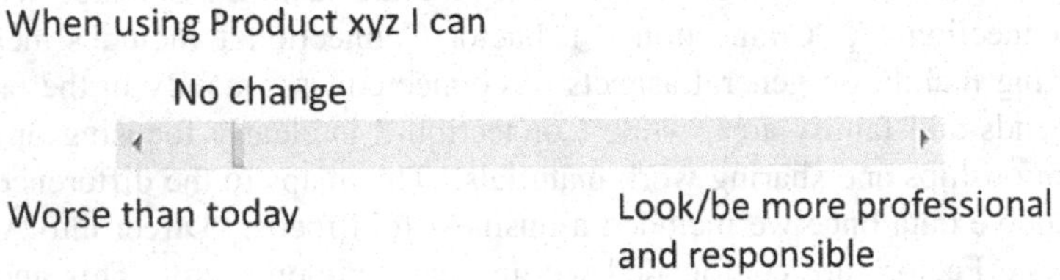

When using Product xyz I can

No change

◄ | ►

Worse than today   Look/be more professional
                                     and responsible

Fig. 1. Schematic view of an item in the Cool Measures Instrument. Initially, the slider control is positioned at "No change". The participant may move the slider to the left side ("worse than today") or to the right side (subjective rating of how much the considered product helped to influence the rated dimension positively).

An example for a typical results overview is displayed in Figure 2. In addition to the determination of a coolness-score (overall and for the single dimensions), the cool measures instrument is a perfect tool to use to begin an in-depth conversation with the participant about the product they just experienced.

The scores determined for the single factors can serve as basis for understanding the coolness of the product and how its coolness could be improved. Since the Cool Concepts were validated and extended, the depth of understanding and guidance goes beyond the literal meaning of the phrases used in the measure. As such, recommendations can be made from this wider knowledge and the design principles that InContext has defined and associated with each factor. In addition, as part of InContext's client work 3-4 field interviews with the product being tested provide additional insight into the meaning of the scores.

Therefore the cool measures provide guidance for design. Considerations for design may emerge based on these scores. Particularly low or high scoring dimensions are likely to stimulate considerations and discussions regarding specific requirements of a product. Low scores indicate requirements that are not met while high scores highlight product properties that obviously contribute to coolness.

Looking at Fig. 2 overall scores are on average indicating that all factors can be improved. Direct/Hassle, the most impactful factor is particularly low indicating an area for improvement. Sensation is also low indicating that sensual delight is missing. If Identity was improved the product would increase in its emotional impact. Any increase in Accomplishment, the second most important factor will significantly increase impact and value. Accomplishment refers fundamentally to anytime anywhere ability to get activities done while on the move in small chunks of time. Getting teams to understand that task accomplishment or task efficiency alone will not significantly raise the score is the task of the UX professional discussing the meaning of the score. As such the scores open the way for design discussions and for generating design ideas that directly map to the cool user experience.

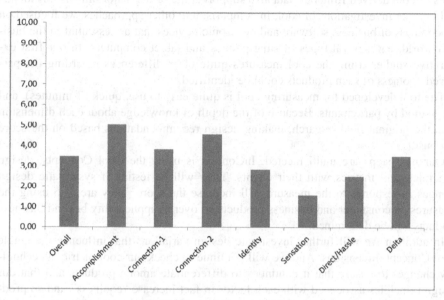

Fig. 2. Example for a results chart

4.4 Validation of the Cool Measure Instrument

To assess validity and reliability of the 40 measures, a validation study with 400 participants was conducted. The study was run with the same procedure as in studies 1 and 2 reported above with 40 measures versus 79. Again, the measures were presented as an online survey with participants from the USA (business professionals in Human Resources, Sales, Finance and Procurement). Gender and age distributions were quite similar to those of the initial studies.

With the data set, the following analyses were conducted: a principal component analysis on the complete data set to investigate if the factors derived from the previous studies can also be found when using the reduced set of measures (i.e. was the measure selection done properly?). The analysis again brought up 7 dimensions explaining 81% of variance, while the factors contributed to explained variance more evenly than in the two initial studies.

To determine the consistency of the subscales (our 7 dimensions), we calculated Cronbach's Alpha for each subscale for the whole dataset as well as for device data and application data only. In each case, the Alpha values are between .91 and .96, meaning that the subscales appear to be highly consistent. This basically means that the measures of the respective dimensions consistently measure the same construct.

5   Discussion

We presented an approach for the development of a metric to measure the experience of product "coolness" grounded in extensive field research. Obviously, the dimensions of cool derived from our data also support some of the major dimensions identified in other investigations of cool. In comparison to other approaches, we focused on the coolness of business software and electronic devices that are essential in the business world, e.g. several types of smartphones and tablet computers. In our first explorative studies using the cool measures quite clear differences regarding the perceived coolness of such products could be identified.

The tool developed for measuring cool is quite easy to use, quick (7-minutes), and understood by participants. Because of the depth of knowledge about each dimension from the original field research, making design recommendations based on the score is robust.

Our next steps are multi faceted. InContext is using the Cool Concepts, design principles, and metrics with their clients. They will be testing if systematic design changes in response to the measure will increase the score. They are also using the measures on consumer and business products so overall applicability beyond business products will be determined.

In addition we will further investigate design variations that influence the single Cool Concept dimensions. And we will continue to check our cool metric as technology changes to ensure that it continues to differentiate among products and that our design principles associated with each factor in fact increase "coolness" and so product success. More data-based insights into those relationships will help to derive well founded design recommendations for business products that will not only be easy to use but will also be cool.

References

1. Warren, C.: What Makes Things Cool And Why Marketers Should Care. Doctoral thesis, Leeds School of Business of the University of Colorado (2010)
2. Warren, C., Campbell, M.: What Makes Things Cool? The Role of Bounded Autonomy (Working paper) (2011)
3. Sundar, S.S., Tamul, D.J., Wu, M.: Capturing "cool": Measures for assessing coolness of technological products. Int. J. Human-Computer Studies 72, 169–180 (2014)
4. Pountain, D., Robins, D.: Cool Rules: Anatomy of an Attitude. Reaktion Books, London (2000)
5. Hassenzahl, M.: The effect of perceived hedonic quality on product appealingness. International Journal of Human-Computer Interaction 13(4), 481–499 (2001)
6. Laugwitz, B., Held, T., Schrepp, M.: Construction and evaluation of a user experience questionnaire. In: Holzinger, A. (ed.) USAB 2008. LNCS, vol. 5298, pp. 63–76. Springer, Heidelberg (2008)
7. Lavie, T., Tractinsky, N.: Assessing dimensions of perceived visual aesthetics of web sites. Int. J. Human-Computer Studies 60, 269–298 (2004)

8. Holtzblatt, K.: What makes things cool? Intentional design for innovation. Interactions XVIII (6), 40–47 (2011)
9. Holtzblatt, K.: CHI 2011: The Design of Cool (2011), http://incontextdesign.com/blog/chi-2011-the-design-of-cool/ (retrieved January 21, 2014)
10. Farnsworth, K., Holtzblatt, K., Pai, S., Wagg, K., Held, T., Wylen, E., Lawler Kennedy, S., Kutty, P.: Measuring Product "Coolness" – Developing a Measurement Instrument. In: Case Study Presented at CHI 2014, Toronto, Canada (2014)
11. Beyer, H., Holtzblatt, K.: Contextual Design. Morgan Kaufmann, San Francisco (1997)

From Inexperienced Users to Co-creators:
An Exploration of a Generative Method

Chrysoula Gatsou

Faculty of Fine Arts and Design, TEI of Athens, Athens, Greece
cgatsou@teiath.gr

Abstract. One of the main challenges for improving user experience in systems and artifacts lies in how designers, development managers and IT professionals can cultivate empathy in users. The present study offers an empirical example of how inexperienced users can be involved in the early stages of design process. It examines the findings from a generative technique which employs inexperienced users as co-creators in collaboration with the designer, in a collage session during the early design stages of a mobile tablet application centred on the topic of "first aid". The findings of this study identify five ponts for eliciting users' needs. Both designers and practitioners can benefit from such knowledge.

Keywords: user experience, generative method, co-design, empathic design, inexperienced user.

1 Introduction

The design of artifacts nowadays is more and more complex, since they contain more functions, they make more demands on experience on the part of users and have to take into account various considerations. One of the main challenges for improving user experience in systems and artifacts lies in how designers, development managers and IT professionals can cultivate empathy in users. The increase in mobile communication and personal computing makes additional demands on mobile applications in order that ordinary people perceive technology as beneficial and helpful. Hanington argues that a considerable knowledge of participatory design is vital in broadening the perspective of designers and in illuminating the way in which potential users can contribute creatively to making decisions [8].

Gaver et al. [6] suggest that users should be involved in the design process. They recommend a direct, subjective and empathetic engagement on the part of designers with everyday people, who are normally the main users [6]. Workshop sessions offer designers the opportunity to develop a greater insight into, and understanding of users, so that they can produce more effective designs. Sensitizing designers to the different ways in which individuals complete daily tasks has helped to diminish the gap between users and designers.

A. Marcus (Ed.): DUXU 2014, Part IV, LNCS 8520, pp. 244–252, 2014.
© Springer International Publishing Switzerland 2014

Such approaches are mainly vital to the design of artifacts, because patterns of behaviour, attitudes and personal motivations on the part of users are notable factors in shaping the design and use of artifacts. As a personal, subjective and contextual, *in situ* method, collaging is often used as a component in generative design research. The collage method itself was inspired by the work of Elizabeth Sanders on generative methods and of Bruce Hanington on innovation methods [7, 20].

The aim of any design is to create new solutions. Design becomes a focusing and generative process, in which interpretations of earlier users' experiences, emerging solutions and the gradual understanding of objectives evolves in the form of a dialogue [2,13,22]. The non - specific use of computers and interactive devices began to increase from 1995, whereupon companies recognized the need to acquire a deeper understanding of users. They began to use groups of people possessing different sets of expertise. However, as Preece et al., point out, communication and collaboration among team members is not easy [16]. The reason seems to be that people from various backgrounds have various opinions and various ways of expressing themselves. The lack of a common language creates confusion and becomes a source of resentment and indifference during the exchange of ideas. In the view of Muller, there is a gap between the world of designers and researchers and that of users [15].

1.1   The Role of Inexperienced User in Design

According to Gaver et al. and Sanders, users may be engaged in various roles in the development process [6, 21]. In particular, inexperienced users can be employed as users, testers, informers and design partners. Despite the explosion of technology in mobile communication and personal computing, inexperienced users can feel isolated from this world and a significant divide between expert and inexperienced has arisen. Here we focus mainly on including inexperienced users in the design process as design partners and sources of information. Not all users possess a broad knowledge of interactive technology and may not be able to summarize their unspoken present or future needs in simple terms. It is important to support such people in the design process, because they do not experience interaction with artifacts in the same manner as experts do nor do they have the same insight as experts.

1.2   Co – creation

Co - creation draws on innovative ideas generated by users, researchers, designers and stakeholders in general. It redefines how such persons are brought into the process of value creation and engages them in the various experiences generated in the process [17]. Co-creation in design allows ordinary people to exploit their creativity, if they are helped and encouraged to do so. Design should take place in close connection with the context in which the user operates, so that the users move within a familiar environment and any stakeholders involved operate in a context based on real life [1]. The role of users in the design process is changing. Instead of being the passive object of research, they are now seen as active co-designers and co- creators.

1.3   The Present Study

This paper examines the findings drawn from the application of a generative method which employs inexperienced users as co-creators in collaboration with the designer, in a collage session during the early design stages of a mobile tablet application centred around the topic of first aid. This paper opens with a literature review, the aim of which is to establish the theoretical background to our study. The review deals with approaches which exploit the inspirations of users that are triggered by various generative methods. It then describes the research methodology employed. It analyses the data and offers results which are then discussed, before offering some conclusions.

2   The User Inspiration Approach

There are a great number of different data-collection methods that can be applied to identify user requirements. Hanington has placed the methods in three main categories: traditional, adaptive and innovative [7]. Innovative methods use creative or participatory tools, such as collages, card sorting, diaries, drama or probes [6,8,18]. Innovative methods differ from traditional user-centred design methods, such as surveys and interviews, which give an emphasis to explicit information gathering.

In approaches that require a participatory way of thinking, the user is seen as a collaborator who actively participates in the product design process. This set of approaches focuses on designing in collaboration with users. In the view of Ehn, participatory design is "... *design challenge of fully anticipating or envisioning, use before actual use takes place in people's life-worlds.*" [3]. It also focuses on users' actual, but unexpressed, knowledge, which is usually difficult to assess and describe. Such knowledge thus tends to be ignored by cognitive theory, which has dominated the study of human computer interaction [25]. Participatory design is an emerging practice, which includes non - designers in various activities throughout the planning process. Participatory methods allow all interested parties to contribute directly to the development of an artifact. They allow participants to express themselves directly and actively in the planning process and to identify the needs of the user. Users' behaviors and involvements thus form a framework rooted in everyday life and rest upon emotions and motivations [23]. Thus partipatory design, along with other participatory approaches, goes beyond a number of other design studies and user-centered techniques.

Cultural probes form another technique employed by the user inspiration approach during the design process. The concept of probes was developed by Gaver *et al.*, as a tool for exploring new or better ways of integrating older participants into the everyday life of their communities [6]. Cultural probes were further expanded to facilitate interactions among groups of people in user involvement projects. Research via cultural probes have used cameras, postcards, maps, journals, recording devices, media diaries and various pieces of text and imagery, to elicit personal experiences. Designers thus derive inspiration from the experiences of users and their ideas. In addition, probes give access to participants' everyday lives and personal environment. As Sanders and Dandavate put it, "*If we can learn to access people's experiences, we can make user experience the source of inspiration and design*" [18].

Sanders played an important role in the evolution of participatory product development, in that she proposed the existence of a new approach to design, whereby user involvement should be responsible for the final design [21]. The aim of her research was to improve design through the exploitation of users' experience and she labelled such methods "generative". Such methods help elicit user needs and aid designers in the understanding of user experiences. A new approach therefore "... *should facilitate exchange between the people who experience products, interfaces, systems and spaces and the people who design for experiencing*" [18]. In the new approach, the role of the designer is to be constructive and to encourage users to express their creativity and decide on their own design [20].

Empathy is a key issue in generative methods. In Wright and McCarthy's view, feelings or empathy are the ability to understand what it feels like to be another person – what that person's situation is like from his/her own perspective [26]. Empathic design is combination of techniques, such as the observation of users or co-creation with them. As Fulton Suri notes, in empathic design designers and researchers over time repeatedly develop and, in dialogue with users themselves, check their understanding in creative terms of users' experiences [4].

Koskinen and Battarbee feel that empathic methods work better in the search for concepts that is the preparation for concept design [11]. Furthermore, Koskinnen considers that designers needed to use systematic ways to study experiences and so recommends direct collaboration between designers and users [10]. On the other hand, Fulton Suri points out that the inner states of the user are the most important factor for designers [5]. She argues that empathic design may not allow a systematic approach to research. Earlier, Leonard and Rayport, in addressing this issue, suggested that designers who exercise empathy through the observation of the environment in which users operate acquire the ability to share the feelings of users and so design artifacts that meet real needs [14]. In a generative research session, users are the creators who generate artifacts in collaboration with the designer/researcher, who simply facilitates the expression of their thoughts and ideas.

3   Methodology

3.1   Participants

Our session was designed specifically to include a representative pool of potential users of the mobile tablet application. There were twelve participants (N=12) ranging from 18 to 79 in age (mean age = 41,6 , SD = 20.9, years), seven of whom were men and five women. All of the participants had little or no experience in the use of computers. The users' expressions, the designer statements and collaborative activities of the session were videoed by the researcher.

The participants chosen came from various backgrounds, were of various ages and of both sexes (see Table 1). The reasons behind our decision to engage such a variety of people were various. We wished to generate inspiration derived from the experiences of other persons, we wanted our users to contribute to the design of the application during the collage session, which meant taking account of various perspectives on a topic, and we wanted to track the course of mutual learning among the participants.

Table 1. Age, gender and number of Participants

ID	P1	P2	P3	P4	P5	P6
Age	50	38	26	27	57	79
Gender	M	F	M	F	M	M
ID	**P7**	**P8**	**P9**	**P10**	**P11**	**P12**
Age	52	31	18	45	65	67
Gender	M	M	F	F	F	M

3.2 Procedure

The study was based on empirical material gathered during the collage session in which inexperienced users were involved in a design process. The aim of the user study was to identify concealed needs on the part of users through an exploration of the experiences of the users in their interactions with tablets in particular. During the study, participants made collages and explained why they made them in the way that they did. Having acquired the tools to express themselves, the participants generated information regarding their personal experiences. This phase began with a discussion in which participants were told of the purpose of the session and of the subject and the process. They then moved on to what Sleeswijk Visser *et al.* term "sensitizing"[24]. Sensitizing is a process in which participants are energized, encouraged and motivated to think about and explore aspects of their cultural context relating to the topic of the meeting (Fig.1).

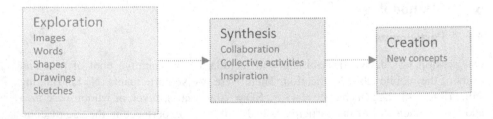

Fig. 1. Conceptual model of the collage session with inexperienced users

Each participant was required to create a collage that expressed the type of expectations and emotions they had regarding a mobile tablet application on the topic of first aid. Participants were required to organize a variety of pictures and words which illustrated the subject of first aid. They were permitted to use paper, crayons, scissors and glue to create in whatever way they liked a collage on this theme. Furthermore, they were free to express ideas and questions regarding their collage and pictures. This they did by drawing on insights taken from their social environment and their activities (Fig 2). An elderly user was confused at the beginning and asked if, in addition to using images, he could sketch or draw on the paper. The user was advised to draw or to sketch whatever he wanted in relation to the theme, to express his feelings. Laseau stated *"the sketches generated are important because they show how we are thinking about a problem, not just what we think about it"* [12]. All participants demonstrated a high level of engagement in this activity.

Fig. 2. Participants during the collage session

4   Results –Discussion

We interpreted the results in a designerly way, that is, we looked for patterns and exceptions, for the creation of semi-factual stories and attempted to capture appealing design ideas. Any demands for objectivity were left aside [9]. Sanders and William note that methods exist for performing a qualitative and quantitative analysis of data produced by generative methods [19]. The most basic methods focus on determining the factors that appear most often in collage or recordings. Such evidence can serve as a starting point from which one may examine the recordings (i.e., the written record of what was stated by the participants during the session) in the search for recurrent themes and motifs. In the view of Sleeswijk Visser *et al.*, a practical way of extracting information from findings derived from experiential material is to collect carefully selected extracts or instructions from the unprocessed material. Thus ideally the material allows one to interpret the main issues [24].

The summary and combined findings provide a shorter path to the final result, although they represent a map of possible routes and offer an opportunity for the designer to find information and support for his own interpretation and orientation. Various forms of content analysis form an appropriate tool for this. One looks for categories, patterns and themes in the information collected by participants' creations. A simple method is to count the number of times a word or image is used in a collage. The standard procedure of grouping common elements that appear in categories, such as is done in content analysis, is used to identify key issues. In particular, since qualitative research involves samples of smaller size than occurs in a quantitative survey, a large part of the analysis can be done by hand through the use of affinity diagrams [9].

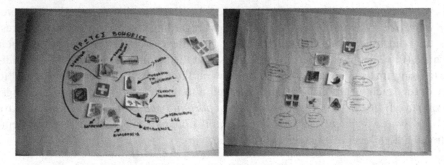

Fig. 3. Participants' posters

The participants generated a total of 14 different design ideas, since some of them created two posters. Analysis of the results showed that "inexperienced users" produced ideas that were more valuable to users. Two design topics became apparent during the session regarding 1) the selection of images preferred by the users and, 2) the way in which users preferred to find information on the topic. The posters offer strong evidence in favour of the effectiveness of convincing design strategies. After the meeting with users, I analyzed the posters in search of design patterns, motifs and surprises (Fig.4) and after the completion of the session I prepared a report on each one of the posters.

Fig. 4. Analysis of the collage session results

Several issues emerged from participants' ideas, which we subsequently classified in three main categories, namely ideas regarding:

- Icon representation
- The mapping of functions
- Navigation

Our study allowed us to identify five main points required for a successful collage creation session.

- Prepare the collage kit carefully. There should be sufficient images and words, all specific and relevant to the topic of collage. A well-structured session leads to the generation of more creative ideas.

- Designers, researchers or facilitators should be flexible in their handling of participants.
- One should to listen all the participants. An apparently irrelevant query may produce new insights.
- Preconceptions and stereotypes should be abandoned and participants' ideas should be given full consideration.
- The diversity of participants should be valued.

5   Conclusions

The results of the evaluation carried out by designers during collage sessions can contribute to the creation of new ideas and to fruitful speculation and reflection on the designs in question. This paper has also illustrated how a collage session can provide vital information for making such a process possible, because such a session offers a forum for communication between users and designers. Collage seessions also assist in finding solutions that may not have occurred to the researcher. The main fruit of the workshops are the posters that present the design ideas conceived by the users involved. We placed the issues that emerged from the ideas of the participants in three main categories: ideas for icon representation, the mapping of functions and navigation.

In addition, we identify five main points in the structuring of a collage session involving inexperienced users required to produce effective results. We found that the empathic mindset created during the dialogue with users, which includes the kind of informal meetings mentioned above, becomes the key driving force in the interpretation of the materials gathered during the experiment, particularly in regard to matters of design.

One of the conclusions to be derived is that collage sessions need both to be fully integrated into the design process, if they are to act as an effective design tool, and into the practices employed by designers themselves, if they are to contribute to the creation of effective interactive applications.

Acknowledgments. We express our gratitude to the participants, who enthusiastically gave their time to allow us to understand the value of their experiences.

References

1. Buur, J., Bødker, S.: From usability lab to 'design collaboratorium': reframing usability - practice. In: Conference on Designing Interactive Systems, New York, USA (2000)
2. Cross, N.: Designerly ways of knowing. Birkhauser, Boston (2007)
3. Ehn, P.: Participation in design things. In: Proceedings Participatory Design Conference (PDC) Experiences and Challenges, Indiana University, pp. 92–101 (2008)
4. Fulton Suri, J.: Empathic design: Informed and inspired by other people's experience. In: Koskinen, I., Battarbee, K., Mattelmäki, T. (eds.) Empathic Design: User Experience in Product Design, pp. 51–58. Edita IT Press, Helsinki (2003)
5. Fulton Suri, J.: Informing our intuition: Design research for radical innovation. Rotman Magazine, 52–57 (2008)

6. Gaver, B., Dunne, T., Pacenti, E.: Cultural probes. ACM Interaction 6, 21–29 (1999)
7. Hanington, B.: Methods in the Making: A Perspective on the State of Human Research in Design. Design Issues 19(4), 9–18 (2003)
8. Hanington, B.: Generative Research in Design Education. In: Proceedings of the International Association of Societies of Design Research, IASDR, International Conference, Hong Kong, November 12-15 (2007)
9. Holtzblatt, K., Wendell, J.B., Wood, S.: Rapid contextual design. Morgan Kaufmann, San Francisco (2005)
10. Koskinen, I.: Empathic Design in Methodic Terms. In: Koskinen, I., Battarbee, K., Mattelmäki, T. (eds.) Empathic Design, User Experience in Product Design, pp. 59–65. ITPress, Helsinki (2003)
11. Koskinen, I., Battarbee, K.: Introduction to user experience and empathic design. In: Koskinen, I., Battarbee, K., Mattelmäki, T. (eds.) Empathic Design, User Experience in Product Design, pp. 37–50. IT Press, Helsinki (2003)
12. Laseau, P.: Graphic Thinking For Architects and Designers, 3rd edn. John Wiley and Sons, New York (2001)
13. Lawson, B.R.: How Designers Think, 3rd edn. Architectural Press (1997)
14. Leonard, D., Rayport, J.F.: Spark innovation through empathic design. Harvard Business Review 75(6), 102–113 (1997)
15. Muller, M.J.: Participatory design: The third space in HCI. In: Jacko, J., Sears, A. (eds.) The Human Computer Interaction Handbook: Fundamentals, Evolving Technologies and Emerging Applications, pp. 1051–1068. Lawrence Erlbaum Associates, Mahwah (2002)
16. Preece, J., Rogers, Y., Sharp, H.: Interaction Design: Beyond Human Computer Interaction. John Wiley & Sons, NY (2002)
17. Ramaswamy, V., Gouillart, F.: The Power of Co-Creation: Build It with Them To Boost Growth, Productivity, and Profits. Free Press (2010)
18. Sanders, E.B.-N., Dandavate, U.: Design for experiencing: New tools. In: O Beeke, C.J., Hekkert, P. (eds.) Proceedings of the First International Conference on Design and Emotion, Delft University of Technology, pp. 87–91 (1999)
19. Sanders, E.B.-N., William, C.T.: Harnessing People's Creativity: Ideation and Expression through Visual Communication. In: Langford, J., McDonagh-Philp, D. (eds.) Focus Groups: Supporting Effective Product Development. Taylor and Francis (2001)
20. Sanders, E.B.-N.: Information, Inspiration and Co-creation. Paper presented at the 6th International Conference of the European Academy of Design, Bremen, Germany (2005)
21. Sanders, E.B.-N.: Design Research in 2006. Design Research Quarterly 1(1), 1–8 (2006)
22. Schön, D.A.: The Reflective Practitioner. How Professionals Think in Action. Basic Books (1983)
23. Schuler and Namioka.: Praticipatory Design: Principles and Practices. Larence Erlbaum, N.J. (1993)
24. Sleeswijk Visser, F., van der Lugt, R., Stappers, P.J.: Participatory design needs participatory communication. In: Proceedings of the 9th European Conference on Creativity and Innovation, Lodz, Poland, pp. 173–195 (2005)
25. Winograd, T., Flores, F.: Understanding Computers and Cognition: A New Foundation for Design. Ablex, Norwood (1986)
26. Wright, P., McCarthy, J.: Empathy and experience in HCI. In: Czerwinski, M., Lund, A., Tan, D. (eds.) Proceedings of the 26th SIGCHI Conference on Human Factors in Computing Systems, pp. 637–646. ACM Press, New York (2008)

From Wearables to Soft-Wear: Developing Soft User Interfaces by Seamlessly Integrating Interactive Technology into Fashionable Apparel

Daniel Gilgen and T. Raune Frankjaer

Trier University of Applied Sciences, Department of Design,
Irminenfreihof 8, D-54290 Trier, Germany
gilgen@hochschule-trier.de, raune@frankjaer.de

Abstract. The development of electronic features for use in apparel has advanced rapidly in recent years, and applications in athletic wear have been particularly successful. However, 'Smart Fashion' has not yet been integrated into everyday garments. In this paper we propose a new approach to the design of interfaces in Smart Fashion, which we refer to as the Soft User Interface (SUI). The ways in which e-textiles physically convey information differs greatly from traditional ways in that information is communicated via graphical user interfaces on computers, smartphones or on WearComp devices. As a result of our research, we advocate the use of iconic and indexical signs for Smart Fashion as these are widely accessible and understood. As an extension to this new interface paradigm, we expect that the harvesting of biometric data, including bodily gestures, will significantly extend the possibilities of SUIs.

Keywords: Smart Fashion, applied semantics, gestural input, embedded electronics, physical computing, wearable networks, hybrid space, interactive technology, Soft User Interface, SUI.

1   Introduction

Interactive technologies have been successfully integrated into clothing in industries in which functionality is very important, such as sports, healthcare, security and safety. Nevertheless, this remains a niche market, and Smart Fashion is not yet common in everyday wear. Electronically augmented fashion is generally known as illuminated outfits that are reserved for stage performances or other special events. In this paper we discuss how Smart Fashion can be integrated into everyday clothing. We examine the concerns that need to be addressed and the design requirements that need to be met for seamless integration of interactive technologies into fashionable apparel.

A cooperative interdisciplinary design research project between the Department of Fashion and the Department of Intermedia Design at the Trier University of Applied Sciences constituted the basis for our investigations. This research, which focuses on psychological design aspects as well as on semiotic and aesthetic issues, commenced in 2011 and will be finalized by the end of 2014.

A. Marcus (Ed.): DUXU 2014, Part IV, LNCS 8520, pp. 253–260, 2014.

The application of new technologies to long-established products like clothing often meets with strong resistance as society has very strict pre-established conceptions about these everyday artifacts. Along with these cultural expectations come certain habits and behaviors that are very hard to challenge, as they are associated with objects for which the patterns of interaction are internalized at a very deep level. These patterns are established over many generations and are passed on during infancy. Thus, different types of clothing and clothing items are highly archetypical, often with concise perceptions and with high iconicity. These archetypes are independent of prevalent fashion trends and, in stark contrast to other technological developments, evolve slowly. There are generally three ways to approach established mental models in the field of new technology:

1.1. The technology can physically disappear into a known product, such as imperceptible embedded sensors that track personal biodata and transmit the data to a medical service. One example is the cancer-detecting bra developed by First Warning Systems [1, 2].

1.2. A novel product category can be designed that is not associated with any preconceptions. The Nike FuelBand, Jawbone's UP and FitBit are examples of this type of product [3, 4, 5]. One could argue that these devices are similar to wristwatches or bracelets; however, the integrated functionality provides a novel experience, so these technologies may be perceived as original and different.

1.3. A known product can be extended using interactive technology. The Sporty Supaheroe Jacket for bicyclists by Utope is a good example of this. The primary function of a jacket is to protect against adverse weather conditions, and the Supaheroe Jacket extends this function by providing increased visibility and the ability to communicate the cyclist's intentions to others using the road [6].

This paper focuses on the third category i.e. applications in the field of smart wearable textiles, which we define as Soft User Interfaces (SUIs). We position SUIs as a subcategory of Wearables. But distinct from WearComp, such as augmented glass technologies, smart watches and digital wristbands, so-called fourth screens rely on text- and image-based communication.

In contrast, SUIs are "embedded computing worn on the body, made of soft and flexible materials, and, being devoid of screens, exclusively rely on non-verbal communication as a mean of interaction." SUIs must be aligned with established attitudes towards clothing and must be simple and intuitive to use. This can be achieved by reducing the symbolic representations in the interface design [7].

2   Nonverbal Communication

With WearComp, as with any screen-based communication, the focus is on text, image and auditory interactions. Thus, although the extent and importance of nonverbal interactions in interpersonal communication is widely recognized, nonverbal communication has not been integrated into human-computer interfaces in Smart Fashion. Between 70–90% of all inter-human communication takes place through wordless clues, which are primarily used to establish and maintain interpersonal relationships [8, 9]. Understanding and applying these patterns of communication is paramount for the development of SUIs, as clothing provides a wide array of non-verbal communicative cues. There are many types of nonverbal communication, and artifactics, proxemics, chronemics, kinesics and haptics are particularly significant for the design of SUIs.

2.1   Artifactics

Artifactics denote the communication and non-verbal signaling that emerges from personal accessories, such as dress or fashion accessories. The choice of what to wear is an efficient means of communicating during social interactions: Clothing not only conveys a message, but it also directly manipulates and influences how we and others establish our identities. Clothing acts as an extension of oneself and can non-verbally communicate a wide array of meanings, including identity, mood and attitude. Identities that are communicated by dress are also influenced by technology and society-wide moral and aesthetic standards [10, 11].

The aesthetics of a garment are important cues for interpreting dress. These include the construction material and usage, manufacture (handmade vs. machine produced vs. high-tech), design and historical references (innovative vs. traditional) and syntax (use of colors, patterns and shapes).

When choosing what to wear, both conscious and unconscious decisions are made. The primary considerations are suitability: Is the clothing suitable for the situation (expected dress code, weather conditions and wearer's persona)? Is it physically suitable (consistent with one's personal style and body shape)? People generally take 10–30 minutes to dress in the morning, but sometimes they take up to an hour (both genders). There is a general unwillingness to complicate the process of dressing by adding the need to configure a dress electronically. In fact, over the last hundred years, clothing development has trended towards greater simplicity and towards clothing that is easier to put on and wear [12].

2.2   Proxemics

Proxemics describes the use of space and orientation within nonverbal communication. Proxemics differentiates between two kinds of space, territorial and personal, the latter being of particular interest in the development of SUIs. This space, termed the Personal Reaction Bubble, can be divided into four groups that are associated with differing distances depending on the situation and the people involved. Intimate distance is used for close encounters, such as embracing, touching, or whispering. Personal distance is used with close friends and family members. Social distance is used among acquaintances and is used in a workplace or school setting, where there is no physical contact. Public distance is used when strangers meet or for public meetings [13].

2.3   Chronemics

Chronemics are concerned with the use of time in the context of human communication interactions. Chronemics is the study of the interaction time that is associated with our formal and informal obligations. However, chronemics also include subjective and personal temporalities [15]. In the design of SUIs, chronemics offer a reliable and easily executable tool for control. For example, the duration of time that a wearer chooses to spend in a place or in proximity to a certain object or person generally reflects the wearer's interest in the person or object. Chronemics are mostly used in conjunction with proxemics. When applying these tools to the design of a SUI, provisions must be made for situations in which the time and body position is out of a wearer's control, such as riding an escalator or sitting in a doctor's waiting room.

2.4   Kinesics

Kinesics is the interpretation of non-verbal behavior as related to movement either of a particular part of the body or of the body as a whole. These include facial expressions, gestures and posture. Only a few gestures are universal, such as the shrug, the 'halt' gesture and pointing, with slight culturalvariations in the execution of the gesture [16]. Facial expressions, however, are to a large extent innate and are therefore often universal and easy to read [17].

Unfortunately, it is difficult to integrate facial expressions into smart fashion because using tracking technology on the face is both conspicuous and uncomfortable. To a lesser extent, this is also true for the use of gloves or fingerings to track hand gestures [18]. Therefore we assume that future e-textiles will have embedded sensors, such as gyroscopes, flex sensors and accelerometers, that will allow the tracking of gestures and posture. To some extent, these sensors can be fashioned by exploiting the properties of soft materials that are used in the manufacturing of garments [19]. Evaluating these data could be important for reading and interpreting nonverbal cues.

In addition to using preconscious bodily gestures to better interpret the user's intentions, certain conventions used in body gesture control could be developed. Such conventions are used in interactions with the multitouch surface of smartphones and tablets. There has been little research into using sign language for bodily interfacing. Existing research focuses on the use of camera-based tracking technology and does not use data directly from the body [20].

2.5   Haptics

Haptics are concerned with the significance of touch and the impressions received through touch. These include vibrations or motion, heat, cold and pressure. Vibration is most commonly used in mobile technologies to convey information unobtrusively. In Smart Fashion, haptic impressions are most commonly used to communicate presence [21]. Although of the utmost significance in the human perception of reality, haptics are not widely used in inter-human communication. In most cultures, the act of touching is used only as a gesture of recognition when meeting or departing or in an intimate situation. Some cultures do not touch at all in public. Another aspect of touch in interfacing is the issue of hygiene, as for public touch-screen displays [22]. Therefore we have not integrated haptics into the SUI as a direct functionality between wearers. However, haptics do provide ample opportunities for recipient-based information mapping. Unfortunately, current technical possibilities are limited, so that impressions will be intrinsically symbolic in nature. However, it is possible that technical improvements in actuators, vibration motors and heating materials will meet the necessary requirements to convincingly communicate an iconical haptic input to the wearer.

3   Levels of Integration

Fashion is one of the oldest ways to express one's personal identity. People are generally willing to accept new fashions, yet new fashions are expected to be uncomplicated to wear and to require no significant learning. In our research, we found that in order to make technology an integral part of everyday clothing, we need to develop a greater awareness of the level of integration. Integration can be subdivided into four main elements that can serve as guidelines for integrating interactive technology into fashionable apparel.

3.1   Signal Level

Signals represent information in different ways, i.e. via symbolic, indexical and iconic representation. Indexical and iconic representation are preferable, as they are more in line with established perceptions and require little or no additional learning. Symbolically represented information is either based on socio-cultural conventions or has to be learned. Due to our ocularcentric perception, the visual signals and display level of the garments are a primary focus. Wearing illuminated apparel draws the observer's attention to the wearer, as the animated light patterns tend to distract from other (non-visual) information. Therefore light-emitting technologies have to be applied very carefully. A well-executed example of this is the electroluminescent fashion Alpha Lyrae by Vega Zaishi Wang. Wang applies the photonic material indirectly to create an ethereal and pleasant effect that does not directly confront the onlooker with an overpowering light source [23]. There are additional signals that can be conveyed through tactile and acoustic cues rather than through visual cues that are also important methods for conveying information. As we are continually aware of tactile impulses, without the need for focused attention, tactile cues have the potential to provide new kinds of wearable ambient displays [24].

3.2   Level of Interaction

Multitouch sensitive devices that have Natural User Interfaces (NUI) have gained popularity in the last 5 years and standards of operation such as swiping and pinching have been established [25, 26]. In fashion technology, comparable standards have yet to be established, with a plethora of suggestions that range from zippers, hooks and velcro to touch-sensitive textile surfaces. As the level of interaction is closely related to the input possibilities, we questioned the ways in which the body, covered with textiles, can be used as an input device. We studied gesture and movement for their potential for intuitive affordances, analyzed the most common approaches and compared the advantages and drawbacks. Our investigations confirmed the expectations that body gestures are socially, culturally and individually determined symbols. However, we believe that with the use of NUIs, more gestures can become "intuitive" as the market becomes increasingly saturated.

3.3   Level of Connectivity

There are many different input options, from the wearer's biometric data as captured by sensors integrated into the clothing, to information from remote locations or interactants. Accordingly, the level of connectivity can vary greatly. It begins in the personal sphere of social interactions between two people and extends to group interactions. However, when remotely extending beyond peer-to-peer (P2P) communication, the need arises for an additional control mechanism to distinguish among remote interactants.

3.4   Level of Privacy

Generally there are two main approaches to privacy in Smart Fashion. First, the signals and signs that are displayed can be completely visible but only be understandable to the wearer due the arbitrary nature of symbolic representation. Alternatively, the signals can be invisible or imperceptible except to the wearer [27].

However, as SUIs aim to extend the function of fashion as a public display, the wearer makes a decision about privacy when choosing to wear a certain garment. If the wearer feels outgoing and communicative, a brighter and more expressive garment can be chosen. If the wearer is in a more introspective mood, more unobtrusive designs can be favored. This user-controlled approach to privacy is in line with current practices for dressing.

4   Discussion and Conclusion / Further Work

Clothing constitutes one of our main cultural assets and is deeply rooted in human history. These traditions influence both clothing design and our perception of clothing. For interactive technology to become a truly integral part of our culture, these preconditions have to be acknowledged and respected. Only a few of the examples that we studied reflect these aspects fully or even partially. Often it is the technical elements that need to be improved substantially for the interactive garments to truly become suitable for every day wear. For example, two important practical considerations are the garment's power supply and washability.

In our analysis of representative examples of Smart Fashion we deduced that apart from the technical specifications, the design of the interface itself is of paramount importance for the acceptance of Smart Fashion. We identified the following parameters that should to be applied to the development of what we describe as the SUI:

The SUI is a subcategory of Wearables, which, in contrast to WearComp, is a physically embedded interface with a textile or other flexible material that can be worn comfortably on the body as the main substrate. The SUI has no screens and is in direct contact with the user. The operation of the SUI relies on biometric and contextually relevant data in conjunction with the nonverbal communication cues of the wearer and other interactants.

An SUI must be as easy to use as any other everyday garment, and the interface should not requiring any additional configuration or training. Consequently, the focus must be on indexical and iconic representations within the user interface. As part of enhanced apparel, an SUI can extend and amplify social interactions on a variety of levels, including interactions with distant environments as well as with interactants. However, when incorporating multiple remote connections, the issue of distinguishability arises. We anticipate the areas of application of this technology to be predominantly in inter-personal communication, although it will introduce novel methods of interaction with surrounding architectural space or to remote locations [28]. Therefore, one challenge in the development of SUIs is for the interfaces to remain understandable to interactants in a larger network. We think that haptics have great potential for information mapping when the technical issues are resolved.

We believe that the application of context-relevant data, and sensor-based data harvesting and evaluation of nonverbal communication cues in particular, has the potential to create a new paradigm for the design of SUIs. To accomplish this, it is necessary to establish the positioning and movement of the body (kinesics) in conjunction with distance (proxemics) and time (chronemics) with regard to a given location. The ensuing seamless integration into everyday apparel should result in a soft human-computer interface.

References

1. Streitz, N., Nixon, P.: The Disappearing Computer. Communications of the ACM 48(3), 33–35 (2005)
2. First Warning Systems, Inc., http://www.firstwarningsystems.com/
3. Nike+ FuelBand SE Activity Tracker & Fitness Monitor, http://www.nike.com/us/en_us/c/nikeplus-fuelband (accessed November 20, 2013)
4. UP by AliphCom dba Jawbone, https://jawbone.com/up/ (accessed January 12, 2014)
5. Flex by fitbit, https://www.fitbit.com/ (accessed March 4, 2014)
6. Sporty Supaheroe jacket for bicyclists by Utope, http://www.utope.eu/sporty-supaheroe_jacket01.html (accessed November 20, 2013)
7. Frankjaer, T.R., Gilgen, D.: Wearable Networks, Creating Hybrid Spaces with Soft Circuits. In: Marcus, A. (ed.) DUXU 2014, Part II. LNCS, vol. 8518, pp. 435–445. Springer, Heidelberg (2014)

8. Hogan, K., Stubbs, R.: Can't get Through 8 Barriers to Communication. Pelican Publishing Company (2003)
9. Argyle, M., Salter, V., Nicholson, H., Williams, M., Burgess, P.: The Communication of Inferior and Superior Attitudes by Verbal and Non-verbal Signals. British Journal of Social and Clinical Psychology 9, 222–231 (1970)
10. Stone, G.: Appearance of the self. In: Human Behavior and Social Processes: An Interactionist Approach, pp. 86–118. Houghton Miffilin, New York (1962)
11. Roach-Higgins, M.E., Eicher, J.B.: Dress and identity. Clothing and Textiles Research Journal 10(4), 1–8 (1992)
12. Christine Frederick, C.: How long does it take your wife to dress? American Weekly (January 14, 1917)
13. Hall, E.T.: The Hidden Dimension. Anchor Books. Random House, Inc. (1990)
14. Bruneau, T.: Chronemics. In: Encyclopedia of Communication Theory. SAGE Publications, Inc., Littlejohn S.W (2009)
15. Doherty-Sneddon, G.: Children's Unspoken Language. Jessica Kingsley Publishers (2003)
16. Knapp, M.L., Hall, J.A., Horgan, T.G.: Nonverbal communication in human interaction. Cengage Learning (2012)
17. Sign Language Ring, http://www.red-dot.sg/en/online-exhibition/concept/?code=1033&y=2013&c=16&a=0 (accessed November 20, 2013)
18. Fraser, G.A., Raab, S.: Posture monitoring system. U.S. Patent 4, 730, 625 (1988)
19. Fox, M., Polancic, A.: Conventions of Control: A Catalog of Gestures for Remotely Interacting With Dynamic Architectural Space. In: Proceedings of the 32nd Annual Conference of the Association for Computer Aided Design in Architecture (ACADIA), San Francisco, pp. 429–438 (2012)
20. Cohen, C.J., et al.: Gesture-controlled interfaces for self-service machines and other applications. U.S. Patent No. 7460690 (2008)
21. Keng Soon Teh, J., et al.: Huggy Pajama: A mobile parent and child hugging communication system. In: Proceedings of the 7th International Conference on Interaction Design and Children, pp. 250–257. ACM, Chicago (2008)
22. Dix, A., et al.: Physicality and Spatiality: Touching private and public displays. In: Workshop on Designing Multi-touch Interaction Techniques for Coupled Public and Private Displays, Napels, p. 8 (2008)
23. Alpha Lyrae by Vega Zaishi Wang, http://www.vegawang.com/ (accessed November 20, 2013)
24. Wisneski, C.A.: The design of personal ambient displays. Diss. Massachusetts Institute of Technology (1999), http://dspace.mit.edu/handle/1721.1/
25. Buxton, B.: Multi-Touch Systems that I Have Known and Loved Microsoft Research. Original (January 12, 2007)
26. Wigdor, D., Wixon, D.: Brave NUI World: Designing Natural User Interfaces for Touch and Gesture. Morgan Kaufmann Publishers Inc., San Francisco (2011)
27. Fajardo, N., Andrew, V.M.: ExternalEyes: Evaluating the visual abstraction of human emotion on a public wearable display device. In: Proceedings of the 20th Australasian Conference on Computer-Human Interaction: Designing for Habitus and Habitat. ACM (2008)
28. Kobayashi, H., Ueoka, R., Hirose, M.: Wearable Forest-Feeling of Belonging to Nature. In: MM 2008, Vancouver, British Columbia, Canada, October 26–31, 2008. ACM (2010)

Beyond Wearables: Experiences and Trends in Design of Portable Medical Devices

Rafael Gomez and Anna Harrison

Queensland University of Technology, School of Design,
Creative Industries Faculty, Australia
(r.gomez,anna.harrison)@qut.edu.au

Abstract. The use of Portable Medical Devices (PMDs) has become increasingly widespread over the last few years. A combination of factors; including advances in technology, the pressure to reduce public health costs and the desire to make health solutions accessible to a wider patient base are contributing to the growth in the PMD market. Design has a clear role to play in the current and future context of the PMD landscape. In this paper, we identify emerging trends in the design of PMDs; including changes in the form, purpose and mode of use, and explore how these trends are likely to fundamentally impact the nature of healthcare and the patient experience from an experience design perspective. We conclude by identifying a research opportunity for design within the healthcare and PMD context.

Keywords: Portable Medical Device, Implantable Medical Devices, Mobile Health, Patient Experience, Experience Design.

1   Introduction

Portable medical devices (PMDs) have become commonplace for many people around the world, and this trend is likely to continue. These devices impact the ways in which people monitor, manage, maintain, regulate and ultimately determine their own health and wellbeing. PMDs play a critical role in health management that can lead to reduced pressure on the healthcare system, curtail unhealthy habits, improve adherence to medical regimes, increase likelihood of improved lifestyle choices and enhance the ongoing experience of health management [1,2]. With the rise of chronic health conditions [3] innovations in this area have the potential to improve and enhance the experience and overall quality of life for patients. PMDs not only allow ongoing, continuous, and unobtrusive monitoring of physiological patient conditions they can also provide more realistic indication of health status and information that is otherwise inaccessible through other means [4]. As PMD technology progresses we are seeing devices shift from operating externally to our bodies to being on our bodies as wearable devices and ultimately merge internally as implantable technologies. At that point the patient experience transforms and we enter an era where products themselves have the power to change not only the patient experience but also ultimately

A. Marcus (Ed.): DUXU 2014, Part IV, LNCS 8520, pp. 261–272, 2014.

the human condition [5]. Implantable medical devices will have the capacity to rewire the human brain, and thus have a substantial impact on physiology, behavior, and emotions and people's overall health and wellbeing – radically changing the nature of healthcare and patient experience. Within the context of this paper PMDs are defined as small, portable (mobile, untethered) wireless computing devices to meet healthcare needs [2,6]. Due to their nature, PMDs enable people to be acutely aware of and monitor their health and wellbeing virtually at any time in any given context. From an experience design perspective, PMDs can be considered as mediators between the user and an external motivation to achieve a positive health outcome. They become a hinge by which patients can achieve a health related goal and permit or prohibit these goals from happening. But as we will discuss, when PMDs move beyond wearable to internal this dynamic changes and the interaction shifts from a conscious tangible experience to an unconscious intangible experience. As technology and other drivers continue to push the boundaries further an important question arises; how will trends in PMDs impact the nature of the patient and health experience? This presents a research opportunity for design, understanding and unpacking this new landscape is a step towards a dialogue that will lead to effective, and appropriate, design strategies for PMDs and healthcare experience. This paper discusses trends that have emerged beyond the current PMD landscape. Through this analysis existing PMDs are categorized along three dimensions, namely; form (dedicated or add-on), purpose (monitor, nudge, advanced diagnostic) and mode of use (external, wearable, internal), with mode of use being a driving factor for significant change. Future vision and directions are proposed and consideration of the potential impacts on the nature of healthcare and patient experience are discussed through the lens of experience design. By better understanding PMDs and impacts of future trends from an experience design perspective; researchers, designers and technology experts can contribute in a more meaningful way to the development of devices that ultimately raise the quality of life for patients now and in the future.

2   The Rise of Portable Medical Devices

It is evidently clear that the proliferation of 'anywhere, anytime' computing [7] has well and truly begun, and its inevitable path toward the medical and health field is already occurring. Devices will no longer just be portable they will soon be wearable and integrated into our bodies. In the not too distant future we will be experiencing medical devices that are embedded into our bodies to track, manage, diagnose and respond automatically and without our knowledge to our physical and physiological conditions. The convergence of the seemingly never ceasing advancement of smaller and more powerful computing with internet capabilities have created an environment in which patients can begin to be more active in their own personal medical and health management through PMDs. Innovations in technology are transforming the health care industry and spurring the development of portable medical devices for health management, tracking, monitoring, diagnosis, treatment and measuring of various health related data [2]. Health systems in many countries around the world are moving towards electronic healthcare systems (e-health) that automatically store personal, sensitive and medical information. These technical advances and developments are creating significant challenges for the industry [8,9] but also generate many opportunities in healthcare. Reducing public healthcare costs is another driving factor. Spiraling costs continue to be a challenging dilemma worldwide and with an ageing population the demand for healthcare will not dissipate anytime soon. In the United States healthcare costs account for 18% of GDP [2] and in Europe the same scenario prevails [10,11]. The current and emerging PMD technologies have the potential to reduce the strain on healthcare spending through better and faster decision-making processes, improve prevention strategies, reduce hospital visits and administrative costs, and improve adherence to treatment plans [2]. The desire to provide healthcare to a wider patient base is a further driver in this area [12]. Current healthcare system is founded on large-scale, capital intensive, centralized networks that demands individuals travel to hospitals and medical facilities. This system has become highly inefficient and PMDs can play a key role in transforming healthcare into a more efficient, patient-centered system. They permit individuals to have instant, on-demand access to their medical needs, health data and powerful clinical decision support tools that empower them to actively participate in their treatment plans. Portable devices also allow people to overcome the limitations of geography in rural areas, people in lower socio-economic settings, people who suffer from mobility difficulties and cultural minorities [2,12,13]. These factors have been driving the advancement of PMDs at an ever-increasing rate. PMDs are not only permeating modern life but will continue to do so for decades to come. The opportunities afforded are encouraging but it is essential to contextualize this within a design framework that situates the patient at the center in order to prepare for the shift in the nature of healthcare and ultimately provide an appropriate and positive patient experience.

3   Experience and Design

For over a decade, the field of design has seen an emerging interest in what has been termed as experience design. Experience design attempts to move past usability, functionality and effectiveness towards a more comprehensive understanding of the overall human-product interaction [14,15,16]. As [17] argues: "Experience design asserts design not to be about products anymore but about the experiences they deliver... meaning and emotion (*becoming*) the prime design objective " [17 p.75]. Users of products in everyday life, although concerned about practical and pragmatic issues, care more about about how products enhance and mediate daily experiences. So when talking about experiences this encompasses: emotions, interactions and user-product-context relationship over time [17,18,19,20]. Experience design is relevant for PMDs as emotional experiences have a significant role to play in how people feel about themselves and about their health and can promote as well as hinder personal health [21]. [22] argues that well designed medical products lead to increased patience adherence to medical and take on a crucial role in patient therapy. Even more relevant perhaps is that if device design does not take into account patient experience this can lead to not only poor health regimes but also reduce people's quality of life and even lead to dangerous medical situations [21]. Within available research there seems to be minimal consideration of dealing with the emotional experience of interacting specifically with PMDs, especially when it comes to healthcare and the patient experience [23]. If the experience of interaction is not taken into account a gap in understanding the full spectrum of the patient experience can arise, as a result leading to inadequately designed services and devices. Research conducted by one of the authors on the emotional experience of portable interactive health and medical devices is one exception [23]. [24] describe two cases in which limited consideration of user experience leads to dangerous and hazardous results. Both cases involved the use of a defibrillator in a real world situation in which the design led to incorrect use of the device. In the first situation a medical team working on a cardiac arrest patient inadvertently delivered an electric shock leaving the patient with profound neurological injuries. The second case was a simulation where physicians were observed powering down a defibrillator when they intended to deliver a shock instead. Both cases appear like simple design flaws but also reveal a deeper issue about the experience. The authors argue that these devices failed because they were not designed to match the needs, cognitive processes, and environments of users [24]. To go one step further it is important to consider the experiential and emotional aspects of the users. For example in both cases stress, anxiety and concern are experiential aspects that can also contribute to incorrect use and errors with the device. Another paper published more recently discusses the importance of applying human factors approach to the medical device field [25]. The paper does a good job of stressing the relevance of including a human centered design approach. The authors go on to suggest the impact of the context of the experience as an important element of the relationship between user and product that is currently missing in studies of medical device design. Although [25] make a concerted effort to try and raise the level of design in the medical device industry by incorporating usability principles, if we are to truly acknowledge the complexity of user interactions with medical devices a broader experience design approach is needed. To better understand and design for the patient experience it is important to consider the latest in design research and knowledge. The experience design approach offers a perspective that encapsulates broader issues of experience design that form a part of the complex user-product relationship. Current and future PMDs should be designed appropriately to support the quality of life of people as they are implicated in influencing the way patients relate to their own health and wellbeing and can facilitate or inhibit positive experiences.

4   Trends in the Portable Medical Device Landscape

As PMDs continue to flourish there are some trends that are becoming evident. Instead of classifying these trends purely on technical capabilities the approach taken here is to view them along three interconnected dimensions, namely: form (dedicated or add-on), purpose (monitor, nudge and advanced diagnostic) and mode of use (external, wearable, internal). By looking at the existing literature from this novel perspective, several trends emerging in the PMD landscape can be observed and particular aspects in relation to the potential impact on the nature of healthcare and the patient experience can be identified.

Form. The first observed trend is related to the change in form of PMDs [26]. Here the form of health related technologies is broken into two types; dedicated devices for specific medical needs and add-ons to existing technologies that permit users to perform medical related functions that would otherwise not be able to be performed with a single device. Ever since the pacemaker, first used in 1959 [9] there have been a multitude of dedicated portable medical devices. More recently a multitude of manufacturers are developing PMDs for various needs such as diabetes and heart disease through to health and fitness devices for everyday use [2,12,27]. This area of the medical field is evolving rapidly but is also being absorbed in some cases by the development of add-on technologies. Health related add-ons are becoming more and more prevalent. One type that is growing rapidly is health related apps on mobile devices. There are apps that target almost any conceivable area of the health area including chronic conditions, telemedicine, remote monitoring, data capture, electronic records, e-prescribing, and health and fitness [2]. Services like WebMD are another form of add-on that have become available to patients on mobile devices, making self-diagnosis easily accessible to the billions of people around the world who now carry a mobile phone. Peripheral products that attach to existing mobile devices and provide functionality not possible with the original device alone are another type of add-on technology. Example include a peripheral that attaches to a mobile phone for blood glucose monitoring and an eye testing device that attaches to a mobile phone camera [28,29].

Purpose. As PMDs have increased in variety so have the ways in which they are used. The second trend is classified according to the purpose that PMDs serve including monitoring, nudging and advanced diagnostics. PMDs used for monitoring medical information have been around for some time with electrocardiogram (ECG) and electroencephalogram (EEG) being some of the first portable devices used [30]. The AMON (advanced care and alert portable telemedical monitor) consists of a monitoring and alert system for high-risk cardiac and respiratory patients [31]. Recently monitoring functions have moved into the health and fitness area and can log data about people's exercise regime, habits and patterns with the Fitbit range of products and the Jawbone fitness tracker being examples of popular devices in this area. Beyond monitoring and data logging, PMDs have moved into what has been referred to as 'nudging' or persuasive functions [32]. A nudge refers to the ways in which a device motivates or prompts users to perform activities that improve the life of the individual and encourage them away from potentially harmful choices and nudge them towards healthy decisions. For instance, UbiFit transforms the background wallpaper on a mobile phone into a garden. Physical movement keeps the garden alive, thus encouraging users to be physically active and keep the garden nourished [33]. Another example is the Vito television remote control that offers viewers alternatives to watching TV including viewing "to do" lists and playing physical games [32]. A third group of PMDs are defined as advanced diagnostic devices. These devices support complex healthcare applications and enable continuous provision of health and medical needs by monitoring the patient, environment and context and respond accordingly. Some of the vitals signs these devices can monitor include electromyogram (EMG), (ECG), activity, mobility, falls, respiratory rate, heart sounds, blood glucose levels, oxygen saturation, body or skin temperature and galvanic skin response [34]. The Cardionet wearable system monitors patient heart rate, ECG and other data to help physicians diagnose and support patients suffering from arrhythmias [34]. [35] outline recent developments in ingestible medical devices that offer non-invasive alternatives to traditional endoscopy or surgery for diagnosis and treatment of gastrointestinal disorders.

Mode of Use. The ways in which PMDs are utilised have changed over the years from devices that are external to ones that are worn on the body to more recent devices that exist internally. Each change in mode has moved the device closer to the patient from fixed medical systems to mobile, wearable and ultimately implantable devices. The initial wave of PMDs were external to the body (with a few exceptions). As micro-electronics and textile technology evolved wearable computing became common. Wearable computing is similar to portable or mobile devices but the term wearable suggests that the support environment is either the human body or a piece of clothing [27]. In this way wearable devices are closer in proximity to the body and have a different relationship to the person. Current developments in this area include implantable devices, which significantly alter the relationship of patient and device. The technology required for more modern implantable devices is also changing and impacting the user experience at a fundamental level as these devices, working at the nanoscale in some cases [36], are used for a variety of therapeutic or life-saving functions ranging from drug infusion and cardiac pacing to direct neurostimulation. Implantable devices can automatically and directly alter a patient physically, physiologically and in many cases without any patient interaction [8]. It is this third dimension that is interesting to discuss in terms of the health experience. This presents designers with a unique challenge because as devices move from external to wearable to internal, the ways in which we relate and interact with devices changes significantly. Implantable devices have the capacity to modify the patient's condition without the patient even knowing. This is a distinct change in user-product relationship that requires a new way of defining and evaluating the health experience. Form changes and transformations in purpose are relevant to outline but it is the change in mode of use that will perhaps have the biggest impact on the nature of healthcare and the patient experience. As dedicated and add-on devices begin to be implanted in our bodies performing monitoring, nudging and advanced diagnostic functions without patient interaction or awareness, it is crucial to begin to explore opportunities and question the role that design plays in this scenario.

5   Future Visions for Potable Medical Devices

As we move from the current state to a future vision some radical changes in the ways that patients experience PMDs can be envisaged. We have identified three dimensions that have recently evolved and following these trajectories we discuss the ways in which the next generation of PMDs impact the nature of healthcare and the patient experience.

Impact on Nature of Healthcare. Figure 1 outlines changes in the nature of healthcare in the future [2]. The current state of patient needs involves fitness, healthy living and wellbeing with a focus on home and remote monitoring and active access of health information by patients.

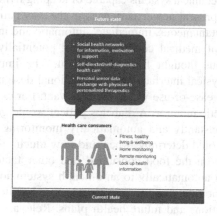

Fig. 1. Current and Future state of patient healthcare (adapted from [2 p.11])

The future of the patient experience is predicted to include social health networks for information access, support and motivation; self-directed and self-diagnostics capabilities for devices, personalised therapeutics and personal sensor data exchange with physicians. The future of healthcare will see the development of health capabilities with the capacity to capture and analyse self-reported data alongside objective behavioral and contextual information to extract meaning that positively impacts an individual's health status and well being [2]. This future vision provides a view on the nature of healthcare with the proliferation of PMDs in the near future. Similarly, [37] discusses the ways in which advanced wearable medical devices may impact the nature of healthcare. Patients interact via dedicated wearable technology as well as a variety of add-on gadgets functioning as sensors or data recorders continuously monitoring patient vital signs. The idea of traveling to a doctor's clinic will be an option of last resort as medical professionals and caregivers engage with patients remotely and provide health diagnosis based on data gathered from wearable devices. Patients will receive virtual and remote care in a variety of ways with virtual clinics providing urgent care through videoconferencing between patient and caregivers. For complicated cases wearable devices will be used to monitor specific conditions and alert emergency services while virtual procedures will become the norm as doctors will be able to use a variety of sensors to treat a patient without patients leaving the comfort of their own home. As we have identified it is likely that beyond wearable devices the forthcoming generation of devices will be more intimately integrated within the patients' bodies. Once PMDs move from the external to the internal a new dynamic begins to evolve. Internal devices verge on the concept of the 'cyborg' – a chimera of living organism and machine [9]. As identified earlier, implantable devices have the capacity to monitor, log and detect changes in the physical and physiological condition of the patient and control parts of the body autonomously and remotely. Although in their infancy, implantable device technologies are functioning at a high level of complexity with some devices designed to compensate for reduced sensory perception through to complicated technical systems capable of keeping living organisms alive [9].

Implantable devices present new experiences in the way patients manage and interact with healthcare. Instantaneous, immediate, automatic and involuntary interactions with the management of medical conditions could potentially occur anytime, anywhere without conscious thought from the patient. The implantable device itself would not include a physical interface and so traditional design issues regarding usability, functionality and ease-of-use would be irrelevant. For example consider a fully implantable smart diabetic monitor. A diabetes patient would go about their daily life while the device is constantly and automatically monitoring blood-glucose levels. Over time the device would determine when and how much insulin is required in the bloodstream depending on the food consumed and other factors. The device could upload this information automatically to an e-health system so that the patient's diet and information could be monitored to provide accurate longitudinal data for medical checkups, recommendations and future health plans. Relevant information about adjustments to diet and exercise could be delivered to the patient if a particular threshold was reached. In an emergency the implantable device could automatically alert emergency services and accurately pinpoint the location of the patient. It could also monitor the patient during this period and inform emergency personnel of any critical data that needs to be immediately addressed when they arrive for treatment. Another scenario could be a future implantable cardiac defibrillator device, early versions of which are currently available [8]. More advanced designs could have the capability to monitor heart rhythms and deliver small electrical shocks to adjust irregularities. Patients could go about their daily activities and the device would autonomously control irregular patterns in rhythms and even respond instantaneously to early signs of more severe heart problems and prevent the onset of a heart attack. Longitudinal data regarding could be monitored and logged to an external e-health network and analysed by a medical professional. Personal exercise and activity programs could be designed for the patient in response to the data history recorded. As technology progresses and PMDs begin to evolve opportunities exist for other scenarios. Devices implanted directly onto the brain could be used for treatment of conditions such as chronic pain, tremors and Parkinson's disease [9]. A range of biosensors used to measure biological phenomena and send data elsewhere for storage or analysis are also potential implantable systems [8]. Ingestible pills that enable inspection of cancerous growths in the intestinal wall and permit visual assessment of the overall health of the gastrointestinal tract are another form of implantable device [35]. All of these scenarios provide a window into the various ways in which PMDs have the potential to change the nature of healthcare. From a design perspective it is important to begin to consider how this shift impacts the experience of interaction and identify the ways design can be applied to positively contribute to these visions.

Impact on Patient Experience. As PMDs evolve in form, purpose and mode of use not only does the nature of healthcare transforms so too does the patient experience. From an experience design perspective how do these changes impact the patient experience? Once we move from external to wearable to internal, the design experience – as we traditionally know it – transforms completely. Issues relating to tangible factors such as usability, physical button layout, interface design and so on almost disappear when it comes to internal devices. With devices that are internal it becomes all about the experience, or rather, what experience the device is programmed to deliver. As examined in the previous section fundamental aspects regarding the nature of healthcare changes as we move from external to wearable to internal (Section 5.1). Here we will propose ways in which the patient experience transforms through the lens of experience design. Table 1 illustrates the different ways that PMDs impact aspects of the patient experience. The top row outlines the modes of use as outlined previously including external, wearable and internal. For external type devices the interface that patients deal with are usually tangible and often include some sort of GUI. The device responds to the user input and as such can facilitate user intention or goal and mediate experience. Since the patient is driving the experience they are also aware of the interaction that is occurring and has a high degree of control. For wearable devices the interface is also tangible and may include a GUI but controls can sometimes be small or non-existent. Due to the nature of wearable devices, the device can respond to the user input but can also respond to the external context including environment, social setting, time of day, and so on; in other words wearable technology lends itself well to be context sensitive [38].Wearable devices can mediate a users intention or goal but over time the interaction between can fade into the background, as there is only some degree of control on behalf of the patient. With implantable devices the experience between user and device changes in various ways. From a design perspective the biggest change is driven by the fact that implantable devices have no tangible interface since they are internal, but do have the potential to include an external GUI. One of the unique characteristics about implantable devices is that they not only have the capacity to *respond* to the patient's physiological, physical and internal conditions, they also have the capacity to *control* the patient and as a result not only mediate but also direct the experience. The device can continuously perform its function autonomously and so users can easily become unaware of its presence, as they are no longer controlling or managing the interaction. As healthcare merges with our internal physiological and physical body through devices that are implantable, intangible, and no longer consciously controlled by the user – what role will design play? These changes to patient interaction have clear and significant impacts on the nature of healthcare and the patient experience. The challenge is to identify the opportunity for design and to explore the ways design can engage effectively in this future scenario.

Table 1. Portable medical device experience according to PMD changes

Distance to body	External	Wearable	Internal
Interface	Tangible, graphical user interface (GUI)	Tangible, GUI	Intangible, GUI
Device response condition	Responds primarily to patient input	Responds to patient input and context	Respond to internal condition of patient
Experience potential	Can mediate experience	Can mediate experience	Can mediate and control experience
Patient awareness	Conscious device interaction	Interaction fades into subconscious	No longer aware of device interaction
Patient control	High degree	Some degree	Minimal to none

6   Conclusion: A Dialogue on the Experience and Trends in Design of Portable Interactive Devices

Devices that assist in patient healthcare should be designed to support the ongoing health and medical needs and overall quality of life for patients through effective user-device experience. PMDs play a critical role in healthcare that can lead to reduced pressure on the healthcare system, curtail unhealthy habits, increase the likelihood of improved lifestyle choices, enhance the user experience and ultimately raise the quality of life [2]. Designers need to be aware of the future trends in the PMD landscape and should apply experience design approaches to design effective, appropriate and positive user-product interactions and facilitate better healthcare and patient experiences [17,18,19,23]. This paper has identified some emerging trends in the design of PMDs; including changes in the form, purpose and mode of use, and explored how these trends are likely to impact the nature of healthcare and the patient experience from an experience design perspective. When PMDs evolve beyond wearable to implantable, and their mode of use changes from conscious to sub-conscious to no awareness of device interaction [39], patients will enter an era in which the very products themselves have the power to change the human condition [5]. Implantable devices will have the capacity to substantially impact physiology, behavior, and emotions as well as people's general health and wellbeing [2,5,9] ultimately rewiring the human brain. By addressing how people relate and interact with current and future PMDs, they can be better designed to suit the needs, requirements, wants and overall demands of patients within the healthcare system. Appropriately designed PMDs can permit patients to make informed decisions about their health and chronic conditions, take responsibility for their personal health management, motivate patients to make the right choice at the right time about their health, reduce the stress of managing chronic health, enhance experience and improve the overall quality of life for patients. From a design perspective there is a research opportunity to explore and better understand the ways these devices facilitate experiences for people in everyday life. Understanding the trends and the potential PMDs have to impact the nature of healthcare and the patient experience is a first step towards initiating a dialogue that will lead to effective and appropriate design strategies for PMDs in this new landscape.

References

1. Kilian, J., Pantuso, B.: The Future of Health Care Is Social (2009),
   http://www.fastcompany.com/future-of-health-care
2. Greenspun, H., Coughlin, S.: mHealth in an mWorld: How mobile technology is transforming health care. Deloitte Center for Health Solutions, Washington (2012)
3. Geneau, R., Stuckler, D., Stachenko, S., McKee, M., Ebrahim, S., Basu, S., Chockalingham, A., Mwatsama, M., Jamal, R., Alwan, A., Beaglehole, R.: Raising the priority of preventing chronic diseases: A political process. Lancet 376, 1689–1698 (2010)
4. Hung, K., Zhang, Y.T., Tai, B.: Wearable Medical Devices forTele-Home Healthcare. In: 26th Annual International Conference on the IEEE EMBS, pp. 5384–5387 (2004)
5. Carr, N.: The shallows: What the Internet is doing to our brains. WW Norton & Co. (2011)
6. Mirza, F., Norris, T., Stockdale, R.: Mobile technologies and the holistic management of chronic diseases. Hlth. Inf's. J. 14, 309–321 (2008)
7. Jones, M., Marsden, G.: Mobile interaction design. JohnWiley & Sons, Chichester (2006)
8. Burleson, W., Clark, S., Ransford, B., Fu, K.: Design Challenges in Secure Implantable Medical Devices. In: ACM/IEEE DAC 2012 Conference, pp. 12–17 (2012)
9. Giselbrecht, S., Rapp, B., Niemeyer, C.: The Chemistry of Cyborgs—Interfacing Technical Devices with Organisms. Angew. Chem. Int. Ed. 52, 13942–13957 (2013)
10. The Economist: The Future of Healthcare in Europe (2011), http://www.janssen-emea.com/sites/default/files/The-Future-Of-Healthcare-In-Europe.pdf
11. Chaytor, S., Staiger, U.: Future of Healthcare in Europe – Meeting future challenges: Key issues in context (2012), http://www.ucl.ac.uk/public-policy/public_policy_publications/FHE-print.pdf
12. West, D.: Improving Health Care through Mobile Medical Devices and Sensors (2013), http://www.brookings.edu/~/media/research/files/papers/2013/10/22%20mobile%20medical%20devices%20west/west_mobile%20medical%20devices_v06.pdf
13. Mechael, P.: The Case for mHealth in Developing Countries. Inn's: Tech, Gov's, Glob'n 4(1), 105–118 (2009)
14. Desmet, P., Hekkert, P.: Framework of product experience. Int. J. Des. 1, 57–66 (2007)
15. Overbeeke, C., Djajaningrat, J., Hummels, C., Wensveen, S.: Beauty in Usability: Forget about ease of use. In: Green, W., Jordan, P. (eds.) Pleasure with Products: Beyond Usability, pp. 9–18. Taylor and Francis, London (2002)
16. Schifferstein, H., Hekkert, P.: Product Experience. Elsevier, Amsterdam (2008)
17. Hassenzahl, M.: Experience Design: Technology for all the right reasons. Morgan & Claypool, California (2010)
18. Gomez, R.: The evolving emotional experience with portable interactive devices. PhD thesis, Queensland University of Technology, Brisbane (2012)
19. Gomez, R., Popovic, V., Blackler, A.: A framework to better understand emotional experiences with portable interactive devices: Preliminary trial. In: 5th International Congress of IASDR, Tokyo (2013)
20. von Saucken, C., Michailidou, I., Lindemann, U.: How to Design Experiences: Macro UX versus Micro UX Approach. In: Marcus, A. (ed.) DUXU/HCII 2013, Part IV. LNCS, vol. 8015, pp. 130–139. Springer, Heidelberg (2013)
21. Mayne, T.: Emotions and health. In: Mayne, T., Bonanno, G. (eds.) Emotions: Current Issues and Future Directions, pp. 361–397. Guilford, New York (2001)

22. Gloyd, D.: Positive user experience and medical adherence. In: International Conference on DPPI, pp. 17–21. ACM Publications, New York (2003)
23. Gomez, R., Popovic, V., Blackler, A.: Emotional experience with portable health devices. In: 7th International Conference on D&E, Chicago (2010)
24. Fairbanks, R., Wears, R.: Hazards with medical devices: the role of design. Ann. of Emerg. Med. 52, 519–521 (2008)
25. Sharples, S., Martin, J., Lang, A., Craven, M., O'Neill, S., Barnett, J.: Medical Device Design in Context: A Model of User-device Interaction and Consequences. Displays 33(4-5), 221–232 (2012)
26. Ahmadvand, A., Fayaz-Bakhsh, A.: Mobile Devices and Applications for Health: An Exploratory Review of the Current Evidence with Public Health Perspective. Ira'n. J. of Med'l. Inf's. 1(2), 6–14 (2012)
27. Glaros, C., Fotiadis, D.: Wearable Devices in Healthcare. In: Hutchison, D., Shepherd, W.D., Mariani, J.A. (eds.) Intelligent Paradigms for Healthcare Enterprises. STUDFUZZ, vol. 184, pp. 237–264. Springer, Heidelberg (2005)
28. McCurdie, T., Taneva, S., Casselman, M., Yeung, M., McDaniel, C., Ho, W., Cafazzo, J.: mHealth Consumer Apps: The Case for User-Centered Design. Biomed. Instrum. Tech. 46, 49–56 (2012)
29. Dolan, B.: 7 medical phone peripherals you should know, (2011),
    http://mobihealthnews.com/12062/
    7-medical-phone-peripherals-you-should-know/6/
30. Bai, J., Zhang, Y., Shen, D., Wen, L., Ding, C., Cui, Z., Tian, F., Yu, B., Dai, B., Zhang, J.: A portable ECG and blood pressure telemonitoringsystem. IEEE Engineering in Medicine and Biology Magazine 18(4), 63–70 (1999)
31. Anliker, U., Ward, J., Lukowicz, P., Tröster, G., Dolveck, F., Baer, M., Keita, F., Schenker, E., Catarsi, F., Coluccini, L., Belardinelli, A., Shklarski, D., Alon, M., Hirt, E., Vuskovic, M.: AMON: A wearable multiparameter medical monitoring and alert system. IEEE Trans. Inform.Technol. Biomed. 8(4), 415–427 (2004)
32. Consolvo, S., McDonald, D., Landay, J.: Theory-driven design strategies for technologies that support behavior change in everyday life. In: CHI 2009, pp. 405–414 (2009)
33. Byrne, R., Eslambolchilar, P.: Encouraging an Active Lifestyle with Personal MobileDevices: Motivational Tools and Techniques. In: First International Workshop on Nudge & Influence Through Mobile Devices, MobileHCI 2010 (2010)
34. Chan, M., Estve, D., Fourniols, J., Escriba, C., Campo, E.: Smartwearable systems: Current status and future challenges. Art. Intl. in Med. 56(3), 137–156 (2012)
35. Chen, I.-M., Phee, S., Luo, Z.: Personalized biomedical devices & systems for healthcare applications. Front's. of Mech. Eng. 6(1), 3–12 (2011)
36. Wallace, G., Higgins, M., Moulton, S., Wang, C.: Nanobionics: The impact of nanotechnology on implantablemedical bionic devices. Nanoscale 4, 4327–4347 (2012)
37. Schroetter, J.: The Future of Wearable Computing in Healthcare (2014),
    http://www.mdtmag.com/blogs/2014/01/future-wearable-
    computing-healthcare
38. Lukowicz, T., Kirstein, G., Troster, G.: Wearable systems for health care applications. Meth. Inf. Med. 43, 232–238 (2004)
39. Lookout.: Mobile Mindset Study (2012),
    https://www.lookout.com/resources/reports/mobile-mindset

On Feelings of Comfort, Motivation and Joy that GUI and TUI Evoke

Julián Esteban Gutiérrez Posada, Elaine C.S. Hayashi, and M. Cecília C. Baranauskas

Institute of Computing, University of Campinas (UNICAMP)
Av. Albert Einstein, 1251, 13083-970, Campinas-SP, Brazil
{jugutier,hayashi,cecilia}@ic.unicamp.br

Abstract. New ways to interact with technology are gaining ground over the familiar Graphical User Interfaces (GUI). The Tangible User Interfaces (TUI) are one example of this. However, while it may seem intuitive that such interfaces should evoke rather positive responses from users – e.g. feelings associated with pleasure – little has been studied in this sense. In this challenge of understanding the feelings that GUI and TUI have the potential to evoke, we present our findings from a research that involved more than a hundred people. The research question that guided our endeavors was: What are the relations between the feelings of joy, motivation and comfort when using TUI and GUI? We analyze the results and discuss some hypotheses to explain the behavior observed.

Keywords: Feeling, Comfort, Motivation, Joy, TUI, GUI, Kodu, Scratch.

1   Introduction

Advances in research in Tangible User Interface (TUI) have inspired diverse researchers, who are trying to understand the differences in users' responses when they interact to TUI and to Graphical User Interface (GUI). While statistics on impacts on productivity and cognitive development are important information, a research opportunity that still offers ground for further investigation is related to the type of feelings that those interfaces can evoke. As Norman [13] argues, "attractive things work better". Since usability and the efficacy of objects or systems are not always enough to determine their success or appreciation, we must also consider the affectibility - i.e., the affective or emotional aspects of interaction [6]. In this sense, this work reports on our endeavors to understand the feelings of comfort, motivation and joy that the different interface styles TUI and GUI may evoke.

Xie et al. [19] have found that, although children's self-reports of enjoyment are similar for TUI and GUI, they took longer and had more difficulty completing puzzles when interacting with GUI. As Ishii et al [8] explain, GUIs can be powerful, but they are not consistent with our interactions with the rest of the physical world. The study from Patten and Ishii [15] suggest that TUI provides better opportunity, when compared to GUI, for task recall and problem solving.

A. Marcus (Ed.): DUXU 2014, Part IV, LNCS 8520, pp. 273–284, 2014.

Besides the work of Xu [20] comparing enjoyment in children when interacting with TUI and GUI, Horn et al. [7] investigated other facets of affectibility aspects. They found that TUI was more inviting, more supportive of active collaboration, and more child-focused than the mouse-based interface. GUI and TUI were equivalently apprehendable and engaging. Those feelings, however, have been treated isolatedly in each separate research. This leads us to the research question that guided our study: what are the relations between the feeling of Joy, Motivation and Comfort when using TUI and GUI?

Historically, the Xerox Company introduced the first generation of Graphical User Interfaces (GUI) in 1981 [9]. The GUI allows the user to view digital information through one or more screens, and interact with it via remote controls such as keyboards, mouse and more recently through touch screens [8].

Ten years later, in 1991, Mark Weiser, employee of Xerox company, published an article with a new vision entitled "Ubiquitous Computing"; in this vision, he tries to make the computer, as it is traditionally known, hidden from the user, almost invisible. One way to achieve this invisibility of computers is with an interface type called Tangible User Interface (TUI), which has been investigated in deep by authors like Ishii [8, 9, 10]. The TUI allows users to manipulate physical objects, and through this manipulation the computer is able to change its internal state, subsequently causing a response or feedback to the user [4], [18], [19]. In other words, TUI makes a connection between physical objects with digital elements, thus providing the possibility of directly manipulating these elements [3].

We agree with the authors Doering et al. [3], who say that the TUI does not fit all situations; however, we also agree with the benefits that this type of interface may have in specific contexts, such as education. This idea is shared by authors such as: Garzotto and Gonella [5], Horn et al. [7], Strawhacker and Sullivan [17], Sylla[18] and Xu [20]. While many agree on the potential of TUI, there is still a great research opportunity on the investigation of the affective responses that GUI and TUI might evoke. In this sense, the research question that we presented and that guides our work should manage this opportunity.

The aspects of affective responses that we cover in our study are related to the feelings of Comfort, Motivation and Joy. Bernstein [1] defines Motivation as "an inner state that energizes an individual toward fulfillment of a goal". We understand that this should be an important response from users, as it should make the users continue using the application and fulfilling its tasks (e.g. an educational goal). Hence, motivation should not only stimulate users but also should indicate the success or failure of an application or type of application/interaction style.

Some authors (e.g. [2]; [16]) who study emotional responses adopt the PAD emotional state model. PAD stands for Pleasure, Arousal and Dominance. In our context we can associate arousal (excitement in the use of an application) with the Motivation of use. Pleasure could be associated with the feeling of Joy, as Joy is defined by the Oxford Dictionary [14] as "a feeling of great pleasure and happiness".

Another aspect of Dominance is the feeling of Comfort (e.g., when we dominate/feel powerful over an application, we usually feel comfortable in the use of it). For sake of simplicity, we provided easier definitions for each of these feelings, as we show in the next section.

This work investigates the relations between the feelings of joy, motivation and comfort of different user profiles when using TUI and GUI. The paper is organized as follows: in section 2 we describe the study context and method. In section 3 we present the results and we discuss them in section 4. Section 5 concludes this paper.

2   The Study Context and Method

This research was conducted in the context of an HCI discipline in the University of Campinas (UNICAMP), in São Paulo State, Brazil. It occurred during two academic semesters in 2013 as part of the design and development of user interfaces projects, in which the students had the role of designers.

2.1   Participants

Besides the students enrolled in the discipline, we managed to include other participants, who contributed as end user evaluators of the projects. In total, we had one hundred and nine people participating.

In the first semester of 2013 (2013A) we had a total of 69 people involved, with an average age of 23 years old (a maximum age of 59 years old and a minimum age of 14). In the second semester of 2013 (2013B) there was a total of 40 people. The average age was of 23 years old (a maximum age of 52 years old and a minimum age of 15). The age distribution of the whole set can be seen in Figure 1.

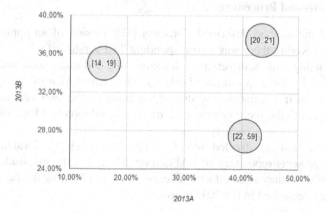

Fig. 1. Age range of the participants

As can be seen in Figure 1, the data of each semester will be treated separately, although shown in the same graph, with the intention to compare and identify any indications of trends.

Figure 1 shows the distribution of the age of the participants: for the 2013A is 11 (15.94%) people aged between 14 and 19 years old, 30 (43.48%) people aged between 20 and 21, and 28 (40.58%) people aged between 22 and 59. For the 2013B, there are 14 (35.00%) people aged between 14 and 19 years old, 15 (37.50%) people aged between 20 and 21, and 11 (27.50%) people aged between 22 and 59.

2.2   Method

In both semesters, the students from the HCI course were asked to choose an existing GUI application and modify it in a way that it would receive external events as inputs. Such external events should be in the form of physical objects being presented to the camera. In other words, their primary task was to take a GUI application and develop its TUI version.

In one semester the students were invited to choose an application among the many available for the Scratch[1] platform. In the other semester, the students chose among the applications available for Kodu[2] platform. Both Scratch and Kodu offers mainly educational solutions and underneath both lays the purpose of bringing programming language closer to children's world. Our objective was to investigate the affective responses from users towards the GUI and TUI versions of a same application. The platform of the original GUI version should have no or little impact on the results. In order to control also this factor we had the two courses working with a different platform (Scratch and Kodu). After developing the TUI applications, the designers were asked to invite other end users to interact with both GUI and TUI versions. After interacting with both versions, designers and end users answered a questionnaire.

2.3   Materials and Procedure

As a result of the method described, for each GUI version of an application (be it from Scratch or Kodu), there was a correspondent TUI version of it.

After interacting with both versions, designers and end users answered a questionnaire composed by three questions (Table 1). The central idea of the questionnaire was to determine, if it existed, any difference between the two versions, GUI and TUI, with respect to the feelings that were evoked in relation to Motivation, Comfort and Joy.

In 2013A, the students, divided into 10 groups, had to select a Scratch 1.4 application from the projects repository of SAPOScratch[3]. In 2013B, the students were divided into 5 groups; they selected an application made in Microsoft Kodu to make the same procedure requested in the 2013A group.

---

[1] http://scratch.mit.edu/scratch_1.4/
[2] http://research.microsoft.com/en-us/projects/kodu/
[3] SAPOScratch, is an educational program, product partnerships between "Portugal Telecom" and "Massachusetts Institute of Technology" (MIT) since 2008.
     http://kids.sapo.pt/scratch/channel/toploved

Table 1. The questionnaire

With which version did you feel more Comfortable?   *(which application evokes a greater sense of comfort in use)*   ( ) GUI ( ) TUI ( ) Indifferent ( ) None   **With which version did you feel more Motivated?**   *(which application evokes a greater desire to continue using it)*   ( ) GUI ( ) TUI ( ) Indifferent ( ) None   **Which version caused more Joy?**   *(The application that evokes a greater sense of pleasure in use)*   ( ) GUI ( ) TUI ( ) Indifferent ( ) None

In both semesters, the groups should use the computer vision framework called ReacTIVIsion[4] [11] to implement the TUI version. ReacTIVision is a framework for, among other things, the fast and robust tracking of Fiducial markers attached onto physical objects. This implies that with the TUI version, the user must use different Fiducial markers to associate objects to interact with the system (the markers must be attached to physical objects). Fiducial marks are figures that represent unique codes that can be identified by the computer.

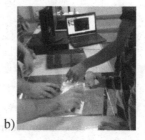

a)   b)

Fig. 2. The codes to associate objects to interact with the system

Figure 2 illustrates this activity and depicts students interacting with physical objects to obtain a response from the application (either Kodu or Scratch) via a monitor. Of course, this output could be projected onto the glass table (shown in Figure 2b) where students interacted, but that was not a requirement of the project.

In 2013A, each group of students had to implement a Java application that communicates ReacTIVision Framework with Scratch 1.4, through the Scratch resource called "Remote Sensor". In 2013B, each group of students received a developed app, which communicated ReacTIVision Framework with Kodu, by sending keyboard events. An open source version of these applications is available on the website of our research group: http://styx.nied.unicamp.br:8080/interhad/products.

In the next section we present the results of answers to the questionnaire and discuss possible interpretation for them. In order to make it clearer to the reader, we will refer to the projects created in 2013A as "ScratchP", and the projects created in 2013B as "KoduP".

---

[4] http://reactivision.sourceforge.net/

3   Results

The next three subsections present results of the questionnaire regarding the focus on each of the feelings of our interest (Comfort, Motivation, and Joy).   For each feeling we present four graphs which show the data: (a) From all participants of that semester; (b), (c), and (d) separated by the different age groups.   In the sequence we discuss the relationship observed between these feelings.

3.1   Comfort Feeling

For the sake of simplicity, the questionnaire defined to the users the feeling of comfort as: "The application that evokes a greater sense of comfort in use".   Surely it is a simplistic definition for a feeling, but this provides a common basis to all users. Our intention is to align participants' idea on the feeling of comfort when making a decision regarding the application that best evokes that feeling.

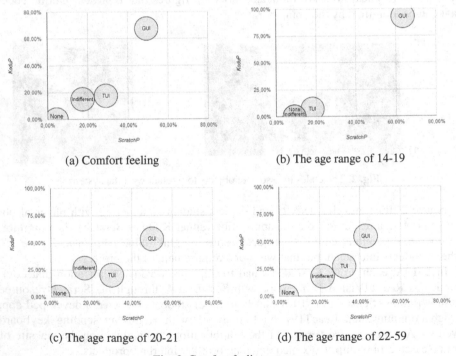

(a) Comfort feeling   (b) The age range of 14-19

(c) The age range of 20-21   (d) The age range of 22-59

Fig. 3. Comfort feeling per age

Figure 3 shows the percentage values of the number of people who felt more comfortable with each option (GUI, TUI, Indifferent and None) in each project; Figure 3a shows the results associated with the feeling of comfort considering all users who participated in the study. In the project with Scratch (ScratchP), 34 (49.28%) users considered the GUI version as the version that evokes a greater sense of comfort. In the project with Kodu (KoduP) 27 (67.50%) users felt more comfortable using the GUI version. That is, the two groups considered the GUI version as the version that evokes greater sense of comfort. If we analyze the TUI version, we see that 20 (28.99%) and 7 (17.50%) people considered it to be the most comfortable, in the projects with Scratch and Kodu respectively. The reason for this preference may be related to the previous exposition of users to the amount of movement required by GUI, in comparison with the TUI versions, which require different physical interaction.

More important than indicating the percentage values or the number of people for each option, we want to highlight the options movement along the three graphs (Figures 3b, 3c, and 3d). These Figures show the behavior of the "feeling of comfort" for each different age ranges. The three charts are on the same scale in both axes, so it is possible to make some observations visually. It is true that we cannot generalize this behavior; however some aspects are evidenced. The GUI version remains the version that best evokes the feeling of comfort. When we look at the older age groups, we can see that the GUI version loses ground to the TUI version and to Indifference. One possible explanation for this latter behavior is that the younger participants in this research are very familiar with computers and their predominant model of user interaction today is through GUI. In contrast, the older participants seem to feel less comfortable with these versions and begin to see the TUI versions as more natural for them.

3.2   Motivation Feeling

The questionnaire defined the feeling of motivation as: "The application that evokes a greater desire to continue using it", for the sake of simplicity.

As we can see in Figure 4a, the results of motivation presents a different picture compared to the results regarding comfort. The TUI version was selected in the project with Scratch by 44 (63.77%) of the people, and in the project with Kodu by 20 (50.00%) of people. In contrast, the GUI version was selected by 10 (14.49%) and 11 (27.50%) people in the two projects respectively, not far from the results shown by the Indifference option, 7 (10.14%) and 9 (22.50%) respectively.

With respect to the behavior of different ages people, we can see that the TUI version was always selected as the version that best evokes the feeling of motivation, for all age ranges. The GUI version seems to lose its ability to motivate groups of older participants. The option of Indifference starts among the least preferred choices (Figure 4b) but gains space and even surpasses the GUI version (Figure 4d). Looking at Figures 4b, 4c and 4d we can observe the opinion of the different age groups about the feeling of motivation for both ScratchP and KoduP applications. First consider the x axis, which represents ScratchP: the TUI version remains more or less stable, being the preferred choice for the first two groups (age groups between 14-19 and 20-21).

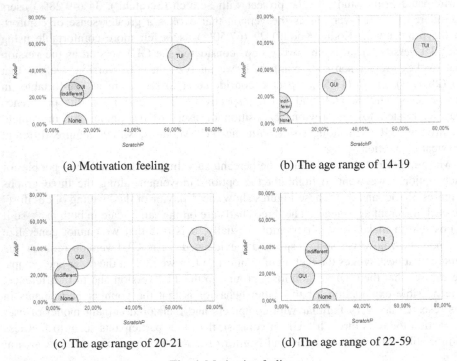

(a) Motivation feeling

(b) The age range of 14-19

(c) The age range of 20-21

(d) The age range of 22-59

Fig. 4. Motivation feeling

However, it falls 22.7% for the older group. Regarding the y axis - KoduP - the percentage value decreases less abruptly, but is still visible in the graphs. The biggest change is between the first age group and the second (10.48%). A possible explanation may be the need of physical activity required by the TUI version, which encourages them to continue using the application while   the GUI version does not present novelty. It is worth noticing the decrease in the last three figures, where the GUI version remained the option that least evokes the feeling of motivation. Regarding the decline of TUI option in the last two figures, one might speculate that this is due to the inability of younger people to be as effective with the required physical activity as they are with the keyboard.

3.3   Joy Feeling

For simplicity, the questionnaire defined the feeling of Joy as: "The application that evokes a greater sense of pleasure in use". With regard to the feeling of joy, we can observe that the TUI version has shown a greater ability to evoke this feeling, 31 (44.93%) people and 17 (42.50%) in the two projects respectively, selected the TUI version; in contrast with 14 (20.29%) and 7 (17.50%) people who selected the GUI version, in the same two projects. In general terms (Figure 5a) the number of people who marked the Indifferent option exceeds the number of people who select the GUI version. People who marked the Indifferent option are 19 (27.54%) and 16 (40.00%) in the two projects respectively.

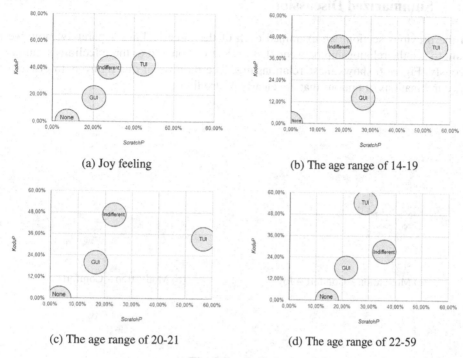

(a) Joy feeling

(b) The age range of 14-19

(c) The age range of 20-21

(d) The age range of 22-59

Fig. 5. Joy feeling

Another interesting result is observed when we look the option of Indifference in the other age groups. Figure 5b shows the Indifference option has the same percentage of choices the TUI version has, in relation to the project with Kodu. However, the difference in the percentages between Indifference and TUI are greater in relation to the project with Scratch. A possible explanation may be found in the applications environments (Kodu and Scratch). The Kodu environment is visually more appealing than Scratch, and may invite interaction with it.

In the next age group (Figure 5c), the Indifference option exceeds the option of TUI version; 46.67% and 33.33% respectively in KoduP.. While for KodyP the distance between "Indifference" and TUI is small, for ScratchP the distance between the same two is bigger. Although there are percentage differences, the behavior and the explanation may be similar for the younger group. Finally in the older age group (Figure 5d), the situation changed drastically, the TUI version options with 54.55% far exceeds the other options (Indifference 27.27%, 18.18% GUI version, and None 0.00%) in the project with Kodu, while the option of Indifference (35.71%) narrowly exceeds the other options (28.57% in the TUI version, GUI version 21.43% and None 14.72%) in the project with Scratch. In other words, the result indicates that for the older group - compared to other age groups - the TUI version is the one that least evokes the feeling of joy when using Scratch.

4   Summarized Discussion

In the previous section, we examined each of the three feelings separately; now we want to see the relationship between these selections on two or three feelings simultaneously. Figure 6 shows these relationships. The purpose of this figure is to observe the combinations of options that are clearly protruding.

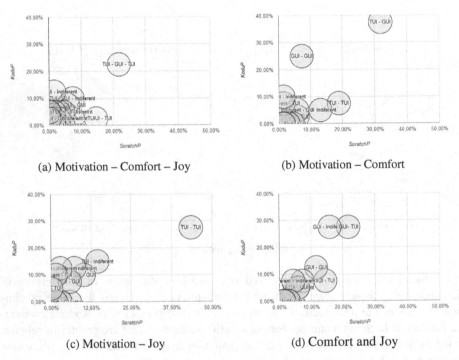

(a) Motivation – Comfort – Joy   (b) Motivation – Comfort

(c) Motivation – Joy   (d) Comfort and Joy

Fig. 6. Relationship of the three feelings

Figure 6a shows the combination of options with greater selection with respect to the feelings: Motivation, Comfort and Joy. Note that the order, in which the feelings were cited, should be the order in which the options on each circle in the figure should be interpreted (e.g: TUI-GUI-TUI, The version that best evokes Motivation feeling is TUI, the Comfort feeling is GUI, and the Joy feeling is TUI). Observing this same combination, we have: 15 (21.74%) and 9 (22.50%) of the people involved in projects with Scratch and Kodu, agree on three things: a) TUI version evokes the greatest motivation, b) the GUI version evokes greater comfort, and c) the TUI version causes the greatest joy. As we can see in Figure 6a, there are no other combinations that stand out from the other options. In Figure 6b, we see that there are two other options that attract attention: a) relative only to ScratchP is TUI-TUI, which tells us that 13 (18.84%) of the participants in the first semester agree that the second version that best evokes the feeling of Motivation and Comfort is the TUI version;

b) in relation only to KoduP is GUI-GUI, which tells us that 10 (25.00%) of the participants of the second semester agree that the second version that best evokes these feelings is the GUI version. But independent of the application, the best combination is TUI-GUI, with more than 31.00% of the participants in each semester. In Figure 6c and 6d, we can see the Indifferent option between the combination that is highlighted, and it appears replacing the TUI version (i.e. Figure 6c: the best combination TUI-TUI, the following TUI-Indifferent; Figure 6d: the best combination GUI-TUI, the following GUI-Indifferent).

5   Conclusion

The research question we wanted to answer was: what are the relations between the feelings of Joy, Motivation and Comfort when using TUI and GUI? In this sense, our objective in this research was to better understand the relationships between the feelings of Comfort, Motivation and Joy evoked in users when interacting with GUI and TUI applications. In order to achieve this objective, we gathered the participation of more than one hundred people over the period of two semesters experimenting applications developed in educational contexts. The paper investigated affective responses with regard to two different interaction types: GUI and TUI.

The results were analyzed both in a general view and also in the perspective of different ages groups. Under the general view, the interaction type to evoke most Comfort was GUI, but TUI seems to be the preferred type in regards to Motivation and Joy (although sometimes Indifference was also chosen in relation to Joy). The analyses among different age groups provide us with some insights on what can be considered as relevant to these groups.

We are aware of the need to extend the study to other contexts; however, the evidence shows a greater sense of motivation and joy related to the TUI versions. This leads us to believe in the potential of TUI to be used in educational contexts. Further work involves a deeper investigation using different TUI architectures (e.g. different sensors, objects) in order to have other combination types of interaction.

Acknowledgements. This work was partially funded by CNPq (#160819/2013-0) and CAPES (01-P-1965/2012). We also thank the undergraduate students of the HCI discipline during two academic semesters in 2013 and the University of Quindío.

References

1. Bernstein, D.: Essentials of psychology. Cengage Learning, Belmont (2013)
2. Bradley, M.M., Lang, P.J.: Measuring emotion: the self-assessment manikin and the semantic differential. Journal of Behavior Therapy and Experimental Psychiatry 25(1), 49–59 (1994)
3. Doering, T., Beckhaus, S., Schmidt, A.: Towards a sensible integration of paper-based tangible user interfaces into creative work processes. In: CHI 2009 Extended Abstracts on Human Factors in Computing Systems, pp. 4627–4632. ACM, Boston (2009)

4. Fishkin, K.P.: A taxonomy for and analysis of tangible interfaces. Personal and Ubiquitous Computing 8(5), 347–358 (2004)
5. Garzotto, F., Gonella, R.: An open-ended tangible environment for disabled children's learning. In: Proceedings of the 10th International Conference on Interaction Design and Children, pp. 52–61. ACM, Michigan (2011)
6. Hayashi, E.C., Baranauskas, M.C.C.: The Affectibility Concept in Systems for Learning Contexts. International Journal for e-Learning Security (IJeLS) 1(1/2), 10–18 (2011)
7. Horn, M.S., Solovey, E.T., Crouser, R.J., Jacob, R.J.: Comparing the use of tangible and graphical programming languages for informal science education. In: Proceedings of the SIGCHI Conference on Human Factors in Computing Systems, pp. 975–984. ACM (2009)
8. Ishii, H., Lakatos, D., Bonanni, L., Labrune, J.B.: Radical Atoms: Beyond Tangible Bits, Toward Transformable Materials. In: Interactions, vol. 19(1), pp. 38–51. ACM (2012)
9. Ishii, H., Ullmer, B.: Tangible bits: towards seamless interfaces between people, bits and atoms. In: Proceedings of the ACM SIGCHI Conference on Human Factors in Computing Systems, pp. 234–241. ACM (1997)
10. Ishii, H.: The tangible user interface and its evolution. Communications of the ACM 51(6), 32–36 (2008)
11. Kaltenbrunner, M.: reacTIVision and TUIO: A tangible tabletop toolkit. In: Proceedings of the ACM International Conference on Interactive Tabletops and Surfaces, pp. 9–16. ACM, Banff (2009)
12. Norman, D.A.: Cognitive engineering, User centered system design, pp. 31–61. Laurence Erlbaum Associates, Inc. Publisher, New Jersey (1986)
13. Norman, D.A.: Emotion & design: Attractive things work better. In: Interactions, vol. 9(4). ACM (2002)
14. Oxford Dictionaries Language matters, http://www.oxforddictionaries.com
15. Patten, J., Ishii, H.: A comparison of spatial organization strategies in graphical and tangible user interfaces. In: Proceedings of DARE 2000 on Designing Augmented Reality Environments, pp. 41–50. ACM, New York (2000)
16. Russell, J.A., Mehrabian, A.: Evidence for a three-factor theory of emotions. Journal of Research in Personality 11, 273–294 (1977)
17. Strawhacker, A., Sullivan, A., Bers, M.U.: TUI, GUI, HUI: is a bimodal interface truly worth the sum of its parts? In: Proceedings of the 12th International Conference on Interaction Design and Children, pp. 309–312. ACM, New York (2013)
18. Sylla, C., Branco, P., Coutinho, C., Coquet, E.: TUIs vs. GUIs: Comparing the learning potential with preschoolers. Personal and Ubiquitous Computing 16(4), 421–432 (2012)
19. Xie, L., Antle, A.N., Motamedi, N.: Are tangibles more fun?: comparing children's enjoyment and engagement using physical, graphical and tangible user interfaces. In: Proceedings of the 2nd International Conference on Tangible and Embedded Interaction, pp. 191–198. ACM, Bonn (2008)
20. Xu, D.: Design and evaluation of tangible interfaces for primary school children. In: Proceedings of the 6th International Conference on Interaction Design and Children. ACM, Aalborg (2007)

The Wearable Self: Braiding a Feminist Critique within a Somaesthetics Framework for Design

Emily Ip, Wynnie (Wing Yi) Chung, Sunmin Lee, and Thecla Schiphorst

Simon Fraser University, School of Interactive Arts & Technology,
Suite 250-13450 102 Ave. Surrey, British Columbia V3T 0A3, Canada
{eip,wyc14,sla38,thecla}@sfu.ca

Abstract. This paper describes the exploratory design process of Wo.Defy, a bioresponsive wearable garment that integrates interaction design with feminist critique through an emphasis on intimacy, self-agency and self-reflection. Our research is based on a Somaesthetics framework addressing values of self-experience, poetics, materiality, and interaction semantics. Wo.Defy critically engages concepts of cultural history and identity to develop a richer understanding of design for the self. Our research design is informed by the historical precedent of the Self-Combing Sisters, a suffragette group in early 20th century Chinese society, who challenged the traditional Chinese status quo of gender roles and social conceptions of pre-arranged marriages through their chosen dress and styling of their hair. Wo.Defy contributes to the design discourse of wearable, embodied interaction by integrating cultural historical research into contemporary wearable design practice, braiding a feminist HCI agenda within a somaesthetics framework.

Keywords: Bioresponsive Wearable Technology, Somaesthetics, Feminist HCI, Embodied Interaction, Cultural Research, Breath interaction, Kinetic Response, Design for the Self, Materiality, Silk, Hair.

1   Introduction

Framed within somaesthetics [19], [20] and an HCI feminist agenda [2], this paper applies cultural historical research expressed as a set of design features to further enrich the design of user experience within interactive wearable technology.

Cultural history is a backbone that shapes our personal experience of society. It forms and greatly influences political values that indirectly affect the behaviour, beliefs, attitudes, and styles of the people within it. Clothing is a cultural artifact that reflects socio-cultural values including personal attitudes of self-selection, -preference and identity. Clothing portrays both personal and cultural expression and can represent the tension between self-agency and self-assimilation within larger cultural expectations. Within HCI, new technological developments continue to shape perspectives of how people explore, experience, and interact with their cultural surroundings. However, culturally oriented research within HCI, often focuses on representing the larger external cultural expression [6], [12], while the presence of the internal voice of the self within culture is often limited or even forgotten, due to the vast

A. Marcus (Ed.): DUXU 2014, Part IV, LNCS 8520, pp. 285–296, 2014.

attentional focus and distraction that exists in the world outside of ourselves. Our research explores how interactive clothing can support attentional focus to our own bodystate within a cultural context. Functioning like a second skin layered on the surface or our body, our garments can mediate communication between our own self-sensing and our surrounding environment. We have designed Wo.Defy, an interactive wearable garment, to bridge the experience of the self as mediated by technology with our own cultural influences. The word "Wo" means "I" in Chinese; explored through elements of self-connection, intimacy, self-actuation and the interplay of fabrics, micro-controllers, and sensors, Wo.defy reveals subjective and personal data through the control of the wearer, contributing to a richer understanding to the concept of self agency and self advocacy. We evaluate our prototype from the perspective of a Research through Design methodology. Our Wo.Defy garment embeds bio-sensing technology to cultivate somaesthetic interaction that supports self-awareness and self-reflection within a specific cultural context. Our design process incorporates cultural narrative to inspire and develop a set of design features that express critical design choices that can be integrated into interaction design experience.

The objective of Wo.Defy is to develop a bioresponsive dress that incorporates a culturally enriched, interactive wearable narrative that elicits self-reflection and dialogue. We frame our design research within the context of somaesthetics [17] integrating an HCI feminist agenda [2] through a cultural historical context. Based on a somaesthetic framework for interaction design, Wo.Defy 1) highlights the self-experience of the wearer, 2) formulates poetics derived from metaphors of cultural appropriation, style, and history, 3) integrates materiality using silk, human hair, and responsive soft-circuits, and 4) develops interaction semantics based on self-agency through incorporating breath and kinetic movement. By integrating a somaesthetics framework through the lens of a feminist agenda within HCI, we highlight historic cultural references that integrate our design choices. Our design choices support the values of Pluralism, Advocacy, Embodiment, and Self-disclosure as articulated in Bardzell's Feminist HCI [2]. We articulate a set of design features that support our research design goals of ameliorating self-awareness and self-reflection within a cultural context. Our design focuses on transformation of the self through user-experience contributing to the discourse of embodied interaction by braiding a somaesthetic framework with feminist HCI principles in the context of cultural HCI.

2   The Self-combing Sisters

Wo.Defy is informed by the historical precedent of the Self-Combing Sisters. *Zì shū nǚ* (自梳女) translates as the "Self-Combing Sisters" in Chinese [15], [18], [21]. Residing in the southern Canton Province in China from late 1800s-mid 1900s, this suffragette group challenged the traditional Chinese status quo towards gender roles and the customs of pre-arranged and arranged marriages. Resisting domestication, many of these women held employment within silk weaving factories, which transformed them into contributors to the financial welfare of the household [21]. Through celibacy and pursuit of personal and economic independence, the

Self-Combing Sisters repositioned their roles in society: women as fulfilling econom-ically and individually self-sufficient social roles outside the bounds of marriage.

The Self-Combing Sisters advocated for a social and personal claim to self-choice regarding marriage and work. Their desire to remain un-married and to work in facto-ries as individual benefactors provided them with a kind independence and economic status. This was socially expressed through the distinctive aesthetic appearance of their hair: a bounded bun or plait of a married woman, signifying their 'marriage to the self', a reference to turning inward to protect the self from cultural demands and also a concealment of the female semblance of youth, beauty, sensuality, and seduc-tion [18], [22]. For these women, the self-binding hair ritual inversely signified freedom from being restrained by marriage.

The design process of Wo.Defy takes as inspiration the self-responsive and critical reflection of the Self-Combing Sisters by embedding the values and daily practices through the selection of form, material, and the development of its interaction model. The cultural history of the Self-Combing Sisters articulates a foundation for the design concept and construction of the wearable dress, Wo.Defy.

3   Designing for Somaesthetic Experience

Somaesthetics, a concept originated by Richard Shusterman a contemporary pragmat-ist philosopher, values the role of body experience (or soma) in aesthetic appreciation [19]. Shusterman considers somaesthetics within three categories; analytic somaes-thetics, pragmatic somaesthetics, and practical somaesthetics. Analytic somaesthetics consists of descriptive studies of our bodily perceptions and somatic practices and their usages in cognitive, social, and cultural aspects. Pragmatic somaesthetics, on the other hand, involves a normative inquiry into specific disciplines to improve our bodi-ly experience and encourage the comparative critique. Practical somaesthetics focuses on concrete bodily practices by aiming at somatic self-improvement.

The narrative of the Self-Combing Sisters demonstrates both a pragmatic and prac-tical somaesthetics of self-reflection and self-regulation. Shusterman argues for the value of employing somaesthetics in designing for body consciousness, which estab-lishes a critical perspective on the socio-cultural influences influencing design prac-tice [20]. Wo.Defy explores paying attention to our physiological state in order to access self-awareness and self-reflection. This concept is supported not only by pragmatist philosophy but also by physiological research which indicates that direct-ing attention to one's bodystate supports self-knowledge and can lead to higher-levels of physical, cognitive and emotional performance in our daily lives [4], [5], [19].

Our design research contributes to concepts of self-advocacy through the integra-tion of design principles that support design for the self.   Our work with body-based somatic practices can provide new insights within user experience design in HCI [16]. Wo.Defy contributes to the design discourse of wearable, embodied interaction by integrating cultural historical research into contemporary wearable design practice, braiding a feminist HCI agenda within a somaesthetics framework.

4 Emphasis on Feminist Interaction

Within Somaesthetics, our lens of Feminist HCI highlights an agenda that supports the values of Pluralism, Advocacy, Embodiment, and Self-disclosure within the interaction design process [2]. While, the Self-Combing Sisters illustrate attitudes and traits of such an agenda, their contribution to reconstructing social identity has not been explicitly acknowledged within Chinese cultural history. Nevertheless the *Nǚquán zhǔyì* (女權主義) translates as 'the viewpoint of powerful women' [13].

Wo.Defy aims to embed the attitude of the Self-Combing Sisters *Nǚquán zhǔyì* into wearable design and embodied interaction. We develop and implement a set of design features influenced by the cultural history of the Self-Combing Sisters.

The Self-Combing Sisters' stance against arranged marriages transformed cultural models within their own community, advocating for a greater range of personal choice regarding self-agency and identity. The controversial actions of the Self-Combing Sisters separated them from their family and community. Without a husband and children the Self-Combing Sisters were able to devote their time to silk-weaving in the factories leading to economic independence and stability. This ultimately enabled these women to 'give-back' and even maintain economical support for their extended family and community. As their circle of independence led to providing much needed economic support to their local families and community, the community in turn was able to recognize and accept the way of life of the Self-Combing Sisters. This historical narrative illustrates the feminist principles, of *advocacy* for their life-style, *self-disclosure* and *embodiment* (represented in part through their choice of hair style and dress), leading ultimately to cultural *pluralism* in their communities' acceptance of their agency, life-style and identity. While striving for gender equality, the underlying intention of the Self-Combing sisters was to maintain control of their own bodies, identities, and sexual choices. Their advocacy and evidence of self-disclosure is visibly recognized through the choice in their physical appearance (how they wore their hair), their choice in marital status and their lifestyle choices, working in the silk-factories to increase economic independence for themselves and their families.

Shusterman articulates a similarly framed somaesthetics critique integrating a feminine aesthetic and representation of the female body, inciting "women to self-examine and self-maintain her somatic feelings for a better control, the familiarization of her body, and the transformation into somatic knowledge" [19]. Braiding a somaesthetic framework within feminist HCI principles in the context of cultural HCI, we appropriate the concept of hair and clothing and its intimate relationship with the body, drawing inspiration from the Self-Combing Sisters narrative to design for wearable technology.

While feminist discourse has existed within critical theory for over half a century, a focus on Feminist HCI has emerged only recently with Bardzell's introduction of a design agenda that acknowledges feminism as a lens within technology design. A subsequent CHI workshop in 2011, *Feminism and Interaction Design* resulted in a number of workshop papers, including Ascencao's [1] interactive audio-visual installation, 'Euphoric Femme', which aims to ameliorate attitudes and create a discourse around female sexual subjectivity and Lehtinen's [14] evaluation of feminist interaction design in HCI which examines vibrator design, providing an analysis of preferences in technology and sexuality.

Wo.Defy integrates a Feminist design agenda through its incorporation of Pluralism, Advocacy, Embodiment, and Self-disclosure. Both Pluralism and Advocacy are
incorporated within the conceptual design of Wo.Defy as an exploratory process
involving socio-historical research, while Embodiment and Self-Disclosure are incorporated into the material design and use of breath sensors and soft-sensor actuators to
both reveal and conceal bodydata. Our design has stemmed from a desire to incorporate critical reflection based on the historical socio-cultural example of the Self-
Combing sisters. Inspired by the narrative of the Self-Combing Sisters [15], [18], [22]
we provide a design context that includes the craftwork of silk weaving and the
integration of human hair, as referenced in their socio-historical agenda. Through
investigating and evaluating historical precedents of identity construction, Wo.Defy
highlights the use of critical reflection as a design strategy and catalyst for interaction
design that promotes self-change and agency.

5   Somaesthetics in Cultural HCI

Culturally oriented research within HCI, often focuses on representing the larger
forces of cultural expression [6], [12], while the presence of the internal voice of the
self within culture is often set aside, due to the vast attentional focus in the world
outside of ourselves. Our research explores how interactive clothing can support
attentional focus and self-reflection with our own bodystate while maintaining a
cultural context.

Self-reflection requires paying attention to one's self-experience in the world. Our
sense of self can be considered as a set of blueprints that influence our perspective
and attitude for our own behaviour, decisions, and interactions towards our surrounding environment [10]. An ability to accurately attend to and reflect upon the various
aspects of one's emotional and physical well-being is crucial for a higher development in cognitive, emotional and physical ability [9].

Bio-medical studies show that a shift of attention between external and internal
happenings can be supported by 'distraction', which diminishes external stimuli for
an emphasis on internal information. Thus, self-awareness can be induced through
focus on the self's physiological reactions and psychological state [4]. Wo.Defy
fosters an interactive experience using breath sensors that focus the wearer's attention
on their breathing patterns. The technique of focusing attention to affect change in our
bodystate is a core pragmatic strategy of somatic practice. We apply a somaesthetics
framework in the conceptual development of the bioresponsive dress Wo.Defy [17].
Somaesthetics can support somatic connoisseurship (the development of somatic
knowledge) to support interaction design within the field of HCI [16]. Wo.Defy
adopts a Somaethetic design that braids a feminist HCI agenda within a somaesthetics
framework through the lens of feminist interaction [2].

6   Wo.Defy: Defying Expectation

Wo.Defy is a bioresponsive wearable dress that explores the somaesthetics of sensory
interaction. Wo.Defy incorporates techniques of self-awareness by directing attention
to the wearer's breath which in turn actuates kinetic changes in the garment's material

properties revealing and concealing fabric layers in the front pelvic regions of the garment. Historical research on the Self-Combing Sisters dress and work habits is used as inspiration to select material, form, color, textures, and symbols for the wearable design. The integration of cultural associations drawn from the Self-Combing Sisters constitute a somaesthetic framework for the design of Wo.Defy, including: 1) the self-experience of the wearer, 2) poetics derived from metaphors of cultural appropriation, style, and history, 3) integration of materiality using silk and human hair 4) development of interaction semantics based on self-agency through incorporating breath and kinetic movement.

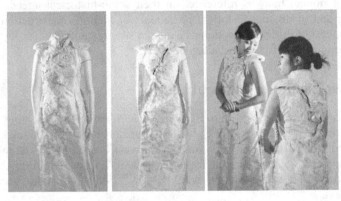

Fig. 1. Fig. 2. Wo.Defy 2012-14

7   Poetics in Design and Interaction

Wo.Defy borrows from the culturally rich background of the Self-Combing Sisters. Wo.Defy collects physiological breath data to both reveal and conceal body state. Inspired by the practice of Noh Theatre, Wo.Defy reveals the wearer's internal emotions through inner body rhythm expressed through the act of breathing [7]. A custom made breath-band embedded with a piezo force sensor and a soft circuit band wraps around the wearer's chest capturing the amplitude of each breath. This enables the wearer to noticing shifts between behavioural (autonomous) breathing and sensory breathing can illustrate shifts in body state [3], [8]. Wo.Defy supports a design concept of self-disclosure and embodiment [2].

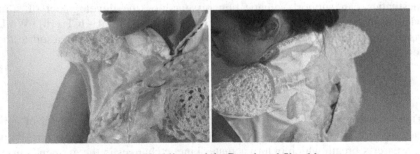

Fig. 2. The Neckline and the Broadened Shoulders

Wo.Defy incorporates elements of gender blurring, which is reinforced by the widened shoulder pad of the traditional qípáo (旗袍), a wedding garment traditionally worn by Chinese women. The widened shoulder pad incorporates a symbolic reference to 'shouldering' economic responsibility and independence typically a role held by the male family members. This was physically indicated through attributes of broader shoulders and a higher ranking in the family hierarchical structure. The traditional qípáo wedding dress worn by Chinese women has a right-overlapping neckline. Wo.Defy inverts this neckline incorporating a left overlapping neckline reserved for the male thus appropriating and blurring gender roles and identity. Traditional Chinese heritage maintains a structure of the male standing on the left and the woman on the right. Wo.Defy appropriates these cultural gender designs to mirror a counterposition in social and family structure, representing the economic and financial contribution of the Self-Combing Sisters [2].

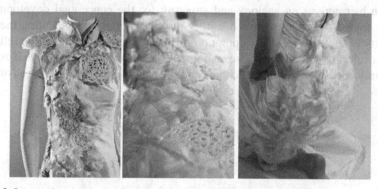

Fig. 3. Integrating a palette of white as a cultural critique towards agency and sexuality

The white colour of Wo.Defy again blends contrasting symbolic meaning across East and West cultures. In Chinese culture, white is seen as a mournful colour that signifies the ending of a life and is often worn in funerals; on the other hand, white suggests purity in the Western culture and is often worn in weddings and baptisms to symbolize a gateway between innocence and self-actualization. As such, the Wo.Defy garment signifies a 'death' of normative cultural expectations, and the critical act of 'marrying the self' as a constructive stance towards self-agency. Wo.Defy also acknowledges pluralism [2] by bridging a cultural critique between East and West. The designers replaced the lucky red and gold colour palette of a Chinese wedding with an 'unlucky' white colour. This contextualizes the traditional wedding qípáo dress as a commentary on the burial of normative beauty associated with pre-arranged marriage and pre-ordained sexual relationships that were eschewed by the Self-Combing Sisters.

8   The Materiality of the Self within Cultural History

Materials are selected based on their literacy, agency and sensitivity to cultural background, body, and mind. The Self-Combing Sisters were favoured in the silk factory during the industrial revolution in China because of their freedom from domestic obligations and contributed to significant economic growth in the Southern Canton province of China around the late 1800s [21].

Various forms of raw silk are hand-sewn within the design construction of Wo.Defy to symbolize the versatility of the Self-Combing Sisters, represent their craftsmanship in the silk-weaving arts, and honour their constructive contribution to their community. The foundational layer of the wearable garment is made of dupioni silk fabric layered with hundreds of hand-sewn silk chiffon flowers that lay organically from the central torso and spreading downward toward the feet of the dress. Extending from the left neckline to the waistline of Wo.Defy is a small black strand of human hair interwoven into a long braid of white silk fibers. The progressive transition from the black human hair to the white raw silk fiber visualizes a process of concealing beauty and resisting pre-arranged sexual relationships in favor of a self-disclosure that both acknowledges agency, celibacy and self-sufficiency.

Human hair acts as an analogy and structure for the conceptual development of Wo.Defy since hair narrates one's life story through literally documenting the health and vitality of the body. The incorporation of black hair with white silk parallels life to death cycle, the concealing to revealing self-state, and the advocacy of resisting external influences in favor of self-choice and the acknowledgment of pluralism [2].

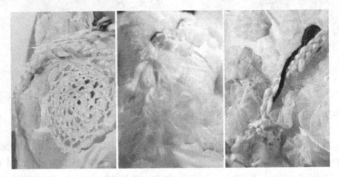

Fig. 4. The interwoven silk fibers, fabric (organza & chiffon), human hair

9   Interaction Semantics

The Lilypad Arduino board on the left chest collects the hidden and underlying breathing pattern of the wearer. The expansion and contraction of each breath is translated as a pulsating light pattern on Wo.Defy. The light-emitting diodes illuminate as the chest expands to compress against the force sensor and dim as the chest contracts to loosen the tension towards the force sensor.

The Arduino Uno microcontroller board on the back of the garment captures the slightest movement of the wearer with a Lilypad tri-axis accelerometer located on the vertebrae. When the wearer generates any motion, the servo motors pull upward on a collection of translucent threads which connect to a bed of silk chiffon flowers throughout the dress. The contracting and dilating silk chiffon flowers caused by the kinetic input draws a metaphor to the contraction of pubococcygeus muscles. This references the female body advocating personal choice.

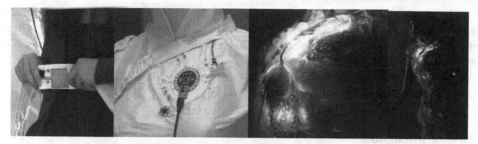

Fig. 5. (Left) The breath chest band containing the squared FSR sensor transmits pressure data to the Lilypad Arduino microcontroller. (Right) The LEDs illuminate based on the values sent from the Lilypad Arduino microcontroller board.

Fig. 6. The shoulder shells house the 2 servomotors that pull on the organza flowers

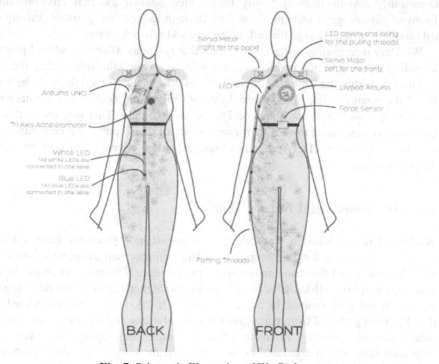

Fig. 7. Schematic Illustration of Wo.Defy

The synchronous expression and artistic mimicry of the physiological information considers the bioresponsive dress as a 'sister' who fosters an opportunity for self-disclosure. The acts of illuminating/opening and dimming/concealing of visual expressions on Wo.Defy enact as self-control and self-agency through self-experience. Anthropomorphic expressions are reflected in the lights that illuminate and flowers that contract and expand on the surface of Wo.Defy.

10   Conclusion

Wo.Defy contributes to the design discourse of wearable, embodied interaction by integrating cultural historical research into contemporary wearable design practice, braiding a feminist HCI agenda within a somaesthetics framework. Wo.Defy is informed by the cultural narrative of the Self-Combing Sisters' conscious design of their own lives. Based on a somaesthetic framework for interaction design, Wo.Defy 1) highlights the self-experience of the wearer, 2) formulates poetics derived from metaphors of cultural appropriation, style, and history, 3) integrates materiality using silk, human hair, and responsive soft-circuits 4) develops interaction semantics based on self-agency through incorporating breath and kinetic movement [17]. By integrating a somaesthetics framework through the lens of a feminist agenda that supports the values of Pluralism, Advocacy, Embodiment, and Self-disclosure within HCI [2], we highlight historic cultural references that integrate our design choices. Our design consciously reveals internal bodily information against external environments in forms of physiological and emotional data through the reactive garment, raising critical questions around design for self-awareness and self-reflection.

Wo.Defy incorporates material signifiers that reference Chinese cultural practices; including its construction of black human hair and white silk, referencing the life to death cycle within the Chinese culture. Self-disclosure is designed through the visibility of the wearer's states incorporated through the breath sensor, accelerometer and the kinetic response of the floret designs to the bio-data. This references the Self-Combing Sisters stance toward their own agency of their bodily and economic choices. The design of Wo.Defy embodies these historical concepts through its material design process.

11   Discussion and Future Work

Wo.Defy has combined a framework of somaesthetics practices with a feminist agenda to advocate for design practices that support self-awareness, -reflection, and -disclosure and that can ameliorate user experience. Directing attention to one's bodystate supports self-knowledge and can lead to higher-levels of physical, cognitive and emotional performance in our daily lives [4], [5], [19]. Our initial qualitative data has been gathered from participants at 6 exhibitions and has indicated that a cultural historical narrative can create a legible context for shaping user awareness of their own state within a cultural context. Participants used a talk aloud process that reflected upon their experience of self-revealing and self-concealing expressions through bioresponsive technology based on breath. Our initial findings support our goals of furthering our design research by crafting a qualitative somaesthetic instrument to further understand how wearable technologies and biosensors can support the development of our attentional skills. As highlighted by Shusterman [19], the application of somaesthetics toward designing technology that supports attention to one's own state can lead to knowledge for an increase in everyday emotional, physical and cognitive well-being and performance. In our next stage of research we will iterate the prototype and develop an evaluation strategy to assess breath input as a mechanism to address self-observation. This is an application of pragmatic and practical somaesthetics strategies in interaction design for user experience and has the potential to reinvigorate bodily understanding and practice within human computer interaction.

References

1. Ascencao, T.: Euphoric Femme an interactive media art installation exploring women's sexual subjectivity. In: CHI 2011 Feminism and Interaction Design Workshop (2011)
2. Bardzell, S., Feminist, H.C.I.: Taking Stock and Outlining an Agenda for Design. In: Proceedings: 28th ACM Conference on Human Factors in Computing Systems (CHI 2010), pp. 1301–1310 (2010)
3. Boiten, F.A., Frijda, N.H., Wientjes, C.J.E.: Emotions and respiratory patterns: Review and critical analysis. International Journal of Psychophysiology 17, 103–128 (1994)
4. Cioffi, D.: Beyond Attentional Strategies: A Cognitive-Perceptual Model of Somatic Interpretation. Psychological Bulletin 109(1), 25–41 (1991)
5. D'Argembeau, A., Jedidi, H., Balteau, E., Bahri, M., Phillips, C., Salmon, E.: Valuing One's Self: Medial Prefrontal Involvement in Epistemic and Emotive Investments in Self-views. Cerebral Cortex 22, 659–667 (2012)
6. Heimgartner, R.: Reflections on a Model of Culturally Influenced Human-Computer Interaction to Cover Cultural Contexts in HCI Design. International Journal of Human-Computer Interaction 29(4), 205–219 (2013)
7. Homma, I., Masaoka, Y., Umewaka, N.: Breathing Mind in 'Noh'. Breathing, Feeding, and Neuroprotection. pp. 125-134 (2006)
8. Homma, I., Masaoka, Y.: Breathing Rhythms and Emotions. Experimental Physiology 9, 1011–1021 (2008)
9. Johnson, M.K., Nolen-Hoeksema, S., Mitchell, K.J., Levin, Y.: Medial cortex activity, self-reflection and depression. SCAN 4, 313–327 (2009)
10. Johnson, S.C., Baxter, L.C., Wilder, L.S., Pipe, J.G., Heiserman, J.E., Prigatano, G.P.: Neural correlates of self-reflection. Brain 125(8), 1808–1814 (2002)
11. Kallio, T.: Why We Choose the More Attractive Looking Objects - Somatic Markers and Somaesthetics in User xperience. In: ACM DPPI 2003, Pittsburgh, PA, USA, pp. 142-143 (2003)
12. Kamppuri, M., Bednarik, R., Tukiainen, M.: The expanding focus of HCI: case culture. In: Proceedings: 4th Nordic Conference on Human-Computer Interaction: Changing Roles (NordiCHI 2006), pp. 405–408 (2006)
13. Ko, D., Wang, Z.: Introduction: Translating Feminisms in China. Gender & History 18(3), 463–471 (2006)
14. Lehtinen, V.: Negotiating Technology Design and Female Sexuality. In: CHI 2011 Feminism and Interaction Design Workshop (2011)

15. Li, J.M.: Dec-hair-ation - A Lively Perspective into China's Zishunv. Women of China. 43-45 (2009)
16. Schiphorst, T.: Self-Evidence Applying Somatic Connoisseurship to Experience Design. In: CHI 2011 Extended Abstracts on Human Factors in Computing Systems (CHI EA 2011), pp. 145–160. ACM, NY (2011)
17. Schiphorst, T.: Soft(n): Toward a Somaesthetics of Touch. In: CHI 2009 Extended Abstracts on Human Factors in Computing Systems (CHI EA 2009), pp. 2427–2438. ACM, New York (2009)
18. Shao, Y.F.: Origins behind the customs, composition, and basic characteristics of Zishunu. Cultural Heritage (Wen Hua Yi Chan). pp. 143–151 (2012)
19. Shusterman, R.: Body Consciousness: A Philosophy of Mindfulness and Somaesthetics. Cambridge University Press, New York (2008)
20. Shusterman, R.: Soma, Self, and Society: Somaesthetics as Pragmatist Meliorism. Metaphilosophy 24(3), 314–327 (2011)
21. Stockard, J.E.: Daughters of the Canton Delta: Marriage Patterns and Economic Strategies in South, pp. 1860–1930. Standford University Press, California (1989)
22. Wang, L.J.: On the Study of the Self-Bunning Ladies. pp. 66–67 (2011)

Throwing a Smile: Using Smile Icons to Design Social Interfaces

Kyoko Ito, Shumpei Hanibuchi, and Shogo Nishida

Graduate School of Enginering Science, Osaka University, Osaka, 5608531, Japan
ito@sys.es.osaka-u.ac.jp

Abstract. A social interface is defined as that which allows for the visualization of potential social relationships between a human and an object, or between humans. In this study, we focus on facial expression, because it is an important source of non-verbal information. We aim to apply this study in designing a social interface. More specifically, we are concerned with the functions of smile. We have designed a "smile icon" as a way of carrying the visual information that the sender is smiling , and developed an experimental system. We have conducted an experiment of conversation between two persons, using TalkWithSmile. The results of the experiment show that the use of smile icons leads participants in a conversation to form the impression that the conversation is more active than otherwise. In the near future, we will expect more experimental trials and investigate the boundary between the condition in which the smile icon facilitates a conversation and the condition in which it does not.

Keywords: Smile icon, social interface, interface design, conversation, tabletop.

1 Introduction

Recently the concept of social interface has been widely investigated in the study of human interfaces[1][2][3][5][4][6]. A social interface is defined as that which allows for the visualization of potential social relationships between a human and an object, or between humans.

In this study, we focus on facial expression, because it is an important source of non-verbal information. We aim to apply this study in designing a social interface. More specifically, we are concerned with the functions of $smile$[7][8][9][10][11]. Smile is a facial expression and has distinctive emotional and social meanings. The social functions of smile are important for designing social interfaces. A smile often facilitates a conversation or interac tion, but it only exists in a moment. It is then desirable for a good social interface to emphasize and preserve that messages are sent with a smile. There are some related studies on social interface[12][13][14]. We develop a system on which users can send and receive messages with the information that they are smiling, and the system can emphasize this information. We call the 'sender' the person who presents a smile facial expression and the 'receiver' his or her interlocutor.

A. Marcus (Ed.): DUXU 2014, Part IV, LNCS 8520, pp. 297–307, 2014.

Fig. 1. A smile icon

2   A Proposal of Smile Icon for Social Interface Design

2.1   Utilization of Smile Icon

We have selected the use of smile icon (Fig.1), on the basis of considerations provided in the previous studies[15][16][17][18]. As for the utilization of smile icon, the followings are considered: "Timing for the presentation of smile icon" and "Additional moving of smile icon."

As for the timing for the presentation of smile icon, a smile icon is presented immediately after a sender expresses smile. It would lead to the receiver's awareness of the message that the sender sends.

As for the additional moving of smile icon, a reference, TableTalkPlus, reports that an animation moving could affect the users' actions and the impressions on conversation.

In this study, the place for the presentation of smile icon is set on the table, for it is one of the common places for conversation.

2.2   Design and Development of an Experimental System

We have designed a *smile icon* as a way of carrying the visual information that the sender is smiling , and developed an experimental system, consisting of a smile detection subsystem and a smile icon presentation subsystem . When two persons sit at a table and have a conversation, the system shows a smile icon on the table immediately after a person makes a smile and the system detects it. We name the system "TalkWithSmile."

For the hardware setting, a monitor is set on the table, as the simulation of a table. The experimental settings of face-to-face and voice situations are shown respectively in Fig. 2 and Fig. 3.

As the software setting, a smile detection subsystem recognizes a user's smile via the movie captured by a video camera; this is; on the basis of the coding of 'pleasure' facial expression by JACFEE[19]. The user sets three markers on the face (Fig. 4) and the camera for smile recognition periodically detects the smile angle in each 33 ms.

The threshold value for smile recognition is decided from two values, $\alpha(SA = 0\%)$ and $\beta(SA = 100\%)$ on the basis of the previous study[20].

$$T = \frac{\alpha + \beta}{2}$$

Fig. 2. Face-to-face situation

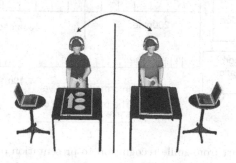

Fig. 3. Voice situation

The time chart (from the recognition of smile to the presentation of smile icon) of both subsystems is shown in Fig. 5.

3   A Conversation Experiment with TalkWithSmile

3.1   Purpose

We analyze how the place of smile icon (moving) affects the users and consider whether the smile icon presentation can be a kind of social interface. In order to consider which stimulus in the smile icon affects users and what influences it has on users, we design a comparison experiment. The ways of stimulus are two points: with a smile icon or without a smile icon, and a moving or a resting smile icon. In this experiment, we have two situations as *face-to-face* and *voice*. Taken together, there are six conditions in the experiment. (Fig. 6) Each condition includes a condition of presentation and a condition of the state of smile icon. The conditions are shown in Table 1.

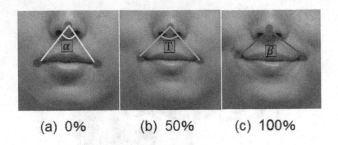

(a) 0%   (b) 50%   (c) 100%

Fig. 4. Smile angle and threshold value

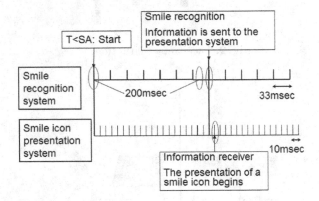

Fig. 5. Timechart from smile recognition to presentation of a smile icon

3.2 Analysis

We design three points for the analysis.

(A) How the presentation of the smile icon affects the impression on the conversation

(B) How the presentation of the smile icon affects the users' facial movements

(C) How the moving of the smile icon affects the users' thoughts on the conversation

With regard to (A), we use factor analysis by Semantic Differential Method[21] to concretely capture the common semantic space by users' evaluations with paired adjectives. Forty nine paired adjectives[22][23] are used in the evaluations (Seven point-Rickard scale; -3 to +3). Excluding the paired adjectives whose scores are under 0.4, the factor analysis is repeatedly computed. With regard to (B), it is assumed that the smile icon would lead the change of users' facial expression actions. The number of *smile* facial expressions is counted as the number of *smile* that is kept over T and longer than $200ms$. The *smile* expression keeping time is counted as the period between when SA is over T and when SA

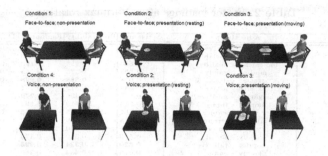

Fig. 6. Six conditions of the experiment

Table 1. Each condition's stimulus

#	Situation	Ways of presentation of smile icon	User's own smile	Interlocutor's own smile	Smile icon presented by interlocutor	Moving of interlocutor's smile icon	Smile icon presented by the user	Moving of user's smile icon
1	Face to face	No	×	○	×	×	×	×
2	Face to face	Resting	×	○	○	×	○	×
3	Face to face	Moving	×	○	○	○	○	○
4	Voice	No	×	×	×	×	×	×
5	Voice	Resting	×	×	○	×	×	×
6	Voice	Moving	×	×	○	○	×	×

○ : comfirmable by sight,   × : non-comfirmable by sight

is under T. With regard to (C), in order to analyze whether the users could feel the difference between the moving smile icon and the resting one, the users are asked after the six conditions, "Did you feel the difference between the moving and resting?" The answer is entered in the free statement.

3.3 Method

- **Participants**
  Thirty students (16 men and 14 women, ages from 20 to 28) participate in the experiment. The students are divided into 15 groups. The interlocutor is not a complete stranger to the students and it is the first time for them to user TalkWithSmile.
- **Task**
  The task is set as a 'joint remembering dialogue' [24][25] about the video they watch. The content of the video is 'Usavich' [26], which is a movie about the rabbits. A movie takes about 1 minute and 30 seconds. Six movies are ready for the experiment. A user watches all six movies in the same order.
- **Experimental flow**
  (i) **Explanation:** Users hear the outline of the experiment.
  (ii) **Initial Settings:** Users set three makers on their faces, and the value of the threshold T is set.

Table 2. Factor loadings after Varimax rotation

	Adjective pairs	Activeness	Preferability	Familiarity	Tidiness
	inactive - active	0.679	0.400	0.156	0.019
	introspective - sociable	0.663	0.255	0.170	0.227
	unhealthy - healthy	0.660	0.235	0.190	0.279
	modest - gaudy	0.658	0.375	0.253	-0.228
	static - dynamic	0.658	0.388	0.028	-0.097
	passive - active	0.641	0.372	0.231	0.249
	negative - positive	0.619	0.406	0.270	0.023
	boring - funny	0.589	0.519	0.292	-0.131
Activeness	weak - strong	0.582	0.345	0.065	0.186
	weak-minded - strong-minded	0.578	0.306	-0.110	0.180
	quiet - noisy	0.571	0.240	0.099	-0.323
	lonely - social	0.570	0.510	0.176	0.030
	quiet - talkative	0.520	0.324	0.223	0.026
	gloomy - sunny	0.475	0.434	0.260	-0.166
	insensitive - sensitive	0.462	0.078	0.231	0.381
	tired - energetic	0.458	0.313	0.333	-0.058
	unsociable - sociable	0.457	0.369	0.251	0.153
	focused - distracted	0.443	-0.291	-0.072	-0.390
	unreliable - reliable	0.421	0.193	0.285	0.376
	cowardly - brave	0.415	0.309	0.205	0.051
	bad - good	0.298	0.753	0.210	0.136
	hated - liked	0.257	0.685	0.346	0.021
	uncool - cool	0.358	0.663	0.366	0.027
	unsatisfied - satisfied	0.484	0.655	0.217	0.074
	unfree - free	0.295	0.651	0.065	0.084
Preferability	uncomfortable - comfortable	0.347	0.618	0.401	0.074
	unfunny - funny	0.375	0.602	0.224	0.000
	unfriendly - friendly	0.278	0.573	0.313	0.059
	hard - soft	0.331	0.565	0.223	-0.137
	cold - warm	0.364	0.554	0.476	-0.021
	unstable - stable	0.188	0.552	0.169	0.360
	stubborn - open	0.194	0.542	0.124	0.288
	obstinate - flexible	0.224	0.458	0.151	-0.227
	glum - cheerful	0.407	0.434	0.221	-0.071
	harsh - kind	-0.005	0.352	0.695	0.178
Familiarity	unkind - kind	0.252	0.312	0.608	0.149
	selfish - compassionate	0.218	0.285	0.608	0.400
	unhappy - happy	0.276	0.483	0.545	-0.158
	annoying - pretty	0.142	0.266	0.528	0.070
	ugly - beautiful	0.099	0.048	0.488	0.256
	lazy - serious	-0.132	-0.030	0.020	0.733
Tidiness	untidy - tidy	0.144	-0.008	0.176	0.710
	dirty - clean	-0.016	0.236	0.398	0.581
	irresponsible - responsible	0.297	0.096	0.247	0.547
	imprudent - prudent	-0.079	-0.143	-0.028	0.545
	dull - bright	0.426	0.056	-0.019	0.440
	Sum of squares of factor loading	8.346	8.148	4.234	3.747
	Contribution of factor ()	18.144	17.714	9.205	8.145
	Cumulative contribution ratio ()	18.144	35.858	45.063	53.208

(iii) Practice: Using TalkWithSmile, users practice the use of the system and have a free conversation.

(iv) Watch a Movie: Users watch a movie.

(v) Conversation: Users converse on the story of the movie for five minutes.

(vi) Answer a Questionnaire: Users are asked to answer a questionnaire to describe the impression on the conversation with 49 paired adjectives.

(vii) Give the Users' Thoughts: Users repeatedly conduct from (iv) to (vi). After the sixth condition, users answer the question: of "Did you feel the difference between the moving and the resting smile icon?" in a free statement.

A user talks about a movie in all the six conditions and the order effect is offset by counterbalancing the order. The condition in which a user watches a movie is randomly set.

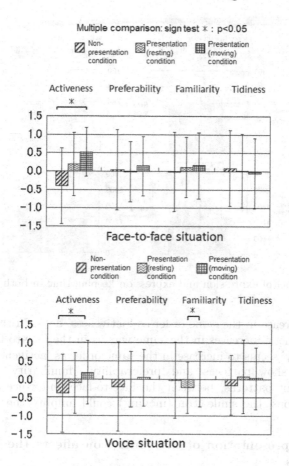

Fig. 7. Factor scores in both situations

3.4 Results

(A) How the presentation of the smile icon affects the impression on the conversation

– **Factor Loadings**
  Table 2 shows the results of factor analysis. Four factors are regarded as valid values and a simple structure is made on the basis of the factor loadings. The cumulative contribution ratio is 53.2%. We call the first, second, third and forth factors 'activeness', 'preferability', 'familiarity' and 'tidiness'.

– **Factor Score**
  As for the factors extracted by the factor analysis, Fig. 7 shows the results of the average score in the face-to-face and voice situations. In the face-to-face situation, the score for 'activeness' increases in the order of non-presentation, presentation(resting) and presentation(moving). 'Familiarity'

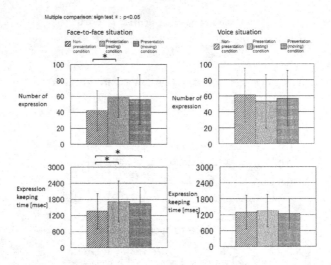

Fig. 8. Number of expression and expression keeping time in both situations

seems to increase in the same order as 'activeness' does. In the voice situation, 'activeness' increases in the same way as in the face-to-face situation. 'Preferability' seems to increase in the same order as 'activeness' does.

'Activeness' show patterns, and 'preferability', 'familiarity' and 'tidiness' show different patterns, between the face-to-face and voice situations. In both situations, the smile icon (moving) could amplify the impression of 'activeness.'

(B) How the presentation of the smile icon affects the users' facial movements

Fig. 8 shows the number of 'smile' facial expressions and the expression keeping time.

In the face-to-face situation, users share the table and directly see their own smile icon. As a result, users might try to present their own smile icon and increase the number of facial expressions and the expression keeping time. On the other hand, in the voice situation, users do not see the interlocutor's face and their own smile icon. As a result, the number of facial expressions and the keeping time might not dynamically increase or change.

(C) How the moving of the smile icon the users' thoughts on the conversation

The results of the free statements imply that; twenty four users out of thirty have more positive impressions on the presentation of the moving smile icon than those of the resting one. Many have said "felt more familiar", "could receive the interlocutor's feelings", "felt the presence", "felt the enjoyment", and so on. The moving smile icon might lead to stronger awareness of the sending of message and increase the familiarity of and a sense of unity with the interlocutor.

4 Conclusion

We have proposed the use of 'smile' as a future type of social interface in this study.

We have designed a "smile icon" as a way of carrying the visual information that the sender is smiling , and developed an experimental system consisting of a smile detection subsystem and a smile icon presentation subsystem . When two persons sit at a table and have a conversation, the system shows a smile icon on the table immediately after a person makes a smile and the system detects it. We name the system "TalkWithSmile."

We have conducted an experiment of conversation between two persons, using TalkWithSmile. The number of participants is thirty, and they are divided into fifteen pairs. Each pair is asked to perform the task of "joint remembering dialogue": they watch a one-minute movie, and then discuss about it with TalkWithSmile. On the basis of the results of the questionnaire, it is shown that the use of smile icons led the participants to have the impression that their conversation was active.

The results of the experiment show that the use of smile icons leads participants in a conversation to form the impression that the conversation is more active than otherwise. Thus, we have confirmed an important social function or meaning of smile: activating a conversation. The method we have proposed in this study increases the quantity of messages by emphasizing their active aspect, i.e., the information that it is sent with a "smile." It also helps a person to recognize that the interlocutor shows a positive attitude to her. In the near future, we will expect more experimental trials and investigate the boundary between the condition in which the smile icon facilitates a conversation and the condition in which it does not. A person does not always want to be in the condition where her conversation is activated. The ultimate goal of our study is to figure out what interface is best suited for sending and receiving different non-verbal information in different conditions, with reference to other studies[28][28][29][30][31].

References

1. Takeuchi, Y., Okada, M., Sumi, Y., Suzuki, N.: An Approach to Social Interface Studies. Journal of Human Interface Society 7(1), 1–10 (2005) (in Japanese)
2. Kujiraoka, T.: Various Aspects of Primitive Communication. Minerva Publishing (1997) (in Japanese)
3. Kushida, S.: Transmission and Commune on Unison -description of copyright on conversation. In: Tani, Y. (ed.) Nature of the Communication Magazine. Shin-yo-sha (1997) (in Japanese)
4. Malinowski, B.: The Problem of Meaning in Primitive Languages. In: Odgen, C.K., Richards, I.A. (eds.) The Meaning og Meaning, Harcourt, Brace and World, pp. 296–336 (1923)
5. Garey, J.M.: Communication as Culture. Umwin Hyman (1989)
6. Tnannen, D.: You Just Don't Understand: Women and Men in Conversation, New York, Qull (2001)

7. Fridlund, A.J.: Human Facial Expression: An Evolutionary View. Academic Press, San Diego (1994)
8. Ekman, P.: Strong Evidence for Universals in Facial Expressions: A Reply to Russell's Mistaken Critique. Psychological Bulletin 115, 268–287 (1994)
9. Vrugt, A., Eechoud, M.V.: Smiling and Self-Presentation of Men and Women for Job Photographs. European Journal of Social Psychology 32, 419–431 (2002)
10. Hosoma, H.: Preliminary Notes on the Sequential Organization of Smile and Laughter. In: Hattori, H., Kawamura, T., Idé, T., Yokoo, M., Murakami, Y. (eds.) JSAI 2008. LNCS (LNAI), vol. 5447, pp. 288–293. Springer, Heidelberg (2009)
11. Shimizu, A., Sumitsuji, N., Nakamura, S.: Why does human laugh? - Psychophysiology of laughter. Kodansha Ltd., Publishers (1994) (in Japanese)
12. Ohshima, N., Okazawa, K., Honda, H., Okada, M.: TableTalkPlus: An artifact for promoting mutuality and social bonding among dialogue participants. Journal of Human Interface Society 11(1), 105–114 (2009) (in Japanese)
13. Watanabe, T., Ogikubo, M., Ishii, Y.: Visualization of Respiration in the Embodied Virtual Communication System and Its Evaluation. Journal of Human Interface Society 3(4), 319–326 (2001) (in Japanese)
14. Tanaka, D., Yoshida, K., Yoshiike, Y., Ravindra De Silva, P., Okada, M.: Peepho: Captivation of the Natural Expressions that Emerged from the Interaction. In: Proceedings of the Human Interface Symposium 2010, pp. 649–652 (2010) (in Japanese)
15. Takehara, T., Sato, N.: On difference of impression conveyed by messages with or without face mark. Journal of Japanese Academy of Facial Studies 3(1), 83–87 (2003) (in Japanese)
16. Takehara, T., Sato, N.: Facilitation effect of emotional communication by face mark of happiness. Journal of Japanese Academy of Facial Studies 4(1), 9–17 (2004) (in Japanese)
17. Takehara, T.: Effect of emotion recognition due to the use of face marks on different generations. Journal of Japanese Academy of Facial Studies 7(1), 41–51 (2007) (in Japanese)
18. Yuasa, M., Saito, K., Mukawa, N.: Brain Activity Associated with Emoticons: An fMRI Study: Effects of Facial Expressions in Personal Communications over Computer Network. The Transactions of the Institute of Electrical Engineers of Japan. C, A publication of Electronics, Information and System Society 127(11), 1865-1870 (2007) (in Japanese)
19. Matsumoto, D., Kudoh, T.: Japanese Feeling World -solve the Mysterious Culture Puzzle. Seishin Bookstore, p. 39 (1996) (in Japanese)
20. Ishi, H., Gyoba, J., Kamachi, M.: Analyses of the Relationship between Facial Impression and Perceived Intensity of Smile. Journal of Japanese Academy of Facial Studies 3(1), 5–11 (2003) (in Japanese)
21. Masuyama, E.: Measure Image which Come to Mind -Semantic Differential Theory and Application. ISS Co., Ltd, (1996) (in Japanese)
22. Inoue, M., Kobayashi, T.: The Research Domain and Scale Construction of Adjective-pairs in a Semantic Differential Method in Japan. Japanese Journal of Education Psychology 14, 123–132 (1985) (in Japanese)
23. Kim, K.: An Exploratory Study of Impression Formation in Computer-mediated Communicaiton. Japanese Journal for Social Psychology 14, 123–132 (1999) (in Japanese)
24. Okada, M.: Human and Robot Interaction and Embodiment on Communication. Gendai-Shiso 36(16), 300–311 (2008) (in Japanese)
25. Mizutani, N.: From "sympathized communication to "dialogue". Japanese language 12(4), 4–10 (1993) (in Japanese)

26. USAVICH, http://www.mtvjapan.com/usavich/top (Febraury13, 2014)
27. Matsushita, Y., Okada, K.: Collaboration and Communication. Kyoritsu Shuppan (1995) (in Japanese)
28. Matsuda, K., Nishimoto, K.: HuNeAS: Supporting Information-sharing and Activating Human Network by Exploiting Spontaneous Encounters in An Organization. Journal of Information Processing Society of Japan 43(12), 3571–3581 (2002) (in Japanese)
29. Matsubara, T., Usuki, M., Sugiyama, K., Nishimoto, K.: Raison D'etre Object: A Cyber-Hearth That Catalyzes Face-to-face Informal Communication. Journal of Information Processing Society of Japan 44(12), 3174–3187 (2003) (in Japanese)
30. Siio, I., Mima, N.: Meegint Pot: Informal Communication Support by Ambient Display. Interaction 2001 Papers, pp. 163-164 (2001) (in Japanese)
31. Tsujita, H., Tsukada, K., Siio, I.: InPhase: Evaluation of a Communication System Focused on Happy Coincidences of Daily Behaviors. In: The Proceeding of CHI 2010, pp. 2481–2490 (2010)

User Experience Milestones

Structuring the Development of Experience Products

Simon Kremer, Ioanna Michailidou, Constantin von Saucken, and Udo Lindemann

Technische Universität München, Institute of Product Development, Germany
{kremer,saucken,michailidou,lindemann}@pe.mw.tum.de

Abstract. The approach of User Experience (UX) can help to create a unique selling proposition in mature markets like the automobile industry by meeting motives of users and evoking positive emotions. Yet, the User Experience goal is not continuously implemented in existing product development processes. In this paper we discuss the question: How can a continuous focus on the user's experience with a new product and the demands of a heterogeneous and mostly technical development process be brought together. We suggest six continuous, consistent, evolutionary UX milestones for the development of successful experience products. These milestones embody the intended UX, accompany the developers and evolve from a rough UX orientation, to more and more detailed user stories, to physical prototypes, the final product and its UX evaluation. By defining six UX milestones as compulsory checkpoints we facilitate the anchorage of UX aspects in established development processes.

Keywords: Management of DUXU processes, Product development processes Emotional design, Storytelling, UX methods and tools.

1 Introduction

1.1 Motivation for User Experience (UX)

Companies in many industrial sectors, e.g. in the automotive industry, are facing great challenges due to competitive environments in mature markets [1]. In addition, crucial changes considering the requirements of customers and their behavior when using a product can be observed. While traditionally requirements were limited to pragmatic aspects like utility and usability these factors are not sufficient anymore when it comes to convincing the customer with unique selling propositions. The demands of customers are expanding [1].

Consequently new ways of creating differing products and meeting real customer needs have to be found. Under these circumstances the approach of User Experience (UX) widens the scope of product development in science and industry by including non-technical, emotional and psychological values [2]. Don Norman states: „It's not enough that we build products that function, that are understandable and usable, we also need to build products that bring joy and excitement, pleasure and fun, and yes, beauty to people's lives." [3].

A. Marcus (Ed.): DUXU 2014, Part IV, LNCS 8520, pp. 308–318, 2014.

At the same time new technologies create great chances for providing more than just bare functionality [1]. Technological innovations can help to meet and exceed increasing customer demands. And products which consequently evoke positive emotions provide novel opportunities for convincing potential customers and satisfying existing ones.

1.2   Initial Situation

In reality there is often a gap between the potentials for User Experience due to technological advance on the one hand and the transformation of these potentials into actual products in real development processes on the other hand. The arousal of User Experience is very much dependent on intangible factors like subjective and affective characteristics of the user or the specific context of the product usage [2]. Nevertheless, possibilities for the emergence of positive experiences can be designed by keeping the user in focus throughout the whole development process [4] and creating products that satisfy and exceed real customer needs [5]. But analyzing real projects in automotive industry, we observed that the focus on the user and connected analysis results "get lost" on the way from research to development. Due to established practices the technological perspective predominates in product development. The impact of technological innovations and technical solutions on the customer benefit is often not constantly considered. The UX goal is not continuously implemented.

As an example from the automotive industry, e-mobility is such an innovative field that offers possibilities for generating new User Experiences. Electric cars create great chances for experiencing a new way of driving. But in many electric cars of the first generation the experience already fails when starting the car. As traditional sound feedback is missing and no consistent feedback is presented the driver is left alone with his concern: Is the car switched on? Instead of using the technological potential to fascinate the user, he gets frustrated.

1.3   Goal

We need to find a way to integrate the concept of User Experience into product development processes in order to exploit the potentials of technologies and implement experience ideas into products. Analyzing projects in automotive industry, we observed potentials in the following fields that we want to address with our approach:

Naming the Customer Benefit. Today User Experience is still often considered as a marketing aspect which is added after the actual product development. Hence technological potentials for increasing the customer benefit are neglected. The communicated experience is not consistent. We propose to define the intended UX in an early stage and determine it as a design goal itself.

Maintaining Initial Experience Ideas. Often no overarching story exists in a development process that represents the user's view on the product interaction. As a consequence, experience ideas gathered in early development phases are not present anymore during product implementation. Furthermore, separate experience ideas often lose their intended effect when being integrated into one product.

Creating Reproducible Experience Products. Fascinating products are already developed today. Yet, they are often based on random ideas and great performances of certain people involved. Creativity of engineers and designers will still be needed. But we aim at joining individual performances in a continuous development process - planning User Experiences more systematically.

In this paper we present UX milestones to structure the development of successful experience products. The approach is based on milestones which are a common tool in project management. Traditionally these milestones are predefined checkpoints where certain development objectives have to be achieved. We adapt this tool, defining six UX-related milestones that evolve from a strategic UX orientation to the final product and its experience evaluation by real users. We recommend that these UX milestones have to be fulfilled at defined points in the development process besides technical aspects before starting with the next development stage.

Furthermore, the milestones represent the user-product-interaction during the entire development process and help designers in creating a mental model of it. The idea of this approach is to connect different development steps to each other without losing the customer requirements. By this means we facilitate UX to become an integrated part of product development processes.

2   Background

Before the UX milestone approach is described in detail the reasons for the status quo and the consequential implications for our methodology are presented. Several specific characteristics and requirements of User Experience Design (UXD) on the one hand and existing product development processes on the other hand have to be considered when bringing the two perspectives together. Important factors were gathered from literature and the analysis of development processes in the automotive industry. The issues were supplemented with ideas of how to address these challenges with our concept.

2.1   User Experience Design (UXD)

Focus on New Aspects. UXD extends the view on product usage towards new aspects like emotions and excitement [2]. Therefore, not only the product on its own but the interaction with the user and the context as well as its evaluation by the user is strongly considered [1], [2]. In our approach the user's point of view on his encounter with the product is represented by the UX milestones. By handing on these representations from one development phase to another, the user remains in focus.

UX Requirements Harder to Define. Compared to technical requirements the various factors influencing UX are more difficult to specify. Hence engineers tend to neglect the user motives during technical implementation. We suggest presenting the UX goal in a coherent evolving story, simultaneously to the development of technical aspects.

Many Different Perspectives on UX. The existing UX definitions range from a marketing perspective to psychological needs fulfillment [2]. We want to provide a pragmatic approach for product development helping all disciplines involved to take a common user's perspective and design products accordingly.

No Consistent UX Process. There are a lot of methods supporting the creation of experience possibilities but no suggestions for an ongoing UX development process. With the UX milestones we present a step towards a continuous UX Design.

2.2   Product Development Processes

Focus on Technology. Today products like automobiles are mostly designed from a technological perspective. It is challenging to bring in the user's motives. Therefore they have to be connected to and translated into technical requirements.

Product and Process Complexity. Handling complexity is a main challenge in product development. Accordingly we have to be careful not to add even more complexity by introducing UX factors. Instead we present overarching user goals making it easier for product designers to focus on a common theme. By this means the complexity of the product received by the user should be reduced as well.

Many People Involved in Process. In big companies such as car manufacturers a huge amount of people from different disciplines (e.g. psychology, engineering, industrial design, informatics) is involved in product development. Each person has clearly defined competences and duties - focusing on his own perspective and his specific task rather than on the real user. With the UX milestones we want to connect the different development steps without losing the customer requirements.

Established Processes. Existing processes in automotive industry and other mature industrial sectors are mostly well established and optimized regarding traditional aspects like time, costs and technology. Therefore the recommended UX milestones are designed to be integrated into these existing development processes.

2.3   Integration of UXD into Product Development Processes

As a result of the diverse influencing factors the idea of UX is not yet continuously implemented in reality of product development. More specifically the real user and his motives as well as corresponding UX requirements are hardly represented in actual product development processes.

3   Approach

In order to enable a continuous, systematic creation of User Experiences and its integration into existing development processes we introduce User Experience milestones, marking the end of development phases on the way to successful experience products. The approach is based on the traditional project management tool of milestones. Therefore, the basics of this method are pointed out before our adaption to the field of UX is presented.

Milestones are a common instrument in project management. They are defined as key events, having a special significance within a process [6]. By means of milestones the overall process is structured [7]. Every project phase is completed with a pre-defined milestone [8], [9]. Two specific characteristics of milestones can be stated [8], [9], [10]. Firstly, they are used as an orientation and controlling tool. The milestones represent important intermediate results regarding aspects like costs, time and performance. These outputs can then be compared to the target planning which was done before the project start. Trend analysis can be used to predict the achievements of objectives. Secondly, milestones are designated decision points in a project where the course of action can be adjusted. Regarding product development e.g. promising ideas, concepts or generated solutions are selected to be developed further at the milestones while others are discarded. Summing up, milestones are scheduled points in projects where previously defined targets have to be reached. Due to many similar projects in reality milestones are often standardized and institutionalized [9].

In our approach we adapt the milestones to User Experience Design. Six UX milestones outline important steps towards systematically planned experience products. Three main characteristics and advantages of the methodology can be named:

Representing UX Progress. Similar to traditional aspects which were explained before also the progress of UX development is now reported. The UX milestones represent the user's perspective and user's goals throughout the project and have to be fulfilled at pre-defined points in the development process. Hereby we provide a possibility to continuously anchor the idea of UX in product development processes.

Evolving Milestones. By structuring the development process into six phases, each one finishing with a UX-related milestone, we help every designer understanding his defined position and role in the overall project without losing the initially intended UX focus. In every phase the previous milestone is evolved to the next level. As a result, every designer has the same background information and goal to work on. Each milestone can be used in the following steps as an inspiration as well as a reference for evaluating new solutions with respect to UX requirements.

Linking UX with Technical Aspects. To solve the conflict between User Experience Design and existing product development processes (see chapter 2) the UX milestones are linked to technical aspects. In this way the experience concepts can be embedded into traditional processes and implemented into actual products.

In the following each of the six consecutive UX milestones is presented in detail. The approach is illustrated with an automotive use case from our research project.

3.1   UX Framework

Description. Motives of potential customers and chances for User Experience are clustered in the first milestone: the UX framework. The framework symbolizes and visualizes opportunities for creating potential User Experiences with a product. Figure 1 shows an example for a framework in the field of electro-mobility, coming out of our project with the automotive industry. User motives are represented in the form of "I…"-sentences. In order to specify the framework, further explanations about the product context or first ideas can be placed around the clustered UX chances. A framework is a rather strategic, abstract tool and can also have other formats like a mood board, brand image etc. In addition to established objectives like target costs, schedules, technologies or market segments the UX framework defines a rough orientation for further development phases in which it evolves into concrete experience concepts and their realization.

Important Aspects. The framework has to be based on the analysis of real users. Besides this, technology and market aspects have to be considered. Whereas traditionally product development is mostly problem-oriented, the UX framework concentrates on potentials in order to derive positive User Experiences.

Additional Elements. Customer profiles representing potential users have to be attached to the framework. This is an important aspect, as according to different user groups the UX chances can be interpreted differently.

Next Steps. Whereas in today's projects these initial chances are often not present anymore when it comes to technical implementation stages, we suggest to hand on the framework as an overarching goal throughout the whole development process. Ideas within the framework are used as a basis for the creation of experience stories (chapter 3.2).

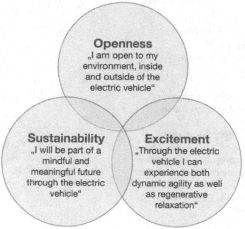

Fig. 1. UX Framework: Clustered chances of electric vehicles

3.2   UX Story

Description. At the second milestone a story describes a positive User Experience within the framework. Supporting the exploration and communication of new concept ideas the story is outlined in a rough story plot and contains exemplary characters [11], [12]. The story is basically a textual description supplemented with pictures. Figure 2 shows an extract from the story of the *Heartbeat*, an automobile interface developed by Löhmann et al. [13]. The concept addresses the chance for excitement by experiencing agility and relaxation, as it is described in the UX framework for electro-mobility (figure 1). Instead of just naming the idea of an electric vehicle that provides a natural energy feedback a possible experience is written down in a story. In this way a story helps all people involved in the following process to have a common understanding of the intended product interaction. We suggest that compulsory experience stories for all concept ideas have to be developed and evaluated before the UX milestone. At this point promising concepts are chosen to be developed further.

Important aspects. The story visualizes the basic characteristics of the intended positive user-product-interaction but is yet not connected to a specific technology. Instead, focus is set on emotions and motives of the user.

Additional elements. A virtual integration concept specifies the product functions that are addressed with one experience story and explores the integration of different stories into a final product concept. As well, first technical parameters which are critical for the emergence of an intended experience are derived from the story (in case of the *Heartbeat*: e.g. interface reachable for driver and consistent energy feedback by pulsation).

Next Steps. Complementary to technical requirements the story is handed on during the development process. The matching of subsequent technical implementation with the story has to be guaranteed and checked at all times in order to meet users' motives and goals.

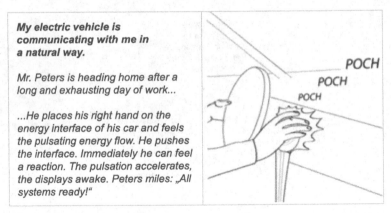

My electric vehicle is communicating with me in a natural way.

Mr. Peters is heading home after a long and exhausting day of work...

...He places his right hand on the energy interface of his car and feels the pulsating energy flow. He pushes the interface. Immediately he can feel a reaction. The pulsation accelerates, the displays awake. Peters miles: „All systems ready!"

POCH
POCH
POCH

Fig. 2. UX Story: The idea of a natural energy interface in an electric vehicle

3.3   UX Storyboard

Description. The positive experience described in the story is specified at the next milestone: The UX storyboard describes the intended usage and experience step by step. Pictures illustrate the user-product-interaction. By that means important experience aspects are transparently documented for the ongoing process. An extract from the storyboard of the *Heartbeat* [13] is shown in figure 3. Actions of the exemplary character and reactions of the energy interface are presented. In order to provide a precise experience goal, every detailed technical concept description has to be complemented with such a storyboard before starting with the implementation process.

Important Aspects. Whereas the story explains a rough experience idea, the storyboard depicts a detailed interaction process in a specific usage context. First experience mock-ups are used to evaluate and iteratively adapt the drafted storyboard before the milestone.

Additional Elements. The storyboard has to be translated into detailed technical requirements in order to be accepted by and applicable for developers. An advanced integration concept considers the interplay of different experience drafts as well as implementation aspects like usability and packaging. Storyboard, integration concept and technical requirements affect each other and have to be adapted accordingly.

Next Steps. The storyboard forms the basis for the subsequent implementation of the experience concept. Technical specification sheet and storyboard are passed on simultaneously until the end of the project.

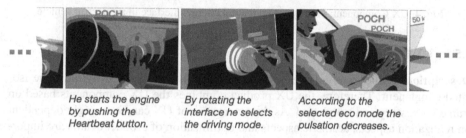

He starts the engine   By rotating the   According to the
by pushing the   interface he selects   selected eco mode the
Heartbeat button.   the driving mode.   pulsation decreases.

Fig. 3. UX Storyboard: Intended interaction with a natural energy interface in an el. vehicle

3.4   UX Components

Description. After having planned the User Experience possibilities, physical prototypes are developed in detail. In an iterative implementation process the prototypes are frequently evaluated by real users. At the end the UX components realize the intended experience and roughly define dimensions and design. In case of the *Heartbeat* the prototype provides multimodal feedback about the status of the car and the remaining range [13]. The visual energy scale and the haptic pulsation vary depending on the selected driving mode and the current speed of the car (see figure 4). After the previous analyzing and conceptual milestones, the UX components mark the first point in the development process where a physical representation of the experience concept has to be presented.

Important Aspects. Usually the implementation is executed based on the requirements list. But special attention has to be paid to not losing UX chances when solving technical problems. Hence, the technical realization not only has to meet technical requirements but also represent the content of the storyboard.

Additional Elements. All components have to be integrated into one product in the next step. Therefore, the prototypes are not developed separately. The integration concept connects the UX components with each other.

Next steps. The final prototypes are used as input for the serial development.

Fig. 4. UX Component: Prototype of a natural energy interface in an electric vehicle

3.5   UX Product

Description. Rather rarely a user-product-interaction is influenced by only one isolated component. Therefore, the UX product combines the UX components based on framework, story and storyboard. As the emergence of UX can be strongly dependent on realization aspects, aesthetic aspects and optimization of product details are important factors which have to be considered before this milestone. Focus is put on a homogeneous look and feel. Finally the product should embody the story behind it and facilitate a positive User Experience by itself without any further explanations. Figure 5 shows the *Heartbeat* integrated into the dashboard of a vehicle [13].

Fig. 5. UX Product: Natural energy interface integrated into the dashboard of an electric vehicle

Important Aspects. When the different components are combined in the final product it is very important to concentrate on the global User Experience. Even if each function creates a valid experience possibility a bad integration can ruin the overall product experience.

Additional Elements. Additionally the marketing concept is developed. Compared to traditional processes it is not only based on the product. Framework, story and storyboard can also serve as input for the communication of the intended User Experience.

Next Steps. The product is now used by the customer in the real world.

3.6   Proof of UX Concept

Description. Finally the matching of the intended User Experience (framework, story, storyboard) and the actual User Experience (user-product-interaction) can be evaluated with real customers in a real context. The proof of concept consists of structured experience reports, addressing the question: Do User Experiences emerge in real usage situations? Exemplary statements from users of the *Heartbeat* [13], confirming the arousal of an intended experience, are shown in figure 6.

Important Aspects. The traditional evaluation of technical characteristics and usability is enhanced by testing UX-related aspects like the fulfillment of users' motives.

Next Steps. The proof of concept can be used as starting point for product modifications or as input for following projects.

U21: *"The car...*   U15: *"You can*   U05: *"It feels like interacting*
becomes alive."   *feel the car!"*   *with a living being."*

Fig.6. Proof of UX Concept: Experiences of users when interacting with the energy interface

4   Conclusion

The idea of User Experience provides great opportunities for creating fascinating products that meet the motives of real users. But in reality of product development the potentials for UX are often not exploited. Reasons for this can be found both in the special characteristics of UX Design as well as in the properties of traditional development processes.

We introduce UX milestones that represent the intended customer benefit throughout a product development project. As the first milestone the UX framework provides an overarching goal and a rough development direction. Within this framework stories describe possible experience concepts. These concepts are then specified in form of storyboards, describing an interaction step by step. The storyboards are transformed into physical prototypes before the components are integrated into a final product. Finally the occurrence of experiences with the product is tested in a realistic context.

The evolving milestones ensure a continuous focus on the initially intended User Experience during the development process. At these predefined points not only technical factors but also compulsory UX requirements have to be fulfilled in order to proceed with the project. A consequent experience goal is provided for all people involved in a development project and important decisions about the ongoing development process are influenced by the UX milestones. In this way possibilities for the emergence of positive User Experiences can be planned systematically.

Our approach was developed and evaluated during an interdisciplinary research project in the automotive industry. The feedback was very positive. Yet, the approach has to be specified and evaluated in real development projects and other branches. The concept of UX milestones is designed to be integrated into existing processes. It is adaptable to different development situations. But the specific points where the milestones should be included compared to existing aspects are to be defined in detail. In addition, the approach has to be supplemented with detailed development steps, appropriate methods for each stage and roles involved in the process.

References

1. Hassenzahl, M., Tractinsky, N.: User Experience A Research Agenda. In: Cakir, A. (ed.) Behaviour& Information Technology, vol. 25(2), pp. 91–97. Taylor & Francis, London (2006)
2. Roto, V., Law, E., Vermeeren, A., Hoonhout, J.: User Experience White Paper - Bringing Clarity to the Concept of User Experience (2011),
   http://www.allaboutux.org/files/UX-WhitePaper.pdf
3. Norman, D.A.: Introduction to this special Section on Beauty, goodness, and usability. In: Moran, T.P. (ed.) Human-Computer Interaction, vol. 19(4), pp. 311–318. Taylor & Francis, London (2004)
4. Norman, D.: Emotional Design - Why we love (or hate) Everyday Things. Basic Books, New York (2005)
5. Kim, J., Park, S., Hassenzahl, M., Eckoldt, K.: The Essence of Enjoyable Experiences: The Human Needs – A Psychological Needs-Driven Experience Design Approach. In: Marcus, A. (ed.) Design, User Experience, and Usability, Pt I, HCII 2011, Part I. LNCS, vol. 6769, pp. 77–83. Springer, Heidelberg (2011)
6. DIN (German Institute for Standardization): DIN 69900:2009-013.40. Beuth, Berlin (2009)
7. Lindemann, U.: Methodische Entwicklung technischer Produkte. Springer, Berlin (2007)
8. Litke, H.-D.: Projektmanagement - Methoden, Techniken, Verhaltensweisen. Hanser, München (2007)
9. Bea, F.X., Scheurer, S., Hesselmann, S.: Projektmanagement. Lucius & Lucius, Stuttgart (2008)
10. Horsch, J.: Innovations- und Projektmanagement. Gabler, Wiesbaden (2003)
11. Quesenbery, W., Brooks, K.: Storytelling for User Experience. Rosenfeld Media, New York (2010)
12. Michailidou, I., von Saucken, C., Lindemann, U.: How to create a User Experience Story. In: Marcus, A. (ed.) DUXU/HCII 2013, Part I. LNCS, vol. 8012, pp. 554–563. Springer, Heidelberg (2013)
13. Löhmann, S., Körber, M., Landau, M., Butz, A.: Heartbeat - Experience the Pulse of an Electric Vehicle. Submitted Paper for DIS 2014. ACM Press (2014)

Not So Fun? The Challenges of Applying Gamification to Smartphone Measurement

Michael W. Link[1], Jennie Lai[2], and Kelly Bristol[3]

[1] Nielsen, 3784 Ardsley Ct, Marietta, GA, USA, 30062
[2] Independent, 105 Duane St, New York, NY, USA, 10007
[3] Nielsen, 501 Brooker Creek Blvd, Oldsmar, FL, USA 34677
{michael.link,Kelly.Bristol}@nielsen.com, Lai.Jennie@gmail.com

Abstract. Gamification and engagement techniques (points, status, virtual badges, and social-sharing) are applied to a mobile and on-line data collection tool to determine if these approaches can improve respondent compliance with a requested task: recording their television viewing over the course of several weeks by increasing their engagement with the app. In a series of tests, we demonstrate that virtual badges appear to be a salient and positively viewed technique for app engagement among teens and younger adults. However, not all of these approaches have positive impact especially with older adults and, in the end, do not improve compliance with the primary task.

Keywords: smartphones, mobile apps, gamification, motivation, user engagement.

1 Introduction

"Gamification" can be broadly viewed as the concept of applying game-design thinking to non-game applications to make them more engaging and improve motivation for targeted behaviors. For measurement researchers, "gamification" may be viewed through a more focused lens as the process of applying the psychological and sociological drivers of game play to behavioral and attitudinal measurement tasks in order to improve respondent engagement and compliance[1]. Gamification has proliferated in recent years throughout the marketing industry, and by extension, to market research -- less so in more traditional survey research markets. But while both disciplines seek to promote engagement for their respective needs, marketing uses gamification to keep consumers returning to a product or service (e.g., airline loyalty programs), while opinion and behavioral research is exploring its use to engage panelists to respond and comply fully with an information-gathering task. The collection of valid and reliable information from the public requires that respondents be motivated to both participate in and comply fully with the tasks involved in the measurement process. Traditionally, respondents have been offered monetary incentives. While perhaps still necessary to initially capture the attention of prospective respondents, monetary incentives do little to engage them in the longer-term. This is where game-based approaches may offer a new and innovative way of motivating participants.

A. Marcus (Ed.): DUXU 2014, Part IV, LNCS 8520, pp. 319–327, 2014.

There are two key concepts at work in gamification [2]. First, "game mechanics," which refers to the actions, tactics, or mechanisms used to create an engaging and compelling experience for respondents. This can include use of points, levels, challenges, leaderboards, virtual goods, gifts/charity, etc. to drive the desired behavior for engagement with and ultimately achievement of a given task. For example, virtual badges have been shown to have a range of utilities, from reinforcing goal setting, increasing compliance with instructions, denoting reputation/status/affirmation, and fostering group identification [3]. In contrast, "game dynamics" refers to the motivations that are tapped into as a result of the gamified experience, thereby driving continued participation by the respondent. These include motivational elements such as achievement, self-expression, competition and altruism. The choice of gaming tactics is an important one. Researchers need to understand the motivations they are trying to trigger so that they can utilize the appropriate game mechanics in turn. In doing so, however, researchers need to take care not to change or influence the attitudes, behaviors, or phenomena they are trying to measure.

Although gamification techniques tied to monetary or tangible rewards (such as point systems for panel participants to earn cash or goods over time or lottery drawings for survey participants), little research has looked at the use of gamification techniques to tap into intrinsic motivations -- that is, activating game dynamics without the use of monetary or tangible rewards. One such study applied a "gamified" approach to an online survey, utilizing a respondent avatar operating in a virtual world with the goal of answering survey questions to move the action forward [4]. While many of the participants reported that the approach was engaging and fun, it was also viewed as being more difficult to navigate, took longer, and produced greater survey break-offs than did the more traditional online survey design.

Here we examine a somewhat different set of game mechanics (points, status, virtual badges) and engagement techniques (social sharing) in order to test their effectiveness in motivating and engaging respondents to utilize a data collection mobile app over different timeframes.

2   Methodology

A succession of three experiments was conducted between January 2012 and May 2013, examining the impact of various gamification and engagement techniques on respondents' use of a smartphone/online-based activity diary. The features tested includes points for completing various tasks; "status" upgrades based on the number of points earned; virtual badges for both task completion and longevity in the measurement panel; and ability to post activities to interact with others in a newsfeed, on Facebook, and/or via Twitter. The three studies consisted of an initial convenience sample of "friends and family" using a split-sample design to test basic concepts, followed by two probability samples of the general public (see Table 1 for details).

User engagement was assessed using a number of different techniques across the studies, including (1) analysis of the paradata generated within the app by the users behavior and interaction with the app; (2) structured debrief web survey; and, (3) in-depth interviews conducted either via telephone or in-person.

3   Key Findings

The app use studies were conducted in sequence, with learnings from preceding tests used to enhance subsequent versions.   We consider the key findings from each in turn.

Table 1. App Version, Study Design, Game Features, & Evaluation Methods

App Ver.	Respondent Population	Sample Frame / Recruit Mode (n)	Field Period	App Interfaces	Features Tested	Evaluation Methods
V1	Friends & Family (one per home) w Internet or mobile device[1]	Employee listing / Email recruitment (n = 250)	6 weeks (1/17/12-2/27/12)	• iOS app	• Points • Levels • Badges • Social Sharing (Internal Newsfeed)	• App Usage Behavior • Follow-up Survey • Follow-up Telephone Debriefs
V2	Adults aged 18+ (one per home) w Internet or mobile device[1] in Birmingham, AL, USA & Little Rock, AK, USA	Landline & Cellphone Listings / Telephone Recruitment (n = 150)	2 weeks (8/2/12 - 8/15/12)	• Android app • iOS app • Web	• Badges • Social Sharing (Facebook Newsfeed)	• App Usage Behavior • Follow-up Survey
V3	Adults aged 15+ (all in home) with Internet or mobile device[1] in Birmingham, AL, USA & Dallas, TX, USA	Home address Listing / Mail & Telephone (n = 464)	2 weeks (5/9/13-5/24/13)	• Android App • iOS app • Web	• Badges • Social Sharing (Facebook, Twitter)	• App Usage Behavior • Follow-up Survey • In-person Interviews

3.1   Version 1

The initial study utilized only an iOS-based smartphone app with a convenience sample of "friends and family" of Nielsen employees across the United States and was conducted over a 6 week time period [5]. A split sample design was used in which half of the respondents were provided with a full-feature app on the first day, which allowed users to earn points & advance "levels" by completing specific activities such as accessing the app or responding to push notifications; and earn virtual badges within the app for specific viewing activities such as entering their first 'live' viewing or retrospectively recalling entries they did not report in the moment (they were not told, however, explicitly how to earn badges -- this was to keep a sense of "mystery" and encourage the users to explore the app features.), and an internal newsfeed for sharing their viewing with other app users. We call this the "Full App" group. The second group started the study with an app that had no gamification features. They used this version for the first two weeks, and then were sent an app upgrade which activated the game mechanics (points, status, & badges). Two weeks later, they received a second upgrade which activated the social sharing newsfeed. We refer to this as the "Sequential App" group.

Looking at the number of television viewing hours recorded on average by week for the two groups, three key findings emerge. First is a general decline in participation across the 6 week study by all participants -- with a greater decline between weeks 1 and 2 and a more gradual fall-off from weeks 2 through 6. Based on data from Nielsen's ongoing TV ratings services, we would expect the 6 week trend to be relatively flat with some minor variation. The conclusion, therefore, is that gamification and engagement elements did not appear to drive long-term compliance with the primary data collection task.

Second, the number of hours recorded for the Full App and Sequential App groups was nearly identical for weeks 1 and 2 (week 1: 10.3 hours Full App, 10.2 hours Sequential App; Week 2: 7.3 hours for both). This indicates that neither the game nor social features appears to have had an effect in engaging respondents to record their viewing. In other words, it made no difference whether respondents did (Full App) or did not (Sequential App) have these features in their version of the app (though the age group of these users was skewed older than the general U.S. population given the convenience sample of Nielsen employees).

Third, and perhaps most important, when the game features were introduced to the Sequential App group at the start of week 3, their average viewing per week increased (7.3 hours to 8.0 hours), while those in the Full App group declined slightly (7.3 hours to 7.2 hours). During the subsequent weeks (3 thru 6) both groups saw viewing hours decline, but the Sequential App group drop-off was less -- especially once the social sharing elements were added at the start of week 5. By week 6, those with the Full app recorded, on average, 4.8 hours of viewing per week compared to 6.4 hours for the Sequential App group. The takeaway is that by introducing game and social mechanics sequentially, the user experience was "freshened" over time compared to those who received these features at the start and as a result appears to have slowed the rate of decline in compliance with the viewing entry task.

Virtual badges were viewed by respondents as the most liked game component, with younger respondents (aged 18-29, 54%; aged 30-39, 48%) being more likely to say in a follow-up debrief survey that they loved or liked the feature, compared to older adults (aged 40+, 28%). In terms of race/ethnicity, positive reactions (loved or liked) to virtual badges were higher among African American respondents (83%) and Asian Americans (73%), than among Hispanics (54%), or non-Hispanic Whites (39%). Moreover, a majority (60%) of Asian Americans said that the virtual badges were very or somewhat encouraging their continued participation in the study. When asked about their experience in using the app during the debriefing interviews, these users wanted to learn how to earn points or badges and opportunity to earn them over the course of the study period otherwise these features would be viewed as "pointless." More importantly, they preferred to be rewarded for watching more TV or a specific program rather than their reporting behavior (they cited other apps that rewarded them for watching specific programs as intended for marketing purposes). This approach, however, would have a clear biasing effect by influencing the behavior we were trying to measure. One of the potential complexities of using gamification approaches is, therefore, how to apply them effectively to secondary tasks such that there is respondent motivation to comply with the primary task as well -- yet not change the actual behavior or attitudes being measured.

In contrast to the more positive views of some of the gamification elements, the social sharing newsfeed was utilized by very few respondents: approximately 20% accessed the feature and only 3% posted any viewing content to the feed. In debrief interviews, respondents remarked: "I want to invite friends and family so I can share viewing and compete for badges, points, etc." and "I don't want to share what I'm watching with people I don't know."

3.2   Version 2

Given the lack of apparent efficacy of the points and status approach in Version 1, we dropped these elements and focused solely on virtual badges as the gamification technique in Version 2 of the app [6]. In particular, using virtual badges to "reward" individuals for engaging with the app rather than the amount of viewing they recorded.. Respondents could earn badges by 1) completing instructional tasks such as completing the app tutorial or accessing the 'info' button customized for specific app activities; and 2) exploring various components of the app such as the home screen or checking their viewing entries (in hopes of jogging their memory of entering any viewing they may have forgotten). Taking into consideration the feedback from the first version, respondents were provided instructions on how to earn the badges once they accessed the "virtual trophy case" within the app and also shown the number of badges they could potentially earned over the course of the two-week study period.

In terms of social-sharing, we eliminated the internal app-user only newsfeed and instead allowed respondents to post a generic message to Facebook about their televisions viewing (e.g., "Bob Smith is watching Comic book Heroes"). This approach was an attempt to allow individuals to share their activity with people in their own social network while minimizing any potential biasing effects this might have on their viewing behavior by not allowing those network friends to comment within the app -- any comments were kept with the individual respondent's Facebook account.

Looking at the virtual badges earned during this field period, all respondents received the badge for registering the app ("Rock the Registration") as a way of introducing them to the badge concept. The next two highest earned badges were for accessing all four major modules within the app ("Hide & Seek," 65% of users) and completing their first (of four) brief, five-question survey posed during the field period ("Reporter," 64%). Both of these related to first-time, high-level exploratory behaviors. The lowest earned badges involved checking their viewing entries for accuracy ("Editor-in-Chief, 21%) and completing 3 of the 4 brief surveys posed during the two week collection ("Correspondent," 13%). These reflected either more detailed types of behaviors or repeated activities. It appears, therefore, that a majority of respondents did partake in the initial, high-level exploration of the app and its features, yet only a much smaller percentage had deeper, longer-term interactions with many of the app features.

Age differences in acceptance of the badge feature were clear in the surveys conducted after the first badge was earned and after the last badge was earned. All (100%) of the respondents aged 18 - 35 said they were "excited" about receiving the badge in both surveys. Among those 36 and older, 87% said they were excited after the first badge, however, this number dropped to 72% when asked about the last badge -- so interest was more on the wane among the older respondents.

In terms of social-sharing, the results were similar to those seen in Version 1 with very few respondents accessing this feature and far fewer still pushing content to their Facebook social feed.

3.3   Version 3

The final version of the television viewing app continued the focus on virtual badges, but with an eye towards encouraging younger respondents to engage with the app from start to end of a two-week study period (with emphasis on those aged 15 to 24, the demographic which is often the most difficult to get to comply with data collection tasks) -- the group seen in the first two tests as most likely to be engaged by this approach. A total of 15 badges were designed focusing on obtaining greater compliance with high-value activities such as registering the app at the start of the study, completing instructional tasks and reporting their viewing regularly or completing custom surveys during the study in hopes of sustaining their motivation throughout the two-week period.

Social-sharing options were also included in this version given the increasing popularity and growing number of social media sites. Like version2, respondents could post (but not receive within the app) a message about their viewing activity on Facebook. Version 3 also included a similar option to post to Twitter and allowed respondents to tailor their messages rather than a generic message from the first two versions.

Assessing the impact of the gamification features, younger age groups (particularly those aged 15-24) found the virtual badges to be of greater value and interest than did older adults. Just under 95% of this younger group indicated that the virtual badges helped them to understand how the app worked, compared to 60% of those aged 50 and older. Likewise, 82% of respondents aged 15 to 24 years indicated that they consciously tried to earn badges, versus just 34% of adults aged 50 or older. Younger respondents also said that the badges motivated them to enter television viewing more regularly -- the critical task for the study: 82% versus 26%. A majority across all age groups felt that earning badges was not difficult.. This finding aligns with in-person debrief results that found younger age groups were very engaged in the badges; however, most of other age groups did not see badges as a very useful engagement feature.

In terms of social-sharing, 68% of users did not think the social sharing feature (Facebook or Twitter) were important to them, while only 3% of respondent thought that they were very important. About 20% of users did not even have FB/Twitter account. These findings were fairly consistent across age groups. The figures indicated that Facebook and Twitter were considered less important in the TV viewing as the motivation to participate in the study (they preferred not to share what programs they watch or how much TV they watch with their social network online).

Based on the in-person debriefing interviews conducted with 15 participating households in Birmingham and Dallas, younger respondents aged 15-18 in multi-generational homes were far more engaged with the badge feature than the adults (i.e., parents or grandparents). The minors across these homes consistently reported they deliberately tried to earn all the badges in the app and were "frustrated" when they couldn't earn them all. However, some also admitted while they liked earning the badges but that did not necessarily motivate them to report their viewing consistently throughout the study period. In fact, the parents played a key role in reminding them to enter what they watched in the app. While this version of the app achieved the objective of using badges as an instructional tool by helping the respondents learn the features of the app but it did not seem to influence their reporting behavior.

4   Conclusions

Despite the finding that younger participants reported liking the virtual badges and found them useful for instructional purposes, there was no corresponding improvement in television viewing recording for this group compared to others age groups (looking simply at the regularity of their app entries, not the amount of viewing). In this case, therefore, respondent perception and behavior were not apparently aligned and as a result, the gamification features did not have the desired effect of improving consistency in reporting. Given the evidence across the three studies, therefore, the final recommendations were to either remove all gamification features or to add monetary rewards when badges are earned (e.g., incremental incentive) -- a recognition that any intrinsic motivation generated by the use of virtual badges was insufficient in and of itself to motivate respondents to comply fully, over time with the primary data collection task.

Based on these studies we can draw the following initial conclusions about the use of gamification techniques to improve respondent engagement:

Techniques Work Differently across Populations: People differ in the types of game mechanics and dynamics that motivate them. In particular younger adults, Blacks, Asians and Hispanics responded more favorably to some of the gaming techniques (in particular virtual badges) than did older adults and Whites. No single approach, therefore, will work equally well across different subgroups of the population.

Gamification Appears to Work Better with a Longer-Term Panel Survey than a One-Time Survey: Game mechanics appear to have their optimal impact in terms of potentially changing the pace or "freshening" a longer-term measurement experience. Although the techniques could be employed for a stand-alone survey, it is doubtful that the time and cost of developing these techniques in such an instance would be worthwhile.

It is Important to Measure the Desired Outcome Behaviors not Just Assess Respondent Engagement of Gamification Features: In all three studies, when asked, younger adults and teens tended to give certain gamification mechanics (in particular virtual badges) high marks. They even stated that they felt motivated by receipt of the virtual badges. This did not, however, translate into more consistent compliance with the primary task they were asked to undertake.

Techniques Should Motivate Respondents to Achieve the Measurement Tasks, but not to Drive or Change the Behavior or Attitudes that are being Measured: This is an obvious, but critical insight. While marketers can utilize gamification techniques to directly drive consumer purchase behavior, researchers need to motivate respondents to complete the measurement tasks without inadvertently encouraging or changing what it is they are trying to measure.

Gamification is a powerful motivational tool in marketing. While it may one day have a similar impact in attitude and behavioral measurement, the goals and mechanics need to be thought through carefully to ensure that respondents are motivated to comply with the measurement tasks and are not driven simply to win the "game." There are promising results for engagement, particularly with traditionally hard-to-engage groups (i.e., younger adults, racial/ethnic minorities); however, there are also challenges to effectively implementing these techniques to influence compliance with primary (rather than simply secondary) data collection tasks and do so without jeopardizing the critical information being gathered.

References

1. Link, M.W., Donato, P.: Engaging Consumer Panelists Through Gamification. Marketing News by the Advertising Marketing Association,
   http://www.marketingpower.com/ResourceLibrary/MarketingNews/P
   ages/2013/2-13/consumer-panels-purchasing-behaviors-
   gamification-behavior-motivations-consumer-measurement.aspx
   (February 2013)
2. Lai, J., Link, M.W.: Emerging Techniques for Respondent Engagement: Leveraging Gamification Techniques for Mobile Application Research. CASRO Journal 2012-13 (2013), http://bit.ly/123gmpr

3. Antin, J., Churchill, E.: Badges in Social Media: A Social Psychological Perspective. Paper presented at 29th CHI Conference on Human Factors in Computing Systems, Vancouver, BC, Canada (2011)
4. Downes-Le Guin, T., Baker, R., Mechling, J., Ruyle, E.: Myths and Realities of Respondent Engagement in Online Surveys. International Journal of Marketing Research 54, 613–633 (2012)
5. Link, M.W., Lai, J., Vanno, L.: Smartphone Applications: The Next (and Most Important?) Evolution in Data Collection. Paper presented at the 67th Annual Conference of the American Association for Public Opinion Research, Orlando, FL, May 17-20 (2012)
6. Lai, J., Bristol, K., Link, M.W.: Unlocking Virtual Badges as the Key for Respondent Engagement in Mobile App Surveys. Paper presented at the Annual Meeting of the Midwest Association for Public Opinion Research, Chicago, IL (2012)

The Power of Negative Feedback from an Artificial Agent to Promote Energy Saving Behavior

Cees Midden and Jaap Ham

Eindhoven University of Technology Department of Human-Technology Interaction PO Box 513, 5600 MB Eindhoven +31 40 247 3446

c.j.h.midden@tue.nl

Abstract. In this paper we analyze the role of negative feedback as provided by artificial agents. We examine the hypothesis that negative feedback offers substantial potential to enhance persuasive interventions aimed to change behavior. This hypothesis is tested based on a review of several studies using the same experimental paradigm that includes a virtual washing machine, in which users have to make choices how to program the washing machine. The studies show how the provision of positive and negative feedback influences these choices under various experimental conditions. Results show that negative feedback can be more effective than positive feedback, also independent of the presence of positive feedback. Negative feedback is in particular effective when the feedback is social instead of factual. Furthermore, the analysis suggests that the effect of negative feedback is enhanced under conditions of task similarity, which stimulate using the feedback for performance improvement. Finally, we show that negative feedback is superior to positive feedback under multiple goals conditions.

Keywords: Persuasive technology, artificial social agents, social evaluation, sustainability.

1 Introduction

The exhaustion of natural resources and the threats of growing CO_2-emissions and climate change effects have urged nations worldwide to seek for substantial reductions in energy consumption. Although technological solutions like more efficient systems and devices and the development of renewable energy sources are of great importance, consumer behavior plays a crucial role in bringing down the level of energy consumption. Influencing consumer behavior to promote energy conservation has become an important target of national and international policy efforts. Thereby, the question which instruments should be applied to promote energy conservation behavior has become highly relevant.

Recent reviews (e.g. 1) have evaluated the effects of interventions to promote energy efficient behavior. Raising people's awareness of energy consumption by providing tailored feedback about their energy consumption (for example in kWh) can promote the achievement of behavioral change. The results are mixed though. Weak linkages between specific actions and energy outcomes caused by low feedback

A. Marcus (Ed.): DUXU 2014, Part IV, LNCS 8520, pp. 328–338, 2014.

frequencies (e.g. once month) and insufficient specificity of the feedback (e.g. household in general vs. specific person or specific devices) are underlying these findings. Recently, technological solutions have created new opportunities to improve feedback efficacy by embedding it in user-system interactions. That is, energy use is almost always the outcome of an interaction between a user and some energy-using device. Intervening in these specific interactions could improve the quality of feedback substantially. Some evidence supports this claim. McCalley and Midden (2) demonstrated in several studies that interactive forms of feedback could be effective to enhance energy efficient use of devices like a washing machine. By adding an energy meter to the user interface of a washing machine they achieved 18% of energy conservation both in lab and field studies. Basically, their approach entailed giving factual feedback in terms of kWh consumed as a function of programming choices made by the user, like water temperature, spinning speed or the duration of the washing cycle.

This work was followed up by new attempts to increase the persuasiveness of the system through the introduction of social feedback (e.g. 3, 4). We examined whether social feedback can add to the promotion of pro-environmental behaviors such as energy conservation in the home. Social reinforcement has been applied widely in many domains such as child education, therapeutic programs, health behavior and social interaction as a mechanism for behavioral change (2). Social praise and compliments operate as positive incentives. In previous studies we demonstrated how the effectiveness of social reinforcements as delivered by human actors, can successfully be provided by an intelligent system (see 4 for an overview).

Surprisingly, social feedback by smart computer agents has mainly focused on positive social feedback. One of the exceptions is research by Bracken, Jeffres, and Neuendorf (5), which studied the influence of praise or criticism in feedback by a computer on user experiences (e.g., motivation). Many researchers seem to assume that positive feedback is more effective than negative feedback. There are some legitimate reasons for that. In our own research we found that direct feedback that constrains user choices may lead to reactance responses, which are detrimental to message adoption and behavioral change (6). Also negative information may not work, because it does not specify, by itself, how a person should respond. Yet, in the current paper we conjecture that the effects of negative social feedback are underestimated and can contribute substantially to effective interventions to change behavior. Although negative feedback may be less pleasant for the user, there are reasons to expect significant outcomes from negative feedback.

In a more general sense negative events show, almost universally, a higher impact than positive events and bad information is usually processed more intensely than positive information (7). In an evolutionary sense negative information is more valuable for adaptation than positive information. Ignoring danger is in general more threatening for survival than missing a positive opportunity. One could say that negative information has a higher level of diagnosticity (8). One accident may make a system unsafe, while long periods of flawless functioning are necessary to create a feeling of safety. Information diffusion studies show that bad news travels faster through networks than positive news (9). Similar patterns can be observed regarding feelings of trust. Trust is an important social emotion that allow individual to accept risky decisions that may produce positive outcomes, but also negative outcomes.

The saying, trust comes on foot, but leaves on horseback' suggests that it may require a lot of effort to build trust, but a single disappointing experience may breakdown a trustful relationship. This prominence of negative information is also predicted by Prospect theory (10), which suggests that potential negative consequences have a higher impact on decision making than potential positive consequences. Negative information can also be important because it signals a need for change, thereby feeding the self-regulatory system, through which an individual can adapt to changing circumstances (11).

Following this reasoning we included negative feedback in our persuasive feedback studies and expected negative feedback to contribute to the persuasive impact of the feedback. Although this issue was initially not at the core of our attention in most of those studies, we found remarkable results on the distinction between positive and negative feedback. In the current paper we reanalyzed our studies with this specific hypothesis in mind. First, we show in Study 1 and 2 how negative feedback influences behavior change. We show how it worked in combination with positive feedback and separate from positive feedback. Next, we discuss the results of Study 3 showing that negative feedback is in particular effective when the context offers an opportunity for adaptation and learning based on the feedback. Finally we present in Study 4 new data that suggest that positive feedback is in particular effective when a single goal has been activated, but fails under conditions of multiple goals. Negative feedback, by contrast, is not only effective when a single goal has been activated, but retains its effectiveness when multiple goals force the user to make trade-offs.

2   Study 1: Social vs. Factual Feedback and Feedback Valence

In our first study (3) about the persuasive effects of feedback on behavior by a smart social agent we set up an experiment in which subjects received social feedback from an artificial robotic agent while carrying out tasks in which they could conserve energy. More specifically, we tested the effects of social feedback compared to factual feedback, the effect of positive vs. negative effect and thirdly the effect of low vs. high perceived agency as characteristic of the feedback source. The latter effect is not relevant for the current paper and will not be discussed here. Thirty-three participants were randomly assigned to one of three experimental conditions. The experimental procedures have been explained elsewhere in detail (3). In short, participants completed 10 washing trials in which they programmed the washing machine (see Figure 1) by making various choices such as for water temperature and spinning speed. They received the factual feedback from the computer system displaying the amount of electricity (in Kwh) consumed. The feedback was presented through a little led-indicator on the display. In the social feedback condition the feedback was provided by a little robotic agent, which is known an iCat, produced by Philips corporation (ref) in the form of stylized head of a cat that was able to display social expressions by moving lips, eyes, eyelashes and eyebrows and by playing speech files. For all participants, a simulated washing machine, a copy of a current model on the market, was presented., while the social feedback was provided by the iCat and selected from a repertoire of six positive and six negative evaluative expressions like fantastic, good, bad or awful.

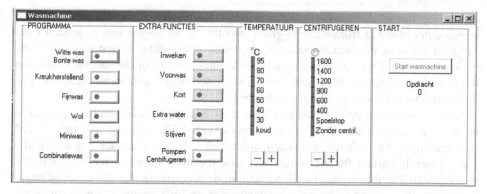

Fig. 1. The virtual washing machine interface

The results supported our expectations. The participants who received social feedback saved more energy than the participants who received the factual feedback. More importantly for the current analysis, findings showed a feedback valence effect. More specifically, these findings showed that the greatest changes to conservation behavior were achieved after negative feedback (compared to positive feedback). In addition we found an interaction indicating that the negative feedback effect was strongest when the social artificial agent, the iCat, provided it.

3   Study 2: Negative Feedback Only

Before drawing firm conclusions, a second study was performed first to replicate these results and second to test whether the negative feedback effect would also occur independent of the positive feedback. Therefor in Study 2 feedback valence was manipulated in a between-subjects design (3). So, while in Study 1 participants could receive both positive and negative feedback, in Study 2 they got either positive or negative feedback. Like in Study 1 factual feedback and social feedback were tested between-subjects. However, we also adapted the factual feedback condition to control for a potential confound between the social nature of the feedback and the evaluative nature of the feedback. On could argue that the social feedback was more effective, not because of the social nature of the feedback, but instead, because it was more directly evaluative compared to the factual feedback. To control for this potential confound we substituted the factual feedback with the led kWh-indicator for one that used colored lighting to provide factual feedback with red light for negative feedback and green light for positive feedback, both at 6 levels of intensity. In the negative feedback condition, factual evaluative feedback was given when participants used more energy than the middle of the scale. This was done by gradually changing the color of the screen from white to red and back within 3 seconds. In addition, an unpleasant sound (a buzzer) was played through the speakers for one second. The strength of the red color and the loudness of the sound depended on the amount of energy consumed by a participant's settings. If e.g. a setting used much energy, the screen changed color to dark red, and a loud buzzer sounded. In positive feedback conditions, factual evaluative feedback was given in an identical fashion, but now the screen color changed from white to green, and the sound played was a pleasant ring. Level of detail of the factual-evaluative feedback was similar to that in social feedback conditions. This setup equalized the evaluative nature of the feedback between the conditions, but kept the distinction between social and non-social feedback. For the remainder the setup was similar to Study 1.

Results were in support of the conclusions of Study 1. Social feedback proved to be more effective than factual feedback, both with kWh indicator and the colored light condition. The difference between both types of factual feedback was not significant. More important for the current analysis, the main effect of feedback valence was replicated in this between subjects design, demonstrating that the effect of negative feedback occurred without the availability of positive feedback. Furthermore we found the same interaction indicating that the effect of negative feedback was strongest for social feedback compared to factual feedback. The latter single effect proved to be non-significant. Moreover it seemed as if the positive feedback encouraged participants to enhance their energy consumption. Thus, this last finding suggests that while people may feel pleased by a system that offers compliments, this does not ensure that the user may also change her or his behavior. In particular this may happen when multiple goals have been activated. We will address this issue in Study 4.

Together Study 1 and 2 demonstrated the effectiveness of negative feedback and in particular when the feedback was social in nature. These rather surprising effects of negative feedback evoked the question why these effects occurred. This was the reason for setting up Study 3 in which we explored conditions that facilitated the working of negative feedback.

4   Study 3: Learning from Negative Feedback

We argued that an important reason for the effectiveness of negative feedback is that negative feedback is especially useful in situations that allow people to avoid aversive consequences by learning from previous experiences. It has been argued that negative feedback is not effective because, in contrast to positive feedback, it does not learn how to avoid the negative consequences (12). In other words it would not stimulate learning sufficiently. Consistent with this explanation also in other fields similar hypotheses have been tested. Earlier research in the domains of risk management (13) suggested that people seek information about impending dangers only when they see a possibility to avoid negative consequences. In line with these findings, we argue that the effects of negative feedback will be moderated by the extent to which options are available to avoid negative consequences. This could for instance be the case when tasks that people have to perform are relatively similar (as compared to tasks that are dissimilar). In such a task context feedback can provide better options to learn from previous negative experiences because these may offer indications for improvement in follow-up tasks. So, we argued that task similarity would enhance the effects of negative feedback. Therefore, in Study 3 we investigated the hypothesis that the persuasive effect of negative social feedback vs. positive social feedback as provided by an artificial social agent will be enhanced under conditions of high task similarity in comparison to low task similarity (14).

In this study in which 120 participants participated we manipulated in a 2x2 design high vs. low task similarity and positive vs. negative social feedback by the artificial agent. The experimental setup followed the setup and procedures of Study 1 and 2. Task similarity was manipulated by distinguishing a set of washing tasks with high similarity vs. one with low similarity. This distinction was based on a pretest in which we asked 27 participants to sort 16 washing tasks on similarity. The outcomes of the pretest were used to compose a set in which subsequent tasks were rather similar vs. a set in which subsequent tasks were rather dissimilar. So, the 16 tasks were the same in both conditions, but only the order of the tasks was different to induce the desired effect. For example, in the high similarity condition tasks including the same type of material, for instance woolen or cotton wear.

The results confirmed again the main effect of feedback valence showing a higher level of behavior change as a result of negative feedback. Moreover, a significant interaction was found showing that the effects of negative feedback, compared to positive feedback, was enhanced in the task similarity condition, thereby supporting our hypothesis.

In sum, this study showed that negative feedback is able to contribute to behavior change interventions if the right learning conditions are met. In the next section we will argue that negative feedback can also compensate for weaknesses of positive feedback.

5   Study 4: Serving a Single Goal vs. Multiple Goals

Without doubt, lack of clarity about the role of set goals has been one of the major reasons why results of feedback have been mixed in the past (15). It was often presumed that energy feedback would allow users to see where they stood in relation to their energy consumption goal and thus would automatically seek to reach it. However, residents may or may not have had an active goal to save energy, and of those that did, many may have given this goal a lower priority than other goals, such as comfort or convenience. In fact, the earlier studies that evidenced some success of energy feedback either assigned a specific energy saving goal to subjects and requested various forms of commitment to the assigned goal (2, 16, 17) or were likely to have unknowingly triggered an energy saving goal in the subjects prior to the experimental treatment (e.g. 18). Those that did not engage the user in some form of goal setting showed no success of lowering consumption through feedback. Possibly others were likely to have unknowingly triggered an energy saving goal in the subjects prior to the experimental treatment (18).

The relevance of goal setting has also been demonstrated for persuasive technology using smart agents. The study by (2) illustrated that goal setting can be a highly effective means of assuring response to feedback in the washing machine paradigm as also used in the Studies 1-3 of the current paper.

In spite of the significance of these results, we should wonder to what extent these results match real life circumstances. As far as we know, studies that investigated goal setting in relation to the effectiveness of feedback, regarded only single goals, that is a goal to conserve energy was set, or activated, or not. In real life however, people usually have multiple goals when making decisions to conserve energy. Even more, energy conservation is usually not the prime goal for using appliances. Most of the time, actions will connect to other major goals like heating the home, cooling foodstuffs or cleaning the laundry. One may wonder how the presence of these other goals could affect the pursuit of a conservation goal? In general, it seems likely that if a user has to divide his or her attention between multiple goals, each goal would receive less attention. In particular, this will be the case if goals are not compatible, which forces a user to make a trade-off between the achievement of both goals. We suggest that for many users the prime need for using energy will dominate the goal to conserve energy. In others words when people have to make a choice, often energy conservation will not prevail. Actually, this may be a reason why adoption of sustainable technology in general is hampered. Producers of sustainable technology improve a product attribute of secondary significance for the consumer, the exception being the case that resource conservation is among the dominant goals of action (15).

If consumers would tend to weigh their prime goal of use higher than the conservation goals, what could be the effect of feedback? Most likely, the user will be more alert on the achievement of the prime goal rather than the conservation goal. That is why we hypothesized that positive feedback on the conservation goal could generate a response that turns attention away from the conservation goal and towards the prime goal. After all, positive feedback may suggest that the conservation goal has been achieved to a reasonable extent. Most likely, negative feedback will not induce that conclusion to the same extent.

Note, that in all three preceding studies that we described in the current paper actually multiple goals were present. We asked our participants to perform washing tasks to clean the laundry in proper way. In addition we asked them to conserve as much energy as possible. Thus, our participant had to make the tradeoff between the two goals. This may be one of the explanations why negative feedback works. One might even reason that in most studies on energy feedback this trade-off of multiple goals has played a role in the decisions of users. In most cases, however, this decision aspect was not articulated in the research. This could also be part of the explanation why the results of feedback studies have been mixed.

On the basis of these considerations on the relationship between multiple goals and feedback, we hypothesized that in a multiple goal situation in which a conservation goal competes with a goal of use, negative feedback may exert stronger effects on the achievement of conservation goals compared to positive feedback (Hypothesis 1). Furthermore we expected that participants aiming for a conservation goal while a (consumption) goal was also activated, would consume more electricity than participants who are aiming for a conservation goal only. (Hypothesis 2). Finally, we expected to replicate the finding of higher savings as a result of negative feedback compared to positive feedback (Hypothesis 3).

5.1   Method

Participants and design. 73 participants (35 men and 38 women), all students at Eindhoven University of Technology, were randomly assigned to one of four experimental conditions: 2 (feedback condition: single goal activated vs. multiple goals activated) x 2 (feedback type: positive vs. negative). In addition, each participant completed 10 washing trials, which composed the 10 levels of our third independent variable.

Materials and procedure. The experimental procedure was identical to that of Study 1, except that only social-evaluative feedback was given and goal setting was manipulated. The expressions and behavior of the iCat were similar to the previous studies.

Participants were asked to complete the washing trials on the simulated washing machine panel that was presented on the screen. In the multiple goal condition two goals were assigned: clean your clothes and save energy.   In the single goal condition they were only requested to save energy. Each participant completed a practice washing trial and the ten real washing trials, which were identical for all of the participants. For each trial, participants were instructed to complete a specific type of washing task (e.g., "wash four very dirty jeans").

After the participants completed all trials, they answered several demographic questions, were debriefed and thanked for their participation.

To be able to distinguish the effects of positive and negative feedback we calculated an index based on total number of actions of users in the user interface. So, we not only included the final choices per trial, but all the preceding programming choices. As explained, these were all followed by social feedback, either positive or negative. The index subtracted for each action the following choice, in terms of energy consumption effect, from the current choice, thereby indicating whether the feedback resulted in a higher or lower energy consumption score for the next following choice. This procedure was similar to those in the previous studies.

5.2   Results

The electricity consumption score was analyzed using a 2 (goal: single vs. multiple) x 2 (feedback type: negative vs. positive) mixed model analysis, controlling for multiple observations per participant. Analyses confirmed our expectations regarding Hypothesis 1 and 3. The main effect of the goal factor did not reach significance (Single goal M = -0.11, SD = 0.01; Multiple goal M = -.09, SD = 0.01), $F(1, 59,342) = 2,186$, $p = 0.14$). More specifically, these analyses indicated that participants who had been provided with positive social feedback saved less energy (M = .-.05, SD = .009) than participants who had been provided with negative (social) feedback (M = −.16, SD = .01), $F(1, 557,676) = 80,586$, $p < .0001$. Secondly, these analyses confirmed the interaction between feedback valence x # of goals, $F(1, 557,676) = 4,863$, $p = .0.028$ (see Figure 2). Specific comparison within the mixed model analysis (using Bonferroni adjustments for multiple comparisons) showed that the simple effect of positive feedback significantly reduced under multiple goal conditions compared to single goal. This effect did not occur for negative feedback. Negative feedback was effective in saving energy under single goal conditions but remained so under multiple goal conditions.

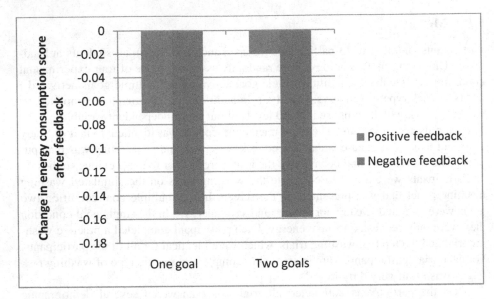

Fig. 2. Change in energy consumption score after positive vs. negative feedback under one vs. two goal conditions in Study 4

6   Discussion

In general, our findings demonstrated that people are sensitive to social feedback as provided by an artificial agent. Apparently, persuasive artificial agents are able to create behavior change among human users. In contrast to earlier work that focused primarily on praise, our feedback interventions included both positive and negative feedback (Study 1). The effect of social feedback on energy conservation should therefore be considered as the joint effect of both positive as well as negative feedback. Interestingly however, our analysis on the level of single programming acts within trials, suggested that the direct influence of negative feedback on following programming choices was greater than the effect of the positive feedback. Furthermore Study 2 demonstrated convincingly that providing negative feedback only is more effective than providing positive feedback only. This finding suggests that the effectiveness of negative feedback is not dependent on the presence of positive feedback. It is however related to the social nature of the feedback. The effects of negative feedback were especially noticeable for social feedback and less for factual feedback. Apparently, the social nature of the feedback amplifies the difference between positive and negative feedback. Results of Study 3 indicated that negative feedback was effective especially when tasks were relatively similar—as is the case of many of the daily routine tasks people perform. Enhanced task similarity creates a context in which the feedback can immediately be employed for improving performance. In this sense negative feedback contributes to self-regulatory action by the user. This function is weaker when the context does not offer opportunities for performance improvement based on the negative feedback. This process may have influenced the effectiveness of negative feedback in most of our studies using the washing machine paradigm. This paradigm offers a structured environment in which users are requested to make specific choices while using a well-defined interface. In this context it becomes easily clear for the user how to enhance performance when this is indicated by the feedback. In ill-structured environments, it could be necessary to offer the user additional cues how to improve performance.

The effects of positive feedback were relatively minor in our studies. Moreover, it seemed as if the positive feedback encouraged participants to enhance their energy consumption. However, this was not generally the case. Thus, while people may feel pleased by a system that offers compliments to a user, an effect that has also been observed in other studies (e.g. 19), this does not ensure behavior change. In particular, this may hold if a user has other goals to achieve, like in our case cleaning the laundry. In making the trade-off the user may decide to stop focusing on the goal that already received positive feedback. Possibly this effect is also influenced by the goal hierarchy. On might expect that the higher goal will be pursued to a greater extent when a trade-off has to be made. Future research could further examine this factor.

In our introduction we have discussed the debate about negative feedback and negative information in various research areas. Our results support the notion that negative feedback can be effective in informing people about their performance or about the need to change actions. One might wonder whether this effect is influenced by the artificial nature of the feedback sources in our research compared to human sources in many other studies. Possibly, people can more easily accept negative information from a non-human source than from a human source. Although our reactance studies showed that also artificial agents could evoke reactance, it seems plausible that tendencies to respond defensively are weaker when the feedback originates from an artificial agent. This is one of the challenging questions that lie ahead in exploring and optimizing the persuasive power of artificial agents.

References

1. Abrahamse, W., Steg, L., Vlek, C., Rothengatter, T.A.: review of intervention studies aimed at household energy conservation. Journal of Environmental Psychology 25, 273–291 (2005)
2. McCalley, L.T., Midden, C.J.H.: Energy conservation through product-integrated feedback: The roles of goal-setting and social orientation. J. Econ. Psychol. 23, 589–603 (2002)
3. Midden, C., Ham, J.: Using negative and positive social feedback from a robotic agent to save energy. In: Conference Proceedings of Persuasive 2009, Claremont, USA. pp. article no.12. Springer, Heidelberg (2009)
4. Midden, C.J.H., Ham, J.R.C.: Persuasive Technology to promote pro-environmental behaviour, in. In: Steg, L., van den Berg, A.E., de Groot, J.I.M. (eds.) Environmental Psychology an Introduction, West-Sussex / UK (2013)
5. Bracken, C.C., Jeffres, L.W., Neuendorf, K.A.: Criticism or praise: The impact of verbal versus text-only computer feedback on social presence, intrinsic motivation, and recall. CyberPsychology and Behavior 7, 349–357 (2004)

6. Roubroeks, M., Ham, J., Midden, C.: When artificial social agents try to persuade people: The role of social agency on the occurrence of psychological reactance. International Journal of Social Robotics 3, 155–165 (2011)
7. Rozin, P., Royzman, E.: Negativity bias, negativity dominance, and contagion. Personal SocPsychol Rev. 5, 296–320 (2001)
8. Slovic, P., Finucane, M.L., Peters, E., MacGregor, D.G.: Risk as analysis and risk as feelings: Some thoughts about affect, reason, risk, and rationality. Risk Analysis 24, 311–322 (2004)
9. Naveed, N., Gottron, T., Kunegis, J., Che Alhadi, A.: Bad news travels fast, A content-based analysis of interestingness on twitter. In: Proceedings of the ACM Web-Sci. (2011)
10. Kahneman, D., Tversky, A.: Prospect theory: An analysis of decision under risk. Econometrica 47(2), 263–291 (1979)
11. Baumeister, R.F., Bratlavsky, E., Finkenauer, C., Vohs, K.D.: Bad is stronger than good. Rev. Gen. Psychol. 5, 323–370 (2001)
12. Skinner, B.: Utopia through the control of human behavior. In: Rich, J.M. (ed.) Readings in the Philosophy of Education. Wadsworth, Belmont (1972)
13. Rogers, R.W., Prentice-Dunn, S.: Protection motivation theory, Gochman, D.S. (ed.). In: Handbook of Health Behavior Research 1: Personal and Social Determinants, ch. 6. Plenum Press, New York (1997)
14. Ham, J., Midden, C.: A persuasive robotic agent to save energy: The influence of social feedback, feedback valence and task similarity on energy conservation behavior. In: Conference Proceedings of Social Robotics, Singapore (2010)
15. Midden, C.J.H., Kaiser, F.G., L McCalley, L.T.: Technology's Four Roles in Understanding Individuals' Conservation of Natural Resources. Journal of Social Issues 63(1), 155–174 (2007)
16. Becker, L.J., Seligman, C.: Reducing air conditioning waste by signaling it is cool outside. Personality and Social Psychology Bulletin 4, 412–415 (1978)
17. van Houwelingen, J.H., van Raaij, W.F.: The effect of goal-setting and daily electronic feedback on in-home energy use. Journal of Consumer Research 16, 98–105 (1989)
18. Seligman, C., Darley, J.M.: Feedback as a means of decreasing residential energy consumption. Journal of Applied Psychology 62, 363–368 (1977)
19. Fogg, B.J.: Persuasive technology: Using computers to change what we think and do. Morgan Kaufmann, Amsterdam (2003)

Emotion, Affectivity and Usability in Interface Design

Renato Nascimento, Carlos Dias Limeira, André Luís Santos de Pinho,
and José Guilherme Santa Rosa

Laboratório de Ergodesign de Interfaces, Usabilidade e Experiência do Usuário
Universidade Federal do Rio Grande do Norte, Natal, Brazil
{renatus.oliveira,carloscafedias,jguilhermesantarosa}@gmail.com,
pinho@ccet.ufrn.br

Abstract. The intent of this paper is to provide an overview of the influence of emotion, affection and feelings during the contact between users and interfaces. Definitions of each of the aspects and relations established between them, and perceived usability and user satisfaction are presented. It was concluded that the process of interface design should include analyzes of the context, objectives and specific features and requirements.

Keywords: emotion; affectivity, usability, interface design.

1 Introduction

This paper presents aspects of human cognition and discusses their impact on human - technology interaction.

Every day we formulate complex judgments about people and objects with which we interact, expressing different emotions to different situations. The impact caused by our sensations, emotions and perceptions can directly affect our interest in using a product or system, their usefulness in estimating and evaluating their. Thus, an individual becomes fruit of their internal complexity, influenced by the world around him/her and the impact of material and affective experiences that help to create their own identity set your impressions and preferences.

A product or system may have different features that can be classified into three red categories [8]:

- practical function: relation at the physiological level, established from the initial contact of the object with the human senses;
- aesthetic function: relation in the sensory level, the perception of the object during its use. Here, the proper development of the aesthetics of a product can improve the perception of performance and contribute to the vested interest of the consumer / user;
- symbolic function: relation establishing connections with the experiences and sensations ever experienced by the user, determined by the acquired psychological and social aspects. Derives from the aesthetic elements contained in the product that create associations with ideas (memory status, satisfaction, pride).

A. Marcus (Ed.): DUXU 2014, Part IV, LNCS 8520, pp. 339–346, 2014.

In order to systematize the types of product configurations use, Lobach (2001) proposed two principles:

- the practical-functional: the products in which predominate objective, utilitarian relationship;
- functional: the products in which there would be a predominance the subjective relationship of signification.

It is noteworthy that, historically, research and development in design always allocated more attention to identifying practical and objective needs of users than the emotional, psychological, social and cultural needs of users during the design of a product or system. This often happens because usually the designer works during the design process in order to "idealize" users and their characteristics without actually making contact with them [8].

2   Emotion Design

Over time, the needs of individuals become more dynamic, amplified by factors related to product use (ergonomics) or cultural and velocity information and the generation of new products and services. Some authors justify the existence of a wide range of industrial artifacts and their variations thanks to the emergence of new human needs, in which "the range of products offers consumers a degree of choice and gives them sense of individuality" [6]. It is noteworthy also that the products can be more than the sum of their duties, satisfying certain emotional needs in people [9].

In humans [7], emotions are essential elements of life, being crucial for making everyday decisions. Interact through them to the stimuli received in the world, helping to assess situations as being good or bad, safe or dangerous [9]. And in contemporary society marked by consumerism, products become true living, objects capable of changing our emotional state and have its own personality [7].

Maslow grouped an individual's basic needs into eight categories [1]:

- Physiological: hunger, thirst, bodily comforts etc.;
- Safety/security: being out of danger ;
- Social: affiliate with others, be accepted;
- Esteem: to achieve, be competent, gain approval andrecognition;
- Cognitive: to know, to understand, and explore;
- Aesthetic: symmetry, order, and beauty;
- Self-actualization: to find self-fulfillment and to realize one's potential;
- Transcendence: to help others find self-fulfillment and to realize their potential.

From 1990s, with increasing investments in user research begins to emerge - with force on the international stage design - a field called "emotional design", which seeks to investigate and understand the role of emotions in the relationship between man and objects. Thus, enabling designers to design more efficient and unique solutions, either in the design or improvement of products and spaces physical interfaces or virtual environments, avoiding or arousing certain emotions in people from their use [11].

In the real world, emotions are neither predictable nor controllable, it is not possible, for example, the designer to add emotions to manufactured objects. But from studies investigating the emotional attachment between human and products or systems, fosters is a scientific field that seeks to formulate statements about the user experience with the product. From the investigation of emotions and other aspects of human cognition is possible to awaken or avoid certain emotions evoked during contact with the product. So emotional design [11] is rather a holistic approach to the needs and desires of the user than a mechanism for handling their experience [11].

It should be emphasized that some research that have been developed in recent decades have brought important contributions to the theories and proposed new field of emotional design:

2.1   Donald Norman and the Three Levels of Design

Among all animals, we humans are more complex: brain structures that possess and enable us to respond to stimuli in the world we live in, give us the amazing ability to reflect on it and what we learn from such experiences and thus evolve and overcome biological inheritance [9]. Thus, according to Donald Norman theory, there are three levels of processing of the human brain, operating continuously in our relationship with objects. Transporting levels for the universe of design, it suggests specific strategies in order to work with each of them in particular ways.

- visceral level: preconscious automatic layer, linked to the appearance in which form first impressions about the object. This layer is related to physical aspects (physical sensation, texture and weight of materials) and the first impression of a product;
- behavioral level: the layer that controls the behavior that is related to the use and performance of the object or system. It is also associated with function, ease of understanding of the product, usability and how it is physically felt by the user, and effectiveness and efficiency;
- reflective level: conscious and contemplative part of the brain that considers the rationalization and intellectualization of something. It is related to a subjective point of view, covering cultural and individual characteristics, affective memory, construction of meaning, self-image, personal satisfaction, memories. Designing this level requires embedding meanings to products such as pride and satisfaction.

It is noteworthy that our interaction with objects of day-to-day [9] reflects the three levels of design in many different ways: some objects are enjoyed only by the visceral impact of its appearance (visceral design), others worshiped solely by their function and use (behavioral design) and others to create an image of self-confidence, identity, fun (reflective design). The levels comprise human brain structures ranging from the lower layer (sensory) to more complex and higher (reflection). There is a temporal issue: the visceral and behavioral levels reflect the "now"; the reflexive can extend much longer, providing long-term relationships, deeper and long lasting [9].

In developing a product a designer should keep in mind that any real experience involves all three levels, and there should be a balance of forces, where each level

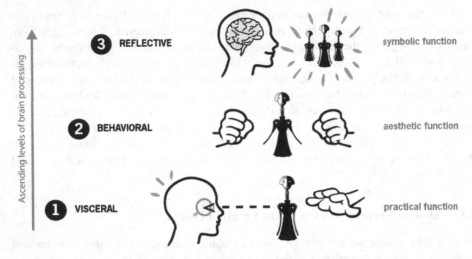

Fig. 1. Levels of brain processing and their functions

has a different role in intellectual functioning, each requiring a different approach for this professional design. The three interacting components, modulating each other and combine the same time, emotion and cognition [9].

2.2   Patrick Jordan and the Four Pleasures

Humans are always in the search for pleasure, and the artifacts they use can be considered as sources of pleasure [7]. In his book "Designing pleasurable products", Patrick Jordan [7] establishes a relationship between pleasure and the use of the product, seeking to understand how people relate to the products, and what kinds of pleasure arises from that relationship. According to the theory of Jordan [7] products may show four types of pleasure from its use:

- Physiological Pleasure. Related to the body and the senses: touch, smell, hearing, sight, and taste, in addition to sensual pleasure;
- Social Enjoyment: related to the pleasure derived from the interactions between humans, and how these products act as facilitators and motivators in these social relations;
- Psychological Pleasure: concerning reactions and psychological state during interaction with the product. The success in performing tasks or in finishing it ends up generating states like excitement or relaxation;
- Ideological Pleasure: related to reflection on experience, and the combination of the person's values (moral values) with the values embedded in the product (cultural values).

The model proposed by Jordan suggests a systematic classification of sources of pleasure in order to assist designers in their projects. Besides contributing to the understanding of how design can awaken pleasure in people, their research also influenced the development of methodologies and techniques for professionals [10]. According to this theory the needs of users on the products go through a hierarchy of levels that need to be satisfied, starting at the lowest point "functionality" (what one expects the product to comply), through the middle level "usability" (the ease in using such a product) until you reach the apex of the needs that would be the "pleasure" (maximum stage that goes beyond functionality and usability - creating a deeper relationship between user and object).

From the above theories and seeking a better understanding of the topic it is shown below a comparative framework that seeks to relate the authors from an order of events: the functions displayed by the products in contact with the user will interact with certain levels of processing in the human brain that require the different design strategies.

Table 1. Relationship between the functions of the object, brain levels and types of pleasure

Löbach	Norman	Jordan
practical function	visceral level	physiological pleasure
aesthetic function	behavioral level	social enjoyment
symbolic function	reflective level	psychological / ideological pleasure

Perception. Perception is the process by which people decode the stimuli (information) received through the five senses (touch, smell, sight, hearing and taste). Our perception is conditioned by social influences, as well as the physical and psychological conditions that surround us. Perception determines what is seen and what is felt, influencing our buying behavior. The perception tends to be a selective process, as we cannot be aware of all inputs simultaneously. Since humans are bombarded by messages you see and hear on a daily basis, it tends to select almost intuitively what interests you most, conditioned by the social and cultural environment for their physical and psychological [3] conditions.

Sentiment. Sentiment is also often confused with emotion. Unlike emotions (and moods) [1], sentiments are not states of an individual, but assigned properties of an object. When people say that they "like" an interface or find an interface to be "frustrating," what they really mean is that that they associate the interface with a positive or frustrating emotional state; in other words, they expect interaction with the interface to lead to positive or frustrating emotions [1].

Memory. Emotion's effect on attention also has implications for memory. Because emotion focuses thought on the evoking stimulus, emotional stimuli are generally remembered better than un- emotional events [1].

Color. Can clearly be designed into an interface with its mood influencing properties in mind. Warm colors, for example, generally provoke "active feelings," while cool colors are "much less likely to cause extreme reactions" [1].

Sound, Voice and Music. Aspects of audio such as timbre, pitch and speech rate, instruments, rhythm and melodies of songs and background envelope, frequency and duration of sounds for the warning and audible feedback can interfere with the perception of the users towards the system and the experience of user.

Gestures. Models and patterns of gestural interfaces when designed properly can facilitate the use of a system and contribute to a positive perception and acceptance of the system by users - making it more enjoyable and intuitive to use and increase over-all user satisfaction during interaction with the system.

Typography. The choice of typography can contribute positively or negatively both in speed reading and understanding the message and perceived credibility. For exam-ple, an annual report on the sales of a company written in sans comics can interfere with the credibility of the document. Also, characters in smaller size may require more effort users to read and therefore the satisfaction when using the system.

User Experience. The user experience is the totality of effects felt internally by a user as a result of the interaction - which can start even before visual contact (due to possi-ble expectation or idealization) [4] and also during and after the interaction - where after use reflections on lived experience occur. Therefore, the user experience is re-lated to the cognitive, physical and emotional processes, and also depend on the con-text of use and variables such as temperature range of environment, lighting, noise, social relations, among others. Usability clears the way for a good experience by eli-minating troublesome interface distractions, but a great experience stems from some-thing more of an awareness of why people could or do care [1].

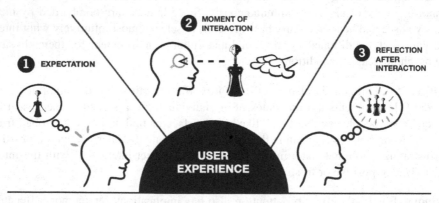

Fig. 2. Flow of user experience

Neuroergonomics. To Parasuraman [10] while Ergonomics (or Human Factors) refers to the study of the relationship between adaptation of technology to humans in the workplace and in other real-world contexts and neuroscience to the study of brain struc-ture and function the area called Neuroergonomics focuses on research on the relation-ship of neural substrates of perceptual, cognitive and motor functions, such as vision, hearing, movement, decision making and planning in the use of technologies. Among the topics and application areas Neuroergonomics highlighted by Parasuraman [10] mentioned: the interaction of humans with computers, devices and environments: at work, at home, at leisure, in rehabilitation activities, for the sake of accessibility; the use of products and operating vehicles such as airplanes, cars, trains and ships. It is worth noting, though, that both the aforementioned technological advances as the development of new research in neuroergonomics have brought contributions to the body of knowledge and theories of cognitive psychology, neurosciences and ergonomics - pushing the boundaries of what was hitherto considered as cash black (set of unobservable mental processes and not considered by behavioral psychology in the 70s).

Accordingly, in the context of interaction, perception occurs through a series of reactions to physical, psychological and emotional stimuli, where once senses and interpreted through cognitive processes of our psychology, we assign meanings things, and experiences. This process allow, for example, to qualify an experience as satisfying or frustrating. And therefore, continuous and long-term mode, which operates the same way for the construction of knowledge and world view, also acts to influence the meaning that is given to a service, product, or brand, and establish a good or bad relationship with an institution.

Therefore, when considering the interaction of the universe as a whole, the mutuality of relationships between user and context, and to project to the experience and, above all, for its quality, it is essential to consider the user's perception, the way we react to varying stimuli from the environment and interacts with a context.

3   Conclusion

The results obtained from the literature survey and the reflections made in this study suggest that there is strong relationship between systems considered by users as easy usability and suitability of the characteristics of the interfaces to aspects such as pleasure, emotion, memory and feeling. Therefore, it is recommended that the user interface is designed from surveys about cognitive, psychological, physical and cultural aspects of the users. Also that experimental research should be conducted to verify and to analyze the relationship between the aspects mentioned and usability of a system or product it is suggested.

References

1. Brave, S., Nass. C. Emotion in human-computer interaction. In: Jacko, J.A., SEARS, A. The human-computer interaction handbook, pp. 81--86. L. Erlbaum Associates Inc. Hillsdale, NJ (2003)
2. Cardoso, R. Uma introdução ao design. Blucher, São Paulo (2008)
3. Cobra, M. Vendas: como ampliar seu negócio. Marcos Cobra, São Paulo (2001)
4. Cybis, W., Betiol, A. H; Faust, R. Ergonomia e Usabilidade. conhecimentos, métodos e aplicações. 2 ed. Novatec Editora, São Paulo (2010)
5. Figueiredo, C. M., BUCICH, C.C. O conceito de prazer na relação entre usuário e o produto. São Paulo, Bauru: XII SIMPEP, São Paulo (2005)

6. Forty, A. Objeto de desejo – design e sociedade desde 1750. Cosac Naify, São Paulo (2007)
7. Jordan, P. Designing pleasurable products. Taylor & Francis, London (2000)
8. Löbach, B. Design industrial: bases para a configuração dos produtos industriais. Editora Blucher, São Paulo (2001)
9. Norman, D. A. Design emocional: por que adoramos (ou detestamos) os objetos do dia-a-dia. Rocco, Rio de Janeiro (2008)
10. Parasuraman, R. & Rizzo, M. Neuroergonomics: the brain at work. Oxford University Press, New York [2007]
11. Tonetto, L. M., Costa, F.C. X. Design Emocional: conceitos, abordagens e perspectivas de pesquisa. Unisinos, São Leopoldo (2011)

New Methods for Measuring Emotional Engagement

Andrew Schall

SPARK Experience, LLC
Bethesdsa, Maryland, USA
andrew@sparkexperience.com

Abstract. Truly understanding the feelings of a user has always been a dream of user experience (UX) researchers. Current methods for understanding emotional response has been limited to self-reporting from study participants or qualitative methods such as surveys or focus groups. New biometric and neurometric devices allow us to collect behavioral data in ways that were not previously practical for user researchers. This paper will provide an overview of these new technologies and how they can be applied to the study of emotional responses during user experience evaluation.

Keywords: Emotion research, emotional design, user experience, physiological measurements, biometric, neurometric, EEG, eye tracking, GSR, facial response analysis.

1 Introduction

Truly understanding the feelings of a user has always been a dream of user experience (UX) researchers. Are they enjoying the experience? Are they frustrated? Are they truly interested and engaged? The broader definition of user experience has grown to extend beyond basic usability. Understanding how a user truly feels in reaction to an experience can help us to optimize specific aspects of the design to exude certain specific emotional states.

Standard user research methodologies rely on either observing the user, or by directly asking the user for input. A common way to address emotional and cognitive aspects in user experience testing today is through retrospective self-report where users are asked to describe or answer questions about their experience after it has been completed, either verbally or through a questionnaire [1]. While these methods are commonplace, they rely too heavily on the highly subjective nature of participant's interpretation and recollection of their emotions. They are also too limited in their capacity to identify changes in emotional or cognitive processing over the course of a test, unless the user is constantly interrupted with questions, which would have a negative impact on the authenticity of the user experience.

The ability to capture biometric and neurometric measurements has existed for over 100 years, predominantly in an academic or clinical setting. Skin conductance,

A. Marcus (Ed.): DUXU 2014, Part IV, LNCS 8520, pp. 347–357, 2014.

respiration, electrical brain activity, pupillary size and cardiovascular activity have all been reported to vary in response to factors such as task difficulty, levels of attention, experiences of frustration and emotionally focused stimuli. Biometric and neurometric measurements have been in use by the cognitive psychology and neuroscience fields for decades, however the extreme complexities in both data collection and analysis have previously made these techniques impossible for those outside of academia or these highly specialized fields. It has been proposed that physiological data might be a valuable tool for user experience testing, as it could help identify significant events in cognitive and emotional behavior [2].

New biometric and neurometric devices, which are practical, reasonably priced, and suitable for UX practitioners, have evoked both a substantial amount of enthusiasm and skepticism. Biometric and neurometric measurements allow us to collect behavioral data in ways that were not previously possible. Researchers can use these measurements when they are interested in understanding the user's emotional reaction at a certain point in time such as when a specific stimulus is displayed, or to catch the overall emotional reaction over a longer period of time that can include the entire interaction with the stimulus. The primary objective of this paper is to provide an introduction to biometric and neurometric tools that can be used by the user experience research community. A secondary goal is to address the specific benefits and challenges of these new tools to accurately and reliably deduce emotional responses in UX research.

2   Physiological Measurements for User Experience Research

There are numerous biometric and neurometric tools and measurements that can be used to gain a deep understanding of human cognition and emotional response. However, many of these such as fMRI (Functional Magnetic Resonance Imaging) MEG (Magnetoencephalography), PET (Positron Emission Tomography) are extremely expensive, highly intrusive, and go well beyond the skillsets of a typical user researcher. This paper focuses entirely on tools that are accessible to those in the UX field including the use of eye tracking, GSR (Galvanic Skin Response), EEG (electroencephalography), and facial response analysis.

2.1   Eye Tracking

Eye tracking is a methodology that helps researchers understand visual attention. Using eye tracking we can detect where users are looking at a point in time, how long they look at something, and the path that their eye follows. Eye tracking has been applied to numerous fields including human factors, cognitive psychology, marketing, and the broad field of human-computer interaction [3].

We are at the beginning of a golden age for eye tracking in user experience research. Most major academic and commercial labs have an eye-tracker, or plan to purchase one in the near future. The primary reasons for this increase in adoption have been ease of use for the researcher and being considerably more participant-friendly. In the past, eye tracking has only been accessible to those with a highly advanced understanding of human physiology, engineering, and computer science. Users of these systems had to have extensive training in order to properly operate the equipment. Making sense of the data was extremely cumbersome and time-consuming, requiring researchers to do analysis by hand.

Advancements in remote eye tracker technology now make it possible to calibrate the equipment with the participant's eyes easily in a matter of seconds [4]. Eye trackers today are extremely accurate, can track a diverse population, and retain their calibrations for long periods of time. The operation of eye trackers today requires significantly less training and does not require a dedicated technician during use.

Gone are the days of clamping down a participant's head into a vice and sticking a bite bar into their mouths. Today's eye tracking technology has been miniaturized and integrated into computer monitors (see Figure 1) or as standalone devices no longer physically connected to the participant. The technology is so covert that participants would have no indication that they are being tracked except for the brief calibration that takes place before the beginning of the study session. As researchers, we want the eye tracker to be completely unobtrusive; we want participants to forget that it is even there.

Fig. 1. Tobii T60 Eye Tracking System (Source: Tobii Technology)

Eye tracking is a powerful tool for user researchers and when properly used can provide insights unachievable by other research methods. The most obvious but unique ability of the eye tracker is that it can track the location of a participant's eyes.

The visual hierarchy of an interface dictates what a user will pay attention and when. This sequence of visualizations can be critical for both the usability of a system and consumption of content. Our visual field is constantly bombarded by a variety of stimuli. We are overloaded and overwhelmed by visual information and constantly resort to prioritizing what we choose to pay attention to. In order to measure the effectiveness of content researchers need to determine what users are looking at and what they choose to engage with.

In trying to understand what users decide to pay attention to we can't always rely on the participants to accurately tell us. Participants are terrible at self-reporting where they looked. For the most part, this is due to our eyes often moving involuntarily and the limits of our short-term memory. Guan et al. [5] measured the extent to which participants did not discuss elements that they in fact visually attended to. They labeled these as omissions. Participants had omissions 47% of the time, meaning that almost half of the time they did not mention elements that they looked at. Omissions may have occurred because participants forgot about seeing the elements, or perhaps simply because they just didn't think or care to mention them. It should also go without saying that a researcher can't simply ask a participant if they noticed a certain on-screen element. This action draws the participant's attention directly towards something that they may or may not have originally seen. This inherently and irreversibly biases the participant and no confident answer can be obtained. Eye tracking provides an objective running commentary of where the individual looks without any need for participants to verbalize what they have seen.

Eye tracking is an essential tool to combine with any biometric or neurometric measurements. These measurements are useless unless they are analyzed in context of what the user is observing. Time-locking eye tracking data with these measurements is key to understanding exactly when a participant was looking at something at exactly what they were seeing.

2.2 GSR

Galvanic skin response (GSR) has long been used as to measure physiological arousal [6]. GSR can provide researchers with a spectrum of states from being high aroused/engaged/stressed to a state of noninterest/unengaged/relaxed. This measurement is ideal for detecting situations where a user is having difficulty using an interface and increasingly becomes frustrated and stressed. For applications designed to keep a user actively engaged or interested, GSR can help measure the intensity of their engagement as well as how long it can be sustained. GSR is incapable of representing a broader set of emotional states such as EEG or facial response analysis, which can both detect levels of valence (positive to negative emotions).

The measurement of GSR is dependent on the levels of sweat within the skin. The more sweat produced, the higher the level of electrical conductance that can be measured. In order to obtain the galvanic skin response, a small electrical current is passed through the skin using a pair of electrodes. The soles of the foot or palms are a recommended location for these electrodes due to the higher amount of sweat produced by these areas. However, in user experience research it would be prohibitive to use these areas of the body to measure skin conductance. Newer devices such as the Shimmer3 (see Figure 2) are far less intrusive and allow for total freedom of movement while interacting with devices. According to Shimmer [7] their new GSR module, "brings an effective way to measure activity, emotional engagement and psychological arousal in lab scenarios and in remote capture scenarios that are set outside of the lab." In addition to participant comfort, the device is also fairly stress-free for researchers who want to quickly setup and gather data. The device includes a built-in Bluetooth receiver that can easily be paired with a laptop and software is provided for visualizing the GSR data.

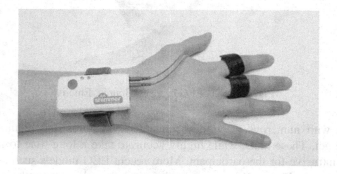

Fig. 2. Shimmer 3 GSR Unit (Source: Shimmer)

Researchers should be aware that the results from GSR do not correspond with a response to a stimulus in real-time. GSR can produce response latencies between 3 to 6 seconds from the response to a stimulus [8]. Therefore it is not recommended to use GSR to identify the exact moment when a response was triggered. Instead, researchers should analyze the response over a period of time, for example the duration of a task or the presentation of a stimulus, and then compare the result to other such units. For all biometric measurements, but especially with GSR, it is critical to obtain a baseline measurement prior to the presentation of stimuli. Participants will vary in terms of their typical level of sweat output and their emotional state (e.g. feeling anxious) when they arrive at the test facility. By establishing a baseline it provides a point of comparison between their state prior and after a stimulus has been shown.

2.3 EEG

EEG measures electrical activity in the brain by placing electrodes along various points along the scalp. The signals obtained from these electrodes are represented by waveforms reflecting voltage variation over time [9].

EEG raw data is measured at the millisecond level and can be directly attributed to stimuli effects in real-time. EEG units traditionally used in academic settings use

Fig. 3. Emotiv EEG headset (Source: Emotiv)

a skullcap with numerous electrodes connected via wires and require the use of conductive gel. These units, while highly accurate take a long time to setup and are extremely intrusive for the participant. More recent EEG models such as the Emotiv EEG headset (see Figure 2) are completely wireless and use over-the-counter saline solution to provide conductivity for the electrodes. These headsets can be worn comfortably during a user experience test and minimally interfere with a participant's natural behaviors. The trend towards less expensive, lighter weight, and totally wireless solutions will make EEG even more practical for UX researchers within the next few years.

Lee and Tan [10] found through their interactions with other HCI researchers that there is a concern over lack of domain knowledge and because of the high cost of owning and maintaining the EEG equipment. While EEG headsets are not mind reading devices, they can give us an accurate sense of what a participant is feeling. Emotional states can be complex. We often feel a composite of emotions at any given time and those emotions can be internalized and unrelated to what is being shown on the screen.

It is true that correctly interpreting the meaning of EEG waveforms and translating that data into emotional states is extremely complex and likely out of the expertise of a UX researcher. However, new analysis tools such as Emotiv's Affectiv Suite [11] processes the raw EEG data and produce visualizations that correspond with a standardized set of emotional states (e.g. engagement/interest, frustration, happy/sad, etc.)

2.4   Facial Response Analysis

Facial coding is the systematic analysis of facial expressions. Research on facial coding dates back to studies by Charles Darwin who concluded that common facial expressions are universal. In the 1970s, psychologist Paul Ekman's early work identified the universality of six core emotions. He also is well known for popularizing a facial action coding system (FACS) that systematically describes facial expressions and movements12.

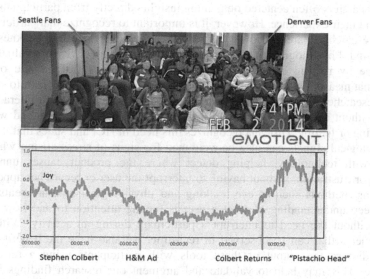

Fig. 4. Facial Analysis Software (Source: Emotient)

Companies like Affdex [12] and Emotient have developed new software that can be used to analyze a user's emotions by examining their facial reactions. These systems use computer algorithms that take video from common webcams as inputs and provide frame-by-frame emotion metrics as outputs [13]. Webcams are already commonly used to capture nonverbal behavior and audio from participants in user experience studies. Using facial analysis is one of the least intrusive methods for capturing emotional reactions in an automated manner. Both companies claim that they are able to capture subtle emotions from only small facial muscle movements called facial action units. The ability to capture these less expressive types of emotions or varying levels of valence is critical for user experience research where participants do not always have a strong outward reaction to stimuli.

3   Benefits of Physiological Measurement to User Experience Research

User experience testing, which has its grounding in usability testing has traditionally not focused on measuring emotions. Usability testing has often focused on efficiency and easy of use. Researchers didn't always concern themselves with whether the interface was enjoyable to use or caused any other emotional response. More recently as those in the field of HCI have expanded their viewpoints to a more holistic view of user experience, finding a way to measure emotion has become increasingly important. A primary limitation has been the inability to accurately measure emotional response in a practical, accurate, and minimally intrusive way.

UX research is often centered on gaining insights directly from participants to truly understand their experience. However, it is important to recognize that participants (as well as researchers) are not always objective, and fall prey to the weakness of the human mind. Physiological measurements remove the subjectivity of evaluating user experience by relying exclusively on quantitative metrics that are the output of devices that measure primarily involuntary, often subconscious responses to stimuli.

UX researchers frequently need to balance the need for a user to interact with a system without constantly being interrupted, with the need to understand what they are thinking or feeling. Diricana recognizes this need in HCI and states that, "Changes in physiological signals can also be examined for signs of stress arising while users interact with technology, helping detect where the product causes unnecessary irritation or frustration, without having to interrupt the user or record her appearance." [14] Using methods such as eye tracking and physiological measurements we can gain a deep understanding of what a user is paying attention to and how they are feeling without the need to interrupt a participant during an activity. With certain measurements that can be observed in real-time, we also have the benefit of being able to discuss the output of these tools with participants using a retrospective technique. This may help to validate and augment our research findings based on what the physiological data is telling us and what we can learn from discussing these findings with participants. We still need to have a dialogue with participants because the physiological data tells us what they were looking at and what they were feeling, but it ultimately does not tell us why they were feeling that way.

The benefit of using multiple types of bio/neurometric devices is that we can learn different things from different devices. Valence is a measure of the positive or negative nature of the participant's experience with the stimulus. Using EEG and facial response analysis we can measure whether the participant is having a relatively good or bad reaction to their experience. GSR and heart rate cannot measure valence, but are a good indicator of a participant's level of arousal, which depending on the reaction, can tell us whether they are feeling stressed, engaged, or relaxed. Another benefit of using multiple types of measurements is that we can often use them to validate or invalidate each other. For example, if our facial analysis data is strongly indicating that our participant is experiencing great happiness, but the EEG data is indicating high levels of sadness we know that one of the measurements is likely reporting incorrect information.

4   The Challenges of Measuring Emotions

When biometric measures are applied either in a controlled lab or in real environments, there are many issues that must be considered. Conducting these types of studies in a real world environment presents several additional challenges and data quality can be a significant issue [14]. However like any lab-based study, we are faced with the artificially of a controlled environment that ignores all of the potential stimuli a user would likely experience in the real world. Ultimately, it becomes a trade-off for the research team as to what is most important to understand in their study.

Today applications are not only accessed through computers, and are available on a variety of platforms from tablets to smartphones, and even wearable devices. These mobile devices have previously made it difficult to collect physiological data outside of the lab environment. However, great progress has been made in this area over the last few years. Eye tracking vendors such as Tobii and SMI have recently developed wireless glasses that can be used to track participants' eyes. These may not be unobtrusive enough for users to completely forget that they are taking part in a study, but they are practical enough to allow for free body movement during the session. Similar progress has been made in the field of EEG with products such as the Emotiv EEG headset. New GSR units have recently become available including the Shimmer3 unit that measures both electro dermal activity as well as heart rate.

Even with new, more versatile equipment, UX researchers will need to possess the technical competence required to set up and operate advanced equipment and ensure a rigorous process is in place to collect accurate data. Pilot testing is essential to these types of studies to determine if the equipment is properly configured and outputting the expected type of data. Equipment must be carefully calibrated with each participant and baseline measurements should be taken to account for variations between individuals. Physiological studies also require higher sample sizes than typical qualitative research projects.

Another challenge lies in the interpretation of data, since the same kind of physiological responses may be observed for different mental states, such as frustration, surprise or increased cognitive effort. Therefore, a correct interpretation requires knowledge of the context in which the data was obtained. In order to better understand the results, it is thus advisable to record additional observations along with the physiological measurements, such as comments, observed behaviors and subjective ratings of events [15].

5   Conclusion

The ability to capture the emotions of our users is becoming an increasingly important aspect of user experience. Users are no longer satisfied with interfaces that simply meet their basic needs in terms of usability. Existing methods of measuring emotional response are flawed and rely too much on self-reporting and other highly subjective measurements. There is an inescapable need to find new ways to objectively measure the complex emotional experiences that result from interacting with digital products. The biometric and neurometric devices discussed in this paper have been identified as having the highest potential for application to HCI research. All of the devices have the capability of being integrated into the existing methods used by user researchers to measure user experience.

The benefits of these tools also come with significant challenges for user researchers. All of these tools originate from unfamiliar fields such as human physiology and neurology, which can be intimidating and potentially risky for those in HCI to adopt. Significant investment is required to purchase the necessary equipment and to employ researchers with a sufficient level of understanding in physiological measurement. Additional time is required to analyze the abundant amount of data that comes from these measurements and then to extract meaning that can be useful for user experience designers.

There are still significant challenges to implementing these new measurements, however the current generation of tools is considerably more economical and practical for UX researchers than ever before, and all indications are that this trend will continue over the next several years. Eventually we will reach a point where collecting physiological data that helps us understand our user's emotions will become commonplace. This eventual enlightenment will bring about interfaces that can be crafted to evoke specific emotional experiences from our users.

References

1. Sherman, P.: How Do Users Really Feel About Your Design? (2007), http://www.uxmatters.com/mt/archives/2007/09/how-do-users-really-feel-about-your-design.php
2. Ward, R., Marsden, P.: Physiological responses to different WEB page designs. International Journal of Human-Computer Studies 59, 199–212 (2003)
3. Schall, A., Romano Bergstrom, J.: Eye tracking in user experience design. S.l. Morgan Kaufmann Publisher (2014)
4. Tobii Technology, An introduction to eye tracking and Tobii Eye Trackers (2010), http://www.tobii.com/Global/Analysis/Training/WhitePapers/Tobii_EyeTracking_Introduction_WhitePaper.pdf
5. Guan, Z., Lee, S., Cuddihy, E., Ramey, J.: The Validity of the Stimulated Retrospective Think-Aloud Method as Measured by Eye Tracking. In: Grinter, R., Rodden, T., Aoki, P., Cutrell, E., Jeffries, R., Olson, G. (eds.) Proceedings of the SIGCHI Conference on Human Factors in Computing Systems, pp. 1253–1262. ACM Press, New York (2006)
6. Picard, R., Scheirer, J.: The Galvactivator: A glove that senses and communicates skin conductivity. Paper presented at Proceedings 9th Int. Conf. on HCI (2001)
7. Shimmer. Motion, Galvanic Skin Response and Optical Pulse captured from one device (December 11, 2013) (press release)
8. Park, B.: Psychophysiology as a Tool for HCI Research: Promises and Pitfalls. In: Jacko, J.A. (ed.) Human-Computer Interaction, Part I, HCII 2009. LNCS, vol. 5610, pp. 141–148. Springer, Heidelberg (2009)
9. Niedermeyer, E., da Silva, F.L.: Electroencephalography: Basic Principles, Clinical Applications, and Related Fields. Lippincot Williams & Wilkins (2004)
10. Lee, J.C., Tan, D.S.: Using a low-cost electroencephalograph for task classification in HCI research, p. 81. ACM Press (2006)
11. Emotiv.com (2012), EEG Features, http://emotiv.com/eeg/features.php (accessed: Decmeber 11, 2013)

12. Picard, R.W., Vyzas, E., Healey, J.: Toward machine emotional intelligence: Analysis of affective physiological state. IEEE Transactions on Pattern Analysis and Machine Intelligence 23(10), 1175–1191 (2001)
13. Kanan, E.: Exploring the Emotion Classifiers Behind Affdex Facial Coding. (whitepaper) (2013)
14. Diricana, A., Göktürk, M.: Psychophysiological Measures of Human Cognitive States Applied in Human Computer Interaction. Paper presented at World Conference on Information Technology. Elsevier (2011)
15. Madrigal, D., Mcclain, B.: Testing the User Experience: Consumer Emotions and Brand Success: UXmatters (2009),
    http://www.uxmatters.com/mt/archives/2009/10/testing-the-user-experience-consumer-emotions-and-brand-success.php
    (accessed: December 12, 2013)

Does Social User Experience Improve Motivation for Runners?

A Diary Study Comparing Mobile Health Applications

Frank Spillers[1] and Stavros Asimakopoulos[2]

[1] Experience Dynamics, Inc, 1827 NE 44th Avenue Suite 250, Portland, Oregon 97123 USA
frank@experiencedynamics.com
[2] Faculty of Communication and Media Studies, National & Kapodistrian University of Athens,
5 Stadiou Str, GR 105-62, Athens, Hellas
sasimako@media.uoa.gr

Abstract. In efforts to enhance the user experience (UX), mobile fitness applications are beginning to incorporate gameplay mechanics and social elements in their design. Unlike the more traditional health applications, m-health applications can provide a richer social user experience that caters to mobile usage contexts, such as fitness. In this paper we discuss to what extent *gamification* and *social elements* improve user motivation and lead to *short-term* positive behavior change. We examine the efficacy of social features in three different m-health running applications with varying levels of social and gamification functionality, each supporting the core task of tracking a user's running activity. Data was collected over a week from 15 mobile app users and runners based in the USA with an online diary study followed by short interviews. The analysis of the diary entries indicates that apps can provide motivation to maintain or increase physical activity, but that the usability, design and feature richness of social and gamification elements negatively impacted user adoption. Moreover, the adoption of social elements, was impacted by interface usability, integration with new music services like Spotify, accuracy of the GPS and so on. The results show that *intrinsic motivation* and *individual goals* can enhance short-term positive behavior change, an important dimension for the design of m-health apps. In addition, many users were comfortable with social UX elements, but social elements in and of themselves did not contribute to motivation in running due to the design and usability of each apps social UX strategy. The results from this study will be useful for designers of m-health apps in formulating appropriate design strategies for incorporating social and game mechanics into mobile UX strategy.

Keywords: Social user experience, Ramification, Mobile usability, Intrinsic motivation, Behavior change, mHealth.

A. Marcus (Ed.): DUXU 2014, Part IV, LNCS 8520, pp. 358–369, 2014.
© Springer International Publishing Switzerland 2014

1   Introduction

As mobile health (m-health) applications become more prevalent, it is imperative that they work for their users. The relationship between user motivations and social behavior in the context of m-health applications is important, since access to fitness and behavior change is on the rise [1, 2, 3, 4]. [5] report that half of adults in the United States do not engage in recommended levels of physical activity, despite established health benefits. Recent research by [6] found that mobile users favor mobile tracking tools, as evidenced by the rapidly increasing number of m-health apps in Apple's App Store. Several guidelines exist for designing technological apps that engage, motivate, and support behavior and attitude changes [7, 8, 9]. The guidelines that are more closely related to mental wellness apps include [10] 7 guidelines for behavior change: (1) remind people who they want to be, (2) foster an alliance (empathy, coinvestigation, joint problem solving), (3) apply social influence, (4) show people what they could lose, (5) put the message where the action is, (6) raise emotional awareness, and (7) reframe challenges. Gamification, that is, using game-like elements has also been proposed in the domain of wellness apps to increase adherence and engagement [11, 12, 13]. However, the guidelines are mostly based on apps promoting physical health and thus they may not be directly applicable to m-health running applications. Moreover, despite the increasing amount of work published on the technological side and adoption of m-health [2, 4], research on the usage and social user experience (UX) strategies of m-health applications remains limited. For example, [4] found that the most common technology-enhanced features in weight loss mobile apps were barcode scanners (56.7%) and a social network (46.7%) and that behavioral strategies that help users improve motivation, reduce stress, and assist with problem solving were generally missing across apps.

Several observations can be made about existing studies on m-health adoption. Firstly, studies of m-health usage and usability among users have been limited [14]. Secondly, most of these studies have developed their adoption models based on general guidelines [10] and have mainly studied the adoption of m-health based on users' intention to adopt or not adopt m-health applications. Lastly, most existing m-health adoption studies have neglected using motivation variables and social elements and their influence on m-health usage activities. Therefore this study aims to investigate the relationship between motivation and social UX variables with m-health usage activities among users of applications used for fitness purposes, specifically running.

1.1   Mobile Applications User Adoption

For mobile fitness applications to achieve some degree of success in today's market they must appeal to as many users as feasibly possible. So designing applications in a manner that provides the same UX (e.g. useful, social, and entertaining) to all users irrespective of user motivation, experience or skill is becoming the focus of modern day m-health research. Traditional design is well suited to covering particular clusters of users' fitness goals (e.g. hardcore, casual) as an app developer's perception of what makes a good application is sure to appeal to someone. However, users who do not fall within these designer perceptions are likely to be excluded; they may initially be interested in the fitness concept but are turned off by its execution (e.g. too easy, too hard), confusing game mechanics or particular design choices (e.g. easy, medium and hard difficulty settings). The designer will try to envisage such changes in the application and adapt the design to reflect them so to ensure the application remains appealing throughout its usage.

1.2   Motivation in Mobile Fitness: Dynamic and Social

Preferably m-health applications for fitness should be capable of dynamically adjusting to usage given that mobile interactions are situated in fluid social and physical environments. Past literature suggests that user motivations can influence their decisions to adopt a particular technology. Motivations can be categorized as intrinsic or extrinsic motivations [15]. Extrinsic motivation is defined as "the performance of an activity due to it being perceived to be instrumental in achieving valued outcomes that are distinct from the activity itself" [16]. Intrinsic motivation "refers to the performance of an activity for no apparent reinforcement, other than the process of performing the activity per se". Examples of intrinsic motivations include perceived fun, ease of use, enjoyment and playfulness. Extrinsic motivations include the perceived benefits gained from using the technology. [16] and [17] found that motivation variables have a positive and significant relationship with Internet usage. Similarly, studies have found that extrinsic and intrinsic motivations can influence the adoption of technologies such as mobile chat services [18], electronic service [15] and mobile internet [19]. Although past studies have focused on these motivation variables in Internet usage activities, literature on the relationships between user motivation variables, social UX and m-health activities remains sparse. Why does the user want to use a mobile application for fitness? Is it for the challenge, the fun of it all, to lose weight, track performance or perhaps to leverage social dynamics to influence performance? In order for m-health applications to design changes that are positively motivating for the user, we need to understand the primary psychological motivators and social needs of that user.

2   Research Questions and Study Methodology

The results of our diary study cover the largely neglected issue [20, 2] of user motivation with social UX on m-health applications. User motivational goals represent a key 'lens' for understanding the impact of social patterns and behavior, and for developing a social UX strategy designed to achieve positive behavior change. We compared

social effects of three widely used m-health applications for tracking fitness user behavior via a diary study as a means of framing motivational goals, and critically, as a
vehicle for bringing about behavioral change. The main research questions are as
follows: (a) Do social features add value to mobile UX? (b) Does gamification add
value to mobile UX?, and (c) Does intrinsic motivation impact the use of social UX
features?.

2.1   Sample and Procedure

Three groups of five experienced iphone app users (15 participants in total) based in
the USA used the following applications, in order to determine if the apps social elements improved motivation: Digifit (little or very light social features), Endomondo
(social features with light gamification), and Runno (social features with heavy gamification). Data were collected from 3 sources: (1) online questionnaires completed at
baseline, after one week's use, (2) interviews conducted at the end of the week's use,
and (3) the usage log of the three apps. Participants completed a 7-day online diary
study [21] and the Stanford Brief Physical Activity Survey [SBAS, 22] followed by
short individual interviews. Participants were purposefully recruited from different
US regions (West coast, Midwest and East coast) with a mean age of 29 years (8
males and 7 females). Study inclusion criteria were: (1) use mobile applications for
their fitness needs, and (2) interested to improve their general fitness goals. Exclusion
criteria were: (1) known medical conditions or other physical problems requiring
special attention in an exercise program, (2) severe hearing or speech problems, and
(3) current participation in lifestyle modification programs or research studies. Participants were self-described runners or included running as part of their work-out (e.g.
weight training, cycling) on average 5 days a week. Listening to music while exercis-
ing and tracking their performance/fitness levels has been mainly reported to be the
main use of users' apps, whereas 40% of them regularly use gadgets. Moreover, all
participants are using Facebook and the majority (75%) of them is comfortable sharing their fitness activities on Facebook or other social media platforms. Participants
were screened by phone and email and given information about the study, including
the requirements of installing the applications in their mobile, daily use of the fitness
applications as well as the diary notes for the 7-days study period. A survey questionnaire and short interview guide was developed to test the research questions in this
research. The diary was designed such that participants had to log data; even if it was
a non-exercise day (SurveyMonkey logic-branching technology was used). Daily
goals based on self-reported steps were relayed by the application, along with immediate and motivational feedback. The interviews focused on prompts and questions
regarding the benefit of physical activity, barriers to increasing physical activity, usefulness of the game included in the applications, and social support for physical activity. SBAS was used to obtain a quick assessment of the usual amount and intensity of
physical activity that a person currently performs throughout the day. The SBAS contains two items. The first item describes different kinds of on-the-job activity, while

the second item describes various leisure-time activities. The participants did not differ significantly in terms of leisure and on-the-job activities. At the end of the study, each participant was compensated with a $100 incentive.

2.2   Analysis and Results

Our analysis of results show that mobile fitness applications can help: increase confidence, achieve specific goals (e.g. lose weight), and improve wellbeing. All users reported the need to track and view results details easily and accurately (duration, distance, calories, pace, time frame), while multi-mode interaction (e.g. voice feedback, music library) increase motivation. Social UX features, including gamification features, in the apps were not necessarily helpful to users in achieving their fitness goals. Specifically, Digifit users were motivated by general tracking features of the app as well as features such as auditory milestone feedback eg "1 mile reached" (see Table 1).

Table 1. Digifit users' quotes summary

Issues	User quotes
Motivation/Social	"Don't share workout, more personal thing" "Share a really good run with friends (share something proud of)" "Want app i want to do 115 lbs, what exercises and for how long and give me suggestions for what do" "Share: useful to support other folks (would) - done it more informal (not used an app- some friends have an app they use)" "Metrics helps motivate you- something to compare it to" "would share if pretty run on beach (something nice) or if decent time (achievement) if slow i wouldn't share"
Usability	"When tracking wasn't sure how to pause the app; needs stop and resume (didn't know- hear beating, didn't know had to slide over to pause or stop). Better if said pause and stop." "I tried to restart half way through- manually entered... (recorded MayMyRun and used that data)" "A bit leery of some of the quoted nutrition facts -- seem unrealistic/incorrect"

Digifit users, without social UX, exhibited positive behavior change, as the following user extract illustrates:

"I ate light meals throughout the day. Everything was fresh and healthy. I did not snack on junk food, I decided I will try to increase my workouts my increasing the amount of time per workout by about 15-20 minutes."

Usability or technical issues such as "wasn't sure how to pause the app" or "missed speed per mile initially" were as important to the overall experience, regardless of social UX-- across all apps in our study. Endomondo users indicated that sharing to Facebook (a key social feature on the app) was most relevant if they could share something they were proud of, like a milestone. Endomondo's UX strategy does not account for this social effect (see Table 2).

Table 2. Edmodondo users' quotes summary

Issues	User quotes
Motivation/Social	*"Challenge helpful- push your goal"* *"Friend joined same gym- good to keep track of each other (friend attempted to download not sure if successful- they use SMS to keep track)- motivational tool, goals very good to stay on track"* *"Yes. Having friends within the app provides the opportunity to compare and compete"* *"Challenges seemed like advertisements- never participated in those before- people at 96 miles"* *"Duration and history Fitbit doesnt have; never seen option to share"* *"No one seemed interested- everyone bombarded sharing these days"* *"If had a group- i could see if motivated- -- depends what want to share (Routes and GPS not share with strangers)"* *"Wanted more customization- run intervals- would love to tell me when ready (music in ears can't hear)"* *"Doesn't share- sharing feels braggy (feels like bragging)"* *"It has increase my motivation because I am able to compare my workouts with others"* *"Good to compare to other people- other motivation"* *"Would be more inclined to share a specific goal than every work out- - some gold, elite status (level reached)- that would be motivational"* *"Challenge- wasn't connected to it- wasn't relevant"* *"I like the community aspect and the prizes being offered, but I think the potential for cheating is huge"* *"Badges for how many steps taken (milestone)-- share more being proud of myself- not to show off"*
Usability	*"Also if had band on arm to hold it (if lighter weight or band would be good tool overall)"* *"General fitness; Running workout- if did it separately it helped"* *"I like it for mapping the run, tracking the time- no hiccups- not into Calorie counting"* *"If get feedback pushes you harder-the fitness test pushes me to run a faster mile"* *"I would like to be able to track an indoor run with possibly a foot pod or other device attached to my shoe"* *"Gym chart has been my favorite because it is customizable and has a very simple interface for tracking weightlifting gains and exercises"* *"There are no annoying ads or push notifications prompting me to do things I dont want to do. It simply replaces carrying around a notebook, plus I can export a graph of my progress"*

We conclude that connecting a mobile app to Facebook is not enough, whereas balancing goal setting with a strong privacy and sharing experience can provide a better user experience, as evidenced by this user concern:

"I was horrified to see the awful privacy settings on my profile! It was like Facebook - and that is not a compliment - with each of many settings NOT private by default! Bad, bad, bad. I had to reset them all manually."

Runno users on the whole understood the gamification aspects of the application, but felt it was boring, irrelevant or misplaced (see Table 3). This does not mean gamification is not valuable in health applications, but that how it is experienced is highly relevant. [23], for example, found gamification to be extremely valuable in stress reduction and increasing wellbeing.

Table 3. Runno users' quotes summary

Issues	User quotes
Motivation/Social	*"Games and minigames part didnt quite get it. Video seemed really interesting... (points and path tried to do it didn't do anything)."* *"Played it once and it's not for me- on Fuel band they had it- i played it once that was it. Like idea, need more interactive aspect (Fuelband reach 75,000 goal) want to see some kind of graphical interface to motivate you."* *"Virtual tokens don't mean anything to me!"* *"Like Hitman: Absolution (you can create your own challenge- kill someone in 4 minutes)- for group motivation to achieve a goal... use for group motivation - use competition as motivation...."* *"Main thing want from app: Timing, Interval training"* *"Didn't see gamification at all!!"* *"Doesn't connect to Spotify (use that all time now- more variety)"* *"They should strengthen the social aspects and the minigame- make it more motivational so it's worth doing it... good to play against friends would be good."* *"Dont share- none of my friends using app- dont feel like broadcasting to FB-- but if friends were in-app would do it. Would be motivating- would be competing."* *"Invited friends- a lot of fun (motivating each other- sharing progress with each other)"*
Usability	*"Few labels off- meters change read as Kilometers"* *"Didn't feel it was that accurate (Calorie) was going regardless of vigor of activity- questioning whether accurate"* *"More complicated than needed to be."* *"Got message said enough time to record- after 40 minutes-- what??!* *"Graphics were too simple and plain, looked cheap."* *"No shortcut from main menu."* *"I am game player but i have never combined fitness and games together- too much time, felt like i was wasting time.."* *"Music player- couldnt play custom list- big disadvantage"* *"GPS- not able to track location.."*

However, for Runno users in addition to poor game design, usability and technical issues overshadowed any benefits of social UX.Users found the relevancy of game mechanics at issues as well as the intuitiveness of the design. Runno required considerable time and effort to comprehend, users complained:

"I am busy in the morning when using fitness apps...I am a game player but I have never combined fitness and games together- this took too much time, felt like I was wasting time."

Runno users reported confusion with the gamification features in the application and complained that the features were not compelling, or were designed for children. In particular, users experienced frustration arising from a failure to know how a game challenge is to be completed as well as the complexity of the game dialogue and terminology used.

"No, it did not do anything better than my current app. It also looks worse and the music playing aspect is horribly designed. I want to be able to play a playlist I have, not just play one song or create my own playlist from within the app. The interface seems outdated!"

Usability and technical issues combined with a poorly designed social UX, can lead to a negative impact on users' motivation. Inaccuracy of statistics (feet/miles) or inability of the app to locate GPS signal, crashes or freezing also caused users to become discouraged.

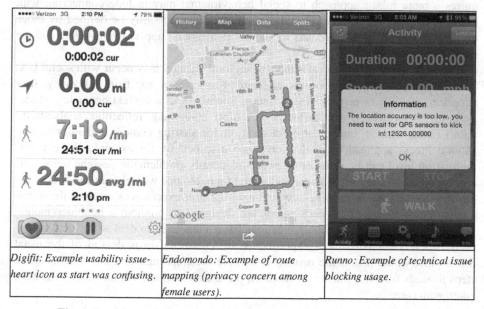

| Digifit: Example usability issue- heart icon as start was confusing. | Endomondo: Example of route mapping (privacy concern among female users). | Runno: Example of technical issue blocking usage. |

Fig. 1. Example of issues impacting UX of the fitness apps used in the study

Our results indicate that social UX does not lead to social user behavior per se, but rather is linked with relevant fitness and healthcare goals: performance, progress, reduced stress, calories burned and accomplishments. Social features users found missing in the social apps (Endomondo and Runno) include: progress-based advice; selective group suggestions for improvement; comparing performance with selective friends and peers; creating your own fitness challenge to share selectively.

3   Discussion

This study reveals that running apps designed to track a runner's activity can influence intrinsic motivation regardless of social or gamification elements. It is our belief that social UX if designed with a high degree of usability, can only improve upon motivating aspects of an app. For example many users were excited by game play and social features outside of the usage of the apps in the study. Several users suggested that the apps should behave like popular games they play (eg. a feature to create your own goals). It is clear that, if designed poorly, social UX might even detract from the value of the app entirely, as in the case of the Runno app.

Our study showed that users are more likely to engage in m-health activities if they perceive them to be motivating. The results highlight the potential for m-health apps assisting users in mobile contexts. New advances in technology enabling biofeedback devices that do the tracking ambiently for users are promising. Many of our users reported that automatic tracking from devices like Nike Fuelband were positive over existing 'self-tracking' apps [1]. Designing social experiences for m-health apps requires a more robust approach to social behavior that may include connecting with existing social networks, like Facebook, but can not necessarily be defined by those existing models of what it means to share-- if a mobile app is to provide a unique experience to its users.

The study further demonstrates that 'behavioral change' may occur with social UX, but cannot exclusively rely on social features to save an app from relevancy, user adoption, usability or privacy design issues. Social UX as a context-dependent strategy is highly associated with different user motivations (e.g. reflection, goals attainment) rather than an implicit user motivation for sharing content and information. Mobile fitness applications evaluation could also benefit, for example if the users' motivation level can be assessed in order to identify problematic designs before the app is released. The role of game and social technologies will play in the fitness industry is certain to create some new and exciting user experiences, such as the therapeutic (i.e. biofeedback), where games are designed to promote a healthier mental well being. However m-health applications have a tendency to deal with 'ideal' situations, where the environment experiments are conducted in is devoid of the usual factors that would distort the results. It is therefore important that the next tentative steps towards fitness applications based on the users' motivational and social state are taken with care.

4   Conclusions and Future Enhancements

This research demonstrates that gamification and social UX variables in general do not have significant relationships with m-health fitness usage activities. This is one of the first known studies that examine the relationships between social and motivation variables with m-health activities among experienced users. The results from this study also contribute to existing studies by highlighting how different motivation and social variables may influence the three m-health applications differently. In contrast to most current m-health applications, it appears that most runners are interested in sharing if it is relevant to a small goal (with a buddy) or if it is a milestone (to a wider audience). None of the major running apps on the market today address this social effect. These challenges highlight a primary issue for designers of m-health applications: understanding users' activities-in-social contexts. Furthermore, applications that facilitate long-term health behavior change can be assisted by the motivating potential of mobile apps. Participants appreciated the structured approach in using their application while running, and felt that these features would increase their motivation. Skepticism toward the design of gamification elements (in the form of rewards or game-like elements) was expressed by participants of the Runno app, with the concern that too much time would be wasted playing instead of running. This points to gamification taking an ambient role in the usage experience, a strategy that the Nike+ app employs.

Notwithstanding that many of the participants were already somewhat familiar with mobile applications for fitness -which may have facilitated the adoption of the app and learning the skills - the patterns observed reflect near as close to reality usage patterns, as the participants were the direct target groups of the apps. Future studies can extend this scope to include users from other countries and conduct cross-cultural comparisons as well with different mobile platforms (e.g. Android). A comparison between developed and developing countries will improve the generalizability of this research. Future studies can consider measuring the diffusion of m-health usage activities across time, and investigate whether motivation (and perhaps demographic) variables change at various stages of m-health fitness and self-tracking activities. Attention to design and users for long-term positive behavior change should form part of a longitudinal study to increase rigour of the results and as part of a larger research initiative. Lastly, additional adoption factors such as self efficacy, security as well as the desire of an individual to engage in physical activity because of external rewards [24, 19] have not been included in this study and these issues can be the focus of future research.

Our findings provide a good starting point for continuing research on motivation and social feature support for fitness applications. Given the short-term behavior change reported by participants using the three applications, it appears that users are motivated to use fitness apps but for social UX to improve their experience, will require thinking about the social elements beyond social media and more in line with the social habits and sensitivities of user behavior.

Acknowledgements. Special thanks to all users who participated in this study. This research was not reviewed by an Institutional Review Board and has not received financial support from any other source.

References

1. Trevorrow, P., Fabri, M.: Running to behavior change. In: Marcus, A. (ed.) DUXU/HCII 2013, Part III. LNCS, vol. 8014, pp. 585–593. Springer, Heidelberg (2013)
2. O' Reilly, A.G., Spruijt-Metz, D.: Current mHealth Technologies for Physical Activity Assessment and Promotion. Annual Journal of Preventive Medicine 45(4), 501–507 (2013)
3. Fabri, M., Wall, A., Trevorrow, P.: Changing Eating Behaviors through a Cooking-Based Website for the Whole Family. In: Marcus, A. (ed.) DUXU/HCII 2013, Part III. LNCS, vol. 8014, pp. 484–493. Springer, Heidelberg (2013)
4. Pagoto, S., Schneider, K., Jojic, M., DeBiasse, M., Mann, D.: Evidence-based Strategies in Weight-Loss Mobile Apps. Annual Journal of Preventive Medicine 45(5), 576–582 (2013)

5. Healthy People: Physical activity and fitness (2010),
   `http://www.cdc.gov/nchs/healthy_people/publications.htm`
   (retrieved)
6. Liu, C., Zhu, Q., Holroyd, A.K., Seng, K.E.: Status and trends of mobile-health applications for iOS devices: A developer's perspective. The Journal of Systems and Software 84, 2022–2033 (2011)
7. Fogg, B.J.: Persuasive Technology: Using Computers to Change What We Think and Do. Morgan Kaufmann, USA (2003)
8. Oinas-Kukkonen, H., Harjumaa, M.: Persuasive systems design: Key issues, process model, and system features. Communications of the Association for Information Systems 24(1), 485–500 (2009)
9. Consolvo, S., McDonald, D.W., Landay, J.A.: Theory-driven design strategies for technologies that support behavior change in everyday life. Presented at the 27th International Conference on Human Factors in Computing Systems (CHI 2009), April 4-9, pp. 405–414. ACM, Boston (2009)
10. Morris, M.: Motivating change with mobile: seven guidelines. Interactions 19(3), 26–31 (2012)
11. Deterding, S., Dixon, D., Khaled, R.: Gamification: Toward a Definition. In: CHI 2011 Gamification Workshop Proceedings, Presented at Annual Conference on Human Factors in Computing Sydtems (CHI 2011), Vancouver, BC, May 7-12, (2011)
12. Mueller, F., Peer, F., Agamanolis, S., Sheridan, J.: Gamification and exertion. In: Proceedings of the Workshop on Gamification at the Conference on Human Factors in Computing Systems (CHI 2011), Vancouver, BC, May 7-12 (2011)
13. Thin, A.G., Gotsis, M.: Game-Based Interactive Media in Behavioral Medicine: Creating Serious Affective-Cognitive-Environmental-Social Integration Experiences. In: Marcus, A. (ed.) DUXU/HCII 2013, Part II. LNCS, vol. 8013, pp. 470–479. Springer, Heidelberg (2013)
14. Brown, W., Yen, P.Y., Rojas, M., Schnall, R.: Assessment of the Health IT Usability Evaluation Model (Health-ITUEM) for evaluating mobile health (mHealth) technology. Journal of Biomedical Informatics 46(6), 1080–1087 (2013)
15. Hsu, M.H., Chiu, C.M.: Internet self-efficacy and electronic service acceptance. Decision Support Systems 38(3), 369–381 (2004)
16. Teo, T.S.H., Lim, V.K.G., Lai, R.Y.C.: Intrinsic and extrinsic motivation in Internet usage. Omega 27(1), 25–37 (1999)
17. Teo, T.S.H.: Demographic and motivation variables associated with Internet usage activities. Internet Research 11(2), 125–137 (2001)
18. Nysveen, H., Pedersen, P.E., Thorbjørnsen, H.: Explaining intention to use mobile chat services: moderating effects of gender. Journal of Consumer Marketing 22(5), 247–256 (2005)
19. Kim, H.W., Chan, H.C., Gupta, S.: Value-based adoption of mobile Internet: an empirical investigation. Decision Support Systems 43(1), 111–126 (2007)
20. Segerstahl, K., Oinas-Kukkonen, H.: Designing personal exercise monitoring employing multiple modes of delivery: Implications from a qualitative study on heart rate monitoring. International Journal of Medical Informatics 80, e203–e213 (2011)
21. Elliot, H.: The use of diaries in sociological research on health experience. Sociological Research Online 2(2) (1997),
   `http://www.socresonline.org.uk/socresonline/2/2/7.html`

22. Taylor-Piliar, R.E., Norton, L.C., Haskell, W.L., Mahbouda, M.H., Fair, J.M., Iribarren, C., Hlatky, M.A., Go, A.S., Fortmann, S.P.: Validation of a new brief physical activity survey among men and women aged 60-69 years. Annual Journal of Epidemiology 164, 598–606 (2006)
23. Spillers, F., Asimakopoulos, S.: Help me relax! Biofeedback and gamification to improve interaction design in healthcare. In: 8th International Conference on Design & Emotion, London, UK, September 11-14, vol. 41 (2012)
24. Venkatesh, V., Morris, M.G.: Why don't men ever stop to ask for directions? Gender, social influence, and their role in technology acceptance and usage behavior. MIS Quarterly 24(1), 115–139 (2000)

Motive-Oriented Design

Helping Automobile Engineers to Take the User's Perspective!

Constantin von Saucken, Ioanna Michailidou, Simon Kremer, and Udo Lindemann

Technische Universität München, Institute of Product Development, Germany
{saucken,michailidou,kremer,lindemann}@pe.mw.tum.de

Abstract. Modern car interiors are often overloaded and not self-explanatory. We supported running development projects within car industry and observed the following reasons: Similar functions are developed in different departments without a sufficient coordination and integration into the car. Functions are arranged according to technologies. Engineers have trouble with putting themselves in a user's position. Therefore, we present a motive-oriented approach: It supports engineers in taking the user's perspective by tools for investigating users' motives, clustering them in use scenarios, matching them with functions, illustrating them in an understandable way and running real-user tests.

Keywords: Emotional design and persuasion design, management of DUXU processes, mental model design, metaphor design, usability methods and tools.

1 Introduction

1.1 Motivation

User-centered design aims at improving the user's experience with a product – making it useful, usable and joyful. The real-world user should always be considered within the development process: by user insights, field observations and several evaluation loops. His needs and problems should be taken seriously [1].

In reality of automotive industry, engineers often design their products from a technological perspective. Products are developed on the basis of new technologies unaware of the impact on and benefit for the customer.

As a consequence, interfaces are mostly designed too complicated for most inexperienced users. Many different interface elements are all available at any time – even if they cannot be used in a specific situation, e.g. parking assistant while driving on the motorway or Cruise Control while driving in the city. Furthermore, the labeling of these elements is often poor – showing the abbreviated function or technology name, e.g. AC for air condition and not self-explanatory symbols like a snowflake.

When it comes to evaluating, engineers tend to see themselves as the potential user and design functions and interfaces accordingly. This perspective can be so extreme that real users who do not get on with the product get labeled as incapable, as if it was their own failure [1].

A. Marcus (Ed.): DUXU 2014, Part IV, LNCS 8520, pp. 370–377, 2014.

Fig. 1. Overloaded, not self-explanatory car interior, © by automobilemag.com

1.2   Goal

To meet these challenges, we want to support developers taking the customer's perspective by three integrated approaches:

Determine User Motives. Developers should always be aware of real users, what they want and what they are (not) able to handle. Therefore, the developer needs methods and tools to determine user motives based on real customers, trend reports and further sources.

Reduce Perceived Complexity. We see a high potential in reducing the perceived complexity of interfaces. Instead of mapping single functions separately with single buttons, the goal is to rearrange functions according to the investigated user motives. This way, users could easily understand what the fewer buttons are good for.

Provide Consistent Mental Model. We want to support the design of intuitive interfaces providing a consistent mental model. Users should understand them without a specific previous knowledge. We propose the use of metaphors and analogies instead of abbreviations of technology or function descriptions.

1.3   Overview

In this paper we present the motive-oriented design approach to help engineers broaden their perspective to a more user-centered one. In an automotive use case we describe our experiences applying it within a design team. The idea of our approach is to cluster functions and controls according to these user motives. A motive describes the cause of a user to perform an action [2]. For example the motive »delegate driving tasks« motivates the action »activate cruise control«. A motive is more abstract than action goals (»press cruise control button«) and more concrete than psychological needs (»feel secure«).

Furthermore, metaphors and consistent system descriptions allow the easy generation of a user's mental model. With this approach designers get encouraged to handle with the real users by taking their perspective on the product and designing it accordingly. This leads to understandable products that fulfill customer needs [3].

2   Method

We present a five step proceeding for developers to fulfill the motive-oriented approach. Figure 2 shows the first three of them. Starting point is the investigation of user motives and needs. We propose different methods and tools for deriving motives in form of »I want to...« from real users in section 2.1. In the next step these motives are clustered to consistent use scenarios resulting in a story which gives the impression of a solution and its experience (see section 2.2). Based on this story existing and new functions and technologies are selected to be integrated in one interface element. This step is described in section 2.3.

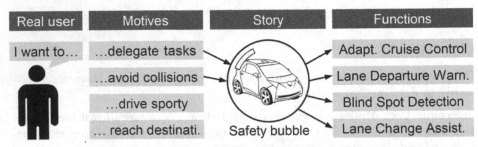

Fig. 2. Overview on motive-oriented approach for clustering functions

After having selected functions that can be integrated based on the story, an interface element needs to be designed accordingly that is easy to understand in order to create a consistent mental model (see section 2.4). Finally, this interface concept, the function cluster and the story as such need to be evaluated with real users. Therefore experience prototypes need to be tested. Section 2.5 explains this final step.

A positive example of a motive-oriented design in existing cars is the driving mode button (see figure 3). Many manufacturers provide an interface element that allows users to select »sport« or »eco« setup. This setup changes numerous settings of the engine and chassis fitting to the motive of »driving sporty« or »driving eco-friendly« but with only one interaction. At the same time, the description is intuitively understandable, even to new customers. Besides this example, we see a high potential for many more motive-oriented interaction concepts to improve the user's experience.

Fig. 3. Driving mode interface as a successful motive-oriented cluster, © by Volkswagen

2.1 Step 1: Get to Know the User Motives

In the first step we suggest methods to derive user motives from interviews and observations but also from literature-based trend research. The challenge is to interpret and translate the collected data and to formulate motives without fixation on existing solutions. The designer needs to uncover the real user needs and motives [3]. He must repeatedly ask for the reasons of a user's statement or behavior until the real desire becomes clear. We suggest the following steps for deriving user motives:

Define User Group. Before observing and asking the user the design team needs to know who the potential user is. Therefore, the market situation needs to be analyzed enriched by future trends: What will future regions, products, competitors and customers look like? We suggest existing marketing methods for this step.

Gather Current State of User Behavior. In this step the goal is to really understand the user defined in the previous step. We could observe several times that engineers tend to see themselves as potential users and therefore think they know whom to design for. But it is highly important to observe and ask real non-expert users from different cultural and social backgrounds. We suggest semi-structured interviews, the »think aloud« method and field operation tests to investigate the user behavior, his needs, problems and wishes.

Structure Data to Derive User Motives. The current state should be sufficiently extensive and thereby too complex to easily overview. For this reason, the insights get structured by paraphrasing and clustering in user motives in form of »I want to...« and corresponding needs, e.g. according to Sheldon et al. [3].

Formulate Chances. Mostly engineers think problem-driven – they are trained to be problem-solvers. In order to create a positive experience it is essential to formulate positively in terms of chances instead of problems. Finally, the user motives get enriched by future trends (e.g. Delphi analysis) based on literature or expert interviews.

As an example we derived the motives »I want to delegate tasks« and »I want to avoid collisions« in our supported industrial project.

2.2 Step 2: Cluster Motives in a Story

In the next step consistent use scenarios are developed which cluster these motives and chances and get illustrated using storytelling. Similar motives fulfilling the same psychological user need [3] are connected by developing a story that describes a positive experience. This story must be kept simple and easy to understand in order to convince other designers and decision makers. Furthermore, these stories must be evaluated with real customers. Finally, the most promising stories are chosen to be implemented.

Cluster Chances and Motives in Use Scenarios. As there should be many motives and chances derived in the first step (we gathered 34 in our project), they need to be further clustered and compared. We suggest to run a comparison in pairs and judge each combination with a value in the range from 0 (low similarity) to 3 (high similarity). Groups of motives with a high inter-relatedness should finally be connected by describing a consistent use scenario.

Create Stories. The most promising use scenarios now get illustrated by creating stories. We suggest applying the proceeding described by Michailidou et al. [4]: After creating the story setting (persona, their motives, environment) the plot is determined (interactions, products, events) and formulated as a text enriched with a sketch.

Evaluate Stories. These stories can afterwards be evaluated with potential users. These users should be selected carefully to ensure to have a representative result. After having read the story, the users are asked qualitatively with an unstructured interview: Did they understand the story? Is it realistic? What are first impressions? Additionally, we suggest running a quantitative questionnaire focusing the upcoming anticipated experience and emotions, e.g. AttrakDiff [5] or PrEmo [6].

Assess and Select Stories. Finally, the decision is made how many and which of the stories are assessed to be implemented in the next stage. We suggest applying a weighted score assessment [7] based on the evaluation results.

As an exemplary outcome we developed the story of a »repelling safety bubble around car« which combines several motives like e.g. »I want to avoid collisions«. This image shall give the impression of a security experience by avoiding any collisions in any direction around the car.

2.3 Step 3: Match Story with Functions and Technologies

The chosen motives now get matched with given technologies and functions. In this step, developers decide which functions and technologies fit to the selected stories. We suggest applying the Design Structure Matrix (DSM) method [8] for this step: in a table (named DMM – Domain Mapping Matrix) functions get listed in the first column, motives in the first row. The design team now decides for each motive which function fulfills it. Extended by the use scenarios, the DMM makes consistent function clusters obvious. In our example figure 4 shows a selection of functions that fulfill the two motives integrated in the »safety bubble« story.

Motives / Functions	Adapt. Cruise Control	Lane Departure Warn.	Blind Spot Detection	Lane Change Assist	Hill Descent Control	Traffic Sign Recogn.	Night Vision	Navigation System	Drowsiness Detection	Automatic Parking	Adjust chassis	Adjust engine setting	Speed Information
...delegate driving	X				X					X			
...avoid collisions	X	X	X	X			X		X	X			
...drive sporty										X		X	X
...reach destinati.								X	X				

Fig. 4. Domain Mapping Matrix linking motives with functions

When the functions and components for integration are determined, the rather abstract story needs to be elaborated to a storyboard [4]. The design team must define every system behavior in every possible use scenario – always with the story in mind. The goal is to develop a system that reacts consistently according to the story. It is highly important also to design every misuse and to consider possible combinations of impacts on the system that could arouse a system failure. The resulting storyboard still needs to be illustrated in a simple way to be tested with real users.

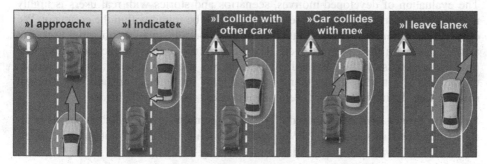

Fig. 5. Use scenarios for the »repelling safety bubble« story

In our industrial application we decided to integrate the existing advanced driver assistance systems (ADAS) »adaptive cruise control«, »lane departure warning«, »blind spot detection« and »lane change assistant« into a storyboard based on the »safety bubble« story showing different use scenarios (see figure 5).

2.4   Step 4: Design Interface According to Clusters

Finally, the user interface must be designed according to the developed story set of technologies, functions and motives. We suggest the use of metaphors to create an adequate mental model and a corresponding, self-explanatory system description.

In our example we suggested to show a protective circle around the car. This circle could have different colors: green for no potential dangers, yellow for potential threads and red for an immediate danger (cp. figure 5). Thereby, the interface could integrate four ADAS buttons. Figure 6 shows a similar implementation of BMW.

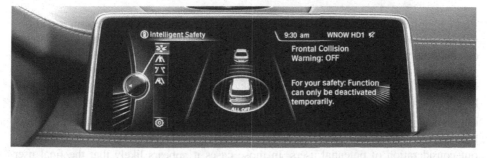

Fig. 6. Interface showing integrated safety systems, © by BMW Group

At this stage it is important to start prototyping the concept and interface taking other systems into consideration as all subsystems need to be integrated in one product in the end. This way, all system prototypes can be tested in a real environment by real users simulating the system behavior, e.g. by applying the »Wizard of Oz« method.

2.5   Step 5: Evaluate Concept with Real Users

The evaluation of developed motives, scenarios and stories with real users is highly important to meet real needs. These users are not to be found within the company. We observe that oftentimes engineers take themselves or colleagues as potential user. But as they deal with their product every day they are not representative and do not see obvious weaknesses. They do hard envisioning real users' problems and reactions on the product and tend to make them responsible, if the interaction fails. We suggest running tests during the whole development process – not only in the end:

Evaluate Stories and Storyboards. The evaluation of stories and storyboards is already described in section 2.2. We propose running qualitative unstructured interviews enriched with quantitative questionnaires (e.g. [5] [6]).

Evaluate Prototypes. We propose building different prototypes for agile testing: rough prototypes in early stages which show the basic function, detailed prototypes in later stages giving an impression of surface, material, design and feedback. These prototypes shall be tested by interviewing experts in the fields of engineering, usability and user experience. Furthermore, we highly recommend testing with inexperienced users by observation and the »think aloud« method enriched with tools used for the story evaluation. The focus of the evaluation lies on qualitative feedback in order to iteratively refine the prototypes.

Evaluate Integrated Product. Different integrated systems in a product finally need to be evaluated with real users. We propose running basic usability tests (visibility, packaging, accessibility), evaluating the integration concept (dissociation of interface elements and systems, no redundancy of functions) and check if the initial story is still preserved in the product. We propose using semi-structured interviews and semantic differentials for evaluating the users' perception and experience.

3   Insights from Industrial Use Case

The exemplary application shown in the sections of this paper is based on a real development project within German car industry, but we needed to adjust the contents due to nondisclosure agreements. We applied this approach in industrial projects and got positive feedback from engineers. The proceeding helped them to overcome fixations on existing solutions and to anticipate the customer's view on and potential problems with their product. During the project we gained several insights:

Challenge of Expressing Added Value. We met engineers that were not able to express the customers' benefit of their system – they »just« fulfilled technical requirements without consideration of potential users. In those cases it appears likely that the final user experience is rather random instead of systematically developed.

Too Late Integration. Oftentimes, interface designers and usability experts were integrated too late into the development process. For that reason, many solutions on the market provide a bad user experience due to an insufficient integration although the isolated system experience and its functionality are good.

Resistance Towards Cooperation. Our approach requires an intense cooperation and integration of systems developed by different departments. This coordination presents a challenge in large companies like car manufacturers and leads to high efforts. We could also observe political resistances towards a collaboration of different departments as there are (like in any company) conflicts of interests and relationships.

4   Conclusion

From the application of our motive-oriented approach within industrial projects we got the feedback that on the one hand the approach has a high potential for improving the company-internal communication and cooperation resulting in a better user experience of singular systems and the overall experience within a car. It helps dealing with customers' motives and helps integrating systems consistently on the story basis. On the other hand, it appears to be very challenging to implement this approach in a large company for the reasons described in section 3.

For this reasons, we need to apply the approach in further branches and companies with different conditions. Furthermore, we want to test other integration methods based on the DSM approach: Instead of investigating motives and clustering functions accordingly, the approach could be used to cluster according to situations or needs.

References

1. Norman, D.: The Design of Everyday Things. Basic Books, New York (2002)
2. Kaptelinin, V., Nardi, B.: Acting with Technology: Activity Theory and Interaction Design. MIT Press, Boston (2006)
3. Sheldon, K., Elliot, A., Kim, Y., Kasser, K.: What is satisfying about satisfying events? Journal of Personality and Social Psychology 80(3), 325–339 (2001)
4. Michailidou, I., von Saucken, C., Lindemann, U.: How to create a user experience story. In: Marcus, A. (ed.) DUXU/HCII 2013, Part I. LNCS, vol. 8012, pp. 554–563. Springer, Heidelberg (2013)
5. Hassenzahl, M., Burmester, M., Koller, F.: AttrakDiff: Ein Fragebogen zur Messung wahrgenommener hedonischer und pragmatischer Qualität. In: Ziegler, J., Szwillus, G. (eds.) Mensch & Computer 2003: Interaktion in Bewegung, pp. 187–196. B.G. Teubner, Stuttgart (2003)
6. Desmet, P.: Measuring emotion: development and application of an instrument to measure emotional responses to products. In: Blythe, M.A., Monk, A.F., Overbeeke, K., Wright, P.C. (eds.) Funology: From Usability to Enjoyment, pp. 111–123. Kluwer Academic Publishers, Dordrecht (2003)
7. Lindemann, U.: Methodische Entwicklung technischer Produkte. Springer, Berlin (2007)
8. Lindemann, U., Maurer, M., Braun, T.: Structural Complexity Management: An Approach for the Field of Product Design. Springer, Berlin (2009)

User Experience Case Studies

A Validation Study of a Visual Analytics Tool with End Users

Heloisa Candello, Victor Fernandes Cavalcante, Alan Braz,
and Rogério Abreu De Paula

IBM Research, Brazil
{heloisacandello,victorfc,alanbraz,ropaula}@br.ibm.com

Abstract. In this paper we describe an user evaluation that aimed to understand how a group of endusers interpret a visual analytics tool in the context of service delivery. It is common for service factories to have an organization devoted to handle incidents. Many incident management systems have strict controls on how fast incidents should be handled, often subjected to penalties when targets are not met. We call Time-Bounded Incident Management (TBIM) those systems, which require clearly defined incident resolution times. In our project, research scientists proposed a method and a visual representation named Workload Profile Chart (WPC) that had as primary goal to understand the area of incident management in a service delivery department. The objective of this visual representation is to help characterizing the performance of TBIM systems and diagnosing major issues such as resource and skill allocation problems, abnormal behavior, and incident characteristics. Researchers wanted to understand if end-users, the quality analysts (QAs), would comprehend the charts and would be able to use them to identify problems and propose effective improvement actions related to TBIM activities. The study was conducted with ten QAs of a service delivery department of a IT company based in Brazil. The data was analyzed using descriptive statistical and qualitative methods. As a result, participants were mainly guided by the axes titles and chart legends to interpret the visualizations, and not always understood what kind of data the chart was displaying. Those results served as insights of how QAs think when analyzing TBIM information in a service delivery department and what improvements in the visual representation tool may be proposed to facilitate their activity. At last we identified evidences of how to design better visual analytics tools based on participant's perceptions and interpretations of color differences and verbal information in chart labels and legend.

Keywords: visual analytics, service design, and user evaluation.

1 Introduction

Systems to deliver and provision services are the key engines of the new global economy where services are increasingly becoming the dominant mode of production. To meet those demands, more and more firms have established mass-scale, complex systems to deliver services using factory-like production methods, or service factories [1]. The modern call center is the typical example of mature implementation of the service factory model, while health, government, and IT services, among others, are just

A. Marcus (Ed.): DUXU 2014, Part IV, LNCS 8520, pp. 381–391, 2014.

starting to deliver services following this approach. It is common for service factories to have an organization devoted to handling incidents, which can be defined as: "any event which is not part of the standard operation of a service and which causes, or may cause, an interruption to or a reduction in, the quality of that service" [2]. They are, by definition, unpredictable and often demand rapid allocation of skilled resources for their resolution and bringing a service back to normal. For example, management of power failures or dangerous situations is an absolutely critical organization in the electric distribution sector. Many incident management systems have strict controls on how fast incidents should be handled, often subjected to penalties when targets are not met. We call Time-Bounded Incident Management (TBIM) those systems, which require clearly defined incident resolution times. Examples of TBIM systems include: fire and ambulance management, some call centers with required maximum resolution times, and most IT service delivery operations of IT outsourcing.

Nowadays, quality analysts know if incidents are handled on time formally and informally. Formally, by metrics available for each service pool; charts from official tools; characteristics of the incident report (e.g. severity); employees who acted incidents (level of expertise). Informally by chatting with people from the team (e.g. dispatchers) to know the root cause of incident and calling the customer to know informally if he is satisfied with the service. So that, many resources have to be consulted to know if the team is solving incidents on time from the internal point of view (e.g. employees are managing to solve the tickets) and for the costumer point of view (e.g. incidents solved according to the time agreement). Despite of being a cumbersome TBIM activity, it is also difficult to track how long the incident report will delay until it reach the right employee for solving. Our visual analytics tool, considers this data to clarify where might be lateness.

In this paper we describe a user evaluation study that aimed to understand how a group of end-users interpret this visual analytics tool in the context of service delivery.

2   Background

Information visualization is defined as "The use of computer-supported, interactive, visual representations of data to amplify cognition" [3]. Spencer [4] completes affirming that "visualization is a process of forming mental model of data, thereby gaining insight into that data". Visualization is a human cognitive activity, not something that a computer does in his views. Thereby, control of information is given over to viewers, not to editors, designers or decorators [5]. To unveil the mental model in every person's mind is a cumbersome activity. Therefore, user experience researchers and designers may dispose what will be formed in people's mind understanding better their contexts and practices in everyday life. Visualizations have their own purpose give insights on data to solve or clarify certain problems. And it posts a critical question: How best to transform the data into something that people can understand for optimal decision-making? [6].

User centered design approaches; such as user evaluation studies may enlighten this question. Hetzler and Turner [7] presented lessons learned from an observational study of an INfovis application. Ins-pire visualization tool uses statistical word patterns to characterize documents based on text content. The purpose of this tool was narrow the number of relevant documents before analysts read them. As a result, analysts found useful to see the main data grouped by similar visualizations and researchers learned that analysts use diverse type of tools to make their conclusions, so that Ins-pire should provide support to other tools and have other features such as to write reports while data analysis.

Toker et al [8] explores the relationship of cognitive abilities, personality, and attention patterns of users have an impact on using different visualization techniques. For doing so, they used eye-tracking studies to identify gaze patterns. Thirty-five subjects participated the study and accomplished three computer-based tasks for a three cognitive measures: verbal, visual and a perceptual speed. The cognitive measure with highest number of effects was Perceptual speed. Among their findings, they discovered that low perceptual speed users tended to access a visualization legend more than high perceptual speed users, suggesting that they should be specifically supported in terms of legend processing. Overall, their analysis show that some of the user characteristics affect user gaze behavior and it was possible to detect this through a variety of eye-tracking measures.

Afterward user studies and have a better understand of people's cognitions to interpret visualizations and their context. Designers may employ multimedia elements to built new or redesigned interfaces to improve user's interpretation of visual and verbal elements. According to Bertin [9]: "A graphic is no longer drawn' once and for all; it is constructed and reconstructed until it reveals all the relationships constituted by the interplay of data". In other words, "the best graphic operations are those carried out by the decision maker itself". He also created a visual grammar to make designers aware of visual elements characteristics when choosing them to compose a graph. In Tufte [10] words "When principles of design replicate principles of thought, the act of arranging information is becomes an act of insight. A more recent study [11] allows individuals may upload data, collaborate and generate visualizations at a large scale in a public website called ManyEyes. This tool also provides a wide range of visualizations types that may help designers to compare and choose appropriate visualizations for different contexts. Those studies have high relevance and serve as basis for future studies in the field. However, more studies are necessary to unveil ways of understanding the huge amount of data available nowadays. In doing so, helping designers to create more effective visual analytics tools.

3   The Visual Analytics Tool: Workload Profile Chart (WPC)

In our project, research scientists proposed a method and a visual representation named Workload Profile Chart that had as primary goal to understand the area of incident management in a service delivery department. The method preprocesses data corresponding to records of incidents (tickets) and plots the spreading of incidents on a log-log chart.

Particularly, the researchers were interested in how to evaluate the performance of a service pool in terms of its compliance with an established Service Level Agreement (SLA) as measured by its performance in those two key variables: the elapsed time since a ticket is reported until its assignment to a support analyst (assignment delay), and the time spent to have the ticket solved and closed by the analyst in charge to handle it (resolution time). Thus, the chart is comprised of the log of the assignment delay (X axis) and the log of resolution time (Y axis), both ranging between 0.1% and 1000% of the time allowance.

The objective of this visual representation was to help characterizing the performance of TBIM systems and diagnosing major issues such as resource and skill allocation problems, abnormal behavior, and ticket characteristics. Researchers wanted to understand if end-users, delivery quality analysts, would comprehend the charts and would be able to use them to identify problems and propose effective improvement actions related to TBIM activities.

The WPC is a density map resulting from the log-log plot and our inspection method takes one of these charts and systematically examines the concentration levels on different areas as defined in Figure 1. High or low concentration of tickets in a particular area corresponds to a set of specific characteristics likely to describe the reality of a service pools and, based on such concentration and an expected level used as reference (a baseline) for each area, a diagnostic is performed.

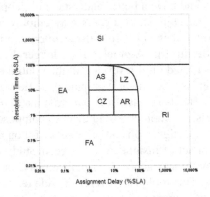

Fig. 1. Different areas of the WPC of the service pool

After analyzing dozens of WPCs, it was detected that high concentrations of tickets in different areas of a WPC are related to different kinds of problems and issues in a service pool. Accordingly, there are eight main areas of interest in a WPC, each of them corresponding to specific issues [12]:

- Comfort Zone (CZ): this area contains tickets that are quickly assigned, resolved and closed. A high concentration of tickets in this area may indicate that the service pool has sufficient resources and most of the tickets have low difficulty to solve, meaning that analysts are typically working in their comfort zone.
- False Alarms (FA): it corresponds to the area covering tickets whose resolution takes less than 1.0% of the SLA resolution time. These tickets are either very simple to solve or they are false alarms (tickets that should not exist) or duplicates. A high concentration of tickets in this area suggests that the performance of the service pool can be improved by automation or by the usage of better monitoring or filtering approaches.

- `Excess Availability (EA)`: tickets in this are quickly assigned but take some time to be solved. A high concentration of tickets in this area may indicate that there are often too many analysts available and ready to immediately start working on tickets as soon as they arrive and are dispatched. Such tickets are also very good candidates for automatic dispatching.
- `Adequate Resources (AR)`: this area contains tickets that meet their SLAs and to which assignments are not immediate but quickly resolved. A high concentration of tickets here may mean that resources are not always promptly available, so assignment takes some time. However, that does not compromise the SLA attainment because most tickets are easily solved without much work.
- `Adequate Skills (AS)`: this area comprises only tickets that meet their SLAs and that require a good amount of effort for their resolution. A high concentration of tickets in this area indicates that resolution tasks can be time consuming and that the SLAs cannot be made tighter without adding more skilled resources to the pool.
- `Limit Zone (LZ)`: this area comprises only tickets that meet their SLAs and that take some time both to be assigned and to be solved. So a high concentration in this area often means that the system is running close to its limit and therefore, resources and skills are being optimally used but with no slack. However, it means a high susceptibility to breakdown when unexpectedly heavy concentrations of incidents occur.
- `Resource Issues (RI)`: this area covers tickets that do not meet their SLA because they were assigned too late. A heavy concentration here often indicates that the service pool does not have enough support analysts or has dispatching issues.
- `Skills Issues (SI)`: this area covers tickets whose resolution took more than the agreed SLA time. A heavy concentration here usually means low skilled resources or a need to renegotiate SLAs.

4 Participants

Ten participants were randomly selected to attend the study. Eight did not know the project and two were familiar with the concept of the chart, but did not use the software to generate it before. All of them work at the same company and have a data analyst position. They have a diverse background in areas such: computing; engineering; math; project management and administration. As part of their everyday routine, they spend most of their time evaluating how their team is solving the incidents based on images and have a weekly meeting to report their analysis. In order to report their findings, they use at least seven to eight types of software. For instance, a software to see the customer metrics, other to generate the charts and tables and another to simulate and report the official data analysis. Usually, they are used to commercial software and prefer to run the analysis and charts on it, and then export to official company tools.

5 Method

The study was conducted with ten quality analysts of a service delivery department of a IT company based in Brazil. The experiment had two parts. First, participants followed a user case scenario [13,14] to explore the visual analytics tool and were encouraged to think aloud [15,16]. Second, they explained the visual representation to the test facilitator, imagining they were explaining it to a member of their own team. Participants also answered a semi-structured interview containing information of their job title and everyday work routine. Overall the study took 45 minutes long per participant. In this paper we are reporting the second part of the study, focused on chart interpretation. Participants were video recorded and signed a consent form allowing data for research proposes. Observation studies were done in situ. Researchers took notes during the user sessions. Additionally, video record files helped to go deep in details for data coding.

6   Data Analysis

The data was analyzed using descriptive statistical methods and qualitative methods. Basic statistical analysis was carried out to analyze the data from the semi-structured interviews. Tables and cross tabulation were applied to compare the results among participants and the use of the system. The restricted number of participants in the study was not enough to ensure the validity of the statistical analysis. Besides, these results did not give us enough evidence of essential chart interpretation trends. Writing on design evidence, Lawson [17] highlights that "we normally measure and express quantities by counting using a numerical system. This leads us to believe that all numbers behave in the same way and this is quite untrue". The same author emphasizes what designers really need is to have a feel for the meaning behind the numbers rather than precise methods of calculating them. (p.71). In agreement with Lawson ideas, a qualitative approach was applied in most of the process.

The data analysis was based on data transformation. Data transformation is a quantification of qualitative data. This involves creating qualitative codes and themes, and then counting the number of times they occur in the textual data. This enables researchers to compare quantitative results with qualitative data [18]. The transcriptions of the video observations, important notes taken during the fieldwork and suggestions given by participants while they were using the WPC were considered. Research questions were established to guide the analysis, such as:

- Does quality analysts understand the topic of the chart?
- Does quality analysts understand the regions of the chart proposed by researchers?
- Does quality analysts understand the structural elements of the chart (color, shapes, axis)?
- Which kind of decisions quality analysts can take based on the visual analytics tool results?
- What improvements can be made in the visual and interactive elements to assist quality analysts perform their data analysis?

These questions were kept in mind while the data was classified and codified. Additionally, issues were also rated as Low (one to three participants mentioned it), Medium (four to eight participants mentioned it) and High importance (over eight participants mentioned it).

7 Findings

Data was organized by categories (or themes) to help in the analysis. About 30 categories were identified in the whole study. The more frequent categories were associated to expectation of ways to add data and representations of their familiar visual analytics tools (seven participants). They also expect another type of chart, based on their previous experience with visual representations (six participants). Understanding was also a prevalence issue. And this category will be detailed here based on the questions previously described above on Section 6. We are also discussing possible improvements in the interface to provide better user experiences with the visual analytics tool and future decision make based on WPC.

7.1 Understanding

Participants were mainly guided by the axes titles and chart legends to interpret the visualizations, and not always understood what kind of data the chart was displaying. Users identified the log-log chart as a not intuitive representation. Six participants had difficulties to interpret it. They are used to decimal scale and not a logarithm scale. They would like to see the numbers not only the percentage on the chart. Three of those participants have their background on project management. Two participants were female, but more investigations are necessary to attest if gender and/or technical background may interfere in chart interpretation. One participant with difficulties on interpreting the chart commented: "I confess that I'm not understanding this chart here. There isn't a type of chart that I have seen before. Our current graphics are limited. We don't accept any value above 100% neither below 0%, and there is also no negative numbers. We just ignore them. I don't understand the values above 100%, unless it is cumulative. But the percentage of resolution time, I can understand up to 100% of my SLA. How do I have points over 100%?"

Four participants understood what is the topic of the chart TBIM but had difficulties to understand the term Assignment Delay. They were not sure if it was the total time or delayed time to reach the dispatcher. They suggested to change the term for dispatcher efficiency, due to the dispatcher job is to assign the suitable ticket to the suitable analyst to solve it. Another participant stated: " What is being measured is down time or full time? If it's considering stopped time, does it measure only the time of break or full time? It should be measuring only one kind time."

WPC was not a static chart. Participants could click on the screen, and they could see a tooltip with given information of that group of tickets position and the region acronym. In the interface, legend and chart were not always in the same view (depending on the resolution screen), which caused misinterpretations of the acronym in the chart. Moreover, not all participants interacted with the chart, and do not know why the chart was divided in parts, and also that each part had a name. (See Figure 2). Two participants stated that the regions (success and fail) from the legend where not identified in the chart.

Researchers named chart regions to help analysts to identify their team performance. In the user sessions, it was possible to validate the terms when participants explained in

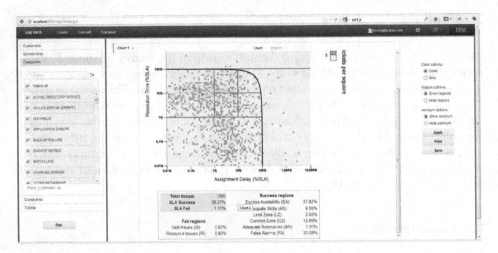

Fig. 2. WPC chart and legend position inside the application interface

their words the meaning of each region. False Alarms (FA) was the most comprehensible term (seven people). Excess Availability (EA) and Resource Issues (RI) were the least comprehensible (eight people). Participants also had problems to distinguish between the regions Adequate Skills (AS) and Adequate Resources (AR). In their view if resources are people, so adequate resources means they have the right skill to solve incidents. Excess availability term generated doubts about what was in excess: resources or skills.

The idea to represent a group of ticket per square, density of tickets per one pixels of the chart, was also difficult to grasp. For users, each square was representing one ticket. Even with color legend displayed beside the chart. Perhaps, they interpreted in this way due to color scale used in the chart. Participants identified colors as level of severity of tickets (red is more severe than green) or time spent to solve the ticket (red took more time to solve than green).

Moreover to assist to understand the chart, and have a better analysis, participants would like to know the SLA agreed within the client, to be able to compare the chart generated to the baseline chart. Further, they also would like to see the ticket life-cycle in the same chart.

7.2 Design Improvements

Observation studies of user sessions assisted the team to have a picture of WPC chart and which improvements were needed to let quality analysts use it as a tool. We describe briefly visual component changes.

Color Scale. The use of color was misleading to understand concepts we were intent to communicate. Not all the participants understood the connection between the labels and the colors in the chart. Graph colors and values were very distinct to represent intensity. A monochromatic color scheme was considered a better choice for the aim to highlight density of tickets per square avoiding the cultural meaning carried by the colors in the previous chart. As Bertin [9] (p.85) affirms:

The use of color cannot be understood unless the notion of color (hue) is distinguished in a rigorous and definitive manner from the notion of value. They are two different sensations, which by nature, overlap. [...] A tone placed on a sheet of paper is therefore defined by two parameters: color (hue/tint) with the categories violet, blue, green [...] and value, defined by the percentage of black in the corresponding gray.

Therefore, we chose to vary the value of a green, instead of coloring the chart with different hues (see Figure 3). Iliinsky [19] agrees with Bertin that color is not ordered, is selective. Order can be achieved by a series of values from one of the scales of the spectrum (warm scale). The eyes mix the colors and order the components according to values. "...It is fantastic for labeling categories and terrible for representing quantities or ranks." [19] p.7.

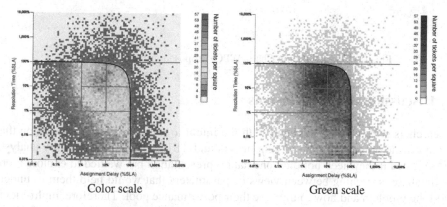

Color scale   Green scale

Fig. 3. WPC charts before and after this study

Visual Configuration. Changes were made in the visual configuration of the tool to clarify what type of data the chart was showing. In agreement with the user studies, participants were guided by wording of titles and legends. Cleveland [20] earlier explored this issue with 55 subjects to understand how people perceive elements in a chart. In his study, participants perceive charts in two levels. First by the overall picture to see what is the subject of the chart and second by the elementary graphical perceptual task. Those sequences of actions were clear in our study.

With the aim to assist analysts to understand both pictures (overall and elementary) of the chart, a redesign of the tool was made. The main title was added to the chart, to help in external identification [9]. The components and legend (internal identification) was redesigned and placed to connect with visual elements in the chart. (see Figure 4). The current interface shows the legend and the chart side by side. Users can highlight the area in the chart with a click on the name of each region in the legend. Below in each region, users have questions to help them analyze the chart with the real number of tickets (decimal), not in log present in the region.

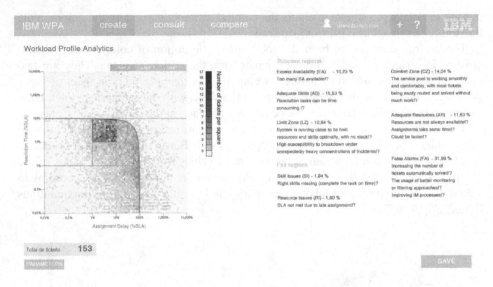

Fig. 4. Workload Profile Chart (WPC) proposed visual configuration

8   Discussion and Conclusions

Researchers created a log-log chart with the intent to find a visual representation that would couple amount of data to help understand TBIM. When users/quality analysts (QAs) tested it they need not only one data representation but wanted to explore more the database, switching between views of parameters that would help them to understand the problem and how to improve their performance pool. Therefore, multi-views of the chart would be necessary to satisfy their object. We are working for the WPC be visualized not only as a 2D chart, but a more interactive visual analytics tool where users can choose their set of parameters.

Although a more interactive tool might be the solution to suit this context, WPC showed information that is difficult to track in the daily basis activities of QAs along with the current tools they use, such as: time of assignment to solve the incident.

It is not easy to evaluate interactive visual analytics tools. So, designers must to think each kind of information should be shown in the screen, and each one should be unveiled when users click, or tap on the screen. It raises questions of what is relevant to the context? What are the primary information to be shown? And what is addiotional information, that users can explore deeply in the data set?

Those results served to have insights of how QAs think when analyzing TBIM information in a service delivery department and what improvements in the visual representation tool may be proposed to facilitate their activity. At last we identified evidences of how to design better visual analytics tools based on participant's perceptions and interpretations of color differences and verbal information in chart labels and legend.

References

1. de Souza, C.R.B., Pinhanez, C.S., Cavalcante, V.F.: Information Needs of System Administrators in Information Technology Service Factories. In: Proceedings of the 5th ACM Symposium on Computer Human Interaction for Management of Information Technology, CHIMIT 2011, pp. 3:1–3:10. ACM, New York (2011)
2. ITIL: Common ITIL Terms, http://itsm.the-hamster.com/itsm4.htm (accessed February 03, 2013)
3. Card, S.K., Mackinlay, J.D., Shneiderman, B.: Readings in Information Visualization: Using Vision to Think. Morgan Kaufmann Publishers Inc., San Francisco (1999)
4. Spence, R.: Information visualization. ACM Press books. Addison-Wesley, Harlow, England (2001)
5. Tufte, E.R.: Envisioning Information. Graphics Press, Cheshire (1990)
6. Ware, C.: Information Visualization - Perception for Design. Morgan Kaufmann, San Francisco (2004)
7. Hetzler, E.G., Turner, A.: Analysis Experiences Using Information Visualization. IEEE Computer Graphics and Applications 24(5), 22–26 (2004)
8. Toker, D., Conati, C., Steichen, B., Carenini, G.: Individual User Characteristics and Information Visualization: Connecting the Dots Through Eye Tracking. In: Proceedings of the SIGCHI Conference on Human Factors in Computing Systems, CHI 2013, pp. 295–304. ACM, New York (2013)
9. Bertin, J.: Semiology of Graphics: Diagrams, Networks, Maps. Esri Press, Redlands (2011)
10. Tufte, E.R.: Visual Explanations: Images and Quantities, Evidence and Narrative. Graphics Press, Cheshire (1997)
11. Viegas, F.B., Wattenberg, M., Van Ham, F., Kriss, J., McKeon, M.: Manyeyes: A site for visualization at internet scale. IEEE Transactions on Visualization and Computer Graphics 13(6), 1121–1128 (2007)
12. Cavalcante, V.F., Pinhanez, C.S., de Paula, R.A., Andrade, C.S., de Souza, C.R.B.: Data-driven analytical tools for characterization of productivity and service quality issues in IT service factories. Journal of Service Research: JSR (2013)
13. Cooper, A.: The Inmates are Running the Asylum: Why High-Tech Products Drive Us Crazy and How to Restore the Sanity. SAMS, Indianapolis (1999)
14. Sharp, H., Rogers, Y., Preece, J.: Interaction Design: Beyond Human-Computer Interaction, 2nd edn. Wiley, Indianapolis (2007)
15. Ericsson, K.A., Simon, H.: Protocol analysis: Verbal reports as data. MIT Press, Cambridge (1993)
16. Nielsen, J., Macks, R.L.: Usability Inspection Methods (1994)
17. Lawson, B.: How Designers Think: The Design Process Demystified, 4th edn. (2005)
18. Creswell, J.W.: Research Design: Qualitative, Quantitative, and Mixed Methods Approaches. SAGE Publications (2009)
19. Iliinsky, N.: Choosing visual properties for successful visualizations, http://public.dhe.ibm.com/common/ssi/ecm/en/ytw03323usen/YTW03323USEN.PDF (accessed February 03, 2013)
20. Cleveland, W.S., McGill, R.: Graphical perception: Theory, experimentation, and application to the development of graphical methods. Journal of the American Statistical Association 79(387), 531–554 (1984)

User Support System in the Complex Environment

Hashim Iqbal Chunpir[1,2], Amgad Ali Badewi[3], and Thomas Ludwig[1,2]

[1] German Climate Computing Center (DKRZ), Bundesstr. 45a, Hamburg, Germany
{chunpir,ludwig}@dkrz.de
[2] University of Hamburg, Department of Informatics, Hamburg, Germany
[3] Cranfield University, Manufacturing Department, Bedforshire, United Kingdom
a.badewi@cranfield.ac.uk

Abstract. e-Science infrastructures have changed the process of research. Researchers can now access distributed data around the globe with the help of e-infrastructures. This is particularly a very important development for the developing countries. User support services play an important role to provide researchers with the required information needs to accomplish their research goals with the help of e-infrastructures. However, the current user-support practices in e-infrastructures in the climate domain are being followed on intuitive basis, hence over-burdening infrastructure development staffs who partly act as human support agents. The main contribution of this paper is to present the environmental complexity with-in the contemporary user support practices of climate science e-infrastructure known as Earth System Grid Federation (ESGF). ESGF is a leading distributed peer-to-peer (P2P) data-grid system in Earth System Modelling (ESM) having around 25000 users distributed all over the world.

Keywords: e-Science, systems, research, user support, help desk, developing countries.

1   Introduction

User support has always been a key topic in Human Computer Interaction (HCI) and other fields as it refers to assistance provided to the users of technology and other products. The user-support process in e-Science infrastructures is an operational process that serves the end-users of e-Science infrastructure in achieving their goals i.e. using e-Science infrastructure (mainly) for their research but not necessarily limited to that. Users are mainly researchers and they accomplish various tasks of research within a specific time-frame via e-Science infrastructures. The user-requests are the inputs to this process and are processed by e-Science infrastructure staffs (also known as user support employees) with the help of tools and methods (whether automated or manual) to service the incoming user-requests, thus meeting the user support needs. However, support staffs in climate e-Science infrastructures, have also other tasks to be done, for instance; programming, strategic planning, node administration and others, apart from servicing end-user requests. This process of operating, maintaining and further expanding the infrastructure, including its data, is iterative in nature as the nature of support in e-Science infrastructure projects. The user support is

A. Marcus (Ed.): DUXU 2014, Part IV, LNCS 8520, pp. 392–402, 2014.

offered in the form of self-help via support websites, online tutorials, wikis or contacting an expert in the form of traditional help-desk [1], [2] and service-desk [3–5].

In this paper, the environmental complexity within the contemporary user support practices of a well-known climate science e-Science infrastructure known as Earth System Grid Federation (ESGF) is presented. The paper then presents the critique of the current user support process in ESGF and finally emphasizes on the need to streamline user-support in e-infrastructures. Moreover, the paper puts forward a recommendation to involve human resources as human support agents from research institutes in the developing countries as a part of remedy to help user support activities in ESGF. The rest of the paper is organized as follows: Section 2 describes the work related to e-Science and user support discipline. Before describing the organization of ESGF and its effects on the user support process in section 4; research methodology is explained in section 3. Finally, section 5 describes the critique of the current user support, followed by conclusion and discussion in section 6 and 7.

2 Related Work

The related work in this paper can be distributed into three sub-sections: e-science, user support, and user support in e-Science discipline.

2.1 e-Science

e-Science infrastructures have been widely deployed to access and share the knowledge, data, computing resources and even human resources to facilitate intra and inter-disciplinary research [6], [7]. There are different names associated to the concept of e-Science. The same concept is popularly known as "e-Science" in Europe and "cyber-infrastructures" in the US. Other names include e-Research, collaboratories, virtual science and Big Data Science [7].

In e-Science infrastructures, as more and more effort is being invested in improving the grid-based technologies like anatomy of data-grid [8], development of middleware, storage of data in grid [7] and socio-structural aspects of e-Science for instance "Virtual Organisations" (VOs), CWE (Collaborative Work Environments), VRE (Virtual Research Environments) [9]; the development in user support is being offered on intuitive basis with a focus on technology oriented methods that dominate the field [10–13]. The organization of user support is mainly based on the past experience, without studying and exploring the factors such as; nature of e-Science infrastructural domains, data application, scientific concerns, consideration of end-user and support staff requirements [14].

2.2 User Support (a.k.a. Help Desk)

User support in IT industry is known to be started in early 1980's with the first "help desk" (HD) that had only a desk, a pen and a telephone used by human support agent [1], [15]. User support allows users to contact support staffs to address particular problem of a user [5]. Service desk is the concept that combined service management studies with the traditional customer support studies that used the term "help-desk" [12]. Until now there are different versions of business service frameworks such as IT Information Library (ITIL) that provides "best practice guidelines" for servicing end-users and customers especially in the commercial corporations and companies locally and globally [16], [17]. Some of these frameworks have been modified and adapted to academic setups such as universities [10], [17] or to governmental administrative bodies [12]. However, these frameworks have yet not been applied to the field of e-Science infrastructures and few studies address the issue of improving user support process of supporting users, keeping economic and human resource factors under control as well as fulfilling the expectations of all the stakeholders. Studying ESGF user support as a use case will contribute to the "service desk" or "customer services" concept in distributed, research oriented, non-commercial environments.

2.3   Defining User Support in e-Science Infrastructures

After examining the notion of user support and e-Science infrastructure individually, the user-support process in e-Science infrastructure can be defined as: The user-support process in e-Science is an operational process that serves the end-users of e-Science infrastructure in achieving their goals. The user-requests initiated by users are the inputs to this process and these user-requests are processed or transformed by user support staff with the help of tools and methods to provide solutions. Hence, meeting the user support needs. This process is iterative in nature as the nature of support in e-Science projects. The end-user support process is an example of a process. The environment is e-Science infrastructures. The mission of this process is servicing and satisfying end-users (of e-Science infrastructures) incoming queries. The constraints are user-support times, support staffs, financial resources, supporting technologies and interfaces. The resources are support staffs team and the support tools. The inputs are user requests / problems. The transformation is to understand the user-requests and provide a solution. The product is end-user support framework that |provides solutions to the users.

Although lots of work has already been invested in the e-Science projects to form and operate a working user-support in e-Science infrastructures, yet there is a need to standardize and systematize user support. This study, through the first empirical investigation of end-user support process in e-Science infrastructure of climate domain, is aimed to fill this knowledge gap by providing a framework for understanding practices in e-Science in general and in climate science in particular. In this paper the elements of organizational structure of a climate e-Science infrastructure, ESGF, is presented.

3   Research Methodology

Case study research is used to depict the current user support practices in e-Science infrastructures [18]. Data collection methods are participatory observation, interviewing, archival analysis, and survey. Triangulating the result is useful to understand the current processes from different angles.

10 Interviews, from ESGF and C3Grid[1] e-Science infrastructures having different backgrounds and roles, are used to explore the current state and to understand the potential weakness in the current system. Participatory observation comes to achieve more understanding to the current processes.

Finally, questionnaire is used to describe the current operations of the support system. Online questionnaire was the method chosen among other methods for this survey since it is quicker, automated and supports complete anonymity of participants [18]. Questionnaire consists of 43 questions. Out of 36 responses received only 25 responses were useful. Despite small sample size of the respondents, it is a significant proportion of the whole targeted population in this case.

4   Organization and Governance of ESGF

In ESGF, software development and project management are done by different institutions that are project partners e.g. LLNL[2] (leading partner), BADC[3], DKRZ[4], ANU[5] and others. The model of an organizational structure of ESGF is shown in figure 1. In the figure, each symbol depicts an entity, having a specific function which is part of a climate e-Science infrastructure organization. The number of each entity may vary from time to time within a particular e-Science infrastructure and from infrastructure to infrastructure in e-Science, thus, creating a dynamic and complex environment. The institutions form the executive part of ESGF headed by principal investigators, technical team leads and the technical development team. An entity representing principal investigator is represented as a rectangle in the figure 1. Similarly, an entity representing a technical team lead including the technical team is represented as a diamond shaped notation in the figure 1. Each of the principal investigators may head different technical teams. There can be many principal investigators from different continents carrying diverse tasks. The executive part of ESGF is responsible for setting the strategic direction and overseeing technical activities of the project. The ESGF technical and maintenance teams are known as administrative bodies. Administrative bodies are a bit different to the concept of administrative domains[6] in such a way that the former includes human resources. Administrative bodies are distributed in Asia, Australia, North America and Europe. Moreover, the forthcoming teams from South America and Africa will be joining soon. Each of these administrative bodies manages one or more nodes. In order to form a distributed

---

[1]   Climate Collaborative Community data and processing grid project.
[2]   Lawrence Livermore National Laboratory, USA.
[3]   British Atmospheric Data Center, UK.
[4]   German Climate Computing Center, Germany.
[5]   Australian National University, Australia.
[6]   A collection of hardware such as computers, databases, networks and other instruments under a common administration thus sharing common policies.

control, the nodes collaborate with other nodes to form a peer-to-peer (P2P) system not only technically but also socially, institutionally and administratively.

The sponsors are represented at the top of the figure 1. In ESGF, sponsors include DOE[7] (main funder), European Commission (EC) and others. For the ESGF operations there are tens of data centers around the globe that are working on data projects represented in the form of an oval in figure 1. The data projects vary in their nature and thematic area within the climate science domain. These data projects are known as data holdings. It is expected that in future the ESGF data archive system will serve the data holdings from the domains other than climate science as well [19]. CMIP5[8] is an example of one of the main projects of ESGF being served by ESGF data archive system represented in the form of a cylinder, in the figure 1. From CMIP5, data has been used to generate IPCC AR5[9] report on the basis of which political decisions are made. Looking at the history of ESGF, one can predict that in future the data holdings will keep on increasing. If users have specific queries about these data holdings then climate specialists are needed to be consulted. This implies that users need to have contact details of persons who can provide guidelines about scientific questions. Entertaining scientific queries is currently not an explicit part of the user support system in ESGF.

A node (represented in the figure 1, at the bottom) may have four different roles or flavors within itself as stated by Cinquini et al. [20]. These flavors are shown by the words "Data, Gateway, Security and Compute" attached to each node (see bottom part of the figure 1). The nodes including their respective flavors are managed by a particular team in an administrative body at a particular location in the world. "Data" stands for data holdings hosted by a node (also known as data node). A number attached the word "Data", for instance (or any of the four words mentioned before) represents the number of data nodes being hosted and maintained by a single administrative body. For example, if there is a label "3Data" it means that there are three data nodes which are managed by a particular administrative body. Every node has at least a data holding(s) part or flavor in it, by default. Additionally, a node may have a gateway "Gateway", a security set-up "Security" and a compute facility "Compute" as shown in the figure 1. A gateway is responsible for representing the data sets available in ESGF system to a user via user interface (UI) to interact with the system.

In ESGF terminology a security part of a node is also known as an identity provider "IdP". Security part of a node is responsible for registration, identification and authorization of a user to ensure that a user is a valid entity who is entitled to access data sets available in the ESGF system. A user accesses a data-set(s) hosted by the ESGF system via its UI "Gateway" from any ESGF node via single-sign on (SSO)[10]. The compute part of node is responsible for computing and visualization in ESGF via High Performance Computers (HPC) in a particular administrative body. The subsystems or system components in ESGF are distributed worldwide. The behaviour of

---

[7] Department Of Energy, USA.
[8] Coupled Model Intercomparison Project – phase 5.
[9] Intergovernmental Panel on Climate Change-Fifth Assessment Report.
[10] SSO facilitates a user to access multiple nodes without providing identification keys (e.g. a certificate) to each node separately.

each component effect each other and the user support system as well. For instance; the network topology of the ESGF P2P network directly influences its management and administration structure.

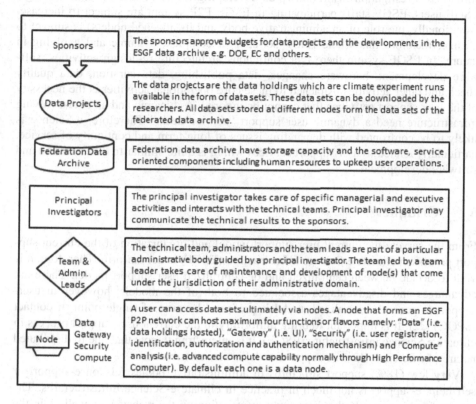

Fig. 1. e-Science infrastructure organization model in climate science domain and its elements

ESGF is stated as: "The Earth System Grid Federation (ESGF) is a multi-agency, international collaboration of people and institutions working together to build an open source software infrastructure for the management and analysis of Earth Science data on a global scale." [21] However, in this ESGF definition, user support services are not explicitly made part of the definition of ESGF. Keeping the anatomy of ESGF P2P data archive system in view, the user support system of ESGF has its sub-units. Though these sub-units are not formally designated as support units within administrative bodies, the support units are implicitly part of administrative bodies. Consequently, from the geographically distributed organization of ESGF P2P network, it is understandable that each and every administrative domain has its own practices of handling user-requests. This observation is also evident from the qualitative cum quantitative inquiry into the user support practices of ESGF undertaken by the authors. The diversity of practices in handling user queries by the user support staff, who themselves are developers of the ESGF system, form different support structures and models in each of the administrative domains, hence making a heterogeneous user support process. Subsequently, the user support system in ESGF does not comply with any set standards of processing user support requests.

From the figure 1, one can anticipate that the numbers of administrative bodies (principal investigation institutions plus developing teams of ESGF), data holdings, ESGF users, ESGF staffs participating in ESGF P2P system are subject to increase. Additionally, the role of an administrative body and its attached node(s) is subject to change, therefore this whole ESGF set-up is a complex, dynamic and evolving in nature. In ESGF system there is a continuous architecture re-design activities, software development, hardware changes, data publishing, data curation, data quality check and other activities. Attached to these core operational activities is the necessity of the user support activities that cannot be ignored. A dynamic and an ever-evolving infrastructure need a dynamic user support "service desk." Therefore, e-Science is likely to be confronted with demanding issues of long-term and continuity of service, particularly related to user support services which is quite similar to data curation and software development.

5   Critique

From the survey, the current user support model and organization of the current support process in climate e-Science infrastructure (ESGF) is not uniform. Therefore, it is vital to decide between centralized and de-centralized user support model. There are advantages and disadvantages associated to both of the models; however in user-support in general, centralized model is preferred because of single point of contact (SPOC) [22]. It is important to bring uniformity in the current user support process in climate e-Science infrastructure (ESGF). It is interesting to note that due to distributed nature of e-Science, the user support model is also distributed.

Very few (18%) support structures in administrative bodies rely on e-support or self-help. e-support is not much in practice in climate e-Science infrastructures. The reason for this is partly the distributed information on the websites as well as in the Wikis which is not completely known to users. On top of this, the information is not updated regularly. e-support should be promoted in climate e-Science projects. A practice should be followed that the users before writing to the help desk, try to get e-support by looking at the associated web sites and Wikis at first, to locate the relevant information.

The update of user-support information on the user support portal(s) should be made regular. A Service Level Agreement (SLA) can be suggested, where the concerned support staff updates the information regularly. The information can be checked by other support staff or a usability expert to make sure that these communication materials are accessible, easy to grasp and are understandable. Since there is no standardized classification into levels of escalation such as Second Level Support (SLS) and First Level Support (FLS); it is important to develop a norm. A support unit must stick to a particular global norm or a standard that may be introduced in the support structure of climate science e-Science infrastructures.

An effort could be made to reduce the time of personal response by introducing FLS employees covering various time-zones. For example, if a user has forwarded a request in Europe then it is vital to reply him/her from a support staff working within European time-zones. The greater the time of personal response, the lesser would be the efficiency of support process and the lesser would be the satisfaction of users. An flexible SLA or a quasi-SLA can be introduced in this case where up to 1 (working) day at maximum could be set as a standard i.e. the maximum time for personal reply. In case a concerned support staff is not available (e.g. on holidays etc.) then ersatz or substitute support staff should be available to service the user-requests in each support unit. This is very much appropriate in terms of showing empathy (building customer confidence in the support process) to the end-user because end-user might get frustrated if s/he does not get a personal reply.

Majority of ESGF employees who do user support (almost 80%) do not use automatic reply mechanism. It is important (in case of a request tracking system) to use automatic reply mechanism. The automatic reply should preferably look like a personalized message and not a machine response. The support process will improve if the reply time between support staff (e.g. between first and second level support staff) can be reduced. This can be achieved by an agreement or introducing a SLA for delegated response. A standard is needed to be defined and the support staffs who receive the delegated user-request might follow the SLA or an agreement. This will improve a delegated response time.

It is important to get the suggestions from users and encourage their participation for a number of reasons: Firstly, their feedback can improve the support process. Secondly, one can get an insight into their level of satisfaction. Thirdly, they may rate the solution suggested by the support staff. Finally, since the number of users is not so high, a personal interaction may create mutual trust, empathy and better relationship amongst end-users and the support staff.

Most of the support staffs (80%) do not collect user statistics and user request statistics. It is important to collect user-statistics to know:

- The users-base (coming from different continents).
- To be able to measure the overall user satisfaction.
- It is important to have statistics in order to measure total number of incoming requests versus resolved requests.
- It is important to try different suggestions to solve similar problem to find out a better solution etc. And to archive these solutions.

The first author has experienced from his participatory observation and meetings with other support staff that, at the moment in e-Science projects, in the support process both "Mailing Lists" (ML) and "Request Tracking tools" (RT) are used in parallel. According to ESGF support staff they need mix of mailing list's features and request tracking tool's features, mostly advantages of both. Therefore, in e-Science support process it is important to decide whether to use either RT or ML or a combination of both. An investigation should be done in this area to get a further opinion of the e-Science support staff and end-users to find out that which communication media is viable in e-Science projects of climate science.

It is important to note that there is no involvement of pure domain scientists in the user support process. It is significant to have a collaboration and exchange or sharing of knowledge between technical experts and pure scientific experts (also known as domain experts). Therefore, there is a need to incorporate scientific experts.

Since there are no dedicated user support employees, the employees of ESGF perform other activities parallel to supporting users. These activities affect support activity or vice versa, therefore it is important to have a dedicated support staff, preferably not as advanced as the current one. For instance, in ESGF top computer scientist are handling the simple and routine user queries. Simple and routine user queries may only be handled by FLS. People from developing countries may be employed to handle simple and routine queries. For the SLS, a norm can be created where a standard could be set in future where a support staff have to plan or reserve part of his/her time as a quota for user support activity. Some priority, recognition or value should be assigned to the user-support time in a working day where one can give as much or more credit to the support activity performed by the user-support staff as other activities that the support staff may perform in parallel. It is important to keep support activity productive and alive. It must be ensured by the support staff that all user queries are addressed properly.

6   Discussion

From the organization of ESGF e-Science infrastructure and the survey results one can say that the staffs who are involved in user-support process are over qualified to undertake first-level support activities which can be categorized as simple and routine. The employees of ESGF may rather be used as specialist for SLS or more levels of user support escalations. The (user-support) process owners who are active human support agents in different parts of the world may be nominated by the executive committee of ESGF from key institutes may recruit and educate the user support staff that may be engaged at the first line of user support as FLS preferably from climate computing institutes or universities in developing countries. The service provided by human support agents will not only be economical but also good for developing countries to not only promote the use of cyber-infrastructure of a particular in the local research arena of a developing country but also to introduce it in university curricula within developing countries. The training of the FLS staff from training countries may be done by the key process owners of the user staff by online sessions and development of instructive guidelines. As there is an upsurge in user queries with the passage of time due to inclusion of new data projects and increase of users of ESGF, it is important to start an initiative at this stage.

The technical and intellectual capacities in the developing countries are immense as already demonstrated by some of high-tech initiatives started there. For instance, formed more than a decade ago, National Database and Registration Authority (NADRA) is a high-tech initiative in Pakistan that proves advancement in IT sector and capability to develop high-tech solutions [23]. Moreover, for the people who reside in a particular region (urban or rural) in developing countries, an adaptive user interface (UI) can be designed that would fit the cultural background, language and interface expectation. Doing so may make it easier for them to get access to data-sets offered by a e-Science infrastructure as well as to get self-help or e-support. A UI can be created by the group of people who will be local human support agents after doing research. Furthermore, the time zones can be covered too, by allocating FLS at different time-zones. Outsourcing of parts of software of an e-Science infrastructure may be engineered in some developing countries economically and effectively.

7   Conclusion

In this study, it is evident from the observations that the user support within e-Science infrastructures in climate science is not being paid attention to and use support needs to be redefined within a complex and dynamic nature of e-Science infrastructures. In climate e-Science infrastructure there is no position of dedicated user support manager. The staffs of e-Science infrastructure are doing other activities apart from user support activities. The employees of e-Science infrastructure in climate domain, who are top computer scientists, are handling simple and routine user enquires. Handling of simple and routine user enquires might be economical to transfer to the institutes in developing countries care of by the staffs of e-Science infrastructure; once the e-Science support process in climate science and other domains is systematized. Currently, the authors are working on a conceptual model to systematize and standardize e-Science use support system in the climate domain. In this paper, a generalized organization structure of e-Science infrastructure, at least in climate domain but not limited to it, is presented. In the future, the authors will observe the effectiveness of transferring front line user support units to various institutes in developing countries.

Acknowledgement. We appreciate the sincere support of DKRZ and ESGF colleagues Dean Williams, Stephan Kindermann and others, including users who took part in our survey.

References

1. Leung, N., Lau, S.: Information technology help desk survey: To identify the classification of simple and routine enquiries. J. Comput. Inf. Syst. (2007)
2. Leung, N.K.Y.: University of Wollongong Thesis Collection Turning user into first level support in help desk: Development of web-based user self-help knowledge management system (2006)
3. Jäntti, M.: Improving IT Service Desk and Service Management Processes in Finnish Tax Administration: A Case Study on Service Engineering. pp. 218–232 (2012)
4. Jäntti, M.: Lessons Learnt from the Improvement of Customer Support Processes: A Case Study on Incident Management. In: Bomarius, F., Oivo, M., Jaring, P., Abrahamsson, P. (eds.) PROFES 2009. LNBIP, vol. 32, pp. 317–331. Springer, Heidelberg (2009)
5. Jäntti, M.: Examining Challenges in IT Service Desk System and Processes: A Case Study (c), 105–108 (2012)
6. Hey, A., Trefethen, A.: The data deluge: An e-science perspective. pp. 1–17 (January 2003)

7. Hey, T., Trefethen, A.E.: Cyberinfrastructure for e-Science. Science 308(5723), 817–821 (2005)
8. Buyya, R., Venugopal, S.: A Gentle Introduction to Grid Computing and Technologies (July 2005)
9. Jirotka, M., Lee, C.P., Olson, G.M.: Supporting Scientific Collaboration: Methods, Tools and Concepts. Comput. Support. Coop. Work (Ci) (January 2013)
10. Graham, J., Hart, B.: Knowledgebase Integration with a 24-hour Help Desk (2000)
11. Leung, N., Lau, S.: Relieving the overloaded help desk: A knowledge management approach. Int. Inf. Manag. ... 6(2), 87–98 (2006)
12. Jäntti, M., Kalliokoski, J.: Identifying Knowledge Management Challenges in a Service Desk: A Case Study. In: 2010 Second Int. Conf. Information, Process. Knowl. Manag., pp. 100–105 (Febraury 2010)
13. Roth-Berghofer, T.: Learning from HOMER, a case-based help desk support system. Adv. Learn. Softw. Organ., pp. 88–97 (2004)
14. Soehner, C., Steeves, C., Ward, J.: E-Science and Data Support Services (August 2010)
15. Kendall, H.: Prehistoric Help Desk!! Support World. Help Desk Institute, pp. 6–8 (October-November 2002)
16. Potgieter, B.C.: Evidence that use of the ITIL framework is effective (2002)
17. Arora, A.: IT Service Desk Process Improvement – A Narrative Style Case Study (2006)
18. Lazar, J., Feng, J., Hochheiser, H.: Research Methods in Human-Computer Interaction. Wiley, Indianapolis (2010)
19. Williams, D.N., Bell, G., Cinquini, L., Fox, P., Harney, J., Goldstone, R.: Earth System Grid Federation: Federated and Integrated Climate Data from Multiple Sources. vol. 6, pp. 61–77 (2013)
20. Cinquini, L., Crichton, D., Mattmann, C., Harney, J., Shipman, G., Wang, F., Ananthakrishnan, R., Miller, N., Denvil, S., Morgan, M., Pobre, Z., Bell, G.M., Drach, B., Williams, D., Kershaw, P., Pascoe, S., Gonzalez, E., Fiore, S., Schweitzer, R.: The Earth System Grid Federation: An open infrastructure for access to distributed geospatial data. In: 2012 IEEE 8th International Conference on E-Science, pp. 1–10 (2012)
21. Williams, D.N.: Earth System Grid Federation (ESGF): Future and Governance World Climate Research Programme (WCRP), Working Group on Coupled Modelling (WGCM)— Stakeholders and ESGF. pp. 1–17 (2012)
22. Middleton, I.: The Evolution of the IT Help Desk: From Crisis Centre to Business Manager in the Public and Private Sectors. MSC Thesis. The Robert Gordon University. Aberdeen, UK (1999)
23. Gelb, A., Decker, C.: Cash at Your Fingertips: Biometric Technology for Transfers in Developing Countries. Rev. Policy Res. 29(1), 91–117 (2012)

Increasing Family Involvement in Elderly Care

Jasper Jeurens, Koen van Turnhout, and René Bakker

HAN University of Applied Sciences
Department of Information Technology, Communication and Media
Ruitenberglaan 26, 6826 CC Arnhem, The Netherlands
jasperjeurens@gmail.com, {koen.vanturnhout,rene.bakker}@han.nl

Abstract. This paper describes the design and field trial of the *Dynamic Collage*, a system which aims support extended family members to take part in the care for an elderly person in a light way manner by sending photos to a digital frame in the elderly home. We evaluated the dynamic collage in a field trial of 4-6 weeks with two families, yielding positive results. Photo-sharing was seen as a valuable contribution by the elderly person and all family members, it provided narrative support for visitors of the elderly and it led to an increased awareness of caregiving behavior and increased cohesion in the family. The study shows there is an opportunity to include Awareness Systems and Persuasive Technology within a participation ecology, which could be beneficial for health care.

Keywords: Persuasive Technology, Awareness System, Health Care.

1   Introduction

Because of reforms in Dutch healthcare which aim for more self-care and a receding government, informal caregiving has become a key theme. Increasingly, adult children or other relatives will have to provide elderly care. Not surprisingly, healthcare institutes have expressed interest in exploring ways of including informal care for residents in these institutes [1,2,3,4]

In cooperation with three healthcare institutes we have set up a case study directed at designing an application that improves relationships between professionals and family of residents. Because of this wide open problem definition, we used 1-10-100 [5] as a method for involving stakeholders in the design process. We used provocative prototypes to collect information and gain a better understanding of the context. We found that in many cases, some family members were highly involved with the care for their partner, mother or father, but most were at a distance. Also, this distance became larger over time.

Therefore, we wished to design an application that might restore the interest and involvement of family members at a distance. The resulting Dynamic Collage [DC] shared many characteristics with Social Awareness systems [6] such as the digital family portrait [7], Astra [8], the social health display [9] and the whereabouts clock [10]. It also exploits principles of persuasive technology [18]. In this paper, we discuss development and design of DC, and show evaluation results. The results suggest

A. Marcus (Ed.): DUXU 2014, Part IV, LNCS 8520, pp. 403–411, 2014.

that DC influences family behavior positively. After discussing the design and evaluation we discuss the relations between the DC and existing work more explicitly.

2   Design Case

2.1   1:10:100; Three Independent, Concurrent Design Cycles

To make sure the design solution would fit the expectations and the (unarticulated) needs of the clients, we used the 1:10:100 method to include them in the design process actively.

1:10:100 promotes 'radical innovation', and allows flexibility throughout the design project by completing the project in three complete, independent, concurrent cycles with an increasing time span. Each cycle consisted of user-centered design steps, determining requirements, creating design solutions and testing the design solutions. The development oriented triangulation framework [12] was used to ensure balance of research within the iterations.

In each design cycle, we presented provocative design solutions to the clients in a quality review board (QRB), in which framing and settling a more specific focus for the next cycle could take place. The outcome of the first QRB led to a focus on improving communication in informal care participants, while the second QRB resulted in a distinction of primary and secondary caregivers, and the identification of an opportunity to include the secondary caregivers (mostly socially or physically remote, passive family members) in the care process [13].

Next we studied the diversity of ways in which family members can take part in family care. It became clear that there is a wide array of things family members can do that have a positive effect on the well-being of a resident in a care home. Family members can provide practical caregiving like cleaning, administering medicine or taking care of laundry, but they can also deliver social-emotional care through paying a visit, taking someone out for a walk or trip, making a phone call or simply "being there" for a person by being physically near1.

We created a framework (figure 1), identifying four phases that influence decision making in informal care participation. First, the personal background, awareness, emotions and personality traits play a role in caregiving: we called this background. Second, family members had to make a decision for an visit or other form of contact. Thirdly, a contact moment took place in one form or the other. Finally, family members made an evaluation or reflection took place.

In a co-creation session, we invited participants to identify and qualify the different connections between the phases. Participants recognized the phases and could provide many stories sketching the connections between the different phases. In the end, the actions in each phase turned out to result in consequences for the others, depicted

---

1   Many definitions for informal caregiving (or the Dutch equivalent 'mantelzorg') exist. For this study, 'Informal caregiving' will be considered in its most broad sense, and can in light of the DFC be considered as 'visiting the elder person'.

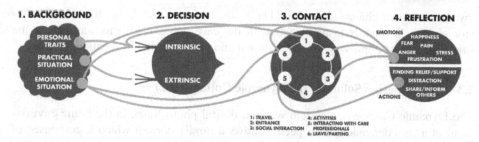

Fig. 1. Framing of the caregiving process and its internal and external relations divided in different steps; Before (condition), During (contact) and After (reflection)

as the gray lines connecting the four separate phases (figure 1); all phases are heavily intertwined. Discussing the framework enabled us to identify the most important motivators for taking part in informal caregiving, including existing problems and opportunities for improvement. We found the presence of strong social ties and social cohesion as a family to be a major motivation for deciding to take part in informal care, and improving cohesion became a core target for the final design.

2.2   Theories for Behavioral Change

The first two cycles of 1-10-100 led to a desire of understanding possibilities to change behavior of relatives surrounding a care dependant elderly person. To gain a quick understanding of theories of behavioral change, we consulted two psychologists. This led to a quick identification of the most important theories in the field and an idea of how they could apply to our work. According to [14], four mainstream theories on behavioral change are the TransTheoretical Model (TTM) [15], the Health Belief Model (HBM)[16],The Social Cognitive Theory (SCT) [17] and the Theory of Planned Behavior (TPH) [18]. All of these theories focus on a context of a personal and big behavioral change. These changes can be triggered by events with a huge impact.

Family relations were dwindling in the families we consulted, so few individual high impact triggers to change behavior exist. Latent guilt, loyalty and shortage of attention and time play a dominant role in these families. These are all elements that fit within the motivation and ability dimensions of Fogg's Behavior Model (BFM) [19]; Lack of motivation spawns from feelings of emotional distance and/or social rejection within the family, whereas physical distance and lack of available time are characteristic for one's disability to join.

Because big impact triggers do not seem feasible in an environment where both motivational and ability issues are apparent, we have chosen for interactions that can be ignored of require very little attention; the individual user experience should blend in their daily lives. This is in line with Fogg's suggestion for a modest approach

towards behavior change in general [11]. Instead of trying to design for radical behavior change in regards to participation in the care process, a focus was put on the
smaller issues of improving the motivational and ability problems mentioned earlier.

2.3   Final Design Solution: the Dynamic Collage (DC)

The Dynamic Collage is a system where a digital photo frame in the home environment of a care dependent elder person shows a family portrait which is composed of
separate pictures sent by family members (figure 2).

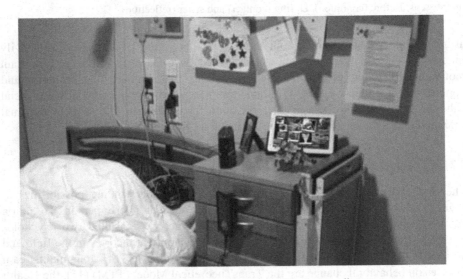

Fig. 2. The DC prototype in context of its surroundings

The composition of the joined portrait is based on data gathered by the system:
members who have participated by visiting will be more visually prominent in the
composition: those pictures have a larger size and are positioned closer to the elder.
When members don't show involvement, their part of the composition will suffer in
size and opacity (figure 3).

Family members can update their part of the portrait only in the event of a trigger:
occurring when someone is around the vulnerable elder person (for example someone
visiting). The result is a composition made from snapshots of 'mundane' moments, all
taken at the specific time of a trigger, rather than the most interesting or precious
events in people's lives. After sending the photos, the new composition will be visible
on the photo frame of the resident, as well as on the mobile phones of the users.

We had 4 goals in mind for the design:

1. Disclosure of informal caregiving behavior to the extended family.
2. Lightweight involvement through contextual photos
3. Supporting commitment and interaction
4. Strengthening social (group)ties

Fig. 3. The composition on the tablet computer. One of the pictures is faded as a result of lacking participation.

3   Field Trial

3.1   Setup

A field trial, using a Wizard of Oz setup [20], was performed to evaluate the effectiveness of the dynamic collage. We wanted insight in changing participation patterns and involvement of the extended family in the care process.

Two test groups took part in the trial. The first group was a family surrounding an 87 year old woman in a nursing home. The eleven participants included all of her four adult children, three of their partners, and all four adult grandchildren. This test group used the dynamic collage for six weeks. The second group was a family surrounding an 88 year old woman who was still living at her own house. This family had sixteen participants, including adult children, adult grand children and their partners. This second test group ran for four weeks.

The families worked with a prototype of the system on a tablet computer. It showed the dynamic collage which was created by the researcher, acting as a Wizard of Oz, behind the scenes. Visiting family members would announce their visit to the wizard, who would inform the family members with a kind reminder to send a picture, which were in turn converted in a dynamic collage during the visit. This setup ran without major problems [13].

We held weekly semi-structured interviews with different participants of each group. We used these interviews to check if participants had been following instructions, and gather their experiences and opinions about the themes involved in the design. In particular we asked participants about the usability of the system, awareness, disclosure, lightweight involvement, and possible unforeseen effects. We held face-to-face interviews with the adult children (4 in both test groups) in the first week and near the end of the trial. We held interviews by telephone with the more distant relatives (grandchildren) in the remaining weeks of the trial.

4 Field Trial Results

(Group) Awareness. Results from the trial suggest the dynamic collage contributed to awareness of the informal caregiving behavior. A notable finding was that, in particular, the family members who participated less in informal care evaluated this awareness positively. The trial showed that family members who considered themselves to be more (socially) distant were now able to predict and see patterns in the informal caregiving behavior of others. When asked about their experience of caregiving awareness, one of our participants, a grandchild in the first group remarked: *"I suddenly realized holy shit, M. is going there 4 times a week"*, showing that the amount of time invested by other family members had sunk in.

More surprisingly, the dynamic collage allowed family members to recognize abnormalities in the weekly routine. The partner of one of the daughters in test group 1 explained *"patterns become visible; I could see that it's Monday: Oh, then I guess this and this person will be there again"*. The awareness of irregularities resulted in information that would otherwise not reach them, as was plain when one of the more active caregivers in group 1 fell ill; *"I found out about things I would never have known about otherwise, like when M was ill"*. While the group dealt with this particular illness adequately, it is likely that such an awareness of caregiving behavior can contribute to keeping the family closer together as a functional group in other cases.

Lightweight Photo Sharing as Narrative Support. Users showed particular effort in making their photos meaningful. This is in line with previous work by Romero et al. [8] that shows how much people value personally targeted effort. The system was designed with the intent to create awareness of people's lives by encouraging sharing photos of 'everyday moments'. However, the trial showed that participant sent photos with a functional goal in mind: helping the visitor in his or her social interaction with the elderly person by having something to talk about. We were surprise how much photos were created and used as a narrative support for the visiting family caregiver.

Biemans and van Dijk [21] reported similar results and suggested the everyday events are of less value for the elderly because, due to the generation gap, they no longer play a part in these everyday lives and therefore have trouble understanding the pictures. The trial in this paper shows that this holds true for sharing towards family members of the same age group as well. This suggests that sharing mundane, everyday events is seen as less valuable even when such photos can be understood by the receiving party. In both studies, the digital photo frame resulted in opportunities for 'food for talk'.

During the design we wondered whether sending photos could be seen as valuable contributions to caregiving. Arguably, a mismatch in invested effort and 'reward' could result in more strained relations, which would be counterproductive to the goal of uniting and connecting the family. Remarkably, the family members from both test groups who were visiting reported the functional use of photo sharing as very helpful and valuable.

This also meant that contributions to our system were less lightweight than intended: because people wanted to make a meaningful contribution (instead of sending a 'random' photo) the act of updating one's picture became a task of some effort. This made the photo itself valuable to both the receiver and the sender. Because of this participants complained about the short turnaround time of the photos: "I think it's somewhat of a waste to put a lot of effort into [making] a picture when it could be replaced the very next day".

Social Connectedness, Group Attraction. Photo sharing also led to an increased sense of connectedness among some of its users. When interviewed, one of the grandchildren mentioned quite literally that the regular sending of photos meant that "the family was now more connected".

The forced, specific timeframe to send photo updates gave all sent photos a 'timestamp' as common attribute. For example, when someone was visiting eight o'clock in the evening, all sent photos would be of an evening atmosphere. This awareness of being involved in the same activities contributed to a sense of unity; "It was really nice to see all the pictures coming in when everyone was having dinner, it was like we're having dinner together".

Changing Family Behaviors. The system succeeded in giving the secondary family caregivers a way 'in' for the care process: although actual visits remained low in number, secondary caregivers contributed with photos which were valued by the elderly person and the primary caregiver. However, we hoped the system would also inspire less active family members to increase their involvement by interaction more with the elderly person outside of the system and this was not achieved. Arguably, such changes in communication patterns within a family need time to settle, but the users did not expect the system to encourage more involvement outside of the system; they reported that the threshold to engage in ways of communication was simply too high.

5   Conclusions

In this paper we discussed the user-centered design and field trial of the dynamic collage, a system that seduces more distant family members to take part in the caregiving process of an elderly person by sending photos to a digital frame at the elderly residence during a visit of another elderly member. These photos turned out to provide food for talk for the visitor and elderly, creating a sense of community and awareness of caregiving in the family that was valued by our participants. The system shares characteristics with Awareness Systems [6] and Persuasive Technology [11] embedded in what Gerard Fisher calls a Participation Ecology [22]. Participation Ecologies are socio-technological systems which support a rich set of smaller and bigger contributions in a joint 'barn raising project'. Participation Ecologies arise in open source communities and other co-creative online systems, such as Wikipedia and Scatch. The Dynamic Collage is a step in this direction. The Dynamic Collage supports multiple roles and contributions and it makes sure these contributions can come together in an innovative, meaningful and positive way.

Because of this, our design efforts move beyond seminal Awareness Systems such as the Digital Family Portrait [7], the Whereabouts Clock [10] Social Health Displays [9]. These examples are information centric awareness systems. Awareness is provided through a display of automatically captured data. The dynamic collage, in contrast, supports awareness as a collateral benefit from a communication centric system. Family members are allowed co-create the dynamic collage, and experience the result - and the benefits for the elderly person and her visitor - as a joint achievement. The idea of participation ecologies provides a useful lens for our efforts to achieve Persuasion as well. For many family members paying a regular visit to the elderly person is, in terms of Fogg's behavior model [19], too demanding on both the axes motivation and ability. We facilitated those family members with a) a trigger to b) a rather undemanding task in terms of motivation and ability (sending a photo). But we did not replace the demanding task with an easier one. In our participation ecology the 'easy tasks' become a visible and valuable contribution to the full process. Both types of users valued this. Visiting family members felt supported and seen, and non-visiting family members appreciated the opportunity to make a contribution.

Clearly, a participation ecology with only two roles may not be particularly rich enough to be sustainable in the long run. Although usage patterns in the field trial stabilized, participants commented on photo-sharing as an activity which they did not imagine doing for a much longer time. Enriching the dynamic collage so that more roles, types of triggers, and types of activities are supported is key. Therefore, we are currently looking further into the field of persuasive interfaces [11], investigating integration with traditional social media infrastructures [23] and searching evaluative measures which can help us to get a sharper eye on relation to motivational goals, persuasion and long-term user experience.

References

1. Ministerie van Volksgezondheid, Welzijn en Sport. De zorg, hoeveel extra is het ons waard? (2012),
   http://www.rijksoverheid.nl/onderwerpen/
   betaalbaarheid-van-de-zorg
2. ActiZ organisatie voor zorgondernemers, Expertizecentrum informele zorg (2007). Samenspel met Mantelzorg publicatienummer (ActiZ publication no. 07.001) (2007),
   http://www.expertisecentrummantelzorg.nl/sma,
   http://www.expertisecentrummantelzorg.nl/
   smartsite.dws?ch=DEF&id=113926
3. Sociaal Cultureel Planbureau, Evaluatie WMO (2010),
   http://www.rijksoverheid.nl/onderwerpen/
   wet-maatschappelijke-ondersteuning-wmo
4. Vilans 'De bewoners en hun familie zijn ons uitgangspunt' (2011),
   http://www.vilans.nl/vilans.net?id=13243

5. van Turnhout, K., Hoppenbrouwers, S., Jacobs, P., Jeurens, J., Smeenk, W., Bakker, R.: Requirements from the Void: Experiences with 1:10:100. In: 19th International Working Conference on Requirements Engineering: Foudation for Software Quality (REFSQ 2013): ICB-Rsearch Report No. 56, Duisburg Essen. Universität Duisbrug-Essen, ICB, pp. 31-40 (2013)

6. Markopoulos, P., De Ruyter, B., Mackay, W.: Awareness systems: Advances in theory. Springer, Heidelberg (2009)

7. Rowan, J., Mynatt, E.D.: Digital Family Portrait Field Trial: Support for Aging in Place, pp. 521–530 (2005)

8. Markopoulos, P., Romero, N., van Baren, J., et al.: Keeping in Touch with the Family: Home and Away with the ASTRA Awareness System, pp. 1351–1354 (2004)

9. Morris, M.E.: Social Networks as Health Feedback Displays. IEEE Internet Computing 9, 29–37 (2005)

10. Sellen, A., Taylor, A.S., Brown, B., et al.: Supporting family awareness with the whereabouts Clock. In: Markopoulos, P., De Ruyter, B., Mackay, W. (eds.) Awareness Systems: Advances in Theory, Methodology, and Design, pp. 425–445. Springer, Heidelberg (2009)

11. Fogg, B.J.: Persuasive Technology: using computers to change what we think and do. Ubiquity, 2002(5)

12. van Turnhout, K., Craenmehr, S., Holwerda, R., Menijn, M., Zwart, J.P., Bakker, R.: Tradeoffs in Design Research: Development Oriented Triangulation. In: Proceedings of the 27th Annual BCS Interaction Specialist Group Conference on People and Computers. British Computer Society

13. Jeurens, J., van Turnhout, K., Bakker, R.: Family in Focus: On Design and Field Trial of the Dynamic Collage. In: Proceedings of Chi Sparks (2014)

14. Aalbers, T., de Lange, A.: The Brain Aging Monitor as Intervention. Draft Radboud UMC, Nijmegen (2013)

15. Prochaska, J.O., Velicer, W.F.: The transtheoretical model of health behavior change. American Journal of Health Promotion 12(1), 38–48 (1997)

16. Rosenstock, I.M., Strecher, V.J., Becker, M.H.: Social learning theory and the health belief model. Health Education & Behavior, 175-183 (1988)

17. Bandura, A.: Social cognitive theory of self-regulation. Organizational Behavior and Human Decision Processes 50(2), 248–287 (1991)

18. Fishbein, M., Ajzen, I.: Predicting and changing behavior: The reasoned action approach. Taylor & Francis (2011)

19. Fogg, B.J.: A Behavior Model for Persuasive Design. In: Persuasive. Claremont, California (2009)

20. Dahlbäck, N., Jönsson, A., Ahrenberg, L.: Wizard of Oz studies—why and how. Knowledge-Based Syst. 6, 258–266 (1993)

21. Biemans, M., van Dijk, B., Dadlani, P., et al.: Let's Stay in Touch: Sharing Photos for Restoring Social Connectedness between Rehabilitants, Friends and Family, pp. 179–186 (2009)

22. Fischer, G.: Understanding, Fostering, and Supporting Cultures of Participation. Interactions 18, 42–53 (2011)

23. van Turnhout, K., Holwerda, R., Schuszler, P., et al.: Interfacing between Social Media, Business Processes and Users. A Design Case Study. In: Proceedings of Chi Sparks (2011)

User Experience of Video-on-Demand Applications for smart TVs: A Case Study

Linda Miesler, Bettina Gehring, Frank Hannich, and Adrian Wüthrich

ZHAW Zurich University of Applied Sciences, Institute of Marketing Management,
Switzerland
linda.miesler@zhaw.ch

Abstract. The convergence of internet and TV and its consequences on TV producers as well as TV users has been a highly discussed topic over the past few years. With the rapid growth of high-speed broadband connections and the development of high-performance TVs, the foundation for the creation and proliferation of smarter TVs enabling the user with a more personalized viewing experience was laid. As a consequence, new business opportunities have opened up and new players have entered the market. Facing a rapidly changing environment with hardly any standards established yet, the consideration of customer satisfaction and user experience plays a major role. Especially in the entertainment industry, user experience is of high relevance and user-centered design an important precondition for service adoption. Therefore, the case study below investigated success factors and barriers which influence usage of a video-on-demand application for smart TVs. Based on a case study of a European video-on-demand service different usability evaluation methods had been applied and combined in order to evaluate and enhance platform performance.

Keywords: smart TV, Video-on-demand, User experience, Usability evaluation procedure, Closed loop.

1 Introduction

As a result of the increasing convergence of internet and TV, smart TVs are gaining popularity around the world, reshaping existing media usage patterns [1].

According to the definition of Shin, Hwang and Choo [2], a smart TV is a television set with integrated internet capabilities. Similar to smart phones, smart TVs allow users an increased control over content and timing and to choose from a more diverse range of content and applications such as video-on-demand [3].

However, a big variety of offerings as well as new market entrants have increased competition and made it difficult for the individual provider to succeed. Before adopting new applications and services, users must recognize their added value compared to existing services [4], which underlines the relevance of the concept of user experience [5] [6] [7].

The research at hand is based on a case study done in collaboration with a cloud-based video-on-demand service provider for the European market. The company was

A. Marcus (Ed.): DUXU 2014, Part IV, LNCS 8520, pp. 412–422, 2014.

founded in 2006 and is part of an international media corporation. They hold multinational license agreements with movie studios in Hollywood and Europe.

The video-on-demand service is offered via various end devices; the main focus, however, is on smart TV apps. The service is pre-installed on the smart TVs of all leading manufacturer brands, which represents an important competitive advantage for the company. It was a key goal of the provider to offer a unique experience to viewers ("Select a movie with a few clicks").

Although the initial position looked promising, the service provider faced the following challenges:

— Demand for the service was low. Only 1.08% of buyers of a new smart TV made use of the service. Of these, only 22.1% were paying customers. The reasons behind the restrained usage were not clear.
— There was a high market risk due to various alternative possibilities for the consumption of video-on-demand on smart TVs (e.g. digital TV of telecommunication providers and cable operators via set-top box, Apple TV etc.) and new players entering the market.

In order to be able to defend their current position and to establish video-on-demand via smart TV apps as standard for movie consumption, it was extremely important for the service to better understand the motives behind the limited use of the service. The present study was conducted for this reason. The specific objectives for the research were the following:

— Identifying and eliminating usage barriers based on an in-depth understanding of user needs, expectations and media consumption behavior
— Establishing an internal control process (closed loop) as a basis for developing and optimizing the service offering
— Helping to increase conversion (with regard to registration and purchases) and consumption rate (with regard to the amount spent per user) for the service as primary goals

Besides the specific goals which were formulated based on the app provider's problems, we further aimed at developing an integrated and generalizable usability evaluation procedure to gain in-depth knowledge about actual user behavior by analyzing existing and newly collected information.

2   Literature Review of Success Factors in smart TV (Application) Adoption and Usage

In order to identify success factors of smart TV applications and smart TVs in general, we conducted a literature review of existing studies. Not surprisingly, research on the adoption and usage of smart TV applications and its success factors is still scarce (as pointed out recently by Shin, Hwang, & Choo [2] or Ko, Chang & Chu [3]). Ko, Chang & Chu [3] distinguished between 21 functions for digital TV application services and found that apps like video-on-demand had the largest direct effect on the users' intention to adopt digital TV application services However, exactly what determines if users adopt and use such services is still an open question.

A few authors already investigated factors that drive the adoption of smart TVs in general [1] [2]. Lee [1] identified six key constructs deduced from several innovation adoption models (e.g., technology acceptance model (TAM), diffusion of innovation theory (DIT)) such as perceived usefulness / perceived ease of use, and perceived risk. However, due to the abstract manner of such concepts it was difficult to derive insights for our specific use case. Concepts like perceived usefulness strongly emphasize the user's utilitarian motives for smart TV adoption and usage. As a matter of fact, as the main goal of watching television is entertainment and relaxation [8], a smart TV also has to fulfil these hedonic user needs. In line with this, Shin, Hwang & Choo [2] formulated the challenge facing the smart TV industry as designing services that are "useful, valuable, enjoyable and, most importantly, user-centred". Their results suggested that usability is not the only important factor for technology adoption, but that utility and hedonism are also important. Hedonism can be fulfilled by both; content and interactive services. Therefore, smart TVs and their applications can be described as convergence of task-oriented and entertainment-oriented technology [2] [4]; the interplay of both creates the "user experience". Firms should not only create products and services which are easy to use, but deliver emotional experiences in order to create value for customers and differentiate from competitors [9]. In the field of entertainment services for mobile devices, Kim, Kim & Kil [4] pointed out the importance of intrinsic motivation for adoption of mobile entertainment services. Zhou [10] also examined the effect of flow experience on user adoption of mobile TV.

To sum up, it was possible to identify four insights from the literature: First, for the adoption and usage of video-on-demand as a specific smart TV application, we differentiate user experience from the technical usability concept. That means, we assumed that not only "effectiveness, efficiency and satisfaction" (cf., definition of ISO [11]) drive adoption and usage, but that user experience as a whole, including its functional and hedonic perspective, needs to be considered. Second, in contrast to existing usability studies that concentrate on user perceptions as determinants of smart TV adoption [1] [2], it was important that the present study focused on actual usage behavior. Third, existing studies mostly focus on the smart TV itself [4] [3], whereas we accentuated our research on one specific application of the smart TV (video-on-demand). Fourth, conclusions from existing studies should be treated with caution since most studies used Korean samples. It is important to remember that the European market does not behave in the same way like the Korean market. Korean consumers are more familiar with innovative technologies than European consumers due to technological advantage of Asian countries.

3   Usability Evaluation Procedure

There are different methodologies regarding usability and user experience evaluation which have proven effective. However, considering the multi-dimensionality of the usability construct, a multi-faceted approach seemed most appropriate. As has been shown, a combination of well-established methods allows the identification of usability problems from different perspectives and leads to better results than adopting only one single method. In addition, each method is capable of identifying usability problems that the other does not, therefore emphasizing the complementary value of the different evaluation methods [12].

Thus, a standard usability evaluation procedure for smart TV applications has been developed by combining several prevalent methods for usability evaluation in order to assess platform usability of the service (Fig. 1). To be able to compare the data collected with different methods, a user's typical "viewing journey" (i.e., registration for the service, searching, buying and watching a movie) was used as an underlying framework.

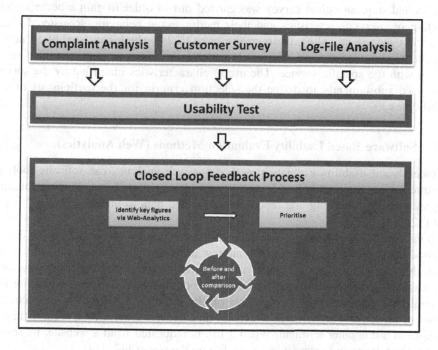

Fig. 1. Usability evaluation procedure

3.1   Service and Complaint Analysis

The assessment of service and complaint requests gives direct indications for difficulties occurring during the usage process. By evaluating service and complaint requests, general areas of concern can be identified which serve as inputs for further analysis.

In the context of the study, existing user complaints and service requests were analyzed to develop preliminary assumptions about factors which might be detrimental for service adoption. A sample (n = 256) of service and complaint requests accrued between May and October 2012 was categorized according to six content categories (registration, new movie releases, movie search, payment, play movie, language) including 15 sub-categories. The categorization gave an indication of major problems users were facing when using the service and provides the basic structure ("viewing journey") for subsequent steps.

It must be taken into consideration, however, that normally only paying customers and users with major problems complain; the others do not take the effort. Furthermore, of the users who are dissatisfied with the service generally only 20-30% complain [13]. This implies that service and complaint analysis is suitable for identifying urgent problems but less for revealing more subtle usability issues.

3.2   Online Survey

In a second step, an online survey was carried out in order to gain a better understanding of user characteristics and their media usage behavior. Registered users were surveyed via an online questionnaire (n = 3'224) which consisted of 57 items, covering media consumption behavior in general as well as perception of and satisfaction with the specific service. The users' characteristics identified by the survey were used subsequently to define the selection criteria for the participants of the usability test.

3.3   Software-Based Usability Evaluation Methods (Web Analytics)

Software-based usability evaluation methods or web analytics use software tools to measure service usage and identify usability problems. It involves collecting, measuring, analyzing, monitoring and reporting web usage data to understand users' behavior [12] [14].

In the case study at hand, log file data from the smart TV app was analyzed during a period of six months in order to find out how users navigate through the service and where breaches in the usage process arise. As data from previous periods was analyzed as well, a server-based log file analysis tool was chosen. Server-based log file techniques record the clicks of each user on the website. A log file is an electronic record of all request activities at a website that updates each time a request (hit) is made from a computer terminal. When a file is requested from a website, its server records the request and enters it into a log file on the server [12] [14].

The data collection process was twofold: First, the data was gathered on an aggregated level by linking the platform to an open source analysis tool. This allowed generating different web metrics (e.g. average time on site, average page views per visit) to measure platform usage and performance. Second, on an individual level, clickstream data was evaluated using approximating techniques. Most frequent user pathways were visualized with the purpose to illustrate users' click behavior and identify deviations from ideal paths. To suit firm-specific specifications, a special tool was developed which generated various reports based on the available log files.

In the usability evaluation procedure, log file analysis was used as a means of giving direction for the subsequent usability test by quickly indicating general usability problems or specific problem pages. By means of the log file analysis, the findings from preceding steps could be quantitatively supported and critical barriers in the usage process be drawn out.

3.4   Usability Test

Based on the preliminary evidence from step 1, in a laboratory usability test potential usage barriers and drivers were analyzed more deeply. Participants were selected based on criteria in accordance with results from the online survey on a typcial user (e.g., age range 30-50 years; moderate level of technical expertise). Sixteen participants without experience with the application were asked to verbalize their thoughts and feelings while solving eight scenarios (i.e., think aloud). The scenarios covered the full range of the viewing experience (e.g., registering for the service, browsing through movies). The test was accompanied by pre- and post-test interviews for further insights (e.g., expectation of video-on-demand service, semantic associations, and subjective satisfaction with usage experience).

4   Discussion of Main Results and Closed Loop Process

4.1   Results of the Case Study

The results of the online survey confirmed preliminary assumptions that the market for video on demand service is highly competitive and the commitment from users to a specific application low. They also emphasized the need for the service in question to design the user experience in accordance with user needs and to deliver a unique experience.

In the context of the service and complaint analysis, user requests were categorized along the viewing journey. Major areas of concern in the usage process turned out to be the login / registration as well as the payment process (e.g., problems with double movie bookings due to delayed remote feedback). Further problems were buffering and playback issues.

The log file analysis provided valuable evidence where breaches in the usage process arose and allowed to quantify their impact. Fig. 2 shows a landscape of the aggregated clickstream data for the video-on-demand service clustered according to the three main processes in the viewing journey 'searching', 'watching' and 'buying'. The ovals symbolize the different pages of the application; the numbers displayed represent the number of clicks on that specific page. The linkages between the boxes show the "jumps" between the pages, indicating the number of users that have taken a particular path. In total, there were 50 jumps of 10'000 different IP addresses. Users with more than 200 clicks were excluded as these most likely were system requests from computers.

Of particular interest were how many users entered the application, how many of them moved from "searching" to "watching" to "buying" as well as determining which stage saw the highest percentage of exits. The results of the analysis showed that first-time visitors are mostly stuck within the searching stage (82.9% of all clicks) and do not advance to the purchase stage. Thus, the majority of exits happen within the search process.

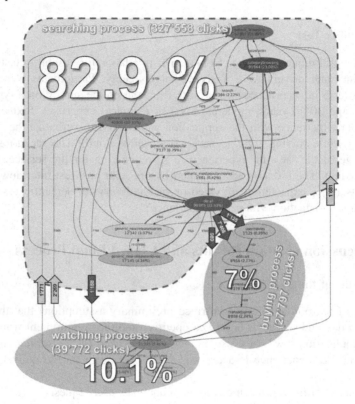

Fig. 2. Clickstream landscape

The usability test revealed some interesting findings on factors impairing the user's viewing experience. General findings were that inconsistent and incorrect wording as well as technical language both influenced user experience negatively. The navigation via remote control was perceived as difficult and was a reason for drop outs. Inconsistent interaction design and information architecture confused users and provoked unnecessary click rates, also impairing user experience.

In terms of the viewing journey mainly two parts of the "journey" stood out negatively during the usability testing. First, during the registration for the application, the interaction between the app and user via remote control impaired customer experience. For example, the response time of the application was very slow and the feedback was delayed after input via remote control, so the user perceived the interaction to be tiresome. Second, during the search phase, the text input via remote control was again a potential usage barrier. The inconsistent interaction design confused the user and resulted in unnecessary clicks: for instance, two buttons/fields were labelled "Back", but they differed in their functions (if user pushes the "wrong" back button, search results were lost). As emotions aroused by interaction with the application are an important component of a positive user experience, we analyzed "think aloud" protocols specifically with regard to emotional statements and categorized the statements as positive or negative emotional expressions. Three fifths of the identified emotional statements had a negative valence. Especially during the registration, negative emotions were elicited. Negative emotions were related to remote control, waiting times and navigation.

4.2   Closed Loop Control Process and Web Metrics

Based on the findings from steps 1 and 2, a concept for a closed loop optimization process was developed. For this reason, relevant key figures which reflect user experience quality and which can be extracted from log files (e.g., average page views per visit, percentage of exits during movie search, conversion rate) were identified and prioritized in order to establish a comprehensive in-house feedback system (Table 1). This serves as a starting point for the implementation of a continuous measurement and control process which allows the provider to evaluate the user interface systematically and to adapt it according to user requirements.

Table 1. Web metrics

General Metrics		
Indicator	Formula	Description
Average time on site/app		Measures how long a user spends time on the app. Time is a good indicator for website efficiency. The goal is not necessarily to reduce time to a minimum, but to optimize website architecture and navigation for a positive user experience.
Average page views		By measuring the average views of a specific page, changes can be tracked over time and irregularities identified.

(Table 1. *Continued.*)

Clickthrough rate (CTR)	$\dfrac{\text{number of clicks to a page}}{\text{number of views per process}}$	By measuring the average clicks to a specific page within the same process (e.g. watching process), it is possible to compare metrics over time and derive improvement measures (e.g. double clicks leading to double bookings in the payment process due to delayed remote feedback).
Jumps		Number of clicks ("jumps") from one process into the next.
Site exits per process		Counting the number of exits in total for a specific process (searching process, buying process, watching process). Exit points may indicate weaknesses in the usage process which should be tackled.
Percentage of high, medium and low frequency visitors		Indicates how often a user returns to the site. User behavior and derived metrics can be analyzed with regard to group differences (e.g. single or returning visitors).
Specific Metrics		
Indicator	Formula	Description
Conversion rate (registration)	$\dfrac{\text{number of registered users}}{\text{number of app accessors}}$	Measures how many users successfully register for the application.
Conversion rate (purchase)	$\dfrac{\text{number of purchases}}{\text{number of registered users}}$	Measures the number of successful purchases compared to the number of registrations.
Consumption rate (average order value)	Ø amount spent / user	Captures the average amount a user spends within a certain time period.

The specific combination of methods in this case study allows a holistic view of the customer experience and is able to measure the impact on key performance indicators (KPIs). The main problem areas with regard to user experience can be identified via survey and complaint analysis. These also form the basis for customer segmentation. The results can be linked to specific elements and pages of the app by means of the log file analysis and their impact can be quantified. Based on the findings from preliminary stages, the usability test can then be focused on the critical topics in order to gain more in-depth insights into the motivational and emotional aspects of the customer experience which are starting point for further development and optimization of the application. To close the loop, the impact of software changes on web metrics can be measured and controlled live, without time-lag, by web analytics techniques.

5   Conclusion

Concluding, by combining qualitative and quantitative methods, it was possible to take the perspective of the user and to optimize the user experience systematically with regard to customer value. While the most common problems in the usage process could be identified via log file analysis, the qualitative analysis delivered the underlying reasons. Based on the assessment of the relevant key figures developed as part of a closed loop feedback process, the service provider can in future quantify and measure the impact of changes in the service on actual user behavior and experience.

References

1. Lee, S.: A Study on Acceptance and Resistance of smart TVs. International Journal of Contents 8(3), 12–19 (2012)
2. Shin, D.-H., Hwang, Y., Choo, H.: smart TV: are they really smart in interacting with people? Understanding the interactivity of Korean smart TV. Behaviour& Information Technology 32(2), 156–172 (2013)
3. Ko, H.-T., Chang, C., Chu, N.-S.: An empirical investigation of the consumer demand for digital television application services. Behaviour& Information Technology 32(4), 397–409 (2013)
4. Kim, K., Kim, G.-M., Kil, E.S.: Measuring the compatibility factors in mobile entertainment service adoption. The Journal of Computer Information Systems 50(1), 141–148 (2009)
5. European Commission, Green Paper – on the online distribution of audiovisual works in the European Union: opportunities and challenges towards a digital single market (July 13, 2011), http://ec.europa.eu/internal_market/consultations/docs/2011/audiovisual/green_paper_COM2011_427_en.pdf (Febraury15, 2012)
6. Foscht, T., Swoboda, B.: Käuferverhalten: Grundlagen - Perspektiven - Anwendungen, 4th edn. Gabler, Wiesbaden (2011)
7. Scherf, K.: IPTV and the Digital Home. A Parks Associates white paper. Parks Associates, Dallas (2009)
8. Rubin, A.M.: Ritualized and Instrumental Television Viewing. Journal of Communication 34(4), 67–77 (1984)

9. Pine, B.J., Gilmore, J.H.: Welcome to the experience economy. Harvard Business Review 76(4), 97–106 (1998)
10. Zhou, T.: The effect of flow experience on user adoption of mobile TV. Behaviour& Information Technology 32(3), 263–272 (2013)
11. ISO, ISO 9241-11, international standard first edition. Ergonomic requirements for office work with visual display terminals (VDTs), part 11: guidance on usability (1998), http://www.it.uu.se/edu/course/homepage/acsd/vt09/ISO9241part11.pdf (August 29, 2012)
12. Hasan, L., Morris, A., Probets, S.: E-commerce websites for developing countries - A usability evaluation framework. Online Information Review 37(2), 231–251 (2013)
13. Schröder, R., Wall, F.: Controlling zwischen Shareholder Value und Stakeholder Value. OldenbourgVerlag, Munich (2009)
14. Wilson, R.D.: Using clickstream data to enhance business-to-business web site performance. Journal of Business & Industrial Marketing 25(3), 177–187 (2010)

Usability Methodological Procedures Applied on an Institutional Site

Lúcia Satiko Nomiso[1] and Luis Carlos Paschoarelli[2]

[1] Institute of Computing, Unicamp, Campinas, Brazil
{lucia.nomiso}@gmail.com
[2] Laboratory of Ergonomics and Interfaces, UNESP, Bauru, Brazil
{paschoarelli}@faac.unesp.br

Abstract. This study is based on the diverse usability methodological procedures, applied during 2008 and 2010, on an institutional site and brief review in 2013. Problems reported by potential users were analyzed and then applied in a redesign of the institutional site. After redesigning, more tests were performed in an attempt to improve the usability of site. In 2013, this institutional site was updated to a new version with reorganized structure and content. Our research presents the changes, the usability improvements applied as well as other advances improved the site significantly.

Keywords: Usability tests, Institutional site, CMS.

1 Introduction

Since the IHC beginning, web designers have been trying to provide access to information, avoiding any embarrassment to final users. This study is part of an essay describing usability methodological procedures results applied over a two-year period on an institutional site of the Graduate Program in Design at Universidade Estadual Paulista, which were intended to improve usability and provide best access to graduation programs. Considering the updates in 2013, a brief review was made to verify if web designers from the institute considered this research recommendation.

The methodological procedures were characterized by steps: Starting with the review theory, which reviews topics of usability followed by laboratory applications and practical simulations with potential users that reported possible usability problems. The stages of development were characterized by prototyping and reanalyzing evaluation results, culminating in a final prototype.

These results were considered satisfactory since it was verified that the use of CMS tools in the development of institutional sites improved their levels of usability. However, the main contribution of this study is to acquire new knowledge resulting from experiments as well as the increase in issues related to interface design, usability and ergonomic information, which collaborate effectively for the development of Ergonomic Design.

A. Marcus (Ed.): DUXU 2014, Part IV, LNCS 8520, pp. 423–433, 2014.

2   Review Theory

2.1   Usability

How well users can use the system is functionally dimensions of usability (Nielsen, 1993):

- **Learnability**: is it easy to learn?
- **Efficiency**: once learned, is it fast to use?
- **Visibility**: is the state of the system visible?
- **Errors**: are errors few and recoverable?
- **Satisfaction**: is it enjoyable to use?

Despite the existence of dimensions of usability, users can quantify all of these measures. Usability dimensions are not standard for all classes of users, for example: inexperienced users will require more learnability whereas expert users need more efficiency.

2.2   Information Architecture (IA)

It is an expression created by Wurman in 1996, as a new discipline emerged with the aim of organizing the information flow making it clear and understandable. (Duque and Vieira, 2008). Information Architecture for a complex site requires two base characteristics: a view from final user and a view from an expert. (Morville, 1998). One classic way to organize and get the initial insights into users' mental model of an information space is to simplify generating good starting for the IA (Nielsen, 2009).

Wireframes has the function of representing schematically all the elements that make up a website. Images, texts, forms, search engines and forms can be outlined in a paper or application making the layout more understandable with its information (Oliveira, 2008).

2.3   Accessibility

In Brazil, there is a national law (number 10.098 2000, chapter VI, art. 47), which regulates the accessibility for all websites that are administrated by the government, including institutional sites. According to SEPRO (Federal Service for Data Processing in Brazil), accessibility is present in a website when the page provides access to information for a large number of users, including users that require assistive technologies such as elderly and mobile users. Especially in Brazil, there are concerns over issues ranging from slow connections to users of outdated browsers and mobile devices. These concerns may not be relevant in developed countries.

The number of visual impairment searches in Brazil is high, according to IBGE (2010), Brazilian Institute of Geography and Statistics, 528.624 recorded users were completely blind and 35.791.488 suffered some visual impairment. Considering the WCAG 1.0 (Web Content Accessibility Guidelines) from W3C, it is possible to improve websites using the three levels of success criteria in the four principles, and develop a website to receive a higher number of users.

2.4   Aesthetic Factors that Increase Website Usability

Attractive things certainly should be preferred over ugly ones (Norman, 2004). Users will prefer attractive features, since other studies reported that screens arranged attractively are easier to use. To improve the attractive level in a website, web developers need to understand typography, worry about font size, legibility and contrast while considering indentation to structure, improving the information displayed on screen.

2.5   Search Engine Optimization (SEO)

SEO must be one of the most important elements for internet strategy (Nielsen and Loranger, 2007). Through a number of strategies, it is possible to improve the position of the site in a search result, when users type in words and phrases (Ledford, 2008). Users create many expectations, so it is necessary for web developers to provide categories, classifying website content in an organized way.

2.6   CMS (Content Management System)

An easy way to connect all of the topics mentioned is using a CMS, which consists of a series of programming pages connected to a database. CMS provides superior flexibility and easy user interface with many options to customize the website and open source code. There are two areas in a CMS: private and public, private representing the management area (administrator area) and publicly visible area (front-end area) (Verens, 2010). Government and institutions in Brazil use this system.

2.7   Usability Tests

Usability tests are used to decrease or eliminate user frustration and create a good relation between organization and user, increasing the quality of product (Rubin and Chisnell, 2008).

- **Heuristic Evaluation:** applied by experts that use criteria of usability. For example the 10 Usability Heuristics for User Interface Design (Nielsen, 1995). Five experts can identify 75% of usability problems (Preece et al 2005).
- **Formative Evaluation:** applied with final users can be tested in a prototype or implementation, framing problems for next iteration of design and evaluating a preliminary effective of the project (Rubin and Chisnell, 2008).
- **Field Study:** applied with final users in a real context with real tasks. Users perform a number of tests with little moderator interaction.

For evaluations with users, it is necessary to test plan and define tasks to be presented to users. The test plan is detailed as follows:

- Purpose, goals, and objectives of the test
- Research questions
- Participant characteristics
- Method (test design)
- Task list
- Test environment, equipment, and logistics
- Test moderator role
- Data to be collected and evaluation measures
- Reports contents and presentation

The best results of usability tests come from testing no more than five users and running small tests. The number of usability problems can be found in the function below (Nielsen, 2000):

$$N(1-(1-L)^n) \tag{1}$$

Where N is the total number of usability problems, L is the proportion of usability problems discovered while testing a single user (average value of L is 31%). A total of 15 users is necessary to attempt to find 100% of the usability problems, and five users are needed to find 85% of the problems, resulting in a good number to fix in a redesign. In the second test, five users will discover most of the remaining 15% of the original usability problems, according to authors.

3   Applying Methodological Procedures on Institutional Site

According to the IHC practice, final users are the main stakeholder to contribute during the design process. Even UNESP has an institutional site for students of design, there is no data concerning usability tests applied during the development of

Fig. 1. Institutional Site (accessed on 21st October, 2009)

current design. This research made its first evaluation in 2008, the results are present in this paper. Consent Terms were signed during the research according to Norma ERG-BR 1002, Code of Ethics of the Certified Ergonomist (ABERGO, 2003).

The first evaluation was a **Heuristic Evaluation** with two experts (5 and 2.5 years of experience), only to map the big problems and elaborate a better test plan. This test was mainly based on 10 Usability Heuristics for User Interface Design (Nielsen, 1995) and other references: (Cybis, 2007) and (Preece et al 2005) generating a list of 21 items to rate user satisfaction, where 5 indicated very satisfied and 1 dissatisfied. The average of satisfaction of all 21 items was 2.28, considered to be a low satisfaction rate.

Table 1. Heuristic Evaluation – answers from an expert

Principle		Satisfaction Level
1	Visibility of system status	(1) (2) (3) (4) (5)
2	Match between system and the real world	(1) (2) (3) (4) (5)
3	User control and freedom	(1) (2) (3) (4) (5)
4	Consistency and standards	(1) (2) (3) (4) (5)
5	Recognition rather than recall	(1) (2) (3) (4) (5)
6	Error prevention	(1) (2) (3) (4) (5)
7	Flexibility and efficiency of use	(1) (2) (3) (4) (5)
8	Aesthetic and minimalist design	(1) (2) (3) (4) (5)
9	Help users recognize, diagnose, and recover from errors	(1) (2) (3) (4) (5)
10	Help and documentation	(1) (2) (3) (4) (5)
11	Easy to learn	(1) (2) (3) (4) (5)
12	Tempting	(1) (2) (3) (4) (5)
13	Grouping / distinction of items	(1) (2) (3) (4) (5)
14	Legibility	(1) (2) (3) (4) (5)
15	Cognitive and perceptual load	(1) (2) (3) (4) (5)
16	Informational density	(1) (2) (3) (4) (5)
17	Adaptability	(1) (2) (3) (4) (5)
18	Compatibility	(1) (2) (3) (4) (5)
19	Clickable is clickable	(1) (2) (3) (4) (5)
20	Attractive Layout	(1) (2) (3) (4) (5)
21	Consistency	(1) (2) (3) (4) (5)

Using an open source Brazilian screen reader, DOX-VOZ, the two experts performed a basic **accessibility test**, based on W3C recommendations in WCAG 1.0. Camtasio Studio 6.0 tool was used to record and map the journey made by the reader, followed by the professionals evaluating pages using an online accessibility validator, daSilva, which is similar to original W3C version, but in Portuguese.

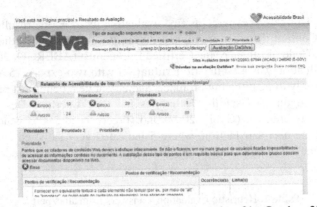

Fig. 2. daSilva accessibility Validator (accessed on 21st October, 2009)

Table 2. Average of errors and warnings in DaSilva validator

Priority 1		Priority 2		Priority 3		Number of evaluated pages
Errors	9.6	Errors	32.6	Errors	1	7
Warnings	27.4	Warnings	99.8	Warnings	87.2	

Screen reader was not able to read menu sub item, due to incorrect HTML tag structure.

Fig. 3. Sequence of navigation using DOX-VOZ (accessed on 21st October, 2009)

The research **Field Study** was applied in two groups: undergraduate students of design as well as postgraduate pupils. The first group was composed of 24 students, 15 males and nine females, average age 20.08 (SD 1.1). The second group was composed of seven students, one male and six females, average age 27.57 (SD 3.82). Camtasia Studio 6.0 tool recorded all users' navigation for each task. A moderator included a series of basic instructions before starting the evaluation.

The questionnaire used for the first group featured three tasks related to postgraduate program applications: Task 1 - Find areas of research, Task 2 - Find registration template and Task 3 - Find postgraduate agenda program.

Table 3. Results from group 1

Task 1		Task 2		Task 3	
Success	45.8%	Success	20.8%	Success	37.5%
Unsuccessful	54.2%	Unsuccessful	79.2%	Unsuccessful	62.5%

The questionnaire used for the second group also included three tasks related to postgraduate activities: Task 1 - Find existing research groups at design program, Task 2 - Find template of a report and Task 3 - Find document to require Master's qualification.

Table 4. Results from group 2

Task 1		Task 2		Task 3	
Success	100%	Success	-	Success	57%
Unsuccessful	0	Unsuccessful	-	Unsuccessful	43%

Task 2 encountered big problems related to browsers, users didn't know how to download a document on computer desktop. In order to avoid any user embarrassment, this task was cancelled. After analyzing recorded videos, it was clear that information in the institutional site was dense, and users had difficulties to find information.

An **Aesthetic factors** evaluation was applied to 20 computer science undergraduate students, two females and 18 males, average age 21.6. The questionnaire had aesthetic factors list with satisfaction indicators, 1 to indicate unsatisfactory and10 to indicate very satisfactory.

Table 5. Results from computer science students

Aesthetic factor	indicator
Typography of page	6.85
General Layout	7.25
Distribution of elements on page	6.9
Page colors	8.25

After evaluations, a redesign of the institutional site attempted to improve information architecture of site and correct usability problems found. Using **Card Sorting** techniques, 15 users collaborated to restructure left menu on institutional site, the new structure reduced 21 items menu to seven items listed below, translated to Portuguese:

- Program (Apresentação do Programa)
- Curriculum (Estrutura Curricular)
- Search Areas (Linhas de Pesquisa)
- Selection Process (Processo Seletivo)
- Agenda/Calendar (Agenda/Calendário)
- Document Templates (Modelos de Documento)
- Students Benefits (Auxílio Discente)

The prototype was developed in Microsoft Expresssion Blend + SketchFlow tool, trial version, and submitted for a **Formative Evaluation** with 11 users, average age 29.09, six females and five males, users are members of a IHC public e-mail group. For this context, two tasks to be done in both environments were selected; prototype and Institutional Site. Task 1 was to find a template of research plan and Task 2 was to find all requirements to conclude a Master's degree in the program.

The prototype also received a satisfaction score bigger than the Institutional Site, in a scale until 10, prototype received 7.91 and Institutional site 4.82. The second version of the prototype was developed in a CMS named Joomla. This CMS was chosen to resolve some problems related to accessibility, SEO (easy application of friendly URLs names) and also given that CMSs have many modules that can be installed easily such as internal search, dynamic menus and a simple management to update content in an organized site structure categorized by topics. For accessibility, CMSs include shortcuts to main content, easy fields to input images alternative texts and recommended HTML structure for a better screen reader navigation.

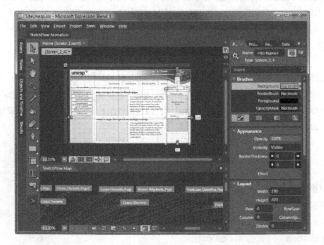

Fig. 4. Microsoft Expresssion Blend + SketchFlow workstation

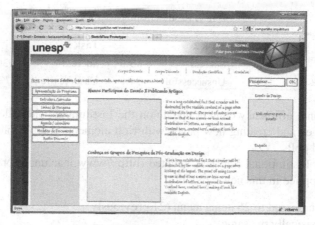

Fig. 5. Prototype version 1

Table 6. Results from Formative Evaluation

Task 1	Success %	Task 2	Success %
Prototype	63.7%	Prototype	72.7%
Inst. Site	72.7%	Inst. Site	45.5%

Fig. 6. Prototype version 2, developed with Joomla

Final Formative Evaluation was applied in the second prototype version. Fourteen users were invited: three females and 11 males, average age 25. Evaluation had three tasks: Task 1 - Find when course was approved by CAPES (Coordination of Improvement of Higher Education Personnel), Task 2 - Find a professor responsible for a specific discipline and Task 3 - Figure out how many disciplines are necessary to conclude the Master's degree.

Table 7. Results from group 1

Task 1		Task 2		Task 3	
Success	100%	Success	86%	Success	93%
Unsuccessful	0	Unsuccessful	14%	Unsuccessful	7%

Joomla aided in a efficiency content update on the Institutional site, allowing edition of existing pages and creating new pages with rich elements such as photos, internal search tool and polls.

In 2013 the Institutional Site was updated (http://www.faac.unesp.br/#42,42), few changes was applied in this new version:

- Left menu increased to 26 items menu (21 previously)
- Content is basically the same
- Breadcrumb, for a better navigation
- Button to increase font (button increases line height, but not font size)
- No friendly URL (http://www.faac.unesp.br/**#42,42**)

4   Conclusion

The evaluations applied between 2008 and 2010 demonstrated usability problems and a number of these are easy to correct. The involvement of end users was most productive and made the difference to correct usability problems. After collecting data, moderators spent additional time talking to users informally so as to gather details on personal opinion and identify different necessities for each user. At this stage it was possible to conclude that information architecture was the big problem. A total of 93 potential users took part in the surveys. The final evaluation on the prototype demonstrated a reduction of user frustration and confirmed the real necessity of end users in usability evaluations. Using Joomla CMS, the corrections were briefly implemented. CMSs have a base structure for websites that already have W3C recommendations on back end code with a friendly development.

All evaluation results are available in the same domain (http://www.faac.unesp.br/#119,441), few changes have been applied in the new version. Left menu increased to 26 items (21 previously), when collected results demonstrated that information architecture was appointed as a big usability problem, and many users were not able to find necessary information on the website. Furthermore, it is expected that this research will contribute to connect issues related to interface design contributing effectively to the growth of the subject.

References

1. ABERGO. Norma ERG BR 1002 Código de Deontologia do Ergonomista Certificado, http://www.abergo.org.br/ (accessed September 16, 2009)
2. Cybis, W., Betiol, A., Faust, R.: Ergonomia e Usabilidade, Conhecimentos, Métodos e Aplicações. Editora Novatec. São Paulo (2007)

3. Duque, L.A., Vieira, A.F.G.: Organização da informação na web: Interfaces para o trabalho colaborativo, Anais do ENANCIB (2008)
4. IBGE - Instituto Brasileiro de Geografia e Estatística 2000, http://www.ibge.gov.br (accessed May 10, 2009)
5. Lei Nacional N° 10.098. Estabelece normas gerais e critérios básicos para a promoção da acessibilidade das pessoas portadoras de deficiência ou com mobilidade reduzida, e dá outras providências 2000, http://www3.dataprev.gov.br/SISLEX/paginas/42/2000/10098.htm (accessed June 20, 2009)
6. Morville, P.: Information Architecture on the World Wide Web, 1st edn. O'Reilly & Associates, Inc. (1998)
7. Nielsen, J., Loranger, H.: Usabilidade na web: Projetando websites com qualidade. Tradução Edson Furmankiewicz e Carlos Schafranski. Campus, São Paulo (2007)
8. Nielsen, J.: 10 Usability Heuristics for User Interface Design (1995), http://www.nngroup.com/articles/ten-usability-heuristics/ (accessed December 09, 2013)
9. Nielsen, J.: Card Sorting: Pushing Users Beyond Terminology Matches. NN/g Nielsen Norman Group (2009), http://www.nngroup.com/articles/card-sorting-terminology-matches/ (accessed December 9, 2013)
10. Nielsen, J.: How Many Test Users in a Usability Study? NN/g Nielsen Norman Group (2012), http://www.nngroup.com/articles/how-many-test-users/ (accessed December 9, 2013)
11. Nielsen, J.: Usability Engineering. Morgan Kaufmann (1993)
12. Nielsen, J.: Why You Only Need to Test with 5 Users. NN/g Nielsen Norman Group (2000), http://www.nngroup.com/articles/why-you-only-need-to-test-with-5-users/ (accessed December 09, 2013)
13. Norman, D.A.: Emotional design: Why we love (or hate) everyday things. TLFeBOOK, New York (2004)
14. Oliveira, L.: Wireframe, documento cada vez mais importante, http://webinsider.uol.com.br/index.php/2003/12/09/wireframe-documento-cada-vez-mais-importante/ (accessed September 15, 2009)
15. Preece, J., Rogers, Y., Sharp, H.: Design de Interação: além da interação homem-computador. Trad. Viviane Possamai. Bookman, Porto Alegre (2005)
16. Rubin, J., Chisnell, D.: Handbook of Usability Testing: How to Plan, Design, and Conduct Effective Tests, 2nd edn. Publishing, Inc., Wiley (2008)
17. SERPRO, Software Livre, http://www.serpro.gov.br/tecnologia/software-livre (accessed June 13, 2009)
18. Verens, K.: CMS Design Using PHP and jQuery. Packt Publishing Ltd. (2010)
19. W3C: Web content accessibility guidelines 1.0, http://www.w3.org/TR/1999/WAI-WEBCONTENT (acessed July 10, 2009)

Interactions around a Multi-touch Tabletop:
A Rapid Ethnographic Study in a Museum

Evelyn Patsoule

BAE Systems Detica
Blue Fin Building (4th Floor), 110 Southwark Street, SE1 0TA, London, UK
evelyn.patsoule@gmail.com

Abstract. Interactive multi-touch tabletops are increasingly making their way into public spaces such as museums, galleries or visitor centres, aiming to support interactions between friends or families. An 'in-the-wild' rapid ethnography was carried out in a museum to explore the interactions between users of different age groups who gather around a multi-touch table and investigate whether the spatial factor affects their behavior. Observations and interviews focused on the factors that attract visitors' attention, the impressions after the first touch and the group interactions. Honey-pot effect, latency times and the tabletop's physical appearance were the main factors that influenced visitors' behavior. Another interesting finding highlighted the importance of sound in attracting visitors' attention. This study identifies implications in developing engaging and usable applications used in real-world settings and provides suggestions on how interactive installations may integrate into a particularly constrained physical context to support and enrich the overall user experience.

Keywords: Multi-touch table; in-the-wild; rapid ethnography; public space.

1 Introduction

Interactive multi-touch tabletops are increasingly making their way into public spaces, such as museums and galleries [6], aquariums [9], tourist information centres [16] and other similar sites, aiming to provide access to multiple users simultaneously allowing for playful interaction [11]. The interplay around a multi-touch table between members of a group in such settings is an issue that has recently begun to be investigated. Previous studies have suggested several solutions for improving user experience while interacting with such installations in public spaces, however the context that these interactions take place can result in different behaviors and expectations from the users [11].

This work explores closely the interactions between users of different age groups who gather around a multi-touch table to interact simultaneously in a particularly constrained physical context: a museum's children-friendly room. More specifically, through a rapid ethnographic study [18], this work tries to identify the ways that people, individually or in groups, approach, behave, organize themselves and interact around a multi-touch table.

A. Marcus (Ed.): DUXU 2014, Part IV, LNCS 8520, pp. 434–445, 2014.

Through thematic analysis, specific patterns and themes are identified, coded, analyzed, and reported, reflecting the entire data set of the study. This aims to explore design considerations and understand ways in which such applications could be developed to invite and encourage diverse groups of people to start interacting, as well as support and enrich their interaction and engage their experience.

Based on these considerations, potential directions on the use of multi-touch tables in real-world contexts are discussed and several recommendations are proposed to designers for developing more engaging and usable applications for such systems.

2   Related Work on Interactive Tables

2.1   In-the-wild vs. Lab Studies

A two-week in-the-wild study [22] was conducted in a museum to investigate how people interact with a tabletop during a visit. Research in public settings has started to emerge and has been used to evaluate new technologies in situ, moving researchers from the usability lab to probe how interactions unfold in a real environment [22].

Although most work in tabletops has been carried out under lab conditions, the importance of studying interactive installations in real environments has been emphasized many times in the past [4; 9; 16; 21; 22; 23]. As opposed to lab studies, findings in real world can map more realistically onto the messy human computer interactions because people are much more unpredictable in such settings [22]. Moreover users can interact more naturally in-the-wild since the researcher's control is absent [22] and the user's attention is on the activity, rather than on the tool [2]. Marshall et al. [16] also highlight that people are often brought to the lab knowing that they are participating in an experiment; they are provided with instructions and someone explains the purpose and functionality of the application to be evaluated. Field studies on the other hand are especially useful in identifying patterns of use, breakdowns, and appropriateness when evaluating a technology [2], something that requires the researcher to be prepared in order to recognize unexpected patterns and events that may occur.

Recent studies undertaken in real world settings such as the home [14], a tourist centre [16] and a museum [11] indicate that people do not always behave in a predefined way, therefore applications designed for such purposes cannot be based on particular specifications. It appears that according to the context, different user experiences can be captured meaning that findings from 'in-the-wild' studies may evoke different design challenges each time.

First Approach. The ways that people notice and approach walk-up-and-use tabletops in public may differ. People may first notice the surface while others using it and then approach for further exploration [21]. Additionally, group members often arrive at different times to a tabletop and some might leave while others continue interacting [16]. This may well be a challenge in a museum where groups of visitors often split up as they enter a room. The honey-pot effect refers to a crowd of people who gathers around a display attracting the attention of others and making it much more likely that they will also notice and approach the technology. Müller et al. [20] argue that the honey-pot effect might be a very powerful cue to attract attention and it has already been observed in several in-the-wild studies [4]. The physical layout in a public space might also influence the way that visitors approach a tabletop and the kind of interactions that take place around it. Koppel et al. [15] introduces many factors to be considered in order to understand the interaction between users and the system, including the location of the display, the architecture of the room or the flow of people. Marshall et al. [17] also suggest that the spatial environment of a public setting can either encourage or constrain social interactions [13].

Engagement. The first impression that a tabletop creates is critical to engaging users in public spaces [10]. Marshall et al. [16] highlight the importance of the first touch, suggesting that users might not give a second chance to the interface if they do not experience a successful initial interaction. Moreover, a walk-up-and-use tabletop should be self-explanatory and clearly indicate its purpose [11] so that people can engage without needing instructions [12]. Encouraging users to further explore the functionality of a walk-up-and-use system in public space and pay more attention to its content might be a challenge [12]. People might just be interested in the technology [16] or curious about how it works and not actually interested in the content it presents [11]. Successful encouraging mechanisms can result in deeper engagement as well as enriched and memorable experiences around a tabletop.

Gestures. Observing the physical actions that people use on a multi-touch table can say a lot about their understanding of the system, from their expectations towards technology to the challenges they might be facing. Marshall et al. [16] point out that previous experience with other interfaces can influence users' initial 'finger-tip' gestures. Additionally, a recent study by Hinrichs and Carpendale [9] investigated the effects that the presence of other people have on the use of gestures and suggested that users demonstrate gestures to other people even if they are strangers.

Interruptions. Interruptions are an unavoidable part of interaction around a multi-touch table especially in public spaces where either groups of friends and families or strangers gather around to interact simultaneously. Fleck et al. [5] argue that interruptions might have a beneficial effect for the ongoing collaboration around a tabletop. As observed in the CityWall study [21] conflicts between strangers encouraged them to interact with each other. However, in other contexts interruptions from strangers may not be perceived positively. In Marshall et al. [16] study there was a case where invasion of one user's personal space while interacting evoked frustration and social discomfort. Studying interruptions is worth examination to understand both the context in which they happen as well as the effects they cause.

3   Study

3.1   The Setting

The study took place on the visitor information centre in Kirkstall Abbey, in Leeds, UK, over a 12-day period at the end of June 2012. Kirkstall Abbey is very popular with tourists and locals as one of the most complete examples of a medieval Cistercian Abbey in Britain[1]. Over the past nine years, the Chapter House of the Abbey has become a visitor centre, including a children-friendly room used as an exhibition area. A Microsoft Surface1.0 SP1[2] sits inside the room, presenting a collection of historical images of the Abbey as well as objects that were used there via a playful application that enables gestures from multiple users.

The room where the Microsoft Surface is located is used for children's activities, such as drawing, dressing up as a monk or building arches of bricks. It also displays exhibits about the history of the Abbey as visual signs or maquettes. The table is placed at the far side of the room next to exhibits A and B (Fig. 1). There is little space around the Surface but chairs can be placed for visitors' comfort and to encourage them to sit and play for longer periods of time.

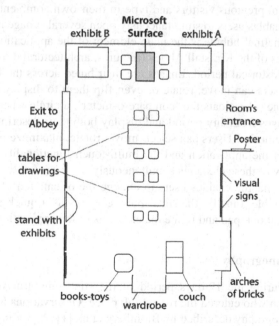

Fig. 1. Layout of the room

---

[1] http://www.leeds.gov.uk/museumsandgalleries/Pages/
Kirkstall-Abbey.aspx
[2] http://technet.microsoft.com/en-us/library/
ee692060(v=surface.10)

3.2   The Application

The Surface Leeds application – designed to support group interactions – was implemented on a Microsoft Surface 1.0 SP1, supporting a set of multi-touch gestures commonly used on interactive surfaces such as dragging, rotating, scaling or flicking.

An initial screen illustrating a 'pebble lake' with sparse ripples draws visitors' attention towards it and encourages their first touch. On tapping the surface, more ripples are generated. At the same time, 4 access points appear in the corners of the screen, representing Microsoft's logo and users can hear a short sound associated with the Microsoft Surface brand. The four corners keep shining and making that sound every 10 seconds for the next 1 minute whether the users touch the surface or not, giving them a hint on where to press in order to start the application.

When users access the main application the screen displays a 'homepage' comprising of four elements: a 'flip view' handle, a 'tips' bubble, a 'show' handle and a 'timeline' bubble. It also presents the Microsoft logo in all 4 corners enabling the users to close the application at any point and return back to the 'pebble lake'.

The 'show' handle on the homepage reveals an 'imageline' from where users can select to view 'image boxes' that include an image (presenting objects of that time), a description and a question card related to the image. On the question card users can see comments from previous visitors and type in their own comment via a keyboard. The application enables users to simultaneously open several 'image boxes'.

The digital 'timeline' bubble is the main element of the application that displays a selection of images of the Kirkstall Abbey (pictures, architectural drawings, paintings, etc.) grouped by historical period. Images are distributed across the table in different orientations but users can move, rotate or even flip them to display a description. In the digital 'timeline' also floats the 'compare-o-meter', a circle where users can drag and drop two images from any period and display both their descriptions to compare the two digital memories. Users can select, move, rotate, maximize or minimize most of the elements of the application and the multi-touch functionality enables them to interact with many of these elements simultaneously.

The 'flip view' handle enables users to change the orientation of all the elements presented on the table. Finally, the 'tips' bubble works as a quick guide illustrating how to zoom in and out, pan and rotate the elements of the application.

3.3   Rapid Ethnography

Observations. During the 12-days period of the study unobtrusive observation of adults and children who entered the room took place. Observations followed the main principles of ethnography described by Blomberg et al. [1]. A guiding framework was developed using findings from previous observations [23; 21; 16; 12]. The researcher was located at different places in order to observe closely or more discretely as well as to take notes of interactions and conversations that could be overheard.

Field notes of how people noticed, approached, gathered around and interacted with the multi-touch surface were taken during the observations. Atmospheric impressions were documented with a series of sketches in the form of diagrams, representing movements around the table. The researcher also recorded the approximate time of each group's interaction, as well as each visitor's gender and approximate age.

The notes were expanded each day, immediately after the observation. Those expanded notes summarized in short paragraphs the distribution of visitors within the room and what people were doing. The focus of observations evolved overtime [7] as the researcher noted each day's interactions, added thoughts and impressions of the day and concluded on aspects to be further studied and observed the following day.

Although video interaction analysis [cf. 8; 24] could have been an easier and more detailed method to capture visitors' interactions, it considered unnecessary. Apart from the fact that video recordings cannot capture the "taste, smell and feel" of the activity [1], being in the field was enough to capture the feeling of the events that were experienced.

Interviews. Observations were coupled with opportunistic interviews and informal discussions that were intentionally semi-structured and open-ended. 18 short interviews of 3-15 minutes length were conducted with a representative sample of visitors (couples, adult members of families or groups of friends). Most interviews took place when visitors left the table but there were also a few cases where interviewees kept interacting after having talked to the researcher. Most of the interviews were carried out individually but when a group of people had interacted together, members of the group were interviewed together. The total number of adults interviewed was 29.

Questions included visitor's motivation to approach the table, difficulties during their interaction, elements they found interesting and general suggestions that could improve their experience. A guiding framework was initially developed and used however through time and as the researcher understood better the setting, more structured and systematic interviews were conducted [1]. All interviews were audio recorded with interviewees' consent, then transcribed and analyzed according to interview questions and emerging recurrent themes.

Gathered Material. Overall, 328 pages of A5 written notes were generated, corresponding to 62 hours of observation. Before the analysis of the data, the notes were divided into sessions. Each session lasted from the moment a single visitor, a pair of visitors or a group of three or more visitors entered the room until they left the room. Even if a person did not notice the table at all, those were also counted as sessions, mainly to report whether the room's layout influenced visitors' ability to notice the interactive display. A grouping of those sessions was identified to assist in the analysis indicating 6 separate types depending on whether the visitors: a) entered the room but did not notice the table at all, b) just noticed or glanced, but did not approach the surface, or passed by without touching it, c) approached and just played with the 'pebble lake', d) approached and tried to understand further what else the application does and e) successfully interacted with the application.

Supplementing the descriptive sessions of each group's interaction, sketches on how people approached the table, positioned or moved around it, as well as the kind of gestures they used with particular interactive elements were collected, supporting the recollection of events and enabling further and more in-depth analysis.

Analysis. The method used to analyze the qualitative data was thematic analysis, following recursively the six phases as presented by Braun and Clarke [3]. Through thematic analysis, specific patterns and themes within the data were identified, coded, analyzed, and reported. This aimed to accurately reflect the content of the entire data set through a rich overall description.

In order to get familiarized with the data all the notes and sketches that collected each day were examined, to identify meanings and issues of potential interest (1st step). Therefore, during the study, some initial ideas and coding schemes had already started taking shape. After the completion of the data collection all interviews were transcribed to compare with the observations as well as deduce further possible themes. The next step was the generation of the initial coding (2nd step) by organizing the data in meaningful groups, identifying potential patterns and themes and then sorting the different codes into these themes (3rd step). Each theme that was identified was intended to capture something important in relation to the overall aim of the study. When a collection of themes and sub-themes was identified, the 4th step was the refinement of those themes. This was achieved through exclusion (where there were not enough data to support them) or merging two separate themes into one (where there was no important difference). After refining the themes and deciding how they fit together, the next step was to determine what aspect of the data each theme captured, in order to start defining and naming them (5th step). The last step (6th step) involved the final analysis and writing up of findings.

4   Findings

Within 293 sessions, 784 visitors were observed, staying in the room from a couple of seconds up to 60 minutes. 241 visitors did not even notice the table, whereas 252 managed to interact with the application. The rest 291 visitors would either notice the table from a distance or would just manage to play with the 'pebble lake'. The mean length of interaction lasted for 7.5 minutes, ranging from a little less than a minute up to 30 minutes. Only 7 sessions lasted 20-30 minutes and most of them lasted for about 3-5 minutes. A small number of visitors were observed coming back to interact again with the table.

Generally, the majority of visitors perceived the application positively and experienced high levels of engagement. Interviews suggested that the table successfully integrates educational and informative content into a playful application, achieving at the same time its purpose as a multi-touch technology. Interestingly, most of the visitors who stayed more than five minutes around the table and were able to actually read some of the content of the application, would immediately leave the room after having interacted, without being interested in looking at other visual signs or exhibits in the room.

The thematic analysis identified a series of themes. The most noteworthy ones are presented below along with quotations from the interviews that supported the observations.

4.1   Noticing and Approaching

What seemed to influence whether people would notice the multi-touch table was mainly its physical appearance (Female, 27: *"To me it looked like a big iPad or something like that...at the beginning it looked like a table game..."*) and the context, as well as whether their natural walking path was directed towards it by other stimuli in the environment. This was confirmed by Müller et al. [19] who argued that public displays installed in specific contexts compete for visitors' attention with other stimuli (like other signs or exhibits). A typical behavior was observed by the younger members of a group who would normally run towards the other side of the room, either to do some drawings or to play with the toys. A considerable number of adults who were visiting alone were observed not entering the room at all and leaving after a quick glance, probably discouraged by the children-friendly nature of the room.

Older adults' postures and attitudes manifested their reservation towards an unknown technology, which would affect their decision on whether and in what way they would approach it. Latency times seemed to also negatively influence whether a visitor would approach or even notice the table. There were occasions where visitors of a group who entered last in the room would immediately approach the other members of their group, who had already moved towards the other side of the room.

Interestingly, whenever the honey-pot effect worked, it could either have positive or negative effects on whether visitors would notice the tabletop. That appeared to mainly depend on whether the effect was created by familiar people or strangers in which case a considerable number of visitors would not even notice it.

4.2   First Touch and Impression

Users' first impressions were clearly affected by previous experience with similar technologies and their expectations towards it. They were often overheard comparing Microsoft Surface to similar technologies they had used before (Male, 45: *"Oh, yeah, I've heard of that before, it's Microsoft's version of a big iPad..."*) and they would also compare it to a computer when they could recognise similar functionalities (Female, 65: *"So, the water screen is something like a screensaver?"*). This finding contradicted with Ryall et al. [23] who suggest that "Users do not view an interactive tabletop as a computer".

A novel finding was that the audible sound of the application after the first touch could give clues, either guiding the users on how to interact or re-attracting their attention to the surface. In some cases, even when visitors had already left the table without being able to initiate the main application, the sound generated 10 seconds after their initial touch on the 'pebble lake' would attract their attention back to the table. However, since no other salient feedback was represented to give a clear indication of what was happening, the sound itself would create more confusion than assistance (Female, 75: *"We were listening to the noise but we couldn't understand what we should do. We gave up because we didn't know what was happening."*).

4.3   Interaction between Visitors

The interactions observed between older and younger members of a group were diverse. In most cases adults would help younger members to interact, by motivating them and giving them instructions or hints. In other cases, adults would either perceive the table as a toy for children and would not pay much attention to it (Female, 40: *"I thought it was something just for children."*) or would be prevented from exploring the application further because children were 'messing around'.

Nevertheless, the multi-touch surface enabled collaborative behaviors between members of a group or even between strangers that reinforce collaborative thinking and playful interaction. Visitors were able to interact, look at things together, read and write collaboratively. In certain cases, members of a group would even create incentives through the application in order to motivate other members to join the interaction.

When interruptions – mainly accidental – occurred, they would be regarded as "part of the game" and would be easily manageable. A few cases were observed where interruptions led to frustration (Male, 50: *"...I got a little bit frustrated (with my kids) because I wanted to read what was on..."*).

The design elements of the interface did not invite special types of gestures so people's gestures on the tabletop seemed to be influenced by their experience with similar interfaces. Additionally, individuals' gestures would reveal different emotions towards the surface [9] or even insecurities around the technology. The interaction gradually unfolded with visitors usually starting interacting with very subtle movements, revealing an initial reservation towards the surface. A few seconds after the first touch, they would increase the expressiveness of their movements [cf. 20] expressing this way their enthusiasm towards the possibilities of the application. People were observed using either one or both hands to interact, depending on the amount of control they desired to have while interacting.

Finally, there were cases where people would implicitly demonstrate their knowledge using exaggerating gestures to demonstrate to other members of their group or even strangers how to interact. This validated the effects that the presence of other people can have on users' behavior and on the use of their gestures [9].

4.4   Usability Issues

Usability problems were mainly observed around cluttered screens, which after accidental touches could interrupt a user's activity causing confusion, tenseness or frustration. Users were frequently observed leaning on their elbows or arms while interacting and accidentally touching the corners of the surface causing interruptions of the interaction, an observation also remarked by Ryall et al. [23].

Usability issues were also related to wrong interpretations and expectations of interactivity. People were observed trying to move or maximize an element that could not be moved or maximized or tapping in a non-interactive element.

5   General Discussion and Conclusions

5.1   Implications for Design

Latency time and splitting up can frequently happen in places such as museums where people of the same group might enter a room at different times [cf. 16] and follow different walking paths, attracted by several stimuli according to their interests. Both the various stimuli in a room and the nature of the room itself can influence the walking path that people will follow or even their willingness to enter the room. It would be advisable to consider the location of interactive displays when installed in public spaces so that other exhibits do not unduly draw attention away from them.

Making people notice and calling them to interact with an interactive display in a public space is not easy [20]. Physical appearance seems to attract attention, meaning that incorporating more visible attractive cues might help people notice an installation easier. What seems to be a particularly hard obstacle for users to overcome before they approach a display is their reservation towards technology. A tabletop's appearance could comprise novel and surprising design elements that intrigue all age groups' interests, stimulating their curiosity and motivating them to use it.

The honey-pot effect might have negative as well as positive outcome on whether people notice and approach an interactive exhibit. It might work negatively on members of a group who enter last, since familiar people who are away from an interactive table may draw attention away from it. Furthermore, strangers around a tabletop might not always attract other visitors' attention; if they do, it is less likely for them to join in. Nevertheless, it would be interesting to intensively explore the causes of this effect in similar contexts.

Interactive displays should not be designed in a way that is too complex for users to understand [cf. 19]. That seems to be more important when it comes to the first touch, which determines whether the user will have a positive experience and continue interacting. Therefore, when the initial interaction is not supported by external factors, such as instructions on how to interact, it seems important for an interactive display to provide this kind of guidance to the users intuitively.

A novel finding in this study highlights the importance of sound in interactive displays in public spaces. It appears that properly indicative sounds, along with visual output, could provide clues to users, either by attracting their attention or by guiding them to successfully interact. Assuming that sound can also add to users' experience, it would be interesting to examine further whether it could work as an additional sensory effect in tabletop interfaces in museums or other public spaces.

Interactive exhibits in museums aim to provide incentives for older and younger users to adopt smooth, collaborative behaviors. This is not always possible especially when one of the members of a group is not interested in interacting. Designers could consider that when designing such applications so that the content is addressed both to adults and children in order to engage all age groups at the same level and mediate their attention leading to a smooth and collaborative interplay.

In a multi-touch tabletop located in public contexts, it is very usual that users' actions might interfere. As Fleck et al. [5] argue, when harmless interruptions happen, they can be beneficial and lead to an overall enjoyable user experience. Nevertheless, accidental intrusions may sometimes cause unpleasant disruptions of the flow of interaction. For that reason, it is suggested for designers to consider whether such applications could be designed in a way that enables freedom of interruptions.

As technology is getting more advanced, users seem to have higher expectations of newly introduced systems. Contrary to a few years ago when they were not surrounded by such technologies, they now inevitably compare similar systems that they are using daily in several ways; functionality, capabilities or ways of interaction. Usability appears to be the main factor that does not meet users' expectations of such technologies. As stated, different expectations and interpretations of interactivity in multi-touch tabletops may result in negative overall experience. Interactive elements could present an indication on how they can be manipulated, giving assistive hints on the functionality, enabling the users to have better control of interaction. Moreover, the interactivity or lack of interactivity of certain elements of the application could be obvious so as not to confuse users on whether they can be operated or not. Providing users better control capabilities through their gestures, without nonetheless restricting the way they interact could enable more pleasant and effective experiences in multi-touch tabletops.

5.2   Conclusions

Multi-touch tabletops in public spaces can constitute a novel form of interaction, upgrading the way that friends or family members function as a group throughout their visit. In a particularly constrained context like the one in this study, interactive displays seem to attract visitors' attention and raise their interest more than the static displays. Provided that they offer educational and informative content through a usable playful application, interactive tabletops could even replace the most uninspiring traditional exhibits, enabling a whole different experience for the group.

This study confirmed findings from previous literature, but it also presented novel outcomes that could be used to assist developers in the design of multi-touch tables in such increasingly technology-intense environments. Taking into consideration all the implications to the design of multi-touch tabletops in similar public spaces, further work could be oriented to this direction.

Multi-touch surfaces in public spaces provide a new tool that could positively influence users' lives, providing to the members of a group the opportunity to speculate and discuss simultaneously a number of themes, enhancing their collaborative thinking and achieving a shared experience.

References

1. Blomberg, J., Giacomi, J., Mosher, A., Swenton-Wall, P.: Ethnographic Field Methods and Their Relation to Design. In: Dchuler, D., Namioka, A. (eds.) Participatory Design: Principles and Practices, pp. 123–155. Erlbaum, New Jersey (1993)
2. Bly, S.: Field Work: Is It Product work? Interactions 4(1), 25–30 (1997)
3. Braun, V., Clarke, V.: Using thematic analysis in psychology. Qualitative Research in Psychology 3(2), 77–101 (2006)
4. Brignull, H., Rogers, Y.: Enticing people to interact with large public displays in public spaces. In: Proceedings of the 2003 INTERACT, pp. 17–24 (2003)
5. Fleck, R., Rogers, Y., Yuill, N., Marshall, P., Carr, A., Rick, J., Bonnett, V.: Actions speak loudly with words: Unpacking collaboration around the table. In: Proceedings of 2009 ITS, pp. 189–196 (2009)
6. Geller, T.: Interactive Tabletop Exhibits in Museums and Galleries. IEEE Computer Graphics and Applications, 6–11 (2006)
7. Hammersley, M., Atkinson, P.: Ethnography: Principles in Practice, 2nd edn., Routledge (1995)
8. Heath, C., Luff, P.: Technology in Action. Cambridge University Press (2000)

9. Hinrichs, U., Carpendale, S.: Gestures in the wild: Studying multi-touch gesture sequences on interactive tabletop exhibits. In: Proceedings of the 2011 CHI, pp. 3023–3032 (2011)
10. Hornecker, E.: Stifter.: Learning from Interactive Museum Installations About Interaction Design for Public Settings. In: Proceedings of the 2006 OzCHI, pp. 135–142 (2006)
11. Hornecker, E.: I don't understand it either, but it is cool Visitor Interactions with a Multi-Touch Table in a Museum. In: Proceedings of the 2008 Tabletop, pp. 121–128 (2008)
12. Jacucci, G., Morrison, A., Richard, G.T., Kleimola, J., Peltonen, P., Parisi, L., Laitinen, T.: Worlds of information: Designing for engagement at a public multi-touch display. In: Proceedings of the 2010 CHI, pp. 2267–2276 (2010)
13. Kendon, A.: Spacing and orientation in co-present interaction. In: Esposito, A., Campbell, N., Vogel, C., Hussain, A., Nijholt, A. (eds.) COST 2102 Int. Training School 2009. LNCS, vol. 5967, pp. 1–15. Springer, Heidelberg (2010)
14. Kirk, D.S., Izadi, S., Sellen, A., Taylor, S., Banks, R.: &Hilliges, O.: Opening up the family archive. In: Proceedings of the 2010 CSCW, pp. 261–270 (2010)
15. Koppel, M., Bailly, G., Müller, J., Walter, R.: Chained Displays: Configurations of Public Displays can be used to influence Actor-, Audience-, and Passer-By Behavior. In: Proceedings of the 2012 CHI (2012)
16. Marshall, P., Morris, R., Rogers, Y., Kreitmayer, S., Davies, M.: Rethinking 'multi-user': An in-the-wild study of how groups approach a walk-up-and-use tabletop interface. In: Proceedings of the 2011 CHI, pp. 3033–3042 (2011)
17. Marshall, P., Rogers, Y., Pantidi, N.: Using F-formations to analyse spatial patterns of interaction in physical environments. In: Proceedings of the 2011 CSCW, pp. 445–454 (2011)
18. Millen, D.: Rapid ethnography: Time deepening strategies for HCI field. In: Proceedings of ACM Symposium on Designing Interactive Systems, pp. 280–286. ACM Press, New York (2000)
19. Müller, J., Alt, F., Michelis, D., Schmidt, A.: Requirements and design space for interactive public displays. In: Proceedings of the 2010 International Conference on Multimedia, pp. 1285–1294. ACM, New York (2010)
20. Müller, J., Walter, R., Bailly, G., Nischt, M., Alt, F.: Looking glass: A field study on noticing interactivity of a shop window. In: Proceedings of the 2012 ACM Annual Conference on Human Factors in Computing Systems, Austin, Texas, USA, pp. 297–306 (2012)
21. Peltonen, P., Kurvinen, E., Salovaara, A., Jacucci, G., Ilmonen, T., Evans, J., Oulasvirta, A., Saarikko, P.: It's Mine, Don't Touch!: Interactions at a large multi-touch display in a city center. In: Proceedings of the 2008 CHI, pp. 1285–1294 (2008)
22. Rogers, Y.: Interaction design gone wild: Striving for wild theory. Interactions 18(4) (2011)
23. Ryall, K., Morris, M., Everitt, K., Forlines, C., Shen, C.: Experiences with and observations of direct touch tabletops. In: Proceedings of the 2006 IEEE TableTop the International Workshop on Horizontal Interactive Human Computer Systems, pp. 89–96 (2006)
24. vom Lehn, D.: Examining "response": Video-based studies in museums and galleries. International Journal of Culture, Tourism and Hospitality Research 4(1), 33–43 (2010)

Skill Specific Spoken Dialogues Based Personalized ATM Design to Maximize Effective Interaction for Visually Impaired Persona

Muhammad Shafiq[1], Jin-Ghoo Choi[1], Muddesar Iqbal[2], Muhammad Faheem[2],
Maqbool Ahmad[2], Imran Ashraf[2], and Azeem Irshad[2]

[1] Department of Information and Communication Engineering
Yeungnam University, South Korea
shafiq.pu@gmail.com, jchoi@yu.ac.kr, yesitsmaqbool@yahoo.com
[2] Faculty of Computing and Information Technology
University of Gujrat, Pakistan
{m.iqbal,imranashraf}@uog.edu.pk,
{fahimrana123,irshadazeem2}@gmail.com

Abstract. Making machines for visually impaired persons is very challenging because they do not receive any useful information through SIGHT. The perception of background activities can be a good supportive mechanism for visually impaired users. In this work we focus on ATMs and propose a new ATM design, i.e., skill specific spoken dialogues based ATM (3s ATM). The personalized ATM design fulfills the requirements of visually impaired people while provisioning services for normal users also. Our proposed ATM is designed to assimilate into conventional ATMs and enable the effective interaction of visually impaired users with the machine. We first analyze the conventional ATM system through heuristics index to simulate its standardized design. For peer evaluation, visually impaired participants carry out the task analysis for simulated systems, i.e., both conventional ATM and 3s ATM. We found that 3s ATM design achieves 47% higher learnablility and 76% better usability than conventional ATMs. Thus we can achieve the machine compliance by overlooking the barriers and needs of the visually impaired persons in design stage.

Keywords: Usability, task evaluation, heuristics index, HCI, 3s ATM.

1 Introduction

Human Computer Interaction (HCI) deal how human interaction become more easy and effective with the help of different human factors (e.g. psychological methods, soft skills) to complex machines. Since, as long as the complexities of machines are exceeded from human ability, applications of human factors become inevitable for designing machine interfaces, to expedite interaction, besides the provision cognitive relief. To implement software's interaction within machine's interface, that is easy to learn and use, but difficult to build. HCI plays important role to make human lives more comfortable, making machines more usable and effective for normal user. However, the role of HCI is more demanding for designing machine interface, which are equally helpful to use for special peoples indeed. According to WHO 285 million

A. Marcus (Ed.): DUXU 2014, Part IV, LNCS 8520, pp. 446–457, 2014.

people are visually impaired worldwide, 39 million are blind and 246 have low vision in 2012. Hence, public systems like "Automated Teller Machine" (ATM) should preferably be designed to make them also useful by the blind user. Visual sense is a BLESSING indeed, user is able to perceive information at a very high speed as compared to other senses. Since, visual sense is able to precede information at one million bits per second. However, on the other hand visual impairment is a DISEASE which referred as the limitation of activities that can be performed with the help of visual sense e.g. blindness. Blindness refers to visual impairment ranging from legal blindness to total blindness. Visual impairment is a disability of severe reduction in vision. It is severe or sometime complete loss of vision. A person whose corrected visual acuity is less than three, they are considered as visually impaired. A visual impaired person can see light but unable to see shapes. Visual impairment has a deep impact on cognitive development of a person. It reduces the ability of person to perform any task. The perception level of blind and partial sighted person is different. The visual input of visual impaired persons is limited and incorrect and the processing speed to process visual input is also very slow. Visual impaired person have to rely more on their memory and other senses that is why these senses become strong. Visual impaired person face difficulty to perform special task since they developed their own strategies to learn/copy and become proficient to fulfill their requirements with the help of self-developed strategies. Human have different senses and they play a vital role to retrieve information from the environment, most important sense that we used to get information is SIGHT. Peoples who are visually impaired have to depend more on their other SENSES to obtain information. Thus, designing machine's interface for almost, 285 million visually impaired peoples as important as for normal user, to support them while interacting with such a sophisticated world of technology. Since, Graphical User Interface (GUI) has made it possible that visual impaired user can use it but they are unable to use them efficiently as required [3]. Growth in GUI development is getting fast with the advent of time. In the earlier days, command line interfaces were used to interact with system but these interfaces are difficult to use, need expertise, boring and missing the element of user friendliness. While, progress in the interfaces development for visual impaired users is very slow, like, provision of ATM services to visually impaired users. In the earlier designs of ATM history speech driven automatic teller machine provide more natural interaction between user and ATM interface [5].Since, Icon based interface are also introduced in these days as an alternative of speech recognition through, MENUS require accessing the interface of ATM [8], [6]. However, unfortunately visually impaired peoples are barren from such a sophisticated technology. Innovations in HCI and spoken language dialogues give a new direction to this discipline for designing suitable specific dialogue system to reveal ATM services, having full support to interact with visual impaired effectively.

2   Problem Statement

The gap between user skills to machine design has challenged the effectiveness of its usability, even for normal person like ATM. ATM has already several barriers including literacy level, awareness, accessibility, multi interfaces and visual impairment. Despite normal user, visual impaired persons unable to handle such terrible multi screens. While, visual impairment is more specific barrier for visually impaired ATM users. This is mostly a variant that depends on individual's SKILLS and different LEVEL of impairment. The differences between individuals include traits, facts of personality, aptitude, skill specificity and performance. Since, language diversity, vision, color recognition, listening strength are also a variant forms of specificity that may vary person to person. A different individual uses different strategies in order to complete same task [7]. The thing need to be focus is to identify universally correct set of interface FEATURES and to design skill specific spoken dialogues for INTERACTION of personalized ATM. Our research problem related to the questions that: (1) How 3s personalized ATM design useful for visual impaired persona? , and (2) How 3s dialogues based technology influence machine usability to its effectiveness?

3   Literature Review

Spoken language dialogue systems as present development in the field of HCI gave new hopes and expectations. Methods introduced by Gudivada et al are used to separate images from text, these methods gives good result but require more processing power [2]. Use of 3D sounds are also very popular which provide audio cues, the main advantage of this approach is that sound come from one direction. These approaches require user to wear headphones in order to present specialized sound. A solution proposed by Yu et al, to access internet by navigation on web, representation of information and accessing graphical information [12]. Visual, audio and hepatic technology used to develop multimodal interface. A model is proposed by McKiel et al that generate audio on mouse position. This system looks perfect but it is unable to tell the position of the pointer on precise objects [13]. Some issues of visual impaired persons are raised by Goble et al that, visual impaired persons don't know what kind of information is given on page, what is the length of page, how to move forward and how to access tables and frames [14]. Speech reorganization is used to identify/match a word, phrase or sentence with the help of finite set of possibilities. Method proposed by Edwards et al for the first time in which blind/visual impaired user can access computer with the help of derived feature of GUI and peripheral devices [15]. Later on the projects by Edwards et al and Petrie et al were launched, the goal behind these projects are to give complete access of windows system by different methods [16],[20]. An interface is proposed by Mynatt et al, in which tree structure is being used through sound, this interface used a specialized tactile hardware in order to keep objects [17]. Researchers done a great job on the development of GUI's and focuses on different factors discussed above to optimize and fulfill the requirements for almost visually impaired user so far. However, visually impaired were not paying attention, exclusively for ATMs. Although ATM systems used in these days are sophisticated and user friendly but are unable to meet the requirement of visual impaired persons, conveniently. The main reason behind them is that the FEATURES essential for visual impaired persons are missing in their graphical user interface.

4   Proposed Framework

Our study is composed of three major phases, first DESIGN of 3s personalized ATM system, second DEVELOPMENT of simulators to be used as test bed for data collection and finally the ANALYSIS of 3s ATM system with conventional ATM system on well-known principles of HCI. Figure 1 exhibit further steps of framework:

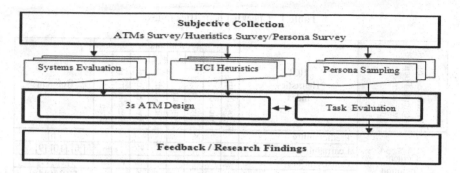

Fig. 1. Study Framework

4.1 Subjective Collection

We have focused four techniques for subjective collection i.e. (1) ATMs SURVEY to simulate the conventional ATM system and subsequently design and simulation of 3s ATM (2) LITERATURE REVIEW for the designing of HCI heuristics index, required for the evaluation of conventional ATM design (3) PERSONA SAMPLING for the representation of visually impaired, and finally (4) TASK EVALUATION to populate the log files with tasks results of participants for ensuing research findings.

4.2 System Evaluation via Heuristics Index

In this stage of our research, as just stated, significant HCI heuristics for 3s ATM design are constituted trough the literature survey for heuristic evaluation of conventional ATM. To rate the significance of heuristics, recommended by HCI experts, we have designed a checklist of HCI heuristics index demonstrated in Table 1, which is intended to design for system evaluation. The system evaluation based on screens and interaction designs of ATM systems, collected through the field survey of two sampled banks, HBL and MCB in December 2013, within the region of Gujrat, Pakistan. This step further constituted of two phases. First, is the 'Interface Analysis' and second, is the 'Interaction Analysis'. The problems found, while ATM systems evaluation were in large. However, due of space limitations some of the sampled issues, concerning interaction and interface design are illustrated in Figure2 and Figure3.

Issues Concerning Interaction Design: (1) Familiarity, Structure, Learnability, Predictability: MCB -ATM process is very obvious, machine interaction starts as long as user insert ATM card, following card validation, machine request for PIN, user follow PIN request, after verifying PIN, machine display option menu to precede transaction. However, HBL machine's behavior is quite different, since after validating card machine display language selection dialogue first, then request for PIN, user follows the request by passing PIN user wait for option menu to display like MCB-ATM experience, thus, time out and card ejected. Since, meanwhile machine is waiting for user action to push ACCEPT button for displaying option menu. Consequently, because of this disparity user perceives machine is out of order.

Table 1. Checklist heuristics index

Interface Components Focused by Experts to Support :	HCI Heuristics Index	Authors								References
		Constantine	Nielson	Dix et al	Norman	Lauessen	Preece et al	Shneiderman	Treu et al	
Content Cognition	Predictability			✓						[6]
	Learnability			✓		✓	✓			[6],[10],[9]
	Consistency		✓					✓		[1],[11]
	Memorability					✓	✓	✓		[10],[9],[8]
	Familiarity		✓							[6]
Handling Information	Recognition		✓							[1]
	Synthesizability		✓							[6]
	Generalizability		✓							[6]
	Visibility	✓	✓			✓				[11],[1],[18]
	Simplicity	✓				✓				[11],[18]
	Subsitutivity		✓							[6]
	Feedback	✓						✓		[11],[8]
	Error indication		✓							[1]
	Standardizibility		✓			✓				[1],[18]
	Responsiveness		✓							[6]
	Safety						✓			[9]
Handling User Interaction	Recoverability		✓	✓				✓		[1],[6],[8]
	Robustness			✓						[6]
	Flexibility		✓	✓						[1],[6]
	User control	✓	✓					✓		[11],[1],[8]
	Customizability			✓						[6]
	Satisfaction					✓				[10]
	Help		✓							[1]
Machine Performance	Effectiveness						✓			[9]
	Efficiency					✓	✓			[10],[9]
	Effort								✓	[4]
	Error Prevention		✓		✓			✓		[1],[8],[18]
Dialogue Design	Universality							✓		[11]
	Aesthetic		✓							[1]
	Conformance		✓		✓					[1],[18]
	Structure	✓								[11]

(2) Visibility, Conformance, Flexibility and Feedback: While, interactions through MCB ATM as long as user request balance inquiry, after accessing database, machine displayed concerning amount over the screen and offer user for getting receipt. User accepts this by passing yes eventually machine generates slip. However, on the other hand HBL ATM process is quite different which may cause users in trouble if slips tray become empty, Since visibility of balance amount become a serious issue if it will not be displayed over the screen unlike MCB.

Event	Sequence Diagrams of ATM Interaction
PIN Entry	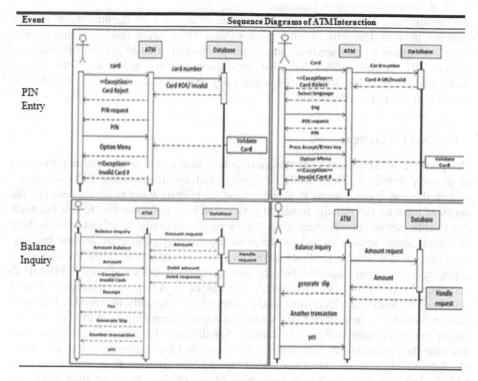
Balance Inquiry	

Fig. 2. Interaction Analysis

Issues Concerning Interface Design: (1) Consistency: Button's metaphore do not match with some others ATM keypad design e.g. ACCEPT for ENTER. (2) Flexibility: Other ATM does not have provision of language selection for user, like MCB while interaction. (3) Recognition: Buttons alignment problem caused user to exclusively determine the right button first, to continue. (4) Predictability: Fast cash menu option's amounts are unpredictable for user to choose from main menu.

Component	ATM Screenshot
Data Entry Keypad (MCB)/ Language Selection (HBL)	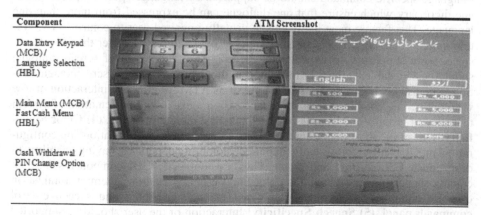
Main Menu (MCB) / Fast Cash Menu (HBL)	
Cash Withdrawal / PIN Change Option (MCB)	

Fig. 3. Interface analysis

(5) Subsitutivity: Numerical format does not seem logical with decimal point, since it does not have to deal with floating point values. Thus, cause confusion and require more key strokes by user while passing required amount of cash. (6) Error Prevention: Unlike HBL yes/no options for error prevention are not available, since if user accidently changes his 4 digit PIN, eventually system does not have any alert to rescue user through confirmation.

4.3   3s ATM Design

The purpose, to device an ATM design in a way that would satisfy the requirements of visually impaired. Thus, while designing skill specific spoken dialogues based system the major issue needs to be addressed on priority basis is how to convey the verity of input by the visually impaired person and how to forward sufficient feedback that enable user to get full orientation. This scenario can only be solved with the help of sound. Since, speech (sound) is the most natural way of communication but systems that provide spoken feedback to the user they are unable to fulfill the needs and capabilities of visual impaired persons and given instructions are very difficult to understand and follow [19]. However, dialogues of 3s ATM design needs to follow skill specific features, which most likely supportive to visually impaired, while interaction, in order to modify or build spoken dialogues according to individual specification are mentioned bellow. **(1) Labels Specificity:** To initiate interaction with machine the position of its components with audible labels, user should be informed. Machine should also let user know, what type of this component is, how to interact with it. For instance at the very beginning of interaction, machine should let user know, where is card reader, and also enable user the way to insert the card. This would, likely to be useful if the interface of card reader, designed similarly to a cone for directing user, to enter card correctly. **(2) Language Specificity:** Language is the most powerful means of human computer interaction. The orientation of audio glances, speech dialogues and environmental sound should be supported with the help of user language. System should also be able to handle speech commands, hot key commands and combination of speech commands within the choice of user language. Language specific command should be supported by language specific speech dialogue dictionary which ensure that one dialogue can be expressed from more than one language. This feature most likely enable visually impaired user to control ATM system more effectively. **(3) Vision Specificity:** Low vision is far better than blindness, since, more supportive to expedite interaction. Thus fount size of screen dialogue should be adjustable by the user to support high visibility. Enabling screen magnification, will also be, highly supportive feature of 3s ATM for effective interaction of low vision user. The combination of sound and vision make a dual presentation of system that support visually and hearing impaired persons, more effectively. **(4) Color Specificity:** One of the most important features of the system is customization and configuration of GUI color for visually impaired, color blind persons having inability to discriminate between red and green. Thus, customizable GUI components may be equally supportive for sighted and color blind users by enabling them customization of color combinations through icon based manual dashboard and speech control commands panel. **(5) Speech Specificity:** Interaction of the user should be supported with the help of dialogue and this is always in the form of audio glances, speech form and environmental sound. System should able to control speech commands, hot key commands and combination of speech commands comfortably. Speech command should be supported by speech command dictionary which ensure that one command can be expressed from more than one method. Using speech synthesizer module that translates machine readable text language to artificial voice dialogues like human speech is a viable solution to seek interaction of visually impaired. This feature enable user to control system effectively and it is equally good for sighted and visually impaired users. **(6) Listening Specificity:** Listening is another subjective skill of visually impaired potential user. This specificity is associated with 3s ATM system by loudness control commands, mode of speech, audio glances, environmental sound and type of speech synthesis output. It is very essential to enable user in order to obtain, review and understand information quickly. Hearing aid is likely to be more useful particularly if the user is hearing impaired? **(7) Proficiency Specificity:** The system should be design proficiency specific and efficient to use, if user has already learned it, then to expedite interaction and chase high productivity should be supportive by the systems through short keys and smart dialogues. **(8) Tangible Specificity:** For effective input and to capitalize user effort, ATM card, key pad and ATM dashboard needed to be redesign for letting user recognize card, buttons and ATM dashboard, through his alternate senses, instead of vision, so that user can touch and feel right key while passing input to the system and right orientation of ATM card while insertion. In addition system should also acknowledge user action through audio glances and spoken dialogues. To help user, embossed dots on number keys should be placed in the design of the keys in such a way, so as not to condense legibility. However shaped and concave key tops may also be helpful in manual interaction for user's having deprived dexterity. To prevent incorrect insertion, cards should also be embossed to at least 2~3 mm, for indentation of correct orientation **(9) Safety Specificity:** The ATM environment should be fool proof to make user transaction more secure and safe. Thus, machine dashboard should be enabled with panic knob to inform security in case of emergency. However, appointment of trustworthy agents outside the cabin may also be useful to keep ATM transactions safe and sound. **(10) Biometric Specificity:** Dealing with Personal Identification Number (PIN) is an issue, for many people, since it is a source of cognitive stress, to remember, recall and enter a 4~6 digits PIN, particularly for visually impaired user. Thus, the solution of these visual and intellectual impairments may also a viable option of enabling biometric authentication in 3s ATM (e.g. fingerprint) instead of using PIN.

4.4   Task Evaluation

In this study, participants sampling constituted to conduct indoor laboratory test. Seven, participants were selected from student population of special education school in Gujrat. Prior task evaluation a task plan was designed, that encompasses three turns, for each turn, every participant has to pass through three task scenarios. A sum of 21 (7 × 3) tasks was evaluated on each simulator for each turn of participant.

The first step of this phase belongs to the SIMULATION of two ATM designs. Initial, is the simulation of conventional ATM design, developed through the analytical survey of ATM systems used by the banking sector of Pakistan and subsequent, is the simulation of 3s personalized ATM design, proposed for visually impaired persona. For peer evaluation, log base event record files are set in both simulated systems,

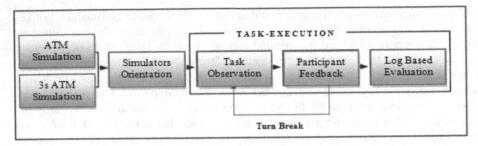

Fig. 4. Task evaluations process

to be used as test bed for visually impaired users, while navigation. Thus, before task evaluation a brief orientation about simulators to the participants was presented. Eventually, number and type of errors, meantime for task completion and task success rate were further analyzed through the task observation and navigation log files to measure the productivity of proposed system relative to the conventional system in practice, using heuristics index. Three task scenarios were designed to evaluate the in lab experiments for sampled participants representing visually impaired persona are: (1) Cash Withdrawal (2) Pin Change and (3) Balance Inquiry. Thus, after finishing, each of the three task scenarios for each of the simulated system, an interview was held during five minutes turn break for participant's feedback related to the effectiveness of system usability,   concerning the execution of task scenario. To measure the productivity of both systems (i.e. ATM and 3s ATM) embedded programs of VB with Metro apps of Windows-8, simulated applications were developed to simulate ATM's realism environment in lab to evaluate each of the systems performance and support for participants, while navigation. Each participant out of the 7 is presented with simulated applications of ATM systems for a sum of 6 task scenarios i.e. 3 for each. The participants have to select the required option in given order of Table 2. This is essential that each simulation is exactly mapped out as to the realism ATM environment. However, for this study we have tried to make its conformance with real milieu, except some inevitable assumptions, for instance biometric specificity and card insertion. Since, while using simulated systems in lab, it is not possible for participants to insert ATM card therefore, we have replaced it with most relevant possible solution, which is card swipe. Once the card is swiped successfully by the participant, main menu emerges, inviting user to select interaction language first, and then, obviously prompt participant to enter their 4 digit PIN which is subsequently verified by matching algorithm of simulators. To choose required option, participant has to press the push buttons adjacent to the screen, similar to the real-life ATM. The design of push buttons for selecting option menu was really crucial, since mouse click option would not satisfy the requirements of this case study for evaluating the performance of visually impaired persona on 3s ATM design. For dual presentation embossed designed numerical keypad was acquired for data entry purpose along with audio glances, so that participant most likely recognizes the concerned keys he/she required. Last but not least, as only viable option to seek function keys in simulators, the ENTER, MINUS and PLUS keys of numerical keypad was utilized for ACCEPT, CANCEL and CORRECTION buttons respectively. Thus, this is what our simulators do.

Table 2. Task scenario

Task Description	Subtasks Involved	
Cash Withdrawal	a)	Trace card insertion area, swipe card, enter pin to login,
	b)	Choose cash withdrawal, enter amount, acknowledge amount, and transaction completion.
Pin Change		
	c)	Do a, and choose pin change option, enter new PIN, confirm this, finish transaction and then re-do a, with new pin and then exit.
Balance Inquiry	d)	Do a, and choose balance inquiry, get balance also record it to the invigilator.

Table 3. Task evaluation construct of 3s ATM simulator

Turn	Task Description	Successful Tasks Sum	Total Tasks	Productivity
1	Cash Withdrawal	3	7	47.61%
	Pin Change	3	7	
	Balance Inquiry	4 = 10	7 = 21	
2	Cash Withdrawal	4	7	52.38%
	Pin Change	3	7	
	Balance Inquiry	4 = 11	7 = 21	
3	Cash Withdrawal	5	7	76.19%
	Pin Change	5	7	
	Balance Inquiry	6 = 16	7 = 21	
	Total	37	63	

4.5   Research Findings

We have observed different barriers by the visually impaired participants while interaction with ATM simulators, since, the lack of sight, inability to read or understand instruction in English, inability to deal with numbers, inability to interact with design and affordability, for instance, inability the way card is handled, particularly with conventional ATM simulator, which was not aimed to design for visually impaired users. Since, this is very obvious reason to understand that our hypothesis become, true when, even a single participant couldn't successful to conduct any task scenario while interacting with conventional ATM design. We also observed most frequent errors on each simulator differ, which indicate that errors are more subjective to the design of ATM and less respective to the user. Since, we frequently observe same participants while conducting wrong digit errors and anagram errors particularly on the conventional ATM, than the 3s ATM design. The results of Table 3 showing that the 3s ATM simulator's productivity is 47.61% greater than the conventional ATM design, exclusively for user's doing first time interaction with the system. However, productivity rate of 3s ATM, stridently increased in 2nd and 3rd turn, to 52.38% and 76.19% respectively. First turn, productivity results reflects that how good enough 3s ATM is supportive to learn, while the productivity results of 2nd and 3rd turn, describes the effectiveness of its usability for visually impaired users. More specifically, these results really strengthen the idea of skill-specific-spoken dialogs based personalized ATM design to maximize effective interaction for visually impaired persona. The method of productivity we adapted to evaluate 3s ATM efficiency factor is:

$$\textbf{Productivity \% = Successful tasks sum/Total tasks} \times \textbf{100}$$

5   Summary

As HCI developed, the ATM system's design should also evolve to acquire the benefits of the new innovations, especially for visually impaired persons, to make this technology equally usable as for as normal users. Through this study, this is very obvious to know that today's ATM systems totally flopped to be used for visually impaired users, since, there are not intended to design by the designers, decisively. The purpose of our study is to raise the awareness among HCI experts for the exclusive requirements and problems of visually impaired peoples into the conventional design of ATM systems. Therefore, in the first phase of our study we design heuristics index based on most significant HCI system's design and evaluation principles. Under the light of heuristics index, subsequently we analyzed the conventional ATM design disparity, which equally affect system's usability by the normal user as special users and also oversight the need/barrier of visually impaired users, indeed. In the second phase of our study, we purposed the 3s ATM to maximize effective interaction for visually impaired persona. The 3s ATM is intended to ensure compliance and assist visually impaired users through: Labels, Language, Vision, Color, Speech, Listening, Proficiency, Tangible, Safety and Biometric specificity, while interaction. In the final phase, through in lab simulated environment, we plane for the evaluation of 3s ATM design to figure out its effectiveness relative to the conventional ATM design. Furthermore, task evaluation is divided into eight steps: developing task plan, sampling participants, preparing tasks, developing simulation, briefing participants, conducting task, logging data and finally converting it into research findings. This research work is specific of its type in a developing country focusing visually impaired persons as important element of society, likely to bring them in the world of sophisticated technology of ATM, and enable them to conduct financial transaction like normal users. Since, task evaluation results reflect that 3s ATM design, constitute a significant compliance to visually impaired participants while interaction unlike to conventional ATM design. Thus, the think need to be focused by the HCI experts is, by overlooking the needs and barriers of visually impaired users, is likely to have adverse effects on taking up the services of modern technology.

References

1. Nielsen, J.: Heuristics evaluation. In: Nielsen, J., Mack, R.L. (eds.) Usability Inspection Methods, pp. 25–62. Wiley, New York (1994)
2. Gudivada, V., Raghavan, V.: Content based image retrieval systems. In: IEEE Computer (1995)
3. Schwerdtfeger, R.S.: Making the gui talk. IBM, ftp://service.boulder.ibm.com/sns/sr-os2/sr2doc/guitalk.txt (1991)

4. Treu, S.: User interface evaluation: A structured approach. Plenum, New York (1994)
5. Rogers, W.A., Fisk, A.D.: ATM Design and Training issues. Ergonomics in Design 5, 4–9 (1997)
6. Dix, A., Finlay, J., Abowd, G., Beale, R.: Human-computer interaction. Prentice Hall, Upper SaddleRiver, NJ (1998)
7. Miller, M.B., Van Horn, J.D., Wolford, G.L., Handy, T.C., Valsangkar-Smyth, M., Inati, S., Grafton, S., Gazzaniga, M.S.: Extensive individual differences in brain activations associated with episodic retrieval are reliable over time. Journal of Cognitive Neuroscience 148, 1200–1214 (2002)
8. Shneiderman, B.: Direct manipulation for comprehensible, predictable and controllable user interfaces. In: Proc. of the 2nd International Conference on Intelligent User Interfaces. ACM Press, NY (1997)
9. Preece, J., Rogers, Y., Sharp, H.: Interaction design. Wiley, New York (2002)
10. Lauessen, S., Younessi, H.: Six styles for usability requirements. In: Dubois, P., Opdahl, A.L., Pohl, K. (eds.) Proceedings of 4th International Workshop on Requirements Engineering: Foundations of Software Quality, pp. 1–12 (1998)
11. Constantine, L.L.: Collaborative usability inspections for software. In: Proceedings of the Software Development 1994. Miller Freeman, San Francisco (1994)
12. Yu, W., Mcallister, G., Murphy, E., Kuber, R.: Developing Multi-modal Interfaces for Visually Impaired People to Access the Internet. Philip Strain Queen's University of Belfast Northern Ireland
13. McKiel, J.F.A.: Method and system for enabling blind or visually impaired computer users to graphically select displayed elements. United States of America Patent Pat. 6,046,722 (April 2000)
14. Goble, C., Harper, S., Stevens, R.: The travails of visually impaired web travellers. In: Proceedings of the Eleventh ACM on Hypertext and Hypermedia, pp. 1–10. ACM (2000)
15. Edwards, A.D.N.: Soundtrack: An auditory interface forblind users. Human-Computer Interaction 4, 45–66 (1989)
16. Edwards, K., Mynatt, E., Stockton, K.: Access tographical interfaces for blind users. Interactions 2(1), 54–67 (1995)
17. Mynatt, E., Weber, G.: Nonvisual presentation of graphical user interfaces. In: Proceedings of CHI 1994. ACM Press, New York (1994)
18. Norman, D.A.: Cognitive Engineering. In: Norman, D.A., Draper, S.W. (eds.) User Centered System Design: New Perspectives on Human-Computer Interaction, pp. 31–65. Lawrence Erlbaum Associates, Hillsdale (1986)
19. Ran, L., et al.: Drishti: An Integrated Indoor/Outdoor Blind Navigation System and Service. In: Proc. 2nd IEEE Conf. on Pervasive Computing and Communications, pp. 23–30 (2004)
20. Petrie, H., Morley, S., Weber, G.: Tactile-Based Direct Manipulation in GUIs for Blind Users. In: Conference Companion to CHI 1995, pp. 428–429. ACM Press, New York (1995)

Consideration for Interpretation of Brain Activity Pattern during Car Driving Based on Human Movements

Shunji Shimizu[1], Hiroaki Inoue[1], Hiroyuki Nara[2], Fumikazu Miwakeichi[3],
Nobuhide Hirai[4], Senichiro Kikuchi[5], Eiju Watanabe[5], and Satoshi Kato[5]

[1] Tokyo Universtiy of Science, SUWA, Japan
Jgh12701@ed.tus.ac.jp, shun@rs.suwa.tus.ac.jp
[2] Hokkaido University, Japan
nara@ssc.ssi.ist.hokudai.ac.jp
[3] The Institute of Statical Mathmatic, Japan
miwake1@ism.ac.jp
[4] Tokyo Medical and Dental University, Japan
nobu@nobu.com
[5] Jichi Medical University, Japan
skikuchipjichi.ac.jp, psykato@jichi.ac.jp, eiju-ind@umin.ac.jp

Abstract. The purpose in this research is to contribute to developing of assistive robot and related-apparatus. Recently, there is a pressing need to develop a new system which assists and acts for car driving and wheelchair for the elderly as the population grows older. In terms of developing a new system, it is thought that it is important to examine behaviors as well as spatial recognition. Therefore, experiments have been performed for an examination of human spatial perceptions, especially right and left recognition, during car driving using NIRS. In previous research, it has been documented that there were significant differences at dorsolateral prefrontal cortex at left hemisphere during virtual driving task and actual driving. In this paper, brain activity during car driving was measured and detailed analysis was performed by segmentalizing brain activity during car driving on the basis of subjects' motion. So, we report the relationship between brain activity and movement concerned with perception during driving in this paper.

Keywords: brain information processing during driving task; spatial cognitive task;determining direction; NIRS.

1 Introduction

Human movements change relative to his environment. Nevertheless, he/she recognizes a new location and decides what behavior to take. It is important to analyze the human spatial perception for developing autonomous robots or automatic driving.

The relation of the theta brain waves to the human spatial perception was discussed in [1][2]. When humans perceive space, for example, try to decide the next action in a maze, the theta brain waves saliently appear. This means we have a searching behavior to find a goal at an unknown maze. From the side of human navigation,

A. Marcus (Ed.): DUXU 2014, Part IV, LNCS 8520, pp. 458–468, 2014.

Maguire et al. measured the brain activations using complex virtual reality town [3]. But, every task is notional and the particulars about the mechanism that enables humans to perceive space and direction are yet unknown. Also, Brain activities concerned with cognitive tasks during car driving have been examined. For example, there was a report about brain activity when disturbances were given to subjects who manipulated a driving simulator. Also, power spectrums increased in beta and theta bands [4]. However, there is little report on the relationship among right and left perception and driving task.

So, we performed experiments in which perception tasks were required during virtual car driving using Near Infrared Spectroscopy (NIRS) [5]. From experimental results, there were significant differences at dorsolateral prefrontal cortex in left hemisphere via one-sample t-test when subjects watched driving movie and moving their hand in circles as if handling a steering wheel [6].

. In addition, we conducted experiments in real-space, which were performed by taking NIRS in the car, and measured the brain activity during actual driving. A purpose in this experiment was to measure and analyze the brain activity during actual driving to compare results between virtual and actual results. As a result, there were significant differences at similar regions [7][8]. In addition, we measured the brain activity of frontal lobe, which is related to behavioral decision-making, during car driving in different experimental design from previous one to verify previous results [9][10].

It is well known that higher order processing, such as memory, judgment, reasoning, etc. is done in the frontal lobe [11]. We tried to grasp the mechanism of information processing of the brain by analyzing data about human brain activity during car driving.   Also, the goal of this study is to find a way to apply this result to new assist system.

So, with the aim of increasing number of subjects and examining more closely the brain activity   concerned with spatial perception and direction determination during car driving, we performed additional experiments.

In this time, the brain activity of same lobe with human spatial perception and direction determination was discussed on the basis on changing direction of the gaze and starting to turn the steering wheel.   Furthermore, we examined the mechanism of information processing of the brain and human spatial perception during car driving.

2   Experiment

2.1   Brain Activity on Virtual Driving

1)   Brain activity on driving movie is shown
The subjects for this experiment were eight males who were right handed. They were asked to read and sign an informed consent regarding the experiment.

An NIRS (Hitachi Medical Corp ETG-100) with 24 channels (sampling frequency 10 Hz) was used to record the density of oxygenated hemoglobin (oxy hemoglobin) and deoxygenated hemoglobin (de-oxy hemoglobin) in the frontal cortex area.

The movie is included two scenes at a T-junction in which it must be decided either to turn to the right or left. In the second scene, there is a road sign with directions. We used nine kinds of movies in about one minute. Before showing the movie, subjects were given directions to turn to the right or left at the first T-junction. They were also taught the place which was on the road sign at the second T-Junction. They had to decide the direction when they looked at the road sign. They were asked to push a button when they realized the direction in which they were to turn.

2) Brain activity on handling motion

In this experiment, measuring was performed by NIRS, made by SHIMADZU Co. Ltd with 44ch. Five subjects were healthy males in their 20s, right handed with a good driving history.

Fig. 1. Recorded movie during measurement

(This picture was view subjects was watched.)

They were asked to read and sign an informed consent regarding the experiment.

The subject was asked to perform simulated car driving, moving their hand in circles as if using a steering wheel. A PC mouse on the table was used to simulate handling a wheel, and NIRS (near-infrared spectroscopy) to monitor oxygen content change in the subjects' brain. NIRS irradiation was performed to measure brain activities when the subject sitting on a chair make a drawing circle line of the right/left hand 1) clockwise, and 2) counterclockwise. The part of measurement was the frontal lobe. The subject was asked to draw on the table a circle 30 cm in diameter five times consecutively, spending four seconds per a circle. The time design was rest (10 seconds at least) – task (20 seconds) – rest (10 seconds) - close rest.

2.2   Brain Activity during Actual Car Driving

1) Brain activity during actual car driving

In general roads, experiments were performed by taking NIRS in the car, and measuring the brain activity when car driven by subjects was went through two different intersections. Six subjects were a healthy male in their 20s, right handed with a good driving history. They were asked to read and sign an informed consent regarding the experiment. In all experiments, measurements were performed by NIRS (Near Infrared Spectroscopy), made by SHIMADZU Co. Ltd [11].

Subjects took a rest during 10 seconds at least with their eye close before driving task and they drove a car during about 600 seconds. Finally, subject closed their eyes for 10 seconds again after task. Then, the brain activity was recorded from the first eyes-closed rest to the last eyes. Subjects were given directions to turn to the right or left at the first T-junction during driving task. They were also taught the place which was on the road sign at the second T-junction. And, they were given the place where they have to go to. So, they had to decide the direction when they looked at the road sign.

A trigger pulse was emitted on stop lines at T-Junctions to use as a measuring stick for the analysis.

Fig. 2. Sample of first T-Junction (This T-junction has no sign.)

Fig. 3. Sample of second T-Junction (This T-junction had a load sign which was shown the direction and place name.)

Also, we recorded movie during the experiment from a car with a video camera aimed toward the direction of movement (Figure. 1). Recorded movies were used to exempt measurement result including disturbances, such as foot passengers and on-coming cars, from analysis. Figureure.2 and figureure.3 shows one sample of T-junction.

2)   Verification Experiment

To conduct verification for experimental results in previous experiment, we per-formed additional experiment which was achieved in a similar way.

In this experiment, experimental course was different from previous one. While previous one was included two T-junctions in which there was road sign at second one and not at first one per a measurement, there were multiple T-junctions. Three were 5 T-junction without road sign and 4 T-junctions with road sing.

Subjects were twelve males who were all right-handed. They drove a car during about 20 minutes after a rest during 10 seconds at least with their eyes close. Subjects were enlightened about turning direction and the place on which road signs was at T-junction during measurement. And, they arbitrarily decided the direction to turn when they confirmed road signs. Also, a trigger pulse was emitted in the same way.

3)   Detailed analysis based on driving behavior

In this analysis, movies aimed toward the direction of movement as well as ones aimed subject movement like ocular motion and arm movement were recorded. This is to analyze brain activity using ocular motion in looking at road signs as a trigger. In previous research we performed, stop line at T-junction was used as a trigger. But, brain activity in T-junction involved movement task such as turning steering wheel, changing neck direction, hitting the brake. So, it is thought that brain activity derived from cognitive tasks was overwritten with brain activity due to movement tasks. Therefore, we tried to analyze brain activity on the basis of ocular motions to examine significant differences with cognitive tasks.

3   Experimental Results

3.1   Brain Activity on Virtual Driving

1)   Brain activity on driving movie is shown

On the whole, the variation in de-oxy hemoglobin was smaller than in the oxy hemog-lobin. However, there was a great increase in channel 18(around #10 area of the dor-solateral prefrontal cortex of the right hemisphere). This might be the variation based on the spatial perceptions

Next, differences were investigated concerning the subject's brain activity. As the first case, it was when the vision was directed after having been told the direction. As the Second, it was when the vision was directed after having been decided the direc-tion under the road sign.

Here, d1 and d2 were defined to analyze measurement data. d1 is the variation of hemoglobin turning of one second at the first T-junction, and d2 is variation of hemoglobin at the second one. From the measurement result, d1 and d2, all of the 269 times of each subject, there were significant differences in oxy hemoglobin 3ch. (p<0.02:

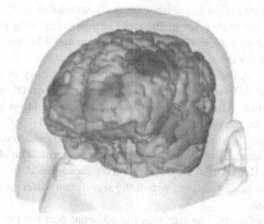

Fig. 4. Brain activity (clockwise)

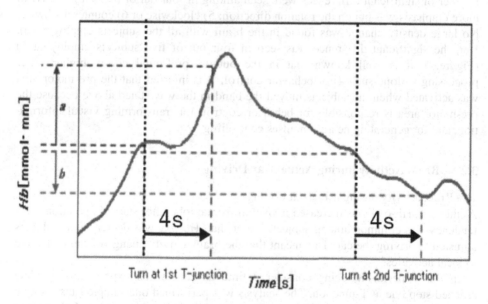

Fig. 5. Analysis method

paired t test) and 20ch. (p<0.03) using NIRS. These regions were corresponded to around #46 area of the dorsolateral prefrontal cortex of the left hemisphere and around #10 area of the dorsolateral prefrontal cortex of the right hemisphere, respectively.

Subjects pushed a button before turning at the second T-junction, so it influenced brain activities. The possibility of a correlation between d2 and the time until the movie was turned at the second T-junction after each subject pushed a button was investigated. Each correlation coefficient of hemoglobin channel was calculated. There was significant difference at only de-oxy hemoglobin 10ch (around #10 area of the dorsolateral prefrontal cortex of the right hemisphere) using paired t test. In only this result, the relationship between pushing a button and d2 cannot be judged.

2)   Brain activity on handling motion

During the motion, the increase of oxy hemoglobin density of the brain was found in all subjects. The different regions of the brain were observed to be active, depending on the individual. The subjects were to be observed 1) on starting, and 2) 3-5 seconds after starting moving their 3) right hand 4) left hand 5)clockwise 6)counterclockwise. Although some individual variation existed, the result showed the significant differences and some characteristic patterns. The obtained patterns are shown as follows. Regardless of 1), 2), 3) and 4) above, the change in the oxy hemoglobin density of the brain was seen within the significant difference level 5% or less in the three individuals

out of all five subjects. The part was the adjacent part both of left pre-motor area and of left prefrontal cortex. Especially, in the adjacent part of prefrontal cortex a number of significant differences were seen among in four out of five subjects. Next, more emphasis was put on the rotation direction: 5) clockwise or 6) counterclockwise. No large density change was found in the brain with all the subjects employing 6). But, the significant difference was seen in four out of five subjects employing 5) (Figure.4). It is well known that in the outside prefrontal cortex higher order processing is done such as of behavior control. It is inferred that the pre-motor area was activated when the subjects moved the hand in the way stated above because the pre-motor area is responsible for behavior control, for transforming visual information, and for generating neural impulses controlling.

3.2   Brain Activity during Actual Car Driving

1)   Brain activity during actual car driving

At the first, Hb-oxy was increased in overall frontal lobe after start of operation. This tendency was common among subjects. After that, Hb-oxy was decreased as subjects adjusted to driving the car. This meant that the brain activity changed from collective to local activities.

In this experiment, being considered time as zero when experimental vehicle reached stop line at T-junction. The analysis was performed one-sample t-test using a and b within the significant difference level 5% or less between zero and about four seconds (Figure.5). Here, a is the variation of hemoglobin turning of one second at the first T-junction. And b is variation of hemoglobin at the second one. As the results, there were significant differences around #46 area of the dorsolateral prefrontal cortex and the premotor area of the left hemisphere brain in turning left(Figure. 6:red). Also,   there were significant differences #9 of the dorsolateral prefrontal cortex of the left hemisphere brain at the turn right (Figure. 7: red).

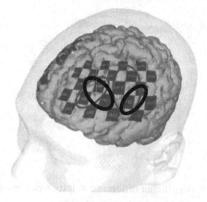

Fig. 6. Significant differences at the turn left

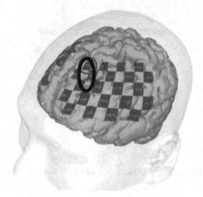

Fig. 7. Significant differences at the turn right

2)   Verification Experiment

Various tendencies among individuals were observed in comparison with results in B. However, there were tendency that oxy-Hb was increased when car turned left or right at T-junctions and oxy-Hb was decreased during going straight

The analysis method was the same as previous one. Though Gaps were shown regions at which there were significant differences, there were significant differences in common region, too (Figure. 6, 7: black). In the analysis, measurement results including disturbance at T-junctions were excluded as analysis object.

3)   Detailed analysis based on driving behavior

The analysis was performed one-sample t-test within the significant difference level 5% or less between brain activity before and after looking at road sign.   Each of sample data for analysis was 1 second.   Also, analysis was performed with respect to each direction which subject had to go at next T-junction. As a consequence of analysis, there were significant differences at interior front gyrus of flontal lobe of left hemisphere without reference of direction (Figure 8 and Figure 9).

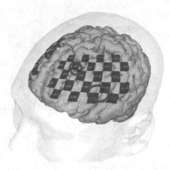

Fig. 8. Significant difference at left direction of road sign

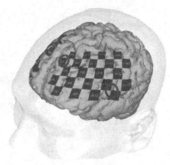

Fig. 9. Significant difference at right direction of road sign

4   Conclusion and Future Work

The hemoglobin density change of the human subjects' frontal lobe was partly observed in the experiments we designed, where three kinds of tasks were performed to analyze human brain activity from the view point of spatial perception.

The NIRS measures of hemoglobin variation in the channels suggested that human behavioral decision-making of different types could cause different brain activities as we saw in the tasks: 1)   taking a given direction at the first T-junction,   2) taking a self-chosen direction on a road sign at the second T-junction and 3) turning the wheel or not. Some significant differences (paired t test) on NIRS's oxy-hemoglobin and less interrelated results between "pushing a button" and brain activity at the second T-junction are obtained.

Furthermore, experimental results indicated that with the subjects moving their hand in circle, regardless of right or left, 1) the same response was observed in the prefrontal cortex and premotor area, and 2) different patterns of brain activities generated by moving either hand clockwise or counterclockwise.

The regions observed were only those with the 5% and less significance level. Possible extensions could be applied to other regions with the 10% and less significance level for the future study. With a larger number of subjects, brain activity patterns need to be made clear. In addition, it is thought to take particular note of participation concerning working memory when car is driven.

Furthermore, it was found that there were significant differences around #44-45 area. It is well known that this region is corresponding to language area. So, it is thought that subjects look at road map to determine direction that they have to go according to word described in road sign.

From results of these experiments, there was significant difference around working memory. So, experiments focusing on relationship turning wheel and working memory will be performed. On the other hand, experiments as to actual driving were required a broad range of perception and information processing. Especially, subjects had to determine   behaves depending on various information at T-junctions, that is, the color of the traffic light, presence or absence foot passengers and so on. And so, we plan to perform more static experiments. we attention to differences on the basis of turning direction and dominant hand. In addition, we will conduct the experiments in which subjects were narrowed down to left-handedness. Furthermore, researches into other human brain activities than spatial perception are to be necessary with accumulated data from fMRI (functional magnetic resonance imaging), EEG (Electroencephalogram), etc.

When compared virtual result to actual ones, there were significant differences around #46 area in both experiments, which were performed in virtual and actual condition, as a common result. It is thought that this result is due to activities of working memory because subjects must to recall memories of movements required for car driving and turning steering wheel. Conversely, there were significant differences around #10 in virtual experiments and around premotor area in actual driving, respectively.   In the virtual case, it is thought to result from inhabitation of task without movement. In the actual case, subjects had to perceive space information in real time. So, it is considered that there were significant differences around premotor area because they always ready up to manipulate steering wheel.

As a future plan, we aim to apply these results to assistive human interface. As a matter of course, we plan to performed additional experiments including the verification of these results. And final purpose is to develop a new system for manipulating wheelchair and information presentation system to assist recognition of information including spatial one during car driving.

References

1. Kahana, M.J., Sekuler, R., Caplan, J.B., Kirschen, M., Madsen, J.R.: Human theta oscillations exhibit task dependence during virtual maze navigation. Nature 399, 781–784 (1999)
2. Nishiyama, N., Yamaguchi, Y.: Human EEG theta in the spatial recognition task. In: Proceedings of 5th World Multiconf. on Systemics, Cybernetics and Informatics (SCI 2001), Proc. 7th Int. Conf. on Information Systems, Analysis and Synthesis (ISAS 2001), pp. 497-500 (2001)
3. Maguire, E.A., Burgess, N., Donnett, J.G., Frackowiak, R.S.J., Frith, C.D., O' Keefe, J.: Knowing Where and Getting There: A Human Navigation Network. Science 280 (May 8, 1998)

4. Lin, C.-T., Chen, S.-A., Chiu, T.-T., Lin, H.-Z., Ko, L.-W.: Spatial and temporal EEG dynamics of dual-task driving performance. Journal of NeuroEngineering and Rehabilitation, 8–11 (2011)
5. Watanabe, E., Yamashita, Y., Ito, Y., Koizumi, H.: Non-invasive functional mapping with multi-channel near infrared spectroscopic topography in humans. Heurosci. Lett. 205(1), 41–44 (1996)
6. Shimizu, S., et al.: Fundamental Study for Relationship between Cognitive task and Brain Activity during Car Driving. In: Harris, D. (ed.) Engin. Psychol. and Cog. Ergonomics, HCII 2009. LNCS (LNAI), vol. 5639, pp. 434–440. Springer, Heidelberg (2009)
7. Takahashi, N., Shimizu, S., Hirata, Y., Nara, H., Miwakeichi, F., Hirai, N., Kikuchi, S., Watanabe, E., Kato, S.: Fundamental Study for a New Assistive System during Car Driving. In: Proc. International Conference on Robotics and Biomimetics, China (2010)
8. Takahashi, N., Shimizu, S., Hirata, Y., Nara, H., Inoue, H., Hirai, N., Kikuchi, S., Watanabe, E., Kato, S.: Basic study of Analysis of Human Brain Activities during Car Driving. In: The 14th International Conferrence on Human-Computer Interaction, 2011, Orlando, Florida, USA (2011)
9. Shimizu, S., Takahashi, N., Nara, H., Inoue, H., Hirata, Y.: Fundamental Study for Human Brain Activity Based on the Spatial Cognitive Task. In: The 2011 Internatinal Conference on Brain Informatics-BI 2011, China (2011)
10. Shimizu, S., Nara, H., Takahashi, N., Inoue, H., Hirata, Y.: Basic Study for Human Brain Activity Based on the Spatial Cognitive Task. In: The Third International Conference on Advanced Cognitive Techonologies and Applications, 2011, Italy (2011)
11. Cockburn, J.: Task interruption in prospective memory: A frontal lobe function? Cortex 31, 87–97 (1995)
12. Watanabe, E., Yamashita, Y., Ito, Y., Koizumi, H.: Non-invasive functional mapping with multi-channel near infrared spectroscopic topography in humans. Heurosci Lett 205(1), 41–44 (1996)

Cross-Platform Product Usability and Large Screen User Experience: A Teleconference System U&E Research

Yinting Zhang, Chuncheng Zhao, Gang Liu, and Ting Han[*]

School of Media and Design, Shanghai Jiao Tong University, China
hanting@sjtu.edu.cn

Abstract. In this paper, researchers focus on product usability and user experience on a teleconference system that was in development, aiming at using a effective method to focus on the whole user experience, looking for product defects and improving the product usability and experience (U&E) in the mid stage of the product development. The main method applied in this study are Users Performance, User Experience Map and CSUQ. The most important finding is that the large screen is the key experience when user interact with the large screen system.

Keywords: Teleconference system; User Experience; Product Usability; Large Screen Experience.

1 Introduction

1.1 Large screen

With the development of information technology, the human-computer interaction (HCI) technology and network technology is developing rapidly. The application of large screen based human-computer interaction technology is applied more and more widely. Screen with big picture, color, high brightness, high resolution display rate in demand by such as network center building, command control center, temporary meetings etc. Large-screen wall displays are becoming a common fixture in command and control environments [12]. As with high resolution, high brightness and color, the size of screen has been a important parameter to describe the large screen device. There are many studies focus on the relationship between the size of screen and users experience, even though they come from different domains. As long as, researchers studied the impact on study performance of screen size. Subjects using a 15 inch screen need less learning time than subjects using a 12 inch screen, with no difference in learning performance [4]. Consumer demand for large screen television sets is on the rise, with sales of 27 inch and larger sets exceeding the most optimistic industry expectations. One reason for this demand may be that a large screen television delivers a different, more enjoyable, more intense viewing experience than a small screen model. This greater intensity may also indicate that large screen viewers experience a

---

[*] Corresponding author.

A. Marcus (Ed.): DUXU 2014, Part IV, LNCS 8520, pp. 469–479, 2014.

sense of presence, a feeling that they are in the environment portrayed on the screen [7]. In some study of Virtual Reality, researchers found that large, curved projection screens yielded better performance than HMDS (head-mounted display) [3]. Besides, some researchers used bio-measurement to proved similar theories. In a comparison experiment, largest screen produced greater heart rate deceleration than the medium and small screens. The large screen also produced greater skin conductance than the medium and small screens [10]. There are relevant study in military domain. Panoramic displays are intended to facilitate a common operational picture between multiple commanders or command centre operators, enabling personnel in the command centre to appreciate the 'big picture' of a tactical situation. Hence, the panoramic display may improve situation awareness and assessment of the situation, facilitate shared mental models, and improve team decision-making [1].

In this study the large screen is applied in a Teleconference system with Cross-Platform Product. The main goal is to prove whether the large screen has positive impact on users experience or not.

1.2   User Experience and Usability

The goal of user experience design in industry is to improve customers satisfaction and loyalty through the utility, ease of use, and pleasure provided in the interaction with a product [11]. High quality user experience (UX) has become a central competitive factor of product development in mature consumer markets [8]. There are so many studies on users experience, but a clear evaluation methods is not exist. So far, user experience studies have mostly focused on short-term evaluations and consequently on aspects relating to the initial adoption of new product designs [5]. The recent shift of emphasis to user experience (UX) has rendered it a central focus of product design and evaluation. A multitude of methods for UX design and evaluation exist, but a clear overview of the current state of the available UX evaluation methods is missing [2].

The study on usability is more complete relatively. Usability inspection is the generic name for a set of cost effective ways of evaluating user interfaces to find usability Problems [9].

1.3   The Present Research

The main goal of this study is to propose a new model for evaluating usability and experience of one new teleconference system. The model contains User Performance, Experience Map, CSUQ. Researchers selected CSUQ to analyze users satisfaction. At the beginning, researchers compared nine questionnaires as Table 1:

In consideration of the system type: a human –computer teleconference system, researchers chose CSUQ to evaluate users satisfaction.

Table 1. Nine questionnaires to evaluat usability

QUIS	Questionnaire for User Interface Satisfaction	Chin et al, 1988
PUEU	Perceived Usefulness and Ease of Use	Davis, 1989
NAU	Nielsen's Attributes of Usability	Nielsen, 1993
NHE	Nielsen's Heuristic Evaluation	Nielsen, 1993
CSUQ	Computer System Usability Questionnaire	Lewis, 1995
ASQ	After Scenario Questionnaire	Lewis, 1995
PHUE	Practical Heuristics for Usability Evaluation	Perlman, 1997
PUTQ	Purdue Usability Testing Questionnaire	Lin et al, 1997
USE	USE Questionnaire	Lund, 2001

2　Method

2.1　Participants

Sixteen participants took part in this study, and all of them were recruited from the general public. Eight were recruited from the person who have been working and eight were recruited from students. The male/female ratio is 5:3, that is ten men and six women. They were aged between 23 to 30 (M=25.87;SD=2.22). Male participants were aged between 23 to 28. Female participants were aged between 23 to 30. The study investigated employment statues and gender. The researchers established three criteria for recruitment: English level, iPad using experience, teleconference using experience .

2.2　Experimental Materials and Device

Experimental Hardware. The experimental site was in a main conference room. The room was decorated specifically for the system. There was an assistant meeting room beside the main one, which was with screen which could be connected with the large screen and act as the remote site. The main experimental hardware devices were a large screen teleconference system which could be touched (developer called it touch wall) and a iPad, the area of touch wall almost took up about two adjacent walls. Moreover, there were some other physical objects-mark pens with different colors and whiteboard eraser providing to participants to use.

Experimental Software. There was an Application on both large screen and iPad, participants could use it to do some interaction.

2.3   User Tasks

The main functions of the teleconference system were made both sides who participant the meeting communicate freely, also made them share their ideas to other people and understand others' ideas by the Cross-Platform Product.

According to these main functions researchers established 29 tasks which covered all the functions. The 29 tasks belonged to 4 section in sequence: (1) Tasks Conducted on Touch Wall, (2) Tasks Conducted on iPad, (3) Tasks Conducted back to Touch Wall and (4) Voice Command. The detail task name are presented in Table 2

Table 2. Tasks names and numbers

1.1	Join a scheduled meeting	2.16.2	Full-screen the document by iPad
1.2	View meeting information from meeting panel	2.17	Annotate on shared document
1.4	Display workspace	2.18	Navigate shared document
1.5	Access group space to open a document	2.19	Unshared the document
1.7	Annotate on the document	2.20	Create sticky notes and share to touch wall
1.8.1	Open active chart	2.22	View touch wall content on iPad
1.8.2	Play active chart	2.23	Download file/screenshot on touch wall
1.9.1	Launch Whiteboard	2.24	View downloaded file/screenshot
1.9.2	Full-screen the whiteboard	3.13.1	Stack sticky notes by color
1.10	Draw on whiteboard	3.13.2	Stack sticky notes by selection
1.11.1	Erase the whiteboard	3.13.3	Move sticky notes
1.11.2	Select something. on whiteboard	3.14.1	Un-stack sticky notes by "un-group"
1.11.3	Scale selected object on whiteboard	3.14.2	Un-stack sticky notes by finger sliding
1.11.4	Move selected object on whiteboard	4	Voice command
1.12	Navigate whiteboard (zoom, pan,)	2.16.2	Full-screen the document by iPad

- Task 1.3, 1.6 and 1.15 was deleted during the experiment, because they were unimportant tasks that could be ignored and had no impact on UX.
- Tasks numbers was not in sequence but tasks was in actual order. Please ignore the numbers order and focus on the task itself.
- 4.Voice command was added tasks and didn't belong to the 29 tasks.

2.4   Experimental Design

Researchers invited a moderator to host the experiment. Moderator had been trained to use the teleconference system before so that moderator known the system very well could get hold of the condition. Participants was invited into the meeting room to do the test one by one. After moderator's introduction about the experiment, the participant was told the names of the tasks and prepared to complete them one by one. Once participants were in trouble, they could try to (1) Conquer the problems all by themselves; (2) Call the moderator for help; (3) Call for a hint; (4)Task failed . During the test processes, the moderator would ask some presupposed questions about users' feeling and thinking (think aloud), the answers were recorded. After participant finish the whole tasks, they was asked to fill CSUQ. At the same time, two cameras were set up in the meeting room, one was set up the left side of the participant to record his or her facial expression and body gesture. The other was set up in the back of the room in order to record the screen of the touch wall so that researcher could judge the progress of tasks. One recorder controlled two cameras and the other recorder seat in the back of room and recorded participants' added details. 16 participants was separated into 6 days, that means there was 2 or 3 participants conducted this test everyday so that researchers could ensure the moderator's physical and mental condition was fine.

2.5   Analytical Method

Users Performance. Users Performance Analysis, researchers could get the data about product performance. On the basis of analyze result researchers could improved the product features accurately and reduce newcomers' learning cost.

User Experience Map. Experience Map was an objective way to analyze users subjective emotion changes according to the times. It helped researchers to get the users Pain Points, Gain Points and Wow Points.

Table 3. Computer System Usability Questionnaire. It is a 1-7 scale from disagree to agree

1. Overall, I am satisfied with how easy it is to use system
2. It was simple to use system
3. I can effectively complete my work using system
4. I am able to complete my work quickly using system
5. I am able to efficiently complete my work using system
6. I feel comfortable using system
7. It was easy to learn to use system
8. I believe I became productive quickly using system
9. System gives error messages that clearly tell me how to fix problems
10. Whenever I make a mistake using system, I recover easily and quickly
11. The information (such as online help, on-screen messages, and other documentation) provided with system is clear
12. It is easy to find the information I needed
13. The information provided for system is easy to understand
14. The information is effective in helping me complete the tasks and scenarios
15. The organization of information on system screens is clear
16. The interface of system is pleasant
17. I like using the interface of system
18. System has all the functions and capabilities I expect it to have
19. Overall, I am satisfied with system

CSUQ Analysis. CSUQ (Computer System Usability Questionnaire) was proposed in Psychometric Evaluation and Instructions for Use. International Journal of Human-Computer Interaction. It is a subjective usability measurement at IBM [6]. The 19 questions show in Table 3.

CSUQ showed users subjective satisfaction of every level of the teleconference system. CSUQ contains 19 questions and analyzed to the 19 questions would revealed whether users were satisfied with system interface, Efficient, Effective, Engaging , Easy to learn, Error Tolerant .

3   Result and Conclusion

3.1   Performance Result

Users Performance included the following aspects

Overall Performance. Sixteen participants were numbered 101 - 116. Researchers watched the recorded video and got statistical data about the total time comparison as Table 4. Table 4 indicated that participant NO.110 spent longest time (1 hour and 4 minutes) to fulfill 29 tasks and participant NO.116 spent shortest time (about 20minites).

Table 4. Measured in hours

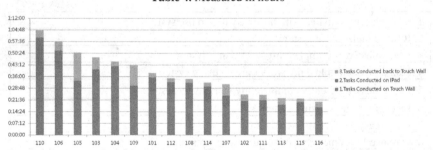

Before researchers started the experiment, they invited a developer of this teleconference system to do preliminary experiment on 16 tasks. The meaning of experiment result was that established the ideal duration (there is no cognition friction between human – computer) of 16 tasks. The ideal duration was a datum line. By means of the comparison with the datum line researchers got difficulty level of 16 tasks for newcomer. Researchers called it Magnification Comparison as **Table 5**.

β (Magnification Comparison)* is the ratio of T1 (mean time) and T2 (Estimated Time), namely

$$\beta = T1/T2$$

Table 5. 1.0 means the task is as difficult as Estimated

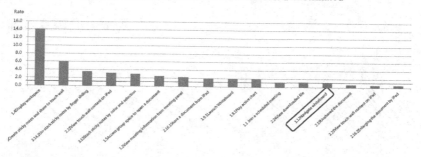

The table indicated that several tasks were harder than estimated some were easier and 3were almost as difficulty as estimated.

Comparison of Control Variables. Researchers classified 16 users into two categories according to their employment statues and gender: Employed group and Students group / Male group and Female group. The result revealed that there is no significant difference between employed group and Students group.

That means the difficulty level of this teleconference system was almost equivalent for all newcomer no matter what his / her gender and work or not, as long as they were proficiency in English and iPad operation and also known something about teleconference system.

Number of Wrong Gestures and Calling for Help. In the process of test, users came up against so many kinds of problems. Researcher systemized the number of wrong gestures when they trying and believe that the number reflected which task was difficult, which interface made users feel confused, which part layout unreasonable as **Table 6.**

Table 6. Numbers of wrong gestures

They could call for a hint to moderator to be provided a simple hint. Researcher systemized the number of the hints. The number showed difficulty level of each task in a qualified sense as **Table 7.**

Table 7. Number of hints

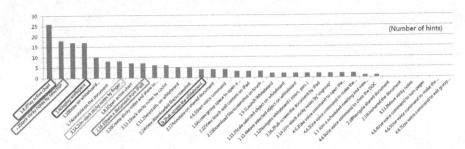

Both the **Table 6** and **Table 7** reflected six tasks were in a high difficulty level. Researchers believed that cognition friction exist in this six tasks: 1.9.2 Full-screen the whiteboard, 3.14.2 Un-stack sticky notes by finger sliding, 1.4 Display workspace, 1.8.2 Play active chart (Switch 2D to 3D), 3.13.2 Stack sticky notes by selection, 2.16.2 Full-screen the document by iPad .

3.2   User Experience Map Result

Researches took the employed group and the students group as an example to how to obtain the key factors of the whole UX. **Table 8** is emotion changes graphic coordinates of participant NO.115. X position represented the time he spent. Y position represented participant emotion changes. Numerical range was -5 to 5. Positive value stood for positive emotion of user such as happy / surprise / praise and so on. Negative values represented negative emotion, for example anxiety / upset / criticism and so on. Researcher recorded each point of emotion change in three ways: facial expression, body language, words. According to these method, researchers judged users' emotion (gave the emotion a score -5 to 5) at some time point and marked a position in coordinates. A Experience Map presented when every position was linked by smooth curve in sequence.

Table 8. Take NO.115 as an example

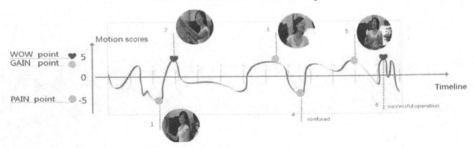

Pain Points, Gain Points and Wow Points were obtained by compare the 8 Experience Maps. All of Points were universal.

Participants revealed negative emotion when the Pain Points appeared usually:

- Meeting with difficult tasks.
- "Exit" button was ambiguous, that means exit menu rather than exit meeting.
- The screen was not sensitive enough.
- Inconsistent interfaces between touch wall and iPad.
- The screen was too big to conduct, the visual range on screen was relatively small.
- Voice commend gave no reaction.

They also gave some positive comments to the function they like.

- Whiteboard contained many functions, "smoothly" was attractive.
- Share a document from iPad was an interesting task.
- The app had clear hint message when sharing a document from iPad.
- Annotate on shared document by iPad.
- Annotate on the document when using marker pen.
- Interacting with the remote site on whiteboard.
- The dynamic effects of active chart.

Participants also gave a compliment to the functions which surprised them.

- Large screen meeting made users feel amazing surprise.
- The process of interacting with the remote site on whiteboard was interesting.
- "Smoothly" on whiteboard was a very useful function.
- The dynamic effects of active chart.
- Annotate on the document when using marker pen and eraser.
- Voice command was intelligent.

3.3 CSUQ Analysis Result

Researchers used SPSS to analyzed the Computer System Usability Questionnaire as **Table 9**. Descriptive Statistics revealed that participants gave weak score on question NO.9, NO. 10 and NO.11. And question NO.17, NO. 7, NO.16, NO.3 got good score.

Table 9. Descriptive statistics

CSUQ Descriptive Statistics	N	Minimum	Maximum	Mean	Std. Deviation	Variance
9 System gives error messages that clearly tell me how to fix problems	16	1	6	2.81	1.377	1.896
10 Whenever I make a mistake using system , I recover easily and quickly	16	2	6	3.63	1.408	1.983
11 The information provided with system is clear	16	2	6	4.44	1.548	2.396
18 System has all the functions and capabilities I expect it to have	16	2	7	5.00	1.414	2.000
12 It is easy to find the information I needed	16	4	6	5.19	.750	.563
2 It was simple to use system	16	4	7	5.38	.957	.917
4 I am able to complete my work quickly using system	16	3	7	5.38	1.204	1.450
8 I believe I became productive quickly using system	16	2	7	5.38	1.204	1.450
5 I am able to efficiently complete my work using system	16	4	7	5.38	.806	.650
1 Overall, I am satisfied with how easy it is to use system	16	3	7	5.50	1.033	1.067
15 The organization of information on system screens is clear	16	3	7	5.69	1.138	1.296
19 Overall I am satisfied with system	16	3	7	5.75	.931	.867
13 The information provided for system is easy to understand	16	5	7	5.81	.544	.296
6 I feel comfortable using system	16	4	7	5.88	.885	.783
14 The information is effective in helping me complete the tasks and scenarios	16	5	7	5.88	.619	.383
17 I like using the interface of system	16	3	7	6.00	1.033	1.067
7 It was easy to learn to use system	16	4	7	6.13	.885	.783
16 The interface of system is pleasant	16	3	7	6.19	1.047	1.096
3 I can effectively complete my work using system	16	4	7	6.25	.856	.733
Valid N (listwise)	16					

Table 10. Factor Analysis

Total Variance Explained

Component	Initial Eigenvalues			Extraction Sums of Squared Loadings			Rotation Sums of Squared Loadings		
	Total	% of Variance	Cumulative %	Total	% of Variance	Cumulative %	Total	% of Variance	Cumulative %
1	5.575	29.341	29.341	5.575	29.341	29.341	4.096	21.557	21.557
2	3.488	18.360	47.702	3.488	18.360	47.702	3.117	16.403	37.960
3	2.677	14.091	61.793	2.677	14.091	61.793	2.388	12.567	50.527
4	2.083	10.962	72.755	2.083	10.962	72.755	2.380	12.529	63.056
5	1.333	7.015	79.770	1.333	7.015	79.770	2.230	11.739	74.795
6	1.048	5.514	85.284	1.048	5.514	85.284	1.993	10.489	85.284
7	.891	4.689	89.973						
8	.683	3.596	93.569						
9	.363	1.911	95.480						
10	.268	1.409	96.889						
11	.200	1.054	97.943						
12	.174	.917	98.860						
13	.144	.757	99.617						
14	.054	.282	99.899						
15	.019	.101	100.000						
16	.000	.000	100.000						
17	.000	.000	100.000						
18	.000	.000	100.000						
19	.000	.000	100.000						

Extraction Method: Principal Component Analysis.

Table 11. Factor Analysis

Principal factor	Variable	
Effective	It was simple to use system	.497
	I can effectively complete my work using system	.890
	I am able to complete my work quickly using system	.834
	I am able to efficiently complete my work using system	.871
	The information is effective in helping me complete the tasks and scenarios	.713
	Overall, I am satisfied with system	.712
Engaging	I believe I became productive quickly using system	.771
	The organization of information on system screens is clear	.670
	The interface of system is pleasant	.778
	I like using the interface of system	.842
Efficient	The information (such as online help, on-screen messages, and other documentation) provided with system is clear	.606
	It is easy to find the information I needed	.940
	System has all the functions and capabilities I expect it to have	.678
Easy to learn	I feel comfortable using system	.598
	It was easy to learn to use system	.870
	System gives error messages that clearly tell me how to fix problems	-.639
	The information provided for system is easy to understand	.927
Error Tolerant	Overall, I am satisfied with how easy it is to use system	.770
	Whenever I make a mistake using system, I recover easily and quickly	.713

There were five principal factors(5Es) of CSUQ: Effective, Engaging, Efficient, Easy to learn, Error Tolerant.

The result of CSUQ showed that users were satisfied with System Interface, Efficient and Easy to learn. And they gave bad score on Error Tolerant.

4   Discussion

The central goal of this study is to propose a novel model to evaluate usability and experience of this new teleconference system.

New technology triggered evolution in people's daily life. Take large screen as an example, it has been applied in many domains such as Military Command. Bigger is better? Interestingly, in this study researchers grasped the key factors that hade impact on large screen users experience. Even though most of the participants thought large screen was a amazing surprise to them, but there are still part of users considered that large screen was too large to conduce and the visual range on screen was relatively small when they operate this system. So it is not 'bigger means better', more appropriateness is better, better experience is better.

The technology of Large screen and Cross- Platform is applying in more and more domains such as education and medical. It is still need to study that how to make this resource plays the biggest role under limited conditions and brings users best experience.

Acknowledgments. This paper is sponsored by Shanghai Pujiang Program (13PJC072), Shanhai Philosopy and Social Science Program (2012BCK001), Shanghai Jiao Tong Universty Interdisciplinary among Hunmnity, Social Science and Natural Science Fund (13JCY02). We thank to the students of Shang-hai Jiao Tong University who contributed to this research. Moreover, we thank Cisco Systems (China) Research & Development Centre for their support.

References

1. H.J.D.C.M.R.F.A.S.P.H.: People in Control. Human Factors in Control Room Design. Manchester, UK (2001)
2. Vermeeren, A.P.O.S., Law, E.L.-C., Roto, V., Obrist, M., Hoonhout, J., Vänänen-Vainio-Mattila, K.: User Experience Evaluation Methods: Current State and Development Needs. In: NordiCHI, October 16-20 (2010)
3. Riecke, B.E., Schulte-Pelkum, J., Bülthoff, H.H.: Perceiving Simulated Ego-Motions in Virtual Reality - Comparing Large Screen Displays with Hmds. Human Vision and Electronic Imaging X 5666, 344–355 (2005)
4. David De Bruijn, S.D.M.: Herre Van Oostendorp: The Influence of Screen Size and Text Layout on the Study of Text. Behaviour& Information Technology 11, 71–78 (1992)
5. Kujala, S., Roto, V., Väänänen-Vainio-Mattila, K., KarapanosE.Sinnelä, A.: Ux Curve: A Method for Evaluating Long-Term User Experience. Interacting with Computers 23, 473–483 (2011)
6. Lewis, J.R.: Ibm Computer Usability Satisfaction Questionnaires: Psychometric Evaluation and Instructions for Use. Human Factors Group 54(786), 1–39 (1993)
7. Lombard, M., Ditton, T.B., Grabe, M.E., Reich, R.D.: The Role of Screen Size in Viewer Responses to Television Fare. Communication Reports 10, 95–106 (1997)
8. Marianna Obrist, V.R., Väänänen-Vainio-Mattila, K.: User Experience Evaluation – Do You Know Which Method to Use?CHI 2009 Special Interest Groups, April 4-9 (2009)
9. Nielsen, J.: Usability Inspection Methods. In: Conferenc Coempanion* CHI 1994, April 24-28 (1994)
10. Reeves, B., Lang, A., Kim, E.Y., Tatar, D.: The Effects of Screen Size and Message Content on Attention and Arousal. Media Psychology 1, 49–67 (1999)
11. Sari Kujala, V.R., Väänänen-Vainio-Mattila, K., Karapanos, A.: Sinnelä: Ux Curve: A Method for Evaluating Long-Term User Experience. Interacting with Computers 23, 473–483 (2011)
12. Stacey, D., Scott, J.W., Rico, A., Carina Furusho, M.L.: Cummings: Aiding Team Supervision in Command and Control Operations with Large-Screen Displays. In: Proceedings of HSIS 2007: ASNE Human Systems Integration Symposium, pp. 19–21 (March 2007)

Author Index